5/93

THE
COLD
WAR
1945-1991

CIA map of Europe in February 1992, two months after the Soviet Union was dissolved

THE COLD WAR
1945-1991

Resources:

Chronology, History,

Concepts, Events,

Organizations,

Bibliography, Archives

Edited by
Benjamin Frankel

A MANLY, INC. BOOK

 Gale Research Inc.

DETROIT • WASHINGTON, D.C. • LONDON

Table of Contents

Preface

The purpose of *The Cold War, 1945-1991* is to provide the reader with an accessible source of information on the events that dominated and defined the second half of the twentieth century. The central theme of the period was the tense, grim rivalry between the United States and the Soviet Union. The Cold War was not merely a political conflict between the two states, although the competition over spheres of influence was a central part of it. Two aspects made the Cold War unique. The first was that is was also a competition between two rival social systems, two incompatible views of man and society. The second was the introduction of nuclear weapons. These two elements combined to endow the Cold War with an apocalyptic air and messianic fervor absent from the usual, and more mundane, competition between states for power and influence. There were many other important developments in the post–World War II world, but all of them, to a greater or lesser degree, were shaped or influenced by the U.S.-Soviet rivalry. The encyclopedia describes, explains, and analyzes the major events of this anxious time.

It does so by examining the careers of the important individuals who played major roles and made unique contributions during the period: they participated in the events, made the decisions, fought the wars, passed the laws, coined the terms of policy and debate, wrote important analyses, mobilized public opinion, or anchored the events of the Cold War in the larger historical sweep. It is no coincidence that very different participants in the Cold War chose similar titles for their memoirs of the period: Dean Acheson's *Witness at the Creation*, Charles Bohlen's *Witness to History*, Whittaker Chambers's *Witness*. The individuals studied in the first two volumes of the encyclopedia were all intimate and active witnesses to the Cold War as it unfolded.

The biographical entries are not full–scale biographical studies. Rather, they concentrate on these individuals' participation in and contribution to the events we call the Cold War. The first volume offers biographical entries on 149 personalities from the United States and Europe. The second volume consists of biographical entires of 134 important figures from the Soviet Union, China, the communist countries of East Europe and Asia, and the Third World.

The encyclopedia also offers, in volume 3, a detailed examination of the major events, concepts, terms, and themes that dominated the Cold War.

It should be remembered that editing an encyclopedia begins with the act of selection, winnowing the thousands of relevant biographies and pertinent nonbiographical entries to a manageable number of a few hundreds. This encyclopedia, like others, is therefore suggestive and representative, not exhaustive or comprehensive.

This reference work serves the reader as a first and a full resource for information on the Cold War. It is organized so that each entry is self contained: terms are explained each time they appear; every entry is accompanied by a detailed bibliography for further research and a list of other entries in which additional pertinent information may be found; the third volume contains a chronology and analytical history of the Cold War, allowing the reader to place individual entries into the larger picture.

The main features of *The Cold War, 1945-1991* are:

— a close study of the careers and contributions of 149 individuals who played an important role in shaping the Cold War. Each entry is followed by a detailed bibliography for further research

— a detailed chronology of the Cold War, listing the major events, conferences, wars, agreements, laws, and more. Each entry is followed by a detailed bibliography for further research

— a narrative analytical history of the period, offering a comprehensive history of the Cold War and analysis of its major events

— a comprehensive thematic bibliography, broken into categories and sub-categories

— a research guide to the archival material, including private papers, public documents, and oral histories relevant to the Cold War

Benjamin Frankel is a specialist in the areas of U.S. national security, defense, and foreign policy; military strategy; and international relations theory. He completed undergraduate work at the University of Tel Aviv and graduate work in political science at the University of Chicago. He is founder and editor of the journal Security Studies.

Mr. Frankel is editor of the books In the National Interest: A National Interest Reader *(Lanham, Md.: University Press of America, 1990)*; Opaque Nuclear Proliferation: Methodological and Policy Implications *(Frank Cass, 1991); and* The Nuclear Proliferation Fact-book *(Washington, D. C.: Congressional Research Service, 1992).*

Acknowledgments

This book was produced by Bruccoli Clark Layman, Inc. Karen L. Rood is senior editor. Dennis Lynch was the in-house editor.

Production coordinator is James W. Hipp. Projects manager is Charles D. Brower. Photography editors are Edward Scott and Timothy C. Lundy. Layout and graphics supervisor is Penney L. Haughton. Copyediting supervisor is Bill Adams. Typesetting supervisor is Kathleen M. Flanagan. Samuel Bruce is editorial associate. Systems manager is George F. Dodge. The production staff includes Rowena Betts, Steve Borsanyi, Barbara Brannon, Teresa Chaney, Patricia Coate, Rebecca Crawford, Margaret McGinty Cureton, Denise Edwards, Sarah A. Estes, Joyce Fowler, Robert Fowler, Brenda A. Gillie, Bonita Graham, Jolyon M. Helterman, Ellen McCracken, Kathy Lawler Merlette, John Myrick, Pamela D. Norton, Thomas J. Pickett, Patricia Salisbury, Maxine K. Smalls, Deborah P. Stokes, and Wilma Weant.

Walter W. Ross and Suzanne Burry did library research. They were assisted by the following librarians at the Thomas Cooper Library of the University of South Carolina: Linda Holderfield and the interlibrary-loan staff; reference librarians Gwen Baxter, Daniel Boice, Faye Chadwell, Cathy Eckman, Rhonda Felder, Gary Geer, Qun "Gerry" Jiao, Jackie Kinder, Laurie Preston, Jean Rhyne, Carol Tobin, Carolyn Tyler, Virginia Weathers, Elizabeth Whiznant, and Connie Widney; circulation-department head Thomas Marcil; and acquisitions-searching supervisor David Haggard.

THE
COLD
WAR
1945-1991

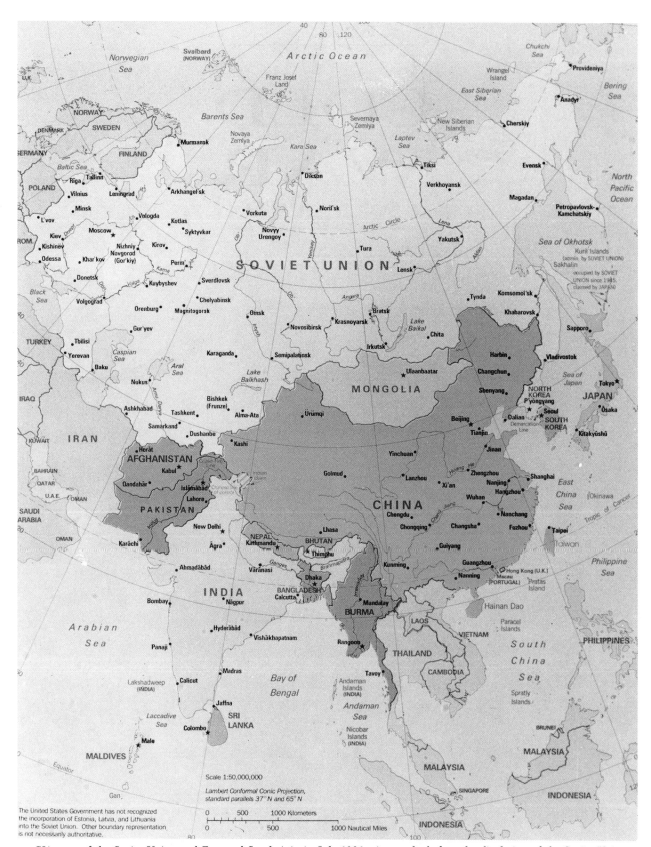

CIA map of the Soviet Union and East and South Asia in July 1991, six months before the disolution of the Soviet Union

Chronology

Prepared by Benjamin Frankel

The chronology lists only events directly related to the Cold War, except in cases where the listing of an event or development is helpful in understanding the context of the Cold War.

1939

AUGUST 23-29	The Soviet Union and Nazi Germany sign a nonaggression pact, the Molotov-Ribbentrop agreement (See **Molotov$_2$**; **Stalin$_2$**)
SEPTEMBER 1	Germany invades Poland. World War II begins
5	**Franklin Delano Roosevelt$_1$** proclaims U.S. neutrality
NOVEMBER 4	U. S. Congress passes Neutrality Act
DECEMBER 14	League of Nations, the post–World War I predecessor of the United Nations Organization (UN), meets for the last time

1940

MAY	U.S. activists supporting American intervention in the war establish Committee to Defend America by Aiding the Allies to marshal support for their position
JUNE	U.S. activists opposing intervention in the war form America First group to marshal support for isolationism
JULY	Interventionist Century Group created
SEPTEMBER 27	Germany, Italy, and Japan sign the Tripartite Pact, creating the Axis

1941

MARCH 11	Lend-Lease Act, which provides weaponry and financial support to any country whose defense is deemed vital to the U. S. interests, is approved by U. S. Congress (See **Attlee$_1$**; **Churchill$_1$**; **Hopkins$_1$**; **Henry Morgenthau, Jr.$_1$**; **Roosevelt$_1$**)
APRIL	Prointervention activists create Fight for Freedom Committee

AUGUST 9–12   At the Atlantic Conference at Newfoundland the United States and Great Britain issue the Atlantic Charter, stating mutual principles supporting self-determination by nations of the world and condemning territorial aggression (See **Churchill**$_1$; **Hopkins**$_1$; **Roosevelt**$_1$)

DECEMBER 7   Japanese planes attack the U.S. Navy in Pearl Harbor, Hawaii

8   **Roosevelt**$_1$ describes Japanese attack as a "day that will live in infamy." The United States declares war on Japan

11   Germany and Italy declare war on the United States; the United States reciprocates

1942

JANUARY 1   Allies – twenty-six nations, principal among them the United States, Great Britain, and the Soviet Union – sign United Nations declaration affirming Atlantic Charter and jointly pledging military and economic action against Axis

AUGUST 12–15   Moscow Conference on Allied military planning, attended by Soviet premier **Joseph Stalin**$_2$, British prime minister **Winston Churchill**$_1$, and U.S. envoy **W. Averell Harriman**$_1$, among others

1943

JANUARY 14–
24(25)   Casablanca Conference between British and American military planners who discuss military strategy and declare that they will seek the unconditional surrender of Axis forces (See **Churchill**$_1$; **Roosevelt**$_1$)

MAY 12–25   The Trident Conference on military strategy in Washington, D.C., between British and U.S. military planning groups (See **Churchill**$_1$; **Roosevelt**$_1$)

29–6/3   Algiers Conference to coordinate British-U.S. operations in the Mediterranean

AUGUST 11–24   Quebec Conference between United States and Great Britain to discuss cross–English Channel invasion of Europe (See **Churchill**$_1$; **Henry Morgenthau, Jr.**$_1$; **Roosevelt**$_1$)

OCTOBER (18)19–
30   Moscow Conference, involving governmental representatives of the three Allied powers. Soviets agree to enter war against Japan after defeat of Germany (See **Eden**$_1$; **Molotov**$_2$)

30   Four Power Declaration on General Security issued in Moscow, calling for an international organization to foster principle of "sovereign equality of all peace-loving states"

NOVEMBER 22–26   **Roosevelt**$_1$, **Churchill**$_1$, and **Chiang Kai-shek**$_2$ meet at the Cairo Conference to discuss war aims in the Far East and surrender terms for Japan

28–12/1   **Roosevelt**$_1$, **Churchill**$_1$, and **Stalin**$_2$ meet at Tehran to discuss Allied invasion of France and Soviet entry into the war against Japan

1944

JUNE 6   Allied forces land on the beaches of Normandy, beginning invasion of Europe

JULY 1–22	Delegations from forty-four nations meet at **Bretton Woods**$_3$, New Hampshire, to design the structure of the postwar world economy. The International Monetary Fund and the World Bank are established
26	General **Charles de Gaulle**$_1$ leads the Free French forces in a victory march down the Champs-Elysées (See **Acheson**$_1$; **Mendès-France**$_1$)
AUGUST	Morgenthau Plan on policy toward Germany, recommending dismantling of German industrial facilities, is prepared (See **Henry Morgenthau, Jr.**$_1$)
21–10/7	Dumbarton Oaks Conference lays foundation for **United Nations**$_3$
SEPTEMBER 11–16	Second Quebec Conference, at which **Roosevelt**$_1$ and **Churchill**$_1$ discuss strategy for ending war
DECEMBER 2–9	**De Gaulle**$_1$ visits Moscow and signs a Franco-Soviet treaty

1945

JANUARY 11	The **Red Army**$_3$ captures Warsaw (See **Gomulka**$_2$; **Stalin**$_2$)
FEBRUARY 4–11	**Roosevelt**$_1$, **Churchill**$_1$, and **Stalin**$_2$ meet at Yalta to discuss terms of German surrender, Soviet participation in the war against Japan, and the boundaries and governments of Eastern European countries (See **Yalta Conference**$_3$)
MARCH 6	Petru Groza forms a communist-dominated government in Romania (See **Gheorghiu-Dej**$_2$)
12	The Soviet Union transfers northern Transylvania from Hungary to Romania
APRIL 12	**Roosevelt**$_1$ dies and is succeeded as U.S. president by **Harry S Truman**$_1$
13	The **Red Army**$_3$ captures Vienna
21	The Soviet Union and the Polish provisional government (the "Lublin Group") sign a twenty-year Treaty of Mutual Assistance
23	**Truman**$_1$ meets Soviet foreign minister **Vyacheslav Michailovich Molotov**$_2$ at the White House. Truman sharply criticizes Soviet behavior in Poland. "I have never been talked to like that in my life," Molotov protested. "Carry out your agreements and you won't get talked to like that," Truman replied
25–6/26	San Francisco Conference: delegates from fifty nations creates the **United Nations**$_3$
30	Adolph Hitler commits suicide
MAY 7	Nazi Germany unconditionally surrenders to Allies, ending war in Europe and Africa. The surrender is ratified by the German government on 9 May
JUNE 29	In a prelude to alliance with Soviets, Czechoslovakia cedes Ruthenia to the Soviet Union
JULY 5	The United States extends recognition to the Polish provisional government
16	The first atomic bomb is exploded successfully at the Alamogordo test site in New Mexico (See **Manhattan Project**$_3$; **Oppenheimer**$_1$; **Teller**$_1$)
17–8/2	**Truman**$_1$, **Churchill**$_1$, and **Stalin**$_2$ meet at Potsdam to discuss the implementation of agreements reached among the Allies during the war and the terms of Japan's surrender (See **Potsdam Conference**$_3$)
15	Marshal Pétain, head of the collaborationist Vichy government, is sentenced to death by the French supreme court. His sentence is later commuted to life in prison, where he dies on 23 July 1951
26	**Churchill**$_1$ is defeated in the British general elections

AUGUST 2	Labour party leader **Clement Attlee**$_1$ becomes Great Britain's prime minister
6	The first atomic bomb is dropped on Hiroshima
9	The second atomic bomb is dropped on Nagasaki
14	Japan announces its unconditional surrender to the Allies, ending World War II (See **Truman**$_1$)
21	Lend-Lease is terminated
SEPTEMBER 2	Japan formally surrenders to General **Douglas A. MacArthur**$_1$ aboard the USS *Missouri*
8	U.S. troops move into South Korea (See **MacArthur**$_1$)
NOVEMBER 4	The largest independent political party, the Smallholders, wins a majority, 245 of 409 seats, in general elections in Hungary (See **Kádár**$_2$; **Rákosi**$_2$)
18	The Communist party wins communist-controlled elections in Bulgaria (See **Dimitrov**$_2$; **Zhivkov**$_2$)
20–10/1/46	International military tribunal at Nuremberg conducts war crimes trials
29	The Yugoslav assembly, elected 11 November, proclaims the establishment of the Federal People's Republic of Yugoslavia, declaring Marshal **Josip Broz Tito**$_2$ prime minister

1946

JANUARY–APRIL	Iran crisis prompted by Soviet attempt to create an "autonomous" Azerbaijani republic that includes parts of Iran. A military confrontation between United States and Soviet Union threatened (See **Acheson**$_1$; **Truman**$_1$)
FEBRUARY 9	**Stalin**$_2$ makes the "Two Camps" speech, declaring impossibility of Soviet coexistence with the West
22	**George F. Kennan**$_1$ transmits the **"Long Telegram"**$_3$ to **Truman**$_1$, interpreting Soviet foreign-policy objectives (See **Containment**$_3$; **Forrestal**$_1$)
MARCH 5	**Churchill**$_1$ makes the **"Iron Curtain" Speech**$_3$ at Westminster College in Fulton, Missouri
28	**Acheson-Lilienthal Plan**$_3$, calling for international control of atomic energy, released
JUNE 3–11/12/48	Japanese war crimes trials
14	**Bernard Baruch**$_1$ presents the American proposal (the **Baruch Plan**$_3$) for the international control of nuclear material and the destruction of nuclear arsenals to the first meeting of the U.S. Atomic Energy Commission
JULY 4	Philippines gains independence from the United States (See **MacArthur**$_1$)
SEPTEMBER 8	Bulgaria abolishes the monarchy and declares itself the Republic of Bulgaria (See **Dimitrov**$_2$; **Zhivkov**$_2$)
30	Twenty-two former high Nazi officials are found guilty of war crimes by an international tribunal at Nuremberg
NOVEMBER 19	The Communist party wins a communist-controlled election in Romania (See **Gheorghiu-Dej**$_2$)
23	French forces bomb Haiphong as the first military move to retain control of colonies in Indochina (See **Mendès-France**$_1$)

DECEMBER 2	The United States and Great Britain agree to "Bizona," an economic merger of their zones of occupations in Germany (See **Adenauer**$_1$; **Erhard**$_1$; **McCloy**$_1$)

1947

JANUARY 19	The Communist party wins a communist-controlled election in Poland (See **Bierut**$_2$; **Gomulka**$_2$)
FEBRUARY 1	Hungary abolishes the monarchy and declares itself a republic (See **Kádár**$_2$; **Rákosi**$_2$)
10	Peace treaties are signed between United States and Axis nations of Finland, Italy, Bulgaria, Hungary, and Romania
MARCH 4	Great Britain and France sign the Anglo-French Fifty Years Treaty of Alliance
12	**Truman**$_1$ announces the **Truman Doctrine**$_3$, which declares that the United States will support "free peoples who are resisting subjugation by armed minorities or by outside pressures"; he requests $400 million in economic and military aid to Greece and Turkey (See **Acheson**$_1$; **Containment**$_3$)
22	**Truman**$_1$ bans communists from serving in the United States government (See **McCarthyism**$_3$)
25	Senator Claude Pepper (D-Florida) attacks the **Truman Doctrine**$_3$ as leading to a conflict with the Soviet Union
30	**Americans for Democratic Action**$_3$ (ADA) announces its support for the **Truman Doctrine**$_3$ (See **Arthur M. Schlesinger, Jr.**$_1$)
31	Former vice-president **Henry A. Wallace**$_1$ charges that the United States wants war with the Soviet Union for Middle East oil
APRIL 7	**De Gaulle**$_1$ declares that Europe must stay out of the Soviet-American rivalry
9	**Wallace**$_1$ attacks **Truman's**$_1$ foreign policy
14	**De Gaulle**$_1$ announces he will reenter French politics as the head of a new party
MAY 13	**Dean G. Acheson**$_1$ resigns as under secretary of state and is replaced by **Robert A. Lovett**$_1$
22	**Truman**$_1$ signs the Greek-Turkish aid bill
31	**Truman**$_1$ signs foreign-aid bill for Europe, Asia
JUNE 5	Secretary of State **George C. Marshall**$_1$, at a Harvard commencement address, announces the **Marshall Plan**$_3$, proposing economic assistance to democracies of Europe to preserve freedom
13	Senator **Arthur H. Vandenberg**$_1$ (R-Michigan), chairman of the Senate Foreign Relations Committee, urges the creation of a bipartisan committee to advise the president and Congress on European reconstruction
16	**Wallace**$_1$ announces his willingness to form a third U.S. political party
27	**Molotov**$_2$, the Soviet foreign minister, discusses with France and Great Britain the possibility of the Soviet Union getting **Marshall Plan**$_1$ economic aid
JULY	The **"X" Article**$_3$, "The Sources of Soviet Conduct," written by **Kennan**$_1$, appears in *Foreign Affairs;* it recommends U.S. **Containment**$_3$ of the Soviet Union (See **Council on Foreign Relations**$_3$)
2	The Soviet delegation walks out of the **Marshall Plan**$_3$ meeting in Paris
3	France and Great Britain invite twenty-two countries to Paris for talks on the **Marshall Plan**$_3$
12	**Marshall Plan**$_3$ conference opens in Paris. The conference is boycotted by Eastern European countries

15	The Morgenthau Plan for the future of Germany is rescinded (See **Henry Morgenthau, Jr.**[1])
26	**National Security Act**[3] passed by Congress, creating the **Central Intelligence Agency**[3] and the **National Security Council**[3] (See **Clifford**[1]; **Forrestal**[1])
26	**James V. Forrestal**[1] is named the first secretary of defense

AUGUST 10	The United States releases the last of the 8 million German prisoners of war
15	India becomes independent. Great Britain continues to rule the Muslim areas of the subcontinent (See **Attlee**[1]). These areas become the Republic of Pakistan in March 1956
31	The communist-led coalition wins a majority of seats, 271 of 411, in semi-communist-controlled elections in Hungary (See **Kádár**[2]; **Rákosi**[2])

SEPTEMBER 2	Inter-American Treaty of Reciprocal Assistance is signed at Rio de Janeiro between the United States and Latin American states
11	**Wallace**[1] again urges the creation of a third U.S. political party for the 1948 general elections

OCTOBER 2	Columnist **Walter Lippmann**[1] concludes his anti–Cold War/anticontainment series of columns, in which he criticized **Kennan**'s[1] notion of **"Containment"**[3]
15	A draft-Eisenhower league is formed to encourage the selection of **Dwight D. Eisenhower**[1] as the Republican candidate for president (See **Nixon**[1])
23	**Ronald W. Reagan**[1] testifies before the House Un-American Activities Committee (HUAC) on communist influence in Hollywood
24	Senator **Robert A. Taft**[1] (R-Ohio) announces his candidacy for the Republican nomination for the 1948 presidential campaign (See **Nixon**[1])
30	Brigadier General Leslie Groves, who directed the **Manhattan Project**[3], testifies that the Soviet Union will need twenty years for the development of its own atomic bomb
30	General Agreement on Tariffs and Trade (GATT), a joint agreement among various nations and the first international trade agreement after World War II, announced in Geneva

NOVEMBER 4	**Lippmann**[1] writes that the Soviet Union had lost the Cold War
15	The Chinese Nationalists, led by **Chiang**[2], ask the United States for $3 billion in aid
21	General Omar N. Bradley replaces **Eisenhower**[1] as army chief of staff
24	Maurice Schuman forms the French cabinet without the communists or Gaullists

DECEMBER 4	Bulgaria alters its name to the People's Republic of Bulgaria (See **Dimitrov**[2]; **Zhivkov**[2])
5	The Communist Information Bureau (**Cominform**[3]) is founded
15	The Progressive Citizens of America attempts to place **Wallace**[1] on third-party ticket in the 1948 presidential elections
17	General Albert C. Wedemeyer, commander of U.S. forces in China, urges increasing United States aid to the Chinese nationalists (See **Chiang**[2]; **Mao**[2])
20	Senator **Taft**[1] attacks the European Recovery Programs
29	**Wallace**[1] launches his 1948 presidential campaign
30	King Michael of Romania abdicates, and the People's Republic of Romania is established (See **Gheorghiu-Dej**[2])
30	**Wallace**[1] calls the **Marshall Plan**[3] "insane"

1948

JANUARY 1	The General Agreement on Tariffs and Trade, negotiated during 1947, takes effect, lowering the trade barriers among the signatory states
6	The American Federation of Labor (AFL) condemns **Wallace**'s[1] presidential effort
16	New York governor Thomas E. Dewey enters the Republican presidential race

22	British foreign minister **Ernest Bevin**[1] announces Great Britain will abandon traditional balance-of-power foreign policy (See **Attlee**[1])
23	**Eisenhower**[1] declares he will not be a presidential candidate in the 1948 elections
25	A **MacArthur**[1] for President campaign is started in Wisconsin
28	Bradley formally becomes the new army chief of staff
30	Mohandas Karamchand Gandhi is assassinated in India by a Hindu nationalist

FEBRUARY 25   A bloodless communist coup takes place in Czechoslovakia, and President Edvard Beneš is forced to nominate **Klement Gottwald**[2] as president (See **Slánsky**)

MARCH 4	King Michael of Romania repudiates abdication
9	Dewey defeats Harold E. Stassen in the New Hampshire Republican primary
10	Czech foreign minister Jan Masaryk dies in fall from a Czech Foreign Ministry window (See **Gottwald**[2])
17	Great Britain, France, Belgium, the Netherlands, and Luxemburg sign the Brussels Treaty for collective defense, precursor of the Western European Union (WEU) and the **North Atlantic Treaty Organization**[3] (NATO)
19	**Marshall**[1] threatens to deny Italy aid if the Communist party wins that country's elections
20	The Soviet Union accuses Yugoslavia of deviating from party discipline (See **Tito**[2])
30	The Soviet Union announces the Berlin Blockade (See **Berlin Crisis, 1948**[3]; **Stalin**[2])
30–5/2	Bogota Conference creates the **Organization of American States**[3]

APRIL 1	The supply operation to Berlin begins (See **Berlin Crisis, 1948**[3])
6	**MacArthur**[1] is defeated in the Wisconsin Republican primary
30	**Organization of American States**[3] charter is adopted

MAY 2	**Eisenhower**[1] reenters the army
14	Israel proclaims its statehood (See **Ben-Gurion**[2])
15	Seven Arab states invade Israel (See **Ben-Gurion**[2]; **Nasser**[2])
26	The Afrikaner-based National party wins elections in South Africa

JUNE 7	The United States, Great Britain, and France recommend the creation of a West German state (See **Adenauer**[1]; **Federal Republic of Germany**[3]; **Schumacher**[1]; **Stalin**[2]; **Truman**[1])
11	By a 64 to 4 vote the Senate passes the Vandenberg Resolution, which approves U.S. involvement in regional defense organizations and leads to American involvement in the **North Atlantic Treaty Organization**[3])
18	Currency reforms are implemented in the American, British, and French zones of occupation in Germany
24	The Soviet Union blockades land access to Berlin (See **Erhard**[1]; **Stalin**[2])
28	Yugoslavia is expelled from the **Cominform**[3] (See **Stalin**[2], **Tito**[2])
30	British forces leave Palestine

July 15	The Democrats nominate **Truman**[1] for president
24	The Progressive party nominates **Wallace**[1] for president
30	The Big Four meet in Moscow to discuss Berlin (See **Berlin Crisis, 1948**[3])

AUGUST 3	**Whittaker Chambers**[1] testifies before the House Un-American Activities Committee, naming **Alger Hiss**[1] as a Soviet spy
5	**Hiss**[1] denies knowing **Chambers**[1]
15	The Republic of Korea (South) is established (See **Rhee**[2])
17	**Hiss**[1] and **Chambers**[1] confront each other before the House Un-American Activities Committee (See **Nixon**[1])
30	Peacetime draft registration begins in the United States

SEPTEMBER 9 The Democratic People's Republic of Korea (North) is established (See **Kim**$_2$)
20 **Curtis LeMay**$_1$ is named head of the **Strategic Air Command**$_3$

OCTOBER 9 **Churchill**$_1$ calls for greater Western assertiveness on Berlin while the West still retains nuclear monopoly
27 The Voice of America is established by Congress to broadcast anticommunist radio programs to Iron Curtain countries

NOVEMBER 2 **Truman**$_1$ is reelected president, defeating the Republican Dewey and Progressive **Wallace**$_1$

DECEMBER 2 **Chambers**$_1$ reveals the existence of the "Pumpkin Papers" – microfilms and copies of secret State Department documents allegedly given to him by **Hiss**$_1$ and which Chambers kept inside a hollow pumpkin on his Maryland farm (See **Nixon**$_1$)
15 **Hiss**$_1$ is indicted by a U.S. grand jury on two counts of perjury
27 Hungarian **Józef, Cardinal Mindszenty**$_2$, is arrested for criticizing the communist regime
29 **Forrestal**$_1$ supports the peacetime draft in the United States (See **Clifford**$_1$)

1949

JANUARY 5 **Truman**$_1$ introduces the Fair Deal, his political agenda
7 U.S. secretary of state **Marshall**$_1$ resigns
13 Chinese communists shell Beijing for the first time in the Chinese civil war (See **Lin**$_2$, **Mao**$_2$)
18 The Soviet Union rejects the Chinese Nationalists' appeal for Big Four mediation in China (See **Chiang**$_2$; **Stalin**$_2$)
19 American and British labor unions withdraw from the World Federation of Trade Unions, accusing the organization of being a communist front (See **AFL-CIO**$_3$; **Congress for Cultural Freedom**$_3$; **Lasky**$_1$)
21 Polish leader **Wladyslaw Gomulka**$_2$ is demoted after being accused of deviating from the party line
*22 (18?) The communist satellite organization, Council for Mutual Economic Assistance (CMEA, also known as COMECON), is established
27 The Greek communists agree to negotiate with government forces if a cease-fire is announced
30 **Stalin**$_2$ announces his willingness to negotiate with **Truman**$_1$ over Berlin (See **Berlin Crisis, 1948**$_3$)

FEBRUARY 2 **Acheson**$_1$ rejects **Stalin's**$_2$ Berlin offer (See **Berlin Crisis, 1948**$_3$)
3 **Mindszenty's**$_2$ trial in Hungary starts
8 Congressmen Karl Mundt (R-South Dakota) and **Richard M. Nixon**$_1$ (R-California) introduce the Mundt-Nixon bill to register communists
15 The WEU meets to fashion a common defense for Western Europe (See **Bevin**$_1$; **North Atlantic Treaty Organization**$_3$)
15 **Acheson**$_1$ refuses new aid to the Chinese Nationalists (See **Chiang**$_2$; **China Lobby**$_3$)
23 The **National Security Council**$_3$ announces its plan to study communist subversion in the United States

APRIL 2 Peace talks begin between the warring factions in China (See **Mao**$_2$; **Marshall**$_1$)
4 Belgium, Canada, Denmark, France, Great Britain, Iceland, Italy, Luxembourg, the Netherlands, Norway, Portugal, and the United States sign the North Atlantic Treaty (See **North Atlantic Treaty Organization**$_3$)

5 Acheson says the United States will arm the **North Atlantic Treaty Organization**$_3$ (NATO)

18 The Republic of Ireland is established

MAY 2 Chinese Nationalist leader **Chiang**$_2$ flees to Formosa (Taiwan)

5 China and North Korea sign a mutual defense treaty

5 Wallace testifies against **North Atlantic Treaty Organization**$_3$

5 The **Federal Republic of Germany** (FRG)$_3$ (West Germany) is established (See **Adenauer**$_1$; **Erhard**$_1$)

12 The Berlin Blockade ends; U.S. airlift continues until 30 September (See **Berlin Crisis, 1948**$_3$)

18 **John J. McCloy**$_1$ is named the first civilian high commissioner in Germany

22 **Forrestal**$_1$ kills himself by jumping out of a window at the Bethesda Naval Hospital

23 The West German constitution takes effect

30 The Soviet ambassador to the United Nations, **Andrei Vyshinsky**$_2$, rejects Western proposal for German reunification (See **Gromyko**$_2$)

30 The German Democratic Republic (East Germany) declares its statehood (See **Ulbricht**$_2$)

31 **Hiss**$_1$ perjury trial opens in New York

JUNE 3 **Chambers**$_1$ admits his own perjury

8 Frank Sinatra, Lillian Hellman, and Charlie Chaplin are accused of being communists

16 **Truman**$_1$ attacks anticommunist hysteria in the United States (See **McCarthy**$_1$; **McCarthyism**$_3$)

19 Communist leader **Mao Zedong**$_2$ declares victory in the Chinese civil war

21 The CIA Act is signed into law (See **Central Intelligence Agency**$_3$; **Clifford**$_1$; **Allen Dulles**$_1$)

29 U.S. occupation forces are withdrawn from South Korea (See **Rhee**$_2$)

JULY 8 Mistrial is declared in **Hiss**$_1$ trial as a result of hung jury

10 The Soviet Union explodes its first atomic bomb (See **Nuclear Proliferation**$_3$)

13 The pope excommunicates communists

21 The Senate ratifies **North Atlantic Treaty Organization**$_3$ treaty

AUGUST 5 The State Department issues a white paper explaining the loss of China (See **Acheson**$_1$)

11 General Omar Bradley is named first chairman of the Joint Chiefs of Staff (See **National Security Act**$_3$)

14 The Christian Democratic Union (CDU) wins West German elections but needs a coalition partner to form a government (See **Adenauer**$_1$)

20 The Soviet Union threatens to invade Yugoslavia (See **Tito**$_2$)

24 The **North Atlantic Treaty Organization**$_3$ treaty takes effect

SEPTEMBER 12 Theodor Heuss nominated first president of West Germany

21 **Mao**$_2$ proclaims China a people's republic

24 **De Gaulle**$_1$ says that France needs its own nuclear weapons

25 The Soviet Union announces the test of its first atomic bomb

OCTOBER 1 The People's Republic of China is established. **Zhou En lai**$_2$ named head of Chinese government. The Chinese announce their desire for diplomatic relations with the Soviet Union

NOVEMBER 6 **John Foster Dulles**$_1$ is defeated as the Republican candidate in New York Senate race

10 **Vyshinsky**$_2$ says that Soviet nuclear weapons will serve peaceful purposes only

14 **Gomulka**$_2$ is expelled from the Polish Communist party

17 The second **Hiss**$_1$ perjury trial opens in New York

DECEMBER 5   The West German chancellor, **Konrad Adenauer**$_1$, says West Germany will rearm if necessary (See **North Atlantic Treaty Organization**$_3$)

8   The Chinese Nationalists abandon the mainland completely, flee to Formosa (See **Chiang**$_2$; **China Lobby**$_3$)

14   Israel transfers the capital from Tel Aviv to Jerusalem (See **Ben-Gurion**$_2$)

16   **Paul H. Nitze**$_1$ replaces **Kennan**$_1$ as director of the State Department's policy-planning staff

18   **Nikita S. Khrushchev**$_2$ is appointed to the Central Committee of the Communist party, Soviet Union

30   The United States decides not to use American troops to defend Taiwan

1950

JANUARY   The United States releases $1 billion in military aid to Western Europe (See **Marshall Plan**$_3$)

11   The United States approves plan to aid **Tito**$_2$ if Yugoslavia is attacked by pro-Soviet Eastern European armies

21   **Hiss**$_1$ is convicted on two counts of perjury in his second trial

23   Jawaharlal Nehru is elected premier of India

23   The Israeli Knesset (parliament) declares Jerusalem the capital of the State of Israel

31   **Truman**$_1$ orders the development of the hydrogen bomb (See **Oppenheimer**$_1$; **Teller**$_1$)

FEBRUARY 1   The Soviet Union demands that Japanese emperor Hirohito be put on trial for war crimes

3   Physicist **Klaus Fuchs**$_1$ is arrested in London for spying for the Soviet Union

9   Senator **Joseph R. McCarthy**$_1$ (R-Wisconsin), in a speech to the Ohio County Women's Republican Club in Wheeling, West Virginia, charges that communists have infiltrated the State Department

10   **Fuchs**$_1$ admits to spying

14   The Soviet Union and the People's Republic of China sign a friendship treaty (See **Mao**$_2$)

16   **Acheson**$_1$ says Cold War requires that the United States aid nondemocratic countries

26   **Wallace's**$_1$ Progressive party holds its convention in Chicago

MARCH 1   **Chiang**$_2$ reclaims Nationalist China's presidency and establishes the Republic of China on Taiwan

1   **Fuchs**$_1$ is sentenced to a fourteen-year prison term

3   France-controlled Saar customs union is formed

8   The Soviet Union announces the successful development of an atomic bomb

9   West Germany calls for a plebiscite regarding the Saar question

15   Poland withdraws from the International Monetary Fund (IMF)

21   Right-wing senators call **Acheson**$_1$ a "security risk"

APRIL 7   The National Security Council produces **National Security Council Memorandum (NSC)-68**$_3$ (See **Containment**$_3$; **Nitze**$_1$)

27   **Tito**$_2$ is reelected premier of Yugoslavia

27   Former president Herbert Hoover states that there should be no communists in the **United Nations**$_3$

MAY 1   The biggest ever May Day parade in Moscow

4   The Soviet Union announces that all German prisoners of war have returned to Germany; West German leader **Kurt Schumacher**$_1$ accuses the Soviets of lying

8 **Truman**[1] orders the establishment of an American military mission in Vietnam (See **Vietnam War**[3])

10 Congressman **Nixon**[1] defends patriotism of physicist **J. Robert Oppenheimer**[1] before HUAC (See **McCarthyism**[3]; **Teller**[1])

19 Great Britain ends most of World War II food rationing (See **Attlee**[1])

JUNE 7 East Germany recognizes the Oder-Neisse border with Poland (See **Ulbricht**[2])

14 Columnist Stewart Alsop predicts an anticommunist revolt in Eastern Europe if the West invades to expel the **Red Army**[3]

15 West Germany enters the Council of Europe

25 North Korea invades South Korea (See **Korean War**[3])

27 UN Security Council approves military aid to South Korea, establishing a fifteen-nation UN force

30 U.S. troops enter **Korean War**[3]

JULY 8 **MacArthur**[1] named commander of UN forces in Korea

17 **Julius Rosenberg**[1] is arrested for spying for the Soviet Union

AUGUST 11 **Ethel Rosenberg**[1] is arrested

23 **Adenauer**[1] and **Schumacher**[1] urge more U.S. troops in West Germany

27 **Truman**[1] forces **MacArthur**[1] to withdraw statements the general made to a Veterans of Foreign Wars convention

SEPTEMBER 9 **Truman**[1] announces plan to raise number of U.S. troops in Europe

12 U.S. secretary of defense Louis Johnson resigns

15 **MacArthur's**[1] forces land at Inchon (See **Korean War**[3])

21 **Marshall**[1] named U.S. secretary of defense

30 **Truman**[1] approves **NSC-68**[3] (See **Nitze**[1])

OCTOBER 1 **MacArthur**[1] drives North Koreans out of South Korea (See **Korean War**[3])

20 **Henry L. Stimson**[1] dies

24 American forces in Korea reach the Yalu River (See **Korean War**[3])

NOVEMBER 1 People's Republic of China enters the **Korean War**[3] on side of North Korea

4 UN forces in Korea are forced into retreat

7 **Nixon**[1] is elected to the U.S. Senate, defeating Helen Gehagen Douglas

17 The U.S. Joint Chiefs of Staff urge West German rearmament (See **Adenauer**[1]; **North Atlantic Treaty Organization**[3])

28 East Germany and Poland formally accept the Oder-Neisse line as border

DECEMBER 10 **Truman**[1] declares state of national emergency because of the **Korean War**[3]

1951

JANUARY 1 France grants the Saar independence

5 Senator **Taft**[1] says the presence of American troops in Korea violates the Constitution

10 **Marshall**[1] recommends universal military service in the United States

FEBRUARY 15 Great Britain nationalizes the steel and iron industries

MARCH 6 The **Rosenbergs'**[1] spy trial starts

19 The European Coal and Steel Community is established (See **Monnet**[1])

29 The **Rosenbergs**[1] are convicted

APRIL 5	The **Rosenbergs**[1] are condemned to death
11	**Truman**[1] fires **MacArthur**[1] for insubordination
14	British foreign minister **Bevin**[1] dies
18	Senator **Vandenberg**[1] dies
19	**MacArthur**[1] delivers his farewell address to Congress, declaring, "Old soldiers never die, they just fade away."
MAY 3	Hearings on **MacArthur's**[1] dismissal open in the Senate
JUNE 21	UN troops push the communist forces out of South Korea (See **Korean War**[3])
25	The Senate concludes the **MacArthur**[1] hearings
27	The State Department suspends China experts O. Edmund Clubb and John Paton Davies, Jr., on security charges (See **McCarthy**[1]; **McCarthyism**[3])
JULY 9	**Adenauer**[1] urges the creation of a West German army
10	Truce talks start in Korea (See **Korean War**[3])
30	"China hand" Davies – U.S. State Department adviser on Chinese affairs – is cleared of security charges against him
AUGUST 9	Senator **Joseph McCarthy**[1] charges twenty-nine State Department employees with disloyalty
23	**Allen Dulles**[1] is named deputy director of the **Central Intelligence Agency**[3]
SEPTEMBER 1	The United States, Australia, and New Zealand sign the ANZUS treaty (See **John Foster Dulles**[1])
8	The war with Japan formally ends with a treaty between Japan and forty-nine other states; the United States and Japan sign a mutual security pact
12	**Marshall**[1] resigns as U.S. secretary of defense
17	**Lovett**[1] named secretary of defense
OCTOBER 16	Senator **Taft**[1] declares his candidacy for the 1952 elections
22	Turkey, Greece join **North Atlantic Treaty Organization**[3]
25	**Churchill**[1] wins general elections in Great Britain, replacing **Attlee**[1] as prime minister
NOVEMBER 11	**Reagan**[1] reelected president of the Screen Actors Guild
27	Cease-fire line established in Korea (See **Korean War**[3])

1952

JANUARY 7	**Eisenhower**[1] announces he will enter the Republican campaign for president
FEBRUARY 25	The **Rosenbergs'**[1] death penalty is upheld by the Court of Appeals
26	**Churchill**[1] announces Great Britain has developed an atomic bomb (See **Nuclear Proliferation**[3])
MARCH 10	The Soviet Union says it wants a German peace treaty
10	**Fulgencio Batista y Zaldívar**[2] seizes power in Cuba
20	Senator **Taft**[1] drops out of the Republican presidential race
29	**Truman**[1] drops out of the Democratic presidential race
APRIL 28	Peace treaty with Japan takes effect
30	**Tito**[2] says Yugoslavia will not join the **North Atlantic Treaty Organization**[3]

MAY 27   The European Defense Community (EDC) is proposed (See **Adenauer**[1]; **Mendès-France**[1])

JUNE 13   **Andrei Gromyko** is named Soviet ambassador to Great Britain

JULY 11   The Republicans nominate **Eisenhower**[1] and **Nixon**[1] as their presidential ticket

26   The Democrats nominate Governor **Adlai Stevenson**[1] of Illinois and Senator John Sparkman of Alabama as their presidential ticket

AUGUST 21   West German leader **Schumacher**[1] dies

OCTOBER 3   Great Britain tests its first atomic weapon

13   The Supreme Court refuses to review the **Rosenberg**[1] cases

24   **Eisenhower**[1] says he will go to Korea to seek peace

NOVEMBER 1   The United States explodes the first hydrogen bomb at a test site in the Marshall Islands (See **Teller**[1])

4   **Eisenhower**[1] defeats **Stevenson**[1] to win U.S. presidency

DECEMBER 2   **Eisenhower**[1] begins a visit to Korea

1953

JANUARY 8   Georges Bidault is named the new French foreign minister

20   **Eisenhower**[1] is inaugurated

24   **Allen Dulles**[1] is named the new **Central Intelligence Agency**[3] director

27   Secretary of State **John Foster Dulles**[1] promises a foreign policy of "righteousness"

MARCH 5   **Stalin**[1] dies of a stroke

6   **Georgi Malenkov**[2] is named the new Soviet premier (See **Khrushchev**[2])

APRIL 7   Big Four foreign minister's meeting (first in almost two years) in Berlin to discuss the status of Germany (See **John Foster Dulles**[1])

21   Roy M. Cohn and David Schine, Senator **McCarthy**'s[1] assistants, return from an investigation of United States Information Agency libraries in Europe

24   **MacArthur**[1] says the United States should attack China

MAY 14   Supreme Court for the second time refuses to hear the **Rosenbergs'**[1] case

JUNE 10   **Eisenhower**[1] rejects Senator **Taft's**[1] isolationism and "Fortress America" doctrine

18   Anticommunist rioting in East Germany; Soviet troops suppress the demonstrations (See **Ulbricht**[2])

19   The **Rosenbergs**[1] are executed

JULY 4   **Imre Nagy**[2] replaces **Mátyás Rákosi**[2] as Hungarian premier; declares a new course of liberalization

9   Senator **Joseph McCarthy**[1] accuses **Allen Dulles**[1] of blocking the investigation of William P. Bundy, a **Central Intelligence Agency**[3] intelligence analyst

24   **Walter Ulbricht**[2] ousts Wilhelm Zaisser, a member of the Politburo and minister of state security, from the East German government

27   P'anmunjon armistice agreement ends **Korean War**[3]

31   Senator **Taft**[1] dies

AUGUST 12	The Soviet Union announces the test of its first hydrogen bomb (See **Nuclear Proliferation**$_3$)
19	A U.S.-sponsored coup in Iran topples populist prime minister **Mohammad Mossadegh**$_2$
19	The populist **Mossadegh**$_2$ government in Iran is overthrown (See **Central Intelligence Agency**$_3$; **Allen Dulles**$_1$)
20	Senator **Joseph McCarthy**$_1$ says the United States should kill communist leaders if U.S. POWs are not returned
22	**Mohammad Reza Pahlevi**$_2$ returns to Tehran in triumph and is installed on the Peacock Throne
31	**Nixon**$_1$ says **Truman**'s$_1$ foreign policy was correct with regard to Korea
SEPTEMBER 13	**Khruschev**$_1$ becomes first secretary of Communist party, Soviet Union
OCTOBER 1	The United States and South Korea sign a mutual defense treaty (See **John Foster Dulles**$_1$, **New Look Policy**$_3$)
20	**Adenauer**$_1$ and the CDU win West German elections
30	**Marshall**$_1$ wins the Nobel Peace Prize
NOVEMBER 13	School textbook commission in Indiana asserts that Robin Hood stories spread communist ideas (See **McCarthyism**$_3$)
24	**John Foster Dulles**$_1$ agrees with **Nixon**$_1$ that Germany and Japan should not have been disarmed in 1946
DECEMBER 6	Prime Minister **David Ben-Gurion**$_2$ of Israel retires
10	**Ho Chi Minh**$_2$ offers to negotiate for peace with the French
16	The Soviet Union announces it will try former **KGB**$_3$-head Lavrenty P. Beria for treason
24	Beria is executed for treason (See **Khrushchev**$_2$)

1954

JANUARY 21	The United States launches the USS *Nautilus*, the first nuclear-powered submarine (See **Rickover**$_1$)
25	Big Four talks open in Berlin
29	The army begins an investigation of Senator **Joseph McCarthy**'s$_1$ assistant David Schine for special privileges he received while in the army
FEBRUARY 10	The West rejects Soviet foreign minister **Molotov**'s$_2$ plan for a fifty-year all-European security pact
10	**Eisenhower**$_1$ opposes American involvement in French Indochina (See **Dien Bien Phu**$_3$; **Vietnam War**$_3$)
18	Big Four Talks end inconclusively
18	**Joseph McCarthy**$_1$ attacks U.S. army for promoting communists (See **McCarthyism**$_1$)
24	Great Britain endorses West German rearmament (See **North Atlantic Treaty Organization**$_3$)
MARCH 1–28	Caracas Conference on policies to stop communism in Latin America
13	Vietminh forces start the attack at **Dien Bien Phu**$_3$ (See **Giap**$_2$; **Ho**$_3$; **Vietnam War**$_3$)
APRIL 5	**Eisenhower**$_1$ declares the United States will not be the first to use the hydrogen bomb (See **Atoms for Peace**$_3$)
7	**Eisenhower**$_1$ says a communist victory in Indochina would set off chain reaction of disaster for the free world (See **Domino Theory**$_3$)

12	**Atomic Energy Commission**$_3$ hearings on **Oppenheimer's**$_1$ political reliability (See **Teller**$_1$)
14	The army says **Joseph McCarthy**$_1$ tried to get Schine special treatment
22	Senator **Joseph McCarthy**$_1$ accuses Secretary of the Army Robert Stevens of communist sympathies; the Army-**McCarthy**$_1$ hearings open
26	Geneva Conference on Korea and Indochina opens

MAY 7	French forces at **Dien Bien Phu**$_3$ are overrun (See **Giap**$_2$; **Ho**$_2$)
8	French seek truce in Indochina

JUNE 9	Army counsel Joseph Welch accuses **Joseph McCarthy**$_1$ of cruelty
13	**Pierre Mendès-France**$_1$ named new French prime minister
17	Army-**McCarthy**$_1$ hearings end
26	**Nixon**$_1$ says **Truman**$_1$ was responsible for the loss of China
27	U.S.-sponsored coup topples leftist Guatemalan president **Jacobo Arbenz Guzmán**$_2$
29	The **Atomic Energy Commission**$_3$ reaffirms **Oppenheimer**$_1$ is a security risk

JULY 20	Geneva Accords divide Vietnam at the 17th parallel, creating North and South Vietnam (See **Ho**$_3$)
21	The French begin withdrawal from Indochina

AUGUST 2	The Senate votes to study the issue of censure for **Joseph McCarthy**$_1$
11	A formal cease-fire is announced in Indochina
30	The French National Assembly rejects French participation in the European Defense Community (See **Mendès-France**$_1$; **North Atlantic Treaty Organization**$_3$;)

SEPTEMBER 6–8	Southeast Asia Treaty Organization (SEATO) is established by the Manila Pact (See **John Foster Dulles**$_1$; **Containment**$_3$)
28–10/23	The Paris Conference on West European defense opens; Western European Union created (See **North Atlantic Treaty Organization**$_3$)
30	Tentative agreement is reached regarding West German military role in **North Atlantic Treaty Organization**$_3$

OCTOBER 6	**Molotov**$_2$ declares that a West German rearmament would make German unification impossible
7	The West German Bundestag approves the London Conference proposals to base British troops in Europe, especially West Germany, to prevent German expansionism (See **Adenauer**$_1$; **Eden**$_1$; **North Atlantic Treaty Organization**$_3$)
23	Paris agreements are signed: West Germany to become sovereign and to contribute twelve divisions to **North Atlantic Treaty Organization**$_3$ (See **Federal Republic of Germany**$_3$)

NOVEMBER 1	**Batista**$_2$ is reelected without opposition in Cuba
5	State Department dismisses China expert Davies (See **China Lobby**$_3$; **McCarthyism**$_3$)
27	**Hiss**$_1$ released from jail (See **Chambers**$_1$)

DECEMBER 2	The Senate votes to censure Senator **Joseph McCarthy**$_1$
2	Mutual defense treaty is signed between the United States and Nationalist China (See **Chiang**$_2$)

1955

JANUARY 12	Secretary of State **John Foster Dulles**$_1$ announces the doctrine of **Massive Retaliation**$_3$ (See **New Look Policy**$_3$; **NSC-68**$_3$)

15	The Soviet Union offers to normalize relations with West Germany if the latter foregoes rearmament
25	The Soviet Union formally ends World War II with Germany
FEBRUARY 8	**Malenkov**$_2$ resigns as Soviet premier and is replaced by Marshal **Nikolai Bulganin**$_2$ (See **Khrushchev**$_2$)
17	Great Britain announces its plan to build hydogen bomb (See **Nuclear Proliferation**$_3$)
21	**Ben-Gurion**$_2$ returns to the Israeli cabinet as defense minister
MARCH 21	The Soviet Union declares it will set up an East European military bloc if West Germany rearms (See **Federal Republic of Germany**$_3$; **Warsaw Pact**$_3$)
APRIL 1	The Senate ratifies the Paris pact, permitting West Germany's sovereignty, rearmament, and membership in **North Atlantic Treaty Organization**$_3$
5	**Churchill**$_1$ retires as Great Britain's prime minister
6	**Anthony Eden**$_1$ become Great Britain's new prime minister
7	**Harold Macmillan**$_1$ becomes the new British defense minister
7	**Eisenhower**$_1$ signs the Paris pact; West Germany enters **North Atlantic Treaty Organization**$_3$
17–24	In Bandung, Indonesia, twenty-nine underdeveloped nations create the **Non-Aligned Movement**$_3$
29	Military clashes begin between North and South Vietnam (See **Ho**$_2$; **Vietnam War**$_3$)
MAY 5	The Allied occupation of West Germany formally ends; FRG becomes sovereign
7	The Soviet Union cancels friendship treaties with Great Britain and France
9	West Germany formally joins **North Atlantic Treaty Organization**$_3$
14	The Soviet Union, Albania, Bulgaria, Czechoslovakia, East Germany, Hungary, Poland, and Romania create the **Warsaw Pact**$_3$
15	The United States, the Soviet Union, Great Britain, France, and Austria sign the Austrian State Treaty, which results in Soviet troops being withdrawn from Austria (See **Warsaw Pact**$_3$)
JULY 18–23	**Eisenhower**$_1$, **Bulganin**$_2$, **Khrushchev**$_2$, **Eden**$_1$, and Edgar Faure meet in the Big Four summit in Geneva (See **Geneva Summit**$_3$)
21	**Eisenhower**$_1$ announces his **"Open Skies"**$_3$ proposal to allow unlimited air reconnaissance for the purpose of verifying arms-control agreements
AUGUST 18	**Ben-Gurion**$_2$ is asked to form a new government in Israel
SEPTEMBER 9	**Adenauer**$_1$ begins talks with the Soviet Union about diplomatic relations between the two countries
13	The Soviet Union and West Germany announce the establishment of diplomatic relations and the repatriation of German POWs
20	The Soviet Union grants East Germany sovereignty and membership in the **Warsaw Pact**$_3$
OCTOBER 26	**Ngo Dinh Diem**$_2$ declares South Vietnam a republic and himself premier
NOVEMBER 21	Middle East Treaty Organization created (See **Baghdad Pact**$_3$; **John Foster Dulles**$_1$)
DECEMBER 18	West Germany wins Saar plebiscite (See **Adenauer**$_1$; **Federal Republic of Germany**$_3$)
29	**Khrushchev**$_2$ rejects **Eisenhower's**$_2$ **Open Skies**$_3$ proposal

1956

JANUARY 25	**Bulganin**$_2$ proposes a twenty-year United States–Soviet Union friendship treaty
26	The Soviet Union returns Porkkala Peninsula to Finland
FEBRUARY 14	**Khrushchev**$_2$ denounces **Stalin**$_2$ in a speech to the 20th Congress of the Communist party, Soviet Union
APRIL 16	The dissolution of the **Cominform**$_3$ is announced
JUNE 4	Voice of America broadcasts **Khrushchev**'s$_2$ "secret speech" (See **Khrushchev**$_2$)
28–30	Riots in Poznan, Poland; more than one hundred killed
AUGUST 16	**Stevenson**$_1$ is renominated by the Democrats as their candidate for the presidency
22	**Eisenhower**$_1$ is renominated by the Republicans
OCTOBER 19	The Soviet Union and Japan resume diplomatic relations
21	"Spring in October" revolution in Poland; **Gomulka**$_2$ becomes first secretary of Polish Communist party
23	The Hungarian revolt begins (See **Gerö**$_2$; **Kádár**$_2$; **Nagy**$_2$)
27	Fighting spreads in Hungary
29	Israel attacks Egyptian forces in the Sinai (See **Ben-Gurion**$_2$; **Nasser**$_2$)
30	**Nagy**$_2$ announces an end to one-party system in Hungary
31	**Nagy**$_2$ asks the Soviet Union to leave Hungary
31	British and French troops land in the Suez Canal zone (See **Ben-Gurion**$_2$; **Eden**$_1$; **Nasser**$_2$; **Suez Crisis**$_3$)
NOVEMBER 1	Hungary proclaims its neutrality and leaves the **Warsaw Pact** (See **Nagy**$_2$)
2	The Soviet army in Hungary moves to Budapest (See **Kádár**$_2$)
4	The Soviet Union invades Hungary and attacks Budapest; **János Kádár**$_2$ installed as Hungary's new premier
6	**Eisenhower**$_1$ wins reelection
7	Cease-fire takes effect in the Suez War (See **Ben-Gurion**$_2$; **Eden**$_1$; **Suez Crisis**$_3$)
8	Anti-Soviet fighting ends in Hungary (See **Kádár**$_2$)
15	UN peacekeeping force arrives in Egypt (See **Nasser**$_2$)
17	**Khrushchev**$_2$ proclaims the Soviet Union "will bury" the West
23	**Nagy**$_2$ is formally arrested by the Soviets
DECEMBER 22	The Soviet Union charges the United States with orchestrating the Hungarian revolt

1957

JANUARY 10	**Eden**$_1$ resigns as British prime minister and is replaced by **Macmillan**$_1$
15	**Gromyko**$_2$ becomes the Soviet foreign minister
FEBRUARY 13	The Senate Foreign Relations and Armed Services Committees refuse **Eisenhower**'s$_1$ request to send American troops to the Middle East (See **Eisenhower Doctrine**$_3$)
27	China announces the "let one hundred flowers bloom" campaign (See **Mao**$_2$)
MARCH 7	**Eisenhower Doctrine**$_3$ endorsed by a joint resolution of Congress
25	The Treaty of Rome establishes the **European Economic Community**$_3$ (EEC), to become effective 1 January 1958 (See **Monnet**$_1$)

APRIL 22

John Foster Dulles[1] says that the purpose of the Eisenhower administration's foreign policy is to "roll back" communism in Europe (See **Massive Retaliation**[3]; **New Look Policy**[3])

MAY 2   Senator **Joseph McCarthy**[1] dies

JUNE 3   **Llewellyn E. Thompson, Jr.,**[1] is confirmed as the new U.S. ambassador to the Soviet Union

17   The Supreme Court says **Acheson**[1] acted illegally in firing State Department "China hand" John S. Service in 1951 (See **China Lobby**[3]; **Luce**[1]; **McCarthyism**[3])

JULY 2   The United States proposes a ten-month nuclear weapons test ban

3   **Malenkov**[2], **Molotov**[2], Lazar Kaganovich, and Dmitri Shepilov (the "anti-party group") are removed from the Central Committee of the Communist party, Soviet Union, after a failed challenge to **Khrushchev's**[2] leadership

AUGUST 19   Neil McElroy is named U.S. secretary of defense

SEPTEMBER 3   China expert Service returns to the State Department

OCTOBER 5   The Soviet Union launches **Sputnik**[3]

30   **Ludwig Erhard**[1] is named West Germany's new vice-chancellor

1958

JANUARY 1   **Ben-Gurion**[2] agrees to form a new government in Israel

9   Soviet prime minister **Bulganin**[2] proposes a summit to include **North Atlantic Treaty Organization**[3], the **Warsaw Pact**[3], and neutral countries

10   **John Foster Dulles**[1] rejects **Bulganin's**[2] offer

27   **Kádár**[2] resigns as Hungarian premier

MARCH 27   **Khrushchev**[2] succeeds **Bulganin**[2] as Soviet premier; retains his position as first secretary of Communist party, Soviet Union

31   The Soviet Union proclaims a unilateral halt to nuclear weapons testing

MAY 3   Vice-president **Nixon**[1] is heckled while on an official visit to Buenos Aires

8   **Nixon**[1] is pelted with fruit in Lima

13   **Nixon's**[1] motorcade is attacked by mob in Caracas

18   The liberal anticommunist **Americans for Democratic Action**[3] urges U.S. recognition of China (See **China Lobby**[3])

JUNE 2   The French National Assembly gives **de Gaulle**[1] power to rule by decree for six months

4   **De Gaulle**[1], on a visit to Algeria, tells the French settlers: "Je vous ai compris!"

17   Hungarians announce that former premier **Nagy**[2] has been executed for his role in the 1956 revolt

JULY 15   **Eisenhower**[1] orders the landing of marines in Lebanon (See **John Foster Dulles**[1]; **Eisenhower Doctrine**[3])

SEPTEMBER 28   A new constitution is adopted in France by a referendum, in which 80 percent vote "yes"

OCTOBER 3	The Soviet Union resumes nuclear testing after the United States and Great Britain refuse ban
DECEMBER 13	**De Gaulle**[1] formally announces for the presidency of the Fifth Republic
17	**Mao**[2] retires as head of China's government
18	**Bulganin**[2] "confesses" to his role in the anti-**Khrushchev**[2] move of 1957 (See **Malenkov**[2])
21	**De Gaulle**[1] is elected first president of the Fifth Republic

1959

JANUARY 1	**Batista**[2] resigns as premier of Cuba and flees the country
2	**Fidel Castro Ruz**[2] takes over in Havana
8	**De Gaulle**[1] is installed as French head of state. The Fifth Republic is established
15 & 25–27	Washington, D.C., and Camp David summit conference between **Eisenhower**[1] and **Khrushchev**[2]
30	**J. William Fulbright**[1] (D-Arkansas) becomes chairman of the Senate Foreign Relations Committee
FEBRUARY 16	**Fidel Castro Ruz**[2] sworn in as premier of Cuba
MARCH	Central Treaty Organization (CENTO) is established (See **Baghdad Pact**[3])
APRIL 9	The Inter-American Development Bank is chartered
15	**John Foster Dulles**[1], ailing with cancer, resigns as secretary of state
18	**Eisenhower**[1] names **Christian A. Herter**[1] secretary of state
MAY 24	**John Foster Dulles**[1] dies
JULY 5	The Saar is reintegrated into West Germany (See **Adenauer**[1]; **Federal Republic of Germany**[3])
SEPTEMBER 17	**Khrushchev**[2] arrives in the United States for talks
19	**Khrushchev**[2] refuses to visit Disneyland
NOVEMBER 3	**De Gaulle**[1] declares France will withdraw from **North Atlantic Treaty Organization**[3] military command
DECEMBER 1	Thomas Gates is named secretary of defense

1960

JANUARY 1	**Khrushchev**[2] announces the Soviet Union will cut the number of conventional troops even if arms-limitation talks with the United States fail
2	Senator **John F. Kennedy**[1] (D-Massachusetts) declares his candidacy for the presidency
3	**Khrushchev**[2] says the Soviet Union still wants a nuclear test ban treaty
10	Secretary of the Army Brucker pledges American defense of the islands of Quemoy and Matsu
FEBRUARY 8	**Nixon**[1] and **Kennedy**[1] win the New Hampshire primaries of their parties
13	France explodes a nuclear device (See **Nuclear Proliferation**[3])
15	**Syngman Rhee**[2] is reelected for a fourth term in South Korea
27	**De Gaulle**[1] says France will give up its nuclear weapons if other countries will

APRIL 5	**Kennedy**[1] defeats Senator **Hubert H. Humphrey**[1] (D-Minnesota) in the Wisconsin primary and becomes the Democratic front-runner
27	**Rhee**[2] resigns the presidency of the Republic of Korea after popular unrest
MAY 1	An American U-2 reconnaissance plane is shot down over the Soviet Union (See **Powers**[1]; **U-2 Affair**[3])
5	**Khrushchev**[2] announces the downing of the U-2 (See **U-2 Affair**[3])
6	The United States claims the U-2 was on a weather research mission (See **Eisenhower**[1])
7	The United States admits that the U-2 was on a spying mission (See **U-2 Affair**[3])
10	Senator **Humphrey**[1] quits the Democratic race
16	Summit talks in Paris between **Eisenhower**[1], **Khrushchev**[2], **Macmillan**[1], and **de Gaulle**[1] break off after **Khrushchev**[2] demands a U.S. apology for the **U-2 affair**[3]
JUNE 14	**De Gaulle**[1] publicly talks about "l'Algéri algérienne" and invites Algerian nationalist rebels for talks (See **Ben Bella**[2]; **Boumédienne**[2])
JULY 5	Senator **Lyndon B. Johnson**[1] (D-Texas) declares for the Democratic nomination for the presidency
13	**Kennedy**[1] is nominated the Democratic candidate for president
14	**Johnson**[1] is nominated the Democratic candidate for vice-president
27	**Nixon**[1] is nominated Republican candidate for president
AUGUST 17	U-2 pilot **Francis Gary Powers**[1] pleads guilty to espionage charges in a Soviet court (See **U-2 Affair**[3])
19	**Powers**[1] is sentenced to ten years in prison
24	The West Germany Social Democrats (SPD) nominate Berlin mayor **Willy Brandt**[1] to run against the CDU's **Adenauer**[1]
SEPTEMBER	**Organization of Petroleum Exporting Countries**[3] (OPEC) is established
OCTOBER 7	Second **Nixon**[1]-**Kennedy**[1] debate, dominated by the question of the islands of Quemoy and Matsu
10	**Truman**[1] says people who vote for **Nixon**[1] can go to hell
NOVEMBER 8	**John F. Kennedy**[1] elected U.S. president
11	Chester Bowles recommends a two-China policy; **John F. Kennedy**[1] disavows Bowles's comments
DECEMBER 12	Ford Foundation president **Dean Rusk**[1] is named secretary of state
13	**Robert S. McNamara**[1], chief operating officer of the Ford Motor Company, is named secretary of defense
31	**McGeorge Bundy**[1], dean of Harvard College, is named national security adviser to the president

1961

JANUARY 1	Senate Majority Leader **Mike Mansfield**[1] (D-Montana) offers to cut the number of U.S. troops stationed in Europe if the Soviets will do the same
3	The United States cuts diplomatic relations with Cuba (See **Fidel Castro Ruz**[2])
20	**John F. Kennedy**[1] takes office
31	**Arthur M. Schlesinger, Jr.,**[1] is named White House speechwriter
MARCH 1	The Peace Corps is founded (See **John F. Kennedy**[1])

3   **Kennedy**[1] proposes the **Alliance for Progress**[3]

APRIL 15   The **Bay of Pigs Invasion**[3]
20   Cuban forces defeat the **Bay of Pigs Invasion**[3]
22   Four French generals – Maurice Challe, Edmund Zeller, Edmund Jouhaud, and Raul Salan – announce their opposition to **de Gaulle**'s[1] policy of Algerian self-determination, and their support of the French settlers

MAY 30   Dominican Republic ruler **Rafael Leónidas Trujillo Molina**[2] is assassinated
31   **Trujillo**'s[2] son is made president
31   South Africa leaves the British Commonwealth, becoming an independent republic

JUNE 3   **Kennedy**[1] meets **Khrushchev**[1] in a summit meeting in Vienna to discuss the American arms buildup and demilitarization of West Berlin
29   Senator **Fulbright**[1] says the United States compromises its foreign policy by its preoccupation with peripheral struggles

AUGUST 4   Great Britain formally requests to be admitted to the **European Economic Community**[3]
13   East Germany forbids its citizens to cross into West Germany (See **Ulbricht**[2])
15   Construction of the **Berlin Wall**[3] begins
17   **Alliance for Progress**[1] created

SEPTEMBER 17   **Adenauer**'s[1] CDU loses its absolute majority in West German election; needs a coalition partner
27   **John A. McCone**[1] replaces **Allen Dulles**[1] as **Central Intelligence Agency**[3] director

OCTOBER 5   General **Maxwell D. Taylor**[1] and **Walt Rostow**[1] go to Vietnam to investigate the military situation
31   **Stalin**'s[2] body is removed from the Lenin Mausoleum

NOVEMBER 14   **Adenauer**[1] forms a coalition with the Free Democrats
14   **Kennedy**[1] sends helicopter companies to South Vietnam (See **Vietnam War**[3])

DECEMBER 10   The Soviet Union and Albania sever their diplomatic relations (See **Hoxha**[2])

1962

FEBRUARY 10   U-2 pilot **Powers**[1] is swapped for Soviet spy Rudolph Abel in Berlin (See **U-2 Affair**[3])

MARCH 2   The United States resumes nuclear testing in the atmosphere
18   The Evian agreement ends the Algerian war (See **Ben-Bella**[2]; **Boumédienne**[2])

APRIL 14   Georges Pompidou succeeds Michel Debré as France's prime minister

JULY 6   Algeria proclaims its independence (See **Ben Bella**[2])

SEPTEMBER 19   General **Taylor**[1], back from a tour of South Vietnam, says the United States is on the road to victory (See **Vietnam War**[3])

OCTOBER 10   Senator Kenneth Keating (D-New York) says the Soviets are building missiles in Cuba (See **Cuban Missile Crisis**[3])
22   **John F. Kennedy**[1] announces a blockade of Cuba until the Soviet Union removes its missiles from the island (See **Fidel Castro Ruz**[2]; **Cuban Missile Crisis**[3])
23   The United States puts its troops on a worldwide alert

24   Cuba blockade goes into effect

25   **Stevenson**[1], U.S. ambassador to the United Nations, shows aerial photos of Soviet missiles in Cuba during a debate at the Security Council

27

       The United States accepts Soviet offer to withdraw its missiles in exchange for an American guarantee not to invade the island (See **John F. Kennedy**[1]; **Robert F. Kennedy**[1]; **Khrushchev**[2])

27   **Franz Josef Strauss**[1], West Germany's secretary of defense, orders raid of the offices of the newsweekly *Der Spiegel*

28   The Soviets begin the withdrawal of their missiles from Cuba

NOVEMBER 2   **John F. Kennedy**[1] confirms that the Soviets are carrying out the dismantling of missile sites in Cuba

20   The blockade of Cuba ends

28   **Adenauer**[1] forced to form a new government without **Strauss**[1], who resigns because of the *Spiegel* affair

DECEMBER 11   New West German government is formed, with **Adenauer**[1] as chancellor (See **Federal Republic of Germany**[3])

1963

JANUARY 1   The Chinese Communist party attacks **Khrushchev**'s[2] doctrine of peaceful coexistence with the West (See **Liu**[3]; **Mao**[2])

7   The Soviets denounce Chinese Communist party

14   **De Gaulle**[1] explains in a press conference that Great Britain's admission to the **European Economic Community**[3] is premature

18   British Labour party's leader **Hugh Gaitskell**[1] dies

29   France blocks Great Britain's membership in the **European Economic Community**[3]

FEBRUARY 14   **Harold Wilson**[1] elected leader of the Labour party

MARCH 10   Former foreign minister Georges Bidault, supporter of the French settlers in Algeria and leader of the anti-Gaullist faction, is arrested in West Germany

APRIL 9   Bidault flees to Rio de Janeiro

23   The West German CDU nominates **Erhard**[1] to succeed retiring **Adenauer**[1]

MAY 1   **Churchill**[1] retires from politics

JUNE 14   The Profumo Scandal: British defense minister John Profumo is discovered to have had an affair with call girl Christine Keeler, who was also seeing the Soviet military attaché to Great Britain. Keeler denies asking Profumo for defense information

16   **Ben-Gurion**[2] resigns as Israel's prime minister and minister of defense

19   Treasury Minister **Levi Eshkol**[2] succeeds **Ben-Gurion**[2]

20   The United States and the Soviet Union announce the agreement to establish a "hot line" between leaders of the two nations

21   **Macmillan**[1] survives a no-confidence vote in Parliament; announces Profumo inquiry

25   The United States, Soviet Union, and Great Britain initial an agreement on a Limited Nuclear Test Ban Treaty (See **Limited Test Ban Treaty**[3])

26   **John F. Kennedy**[1] makes his "Ich bin ein Berliner" speech next to the Berlin Wall

29   **De Gaulle**[1] says France will not sign **Limited Test Ban Treaty**[3]

31   China denounces the **Limited Test Ban Treaty**[3]

AUGUST 5   The United States, Soviet Union, and Great Britain sign **Limited Test Ban Treaty**[3] in Moscow

30   The hot line between Washington, D.C., and Moscow goes into service

SEPTEMBER 21   Soviets reject China's foreign-policy doctrine (See **Liu**[2]; **Mao**[2])

OCTOBER 9   **Macmillan**[1] announces plans to retire as British prime minister

15   **Adenauer**[1] resigns as West German chancellor

16   **Erhard**[1] nominated new West German chancellor

19   Sir **Alec Douglas-Home**[1] replaces **Macmillan**[1] as prime minister of Great Britain

NOVEMBER 22   **John F. Kennedy**[1] is assassinated in Dallas; **Johnson**[1] becomes president

1964

JANUARY 3   Senator **Barry Goldwater**[1] (R-Arizona) declares his candidacy for the presidency

27   France recognizes the People's Republic of China

APRIL 5   General **MacArthur**[1] dies

MAY 28   The Palestine Liberation Organization (PLO) is founded (See **Arafat**[2]; **Habash**[2])

JULY 15   The Republicans nominate **Goldwater**[1] as their candidate for president

AUGUST 2–4   USS *Maddox* and USS *C. Turner Joy* are attacked by North Vietnamese warships in the Gulf of Tonkin

7   The Senate passes the **Tonkin Gulf Resolution**[3]

21   Palmiro Togliatti, leader of Italy's Communist party, dies

26   The Democrats nominate **Johnson**[1] as their candidate for president. **Humphrey**[1] is vice-presidential candidate

OCTOBER 15   **Khrushchev**[2] is ousted from power; replaced by **Leonid Brezhnev**[2] as first secretary and **Alexsei Nikolaevich Kosygin**[2] as premier of Soviet Union

16   **Wilson**[1] defeats **Douglas-Home**[1] and becomes Great Britain's new prime minister

16   China detonates an atomic bomb (See **Nuclear Proliferation**[3])

NOVEMBER 3   **Johnson**[1] elected U.S. president

1965

JANUARY 23   **Churchill**[1] dies

FEBRUARY 7   The United States attacks North Vietnam for the first time, following an attack on a U.S. base at Pleiku (See **Johnson**[1]; **Vietnam War**[3])

MARCH 8   U.S. combat troops land in Vietnam

APRIL 28   **Johnson**[1] sends marines to the Dominican Republic to quell unrest (See **Bosch**[2])

MAY 12   West Germany and Israel establish diplomatic relations; most Arab governments cut ties to Germany

JULY 14	**Stevenson**[1] dies
SEPTEMBER 9	**De Gaulle**[1] says that after 1969 France will not be a part of an integral Western defense (See **North Atlantic Treaty Organization**[3])
NOVEMBER 25	Joseph Mobutu becomes president of Congo in a bloodless coup; the country later changes its name to Zaire (See **Lumumba**[2])
DECEMBER 5	In the first round of the French presidential elections, **de Gaulle**[1] receives 44 percent of the votes, socialist **François Mitterrand**[1] 32 percent, and centrist Jean Lecanuet 16 percent
9	Nikolai Podgorny elected president of the Soviet Union
17	Ferdinand Marcos elected president of the Philippines
19	In the second round of the French presidential elections, **de Gaulle**[1] receives 54.6 percent of the votes, **Mitterrand**[1] 45.4 percent

1966

FEBRUARY 3	An unmanned Soviet spacecraft lands on the moon
10–14	23rd Congress of the Communist party, Soviet Union (See **Brezhnev**[2])
MARCH 7	France formally announces its decision to withdraw from integrated military structure of **North Atlantic Treaty Organization**[3]
12	Indonesian president **Bung Sukarno**[2] is toppled by a coup led by Lieutenant General Suharto
JULY 1	**De Gaulle**[1] announces France's withdrawal from **North Atlantic Treaty Organization**[3]
SEPTEMBER 9	**North Atlantic Treaty Organization**[3] moves its headquarters from France to Brussels

1967

JANUARY 27	A treaty prohibiting the military use of space is signed by sixty-two nations
FEBRUARY 18	**Oppenheimer**[1] dies
APRIL 11	**Andrei Antonovich Grechko**[2] is named the new Soviet defense minister
19	**Adenauer**[1] dies
21	A military coup in Greece topples the government of Stephanos Stephanopoulos to prevent Left-leaning Georgiu Papandreo from coming back to power
MAY 15	Egypt begins to move its forces into the Sinai (See **Eshkol**[2]; **Nasser**[2]; **Rabin**[2])
23	Egypt blocks the Strait of Tiran to Israeli shipping
JUNE 2	A government of national unity is formed in Israel: Moshe Dayan is named Israel's defense minister; Menachem Begin is minister without portfolio
5	Israel attacks the air forces of several Arab countries and launches attacks against Egyptian forces in the Sinai and Jordanian forces in the West Bank. The Six Day War begins (See **Nasser**[1]; **Rabin**[2])
7	Israeli-Syrian fighting begins (See **Assad**[2])
8	Defeated Egypt is willing to accept a cease-fire
9	Defeated Syria accepts a cease-fire

23	**Johnson**$_1$ and **Kosygin**$_2$ meet in Glassboro, N.J. (See **Glassboro Summit**$_3$)
JULY 24	The Canadian government asks President **de Gaulle**$_1$ to cut short his official visit to Canada and leave the country after he announces, in Montreal, "Vive le Québec libre!"
AUGUST 8	Indonesia, Malaysia, Thailand, the Philippines, and Singapore establish the Association of South East Asian Nations (ASEAN)
OCTOBER 10	Bolivia confirms the death of Latin American guerrilla **Ernesto "Che" Guevara de la Serna**$_2$ (See **Fidel Castro Ruz**$_2$)
DECEMBER 2	**Francis Cardinal Spellman**$_1$ dies
27	**De Gaulle**$_1$, in a press conference, explains his decision to impose an arms embargo on Israel at the outset of the Six Day War, by saying that Jews are "un peuple d'élite, sur de lui et dominateur"

1968

JANUARY 5	**Aleksander Dubcek**$_2$ replaces **Antonín Novotny**$_2$ as first secretary of Czechoslovakia's Communist party. Novotny remains president
23	USS *Pueblo* is seized by North Korea (See **Kim**$_2$)
30	The Vietcong launches the Tet Offensive (See **Giap**$_2$; **Johnson**$_1$; **Westmoreland**$_1$)
30	Senator **Eugene J. McCarthy**$_1$ (D-Minnesota) enters the Democratic race for nomination for president
FEBRUARY 1	**Nixon**$_1$ announces his entry into the presidential race
MARCH 12	**Eugene J. McCarthy**$_1$ takes a strong second in New Hampshire Democratic primary
16	Senator **Robert F. Kennedy**$_1$ (D-New York) enters the presidential race
22	Daniel Cohn-Bendit is elected head of a revolutionary student movement at the University of Nanterre, France
30	General Ludvik Svoboda replaces **Novotny**$_2$ as president of Czechoslovakia
31	President **Johnson**$_1$ announces bombing halt in Vietnam; offers to open negotiations with North Vietnam; announces he is dropping out of the presidential race
MAY 2–3	Student riots and takeovers at the Universities of Nanterre and Sorbonne (See **de Gaulle**$_1$)
10	Paris peace talks between the United States and North Vietnam open
13	General strike in France. A crowd of three hundred thousand demonstrates in Paris in support of students' and workers' demands (See **de Gaulle**$_1$)
22	Massive unrest in France, led by students and workers; **de Gaulle's**$_1$ government on the verge of collapse
JUNE 5	**Robert F. Kennedy**$_1$ is assassinated in Los Angeles
12	The Nuclear Non-Proliferation Treaty (NPT) is approved by the UN General Assembly
30	Maurice Couve de Murville replaces Pompidou as French prime minister
JULY 1	The NPT is signed (See **Nuclear Proliferation**$_3$)
15	**Brezhnev**$_2$ announces the **Brezhnev Doctrine**$_3$
AUGUST 8	The Republican party nominates **Nixon**$_1$ for the 1968 elections
10	Senator **George S. McGovern**$_1$ (D-South Dakota) enters presidential race
20	**Warsaw Pact**$_3$ forces invade Czechoslovakia (See **Dubcek**$_2$)
24	The French explode a thermonuclear bomb (See **Nuclear Proliferation**$_3$)

26 The Democratic party convention opens in Chicago
27 Riots in Chicago (See **Humphrey**[1]; **Eugene J. McCarthy**[1])
28 **Humphrey**[1] is nominated by the Democrats; Senator Edmund S. Muskie (D-Maine) is
    nominated as his running mate

NOVEMBER 5 **Nixon**[1] is elected president
        22 USS *Pueblo* is released by the North Koreans

DECEMBER 2 **Henry Kissinger**[1] is named new national security adviser to the president

1969

JANUARY 20 **Nixon**[1] is inaugurated
        29 **Allen Dulles**[1] dies

MARCH 2 Soviet and Chinese military clashes
     18 The United States begins secret bombing of Cambodia (See **Nixon**[1])

APRIL 17 **Gustáv Husák**[2] replaces **Dubcek**[2] as first secretary of Czechoslovakia's Communist party
      27 Following a defeat in a referendum on his idea for reforming the French Sénat, **de Gaulle**[1]
          announces he will no longer exercise the functions of president of the republic.

MAY 10 Pompidou replaces **de Gaulle**[1] as president of France

JUNE 8 **Nixon**[1] announces the "Vietnamization" plan (See **Laird**[1])
     11 Pompidou elected president of France
     20 Jean-Jacques Chaban-Delmas is named the new French premier
     22 Maurice Schumann is named the new French foreign minister

JULY 21 Neil Armstrong walks on the moon
     25 **Nixon**[1] enunciates the Nixon Doctrine in a speech in Guam

SEPTEMBER 1 **Mu'ammar al-Qaddafi**[2] stages a military coup in Libya, driving King Idris into exile,
             and proclaims the establishment of the socialist Arab Republic of Libya
          3 Vietnamese leader **Ho**[2] dies
         28 CDU barely beats SPD in West German general elections; SPD leader **Brandt**[1] tries to
             form a coalition

OCTOBER 15 **Dubcek**[2] is ousted as chairman of the Czech Assembly
        21 **Brandt**[1] is elected chancellor of West Germany
        28 **Brandt**[1] offers to improve ties with East Germany (See **Ostpolitik**[3])

NOVEMBER 9 **Kennan**[1] urges U.S. withdrawal from Vietnam
        24 United States and Soviet Union sign the NPT

DECEMBER 22 Poland agrees to talks with West Germany (See **Brandt**[1])

1970

JANUARY 12 Biafran leaders surrender to the Nigerian government, ending the Nigerian civil war (See
            Gowon[2])
        23 France agrees to British membership in the **European Economic Community**[3]
        30 **Nixon**[1] says the United States will proceed with the Antiballistic Missile (ABM) system
            (See **Strategic Defense Initiative**[3])

FEBRUARY 6   **Kennan**$_1$ says the building of an ABM system jeopardizes chances for arms-control agreements with the Soviet Union in the **Strategic Arms Limitation Talks**$_3$ (SALT)

21   A commission set up to examine the draft recommends an all-volunteer army

MARCH 19   West German chancellor **Brandt**$_1$ meets the East German premier Willi Stoph at Erfurt. The beginning of **Ostpolitik**$_0$

26   Four Power talks are held in Berlin (See **Brandt**$_1$)

APRIL 16   The **Strategic Arms Limitation Talks**$_3$ open in Vienna

30   **Nixon**$_1$ announces the invasion of Cambodia by U.S. troops (See **Pol**$_2$)

MAY 4   Four students are killed at Kent State University by Ohio National Guardsmen during an antiwar demonstration (See **Nixon**$_1$)

JUNE 19   **Edward Heath**$_1$ becomes Great Britain's prime minister after the Conservatives defeat Labour in general elections

26   **Dubcek**$_2$ is expelled from Czechoslovakia's Communist party

29   U.S. ground troops leave Cambodia (See **Nixon**$_1$)

JULY 17   East German leader **Ulbricht**$_2$ wants a summit of the two Germanys (See **Ostpolitik**$_3$)

AUGUST 12   West Germany and the Soviet Union sign a nonaggression pact affirming that existing boundaries between the Germanys, Czechoslovakia, and the Soviet Union are permanent (See **Ostpolitik**$_3$)

12   Senator **Mansfield**$_1$ says the United States can now cut the number of its troops stationed in Western Europe (See **Post-Vietnam Syndrome**$_3$)

SEPTEMBER 1   The Senate rejects a plan to end the Vietnam War proposed by Senators Mark Hatfield (R-Oregon) and **McGovern**$_1$ (D-South Dakota)

23   **Jimmy Carter**$_1$ wins Georgia's Democratic nomination for the governorship

28   Egypt's **Gamal Abdul Nasser**$_2$ dies

OCTOBER 1   The Senate approves the building of antiballistic missiles (See **Strategic Defense Initiative**$_3$)

3   Anwar al-Sadat succeeds **Nasser**$_2$

7   **Nixon**$_1$ announces a new Vietnam peace plan

NOVEMBER 3   **Salvador Allende Gossens**$_2$ is sworn in as president of Chile (See **Frei**$_2$)

9   **De Gaulle**$_1$ dies

15   West Germany agrees to recognize Poland's western boundary (See **Brandt**$_1$)

18   The German-Polish Treaty of Reconciliation is initialed (See **Brandt**$_1$; **Gomulka**$_2$)

DECEMBER 7   **Acheson**$_1$ asks **Nixon**$_1$ to stop **Ostpolitik**$_3$

15–19   Rioting in Polish cities (See **Gomulka**$_2$)

20   **Edward Gierek**$_2$ replaces Gomulka as first secretary of the Polish Communist party

1971

JANUARY 18   Senator **McGovern**$_1$ opens his 1972 presidential campaign

21   **Idi Dada Amin Oumee**$_2$ deposes Ugandan president Milton Obote

FEBRUARY 8   U.S. forces invade Laos

MAY 21   French premier Chaban-Delmas survives a censure motion

JUNE 1   American theologian **Reinhold Niebuhr**$_1$ dies
13   The *New York Times* begins publishing the Pentagon Papers (See **Ellsberg**$_1$)
30   The Supreme Court upholds the right of newspapers to publish the Pentagon Papers (See **Ellsberg**$_1$)

JULY 15   **Nixon**$_1$ announces his visit to the People's Republic of China (See **Kissinger**$_1$; **Mao**$_2$)

AUGUST 15   Nixon announces an end to the convertibility of U.S. currency into gold
16   **Daniel Ellsberg**$_1$ pleads not guilty in the Pentagon Papers case

SEPTEMBER 3   Berlin Treaty signed (See **Brandt**$_1$)
11   **Khrushchev**$_2$ dies

OCTOBER 20   **Brandt**$_1$ wins Nobel Peace Prize
25   The **United Nations**$_3$ admits China to membership, expelling Taiwan (See **Mao**$_2$)

NOVEMBER 15   Soviet spy Rudolf Abel dies
19   Senator **Henry M. Jackson**$_1$ (D-Washington) enters 1972 presidential race

DECEMBER 16   Nationalist rebels in East Pakistan break away from Pakistan, establishing Bangladesh (See **Bhutto**$_2$; **Gandhi**$_2$)

1972

JANUARY 4   Senator Muskie enters the presidential race

FEBRUARY 6   **Llewellyn E. Thompson, Jr.**$_1$, dies
20   **Nixon**$_1$ arrives in China, the first American president to visit China (See **Mao**$_2$; **Zhou**$_2$)

MARCH 7   Muskie wins the New Hampshire primary

MAY 22–30   **Nixon**$_1$ arrives in the Soviet Union for a summit with **Brezhnev**$_2$, becoming the first American president to visit the Soviet Union
26   SALT I interim agreement is signed in Moscow (See **Gromyko**$_1$; **Kissinger**$_1$; **Nixon**$_1$; **Strategic Arms Limitation Talks**$_3$)

JUNE 3   Four Power agreement on Berlin
5   Democratic Southern governors start a stop-**McGovern**$_1$ drive
17   Six men are caught burglarizing the offices of the U.S. Democratic National Committee at the Watergate building
25   **McGovern**$_1$ announces that he has clinched nomination

JULY 12   **McGovern**$_1$ is nominated at the Democratic party's convention in Miami; Senator Thomas Eagleton (D-Missouri) is nominated as his running mate

AUGUST 12   Chinese says the Soviets are behind a plot to kill **Mao**$_2$
29   **Nixon**$_1$ says there was no White House involvement in the Watergate burglary

SEPTEMBER 5   Members of the Black September faction of the PLO seize Israeli athletes at the Munich Olympics, killing eleven of them
14   West Germany and Poland agree to diplomatic relations (See **Ostpolitik**$_3$)

OCTOBER 3   SALT I and the ABM Treaty are signed in Washington (See **Brezhnev**$_2$; **Kissinger**$_1$; **Nixon**$_1$; **Strategic Arms Limitation Talks**$_3$)

NOVEMBER 7   **Nixon**$_1$ is reelected
21   SALT II talks open in Geneva (See **Strategic Arms Limitation Talks**$_3$)

DECEMBER 21   Basic Treaty is signed between West and East Germany (See **Brandt**$_1$)
26   **Truman**$_1$ dies

1973

JANUARY 1   Great Britain joins the **European Economic Community**$_3$
15   United States announces end to offensive military actions against North Vietnam (See **Vietnam War**$_3$)
19   **George Bush**$_1$ is named chairman of the Republican National Committee
22   **Johnson**$_1$ dies
23   **James R. Schlesinger**$_1$ is named **Central Intelligence Agency**$_3$ director
27   Vietnam peace accords are signed (See **Kissinger**$_1$)
28   Vietnam cease-fire is in effect

MARCH 29   North Vietnam releases the last of U.S. prisoners of war

MAY 10   **William E. Colby**$_1$ replaces **James R. Schlesinger**$_1$ as **Central Intelligence Agency**$_3$ director; **James R. Schlesinger**$_1$ is named defense secretary
11   Charges against **Ellsberg**$_1$ are dismissed
30   West Germany and Czechoslovakia normalize ties

JUNE 12   East Germany applies for UN membership
17–24   Washington summit conference between **Nixon**$_1$ and **Brezhnev**$_2$

JULY 3   Opening of the **Conference on Security and Co-operation in Europe**$_3$ (CSCE) in Helsinki

AUGUST 1   **Ulbricht**$_1$ dies
15   Congress imposes a halt on continued U.S. bombing of Cambodia (See **Church**$_1$)
22   **Kissinger**$_1$ is nominated to replace William P. Rogers as secretary of state
30   Saudi Arabia warns of possible oil embargo (See **Organization of Petroleum Exporting Countries**$_3$)

SEPTEMBER 11   **Allende**$_2$ is ousted in a coup (See **Central Intelligence Agency**$_3$; **Pinochet**$_2$)

OCTOBER 6   Yom Kippur War starts (See **Meir**$_2$; **Sharon**$_2$)
10   Vice-president Spiro T. Agnew resigns
15   United States begins major military airlift to Israel
17   The **Organization of Oil Exporting Countries**$_3$ (OPEC) agrees to halt oil exports
20   Saudi Arabia halts oil shipments to the United States
30   **Mutual Balanced Force Reductions (MBFR) Talks**$_3$ open in Vienna

NOVEMBER 27   Congressman **Gerald R. Ford**$_1$ (R-Michigan) is confirmed as vice-president

1974

JANUARY 2   Former U.S. ambassador to the Soviet Union **Charles E. Bohlen**$_1$ dies

MARCH 4   **Wilson**₁ again becomes prime minister of Great Britain, defeating **Heath**₁ in the general elections

APRIL 4   **North Atlantic Treaty Organization**'s₃ twenty-fifth anniversary

25   Portuguese prime minister Marcello Caetano is ousted in a coup

MAY 6   **Brandt**₁ resigns after a high official in his office is discovered to be an East German agent
9   U.S. House Judiciary Committee votes to impeach **Nixon**₁
16   **Helmut Schmidt**₁ nominated to be new West German chancellor
18   India explodes a nuclear device (See **Gandhi**₂; **Nuclear Proliferation**₃)
19   **Valéry Giscard d'Estaing**₁ succeeds Pompidou as president of France
20   Senator **Fulbright**₁ defeated by Dale Bumpers in Arkansas Democratic primary, ending his political career

JUNE 27–7/3   Moscow summit conference between **Nixon**₁ and **Brezhnev**₂

JULY 15   Greek officers in the Cypriot National Guard oust Archbishop Makarios and seize power
20   Turkey invades Cyprus

AUGUST 9   President **Nixon**₁ resigns over Watergate
14   Greece cuts **North Atlantic Treaty Organization**₃ ties over Turkish invasion of Cyprus

SEPTEMBER 4   **Bush**₁ is named U.S. envoy to China
4   United States establishes diplomatic relations with East Germany
8   **Nixon**₁ is pardoned by President **Ford**₁
12   Ethiopian emperor **Haile Selassie I**₂ is ousted in a military coup after a fifty-eight-year rule (See **Mengistu**₂)
16   General **Alexander M. Haig**₁ named **North Atlantic Treaty Organization**₃ commander
19   John Sherman Cooper appointed first U.S. ambassador to East Germany

NOVEMBER 23–24   Vladivostok summit conference between **Ford**₁ and **Brezhnev**₂
29   Ulrike Meinhoff, leader of the West German Baader-Meinhoff gang, is sentenced to eight-year prison term

DECEMBER 14   Political commentator **Lippmann**₁ dies
19   Nelson A. Rockefeller sworn in as vice-president
20   The ruling junta in Ethiopia declares the country a socialist state (See **Mengistu**₂)
26   **Central Intelligence Agency**₃ director **Colby**₁ admits to **Ford**₁ that the CIA spied on U.S. citizens

1975

MARCH 17   **Ford**₁ attacks new isolationism in U.S. foreign policy
20   South Vietnam acknowledges defeat in **Vietnam War**₃ (See **Nguyen**₂)

APRIL 5   Taiwanese president **Chiang**₂ dies
16   The Khmer Rouge takes over in Cambodia, seizing power from the U.S.-backed government of Lon Nol (See **Pol**₂)
30   Saigon falls to North Vietnamese forces; **Vietnam War**₃ is over (See **Giap**₂)

MAY 12   Cambodians seize *Mayaguez* (See ***Mayaguez* Incident**₃)

21   Baader-Meinhoff gang trial opens in West Germany

27   Svoboda removed as president of Czechoslovakia

29   **Husák$_2$,** first secretary of the Czechoslovakia's Communist party, assumes the presidency

JULY 30   Senator **Jackson$_1$** charges the West is retreating from support of self-determination

AUGUST 1   Helsinki Final Act is signed at the end of **Conference on Security and Cooperation in Europe$_3$** talks

23   The Vietnamese-backed Pathet Lao takes over Laos

NOVEMBER 3   **Colby$_1$** and **James R. Schlesinger$_1$** are ousted in a U.S. presidential cabinet shuffle; **Bush$_1$** is named **Central Intelligence Agency$_3$** director; Donald Rumsfeld is named secretary of defense

10   Angola gains independence from Portugal (See **Neto$_2$**; **Savimbi$_2$**)

20   **Reagan$_1$** enters 1976 presidential race

1976

JANUARY 5   **Reagan$_1$** opens presidential race by attacking **Détente$_3$**

8   Chinese premier **Zhou$_2$** dies

20   Secret House report on **Central Intelligence Agency$_3$** activities is leaked and published (See **Church$_1$**)

27   **Bush$_1$** is confirmed as **Central Intelligence Agency$_3$** director

27   Congress forbids continuation of aid to pro-West forces in Angola's civil war (See **Clark$_1$**; **Neto$_2$**)

FEBRUARY 20   SEATO disbands

MARCH 4   Senator **Mansfield$_1$** announces his retirement

16   **Wilson$_1$** announces his intention to resign as British prime minister

18   Senator **Frank Church$_1$** (D-Idaho) enters 1976 presidential race

18   Allan Weinstein's book *Perjury* is published, concluding that **Hiss$_1$** was lying (See **Chambers$_1$**)

APRIL 5   **James Callaghan$_1$** is named new Labour party leader

6   Senator **Jackson$_1$** wins the New York primary

27   Former Soviet defense minister **Grechko$_2$** dies

MAY 9   Terrorist Meinhoff commits suicide in jail

JUNE 23   **Carter$_1$** calls **Ford's$_1$** foreign policy immoral

30   Senator **Goldwater$_1$** endorses **Ford$_1$**

JULY 2   Vietnam formally unites as one nation

14   The Democratic party nominates **Carter$_1$** for president

AUGUST 19   President **Ford$_1$** beats a challenge from **Reagan$_1$** for the Republican nomination; Senator Robert J. Dole of Kansas nominated Republican vice-presidential candidate

SEPTEMBER 9   Chairman **Mao$_2$** dies; succeeded by **Hua Guofeng$_2$**

OCTOBER 6   In a television debate with **Carter$_1$**, **Ford$_1$** blunders, saying Soviets do not dominate Poland

22   China reports a coup attempt by **Mao's$_2$** widow

NOVEMBER 2   **Carter**[1] defeats **Ford**[1], elected president

DECEMBER 3   **Cyrus R. Vance**[1] is named secretary of state

15   **Schmidt**[1] is reelected West German chancellor

16   **Zbigniew Brzezinski**[1] is named national security adviser to the president

1977

JANUARY 6   Charter 77, a Czech human rights group, is formed (See **Havel**[2])

14   Former British prime minister **Eden**[1] dies

17   Theodore Sorensen withdraws as nominee for the **Central Intelligence Agency**[3] directorship

20   **Carter**[1] is sworn in as U.S. president

21   **Carter**[1] pardons Vietnam draft resisters

27   **Carter**[1] orders SALT II negotiations to proceed (See **Strategic Arms Limitation Talks**[3])

MARCH 9   **Carter**[1] says the United States will remove troops from South Korea in four to five years

17   The Baader-Meinhoff trial adjourns after the government admits to having wiretapped the defendants

APRIL 28   Christopher Boyce, a former TRW (U.S. defense industry) employee who passed secret satellite information to the Soviets, is convicted of spying

MAY 5   Former West German chancellor **Erhard**[1] dies

22   **Carter**[1] commencement speech at Notre Dame University calls for Americans to "free themselves of their inordinate fear of communism" and for a new U.S. foreign policy

24   Podgorny is removed as president of the Soviet Union

JUNE 6   The *Washington Post* says the United States is ready to manufacture an enhanced radiation (neutron) bomb

7   Begin's Likud party defeats the Labor party in Israeli elections; Begin to form a new government

16   **Brezhnev**[2] elected president of the Soviet Union

29   **Vance**[1] says the United States will seek full diplomatic relations with China

30   The United States announces plans to deploy cruise missiles

JULY 16   **Deng Xiaoping**[2], Chinese leader purged during the "Cultural revolution," apparently reinstated

AUGUST 1   U-2 pilot **Powers**[1] dies when a helicopter he is flying for a Los Angeles television station crashes

16   **Ford**[1], **Kissinger**[1] endorse the Panama Canal treaties

25   **Reagan**[1] attacks the Panama Canal treaties (See **Carter**[1])

SEPTEMBER 3   Pakistani prime minister **Zulfikar Ali Bhutto**[2] is arrested

7   Panama Canal treaties are signed in Washington, D.C.

18   Three members of the Baader-Meinhoff terrorist group commit suicide in jail

23   **Vance**[1] says the United States will abide by the expiring 1972 SALT I treaty (See **Carter**[1]; **Strategic Arms Limitation Talks**[3])

31   Former CIA director **Richard M. Helms**[1] pleads no contest for failing to testify before Senate

OCTOBER 4	**Conference on Security and Cooperation in Europe**$_3$ follow-up meeting opens in Belgrade
NOVEMBER 7	Sadat accepts Begin's offer to visit Israel
9	Sadat begins an official visit to Israel
DECEMBER 25	Begin, Sadat begin peace negotiations in Egypt
29–1/6	President **Carter**$_1$ visits Poland

1978

JANUARY 10	Antigovernment newspaper publisher Pedro Chamorro is killed in Nicaragua (See **Borge**$_2$; **Chamorro**$_2$)
13	Former vice-president **Humphrey**$_1$ dies
16	New hot-line agreement between United States and the Soviet Union goes into effect, replacing the agreement signed in 1963
24	**Carter**$_1$ reorganizes U.S. foreign-intelligence activities
FEBRUARY 24	Soviet Union asks China to improve relations (See **Deng**$_2$)
24	**Deng**$_2$ is elected chairman of China's Communist party
MARCH	Yugoslavian president **Tito**$_2$ visits the United States
9	Trial of radical terrorists the Red Brigades opens in Italy
10	Congress adopts P.L. 95–242, Nuclear Non-Proliferation Act of 1978
10	**Carter**$_1$ signs the Nuclear Non-Proliferation Treaty (See **Nuclear Proliferation**$_3$)
16	Former Italian prime minister Aldo Moro is kidnapped
17	**Carter**$_1$ warns the Soviet Union against involvement in the domestic affairs of other countries
21–22	Prime Minister Begin visits the United States
APRIL 7	The United States defers production of the neutron bomb
27	Afghan president Mohammed Daud Khan is ousted in a coup and replaced by the leader of the Afghan Communist party, Noor Mohammed Taraki
MAY 9	Moro's body is found in Rome
JUNE 7	**Carter**$_1$ tells the Soviets that they can choose cooperation or confrontation
12	**Vance**$_1$ announces that the United States will not use nuclear weapons against nonnuclear powers who pledge nuclear abstinence
JULY 14–15	President **Carter**$_1$ visits West Germany
18–28	United States and Soviet Union meet in Helsinki to establish rules to curb arms sales
22	Indian officials charge **Indira Gandhi**$_1$ with conspiracy to overthrow government
SEPTEMBER 5–17	Sadat and Begin meet at Camp David; agree on an Egyptian-Israeli peace accord
OCTOBER 10	**Paul C. Warnke**$_1$ resigns as director of the **Arms Control and Disarmament Agency**$_3$ (ACDA), effective 31 October. Ralph Earl III is named interim director

1979

JANUARY 1	United States and China open diplomatic relations

7	Vietnamese forces invade Cambodia, replacing the regime of **Pol**$_2$ with a pro-Hanoi communist regime under **Heng Samrin**$_2$
14	**Carter**$_1$ says that SALT II will be a treaty, not an executive agreement (See **Strategic Arms Limitation Talks**$_3$)
16	Shah **Mohammad Reza Pahlevi**$_2$ flees Iran (See **Khomeini**$_2$)
FEBRUARY 1	Ayatollah **Khomeini**$_2$ arrives in Iran (See **Mohammad Reza Pahlevi**$_2$)
17	China invades Vietnam in response to the Vietnamese invasion of Cambodia (See **Deng**$_2$)
MARCH 15	Chinese forces withdraw from Vietnam
26	Sadat, Begin sign Egyptian-Israeli peace treaty
28	Prime minister **Callaghan**$_1$ loses a no-confidence vote in the British Parliament; elections set
APRIL 6	United States cuts aid to Pakistani because of Pakistani nuclear-weapons program (See **Zia ul-Haq**$_2$)
11	Ugandan exiles supported by Tanzanian troops invade Uganda and oust **Amin**$_2$ (See **Nyerere**$_2$)
MAY 2	Under secretary of state Warren Christopher says the United States will link aid with human rights
4	Conservative **Margaret Thatcher**$_1$ becomes British prime minister
JUNE 18	**Carter**$_1$ and **Brezhnev**$_2$ sign SALT II agreement in Vienna (See **Strategic Arms Limitation Talks**$_3$)
JULY 19	Sandinista rebels take Managua, seize power in Nicaragua; President **Anastasio Somoza Debayle**$_2$ flees (See **Borge**$_2$; **Ortega**$_2$)
AUGUST 30	Pakistan goes ahead with its nuclear program despite U.S. objections
OCTOBER 1	U.S. Canal Zone in Panama dissolves in accordance with the 1977 treaty
22	Shah of Iran comes to the United States for medical treatment (See **Mohammad Reza Pahlevi**$_2$)
NOVEMBER 4	U.S. Embassy in Tehran seized, diplomats taken hostage (See **Carter**$_1$; **Khomeini**$_2$)
21	Muslim fundamentalists burn the U.S. embassy in Pakistan (See **Zia ul-Haq** $_2$)
DECEMBER 12	**North Atlantic Treaty Organization**$_2$ adopts the "two track" policy, uncoupling Europe, especially Germany, from U.S. protection (See **Intermediate Nuclear Forces Treaty**$_3$; **Schmidt**$_1$)
25	Communist Babrak Karmal ousts the Hafizullah Amin government in Afghanistan (See **Brezhnev**$_2$; **Gromyko**$_2$)
26	The Soviet Union invades Afghanistan
28	**Carter**$_1$ warns **Brezhnev**$_2$ of consequences if troops are not withdrawn from Afghanistan
31	**Carter**$_1$ says **Brezhnev**$_2$ lied to him about Soviet intentions in Afghanistan

1980

JANUARY 23	**Carter**$_1$ enunciates the **Carter Doctrine**$_3$ (See **Vance**$_1$)
APRIL 17	Rhodesia becomes Zimbabwe, with **Robert Mugabe**$_2$ as president (See **Smith**$_2$)
24	"Desert I" rescue raid by U.S. forces to free Iranian-held hostages fails

28   Secretary of State **Vance**$_1$ resigns

MAY 4   Yugoslavian president **Tito**$_2$ dies
21–27   About one thousand South Koreans die in political unrest following the arrest of opposition leader Kim Dae Jung

AUGUST 14   Massive strikes in Poland, led by **Lech Walesa**$_2$, at the Lenin shipyards in Gdansk (See **Gierek**$_2$; **Jaruzelski**$_2$)
31   Gdansk Agreements officially recognize the independent trade union Solidarity (See **Gierek**$_2$; **Jaruzelski**$_2$; **Walesa**$_2$)

OCTOBER 23   Nikolai Tikhonov replaces **Kosygin**$_2$ as premier

NOVEMBER 4   **Reagan**$_1$ is elected president
11   **Conference on Security and Cooperation in Europe**$_3$ follow-up meeting opens in Madrid

1981

JANUARY 20   U.S. hostages are released by Iran (See **Carter**$_1$)

FEBRUARY 11   General **Wojciech Jaruzelski**$_2$ replaces **Gierek**$_2$ as Poland's premier

MARCH 30   **Reagan**$_1$ is shot in Washington, D.C.

MAY 10   **Mitterrand**$_1$ elected president of France
13   Assassination attempt on **Pope John Paul II**$_2$

OCTOBER 6   Sadat assassinated in Cairo; succeeded by Hosni Mubarak
18   **Jaruzelski**$_2$ replaces Stanislaw Kania as first secretary of Poland's United Workers' (Communist) party

NOVEMBER 30   Intermediate-range Nuclear Forces (INF) talks open in Geneva (See **Carlucci**$_1$; **Nitze**$_1$; **Shultz**$_1$; **Intermediate Nuclear Forces Treaty**$_3$)

DECEMBER 10   Spain joins **North Atlantic Treaty Organization**$_3$ (effective 30 May 1982)
13   Martial law is imposed in Poland (See **Jaruzelski**$_2$)

1982

JANUARY 4   William P. Clark replaces Richard V. Allen as national security adviser to President Reagan
25   **Mikhail Suslov**$_2$ dies in Moscow

APRIL 2   Argentina seizes the Falkland Islands (See **Jenkins**$_1$; **Owen**$_1$; **Thatcher**$_1$)
3   Great Britain breaks diplomatic relations with Argentina (See **Thatcher**$_1$)
28   The British navy blockades the Falkland Islands
30   United States announces military supplies and intelligence sharing with Great Britain (See **Haig**$_1$; **Kirkpatrick**$_1$)

MAY 2   British ships sink the Argentine ship *General Belgrano* in the Falklands war
9   British forces begin Falkland invasion

JUNE 6   Israeli forces invade Lebanon (See **Gemayel**$_2$; **Sharon**$_2$)

14   Argentinian forces on the Falkland Islands surrender to British forces (See **Thatcher**₁)

25   **Haig**₁ resigns as secretary of state; **George P. Shultz**₁ replaces him

30   Opening of the Strategic Arms Reduction Talks (START) in Geneva (See **Nitze**₁; **Weinberger**₁)

AUGUST 25   U.S. Marines land in Lebanon (See **Shultz**₁)

SEPTEMBER 12–13   **Deng**₂ solidifies his hold over both the party and government in China

17   **Schmidt**'s₁ West German coalition government collapses

OCTOBER 1   CDU's **Helmut Kohl**₁ is elected West Germany's chancellor

NOVEMBER 10   **Brezhnev**₂ dies

12   **Yuri Andropov**₂ named general secretary of the Communist party, Soviet Union

DECEMBER 31   Poland lifts martial law (See **Jaruzelski**₂)

1983

MARCH 23   **Reagan**₁ outlines the **Strategic Defense Initiative**₃

APRIL 18   U.S. embassy in Beirut bombed, killing more than fifty people

JUNE 16   **Andropov**₁ named president of the Soviet Union

JULY 21   Martial law repealed in Poland (See **Jaruzelski**₂)

AUGUST 21   Benigno Aquino is assassinated in Manila

SEPTEMBER 1   The Soviet Union shoots down Korean Airlines flight 007

OCTOBER 9–15   The Kissinger Commission tours Central America

23   U.S. Marine barracks destroyed by a car bomb in Lebanon; 241 Marines are killed

25   The United States invades Grenada (See **Bishop**₂)

30   Raul Alfonsin elected president of Argentina

NOVEMBER 23   The Soviet delegation walks out of the INF talks in Geneva (See **Intermediate Nuclear Forces Treaty**₃; **Nitze**₁; **Perle**₁)

DECEMBER 30   The first nine Pershing II missiles in West Germany become operational (See **Intermediate Nuclear Forces Treaty**₃; **Thatcher**₁)

1984

JANUARY 1   First new U.S. cruise missiles are deployed in Great Britain

11   Kissinger Commission report is released

24   **Reagan**₁, in State of the Union address, urges better United States–Soviet Union relations

FEBRUARY 9   **Andropov**₁ dies

13   **Konstantin Chernenko**₂ replaces **Andropov**₂ as general secretary of the Communist party, Soviet Union

26   U.S. troops withdraw from Lebanon

APRIL 7   Former senator **Church**₁ dies

11	**Chernenko**$_2$ is named president of the Soviet Union
MAY 2	**Andrei Sakharov**$_2$ begins hunger strike
6	José Napoleon Duarte elected president of El Salvador
7	The Soviets boycott the Los Angeles Olympic Games
JUNE 29	Soviets offer negotiations with the United States over nuclear weapons in space (See **Strategic Defense Initiative**$_3$)
JULY 5	**Molotov**$_2$ is reinstated to the Communist party, Soviet Union
17	United States and Soviet Union modernize the hot line
AUGUST 1	Great Britain announces its plan to give up control of Hong Kong in 1997
SEPTEMBER 20	The new U.S. embassy in Beirut is bombed
25	New Zealand prohibits visits by U.S. ships carrying nuclear weapons
OCTOBER 20	The Chinese Communist party approves **Deng's**$_2$ liberalization program
31	Indian prime minister **Gandhi**$_2$ is assassinated; succeeded by her son Rajiv
NOVEMBER 6	**Reagan**$_1$ defeats Walter Mondale in presidential election
DECEMBER 21	Soviet defense minister **Dmitry Fedorovich Ustinov**$_2$ dies
22	Andrei Sokolov is named new Soviet defense minister

1985

FEBRUARY 21	The Soviet Union agrees to international inspection of Soviet civilian nuclear power plants
MARCH 10	**Chernenko**$_2$ dies
11	**Mikhail Gorbachev**$_2$ is named general secretary of the Communist party, Soviet Union
24	Soviet troops kill an American officer in Potsdam
APRIL 26	Member states sign a twenty-year extension of the **Warsaw Pact**$_3$
MAY 20	American John Walker is arrested as a Soviet spy
JUNE 10	United States announces it will continue to abide by the unratified SALT II treaty (See **Brown**$_1$; **Nitze**$_1$; **Strategic Arms Limitation Talks**$_3$)
11	The Senate votes to repeal Clark amendment barring U.S. aid to antigovernment rebels in Angola (See **Clark**$_1$; **Savimbi**$_2$)
JULY 2	**Gromyko**$_2$ is named new president of the Soviet Union; **Eduard Amvrosiyevich Shevardnadze**$_2$ is named foreign minister
SEPTEMBER 12	Great Britain and the Soviet Union each expel twenty-five of the other's diplomats on spying charges
27	Nikolai Ryzhkov replaces Tikhonov as Soviet premier
OCTOBER 6	The United States says **Strategic Defense Initiative**$_3$ research does not violate the 1972 ABM treaty
NOVEMBER 12	General **Jaruzelski**$_2$ resigns as prime minister of Poland and becomes chairman of the State Council (president)

19–21	**Reagan**[1] and **Gorbachev**[2] meet at the Geneva summit conference
DECEMBER 4	National security adviser Robert McFarlane resigns, replaced by John M. Poindexter

1986

JANUARY 1	Spain and Portugal join the **European Economic Community**[3]
FEBRUARY 26	Ferdinand Marcos is deposed in the Philippines; replaced by Corazon Aquino
MARCH 4	The *New York Times* reports former UN secretary-general Kurt Waldheim may have committed war crimes as a Nazi
27	West Germany to undertake **Strategic Defense Initiative**[3] research
APRIL 4	The U.S. government recommends barring Waldheim from entering the United States because of his Nazi past
15	The United States attacks targets in Libya in response to Libyan-sponsored terrorism (See **Qaddafi**[2])
JUNE 8	Waldheim wins the Austrian presidency
SEPTEMBER 19	Italy becomes the second European country to undertake **Strategic Defense Initiative**[3] research
OCTOBER 5	The *London Sunday Times,* quoting an Israeli nuclear technician, reports that Israel has been building nuclear weapons for twenty years (See **Nuclear Proliferation**[3])
11–12	**Reykjavík Summit**[3] between **Reagan**[1] and **Gorbachev**[2] proposes 50 percent cut in long-range missiles
17	Congress approves aid to the **Contras**[3] in Nicaragua
NOVEMBER 3	The press breaks the **Iran-contra Affair**[3] (See **Casey**[1]; **Reagan**[1])
8	**Molotov**[2] dies
20	Karmal resigns as Afghanistan's president
26	John Tower, Muskie, and **Brent Scowcroft**[1] are appointed to investigate the **Iran-contra Affair**[3]
28	The United States formally exceeds weapon limits of the unratified SALT II treaty (See **Perle**[1]; **Strategic Arms Limitation Talks**[3]; **Weinberger**)[1]

1987

JANUARY 28	Oliver Tambo of the African National Congress meets in Washington, D.C., with **Shultz**[1]
FEBRUARY 6	Senator Sam Nunn (D-Georgia) says **Strategic Defense Initiative**[3] testing violates the 1972 ABM treaty (See **Strategic Arms Limitation Talks**[3])
26	The Soviet Union ends an eighteen-month unilateral moratorium on nuclear testing by an underground nuclear test
26	Tower Commission releases report on **Iran-contra Affair**[3]
MARCH 3	Judge William Webster replaces **William J. Casey**[1] as **Central Intelligence Agency**[3] director
23	The United States begins to protect Kuwaiti ships in the Persian Gulf

APRIL 27   The United States bars Austrian president Waldheim from entering the United States because of his Nazi past

MAY 17   Iraqi planes attack U.S. frigate *Stark* in the Persian Gulf
19   The United States begins reflagging of Kuwaiti ships in the Persian Gulf
30   Soviet defense minister Sokolov is fired after Matias Rust, a West German teenager, evades Soviet air defenses and lands a single-engine plane in Red Square

JUNE 4   New Zealand's parliament endorses government policy barring nuclear-powered and nuclear-armed ships from New Zealand's ports
11   **Thatcher**₁ wins an unprecedented third term as prime minister of Great Britain
12   **Reagan**₁ urges **Gorbachev**₁ to tear down the **Berlin Wall**₃

DECEMBER 8–10   Washington summit conference between **Reagan**₁ and **Gorbachev**₂
8   The **Intermediate Nuclear Forces Treaty**₃ is signed, mandating the removal from the European continent of 2,611 intermediate-range nuclear missiles
9   Palestinian Intifada against Israel begins (See **Arafat**₂)
11   Former West German defense minister Manfred Woerner is named new **North Atlantic Treaty Organization**₃ secretary-general
17   **Miloš Jakeš**₂ succeeds **Husák**₂ as general secretary of the Czechoslovak Communist party.

1988

FEBRUARY 8   **Gorbachev**₂ announces Soviet intention to withdraw Soviet troops from Afghanistan
18   Boris Yeltsin is removed from the Soviet Politburo

MARCH 19   Saudi Arabia announces purchase of missiles from China

APRIL 3   Ethiopia and Somalia sign peace agreement (See **Mengistu**₂; **Siad Barre**₂)
14   Geneva Accords on Afghanistan are signed, calling on the Soviet Union to withdraw half its forces by 15 August 1988, the remainder by 15 February 1989 (See **Gorbachev**₂)

MAY 22   **Károly Grósz**₂ replaces **Kádár**₂ as general secretary of the Hungarian Communist party
27   Senate approves the **Intermediate Nuclear Forces Treaty**₃ 95–5
29–6/2   Moscow summit between **Reagan**₁ and **Gorbachev**₁

JULY 3   U.S. cruiser *Vincennes* downs an Iranian commercial jet over Persian Gulf

AUGUST 17   President Mohammad **Zia ul-Haq**₂ of Pakistan dies in a helicopter crash
20   Cease-fire is agreed to in the Iran-Iraq war (See **Hussein**₂)

OCTOBER 1   **Gorbachev**₂ replaces **Gromyko**₂ as president of the Soviet Union
5   President **Pinochet**₂ is denied another term in a referendum in Chile
10   Czechoslovak premier Lubomir Strougal resigns
11   Ladislav Adamec becomes premier of Czechoslovakia

NOVEMBER 8   **Bush**₁ elected U.S. president
23   Miklós Németh becomes Hungary's premier, replacing **Grósz**₂, who had become general secretary of Hungarian Communist party

DECEMBER 1   Benazir Bhutto is appointed Pakistan's prime minister

6 Gorbachev$_2$ announces at the United Nations a plan to reduce Soviet military by five hundred thousand men

14 United States opens talks with the PLO (See **Arafat$_2$**)

22 An agreement is signed between Angola, South Africa, and Cuba about transition to Namibian independence

1989

JANUARY 11 The Hungarian parliament allows freedom of association and freedom of assembly, permitting the formation of independent political organizations and parties

15 Demonstrations are held in Prague to commemorate the twentieth anniversary of the protest-suicides by students following the Soviet invasion of 1968 (See **Havel$_2$**)

18 The Central Committee of the Polish United Workers' (Communist) party allows the banned Solidarity trade union a two-year trial period leading to legalization

19 Yugoslavia's collective leadership chooses Ante Markovic as premier

21 **Václav Havel$_2$** is arrested for inciting protests against the Czechoslovakian regime

23 East Germany's leader Erich Honecker announces a cut of 10 percent in military spending by 1990

26 The Hungarian government allows the exhumation and reburial of the remains of **Nagy$_2$**

26 Six hundred ninety-two Czech cultural figures sign a letter to Prime Minister Adamec demanding the release of **Havel$_2$**

27 Representatives of the Polish government, Solidarity, and the Catholic church meet to negotiate political and economic reforms (See **Walesa$_2$**)

28 **Imre Pozsgay$_2$**, member of the Politburo of the Hungarian Communist party, calls for a reexamination of the 1956 revolt

29 Hungary establishes diplomatic relations with South Korea

FEBRUARY 3 North Korea recalls its ambassador from Budapest

10–11 Hungarian Communist party's Central Committee formally endorses the idea of a multiparty system (See **Pozsgay$_2$**)

15 The Soviet Union completes its military withdrawal from Afghanistan

20–21 The Hungarian Central Committee approves new constitution omitting mention of the leading role of the Communist party

21 **Havel$_2$** is sentenced to nine months in prison

21 Yeltsin, Moscow's former reformist Communist party chief, calls for open parliamentary elections (See **Gorbachev$_2$**)

25 Fifteen thousand Georgians demonstrate in Tbilisi to mark the sixty-eighth anniversary of the Soviet annexation of Georgia

MARCH 1 Six former prominent members of the Romanian Communist party send an open letter to **Nicolae Ceausescu$_2$**, accusing him of discrediting socialism, ruining the economy, and failing to observe the 1975 Helsinki agreement

5 Thousands demonstrate in Moscow in support of Yeltsin's candidacy for parliament

16 Markovic is confirmed as premier by Yugoslavia's federal parliament

23 The revived Independent Smallholders' party in Hungary holds its first national congress

26 Elections for the new Soviet Congress of People's Deputies. Many party and military officials lose to independent candidates. Yeltsin carries Moscow's at-large seat with 89 percent of the vote

APRIL 5 Radio Budapest reports plans to erect two monuments to victims of the 1956 revolt

5 The Polish government and Solidarity reach an agreement on political and economic reforms (See **Walesa$_2$**)

6	Radio Budapest reports that the pullout of Soviet troops from Hungary will begin 25 April and end in late June
17	Solidarity trade union is legalized in Poland
25	Gorbachev removes 110 officials from the Central Committee of the Communist party, Soviet Union
25	One thousand Soviet tanks leave Hungary (See **Gorbachev**$_2$)

MAY 2	Hungary begins to dismantle the barbed-wire barriers on its borders with Austria
4	**Todor Zhivkov**$_2$, Bulgarian Communist party chief, announces land reform plan
5	The Soviet Union announces it had withdrawn one thousand tanks from East Germany
8–9	The Hungarian Central Committee votes to relieve **Kádár**$_2$ of his posts as Communist party president and Central Committee member
11	**Gorbachev**$_2$ announces the Soviet Union will unilaterally reduce its nuclear forces in Eastern Europe by five hundred warheads
17	**Havel**$_2$ is released from prison in Czechoslovakia
25	The new Soviet Congress of People's Deputies elects **Gorbachev**$_2$ as president

JUNE 3–4	The Chinese government orders the suppression of prodemocracy demonstration in Tiananmen Square (See **Deng**$_2$; **Hu**$_2$; **Zhao**$_2$)
4	Solidarity wins a decisive majority in Poland's first free parliamentary elections in almost half a century. The organization wins 92 seats in the 100-seat Senate and 160 of the 161 seats available in the 460-seat Sejm (See **Walesa**$_2$)
16	**Nagy**$_2$ is ceremonially buried in Hungary
19	START negotiations resume in Geneva (See **Nitze**$_1$; **Weinberger**$_1$)
22	The Hungarian Central Committee reorganizes the leadership of the Communist party, creating a four-member presidium with **Grósz**$_2$, **Pozsgay**$_2$, Miklos Németh, and Rezsö Nyers as members

JULY 6	Former Hungarian leader **Kádár**$_2$ dies
6	The Hungarian Supreme Court rehabilitates **Nagy**$_2$ and his associates
11	Bush meets with Solidarity leader **Walesa**$_1$ in Gdansk
19	General **Jaruzelski**$_2$ elected president in Poland
25	President **Jaruzelski**$_2$ invites Solidarity to join the coalition government
29	Mieczyslaw Rakowski replaces **Jaruzelski**$_2$ as head of the Polish Communist party

AUGUST 17	The Soviet Union's Politburo endorses a plan for limited economic autonomy for the fifteen Soviet republics (See **Gorbachev**$_2$)
24	**Tadeusz Mazowiecki**$_2$ becomes the first noncommunist Polish prime minister since the early postwar years. He heads a cabinet in which the communists hold a minority position

SEPTEMBER 9	Yeltsin arrives in the United States for a speaking tour
10	Hungary opens its borders with Austria to allow East Germans to depart. Thirty thousand East Germans reach West Germany in the largest exodus since 1961. Eventually 180,000 East Germans will flee to the West
11	**Mazowiecki**$_2$ nominates a cabinet in which representatives of the Polish Communist party are a minority
18	Hungary establishes full diplomatic relations with Israel, having broken them in 1967

OCTOBER 6	East Germany marks forty years of independence
7	The Hungarian Communist party, which has ruled since 1956, formally disbands, changing its name to the Hungarian Socialist party and adopting a program favoring democratic socialism over Marxism
9	Fifty thousand demonstrators march in Leipzig against the East German regime
9	Supreme Soviet approves bill permitting strikes by workers

16 One hundred thousand demonstrators march in Leipzig against the East German regime

18 The Hungarian parliament rewrites the constitution to allow a multiparty system, scheduling free elections in 1990

18 Honecker, East Germany's Communist party general secretary since May 1971 and head of state since October 1976, is forced to resign both posts and is replaced by Egon Krenz, the youngest member of the Politburo. Also forced to resign are economic chief Gunter Mittag and Joachim Herrmann, chief of propaganda

23 Hungary adopts new constitution and changes name to the Republic of Hungary

23 Between two hundred thousand and three hundred thousand demonstrators march in Leipzig against the East German regime

23 Soviet foreign minister **Shevardnadze**$_2$, in a speech to the Supreme Soviet, criticizes the Soviet invasion of Afghanistan; he also admits that the radar installation at Krasnoyarsk violates the 1972 ABM treaty

25 **Gorbachev**$_2$ renounces the **Brezhnev Doctrine**$_3$

26 **Shevardnadze**$_2$ calls for the dissolution of the **North Atlantic Treaty Organization**$_3$ and the **Warsaw Pact**

NOVEMBER 3 Czechoslovakia opens borders for transit of East German refugees

4 Five hundred thousand East Germans hold a prodemocracy demonstration in East Berlin

7 East German premier Stoph and his cabinet resign

8 Hans Modrow is appointed new East German premier

9 Chancellor **Kohl**$_1$ visits Warsaw

9 East Germany announces the opening of all its borders, including the **Berlin Wall**$_3$

10 East Germany begins to dismantle the **Berlin Wall**$_3$

10 **Zhivkov**$_2$, general secretary of Bulgaria's Communist party since 1954 and president since 1971, resigns

10 **Zhivkov**$_2$ is replaced as general secretary by Petar T. Mladenov, Bulgaria's long-serving foreign minister

12 Adamec, Czechoslovakia's premier, declares that Czechs would no longer require exit visas to leave the country

13 East Germany's parliament, the Volkskammer, confirms Modrow to replace Stoph as premier

17 Modrow disbands the East German ministry for state security

17 Mladenov is elected president of Bulgaria

19 Civic Forum is formed in Prague to serve as an umbrella opposition organization

20 Mass demonstrations in Prague's Wenceslaus Square

23 **Dubcek**$_2$ makes his first public appearance in twenty-one years in a speech to seventy-thousand antigovernment demonstrators in Bratislava, Czechoslavakia

24 **Jakeš**$_2$, who replaced **Husák**$_2$ as head of Czechoslovakia's Communist party in December 1987, resigns along with the party's secretariat. He is replaced by Karl Urbánek

28 Adamec, Czechoslovakia's prime minister since 12 October 1988 and now serving in a caretaker role after resigning on 25 November, pledges to give up the Communist party's fourty-one–year monopoly on power

28 Chancellor **Kohl**$_2$ calls for German federation

30 In a speech in Rome, **Gorbachev**$_2$ calls for a "common European home"

DECEMBER 1 **Gorbachev**$_2$ meets Pope **John Paul II**$_2$

1 East Germany's parliament terminates the Communist party's special status

1–3 Malta summit conference between **Gorbachev**$_2$ and **Bush**$_1$. Gorbachev says that "the characteristics of the Cold War should be abandoned"

3 East Germany's Politburo resigns, including Krenz and Modrow. Krenz remains as general secretary of East Germany's Communist party, and Modrow remains as premier; Honecker and Stoph are expelled from the party

3   Civic Forum, Czechoslovakia's main opposition group, rejects Adamec's proposal for a cabinet headed by him and including non-Communists for the first time in twenty-one years

4   **Gorbachev**$_2$ meets in Moscow with leaders of the **Warsaw Pact**$_3$ nations; the leaders issue a statement condemning the 1968 invasion of Czechoslovakia

6   Krenz resigns as East Germany's head of state and chairman of the council on national defense. He is replaced by Manfred Gerlach as interim president; the council on national defense disbands

7   The East German government announces multiparty elections scheduled for 6 May 1990

7   Adamec leaves the office of Czechoslovakia's prime minister and is replaced by Márian Calfa

7   Former secretary-general **Jakeš**$_2$ is expelled from the Czech Communist party

7   The Lithuanian parliament abolishes the special status of the Communist party

9   Gregor Gysi replaces Krenz as East Germany's Communist party chairman.

10   Calfa is sworn in as Czechoslovakia's new prime minister. He heads a cabinet in which the Communists hold a minority of positions

10   **Husák**$_2$, Czechoslovakia's Communist leader from 1968 to December 1987 and president since May 1975, resigns the presidency

12   U.S. secretary of state **James A. Baker III**$_1$ meets in Potsdam with Modrow

13   The Central Committee of Bulgaria's Communist party expels **Zhivkov**$_2$ from the party

13   The foreign ministers of twenty-four Western nations announce a $1 billion emergency fund for the Polish economy

14   Soviet dissident **Sakharov**$_2$ dies

17   Romanian security forces fire at antigovernment demonstrators in Timisoara (See **Ceaucescu**$_2$)

17   The East German Communist party changes its name from Socialist Unity party of Germany (SED) to Socialist Unity party of Germany–party of Democratic Socialism (SED-PDS)

18   The **European Economic Community**$_3$ and the Soviet Union sign a ten-year commercial agreement

19   Modrow and **Kohl**$_1$ meet in Dresden

20   Lithuania's Communist party votes to declare independence from Moscow

22   **Ceaucescu**$_2$ is toppled after leading Romania for twenty-four years

23   The Brandenburg Gate is reopened in Berlin (See **Berlin Wall**$_3$)

25   **Ceaucescu**$_2$ and his wife Elena are executed

28   The Latvian parliament abolishes the special status of the Communist party

28   Czechoslovakia's parliament elects **Dubcek**$_2$ chairman

29   The National Salvation Front – Romania's provisional government – announces that Romania is no longer a communist state

29   **Havel**$_2$ is elected Czechoslovakia's new president. **Dubcek**$_2$ becomes speaker of the federal assembly

30   Poland alters its name to the Republic of Poland

1990

JANUARY 1   Poland enacts sweeping economic reforms

12   Ion Iliescu, Romania's interim president, bans the Romanian Communist party

15   Bulgaria's national assembly abolishes the special status of the Communist party

18   Czechoslovakia's prime minister Calfa resigns from membership in the Communist party

22   The Central Committee of the Albanian Communist party votes to reform the political process and introduce some free-market reforms (See **Alia**$_2$)

28   The Polish Communist party is renamed the party of Social Democracy of the Polish Republic

FEBRUARY 1   Modrow presents a plan for gradual unification of the two Germanys

2   Alexsander Lilov replaces Mladenov as chairman of the Bulgarian Communist party

3   Andrey Lukanov replaces Georgi Atanasov as Bulgaria's premier

4   The East German Communist party renames itself party of Democratic Socialism (PDS)

5   The East German Communist party becomes a minority party in the cabinet

6   The Bulgarian government announced an end to the Communist party's role in the military and police and the disbanding of the country's secret police

11   At Ottawa Conference foreign ministers of **Warsaw Pact**$_3$ and **North Atlantic Treaty Organization**$_3$ countries, in their first meeting ever, discuss **Bush's**$_1$ "open skies" proposal

13   At Ottawa Conference foreign ministers of the United States, Soviet Union, France, Great Britain, West Germany, and East Germany agree on formal talks to discuss German reunification

20   **Havel**$_2$ meets with **Bush**$_1$ in Washington, D.C.

23   Estonian Supreme Soviet abolishes the Communist party's "leading role"

24   Proindependence nationalists capture most of the seats in elections for legislative and local offices in Lithuania

26   The Soviet Union and Czechoslovakia sign an agreement calling for the phased withdrawal of Soviet troops from Czechoslovakia, to be completed by July 1991

MARCH 8   German Bundestag renounces all claims to German territories given to Poland after World War II

11   Lithuania declares independence from the Soviet Union, changes its name to the Lithuanian Republic, and elects Vytautas Landsbergis president

11   Soviet troops begin withdrawal from Hungary

13   The Soviet Congress of the Peoples' Deputies abolishes the "leading role" of Communist party, Soviet Union

14   **Gorbachev**$_2$ elected first executive president of the Soviet Union

18   The East German prounification Christian Democratic Union–led Alliance for Germany wins elections; the party of Democratic Socialism (formerly the Communist party) receives 16.3 percent of the vote

25   The Hungarian Democratic Forum claims victory in the first round of national parliamentary elections

29   Czechoslovakia changes name to Czechoslovak Federative Republic in the Czech lands and the Czecho-Slovak Republic in Slovakia

APRIL 3   Mladenov elected president of Bulgaria; resigns as secretary-general of Bulgaria's Communist party, which is renamed Bulgarian Socialist party

8   In the second, runoff round of the Hungarian national parliamentary elections, conservative parties win parliamentary majority

9   East German noncommunist parties agree to form a coalition, excluding the Communist party

12   Lothar de Maiziere becomes East German premier

13   The Soviet government admits responsibility for the 1940 Katyn Forest massacre of Polish officers, expressing regret

22   Franjo Tudjman, Croatia's opposition leader, wins the presidency

MAY 1   Protesters jeer **Gorbachev**$_2$ during May Day parade in Moscow

2   New Hungarian parliament chooses Arpád Goncz as acting president. Democratic Forum's leader Jozef Antall is chosen premier

2   The two Germanys finalize agreement on currency unification

2   West German president Richard von Weizacker, on a visit to Warsaw, announces Poland's borders inviolable

3	**North Atlantic Treaty Organization**₃ foreign ministers agree to allow full membership in the organization to a reunified Germany

3   **North Atlantic Treaty Organization**$_3$ foreign ministers agree to allow full membership in the organization to a reunified Germany

4   Latvian parliament votes for independence

5   The Two-plus-Four meeting of foreign ministers opens in Bonn

18   The foreign ministers of East and West Germany sign an agreement detailing the terms of the country's unification

20   Illiescu is elected president of Romania and the National Salvation front wins majority

29   Yeltsin is elected president of the Russian Federation

30–6/3   Washington summit between **Gorbachev**$_2$ and **Bush**$_1$. First state visit by a Soviet leader to the United States

JUNE 7   **Warsaw Pact**$_3$ leaders, meeting in Moscow, announce the West is no longer an "ideological enemy"

8–9   **Havel**'s$_2$ party captures majority in parliamentary elections in Czechoslovakia

14–15   The Romanian government trucks coal miners into the capital to battle antigovernment student rioters and ransack the opposition parties' offices

15   United States suspends economic aid to Romania

17   In a runoff election in Bulgaria, the Socialist (formerly Communist) party gets 211 of 400 seats in parliament

18   European Community suspends economic relations with Romania (See **European Economic Community**$_3$)

21   The West German Bundestag and the East German Volkskammer approve resolution guaranteeing Poland's post–World War II borders

22   East German Volkskammer approves treaty for economic union with West Germany

26   Hungarian parliament votes for the government to negotiate for the withdrawal of Hungary from the **Warsaw Pact**$_3$

JULY 2   Albanian members of Kosovo's parliament declares the province independent from Serbia

3   Party-orthodox Yegor Ligachev condemns Gorbachev's reforms

5   Czechoslovakia's parliament reelects **Havel**$_2$ president

5   Serbia dissolves governing bodies of Kosovo, assuming direct control of the province

6   Mledanov resigns as Bulgaria's premier

8   Albanian government allows emigration of antigovernment protesters sheltered in foreign embassies in Tirana

10   **Gorbachev**$_2$ is reelected party's general secretary

12   Yeltsin announces his resignation from the Communist party

13   The mayors of Moscow and Leningrad resign from the Communist party

16   In a meeting in southern Russia, **Gorbachev**$_2$ and Kohl agree to allow unified Germany to belong to **North Atlantic Treaty Organization**$_3$

30   Albania and the Soviet Union resume diplomatic relations

AUGUST 1   Bulgarian parliament elects opposition leader Zhelyu Zhelev president

15   Russian Federation and Lithuania sign agreement on trade and economic cooperation

31   West and East Germany set 3 October as the official date of German reunification; agree to name Berlin the national capital

SEPTEMBER 5   *Izvestia* publishes detail of the Shatalin Plan by economist Stanislow S. Shatalin for the creation of a Soviet economic union, which includes five-hundred-day schedule for reforming the Soviet economy

11   Prime Minister Nikolai Ryshkov threatens to resign if the Shatalin Plan is adopted

12   Meeting in Moscow, the foreign ministers of the two Germanys and Big Four Powers agree to end the powers' rights and responsibilities in Germany; the agreement also sets 1994 as the date of withdrawal of Soviet troops from the Eastern section of Germany; guarantees the Oder-Neisse as the German-Polish border

17	**Walesa**$_2$ formally declares his candidacy for the Polish presidency
20	West German Bundestag and East German Volkskammer ratify the 31 August agreement on German reunification
24	East Germany withdraws from the **Warsaw Pact**$_3$
30	The Soviet Union and Israel agree to open consulates in Tel Aviv and Moscow, respectively, after breaking off diplomatic relations in 1967; The Soviet Union establishes diplomatic relations with South Korea

OCTOBER 3	West and East Germany unite as the Federal Republic of Germany
15	**Gorbachev**$_2$ is awarded the Nobel Peace Prize for his role in ending the Cold War
16	**Gorbachev**$_2$ presents the "Gorbachev Plan" for economic restructuring of the Soviet Union. The plan does not include the five-hundred-day timetable of the Shatalin Plan. Yeltsin rejects **Gorbachev's**$_2$ plan
19	Supreme Soviet approves **Gorbachev**$_2$ economic plan
31	The parliament of the Russian Federation votes to adopt the five-hundred-day plan

NOVEMBER 14	German and Polish foreign ministers sign a treaty guaranteeing current border as the permanent German-Polish border
21	Heads of **Conference on Security and Cooperation in Europe**$_3$ member states sign the Charter of Paris for New Europe, ending the economic and military division of the continent
23	**Gorbachev**$_2$ offers a new union treaty to govern the relationship between the Soviet central government and the fifteen republics

DECEMBER 7	Bulgarian parliament votes to make Ditmar Popov new premier
9	In runoff elections in Poland **Walesa**$_2$ receives more than 74 percent of the vote
11	Albanian government announces endorsement of independent political parties
20	Shevardnadze surprises the Congress of Peoples' Deputies by announcing his resignation, warning that reactionary forces threaten the Soviet Union
22	**Walesa**$_2$ is sworn in as president of Poland
22	In a vote in Slovenia more than 90 percent of the voters endorses independence from Yugoslavia

1991

JANUARY 2	Soviet elite forces capture buildings in Latvia and Lithuania
13	Soviet troops kill fifteen protesters in Vilnius, Lithuania
13	Russian Federation president Yeltsin signs mutual security pact with the three Baltic states
15	Alexander Bessmertnykh becomes new Soviet foreign minister
19	Croatia places its militia and police forces on alert
20	Hundreds of thousands march on the Kremlin to protest Soviet crackdown in the Baltic states
21	ECC suspends $1 billion in economic aid to the Soviet Union (See **European Economic Community**$_3$)
22	Bush urges Gorbachev to "resist using force" in the Baltics

FEBRUARY 6	Antigovernment riots and strikes take place in Tirana, the Albanian capital
6	Defying **Gorbachev's**$_2$ call, the three Baltic states, together with Georgia, Moldavia, and Armenia, announce they will not particpate in a referendum on the future of the Soviet Union
11	**Gorbachev**$_2$ notifies leaders of the **Warsaw Pact**$_3$ that the organization will cease to exist 1 April
21	Czechoslovakia's parliament begins to pass sweeping legislation on privatization and land restitution

22   Albanian president **Ramiz Alia**$_2$ appoints new government response to prodemocracy demonstrations in Tiranë
25   **Zhivkov**$_2$ corruption trial opens in Sofia
25   Foreign ministers of the **Warsaw Pact**$_3$ nations sign an agreement dissolving the alliance by 31 March

MARCH 1   Tens of thousands of striking miners ignore the Supreme Soviet's demand to go back to work
4–7   Thousands of Albanians flee to Italy and Yugoslavia
11   Thousands march in Bratislava for Slovak independence from Czechoslovakia
15   The United States and Albania resume diplomatic relations, broken off in 1939
16   Serbian president Slobodan Milosevic announces Serbia will no longer recognize the authority of the Yugoslavian federal government
27   The United States withdraws its medium-range missiles from Europe
31   The Albanian Communist party wins the first multiparty elections since World War II, receiving 66 percent of the vote
31   Voters in Georgia overwhelmingly vote for independence

APRIL 4   Georgia declares independence from the Soviet Union
9   **Gorbachev**$_2$ unveils "anticrisis program" to rescue the Soviet Union from disintegration
23   **Gorbachev**$_2$ and leaders of nine Soviet republics agree on a political and economic reform package and modified relationship between Moscow and the republics
24   Hungary's parliament orders compensation for landowners whose land was nationalized under communist rule after 1949

MAY 1   Yeltsin asserts the authority of the Russian Federation over coal mines on Russian territory
4   **József Cardinal Mindszenty**$_2$, who died in Austria in 1975, is reburied in Hungary
6   The Soviet government transfers authority over mines to the Russian Federation
19   Voters in Croatia votes for Croatian sovereignty within a loose Yugoslavian federation
20   **Bush**$_1$ extends waiver to the Soviet Union from the 1974 **Jackson-Vanik Amendment**$_3$
23   Supreme Soviet endorses **Gorbachev's**$_2$ anticrisis program
26   Proindependence candidate Zviad Gamsakhurdia is elected president of Georgia, the first directly elected leader of a Soviet republic

JUNE 12   Yeltsin elected president of Russian republic
17   **Gorbachev**$_2$ and leaders of seven republics sign a new union treaty
19   Soviet troops complete withdrawal from Hungary
19   **Conference on Security and Cooperation in Europe**$_3$ admits Albania
20   The Bundestag votes to move the capital from Bonn to Berlin
21   Soviet troops complete withdrawal from Czechoslovakia
25   Slovenia and Croatia declare independence from Yugoslavia
28   Council of Mutual Economic Aid (Comecon) formally disbands

JULY 1   **Warsaw Pact**$_3$ formally dissolved
1   Supreme Soviet permits sale of state-owned enterprises
20   Yeltsin outlaws political activity in the workplace and government establishments in the Russian republic

AUGUST 19   Tass announces **Gorbachev**$_2$ has been incapacitated in his vacation dacha and is being replaced by Vice-president Gennadi Yanayev as head of the State Committee for the State of Emergency. Troops are positioned in key intersections in Moscow and other cities. Yeltsin denounces coup leaders as traitors

20	Yeltsin is reassured by **Bush**₁ and British prime minister John Majors that Western powers will not recognize the coup leaders as legitimate. Yeltsin addresses a mass rally outside the Russian parliament
20	Estonia declares independence
21	Coup collapses; **Gorbachev**₂ released from house arrest
21	Latvia declares independence
21	Lithuania reaffirms 1990 declaration of independence
21	**Bush**₁ waives the **Jackson-Vanik Amendment**₃ for Romania
22	Latvian and Lithuanian Communist parties are banned
23	**Gorbachev**₂, back in Moscow, replaces top echelon of Defense and Interior Ministries and the KGB
24	Yeltsin recognizes Estonian and Latvian independence
24	Gorbachev resigns as general secretary of the Soviet Communist party; disbands the party's Central Committee; places all party's property under control of the Soviet parliament; dismisses cabinet
24	Ukrainian parliament votes for independence from the Soviet Union
25	Parliament of Belorussia votes for independence from the Soviet Union
25	Yugoslav forces attack Croatia in support of Croatian ethnic Serbs
27	Parliament of Moldavia votes for independence from the Soviet Union
29	Supreme Soviet bans the activities of the Communist party
29	Russian republics sign political and economic treaties with Ukraine and Kazakhstan
30	Parliament of Azerbaijan votes for independence from the Soviet Union
31	Parliament of Uzbekistan votes for independence from the Soviet Union
31	Parliament of Kirgizia votes for independence from the Soviet Union

SEPTEMBER 2	European Community recognizes independence of the three Baltic states. The United States establishes diplomatic relations with them
5	Parliament of Crimea votes for independence from Ukraine
6	Soviet State Council recognizes the independence of the three Baltic republics
6	Leningrad changes its name to Saint Petersburg
7	Croatia and Slovenia declare immediate secession from Yugoslavia
8	Macedonia votes to declare independence from Yugoslavia
9	Parliament of Tadzhikistan votes for independence from the Soviet Union
26	Romanian cabinet resigns
27	**Bush**₁ announces the unilateral elimination of twenty-four thousand U.S. nuclear warheads

OCTOBER 8	**Gorbachev**₂ and leaders of eight republics sign a plan for economic union. Ukraine and Moldavia sign the pact a month later
14	Soviet Union ends all bans on internal travel, to begin 1 January 1992
13	Bulgaria's main opposition party wins national elections
19	Ethnic Albanian legislators declare Kosovo independent from Yugoslavia
22	Ukraine declares the creation of independent armed forces
23	Yugoslav forces attack Dubrovnik in Croatia

NOVEMBER 5	Soviet Union opens its territory to aerial inspection
8	Bulgarian parliament votes for Filip Dimitrov as premier
8	**European Economic Community**₃ imposes economic sanctions on Yugoslavia
15–17	Yeltsin takes control of Soviet natural resources and allows the ruble to float
19	**Shevardnadze**₂ is reappointed foreign minister
25	Soviet republics reject **Gorbachev's**₂ union treaty
25	Congress votes to use $500 million of the defense budget to dismantle Soviet nuclear warheads

27	**Bush**$_1$ declares United States will recognize Ukraine's independence
30	Russia takes control of Soviet foreign ministry and embassies

DECEMBER 1   Ukrainians vote for independence; Leonid Kravchuk is elected president

2   Russia recognizes Ukraine's independence

8   The leaders of Russia, Ukraine, and Belorussia proclaim that the Soviet Union has ceased to exist; they also declare the creation of Commonwealth of Independent States and invite other republics to join

9   **Gorbachev**$_2$ declares the three republics have no right to dissolve the Soviet Union

10   Parliaments of Ukraine and Belorussia ratify the Commonwealth agreement

12   Russian parliament ratifies the Commonwealth of Independent States agreement

12   Former East German leader Honecker seeks refuge at the Chilean embassy in Moscow

14   Kazakhstan, Kirgizia, Tadzhikistan, Turkmenia, and Uzbekistan join the Commonwealth of Independent States

17   **Gorbachev**$_2$ announces that all Soviet central government structures will cease to exist at the end of the year

18   The four Soviet republics in possession of nuclear weapons announce they will implement the cuts agreed upon between **Bush**$_1$ and **Gorbachev**$_2$

19   Yeltsin takes control over the Foreign Ministry, **KGB**$_3$, and Parliament

19   **European Economic Community**$_3$ announces it will recognize Slovenia and Croatia by 15 January 1992

20   Bosnia-Herzegovina applies to the **European Economic Community**$_3$ for recognition as an independent state

21   Eleven former Soviet republics announce they constitute the Commonwealth of Independent States, to begin operations by 15 January 1992. Russia will retain the Soviet permanent seat at the **United Nations**$_3$ Security Council

23   Germany recognizes Croatia and Slovenia

25   **Gorbachev**$_2$ resigns as president of the Soviet Union. The red flag is replaced with the white, blue, and red Russian flag over the Kremlin

The Cold War: A History

Benjamin Frankel

with Neal Rosendorf

A recent book on the Cold War begins with this paragraph:

> Measured by the blood and treasure marshalled and directed in its pursuit, the Cold War must be reckoned among the great epics in human history. Unprecedented quantities of wealth and hundreds of millions of people from nations around the world were absorbed in this endeavor. Unlike Homer's *Iliad* and *Odyssey*, it was not limited to two peoples washed by common waters. It spread and sprawled to the far reaches of the globe, sparking wars – Korea and Vietnam most notably – and siring civil strife along its path.[1]

The Cold War, this great epic, did not break out: it evolved. Sometime during 1945, between the Yalta Conference in February and the Potsdam Conference in July, American leaders began to realize that the United States and the Soviet Union were on a collision course. The Cold War did not replace a warm, cozy relationship between the two countries. The tensions and mutual antipathy between them began much earlier, expressed, for example, by Woodrow Wilson, who, shortly after the Russian Revolution, described the Bolsheviks as representing "nobody but themselves. . . . They have no mandate from anybody. . . . [A] group of men more cruel than the Czar himself is controlling the destinies of that great people."[2] Successive generations of U.S. policymakers accepted Wilson's view.

The 3 March 1918 Brest-Litovsk agreement between the new communist regime in Russia and Germany, and the subsequent Russian exit from World War I on terms favorable to the Germans, only increased American resentment toward the new revolutionary regime, and the administration soon found a way to express its irritation. During the war some seventy thousands Czechs, serving in the Austrian army on the eastern front, deserted.[3] When the Russian Bolshevik Revolution erupted, the Czech soldiers were trapped in Siberia. Wilson contributed American troops to an Allied effort to help the Czechs make it back home. Antirevolutionary White Russian forces, fighting the Red forces, joined the Czech contingent, and as a result the Allied aid to the Czechs had a distinct anti-Bolshevik aspect to it.

Wilson also ordered five thousand American troops to go to the Arctic port cities of Murmansk and Archangel in the summer of 1918 to ensure that large stores of goods the Allies stashed there did not fall into German hands. The American troops found themselves battling with the Bolsheviks for control of the two cities, and in many cases they were joined by White forces engaged in their own antirevolutionary campaign. There was also a dispatch of nine thousand American troops to Siberia to prevent the Japanese from exploiting the revolutionary chaos in Russia as a pretext for expanding into Siberia. The Americans stayed largely neutral between the Red and White contingents, but their presence tended to favor the antirevolutionary forces.[4]

Post–World War I U.S.-Soviet Relations

In the 1920s and early 1930s the United States continued its policy of nonrecognition of the Soviet Union. Rumors of Soviet support for anti-American activities in China and Latin America contributed to further deterioration of relations, and the Soviets were not invited to sign the 1928 Kellogg-Briand Pact. As the Depression deepened, however, Soviet suggestions in 1933 that they might contract to buy over $1 billion worth of goods from the United States prompted the new Franklin D. Roosevelt administration to examine U.S.-Soviet relations.[5] That decision was also prompted by Roosevelt's wish to counterbalance the growing power of Germany and Japan with another world power.[6] In November 1933 the United States and the Soviet Union established diplomatic relations.

The exchange of diplomats, however, did not reduce the suspicion with which the two governments viewed each other. The reluctance of the British and French governments to take a strong stand against Adolf Hitler's Germany upset the Soviets. The failure of Western governments to resist the Fascist-supported rebellion of Generalissimo Francisco Franco in Spain, the British and French acquiescence in the 1938 Anschluss, and the growing tide of appeasement in Great Britain all seemed to confirm the Soviets' fear that the West, rather than gearing up to fight Nazi Germany, was interested in unleashing Germany's military might on the Soviet Union.

But even when Nazi Germany's policies caused the common ground between the Soviet Union and the Western powers to be accentuated, cooperation was difficult to achieve. When Germany's May 1939 occupation of Czechoslovakia prompted Great Britain and France to negotiate a security arrangement with the Soviet Union, the British and French insisted on conditions that were unacceptable to the Soviets. Britain and France wanted the security agreement to absolve them from coming to the aid of Soviet Union in the event Germany invaded and occupied the Baltic States; at the same time, however, both governments insisted that the Soviet Union come to the aid of Belgium and the Netherlands if those countries were attacked by Germany.[7] When Great Britain and France offered security guarantees to Poland, the Soviet Union was excluded from the agreement because of traditional Polish antipathy toward the Russians. Suspicious of the West's intentions, Joseph Stalin decided to trust Hitler and at the end of August 1939 invited Joachim von Ribbentrop, the German foreign minister, to come to Moscow to negotiate a separate German-Soviet agreement.

The shock in the West at the Nazi-Soviet pact and the anger directed at the Soviet Union as a result were even greater than the bitterness generated by the Soviet-German agreement at Brest-Litovsk two decades earlier. Stalin was blamed in the West for encouraging Hitler to attack Poland, causing the outbreak of World War II. Many saw the Nazi-Soviet pact as a vivid demonstration of the cynicism and ruthlessness of Soviet foreign policy, and the naked brutality of its chief architect. The speed with which the Soviet Union moved to occupy the Baltic States, eastern Poland, and sections of Romania confirmed this view of the Soviet Union.

World War II

Even after Germany attacked the Soviet Union in June 1941, in the process becoming an enemy of both the Western powers and the Soviet Union, the differences between East and West, and the

mutual mistrust and hostility, did not subside. Indeed, the very name given to the anti-Nazi collaborative effort – Grand Alliance – is misleading. It is more accurate to describe the 1941–1945 period as a time during which the United States and Great Britain, on the one hand, and the Soviet Union, on the other hand, fought Germany simultaneously. If the term *alliance* means a close coordination of effort and an agreement on the goals and means of that effort, then the relationship among the anti-German partners cannot meaningfully be described as an alliance.[8]

The major contention between the Soviet Union and the Western allies was the issue of the second front. Germany attacked the Soviet Union in one of the largest military moves in history. The German assault consisted of 3.6 million troops, thirty-six hundred tanks, seventy-two hundred artillery pieces, and six hundred thousand vehicles organized into 154 divisions. The Luftwaffe supported the attack with twenty-seven hundred of its planes. The Wehrmacht drove deeply into the Soviet Union, reaching the outskirts of Moscow by October. The Soviets, desperate for help, urged Great Britain and the United States to open a second front in the West to force the Germans to move some of their forces from the eastern front and alleviate the pressure on the Red Army. The United States wanted to accept the Soviet view, but Great Britain, still pained by the massive losses of the wasteful continental ground war fought in World War I, and mindful of the German threat to its imperial possessions, preferred another strategy. Winston S. Churchill wanted the Western allies to fight the German forces in North Africa, then attack the Continent by invading Italy. After deliberations, Roosevelt accepted the British strategy.

The campaign in North Africa and the invasion of Italy were marginal to the defeat of Germany. While British and American forces in North Africa were doing battle with twelve German divisions, the Red Army was engaging close to two hundred. What was especially upsetting to the Soviets was their belief that the German forces in France were inferior to German forces in the East; the Soviets believed those forces could have been overcome without great difficulty by a concerted British-U.S. effort. But the Western allies did not open a second front until June 1944, and by that time the tide of the war had already turned against the Germans, with the war in the East all but decided. The conduct of Great Britain and the United States convinced the Soviets that the Western allies were hoping, in Stalin's words, to have the Soviet Union bled white.

The mutual distrust was deepened by suspicions each side entertained about the possibility of the other making a separate peace with Germany. Talks in Bern, Switzerland, in early 1945, among American, British, and German intelligence officers about the disposition of German troops in Italy — talks to which the Soviets were not invited — made Stalin even more edgy, believing a deal was being struck between his nominal allies and Germany.[9] The mutual lack of trust thus increased as the war drew to a close, poisoning the relationship and making the Cold War all but inevitable.

The Polish Issue

No other issue separated the partners to the anti-Nazi alliance as the Polish issue. Poland had served as a corridor for numerous invasions of Russia from the West. The Soviets, therefore, insisted that the postwar border between the Soviet Union and Poland be the one created by the Molotov-Ribbentrop agreement of August 1939, an agreement giving the Soviet Union large parts of Poland's eastern territories. The British accepted the Soviet view on Poland's eastern border and at the Teheran Conference in late 1943 suggested that Poland be compensated for the lost territories in the east with German territories in the west. The six million Germans who lived in the area between Poland's old western border and the new border on the Oder River would be expelled to Germany. Roosevelt, mindful of the powerful Polish constituency in American politics, could not publicly accept the arrangement, but there was little he could do about it.

The second aspect of the Polish issue separating the Soviets from the Western powers was the nature of the postwar Polish government. The British and the Americans supported the Polish government-in-exile in London (the London Poles), while the Soviets, after 1943, supported a group of pro-Soviet Poles (the Lublin Group). Here, too, the fact that Poland was occupied by the Red Army left the Western allies little choice but to accept the Soviet preferences. At Yalta, Roosevelt was able to extract from Stalin a promise to allow free elections in Poland, but it was clear that the Soviets would do what they wished.

The differences over Poland, and Soviet brutality toward the noncommunist, anti-Nazi Polish resistance, overwhelmed whatever understanding was achieved between the Soviet Union and Great Britain with regard to the postwar world. In the

Balkans, for example, Stalin and Churchill agreed that Romania and Bulgaria would belong to the Soviet sphere of influence, Greece to the British, while Yugoslavia and Hungary would be divided equally between the two. The Soviets demonstrated readiness to live within that understanding by refusing to support the leftist insurgency in Greece and by offering to recognize a reconstituted Greek monarchy. The United States, however, with its anti-imperialist tradition, was never comfortable with the naked power politics of dividing the world into spheres of influence and was reluctant to endorse the British-Soviet understanding.

Great Britain and the Soviet Union reached an understanding on the Balkans. The Western allies, however, made unilateral decisions in North Africa, Italy, and the Low Countries. And yet Great Britain and the United States insisted that the Soviet Union live up to its promise at Yalta to allow free elections in Poland, although the Soviets felt that they should have special privileges in Eastern Europe. The British felt morally obligated to the London Poles, whom they had supported throughout the war. In addition, Polish soldiers performed bravely during the war in the Allied cause, and about 20 percent of the pilots defending Great Britain during the Battle of Britain were Polish.[10] For the American administration, the reluctance to engage in traditional power politics and the influence of the large Polish constituency in domestic politics were reasons to insist on free elections in Poland. As Harry S Truman bluntly told Soviet foreign minister Vyacheslav Michailovich Molotov in a meeting in Washington, D.C., on 23 April 1945, Poland had become the symbol of U.S. foreign policy.[11] Stalin protested that Poland was analogous to Belgium, where the Western allies had established a government without consulting the Soviets, but to no avail.

A compromise on Poland was reached during a visit of Truman's emissary, Harry L. Hopkins, to Moscow. The United States agreed to recognize the Lublin Group as the basis for the provisional Polish government, while the Soviets agreed to include a few representatives of the London Poles and confirm their support for free elections. On 5 July 1945 the United States recognized the provisional Polish government. After the Polish issue was settled, if only temporarily, the Soviets exhibited greater flexibility in their attitudes to the political composition of the governments in Hungary, Romania, and Czechoslovakia.

Less than two weeks after the American recognition of the Polish provisional government, Truman, Churchill, and Stalin met at Potsdam, outside Berlin. One of the major topics of discussion was to be the Soviet entry into the war against Japan. The successful testing of an atomic device at the test site of Alamogordo, New Mexico, on the eve of the conference, however, caused Truman and Churchill to have second thoughts about the advisability of having the Soviet Union participate in the war in Asia because it would provide them claim to a say in postwar political arrangements in Asia.[12] Some members of the American delegation at Potsdam were also hoping the possession of the bomb would give the United States more leverage in dealing with the Soviet Union on Eastern European affairs.[13] With the Polish problem settled, at least temporarily, and with the atomic bomb making Soviet entry into the war against Japan less urgent, the Potsdam Conference saw the settlement of the German problem replace the question of Soviet participation in the war in Asia as the major issue between the United States and the Soviet Union. The Soviets were hoping to extract large reparations from Germany, but the Western allies, mindful of the consequences of the harsh anti-German clauses of the Versailles peace after World War I, objected. The Soviet were also dissatisfied with the division of Germany into occupation zones, since their zone was mostly agricultural, while the heavily industrial areas were under the control of the Western allies.

"Declarations" of the Cold War

The German question and its derivatives became a central topic of superpower relations during the next five years. As the two sides became more entrenched in their positions, and as other divisive issues came to dominate the superpower relationship, the Cold War began in earnest. As two historians write, "By late 1945 it was apparent that Soviet and American policies were no longer joined by even the most tenuous of the strands that had held the wartime alliance together."[14]

Two speeches made at the beginning of 1946 confirmed, and reflected, this new phase of international politics. One historian called these speeches "appropriate declarations" of the Cold War.[15] On 9 February 1946 Stalin made his "Two Camps" speech, in which he declared that communism and capitalism belonged to two different camps, fundamentally incompatible and irreconcilable, and that peace was impossible until capitalism was vanquished and replaced by communism.[16] A month later, at Westminster College in Fulton, Missouri, Churchill declared, "From Stettin in the Baltic to

Trieste in the Adriatic, an iron curtain has descended across the continent." Churchill called for an Anglo-American "fraternal association," a peacetime "special relationship" based on shared heritage, cultural values, and strategic concerns. The purpose of the alliance would be to deny to the Soviets "the indefinite expansion of their power and doctrine."[17]

The image of the international scene portrayed in the "Two Camps" and "Iron Curtain" speeches had been urged upon the Truman administration for the preceding eighteen months by George F. Kennan, a Foreign Service officer who played a key role in elaborating the conceptual framework for United States policy during the Cold War. "Rarely in the course of diplomacy," writes John Lewis Gaddis, "is it given to one individual to express, within the compass of a single document, ideas of such force and persuasion that they immediately change the direction of a nation's foreign policy."[18]

On 22 February 1946 Kennan cabled from Moscow an eight-thousand-word analysis of the Soviet Union to the State Department in Washington.[19] Kennan's Long Telegram became, according to one of his biographers, "one of the two or three most important texts of the early cold war."[20] American effort to normalize relations with the Soviet Union were bound to fail, Kennan wrote, because they were based on the erroneous assumption that Soviet hostility to the West was caused by an understandable if extreme fear of external threats. This assumption led to the belief that it was up to the United States to choose a diplomatic strategy that would overcome Soviet insecurity and assuage Soviet suspicion. However, the Soviet leaders, Kennan pointed out, were traditional Russian authoritarians, like the czars, who found in Marxist dogma "justification for . . . the dictatorship without which they did not know how to rule, for cruelties they did not dare not to inflict, for sacrifices they felt bound to demand." American leaders had to recognize that the Kremlin was "a political force committed fanatically to the belief that with [the] U.S. there can be no permanent modus vivendi, that it is desirable and necessary that the internal harmony of our society be disrupted, our traditional way of life be destroyed, the international authority of our state be broken, if Soviet power is to be secure." If the United States dealt realistically with the problem posed by the Soviet threat, it could be solved "without recourse to any general military conflict." Because the Soviets were cautious and responsive to the logic of force, they would back down if the United States possessed sufficient power and made clear its willingness to use it.

Soviet conduct during 1946 seemed to confirm Kennan's analysis and Churchill's dark picture, as tensions between the United States and the Soviet Union mounted with each passing month. In March, the Iran crisis developed; in April, the Chinese civil war was resumed; April and May saw the intensification of U.S.-Soviet tensions over Germany; in June, the Baruch Plan for the international control of atomic energy was rejected by the Soviets; in August, Soviet efforts to gain control of the Dardanelles brought the two superpowers to the brink of military conflict; in September, Secretary of State James F. Byrnes announced that the United States would stay in Germany indefinitely, if necessary, to make sure the Soviets did not increase their influence there.

The Soviet Union continued to tighten its grip on the Eastern European countries. It also refused to abide by a promise made at Yalta that it would withdraw its forces from northern Iran within six months after the war ended, and in fact the Soviets began to negotiate with the Iranian government on the creation of an "autonomous region" in Azerbaijan. The Soviet conduct in Iran also provided some support for Kennan's argument that the Kremlin would back down in the face of clear and determined opposition. The Truman administration made it very clear that it would not accept continued Soviet presence in Iran and threatened to send American troops to evict the Soviets; the Soviets withdrew in early April. The Soviet Union also backed down from its demand for a shared control of the Turkish Dardanelles Straits, when the United States announced its unequivocal support for Turkey.

Clark Clifford and George Elsey, both trusted aides of the president, summed up the prevailing mood in the administration when they wrote in the Elsey-Clifford Report, prepared at the president's request, that "it is our hope that [the Soviets] will change their minds and work out with us a fair and equitable settlement when they realize we are too strong to be beaten and too determined to be frightened."

"By the end of 1946," writes Kennan biographer David Mayers, "the cumulative impact of Kennan's telegram, Churchill's warnings (for example, the "iron curtain" speech of March 1946), and the George Elsey–Clark Clifford confidential report. . . . confirmed Truman in his instincts about the Soviet Union and the need to treat firmly with it."[21]

The speech, the telegram, and the report dealt in general concepts. Beginning with the enunciation of the Truman Doctrine, policy prescriptions were proposed the following year.

Truman Doctrine

The Truman Doctrine was issued in response to the Greek civil war between the government and local communists, who were receiving aid from Yugoslavia and Bulgaria. Greece and Turkey had traditionally been part of England's sphere of influence, but by early 1947 Great Britain, exhausted from the war and anticolonial agitation throughout its empire, informed the United States that it could no longer maintain its responsibilities in the region and would leave in six weeks.

The Truman administration, alarmed by the what might happen in southeast Europe and the northern Mediterranean when the British left, sought to persuade skeptical congressional leaders of the need for the United States to assume Great Britain's role in the area. On 27 February a dramatic meeting took place between a congressional delegation led by Senate Foreign Relations Committee Chairman Arthur Vandenberg (Republican senator from Michigan), Secretary of State George Marshall, and Undersecretary of State Dean Acheson.[22] "I knew we were met at Armageddon," Acheson later wrote. In what came to be known as the "all-out speech," he recalled that he told the congressmen:

> In the past eighteen months. . . . Soviet pressure on the Straits, on Iran, and in Northern Greece had brought the Balkans to the point where a highly possible Soviet breakthrough might open three continents to Soviet penetration. Like apples in a barrel infected by one rotten one, the corruption of Greece would infect Iran and all the east. It would also carry infection to Africa through Asia Minor and Egypt, and to Europe through Italy and France, already threatened by the strongest domestic Communist parties in Western Europe. The Soviet Union was playing one of the greatest gambles in history at minimal cost. It did not need to win all the possibilities. Even one or two offered immense gains. We and we alone were in a position to break up the play. These were the stakes that the British withdrawal from

the Eastern Mediterranean offered to an eager and ruthless opponent.[23]

Vandenberg and the delegation were convinced that the United States had to assume the responsibilities that Great Britain was abandoning but advised Acheson that the president would have to make a speech to the nation to persuade the public to support this departure from traditional U.S. foreign policy. An interdepartmental committee was immediately set to draft the speech. The speech was more than a request for foreign aid for Greece and Turkey; it enunciated the Truman Doctrine, which set forth what Nathan and Oliver called "the idiom of the debate and the central questions of American foreign policy for twenty-five years."[24]

On 12 March 1947 Truman addressed a joint session of Congress, repeating Acheson's argument. The immediate purpose of the speech was to ask for $400 million in aid to Greece and Turkey, but Truman used the occasion to introduce the new conceptual underpinnings of postwar U.S. foreign policy. U.S. foreign policy would be based on two assumptions: first, U.S. security is inextricably linked with – indeed, it depends on – international peace and order; second, it is the nature of regimes – their internal politics – that determines whether or not they threaten international peace, and totalitarian communist regimes pose the most egregious threat to international order. The conclusion was that in order to protect its own security, the United States would have to take an active interest in the internal politics of other nations. Truman said:

> We shall not realize our objectives.
> ... unless we are willing to help free people to maintain their free institutions and their national integrity against aggressive movements that seek to impose upon them totalitarian regimes. This is no more than a frank recognition that totalitarian regimes imposed upon free peoples by direct or indirect aggression, undermine the foundations of international peace and hence the security of the United States.[25]

Few in the Truman administration intended to implement the Truman Doctrine literally beyond Greece and Turkey. The president's strongly worded speech was seen as a means of winning Congressional and public support for a limited venture.

Marshall and Kennan objected to the doctrine's universalist rhetoric, fearing Truman's speech would be read too literally by the American public and U.S. allies.

The Truman Doctrine may have been hastily improvised to spur domestic support for a limited policy, but it was nonetheless a watershed in the Cold War. Truman served notice on the American public that the United States would no longer stand aloof from European politics; rather, the United States would assume a leading global role commensurate with its power.

The Marshall Plan

After the aid to Greece and Turkey, the first important product of the Truman Doctrine was the Marshall Plan. Europe was devastated at the end of World War II, too poor to initiate a reconstruction effort. A demoralized population and economic chaos, coupled with the strength of the communist parties, especially in France and Italy, caused U.S. policymakers to believe that a real risk existed of Western European nations falling into the Soviet orbit. In the spring of 1947 the Truman administration decided that the United States should finance European reconstruction. The plan, announced by Marshall at a Harvard commencement address in June 1947 and described by Churchill as "the most unsordid act in history," proposed that European nations, including the Soviet Union and Eastern Europe, receive $17 billion over a four-year period. (The amount was later reduced to $13.5 billion.) The Soviet Union refused the aid and prevented Czechoslovakia and Poland, which had expressed considerable interest in the program, from participating.

The United States would not dictate the manner in which the Europeans utilized the funding except to stipulate that it could not be spent on military supplies. Although emphasis was placed on jump-starting Europe's moribund economy, the Marshall Plan, at Kennan's proposal, also contained a covert political element. The Central Intelligence Agency (CIA), created in mid 1947 as part of the National Security Act, was instructed to funnel money secretly to noncommunist political parties, organizations such as churches and labor unions, and newspapers, and other publications. The operation was a success in limiting communist influence on political institutions and in restricting the ability of pro-Soviet organizations to influence public opinion in Western Europe.[26] There was strong bipartisan domestic support for the Marshall Plan, particularly after the communist coup in Czechoslovakia in February 1948. The plan lasted four years and contributed greatly to the resuscitation of the European economy, and the restoration of the Europeans' battered morale.

Kennan played an important role in the planning and implementation of the Marshall Plan. In addition to his introduction of covert activities into the aid program, he was instrumental in the reorientation of the American administration of defeated Germany and Japan from an emphasis on the punitive measures employed since the end of the war to a policy of reintegrating these industrialized states into a Western-inspired global economy. Kennan's advocacy of German and Japanese integration was based on economic reasons but also on his evolving ideas about U.S. policy toward the Soviet Union, which he outlined in "The Sources of Soviet Conduct," published under the pseudonym "X" in the July 1947 *Foreign Affairs*.[27]

The "X" article recapitulated the essence of the Long Telegram and added concrete prescriptions for dealing with the Soviets.[28] Kennan saw the Soviet threat as stemming from a combination of traditional Russian expansionist tendencies and communist messianic ideology. But Soviet expansionism responded to the logic of force, and therefore the Soviet Union could be "contained by the adroit and vigilant application of counterforce at a series of constantly shifting geographical and political points, corresponding to the shifts and maneuvers of Soviet policy."

Kennan did not call for a U.S. response to Soviet attempts to "break out" anywhere along the vast boundary of the Soviet sphere of influence. Rather, assuming that "threats, to be serious, had to combine hostility with capability,"[29] he advocated "strong-point" defense, that is, preventing the Soviet Union from spreading its influence to areas with industrial and military power. According to Kennan there were only five centers of military and industrial power that were important to U.S. national security: the United States, Great Britain, Germany, central Europe, and Japan.

Kennan saw the Soviet threat as primarily political rather than military, and he advocated political and economic programs such as the Marshall Plan to contain that threat. Kennan's views were influential through the end of the 1940s, but a series of Soviet actions and communist victories — among them the Berlin blockade, the Chinese civil war, the communist coup in Czechoslovakia, the detonation of the first Soviet atomic bomb, and the Korean War — was interpreted to mean that the

Soviet Union was more vigorous and expansive than was thought earlier, and caused American leaders to rethink U.S. containment policy.

Following the announcement of the Marshall Plan in June, the United States, Great Britain, and France initiated a series of moves that led to the creation of the West German state. In the fall of 1947 the American and British occupation zones were economically merged into "Bizonia." In February 1948 the United States, Great Britain, France, and the Benelux (Belgium, the Netherlands, and Luxembourg) countries convened in London to discuss the future of Germany. The Soviet Union was not invited to attend. The London Conference ratified the participation of Bizonia and the French occupation zone in the European recovery program. It also called for the Western zones to establish West German political institutions to take control of German political and economic matters.

The intensive U.S. involvement in Western Europe's economic recovery and the move toward the creation of a German state were perceived by the Soviets as hostile policies. The fact that the West implemented these policies without bothering to consult or even inform the Soviets only intensified Soviet suspicions. In response, the Soviet Union, in April 1948, halted Western military supplies to West Berlin. On 24 June, in response to the Western powers' policy of currency reform in the occupation zones, the Soviets imposed a blockade on West Berlin, cutting off all land and water routes to and from the Western sectors of Berlin, which lay deep within the Soviet occupation zone.

While the Western powers were moving resolutely to create a West German state, the Soviet Union faced a challenge to its authority in Eastern Europe by the Yugoslav communist leader Josip Broz Tito. The Soviet Union could neither bring Tito to heel nor topple him, since Tito claimed considerable popular support for his leadership of the anti-Nazi Yugoslav partisans during World War II. This embarrassment made it doubly important for the Soviets to challenge the West over Berlin, where they thought they held the upper hand.

The United States considered and dismissed a plan to break the Berlin blockade militarily. B-29 bombers, from the same groups that had dropped atom bombs on Japan, were sent to England, but these particular aircraft had not been modified to carry A-bombs, a fact the Soviets probably knew.[30] When the implied threat failed, the Truman administration opted instead for a massive airlift of supplies into West Berlin. The airlift was successful in delivering provisions to the Berliners and sustaining them, and in May 1949 the Soviets called off the blockade. Berlin continued to be a friction point between the superpowers, with tensions mounting again in 1958 and 1961.

The Marshall Plan addressed Western Europe's economic and political problems, but it contained no response to the postwar European military balance of power, which favored the Soviet Union. Western European leaders wanted the United States, armed with the atomic bomb, to guarantee their countries' security. The United States was initially reluctant to enter into such a pact. There was still considerable isolationist sentiment in America in 1948, and the Truman administration did not wish to complicate its efforts to obtain congressional support for the Marshall Plan with a debate over the merits of a U.S.-European military alliance. In addition, even among State Department "Atlanticists," who saw Europe as the linchpin of U.S. security, there were those such as Kennan who were primarily concerned with the political and psychological results of Soviet intimidation, not with a full-scale Soviet military invasion of Western Europe, which they viewed as unlikely. The Europeans, however, faced with the Red Army troops poised in close proximity, were not receptive to this line of reasoning.

The United States initially encouraged the formation of the Western European Union (WEU), a defensive alliance between Great Britain, France, and the Benelux nations. Without West German rearmament, however, the WEU did not pose a credible military deterrent to the Soviet Union. With memories of World War II still fresh, Western European nations, especially France and the Low Countries, were unwilling to contemplate the rebuilding of the German military. At the height of the Cold War, at a time when the Soviet Union and international communism appeared to be on the march, Western European countries still perceived Germany to be the more immediate threat. In other words, the United States had to arrange for the containment of Germany before it could see to the containment of the Soviet Union.[31]

North Atlantic Treaty Organization

The Truman administration, therefore, increasingly supported U.S. participation in a Western defense pact and convinced Congress to permit consideration of an alliance if the European nations requested one. That they quickly did, and

with the communist coup in Czechoslovakia and the imposition of the Berlin blockade in the background, the Senate ratified the North Atlantic Treaty Organization (NATO) pact, which was signed in April 1949 by the United States and eleven other nations – the five WEU allies plus Iceland, Norway, Denmark, Canada, Portugal, and Italy. In 1952 Greece and Turkey also entered the alliance.

The central element of the treaty was Article Five, which stipulated that an attack on one signatory was an attack on all. The NATO treaty did not call for or immediately result in an enlarged American troop presence in Europe: NATO was an American guarantee of assistance to its European allies in the event they were attacked by the Soviet Union.

However modest its beginnings, NATO became a central element of the U.S. strategy of containing the Soviet Union. The United States eventually stationed three hundred thousand troops in Europe, with the bulk stationed in West Germany (which joined NATO in 1955), and introduced large quantities of theater nuclear weapons (TNF) onto the Continent. NATO marked the end of over a century and a half of U.S. policy of nonentanglement in European affairs. It was the first U.S. peacetime treaty of alliance since the termination in 1800 of the Franco-U.S. pact that had helped secure American independence in the Revolutionary War. Taken together, the Truman Doctrine, the Marshall Plan, and NATO marked the United States's assumption of global political and military leadership.

In 1949 the United States, despite its possession of nuclear weapons, still lacked a military establishment commensurate with its new role. But events over the next year encouraged the Truman administration to enlarge considerably America's peacetime armed forces.

Between 1947 and 1949 the risk of a Soviet invasion of Western Europe was minimal. Stalin's primary goal during this period was to avoid going to war against the West. The Soviet Union had suffered twenty million deaths during World War II and could ill afford another major conflict. The Soviet leader's secondary goal was to expand Soviet influence in a way that would not provoke a military conflict with the United States and its allies. While war did not break out, the Soviet Union's heavy-handed incorporation of Eastern Europe into its sphere of influence alarmed the West and prompted a large military buildup. The shift from Kennan's concentration on the political nature of the Soviet threat and the response to it, to an emphasis on the Soviet Union's military capacity and its willingness to use it to achieve its ends, gained momentum in 1949 as a result of two events: the "loss" of China to communist insurgents and the Soviet detonation of an atomic bomb.

Chinese Civil War

China had been locked in a civil war between the nationalists, led by Chiang Kai-shek, and the communists, led by Mao Zedong, since the early 1930s. While Japan attempted to conquer eastern China between 1937 and 1945, Mao declared a truce with the nationalists so that both factions could use their troops to resist Japan. The communists' success in fighting the Japanese enhanced their reputation. The Kuomintang (nationalist) government had never achieved wide-spread acceptance in China, and its lackluster record against Japan combined with its reputation for corruption and inefficiency to prevent Chiang from consolidating control. When the Japanese surrendered to the Allies in 1945, the civil war resumed and intensified. The Soviet Union, convinced that the Kuomintang would prevail and less than enthusiastic about the idea of a communist-led China that could challenge Soviet leadership of the international communist movement, concluded a treaty with the nationalist government in 1945.

The United States was split over how to respond to the Chinese civil war. One option was for the United States fully to commit itself militarily and economically to Chiang, a policy supported by the pronationalist "China Lobby," "China-firsters" such as Henry Luce, the influential publisher of *Time* magazine, and powerful conservative senators such as Republicans Styles Bridges (New Hampshire), William Knowland (California), Kenneth Wherry (Nebraska), William Jenner (Indiana), and Democrat Pat MacCarran (Nevada). Another option, encouraged by some of the "China hands" in the State Department who concluded that the Kuomintang was not a viable political ally, was for the United States to abandon Chiang and support Mao. The United States, however, had supported Chiang during World War II, providing him with arms to fight the Japanese. Disengagement at this point would be embarrassing and would incur the opposition of the politically formidable China Lobby. Supporting Mao would mean aligning the United States with communists, which was an unacceptable choice in the late 1940s. Truman's position was made even more difficult by the approaching elections of 1948, which promised to

be very close. In light of the Soviet conduct in Eastern Europe, Republicans were already criticizing Roosevelt and the Democrats for having conceded too much to the Soviet Union at the Yalta Conference. Allowing China to fall into communist hands would only assist the Republicans in their charges that the Democrats were "soft" on communism.

The administration chose a third option of trying to encourage reconciliation between Chiang and Mao. President Truman sent Marshall to China in 1945 to implement the American plan. The Marshall mission lasted until January 1947. Although Marshall was pronationalist, he attempted to play the honest broker between Chiang and Mao. The leaders' mutual distrust, however, derailed the initiative. The Chinese archives have revealed that the Marshall mission was the final opportunity, albeit tenuous, for a positive relationship between the United States and the Chinese communists.

When he returned to the United States in 1947, Marshall was appointed secretary of state by Truman. In office, Marshall emphasized the European recovery and containment, exemplified by the plan which bears his name. This Eurocentric emphasis marked a contraction in the U.S.-perceived security sphere; China, which had been a major focus of U.S. diplomatic and economic interest for well over half a century, was devalued, along with Korea and the rest of mainland Asia. Kennan and most of the State Department believed that a communist victory in China would not affect the U.S.-Soviet balance of power, since the new regime would be more Chinese than communist. However, the State Department's decision to disengage from Chiang was hampered by the residue of pro-Kuomintang sentiment in the United States. In 1948 the Truman administration authorized the China Aid Act as a concession to the China Lobby. The act did not prevent the steady weakening of Chiang's regime, but it did increase the Chinese communists' antipathy toward the United States.

U.S. foreign-policy makers, recognizing that communist takeover in China was probable, hoped to cultivate a cordial relationship with Mao and drive a wedge between the Soviet Union and China. Kennan, the Joint Chiefs of Staff, and General Douglas MacArthur, the military governor of Japan, came together in a rare moment of consensus to formulate the defensive-perimeter strategy for East Asia, which elevated the strategic importance of Taiwan, Japan, the Philippines, and other islands off the Asian coast. This defensive island perimeter was intended to maintain the status quo in East Asia until the anticipated break between China and the Soviet Union occurred, at which time the United States would shift recognition from Chiang to Mao. But the China Aid Act and the domestic political vulnerability of a friendly policy toward a communist government in China doomed this "wedge strategy."

In early Autumn 1949 the Kuomintang government fled mainland China and reestablished itself on the offshore island of Formosa, which was subsequently renamed Taiwan. Mao proclaimed his rule over China on 1 October; the Soviets recognized the new regime one day later. Chiang immediately severed relations with the Soviet Union. On 4 October the United States announced that it would continue to recognize the Kuomintang government of the Republic of China, and twelve days later Secretary of State Acheson declared that the United States would not recognize the communist People's Republic of China (PRC). The United States did not open relations with the PRC until 1972 and did not extend normal diplomatic recognition until 1979.[32]

Beginnings of the Nuclear Arms Race

Less than a month before the communist takeover in China, the Soviet Union stunned the world with its successful test of an atomic bomb. U.S. intelligence estimated it would take the Soviet Union five to twenty years to break the American monopoly on nuclear weapons; many government experts believed that a Soviet A-bomb test would occur later rather than sooner. Immediately questions began to be raised concerning a Soviet "theft" of American nuclear secrets. Several years later it would be revealed, in the midst of an American "Red Scare," that atomic espionage had in fact occurred, but scientists doubt the significance of the contribution espionage made to the Soviet nuclear program. From the Kremlin's perspective, the Soviet possession of nuclear weapons was redressing the strategic imbalance caused by the American nuclear monopoly.

The United States, however, was anxious. Although by mid 1949 the United States had manufactured only a few A-bombs, in the late 1940s it came to rely on its exclusive control of nuclear weapons to compensate for the West's numerical inferiority in nonnuclear forces and to provide a deterrent against the Red Army.[33] In late 1949 and early 1950 the scientists and decisionmakers in the United States engaged in an acrimonious and divisive debate over the direction of American nuclear

strategy. The central question was whether or not the United States should respond to the Soviet bomb by developing the hydrogen, or "superbomb."[34] While they were developing the atomic fission bomb, nuclear physicists had determined that it was theoretically possible to harness nuclear fusion, the process by which the sun generates heat and light, to create a weapon hundreds or even thousands of times more powerful than the A-bomb. Two American scientists who had played leading roles in the development of the atomic bomb took opposing positions on the superbomb question. Edward Teller, who would become known as the "father of the H-bomb," advocated a fusion-weapons program, arguing that even if the United States did not build a hydrogen bomb, the Soviets surely would. J. Robert Oppenheimer asserted that a superbomb was unnecessary. It would be too large to be of any military utility and would be so destructive as to be genocidal. Oppenheimer advocated the manufacture of high-yield strategic and small tactical atomic weapons. Eminent scientists on the scientific advisory committee of the Atomic Energy Commission, among them I. I. Rabi and Enrico Fermi, also advised Truman against the development of the H-bomb. In the end, the Truman administration decided to develop the hydrogen bomb and produce various sizes of atomic weapons. Subsequent historical scholarship has revealed that the Soviet Union in fact decided to develop a fusion weapon before the United States announced its H-bomb project on 31 January 1950.

McCarthyism

Several days after the U.S. announcement, the British government declared that it had uncovered a Soviet spy ring headed by a German expatriate physicist named Klaus Fuchs, who had worked on the allied wartime atomic-bomb project. The British had caught Fuchs passing classified information on nuclear weapons to Soviet agents.[35] Fuchs's exposure touched off another "Red Scare" in the United States. As anticommunist hysteria quickly grew, Joseph R. McCarthy, a little-known junior senator from Wisconsin, dramatically announced during a speech in Wheeling, West Virginia, in early February 1950, that he possessed proof that the State Department employed hundreds of communists. This declaration brought McCarthy instantaneous national attention. The senator began to attack the State Department with increasing ferocity, accusing it of harboring communists and Soviet agents. McCarthy's accusations grew steadily more reckless, reaching new heights in an extraordinary address to the Senate on 14 June 1951, when he accused former secretary of state George C. Marshall of having served Soviet interests throughout his career. "How can we account for our present situation," asked McCarthy, "unless we believe that men high in this government are concerting to deliver us to disaster. This must be a product of a great conspiracy, a conspiracy on a scale so immense and an infamy so black as to dwarf any previous such venture in the history of man." It was Marshall, "this grim and solitary man," who was the pivotal government official in this "strategy of defeat."[36]

McCarthy's red-baiting tactics, in which, without producing any tangible evidence, he accused political enemies and others who disagreed with him of being either outright Communist party members or "fellow travelers," made the Wisconsin senator one of the most feared political figures in the United States. "McCarthyism" was the politics of guilt by association, of the pernicious insinuation, of the baseless accusation.[37]

McCarthy was not the only politician to pursue these techniques, nor did he manufacture the atmosphere in which they flourished. A freshman congressman from California, Richard M. Nixon, had won his first election in 1946 by accusing his incumbent opponent, Jerry Voorhis, of being a communist sympathizer and achieved fame by successfully pursuing the conviction of former State Department official Alger Hiss as a perjurer, when Hiss had denied he had passed secret documents to the Soviets while in the State Department.[38] The Truman administration had initiated a well-publicized loyalty program in 1947 to expose and remove security risks in the government.[39] The Truman Doctrine had framed the threat of international communist subversion in strong, dramatic terms. The Berlin blockade, the communist takeovers in Czechoslovakia and China, the tightening of the Soviet grip over Eastern Europe, the Soviet A-bomb test, and the discovery of Soviet espionage agents in the United States and its allied countries, reinforced and intensified America's growing obsession with domestic communist subversion.[40] The deteriorating East-West relations, the growing tensions, and the heightened ideological content of the conflict between the two nations caused the relations between the United States and the Soviet Union, in the words of John Stoessinger, "to assume the proportions of a struggle between two competing theologies. It had passed out of the realm of ambiguity into a period of moral clichés based on absolute definitions of good and evil."[41]

NSC-68

In the midst of this anticommunist atmosphere, another watershed document of the Cold War appeared. Paul H. Nitze, Kennan's successor as head of the State Department's Policy Planning Staff, authored National Security Council (NSC) memorandum–68, a top-secret reappraisal of U.S. strategic security policy. Although NSC-68 had not been intended as a repudiation of Kennan's policy recommendations, it offered observations and prescriptions considerably at variance with Kennan's. Kennan had argued that to protect U.S. interests and preserve the status quo, it was only necessary to keep Western Europe and other strong-point areas of industrial and military importance out of the Soviets' hands; the loss of strategically peripheral areas would not shift the balance of power. NSC-68 conversely declared that this strong-point defense was not sufficient: "The fundamental design of those who control the Soviet Union and the international communist movement is the complete subversion or forcible destruction ... of the non-Soviet world and their replacement by an apparatus and structure subservient to and controlled from the Kremlin.... Any substantial further extension of the area under the domination of the Kremlin would raise the possibility that no coalition adequate to confront the Kremlin with greater strength could be assembled ... the assault on free institutions is worldwide now, and ... a defeat of free institutions anywhere is a defeat everywhere."

NSC-68 resurrected the idea of "perimeter" defense, aiming to protect all areas outside the present boundary of the Soviet sphere from Soviet encroachment. Perimeter defense became a keynote of containment for the next twenty years, providing the rationale for the U.S. involvement in the Korean and Vietnam conflicts.

Perimeter defense was an expensive strategy, and NSC-68 proposed the means to achieve its ambitious ends. The Soviet Union, NSC-68 stated, had not instigated full-scale war with the West thus far because it could not be assured of victory; this view contrasted with Kennan's assertion that the Soviet threat was primarily political and that they had no intention of militarily confronting the West. Nitze argued that the United States had to place itself on a wartime footing in peacetime to deter the Soviets from launching a surprise attack. Moreover, until the Soviet Union felt confident that it could win a war against the West, it would engage in "piecemeal aggression" in what was coming to be known as the Third World. Thus, the United States would need to develop a spectrum of responsive capabilities to meet Soviet threats at different levels. NSC-68 approved the development of the hydrogen bomb and the production of nuclear weapons of different sizes. The United States, however, would be hobbled if it relied exclusively on mass-destruction weapons, as small-scale Soviet aggression would force the United States to choose between a disproportionately massive response and no response at all. NSC-68 called for a substantial increase in U.S. conventional military capability.

Conventional armed forces are more expensive than nuclear arsenals. While NSC-68 avoided explicit estimates of the cost of the proposed buildup, it implied a more than threefold increase in the military budget, from $13.5 billion to $50 billion. The Pentagon opposed NSC-68 because it would require the government to engage in deficit spending to provide all the necessary funding. President Truman, himself a fiscal conservative, was also reluctant to implement NSC-68's expensive, deficit-producing program.[42] The report was completed in April 1950, but the Truman administration shelved it. However, on 25 June 1950 NSC-68 was revived as North Korean troops crossed the 38th parallel to invade South Korea. The Korean War prompted the Truman administration to adopt the NSC-68 program. "In the decade following the initiation of containment, Korea stands out as the decisive event in the evolution of American policy," writes Robert W. Tucker. "The Korean experience largely determined the form and course that the great transformation in American foreign policy eventually took. . . . Korea put an end to . . . uncertainties."[43]

Korean War

Korea was a Japanese colony prior to World War II. After Japan's defeat in World War II, Korea was divided in two, at the 38th parallel, by the Soviet Union and the United States. Unlike the division of Germany, the United States and the Soviet Union withdrew their forces from Korea. Both North Korea's communist ruler, Kim Il-Sung, and South Korea's leader, Syngman Rhee, claimed sovereignty over the entire nation. Rhee approached the United States about a military operation to unify the two Koreas, but the Truman administration rejected the idea. Stalin, however, apparently authorized Kim to launch an attack. While there is no definitive explanation why Stalin would have

given North Korea the green light, it is likely that the Soviet leader, remembering the Soviet humiliation in the Berlin crisis, saw Korea as an easy target partly because the Pentagon viewed it as strategically unimportant and Secretary of State Acheson had publicly declared it to be outside the West's defensive perimeter.[44] Additionally, it is possible that Stalin was worried that China would become an East Asian Yugoslavia and desire a Soviet foothold in the region.[45]

Whether or not the Soviets supported or approved of the North Korean plan in advance, the Soviet Union was as surprised as the United States by the timing of the attack.[46] Truman's view of the North Korean attack was uncompromising: "Communism was acting in Korea just as Hitler, Mussolini, and the Japanese had acted ten, fifteen, and twenty years earlier. . . . If this was allowed to go unchallenged it would mean a third world war, just as similar incidents had brought on the second world war."[47] Echoing the reasoning offered by NSC-68, Truman did not emphasize Korea's intrinsic strategic value to the United States but rather the fact that making a strong stand in Korea was important as a "symbol of the strength and determination of the West" to resist aggression.[48]

On the 25th, the United Nations (UN) Security Council passed an American-sponsored resolution condemning the North Koreans as aggressors. Two days later the Security Council voted in favor of committing UN member nations to support South Korea in repulsing its northern neighbor. The Soviet envoy to the United Nations was not present to exercise his veto because the Soviet Union was boycotting the United Nations in protest over the organization's exclusion, at the behest of the United States, of the People's Republic of China. The absence of the Soviet UN representative offers a strong indication of the extent to which the invasion's timing had taken the Soviet Union by surprise.

The United States had originally hoped that UN military aid would be limited to air and sea support of the South Korean army.[49] The South Koreans, however, were sent into retreat down the Korean peninsula, and American troops were flown in several days after the initial invasion. Truman had the constitutional authority to involve the United States in a limited "police action" under UN aegis, so he did not ask Congress for a declaration of war. He wanted to avoid an escalation of the conflict, with its inherent risk of world war, that a formal declaration of war would likely precipitate. Truman's decision set a precedent: fourteen years later President Lyndon B. Johnson cited Truman's action as a legal basis for his decision to send U.S. troops into Vietnam.

After suffering a series of setbacks, UN forces under the command of General MacArthur executed a brilliant landing at Inchon and sent the North Korean army reeling back across the 38th parallel. At this point the Truman administration altered its original military objective, the restoration of the prewar status quo, and authorized MacArthur to invade North Korea in order to topple its communist regime. The Chinese had repeatedly warned the United States through intermediaries that they would regard such an invasion as a threat to their national security and would attack if UN forces crossed the 38th parallel, but the administration dismissed these warnings. China sent hundreds of thousands of soldiers across the Yalu River and drove the American forces to the southern tip of the peninsula.

MacArthur, who had assured Truman at a meeting on Wake Island that China would not enter the war in reaction to the invasion of North Korea, began to complain publicly about the Truman administration's prosecution of the war. He especially criticized the administration's policy of limited war, asserting that it would be impossible to achieve UN goals without attacking China. On 20 March 1951 he sent a letter to Republican congressman Joseph Martin, the House minority leader, declaring, "There is no substitute for victory." After warnings failed to silence MacArthur, Truman sacked him on 11 April 1951. The right wing of the Republican party was furious. Senator Jenner of Indiana declared, "The country today is in the hands of a secret inner coterie which is directed by agents of the Soviet Union."[50] MacArthur came back to the United States to a hero's welcome. There were welcome-home receptions and parades for him in cities across the nation, culminating in a ticker-tape parade in New York that dwarfed a similar parade held for Charles Lindbergh two decades earlier. The general then bid farewell in an emotional speech to Congress, telling teary legislators that "old soldiers never die, they just fade away."

Slowly, UN forces counterattacked and pushed the Chinese and the North Koreans back up the Korean peninsula, and by early spring 1951 the lines had restabilized at the 38th parallel. Negotiations between the United States and China began and dragged on for two years before the war came to an end, during the presidency of Dwight D. Eisenhower.

The Korean War appeared to confirm NSC-68's thesis that the Soviet Union would attempt to undermine U.S. security through nibbling attacks on the periphery. The conflict made cogent NSC-68's prescription of an enlarged military establishment as a response to Soviet expansionism; defense spending tripled to about 10 percent of the gross national product (50 percent of all government spending). The Korean War also marked the beginning of "domino theory" thinking. Whereas Acheson's "bad apple" argument concerning the Greek civil war was intended primarily to scare Congress and the American public out of isolationist sentiments, the North Korean invasion caused many U.S. policymakers to fear that a communist victory in Korea would endanger Japan and other U.S. strategic interests in the western Pacific.

The war also extinguished the possibility of an early Sino-American rapprochement; relations were frozen in place, largely because of American ideological rigidity, for the next quarter of a century. The United States allied itself more closely with nationalist China by its decision to have the Seventh Fleet patrol the Straits of Taiwan. The U.S. naval presence was not intended solely to ward off a Red Chinese invasion; Chiang harbored his own irredentist ambitions, and the Seventh Fleet was dispatched to keep the two sides separated. Further south in East Asia, the United States implemented a policy with serious ramifications, although policymakers did not realize it at the time. Two days after the start of the North Korean attack, President Truman ordered the acceleration of military aid the United States was providing to France in its difficult battle against a communist-led insurgency in Indochina, a French colony. The outbreak of the Korean War was a watershed in the history of American involvement in Vietnam.

The Korean War had consequences for American policy toward Europe as well. Soon after the onset of hostilities, the United States decided to rearm West Germany, a decision viewed with anxiety by Great Britain and France. To assuage Anglo-French fears over German rearmament, the United States sent several divisions of U.S. troops to Europe as a guarantee of American protection against Soviet (or German) attack, increased U.S. economic aid to Western Europe, and established an integrated NATO military command led by a U.S. general.

The Korean War also demonstrated the difficulties of using the atomic bomb in limited wars.[51] The use of atomic weapons in the Korean war was first brought up on the evening of the first day of the war, when Truman asked air force chief of staff Hoyt Vandenberg whether the United States could destroy Soviet bases in Asia, and the general replied that it was possible if the United States were to use nuclear weapons.[52] In a press conference on 30 November, following the Chinese intervention in the war, Truman made remarks that could be interpreted as threats to use atomic weapons,[53] especially since they came a few days after speeches by Secretary of the Navy Francis P. Matthews and Major General Orville Anderson, commandant of the Air Force War College, in which both recommended preventive war against the Soviet Union. Truman's statement caused a worried British prime minister Clement Attlee to travel to Washington to dissuade Truman from acting rashly.

While Truman never came close to using nuclear weapons in Korea,[54] the Eisenhower administration, which came to power at the beginning of 1953, was different: it appeared to consider the threat to use nuclear weapons in Korea a logical extension of its New Look strategy, which emphasized the reliance on American technological superiority.[55] The military and officers in the NSC, however, were not eager to use atomic weapons in Korea. They argued that since there were not many suitable military targets in the North, the weapon would not achieve very impressive results, in the process weakening its deterrent effect on the Soviet Union. Eisenhower urged the military, in numerous planning sessions, to consider the use of nuclear weapons, especially if the war expanded into China. As Richard Betts writes, "The record of explicit high-level deliberation over intended use of nuclear weapons in specific situations in Korea is the most extensive in the postwar era."[56]

During the spring of 1953 the administration began an orchestrated campaign of hints and behind-the-scenes messages to Beijing to emphasize its position that unless progress was made at the armistice talks, the United States would consider the use of nuclear weapons.[57] It is not clear to what extent this campaign convinced the Chinese and North Koreans to become more accommodating at the armistice talks and what role other events, such as Stalin's death on 5 March, played in their decision, though Eisenhower and John Foster Dulles were convinced that the veiled nuclear threats were effective in ending the war.[58]

The Korean War also influenced American domestic politics. The military stalemate increased public dissatisfaction with the Democrats, who had been in power without interruption for two decades. A Republican victory in the 1952 presidential election was likely, and the struggle for the Republican presidential nomination provided the last opportunity for the isolationist forces within the Republican party to challenge the nation's assumption of world leadership responsibilities. These forces gathered around the candidacy of Senator Robert A. Taft of Ohio. To thwart this resurgence of neoisolationism, the internationalist forces within the party persuaded Eisenhower, the supreme commander of Allied forces in Europe during World War II and the architect of the Normandy invasion, to run for president.[59] Eisenhower was nominated and went on to defeat the Democratic candidate, Governor Adlai Stevenson of Illinois, in the 1952 presidential election.

U.S. Cold War Policy Under Eisenhower

The new president, after some hesitation, chose as his secretary of state John Foster Dulles, an international lawyer with considerable diplomatic experience. Eisenhower and Dulles were aware of the paralyzing effect the wild accusations of the Republican Right had had on Truman's foreign policy, and were careful not to take on McCarthy and his supporters. They were also aware of the strong anti-interventionist sentiment espoused by a still powerful segment of the Republican party led by Senator Taft of Ohio. The administration responded to the two strands in the party by promising a more ambitious foreign policy than that of its predecessor — rolling back communism rather than containing it — achieved at a lower cost.

Eisenhower described the Truman administration's strategy as "a purgatory of improvisation"[60] and rejected it as too reactive and expensive.[61] There was no coherent matching of means to ends in Truman's approach, no clear understanding of the role of force in international relations, and no indication as to how the administration was going to exploit the virtual U.S. monopoly of nuclear weapons to its advantage. He wanted the United States to regain the initiative in foreign policy while lowering the costs of that policy. He rejected the NSC-68's assumption that means could be found to support the ever-increasing missions and responsibilities for the United States in the world. Eisenhower feared that the growing burden of global responsibilities might turn the American public against the new internationalism.[62] On a deeper level, Eisenhower feared that too expansive a definition of U.S. interests driven by a policy designed to achieve absolute security might distort the nature of the American society and corrupt its institutions.[63] Maintaining a sound economy was as important to the nation's security as building arms. "[L]ong-term security required a sound economy," Eisenhower later wrote. "The relationship between military and economic strength is intimate and indivisible."[64]

In May 1953 Eisenhower ordered a planning exercise code-named "Operation Solarium." Task forces were asked to consider three broad strategic options for adoption by the new administration, each with its own assumptions and recommendations.[65] The first option was the continuation of Truman's containment policy. The second option was deterrence, which meant a more rigid form of containment, involving drawing clear lines around the Soviet sphere, threatening massive, possibly nuclear, punishment if the Soviet Union crossed those lines. The third option was liberation, an active U.S. policy to roll back the Soviet influence from areas already under Soviet control.[66] The administration's New Look strategy incorporated elements from all three options.[67]

But there were tensions between the requirements of an ambitious foreign policy and the desire to reduce its costs. The administration offered to solve them by relying on a strategy of asymmetrical response. Strategies that rely on symmetrical responses to the adversary's challenges aim to minimize risk to the nation's security by accepting higher costs; strategies that rely on asymmetrical responses accept greater risks in exchange for lower costs.[68] Under Eisenhower, the United States would apply its strengths against the adversary's weaknesses, responding to an adversary's hostile action in a manner it saw fit, shifting the nature or the location of the confrontation if necessary. "[W]e cannot counter Communist tactics with their own weapons ... ," Eisenhower wrote.[69] By relying on a wide array of means – technological and nuclear superiority, covert action, diplomatic maneuvering – the administration's twin goals of regaining the initiative and lowering costs would be realized.[70] The Truman administration sought to deter adversaries by emphasizing symmetry: an adversary contemplating hostile action would be certain of a U.S. response tailored to the provocation. The Eisenhower administration, writes Gaddis "sought to combine the certainty of a response with uncertainty as to its nature."[71]

The administration's defense budget reflected the emphasis on economy. The Truman administration had requested $41.2 billion for the Department of Defense for fiscal year 1954. The Eisenhower administration reduced that request to $35.8 billion and for fiscal 1955 requested only $30.9 billion. The army shrank from 1.5 million to 1 million between December 1953 and June 1955. Defense expenditures as a percentage of the budget declined from 65.7 percent in fiscal 1954 to 48.5 percent in fiscal 1961.[72] Defense spending as a percentage of the gross national product declined from 12.8 percent in fiscal 1954 to 9.1 percent in fiscal 1961.[73] There were tensions among the various elements of the New Look strategy, "but they all had the advantage of being cheaper than the symmetrical response strategy of NSC-68."

The first element of the administration's New Look strategy was a greater reliance on nuclear weapons and the threat to use them to deter Soviet or Soviet-sponsored actions against the United States and its interests.[74] Some of the more memorable words associated with the Eisenhower administration – "massive retaliation," "more bang for the buck," "brinksmanship" – were coined by its spokesmen to convey this shift to nuclear reliance. Dulles criticized containment for making the United States rely too heavily on expensive conventional military forces, imposing a heavy burden on the national economy. He argued that the United States should wield its technological superiority to threaten response to Soviet acts of aggression with a devastating retaliation, in Dulles words, "where it hurts, by means of our own choosing."[75] Dulles did not hide that he preferred U.S. reliance on nuclear weapons, reflecting his "often expressed view that somehow or other we must manage to remove the taboo from the use of these weapons."[76] Massive retaliation accepted NSC-68's perimeter-defense strategy while rejecting the memorandum's costly enforcementpolicy prescription of relying on a mix of conventional and nuclear forces.

The second component of the administration's approach was its emphasis on ringing the Soviet Union with American-led defense alliances similar to NATO. The energy Dulles invested in creating anti-Soviet defense alliances – the Baghdad Pact, Southeast Asia Treaty Organization (SEATO), the Korean and Taiwanese mutual-security agreements – and in enhancing agreements the administration inherited from Truman, some of which were negotiated by Dulles – NATO, the ANZUS Pact, and the Japanese agreements – led critics to accuse him of "pactomania."[77]

Yet another important element in the administration's new strategy was its preoccupation with the psychological and rhetorical aspects of diplomacy and politics.[78] There was a great belief in the Eisenhower administration in the importance of posture and appearance and in the power of words. This emphasis in the administration's strategy produced the notions of liberation and roll back and the concept of "captive nations." The containment of the Soviet Union and its influence did not appear to Dulles to be an active and energetic enough a policy for the United States to follow. The 1952 foreign-policy plank of the Republican party platform, authored in large part by Dulles, criticized containment as "negative, futile, and immoral ... abandon[ing] countless human beings to despotism and godless terrorism."[79] With Soviet superiority in conventional forces neutralized by U.S. nuclear superiority, the United States could become more active in encouraging countries that came under Soviet domination to liberate themselves.

Another important ingredient in the New Look strategy was its emphasis on covert action to advance U.S. political objectives.[80] The appointment of Allen Dulles, John Foster Dulles's brother, to head the CIA is an indication of the centrality of covert action to Eisenhower's strategy. The budget of the CIA was increased, as were the number of its employees, foreign stations, and activities. Among the agency's exploits that became public were the successful toppling of the government of the Iranian populist-nationalist leader Mohammad Mossadegh and the reinstatement of Shah Mohammad Reza Pahlevi in 1953. Another CIA success was the toppling of Guatemala's reformer president Jacobo Arbenz Guzmán. Arbenz, the elected president of Guatemala, angered the United States by nationalizing the land holdings of the American-based United Fruit Company and accepting a large shipment of Czechoslovak arms. The CIA provided weapons, training, logistical support, and, at one point, air cover to the right-wing forces of Castillo Armas, who seized power in a coup in 1954. The agency also made attempts on the governments of Indonesia (1958) and Cuba (1960–1961); considered involvement in assasination plots of the foreign leaders Zhou Enlai, Patrice Lumumba, Fidel Castro Ruz, and Rafael Leónidas Trujillo Molina; infiltrated student, labor, and church organizations; funded political parties, newspapers, magazines, and cultural activities; and more.[81] Covert

action offered the administration an effective foreign-policy tool at a fraction of the cost of reliance on traditional military means. Covert action was also a low-cost operation politically in that it allowed the administration to deny its involvement.

The Eisenhower administration placed greater emphasis than the Truman administration on nuclear weapons and initially appeared readier to threaten their use. But two crises in Asia showed the administration to be ambivalent about the actual employment of nuclear weapons.

By the spring of 1954 the French had fought the nationalist insurgency in Indochina, led by Ho Chi Minh's communist Vietminh, for seven years, suffering 92,000 dead and 114,000 wounded. The hopelessness of the French position came to be symbolized by the fight over Dien Bien Phu, where a French garrison of 15,000 was cut off by Vietminh forces and continuously bombarded from the surrounding mountains. France appealed to the United States for help. In response, the U.S. military put together Operation Vulture, a contingency plan involving conventional and nuclear attacks on the Vietminh's positions around Dien Bien Phu.[82] But Eisenhower, unenthusiastic about nuclear use in Indochina, rejected the plan, and Dien Bien Phu fell on 7 May.[83]

A peace conference in Geneva resulted in a cease-fire and the division of Vietnam into North and South along the 17th parallel, pending elections that were to be held in two years but never took place. The United States did not formally accept the Geneva accords and began to act as patron to the South Vietnamese. The United States installed Ngo Dinh Diem, a Catholic Vietnamese anticommunist leader with little popular support, as head of a new government in South Vietnam. Eisenhower, in defending the enlarged American role in Vietnam, warned that Vietnam's loss to communism would ultimately bring down all the Southeast Asian governments, which he likened to a row of dominoes.[84] The United States established SEATO to help preserve regional security and keep the dominoes upright.

In September 1954 PRC artillery units bombarded the Formosan island of Quemoy, killing two American soldiers. Later in the fall PRC forces attacked the Tachen Islands, and in January 1955 communist forces captured the island of Ichiang. Hinting at the possibility of using nuclear weapons, the Eisenhower administration warned communist China not to reclaim the offshore Quemoy and Matsu islands from the nationalist Chinese. Administration officials were apparently not bluffing when they made references to nuclear weapons, but at the same time there was not great enthusiasm about the prospect of their use.[85] It is not clear if the Chinese were deterred by the administration's threats, but Beijing, under pressure from Moscow and Third World countries, adopted a more conciliatory posture, and the crisis was resolved by spring 1955.[86] Although some took the Quemoy-Matsu crisis as a demonstration of the efficacy of brinksmanship, the president did not think war was likely.[87] The crisis, however, did expose the weakness of heavy reliance on massive retaliation – it seemed disproportionate to domestic and Allied critics that the United States should bring the world to the brink of nuclear war in order to defend two tiny volcanic islands. The Eisenhower administration, responding to these criticisms, began a slow evolution in its thinking on credibility and deterrence in general.

While the Eisenhower administration was implementing the New Look, the Soviet Union underwent a decisive transformation with the death of Stalin in March 1953. The two rivals for Soviet leadership, Georgi Malenkov and Nikita S. Khrushchev, who assumed the premiership and the party secretariat respectively, were both dependent on an array of political alliances and did not have the stature or the power to rule in Stalin's autocratic fashion. The Soviet political structure was transformed from an oppressive totalitarian system to a bureaucratic authoritarian one, which it would remain for the balance of the Cold War.

Changes in attitudes toward the West accompanied this relative relaxation of domestic structures. Stalin had charged that the capitalist states sought to encircle and strangle the Soviet Union, the beleaguered bulwark of socialism. In his last year Stalin had "exposed" a "Doctors' Plot," in which a Western group of largely Jewish doctors was accused of plotting to kill him and other Soviet leaders. Khrushchev and Malenkov wanted to relax the tension between the Soviet Union and the West. Malenkov spoke explicitly of peaceful coexistence: "At the present time," he declared, "there is no undisputed or unresolved question that cannot be settled by mutual agreement of the interested countries. This applies to our relations with all states, including the United States of America."

The Eisenhower administration was unsure about the effect of Stalin's death on Soviet policy and reacted coolly to conciliatory Soviet gestures. Dulles dismissed them as a smoke screen to hide the Soviet Union's internal weaknesses.[88] Eisenho-

wer was somewhat more optimistic,[89] but in a speech on 16 April he called on the Soviets to renounce and reverse their entire post–World War II foreign policy. He demanded that the Soviets end their support for revolutionary activity in Asia, allow free elections in Eastern Europe, permit onsite inspection to verify disarmament agreements, and accept Germany's ties to NATO. Eisenhower's speech was published in its entirety in *Pravda* on 25 April, but nothing came of it. Malenkov later expressed his frustration with what he saw as the West's refusal to engage in a meaningful dialogue with the Soviet Union.[90]

Khrushchev emerged in 1955 as the victor of the Kremlin power struggle. Malenkov appeared willing to accept Soviet strategic inferiority in order to free money for improving the Soviet economy. Khrushchev, however, wanted the Soviet Union to attain strategic parity with the West and, soon after gaining control of the government, increased defense spending by 12 percent. Khrushchev also undertook a program of "strategic deception," loud and often dissembling propaganda about Soviet nuclear capability, inflating the actual figures of long-range bombers in the Soviet arsenal. Khrushchev's differences with Maklenkov were not over the need for a more accommodating Soviet foreign policy but rather over means: Khrushchev believed in the advantages of negotiating from a position of strength, and he believed that the Soviet Union should convey an image of strength in order to negotiate with the United States. Khrushchev's policies, and his earthy, blustery style, however, made it difficult for U.S. policy formulators to discern that he was actually keen on reducing tensions.

Despite the bloody Soviet suppression of the 1953 workers' strike in East Germany, Khrushchev's victory over Malenkov, and the creation of the Warsaw Treaty Organization, it was evident that the Soviet Union was adopting a more conciliatory foreign-policy stance. In the United States the 1954 mid-term elections created Democratic majorities in the House and Senate, and the new Democratic leadership was pressuring Eisenhower for a summit with his Soviet counterpart. Prime Minister Churchill, proclaiming that "the great Khan is dead," also urged a summit between the United States and the Soviet Union. In April 1955 the Soviets called for the foreign ministers of the four powers to meet to negotiate the end of the occupation of Austria. The Soviets also made dramatic disarmament proposals and put forward several ideas about the reduction of superpower tensions.

On 18 July 1955 Eisenhower, Khrushchev, and Anthony Eden met at Geneva. In response to the earlier Soviet disarmament proposals, the administration offered the "Open Skies" proposal, which called for frequent inspection overflights of each country's military facilities. The Soviets rejected Open Skies as a plan that would primarily benefit the United States, since the United States knew far less about its adversary's military installations than did the Soviet Union. In fact, the summit failed to yield agreements on any substantive issues. But there did emerge a short-lived "spirit of Geneva," demonstrating the possibility of relaxtion of East-West tensions. The summit's lasting importance was that it signified, according to one of Eisenhower's aides, "the acceptance by the major powers of the common necessity to shun recourse to nuclear war."

Geneva did not lessen U.S. concern about Soviet penetration of the Third World. The Soviet Union began an aid program for developing nations in 1955 that greatly improved its standing in the contested nations on the periphery of the superpower struggle. The United States was having less luck in the Third World. The Eisenhower administration embraced, in principle, anticolonialism and accommodation of Third World nationalism. But it underestimated the durability of nationalism and therefore tended to view with great alarm nationalist movements and leaders who failed to distinguish themselves clearly from communism.[91] The United States had difficulty with the related ideas that not all reformist nationalists were communists and that it was possible to be both a nationalist and a communist. The requirements of containment also tended to limit the administration's freedom of action, as obligations to colonial alliance members such as France and Great Britain, and to pro-Western traditional regimes in Third World countries, at times contradicted the "anticolonial impulse in U.S. leaders"[92] and the traditional anticolonial stance of U.S. foreign policy.

The administration's lack of nuance in understanding contributed to the fact that nations that had little else in common came together in suspicion over U.S. motives. Many Third World nations had little desire to participate in an ideological superpower struggle they felt was not their own; their main concern was gaining or holding onto independence and developing their domestic economies. This concern gave rise to the Non-Aligned Movement in the Third World. At the same time, Great Britain and France became increasingly annoyed with American pronouncements in support of national self-determination, which they saw as an attempt by the United States to improve its standing in the Third World at their expense. The Eisenhower administration's Third World policy thus incurred resentment from both sides. America's reaction to events in the Middle East in 1955–1956 pointed up the contradictions in the administration's approach to Third World nationalism.

Suez Crisis

The United States had long seen the Middle East as a region of strategic importance because of its geographic position as the gateway to the East — and to the West — and its vast petroleum reserves, which were essential to the functioning of Western industry. Great Britain had been the dominant power in the region for almost a century but, as in Greece and Turkey, could no longer maintain its position. The United States, concerned about the spread of Soviet influence, moved to fill the vacuum left as Great Britain withdrew from the region. America's position was complicated by its support for the state of Israel, whose establishment was opposed by the Arab nations of the area.

Much of the administration's concern centered on Egypt's Gamal Abdul Nasser. Nasser was among the leaders of a 1952 coup that had deposed King Farouk and by 1954 emerged as Egypt's strongman. His Pan-Arab message gained a wide appeal throughout the Arab world. Nasser was a nationalist, willing to play East and West off each other in order to obtain aid for his ambitious program to modernize Egypt. The United States recognized this but initially agreed to provide aid in the hopes of increasing American influence.

In 1955 Nasser signed an arms agreement with the Soviet Union. Nasser obtained the Soviet weapons partly to balance the Anglo-American–sponsored Baghdad Pact, an alliance between Great Britain, Turkey, Iran, Pakistan, and Egypt's Arab rival Iraq, and partly to shore up Egyptian defenses against Israeli commando raids into the Gaza Strip. The United States attempted to woo Nasser by offering to help Egypt finance the construction of the Aswân Dam, which would provide cheap electricity to Egyptian agriculture. Immediately the American cotton lobby objected, complaining that cheap Egyptian cotton would undercut their own product. Nasser then recognized the People's Republic of China, which Dulles interpreted as a direct challenge to the administration's policy of ostracizing communist China. The United States responded by withdrawing the Aswân Dam finance offer in July 1956. Several days later, Nasser retaliated by nationalizing the Suez Canal, promising to use the tolls to reimburse the dispossessed shareholders. Although Egypt was within its rights, Great Britain and France were furious and resolved to retake the canal by force. They enlisted Israel in a joint effort to invade the canal zone, and the three nations launched their attack on Egypt in late October 1956.[93] The Eisenhower administration condemned the attack, as did the Soviet Union, which also threatened Great Britain and France with a missile attack if they did not stop the invasion of Egypt. The United States found itself joining with its major rival against two close allies in support of a regime that was getting ever closer to the Soviet Union.

The Soviet Union took advantage of the diversion created by the Suez crisis in order to suppress an attempt by Hungary to leave the Warsaw Pact and declare its neutrality. The United States was in an embarrassing position, as the Hungarians had been encouraged in part by American propaganda broadcasts exhorting them to rise up. The Hungarian uprising was reminiscent of events in East Germany more than three years earlier. In May 1953 East Berlin workers went on a general strike against the communist leadership. The strike quickly spread throughout East Germany, with the encouragement of American radio broadcasts. The Soviets suppressed the strike militarily, while the United States abstained from intervening. Liberation, a key component of the American strategy, was proved empty, as Eisenhower had no intention of challenging the Soviet Union militarily in its own sphere. However, Eisenhower condemned the suppression of the Hungarian uprising and the Soviet threats against U.S. allies but held fast to his determination to coerce the three nations to end their attack against Egypt and withdraw their forces.

Applying diplomatic and economic pressure, the United States was successful in forcing Great Britain, France, and Israel to cease fighting and withdraw from the Egyptian territory they had captured. America's standing in the Third World briefly rose as the result of Eisenhower's stand, but the United States found it difficult to convert this prestige into political gain. France resolved to build an independent nuclear deterrent so that the Soviets would not again be able to threaten it with impunity. NATO unity suffered, healing slowly

and imperfectly, and France would eventualy withdraw from NATO's military command in the 1960s.

The Suez crisis marked the collapse of British power in the Middle East. To compensate, Eisenhower in early 1957 asked Congress to support a program of economic and military aid – including U.S. military intervention – to Middle Eastern nations requesting help against communist aggression. The program, adopted by Congress after extensive hearings, became known as the Eisenhower Doctrine.

De-Stalinization and the U.S.-Soviet Chill

Several months before U.S.-Soviet relations deteriorated as a result of the crises in Hungary and the Suez, Khrushchev had openly and unequivocally repudiated the Soviet leader whose policies had contributed to the onset of the Cold War. In a remarkable speech to the Twentieth Party Congress in February 1956, Khrushchev denounced Stalin's crimes against the Russian people, the Communist party, and the national interest. He asserted that Stalin's cult of personality had made possible the purges and the mass killings of the 1930s. In an apologetic tone to Yugoslavia's Tito, Khrushchev declared that there was more than one road leading to communism. Finally, he felt that Stalin's fear of "capitalist encirclement" and his belief in the inevitability of war with the West had been counterproductive. Khrushchev called instead for a policy of détente, or peaceful competition, between the two adversaries. Khrushchev's de-Stalinization initiative, in the context of the Hungarian uprising and the Suez crisis, presented the United States with a confusing image of the Soviet leader and his intentions. The United States was reluctant to believe that Khrushchev honestly sought a lessening of superpower tensions; the party secretary was too rough in manner for the Eisenhower administration's to view him favorably.

On 4 October 1957 The Soviet Union achieved a major scientific and technological breakthrough, and a stunning propaganda victory, when it launched Sputnik, the first artificial earth satellite. Gaddis writes, "As a revelation of unexpected threat, the shock of Sputnik rivaled only Pearl Harbor and Korea."[94] The Sputnik launch demonstrated that the Soviets were developing strategic-weapons-delivery capabilities similar to those of the United States and that they were mastering the very technology the West relied upon to compensate itself for its inferiority in conventional military forces. This meant that the United States was becoming increasingly vulnerable to attack by intercontinental ballistic missiles (ICBMs) carrying thermonuclear warheads. After Sputnik, Americans began, according to Lawrence Feedman, "to suffer the uncomfortable sensation of being candidates for annihilation in the event of total war."[95] The secrecy that shrouded Soviet technological developments and the realization that there were no defenses against ballistic missiles only increased American anxiety.[96]

The Sputnik launch appeared to confirm the gloomy conclusions of the reports about the state of U.S. defense: the 1955 Killian Report and the 1957 Gaither Report.[97] The pessimistic view of the changing strategic balance between the United States and the Soviet Union found forceful expression in "The Delicate Balance of Terror," an influential article Albert Wohlsetter published in the January 1959 issue of *Foreign Affairs*. The two major themes in the article were that the nuclear balance between the superpowers was becoming precarious and that the United States was facing the possibility of nuclear blackmail.[98] The Soviets' increasing ability to respond in kind to U.S. nuclear deployment raised serious questions about the wisdom of American reliance on massive retaliation, and scholars and defense intellectuals began to offer alternatives to it, emphasizing the need to create a range of responses to Soviet challenges, so that the nuclear option, in the words of Henry Kissinger, "becomes the *last* and not the *only* recourse."[99]

The perception of Soviet military gain brought Democratic contenders for the 1960 presidential nomination and some strategic analysts, such as Kissinger and Nitze, the author of NSC-68, to warn of a growing missile gap that favored the Soviet Union and of the Soviet ability to translate that missile advantage into political coercion.[100] Khrushchev helped this perception along by proclaiming that the Soviet Union would turn out missiles "like sausages." Eisenhower knew, through reconnaissance overflights of the Soviet Union by top-secret U-2 high-altitude spy planes, that the Soviets did not have anywhere near the missile capability that they were claiming. But there was no way for the president to rebut missile-gap critics without revealing the existence of the U-2 and admitting that the United States regularly violated Soviet airspace. The criticism continued and provided the Democrats with a potent campaign issue in the 1960 presidential campaign.

In 1958 the United States faced a series of crises in quick succession. In May, Lebanon's govern-ment requested U.S. aid to suppress a pro-Nasser nationalist rebellion that broke out when the Christian-controlled government announced it would stay in office past its legal term. The Lebanese and Jordanian governments feared that Iraq and Syria might intervene on behalf of the pro-Nasser forces. The United States invoked the Eisenhower Doctrine and, on 15 July, landed 14,300 marines on Beirut's beaches, while the British put some 3,000 troops in Jordan. The marines were met by bemused bathers and bikini-clad women taking the sun,[101] and also by several local drink vendors who came out in force to slake the marines' thirst, and as a result the landing has jokingly become known as the "Coca-Cola invasion." The crisis was resolved when the government stepped down. On the strategic level, however, the Lebanon crisis had more ominous tones. Eisenhower sent a nuclear signal to Moscow by positioning more than 1,100 Strategic Air Command aircraft on take-off alert.[102]

In the summer and fall of 1958 Sino-U.S. tensions over Quemoy and Matsu islands were revived. The PRC once again shelled nationalist positions, prompting another U.S. threat to attack China with nuclear weapons. Although the Soviet Union warned the United States against such an attack, it is not clear how determined the Soviets were in their support of China.[103] Later, the Chinese dismissed the importance of Soviet support in the crisis. The Chinese backed down, and a deep rift secretly opened between the Soviet Union and the PRC. The Sino-Soviet break and the demise of the myth of a "communist monolith" did not become public until 1963.

U.S.-Soviet relations seemed for a time in 1958 to be moving in a positive direction. At the beginning of November the two nations began an informal moratorium on nuclear testing that lasted three years. A week later, however, Khrushchev announced that the Soviet Union would grant East Germany full sovereignty and demanded that the West, which did not recognize East Germany, negotiate with it over access to Berlin. West Berlin, Khrushchev asserted, should become a demilitarized, neutral "free city": the Western allies should evacuate their troops. The United States rejected the Soviet demands and warned that it would preserve its transit rights to Berlin "if need be by military force." For several months the standoff between the superpowers continued. Finally, Khrushchev, seeing no wavering on the U.S. side and anxious over ambiguous statements by Eisenhower that the United States was keeping its military options open, backed down; the Soviet Union rescinded its ultimatum in May 1959. It was a blow to the Soviet Union, which looked with alarm on the continuing rearmament of West Germany and the stationing there of U.S. nuclear weapons.

John Foster Dulles died in early 1959, and Eisenhower decided to become even more active in running his administration's foreign policy. He made several trips to Europe, Asia, and Latin America, and in September played host to Khrushchev during the Soviet premier's visit to the United States. The visit was a great success, and the good will created during the talks between the two heads of state gave rise to what came to be called the "spirit of Camp David." Great hopes were in store for the big-four summit, scheduled to meet in Paris in the spring of 1960, but on 1 May, two weeks before the summit, an American U-2 spy plane was shot down over the Soviet Union.[104] Eisenhower was assured by the CIA that the pilot would follow instructions to commit suicide, destroying the "evidence" that the United States had been violating Soviet air space, but the pilot, Francis Gary Powers, did not carry out his instructions and was captured alive by the Soviets, who produced him as proof that Eisenhower had been lying. Khrushchev demanded a formal apology from Eisenhower and a commitment that the United States would cease reconnaissance flights over the Soviet Union. Eisenhower refused, and the Paris summit collapsed, in the process dashing the fledgling spirit of Camp David.

The administration that had in its final years moved toward lessening superpower tensions, finished its term with a major blunder on its hands and with U.S.-Soviet relations again in a freeze. Tensions flared over crisis in the Congo, when U.S. planes airlifted Tunisian and Moroccan troops in a UN-sponsored operation, supported by the Soviet Union, to assist the central government of Patrice Lumumba. But Lumumba also appealed to the Soviets separately, and Soviet advisers were dispatched to help his government in what Eisenhower saw as a violation of the UN resolution. The new chill in U.S.-Soviet relations found its symbolic expression in Khrushchev's conduct during a debate in the UN General Assembly on 20 September 1960. Khrushchev, sitting with the Soviet delegation, became upset with criticism of the Soviet Union in a speech by British prime minister Harold Macmillan. In anger, the Soviet premier, his face flushed, removed his shoe and alternately banged it on the table and waved it at Macmillan, accompanying his gestures with rude comments.

The picture of the leader of a superpower waving his shoe in the air was etched in many minds as a reminder of the differences between the two nations.

The Kennedy Years

In 1960 John F. Kennedy became the youngest elected president in American history and the first to have been born in the twentieth century. His youthful vigor, in contrast to Eisenhower's image of avuncular, slightly stolid amiability, was a keynote in both his campaign and his foreign-policy style. Kennedy brought to Washington an impressive array of academics and technocrats, a group which became known as the "Best and the Brightest."[105] The new president rejected massive retaliation as a credible strategy to deter Soviet attacks on Western interests. The Soviets were acquiring the ability to retaliate in kind and inflict heavy damage on the United States, making it less likely that the United States would resort to an all-out nuclear attack on the Soviet Union for anything short of a Soviet attack on the most vital American interests. But there were many important American interests in Europe and the Third World that had to be protected from Soviet aggression, and there was thus a need to find a mechanism for a proportional, graduated response to aggression. Kennedy was especially worried about communism making its greatest inroads by appealing to the "hearts and minds" of the peoples of the Third World. Khrushchev had increased the incoming president's concern with a speech in early January 1961, in which he declared Soviet support for "wars of national liberation." In order to turn back the communist challenge, it would be necessary to fight them with their own tools.[106]

Kennedy embraced the idea of flexible response that had been advanced in NSC-68, as well as the significant increases in arms expenditures necessary in order to implement the strategy. The new policy concentrated on improving America's conventional capability; the Kennedy administration's goal was to provide decision-makers with the ability to calibrate U.S. response to any communist aggression. Eisenhower warned in his farewell address against precipitous arms-spending increases. He described a growing "military-industrial complex" and declared, "The potential for the disastrous rise of misplaced power exists and will persist."

Kennedy essentially dismissed Eisenhower's cautionary valedictory. He had appointed the president of the Ford Motor Company, Robert S.

McNamara, as secretary of defense, and McNamara would keep the military and the defense contractors on a tight leash. Kennedy supported the development of an elite counterinsurgency force, the Green Berets. The president was also drawn to covert operations, as Eisenhower had been, but perhaps more because of the glamour than out of a sense of fiscal responsibility. (Kennedy was a fan of Ian Fleming's James Bond thrillers.) With all its talk about a new beginning, the administration's first political-military enterprise looked familiar. It was tried out ninety miles south of Key West, on the island of Cuba, and it was not an auspicious beginning.

Cuba had long had political and economic ties to the United States. Fulgencio Batista y Zaldívar, the dictator of Cuba, ruled with the support of the American government. On New Year's Eve 1959 Batista was toppled from power by lawyer-turned-revolutionary Fidel Castro Ruz. Initially, the United States warily supported Castro's regime in the hopes that it would be no more than mildly reformist. Castro, however, believed that Cuba had to free itself from American domination; also, he was considerably further left-wing than U.S. analysts realized. Castro's policies, which included the confiscation of American-owned property, increasingly alienated the United States. As Castro moved Cuba away from the United States, he developed friendly ties with the Soviet Union, culminating in an extensive Cuban-Soviet trade agreement in 1960. At the beginning of 1961 the Eisenhower administration severed all U.S. diplomatic ties with Cuba.

This was not Eisenhower's sole Cuban legacy to Kennedy. The CIA had been drawing up plans for a seaborne invasion of Cuba, using U.S.-trained Cuban expatriates, who had left when Castro came to power. CIA director Allen Dulles informed the new president of the plan, which was now ready to be carried out, and assured him that it would be successful. Kennedy authorized the CIA plan. In April 1961 fifteen hundred anti-Castro guerrillas landed at the Bay of Pigs with the intention of fighting their way off the beach and disappearing into the mountains to rally Cubans to a counterrevolution. They were pinned down on the beach by Cuban troops and, after suffering heavy casualties, taken prisoner.[107] As reports of the initial failure came back to Kennedy, he called off planned U.S. aerial sorties that were supposed to provide cover to the anti-Castroites. The Bay of Pigs invasion was an unmitigated disaster. Following

Eisenhower's model, Kennedy took full responsibility for the debacle he had authorized.

Still under the cloud of the Bay of Pigs, the president journeyed to Vienna to meet with Khrushchev. The Soviet leader needed a political victory, or at least the appearance of one; critics within the Soviet Communist party were taking him to task over his backing down in 1958–1959 over the Berlin crisis, the U-2 affair, and what they regarded as Khrushchev's willingness to seek accommodation with the United States. Additionally, West Berlin was a major embarrassment. Its location deep within East Germany provided the West with a valuable espionage center and a capitalist showcase in the heart of the Eastern bloc. West Berlin's propaganda value was continually confirmed by the flood of East German immigrants, many of them young and skilled, who used the city as a jumping-off point for resettling in the West. All these factors caused Khrushchev to provoke another crisis over Berlin. He reiterated his earlier demand that the Western allies relinquish their control over the Western sector. The Soviet leader once again threatened to conclude a separate treaty with East Germany that would force the West to negotiate with the Soviet satellite and accord it de facto recognition. The U.S. response was to triple the draft call-up, mobilize reserve units, and initiate a national civil-defense program. U.S.-Soviet tensions continued to rise, and war seemed more likely, until Khrushchev solved the most vexing problem – the embarrassing and debilitating stream of skilled emigrants – by ending the right of transit from East to West Berlin and constructing the Berlin Wall. In taking these steps Khrushchev in effect admitted defeat – the West could not be pushed out of Berlin – and neutralized the most dangerous point of the U.S.-Soviet confrontation. There had been three major showdowns over Berlin between 1948 and 1961, but there were no more for the balance of the Cold War.

The diminution of U.S.-Soviet tensions was only temporary, however. By 1961 the United States had definitively determined through satellite reconnaissance that there was no missile gap – the Soviet Union had overstated its nuclear strength. The Kennedy administration publicized the Soviets' subterfuge, which reassured the American public and the Allies, while further undermining Khrushchev's domestic standing and embarrassing the Soviets before China. The Soviet Union was under pressure to redeem itself in the face of the humiliating U.S. revelation. Khrushchev chose

Cuba as the vehicle for the rehabilitation of the Soviet Union's image.

In October 1962 the Soviet Union possessed fifty operational ICBMs; the U.S. arsenal numbered three hundred. Additionally, the United States maintained a large number of intermediate-range nuclear missiles, such as a battery of Jupiter-C rockets in Turkey, which were positioned close enough to the Soviet Union to pose a direct threat to that country. The Soviet Union shipped its own intermediate-range missiles to Cuba in early autumn 1962, partly to head off a second Bay of Pigs, but mainly to redress the existing strategic imbalance. It is unlikely that Khrushchev intended to use the missiles as anything other than a bargaining chip. The success of this maneuver was dependent on the United States not discovering the existence of the missiles until they were fully operational; at this point the Soviets could brandish them as a threat against the United States, bring the Americans to the bargaining table, and exact concessions. The Soviets underestimated the Americans' aerial reconnaissance capabilities, however – a U-2 plane photographed the intermediate-range ballistic missiles (IRBMs) and intermediate-range missiles(IRMs) being prepared for deployment. On 22 October 1963 Kennedy announced the discovery in a dramatic televised speech in which he declared a strict naval "quarantine" (a "blockade" would have been tantamount to a declaration of war) "on all defensive military equipment" being shipped to Cuba. He warned that the United States would "regard any nuclear missile launched from Cuba against any nation in the Western Hemisphere as an attack by the Soviet Union on the United States, requiring a full retaliatory response upon the Soviet Union."[108]

Kennedy was in part making political hay by taking a strong stand instead of engaging in quiet diplomacy; midterm elections were days away, and the Democrats were under fire for the Bay of Pigs failure and a domestic economic recession. However, it is likely that quiet diplomacy would have encouraged the Soviets to drag their heels, and Kennedy's primary objective was to get the missiles removed from Cuba. These IRBMs and IRMs would double the Soviet Union's strike capability and greatly increase their ability to launch a surprise attack. This public approach boxed Khrushchev into choosing between either capitulating to the United States, or defying the blockade and risking a war that could escalate into full-scale nuclear exchange.

Khrushchev sent Kennedy two letters, one day

apart. In the first he offered to remove the missiles in exchange for the United States's guarantee that it would not invade Cuba. The second letter, the result of domestic political pressure on the general secretary, offered a harder line – as a quid pro quo the United States would have to remove its Jupiter-C missiles from Turkey. The Kennedy administration had been planning to scrap the obsolete Jupiter-Cs. The United States, however, could not be made to look as though it had capitulated to the Soviet Union by removing the missiles from Turkey. The Executive Committee (ExComm), an "inner council" the president had established to deal with the Cuban Missile Crisis, decided to acknowledge the first letter and ignore the second. The president's brother, Attorney General Robert F. Kennedy, followed up the official response with a private meeting with Soviet diplomats. He threatened a U.S. attack if the missiles were not removed, but he informally told the Soviets that the United States would remove the Jupiter-Cs from Turkey soon after the crisis ended on the condition that the Soviet Union not publicize the secret understanding. Khrushchev accepted the deal, and the missiles were soon removed from Cuba.

The Cuban Missile Crisis caused a shift in Soviet foreign policy from strategic deception to a concerted overt effort to reduce tensions between the superpowers. Both Khrushchev and Kennedy were sobered by the episode, in which the United States and the Soviet Union came close to the brink of thermonuclear war; the two nations' policies were brought into some congruence. In June 1963 Kennedy had declared in a speech at American University that the United States's and the Soviet Union's "most basic common link is that we all inhabit this small planet. We all breathe the same air. And we are all mortal." Soon after this speech, the United States and the Soviet Union concluded an atmospheric nuclear test-ban treaty. Superpower relations stabilized and improved throughout 1963.

One of the problems that had dogged the management and resolution of crises was slow, indirect communications; a teletype "hotline" was set up to provide a direct link between Moscow and Washington. The United States began selling wheat to the Soviet Union. The Soviets, who had raised objections to American U-2 overflights and, subsequently, satellite reconnaissance, began to recognize the value of Eisenhower's "Open Skies" proposal when they analyzed their own satellite photographs and were impressed with the quality of the data. This idea of mutual vulnerability as a guarantor of security was a precursor of the mutual assured destruction (MAD) doctrine that would arise in the late 1960s. To be sure, the Soviets still intended to redress the strategic imbalance, which they felt had forced their capitulation to the United States during the Cuban Missile Crisis. A highly placed Soviet told an American, "you'll never be able to do that to us again." The Soviet Union embarked on a program to achieve nuclear parity with the United States; they reached this goal by 1968.

Khrushchev became a casualty of the changing superpower relations in the early 1960s. The People's Republic of China had castigated Khrushchev as foolish for placing missiles in Cuba and cowardly for removing them, prompting a final, open Sino-Soviet split. Similar internal criticism resulted in Khrushchev's removal from power on 15 October 1964 and his replacement by Leonid Brezhnev as party secretary. Although Brezhnev was considerably more conservative than his predecessor in domestic matters, the change in leadership did not alter the evolving Soviet policy toward the West, and a new U.S.-Soviet spirit of détente prevailed. At this juncture the United States intensified its involvement in Indochina.[109]

Johnson and Vietnam

The Kennedy administration had focused its attention on Southeast Asia since the beginning of its term. Indochina had been the subject of Eisenhower's "domino theory" remarks, and Kennedy saw the region as an ideal arena for the use of counterinsurgency tactics. Kennedy considered intervening in a civil war in Laos but decided that this was not the best place to make a stand; the United States and the Soviet Union agreed by early 1962 to neutralize Laos, although this neutrality was not completely successful. Vietnam seemed a more appropriate candidate for U.S. attention. Kennedy sent his military advisor, General Maxwell D. Taylor, and presidential adviser Walt Rostow on a fact-finding trip to Vietnam in 1961. They recommended a large infusion of American combat troops. The president was concerned about violating the 1954 Geneva accords that pledged no outside interference in Vietnamese affairs and about identifying too closely with the troubled regime of Ngo Dinh Diem. Still, Kennedy authorized the deployment of noncombat advisers; by 1963 there were seventeen thousand U.S. troops in Vietnam.

Diem, supported as South Vietnam's leader by the United States, had not built up a popular base.

While personally honest, he was aloof and, as a devout Catholic in a predominantly Buddhist nation, out of touch with his constituents. Additionally, he was an inept administrator, whose attempts at reform were unsuccessful. Particularly unpopular was his "strategic hamlet" policy, based on American advice, which uprooted Vietnamese peasants from ancestral lands and placed them in guarded, centralized villages where they could be shielded from the Vietcong – and more easily controlled by the central regime. Protests against Diem's rule mounted, and South Vietnam became increasingly unstable.

Late in 1963 a group of South Vietnamese generals approached the United States seeking support for an effort to remove Diem and replace him with one of their own. The Kennedy administration had come to view Diem as an embarrassment and an annoyance, as the South Vietnamese leader persistently rejected American attempts to direct his policies. The president approved the planned coup, and in early November 1963 Diem and his brother, Ngo Dinh Nhu, with whom he shared political power, were quickly seized and murdered. Several weeks later, on 22 November, Kennedy was assassinated by a sniper in Dallas, Texas.

Lyndon B. Johnson was a masterful politician who had risen through the Washington ranks to become one of the most powerful Senate majority leaders before serving as Kennedy's vice-president.[110] He possessed a deep sense of justice – the cornerstone of his domestic policy was to be the Great Society, the most ambitious attempt in American history to redress the gap between rich and poor. Johnson perceived several problems as he set about devising strategy.[111] First, he believed in the domino theory and Vietnam's strategic importance to East Asian stability. Second, his planned domestic program was going to be costly and would provoke opposition from the Right; in order to preserve the Great Society, he would have to be invulnerable to charges of appeasement or cowardice, which a disengagement from Vietnam might bring.

Third, the nature and the cost of U.S. involvement in Vietnam would have to be concealed for as long as possible so as not to provide the Right a rationale for slashing the Great Society's budget. As Johnson himself later put it, "I knew from the start that I was bound to be crucified either way I moved. If I left the woman I really loved – the Great Society – in order to get involved with that bitch of a war on the other side of the world, then I would lose everything at home. . . . But if I left that war and let the Communists take over South

Vietnam, then I would be seen as a coward and my nation would be seen as an appeaser and we would both find it impossible to accomplish anything for anybody anywhere on the entire globe." Johnson and his advisers, mainly holdovers from the Kennedy administration, were determined to intervene directly with combat troops in Vietnam. The question was how to justify such a move.

The North Vietnamese provided the solution in August 1964 by attacking two U.S. destroyers in the Gulf of Tonkin, off the North Vietnamese coast. Johnson and McNamara claimed that the attack had been unprovoked. (Later it was revealed that the U.S. ships had been aiding South Vietnamese military operations against North Vietnam.) Johnson asked for and received a congressional resolution – the Tonkin Gulf resolution – authorizing him to take whatever action was necessary to stop North Vietnamese aggression and to aid any SEATO member that requested U.S. help.

The president was not ready to intensify the conflict just yet, however. The 1964 presidential campaign was entering its final phase, and Johnson was portraying himself as a peace-oriented moderate. In contrast to his rival, Senator Barry Goldwater – who had declared that "extremism in the defense of liberty is no vice" and supported the use of nuclear weapons, if necessary, to subdue the North Vietnamese – Johnson flatly stated, "We are not going to send American boys nine or ten thousand miles to do what Asian boys ought to be doing for themselves." An additional brake on immediate U.S. action against North Vietnam was the People's Republic of China's testing of an atomic bomb in October 1964. An American attack would have to be calibrated in terms of force and location so as not to cause China to intervene as it had, with disastrous results for the United States, when MacArthur took American forces north of the 38th parallel during the Korean War. A carefully planned, incremental strategy, to be initiated after the presidential election, was called for.

Johnson won reelection by a landslide. At the beginning of February 1965 the United States began bombing North Vietnamese targets; a month later an intensive bombing campaign code-named "Rolling Thunder" commenced. North Vietnam did not buckle under the bombardment, however, and at the urging of General William C. Westmoreland, the U.S. military commander in Vietnam, the Johnson administration sent 40,000 troops to Vietnam, the first large-scale deployment of a force that would eventually number 540,000. As the United States sank deeper into the Indochi-

nese "quagmire" (as French president Charles de Gaulle had described Vietnam to John F. Kennedy), the Johnson administration responded to a perceived threat closer to home. In late April 1965 the United States sent 23,000 Marines to the Dominican Republic to shore up a right-wing junta that was threatened with a coup by supporters of Juan Bosch Gavino, a leftist noncommunist reformer who had led the Dominican government briefly before he was deposed by the rightist Dominican army. The U.S. intervention was successful in propping up the junta; Bosch later commented, "This was a democratic revolution smashed by the leading democracy in the world." But the United States, still smarting from Castro's success in Cuba, would not risk the creation of another Soviet client state in the Caribbean.

U.S.-Soviet relations remained stable even as the Vietnam War escalated and the United States defended its prerogatives in the Western Hemisphere. Although the superpowers opposed each other indirectly over Vietnam, there were other areas of mutual interest. The People's Republic of China was one such area. After the Sino-Soviet split that had been brewing since 1958 became open in 1963, relations between the two nations, which share the longest border in the world, deteriorated rapidly. With the PRC on the verge of testing an atomic bomb, the Soviet Union had approached the United States with a plan for a coordinated response, possibly including military action, to head off China's acquisition of nuclear capability.

The Soviets, remembering Mao's prodding to attack the United States with atomic weapons during the 1958 Quemoy-Matsu crisis, had good reason to fear that the PRC had an irresponsible attitude toward nuclear strategy. Although nothing came of these discussions, they underlined for the United States that the communist monolith, if there ever had been one, was no more and that the Soviet Union was as concerned as the United States about nuclear stability. U.S.-Soviet apprehensions about an irrational Chinese militancy were not assuaged when the PRC began its Cultural Revolution, a domestic upheaval initiated by Mao in order to stamp out nonorthodox thinking that had become China's version of the Stalinist purges of the 1930s in the Soviet Union. The threat to U.S. and Soviet interests posed by Chinese instability increased further with the PRC detonation of a hydrogen bomb in 1966; the CIA estimated that China would possess intercontinental ballistic missiles (ICBMs) within five years.

The evolving U.S.-Soviet rapprochement combined with American unilateralism during the Cuban Missile Crisis and over Vietnam to cause tension between the United States and its Western European allies. Franco-U.S. relations were the major friction point. De Gaulle had since the late 1950s been looking to develop a European policy independent of the United States, with France as the leading power. The U.S. refusal to share nuclear-weapons technology had led the French to embark on their own atomic-weapons program; they tested an atomic bomb in 1960. De Gaulle cultivated close ties with West Germany, which he envisioned as the backbone of an independent European foreign policy. The French president feared, on the one hand, that the United States might unilaterally trigger a thermonuclear war over a crisis irrelevant to European interests, as had almost been the case with Cuba in 1962, and, on the other hand, that the United States would not be willing to risk an attack on its cities in order to retaliate for a Soviet invasion of Europe. As a result of these concerns France built up its nuclear capabilities and at the same time developed closer ties with the communist world. France completed its move away from the United States by withdrawing from NATO in 1966, although it continued to consider itself part of the Western Alliance.

Great Britain for its part sided with U.S. strategic policy; the Kennedy administration supplied the British with the Polaris submarine-launched ballistic missile (SLBM). That France had not been offered Polaris reinforced de Gaulle's determination to distance his country from the United States. Additionally, the French president vetoed Great Britain's entry into the European Common Market, claiming that Great Britain would be an American pawn in the European Economic Community.

Once the United States and the Soviet Union had concluded that direct confrontation was too dangerous, the reduced superpower tensions allowed differences of strategic interest among members of the Western Alliance to come to the surface. The United States was committed to containing communism globally while avoiding a direct confrontation with the Soviet Union, whereas the Europeans were concerned with maintaining a credible deterrent against the Soviet threat in Europe while avoiding U.S. political and economic domination, or worse, a Soviet-American condominium.

The United States and the Soviet Union moved forward hesitantly in their evolving détente during 1967. After agreeing to a cease-fire between Israel and its Arab adversaries during the June 1967 Six-Day War,[112] the superpowers clashed over Israel's plan, which the United States supported, to take control of the Golan Heights, which belonged to Syria, a Soviet client. The United States sent the Soviet Union one of the most strongly worded messages of the Cold War – "if you want war, you can have war" was the essence of the dispatch, according to McNamara. The cease-fire, with Israel on the Golan, was put into effect. Soon thereafter, in the shadow of the Chinese H-bomb test, Johnson met with Soviet premier Alexsei Nikolaevich Kosygin, had come to power with Brezhnev in 1964, in Glassboro, New Jersey. The summit achieved mixed results. Johnson and McNamara could not convince Kosygin that antiballistic-missile (ABM) programs contributed to instability by encouraging the construction of more and newer offensive missiles to overwhelm the adversary's ABM defenses; Kosygin exclaimed in response to their argument, "Defense is moral, offense is immoral!" (The Soviets would change their thinking on ABMs during the next several years.) However, the premier agreed with McNamara's assertion that the arms race was suicidal and had to be controlled, and soon thereafter the United States and the Soviet Union signed a nuclear Non-Proliferation Treaty. They invited other countries to sign on. China, France, India, Pakistan, Brazil, Argentina, Israel, North Korea, and South Africa declined to do so – all these nations were in various stages of nuclear development and did not wish to limit their future options (France, South Africa, and North Korea have recently announced their readiness to sign the treaty).

U.S.-Soviet détente did not affect the Soviet Union's treatment of its satellites. The Czechoslovak Communist party, under the leadership of Aleksander Dubcek, took steps to liberalize the country economically, politically, and culturally. The Soviets, fearful of the precedent the Czechs were setting in the Eastern bloc, stopped the "Prague Spring" in a bloodless military invasion. Soviet party secretary Brezhnev followed up this crackdown with the Brezhnev Doctrine, which held that the Soviet Union had the right to intervene in order to save socialist nations threatened by "world imperialism." Détente similarly did not influence the course of the Vietnam War. Johnson had hoped that improved relations would encourage the Soviet Union to exert pressure on Ho Chi Minh to end the war on terms favorable to the United States. However, the Soviets saw no reason to aid America – the longer the conflict lasted, the more the United States would be weakened. More-over, Soviet influence over North Vietnam and its nationalist leader was probably not very great. Early in 1968 the Vietcong launched a large-scale attack against both American and Army of the Republic of South Vietnam (ARVN) troops during Tet, the Vietnamese New Year; they inflicted heavy casualties before being driven back. Although the Vietcong decisively lost the battle, the stiff fight they put up after years of massive bombings and ground "search and destroy" missions gave the lie to administration assertions that an American victory was close at hand. Domestically, college students and professors and others who had been protesting since the initial escalation of U.S. involvement stepped up their opposition; dissenters daily stood outside the White House chanting, "Hey, hey, LBJ, how many kids did you kill today?" A dark-horse presidential aspirant who opposed the war, Senator Eugene J. McCarthy, a Democrat from Minnesota, ran against Johnson in the New Hampshire primary and placed a strong second, which the president interpreted as a sign that he had lost his mandate to lead. After Robert F. Kennedy, now a popular senator from New York, also announced his candidacy, Johnson announced that he would not seek nor accept the nomination for another term as president. Vice-president Hubert H. Humphrey headed the Democratic ticket; opposing him was Richard M. Nixon, who had been Eisenhower's vice-president and who had run unsuccessfully against John F. Kennedy in the 1960 election. Nixon declared that he had a plan to bring about "peace with honor," although he did not say how it would be done. The American public, by a bare majority, gave Nixon the opportunity to implement his plan.

Nixon, Kissinger, and Ford

Nixon chose as his chief foreign-policy adviser the Harvard political science professor Henry Kissinger. Kissinger was appointed national security adviser; the State Department, which Nixon viewed distrustfully as a bureaucratic fiefdom with its own political agenda, was to be headed by William Rogers, an old Republican party ally with little foreign-policy experience. Together, Nixon and Kissinger sought to fashion a coherent, pragmatic U.S. diplomacy, which they felt the Kennedy and Johnson administrations had lacked.[113]

Despite considerable differences in background, the president and his national security adviser functioned effectively as a team. Nixon, according to Kissinger, "had an extraordinary instinct for the jugular" that complemented Kissinger's nuanced intellectualism. The two men shared a commitment to pragmatism and stability; Kissinger admitted at one point that, given a choice between order and democracy, he would choose the former.

Nixon, despite his hard-line anticommunist reputation, had demonstrated a willingness to put aside ideological considerations in favor of reasons of state when he called in the mid 1960s for the eventual normalization of U.S. relations with communist China. Kissinger was both a student and an advocate of the realpolitik practiced in the nineteenth century by Klemens Metternich, Viscount Castlereagh, and Otto von Bismarck; the Concert of Europe, with its elegant balance of power, represented the highest achievement of diplomacy in Kissinger's opinion, as it had prevented an all-out continental war in Europe for a century.

Nixon and Kissinger believed that in order for containment to work it had to change with the times. It was no longer feasible for the United States to maintain strategic superiority, as the Soviets had spent the years since the Cuban Missile Crisis building up their strategic nuclear arsenal to approximate parity with that of the United States and constructing a strong navy. The Soviet Union was determined not to be humiliated again as it had been in 1962. Nixon and Kissinger recognized the Soviet achievement, as well as the near-impossibility of undoing it, and concluded that in any event it was unnecessary for the United States to maintain a strategic lead over the Soviet Union — nuclear "sufficiency" would be adequate to maintain American security. Rather than attempt to subdue the Soviet Union, which was an unattainable goal (as was any Soviet effort to subdue the United States), the United States should seek instead to "manage" the Soviet Union. Nixon and Kissinger set out to establish a relationship of détente between the United States and the Soviet Union. The Soviet Union would be encouraged to participate responsibly in global politics through a combination of strategic and economic agreements. The "linkage" of responsible Soviet behavior with the promised rewards of economic benefits, which the Soviet economy needed, and increased international prestige, which the Soviet leadership sought, would provide the engine for "managing" the Soviet Union.

Nixon and Kissinger hoped that with the establishment of détente between the superpowers, the Soviet Union could be persuaded to help the United States extricate itself from Vietnam. However, the Soviet Union consistently described détente as a competitive relationship and saw no benefit in pressuring its client on behalf of its strategic rival. Nixon and Kissinger held that responsible Soviet behavior precluded Third World adventurism, while the Soviets insisted that there was no inconsistency between responsible behavior and attempts to extend their influence in contested regions of the globe. The gap between American and Soviet definitions of détente would prove irreconcilable.

Nixon and his national security adviser planned to establish normal diplomatic relations with the People's Republic of China, both as a means of pressuring the Soviet Union on arms and other negotiations and because, they felt, it was inherently destabilizing for the world's most populous nation to be kept in a state of diplomatic isolation.[114] It had become clear that the Soviet Union and the PRC viewed each other, not the United States, as principal rivals. A series of military clashes along the Sino-Soviet border during 1969 and 1970 underlined America's opportunity to establish an advantageous triangular relationship with the two communist powers. Only Nixon, with his impeccable anticommunist credentials, would be able to initiate relations with China and, necessarily, abandon Taiwan and Chiang Kai-shek's Kuomintang without committing domestic political suicide.

In order to implement this grand strategy, however, the Vietnam conflict had to be downgraded in strategic importance and, ultimately, ended with some sort of face-saving peace agreement. Early in his first term Nixon still held hopes that the Soviets would help the United States exit Indochina. Even so, the president did not count exclusively on a "Soviet card" to further American policy. He ordered a secret large-scale bombing campaign that targeted neutral Cambodia, which the Vietcong were using as a supply route. He announced a policy of "Vietnamization" – the United States would continue to supply arms and matériel to South Vietnam, but American troops would be gradually withdrawn. Vietnamization fit into a larger strategic framework, the Nixon Doctrine, which the president proclaimed in mid 1969. The Nixon Doctrine declared that the United States would maintain existing treaty commitments and provide a shield over American allies threatened by nuclear powers. However, while the United States would furnish military and economic assistance in response to other types of aggression, "we shall look to the nation directly threatened to assume the primary responsibility of providing the manpower for its defense." The Nixon Doctrine was the product of the administration's realist strategy, which called for the reduction of both adversaries and commitments around the world.

Nixon followed the secret bombing of Cambodia with an invasion of that nation in a final drive to eliminate the Vietcong sanctuaries there. Nixon announced the invasion in April 1970 and sparked bitter protests on college campuses across America. At Kent State University in Ohio, National Guardsmen killed four student protesters. Domestic divisions were further deepened in 1971, when Daniel Ellsberg, a former Defense Department analyst, leaked a top-secret government report on the history of America's Vietnam policy through the mid 1960s to the *New York Times,* which published the report as "The Pentagon Papers." The report, which the Nixon administration attempted to have suppressed for national-security reasons, demonstrated that the U.S. government had been misleading the country about its goals and progress in Vietnam. Political and generational tensions threatened the American society and its institutions.

The Opening to China

Nixon and Kissinger nonetheless pressed forward with their plans for détente with the major communist powers. In mid 1971 Kissinger secretly traveled to China for a series of conferences with Chinese foreign minister Zhou Enlai. These talks paved the way for Nixon to announce in July 1971 that he would visit the PRC the following year. Nixon's visit to China was a rousing success. Trade and friendship treaties were signed, diplomats exchanged, and the obstacles to the PRC's membership in the UN were removed. Soon thereafter mainland China replaced Taiwan in the General Assembly and on the Security Council. The Soviets were disquieted by the Sino-American rapprochement and made clear their willingness to host a presidential visit. Nixon took advantage of this diplomatic flexibility and mined North Vietnam's Haiphong Harbor, which Lyndon Johnson had refused to do for fear of inadvertently destroying Soviet shipping and touching off a major superpower crisis. The Soviets, as expected, remained quiescent, even when one of their ships struck an American mine. Soviet premier Brezhnev received Nixon and Kissinger in Moscow in mid 1972. The Soviets were particularly anxious to obtain American technology and agricultural products and to improve economic ties with the United States and the West. Nixon and Kissinger also desired a closer trade relationship between the United States and the Soviet Union, as such ties, they hoped, would give the United States leverage over the Soviet Union and help keep the Soviets responsible (by U.S. standards) in the conduct of their global policy.

Both sides also desired a nuclear arms control agreement as well. While in the Soviet Union, Nixon and Brezhnev signed the Strategic Arms Limitation Talks (SALT I) treaty. SALT I effectively banned antiballistic-missile (ABM) defense systems. The Soviets had finally accepted the argument that McNamara had unsuccessfully pressed upon Alexsei Kosygin in Glassboro several years earlier – MAD, offered the greatest guarantee of nuclear stability through the maintenance of the "balance of terror" between the superpowers. SALT I froze the number of intercontinental ballistic missiles (ICBMs) and submarine-launched ballistic missiles (SLBMs) at current levels, which gave the Soviets a significant numerical advantage. The technologically more advanced United States, however, had developed the multiple independent reentry vehicle (MIRV), which permitted a single launcher to carry as many warheads as the missile could lift, each of which would then proceed on to separate targets. Additionally, U.S. missiles were significantly more accurate than Soviet missiles. Thus, SALT I maintained overall a U.S. numerical superiority – at least until the Soviets developed their own MIRVs, which they did by the mid 1970s. SALT I was seen as an interim agreement; negotiations on SALT II began in 1974, and the treaty was concluded, under the cloud of a renewed Cold War, in 1979.

As part of an economic agreement between the United States and the Soviet Union, Nixon authorized the sale of large quantities of wheat and other grain to the Soviet Union at a low price. The grain sale caused a domestic wheat shortage and caused criticism that Nixon was coddling the Soviet Union. Democratic senator Henry M. ("Scoop") Jackson, an influential politician from Washington who harbored presidential aspirations, began to criticize SALT and the entire policy of détente. Jackson claimed (correctly, as it turned out) that the Soviets would soon obtain MIRV and other technology that currently gave the United States its strategic edge and provided the rationale for allowing the Soviets to retain greater numbers of launchers. He also took aim at U.S.-Soviet trade agreements and the Nixon administration's plan to grant the Soviet Union most-favored-nation (MFN) status. Late in 1972 Jackson demanded that the Soviet Union relax its restrictions on Jewish emigration as the price of his support for the administration's

policy. In the spring of 1973 Jackson and Congressman Charles Vanik introduced an amendment specifically linking Soviet Jewish emigration rights with the granting of MFN status to the Soviet Union. The Jackson-Vanik amendment was passed in 1974, causing the Soviets to claim with some justification that they had been betrayed by Nixon and Kissinger, who had promised that the Soviet Union would receive MFN status. Moreover, Jackson-Vanik was denounced by the Soviets as an intrusion into Soviet domestic policy; the Soviet Union responded to the amendment by reducing the flow of Soviet Jewish émigrés, which had, since the inception of détente, been relatively high. The Jackson-Vanik amendment had the net effect of hurting the group it had been intended to help.

Nixon won reelection in 1972 by a landslide. However, despite the fact that he faced weak competition from the Democrats, the Committee to Re-Elect the President, or CREEP, undertook a dirty-tricks campaign that culminated in an attempt to break into the Democratic party's national headquarters at the Watergate complex in Washington, D.C. The burglars were caught, and a press investigation slowly led up the chain of CREEP command to the highest levels of the White House; Nixon was ultimately implicated. Watergate would eventually cost Nixon the presidency.

Throughout 1972 the United States and North Vietnam engaged in peace negotiations. Shortly before the presidential election Kissinger announced that "peace is at hand." His assessment was premature, however; the North Vietnamese had arrived at an agreement with the United States, but South Vietnamese president Nguyen Van Thieu rejected terms that included the continued presence of communist troops in the South. With the deal foundering because of the South Vietnamese position, the North Vietnamese modified their own terms. After much haggling between the United States and North Vietnam, the North Vietnamese broke off negotiations. Nixon responded in December 1972 with the "Christmas bombing" of Hanoi and Haiphong. The North Vietnamese came back to the bargaining table in January 1973, and within a month a cease-fire was concluded.

The United States withdrew its forces and received in turn American prisoners of war (POWs); fourteen hundred MIAs – soldiers missing in action – remained unaccounted for. Communist troops remained in South Vietnam. The South Vietnamese government, which had long been corrupt and incompetent, was doomed. Its end would come two years later, thus providing the United

States with the "decent interval" that Kissinger had hoped for between the withdrawal of American troops and the South Vietnamese government's overthrow. America's longest war was finally over. When North Vietnam began violating the provisions of the cease-fire, Nixon wanted to implement secret guarantees he had given Thieu of renewed U.S. military assistance. However, Congress had passed the War Powers Act in 1973, which limited to sixty days any military action taken by the president without Congressional consent and which underlined a previous resolution ending all American involvement in Vietnam. With the threat of American reintervention removed, North Vietnam began, as had been expected, to close the noose on the disorganized, demoralized South.

The withdrawal of the United States from Vietnam allowed the Nixon administration to turn to other spheres of strategic interest. While Nixon and Kissinger were willing to reach a modus vivendi with the Soviet Union and the People's Republic of China, they were less tolerant of leftist movements elsewhere. In Chile, an independent Marxist Salvador Allende Gossens had been elected president in 1970. The Nixon administration immediately set about destabilizing Allende's government. After several years of increasing economic and political isolation, the Chilean military staged a coup d'état with at least the indirect aid of the CIA. Allende committed suicide as army troops stormed the presidential palace. General Augusto Pinochet Ugarte assumed control of the Chilean government and held it until 1990, when at last he submitted to a popular vote and lost.

Western Europe had been neglected by the Nixon administration as the president and his national security adviser concentrated on reaching an accommodation with the Soviet Union and the PRC. Nixon and Kissinger became alarmed by what they saw as a dangerous atmosphere of Western European accommodation toward the Soviet Union, although they ultimately took little substantive action to combat this trend. West German chancellor, Social Democrat Willy Brandt, pursued an independent policy of Ostpolitik, a dialogue with the Soviet Union and the Eastern Europe.[115] Brandt's Ostpolitik led to a West German–Soviet nonaggression pact, West German recognition of the Oder-Neisse Line as the permanent German-Polish boundary, Soviet guarantees of permanent access to West Berlin, and, ultimately, formal recognition between West Germany and East Germany, which had long been anathema to the West Germans, who claimed that theirs was

the only legitimate German government. The Four Powers (the United States, Great Britain, France, and the Soviet Union) supported Brandt's efforts. However, Nixon and Kissinger were worried about the left-wing German chancellor's program. Brandt, Kissinger asserted in his memoirs, saw Ostpolitik not as a recognition of postwar boundary divisions but as a means to achieve German unity by cultivating good relations with the Eastern bloc and becoming a cultural and political "magnet" for Eastern Europe. "The question in our minds," wrote Kissinger later, "was which side of the dividing line would in fact be the magnet. We feared that over time, at first imperceptibly, the Communist world would wind up in the stronger position."

The Nixon administration did not oppose Ostpolitik. But Nixon and Kissinger were sufficiently alarmed about frays in the Western Alliance to overcome their usual insouciance toward England, France, and the other NATO allies proclaim 1973 "The Year of Europe." The Europeans were annoyed at the condescension inherent in being assigned a "year"; Nixon and Kissinger's policy did little to accomplish the hoped-for tightening of bonds of the alliance. In part because of the Watergate scandal and crises in the Middle East, Europe and NATO continued to get short shrift from the United States through the end of the Nixon-Kissinger-Ford years, except for a period in 1974–1975 when Kissinger feared that Eurocommunists in Portugal, Italy, and France might participate in coalition governments. Relations between the United States and its NATO allies remained cool until the early 1980s, when there was a convergence of like-minded conservative governments in the United States, Great Britain, and Germany.

In October 1973 Egypt and Syria launched a war against Israel, with the intention of regaining the territories that they had lost in the Six-Day War six years earlier. The Egyptians in particular scored an initial gain by thrusting deep into the Sinai peninsula. The Israelis, aided by an American airlift of supplies, regained their equilibrium and counterattacked. Soon the Israeli Defense Force (IDF) had beaten back the Syrian advance and surrounded the Egyptian Third Army, which was now threatened with annihilation. Egyptian president Anwar Sadat had expelled most of the Soviet advisers in Egypt the previous year and begun to lean toward the United States in the hope that the United States would prevail upon Israel to return captured Sinai. But now, with the Third Army facing destruction at the hands of the Israelis, Sadat called for help from the Soviets. The Nixon administration responded in a two-pronged fashion. The president called a DefCon 3 military alert (DefCon 5 is the lowest state of alert; DefCon 1 is the highest) to deter the Soviets from intervening directly on Egypt's behalf. Next, Kissinger pressured the Israelis not to destroy the Egyptian Third Army, threatening that the United States would allow the Soviets to resupply the Egyptians should the IDF proceed with its planned attack. The Israelis backed down.

When the United States sent arms to Israel, the Arab oil-producing nations leveled an oil embargo on the United States, Western Europe, and Japan. The Japanese and the Europeans were heavily dependent on Middle East oil and adjusted their positions from a pro-Israeli to a pro-Arab orientation. This switch by the Allies angered Kissinger, who saw their policy swing as craven. After Kissinger engaged in a flurry of shuttle diplomacy between Jerusalem, Damascus, and Cairo, the secretary of state (Kissinger had succeeded William Rogers some months earlier) brokered an end to the Yom Kippur War. The oil embargo was lifted, and Kissinger spent the next two years mediating between the Arabs and the Israelis in a "step-by-step" incremental diplomatic process that eventually resulted in the interim Sinai Accords, which in turn set the stage for the dramatic Camp David process during the Jimmy Carter administration.

Throughout 1973 and the first half of 1974 the Watergate issue ate away at the Nixon presidency. As the facts about "slush funds," "hushmoney," and "dirty tricks" came to light, public confidence in Nixon's integrity and fitness for office deteriorated. An unrelated blow to the administration's image was Vice-president Spiro Agnew's plea of nolo contendre to charges of corruption dating back to his tenure as mayor of Baltimore. Setting an ominous precedent for Nixon, Agnew resigned from office in October 1973. House minority leader Gerald R. Ford was chosen by Nixon to replace Agnew. In August 1974, faced with congressional calls for impeachment in response to the Watergate scandal, Nixon resigned from the presidency, and Ford replaced him. Ford told the American public that their "long national nightmare" was over.

The Ford Presidency

Kissinger remained in place as secretary of state (and for a while, also as national security adviser) during Ford's stewardship; thus, constancy in American foreign policy was maintained through the end of 1976. Events in the Third World and elsewhere continued to distract Kissinger from his primary interest, American relations with the Soviet Union. In the summer of 1974 Turkey invaded Cyprus and occupied half of the island in retaliation for the right-wing Greek junta's toppling of the independent and neutral Cypriot government of Archbishop Makarios. The United States managed to alienate the Greeks, Turks, and Cypriots with its clumsy, shifting policy. As Greece and Turkey were both NATO members, anti-American sentiment in these countries threatened to undermine the alliance's defense of the eastern Mediterranean; NATO's position in Greece and Turkey did not restabilize until 1976.

Africa assumed new importance as a strategic hot-spot. Africa had long been viewed by a succession of presidents as a strategic backwater. Only occasionally, as in the attempted secession by the Katanga province from the newly independent Congo Republic (formerly a Belgian colony) between 1960 and 1963, did the United States take an active interest in African politics. The CIA was rumored to have participated in the assassination of Congolese premier Patrice Lumumba, who Eisenhower suspected was a "Soviet tool" – Lumumba had demonstrated hostility toward the mining interests of NATO ally Belgium, which he accused of fomenting the Katanga uprising. Aside from the Congo episode, the United States had devoted little attention to African affairs. The Nixon administration had decided in 1970 to relax the established policy of limited American pressure on white minority regimes in Africa on the assumption that "the whites are here to stay and the only way that constructive change can come about is through them." In 1974, however, the Portuguese colonial government in Angola collapsed with the fall of the four-decade-old Portuguese right-wing government. With independence came a power struggle among black factions. The Soviet-backed Popular Movement for the Liberation of Angola (MPLA) eventually gained control of the country with the aid of thousands of Cuban troops supplied by the Soviet Union. The United States covertly backed the losers in the power struggle. Kissinger denounced the Soviet involvement and requested congressional authorization for a large-scale military aid program for the American-backed factions; he was turned down.

In April 1975 South Vietnam finally fell. Communist troops took control of Saigon, causing a riot at the American embassy there as thousands of panic-stricken Vietnamese who had supported the

United States during the war clamored to be evacuated. The United States had made no provisions for a large-scale evacuation and proceeded with the removal by helicopter of Americans and a small number of Vietnamese. Other less fortunate Vietnamese clung desperately to the helicopters' retractable landing gear as the fleeing Americans ascended from the embassy roof and were crushed when the wheels were raised. America's involvement in Vietnam ended with the return of the helicopters to the aircraft carriers from which they had taken off.

In a violent finale to the U.S. evacuation of Saigon, President Ford ordered a military attack in May 1975 to rescue the thirty-eight imprisoned crew members of the American freighter *Mayaguez,* which had been seized for trespassing in territorial waters by the newly installed communist Khmer Rouge regime in Cambodia. With the United States still smarting from the seizure of the USS *Pueblo* by North Korea in 1968 (when the United States had been forced publicly to admit to espionage before the North Koreans released the crew), and with America's ignominious withdrawal from Vietnam a fresh wound, Ford and Kissinger resolved to take strong action. What was intended to be a demonstration of American decisiveness, however, turned into a comedy of errors – as U.S. warplanes struck a Cambodian port and amphibious forces attacked the island of Koh Tang (the prisoners had been detained there at one point but had been moved to the mainland) at the cost of fifteen American dead, the crew of the *Mayaguez* was being released by the Cambodian authorities. The Ford administration nonetheless received considerable domestic support for the attack; Americans were looking for any manifestation of national strength in which to take pride. It would remain for two later presidents – Ronald Reagan and George Bush – to exploit fully this vein of nationalist sentiment with a sequence of successful military adventures.

Kissinger had been criticized for not making détente – and its political and economic benefits to the Soviets – dependent on the Soviet Union's behavior toward its subject peoples; the Jackson-Vanik amendment had attempted to redress this imbalance and had seriously injured Kissinger's diplomatic efforts. In 1975 Kissinger took advantage of an opportunity at the Helsinki Conference on Security and Cooperation in Europe (CSCE) to mollify his critics. The leaders of the United States, Canada, and all the European nations except Albania (which was encased in self-imposed Stalinist isolation from the rest of the Continent) met in the

Finnish capital to sign a lengthy declaration, over two years in the composing, that officially ratified the post–World War II political order. The Helsinki Agreements declared that the existing European borders were inviolable save through peaceful negotiations; included was a pledge of nonintervention in the internal affairs of member states, which ostensibly precluded anymore Soviet invasions like those of Hungary in 1956 and Czechoslovakia in 1968. Furthermore, the agreements called for the free movement of peoples and ideas both across and within borders. Kissinger supported the declaration on human rights, as it was sufficiently vague in its wording to be harmless to the realist policies the secretary of state continued to pursue. To the surprise of the Western delegations, the subject peoples of Eastern Europe vigorously embraced the human-rights declaration of the Helsinki Agreements, and resistance to Soviet-style authoritarianism, dormant since the suppression of the Prague Spring, began to grow. Helsinki Watch, Americas Watch, and Asia Watch were human-rights advocacy and watchdog organizations established in the aftermath of the CSCE that monitored, often at great risk to reporting members, government compliance with the human-rights principles enunciated in Basket Three. The "Solidarity" coalition of workers and anticommunist intellectuals that grew up in Poland during the early 1980s pointed to the Helsinki accords for its legitimacy. The Soviets for their part cited the agreements on nonintervention in the internal affairs of signatories to ward off criticism of the Soviet Union's repressive policies; the Helsinki human-rights declaration, however, opened a hairline crack in the Soviet Union's belief in its moral imprimatur that would widen into a chasm with the rise of Mikhail Gorbachev and the institution of perestroika and glasnost in the mid 1980s. For the time being, the Helsinki accords and their solidification of Europe's postwar boundaries legitimated the Soviet Union's superpower status on a continent bifurcated into U.S. and Soviet spheres of influence.

In 1976 Ford, the first president in American history who had not been chosen, even as vice-president, by the electorate, gained the Republican presidential nomination after beating back a stiff challenge from former California governor Ronald Reagan. Ford faced off against the virtually unknown Democratic candidate, former Georgia governor Jimmy Carter. In this race of the dark horses, détente was an issue for considerable criticism. The Democrats took the administration to task both for what they claimed were excessive concessions to the Soviet Union during the SALT negotiations and for sacrificing human-rights considerations in favor of cold-blooded realpolitik. These criticisms were mirrored by the claims of the Committee on the Present Danger, a conservative advocacy group opposed to SALT and détente that was the brainchild of NSC-68 author Nitze; ironically, Nitze and the committee would be a major thorn in Carter's side several years later when the ratification of SALT II was being debated in Congress. The two candidates ran neck and neck until Ford committed a gaffe by declaring during a televised debate that Poland was not dominated by the Soviet Union. Carter leapt on Ford's misstatement, claiming that the president, who had a public image as something of a befuddled, amiable bumbler, had a faulty grasp of foreign policy issues. Ford's gaffe combined with the American public's general disgust over Watergate and establishment Washington politics in general – of which the president was undeniably a part – to give Carter a victory in the 1976 election.

The Carter Years

Carter posited himself, not inaccurately, as a political outsider untainted by Washington cronyism and scandal. Indeed, Carter's outsider status and his promises to conduct foreign policy openly and truthfully contributed significantly to his victory over Ford. As a deeply religious Southern Baptist who professed to have been "born again," he sincerely desired to impart a more human emphasis to American statecraft than had been displayed by the preceding administrations. This stance was in contrast to Nixon and Kissinger's secretive style, which had come to inspire considerable distrust among the American public. He declared that his administration would emphasize human-rights concerns, again in contrast to Nixon and Kissinger's cold-blooded realpolitik. Moreover, he argued that the United States had for too long emphasized the Cold War at the expense of the nation's relations with the Third World; his presidency would redress this imbalance.

Carter's lack of Washington connections and his unfamiliarity with foreign policy issues proved to be a double-edged sword, however.[116] The president, at least during his term of office, never possessed a coherent worldview, and his foreign policy formulation suffered accordingly: his diplomacy toward the Soviets, for example, veered from Kissinger-style détente to a frosty "Cold War II" over a three-year period. Additionally, there was a fundamental contradiction inherent in attempting to

stress human-rights concerns and winding down the Cold War – the Soviet Union was among the world's worst human-rights violators, and any U.S. attempt to take the Soviets to task for their transgressions would exacerbate relations between the two superpowers. This contradiction would eventually be worked out in favor of increased tensions between the United States and the Soviet Union, more as the result of an overall worsening of relations than because of an uncompromisingly powerful American commitment to the policing of human-rights abuses.

Carter was also dogged by plain bad luck during his administration – the Iranian revolution and subsequent Teheran hostage crisis, the Soviet invasion of Afghanistan, to name two of the most important examples – that further complicated and undermined his decision-making process.

The Carter administration's vacillating style of diplomacy was in large part both due to and characterized by the president's choice of top policy advisers. Carter appointed as secretary of state Cyrus R. Vance, a top New York lawyer with extensive diplomatic experience in the Kennedy and Johnson administrations. Vance was a classic, nonideological diplomatist who excelled in quiet bargaining and finding common ground with adversaries. The new secretary of state believed that the United States should regard the reduction of the threat of nuclear holocaust as its number-one priority; he was a strong advocate of arms-control agreements with the Soviet Union. Consonant with Carter's appointment of Vance, a liberal foreign-policy "dove," was his choice of Andrew Young as ambassador to the United Nations. Young was a close associate of Carter's from Georgia who was a strong advocate of closer U.S. attention to the Third World as a sphere in its own right. Young was African-American, which sent a message to Third World nations, and Black Africa in particular, that the Carter administration would be more responsive to their concerns than its predecessors had been. Young would eventually be forced to resign his post because of covert meetings with representatives of the Palestinian Liberation Organization (PLO) – a violation of long-standing U.S. policy.

Zbigniew Brzezinski, an expatriate Pole whose family had been uprooted when the communists took control of Poland in 1946, was appointed the new national security adviser, and his views were different from those of Vance and Young. Brzezinski was an old-style "Cold Warrior," who saw the Soviet Union as the principal enemy of the

United States and advocated a confrontational U.S. policy. Brzezinski was inclined to advocate hardline responses to crises; the national security adviser and the secretary of state found themselves at loggerheads over policy recommendations to the president. If Carter had possessed a stronger background in foreign affairs, the contrast between his two top advisers might have provided him a useful dialectic, much as had been the case with Franklin D. Roosevelt, who customarily stood back as his counselors argued among themselves and then made his decision based on his own instincts and imperatives. But Carter did not possess Roosevelt's confidence, and he oscillated between Vance's accomodationism and Brzezinski's confrontationalism toward the Soviet Union. On one occasion, after the secretary of state and the national security adviser provided the president with drafts of a speech on U.S.-Soviet policy that predictably took opposing viewpoints, Carter simply stapled the two drafts together and delivered the speech, much to the confusion of listeners. Brzezinski ultimately won the struggle for the president's ear, following the invasion of Afghanistan by the Soviet Union and the Iran hostage crisis; Vance's moderate counsel seemed ineffectual in the face of Soviet adventurism and Islamic fanaticism.

The Soviets were wary of the appointment of Brzezinski as national security adviser. Their concern increased early in 1977 when Carter responded to a letter sent to him by Andrei Sakharov, a Soviet nuclear physicist who had incurred the wrath of the communist leadership with his criticism of the Soviet Union's foreign policy. The Brezhnev regime denounced the president's action as unlawful interference in Soviet domestic affairs and part of a campaign of provocation taken under the pretense of human rights. The Soviets were confused at the outset by the Carter administration's human-rights emphasis. They briefly hoped, on the basis of their previous fruitful dealings with Nixon and Kissinger, with whom the Kremlin had been comfortable, that the U.S. position was merely the gathering of bargaining chips for the negotiating table, not a serious policy. They were baffled when they discovered that the Carter administration was in fact serious in its criticism of the Soviet Union. They were further confused by the president's apparent naiveté and inconsistency, as the administration continued to its close ties with right-wing dictatorial clients of the United States such as Anastasio Somoza Debayle in Nicaragua, Shah Mohammad Reza Pahlevi in Iran, and Ferdinand Marcos in the Philippines. Because of the Carter administration's inconsistency, the Soviets could legitimately accuse the United States of hypocrisy for turning a blind eye to repression when it suited American strategic interests.

The SALT II Treaty

Nonetheless, negotiations proceeded on the SALT II treaty.[117] Even in this area, however, where much of the groundwork had been laid during the preceding administration, Carter's policy caused a ripple of tension between the United States and the Soviet Union. The 1974 Vladivostok agreement between Ford and Brezhnev had declared that subsequent negotiations would be based on identical ceilings for American and Soviet strategic missiles. Liberal critics in the United States saw this as a license for both sides to increase substantially their arsenals under the guise of arms limitation; conservative critics argued that the United States was conceding too much to the Soviet Union. Carter accepted aspects of both arguments and jettisoned Vladivostok as the basis for U.S.-Soviet negotiations. When the Soviets, who had been counting on the Ford-Brezhnev agreement, were told early in 1977 that the Carter administration had a new proposal, they felt betrayed. The proposed cuts would most affect land-based missiles, in which the the Soviet Union had concentrated most of its strategic nuclear weaponry, while submarine- and air-launched weapons, the American strength, remained virtually untouched. The Soviets angrily denounced the American proposal; still, the SALT II treaty was worked out. The treaty would not be ratified by the Senate, however, as a result of steadily worsening U.S.-Soviet relations over the next two years, culminating in the 1979 Soviet invasion of Afghanistan.

Strategic weapons proved to be a weak link in the Carter administration's policy formulation. The president had difficulty enunciating and following a coherent program concerning which weapons systems to build and which to cancel. He expressed at the outset of his term his abhorrence of nuclear weapons in general, but his decisions were more pragmatic, if not always consistent. Carter canceled the production of the supersonic B-1 strategic bomber, the proposed successor to the aging B-52 Stratofortress, because of its great cost, questionable mission, and dubious design. Carter supported the development of the subsonic, super-accurate – and inexpensive – cruise missile, which could be fired as effectively from the B-52 as from the B-1. The Reagan administration would subsequently build the B-1 in large numbers; the plane turned out to have serious flaws, and the bombers were grounded. While Carter's decision was both sound and defensible, critics maintained with some justification that by unilaterally canceling the B-1, he had squandered its potential as a bargaining chip in arms negotiations with the Soviet Union.

In his decisions on another strategic weapon, Carter exacerbated tense relations with the Western European allies of the United States. The president unilaterally terminated the development of the neutron bomb, a low-yield tactical nuclear device that kills enemy troops with radiation rather than blast, thus leaving the surrounding terrain relatively intact. Western European leaders and Carter's senior advisers had supported the development program as a gesture of reassurance, in the aftermath of bilateral U.S.-Soviet arms agreements arrived at without the consultation of the European allies, that the United States continued to be committed to the defense of its NATO partners. However, Carter found the neutron bomb morally objectionable and ended the project. The Western Europeans were upset over the president's action, especially West German chancellor Helmut Schmidt, on whose soil much of a hypothetical war between NATO and the Warsaw Pact would be waged. The president did, however, go ahead with plans to build the MX ICBM, a ten-warhead, "silo-busting" (that is, so accurate and powerful that it could be used to launch a first strike against opposing strategic weapons hidden in their silos) missile, despite similar moral qualms. After canceling the neutron bomb, Carter responded to West European fears, raised by the installation by the Soviets of new-generation SS-20 intermediate-range ballistic missiles in Warsaw Pact countries, by promising to place cruise missiles and Pershing II IRBMs in Europe as a counterpoise. The move reassured the Allies; however, the SS-20's and Pershing IIs were regarded as destabilizing to the superpowers' strategic balance. These IRBMs would be eliminated through arms negotiations in the late 1980s (the INF Treaty), once relations between the United States and the Soviet Union had warmed as the result of Mikhail Gorbachev's reforms. But Soviet-American relations would become much worse for more than half a decade before they improved.

The DefCon 3 alert during the 1973 Yom Kippur War had underlined the danger inherent in an unstable Middle East. Carter came into office committed to a settlement of the Arab-Israeli conflict, including the Palestinian question. The Carter administration had its greatest, though still equivo-

cal, success during 1977–1979 in its attempts to mediate the confrontation between Israel and its neighbors. Egyptian president Anwar Sadat surprised the world and caught U.S. Middle East experts off guard with his dramatic trip to Jerusalem in fall 1977. Carter, however, recovered quickly and responded with an offer to mediate negotiations between Egypt and Israel. Carter had originally hoped to attain a comprehensive solution to all aspects of the Arab-Israeli conflict, but with both sides displaying considerable intransigence he saw an Egyptian-Israeli accord as an achievable and important first step. The Soviets were locked out of participation in any Middle East peace talks, because its clients in the region – primarily Syria, Iraq, and the PLO – adamantly opposed it. Carter staked his prestige as president on a successful outcome. The exclusion of the Soviets complicated Carter's efforts to draw Syria, a Soviet client and a necessary participant in any comprehensive Middle Eastern peace plan, into the negotiating process. The peace agreement that was ultimately worked out did not include Syria or any other Arab nation except for Egypt. Despite this shortcoming, the Camp David accords were a considerable achievement, as they ended the state of war between the two most powerful states in the Middle East. The signing of the "Framework for Peace in the Middle East" in October 1978 and the Egypt-Israeli peace treaty the following March vindicated the president's policy; ultimately, however, this success could not save his administration, which would ironically be mortally wounded by a Middle East crisis later in 1979.

Carter also made bold strides with equivocal results in Latin America. His general policy, which was supported by both Vance and Brzezinski, called for an end to traditional U.S. paternalism toward its southern neighbors. In this spirit Carter presided over the negotiation of the Panama Canal Treaty, which pledged the return of the Panama Canal Zone to the Panamanians (the actual transfer was to take place in 1999). It was hoped at the time that the canal return would encourage improved U.S.–Latin American relations. The Carter administration further attempted to pave the way for better relations with its diplomatic overtures to communist Cuba; the ultimate goal was the restoration of normalized relations between the two nations. But the presence of Cuban troops in Angola was a growing irritant to the United States, particularly as U.S.-Soviet tensions deepened. The 1979 discovery by U.S. intelligence of a "new" Soviet combat brigade in Cuba – a unit that had been there all along in accordance with a U.S.-Soviet agreement since the termination of the Cuban Missile Crisis in 1962 – killed whatever hopes had been raised of an end to the U.S.-Cuban standoff and additionally contributed to the demise in the Senate of the SALT II treaty.

Elsewhere in Latin America, the Carter administration continued longstanding American support of Somoza's corrupt and repressive regime in Nicaragua, which called into question the sincerity of the president's commitment to human rights. As Somoza's control over the country weakened in the aftermath of the assassination of a popular political rival, the Carter administration attempted to find a "third force" between the unpopular dictator and the left-wing Sandinista coalition, which was dominated by communists. The United States bowed to the inevitable, however; when the Sandinistas toppled Somoza in 1979 the United States, despite reservations, established diplomatic relations with the new government. The next administration would take a different approach toward Nicaragua.

The beginning of 1979 saw the formalization of Sino-American relations, which was explicitly posited by the Carter administration as a strategic flanking maneuver against the Soviet Union. The Soviets noted with annoyance the granting of most favored nation (MFN) status to the Peoples' Republic of China despite the strictures of the Jackson-Vanik amendment – of which mainland China was as much a violator as the Soviet Union. The Soviets were wary about American and Chinese intentions as the latter two countries concluded economic treaties which authorized the sale to the Chinese of military and civilian "dual use" U.S. products such as trucks and scientific technology. Carter hosted a state visit by Premier Deng Xiaoping during which the Chinese leader was treated to an American rodeo. The United States officially severed all diplomatic ties with the Republic of China (Taiwan) and accepted the PRC view that Taiwan was a part of China. Although the ROC's authoritarian government was itself repressive, it allowed greater freedom of speech and of immigration– two U.S. concerns – than the PRC. The Carter administration had once again demonstrated that its commitment to human rights would not be given priority over reasons of state.

The president's ultimate tilt to realpolitik as opposed to morality rebounded heavily against the United States over its relationship with the Shah of Iran.[118] After being restored to the throne following the 1953 U.S.-directed coup against Mohammad Mossadegh, Shah Reza Pahlevi had in the course of two decades consolidated a particularly oppressive authoritarian control over Iran. While the Kennedy and Johnson administrations had held the Shah at arm's length, Nixon and Kissinger saw Iran as an anticommunist, pro-Western bulwark in the Persian Gulf region. They saw Iran as a "policeman" of the region, and the United States sold arms and other goods to the Iranians. With American support, the Shah had launched a modernization program upon a largely unappreciative Iranian public. The Iranians viewed secularization and Westernization as an affront to their religious sensibilities and their cultural heritage; that the United States, which had destabilized the legitimate Iranian government in 1953, was playing a supporting role in the Shah's program only intensified longstanding anti-American sentiment among Iranians. But because American officials' only contacts in Iran were among the government and a small Westernized elite, they had little idea of the intensity of popular discontent and hatred of the Shah's regime. Carter continued the Nixon-Kissinger policy toward the Shah; he traveled to Iran for a New Year's Eve party at the end of 1977 and, in one of the more unfortunate utterances of post-war American diplomacy, declared that "Iran, because of the great leadership of the Shah, is an island of stability in one of the more troubled areas of the world." The CIA took a similar view, concluding in a report in mid 1978 that Iran was not even in a "pre-revolutionary" phase.

Cold War Policy Under Reagan

Jeane J. Kirkpatrick, an academic from Georgetown University appointed UN ambassador by Reagan, provided the Reagan administration with an ideological framework that went beyond instinctive anticommunism. Kirkpatrick developed a thesis distinguishing between authoritarian and totalitarian governments, claiming that the United States was justified in supporting the former and opposing the latter, because right-wing authoritarian regimes, such as the Marcos dictatorship in the Philippines and the Pinochet junta in Chile, could evolve peacefully in a democratic direction, whereas totalitarian regimes, such as the Soviet Union and its satellites, could not. Events in the late 1980s and early 1990s would prove that such generalizations were troublesome. Right-wing dictators such as Marcos, Pinochet, and members of the Argentinian junta relinquished power peacefully, but so did the Marxist Sandinistas in Nicaragua, the leaders of most of the Eastern bloc nations, and the communist leaders of the Soviet

Union. Conversely, China's leaders and Romania's Nicolae Ceausescu, both communist, attempted to cling to power through bloody repression, but so did right-wing autocrats in El Salvador and Guatemala. Nonetheless, Kirkpatrick's thesis provided a rationale for the Reagan administration's abandonment of human rights as an official concern and also for its support for right-wing, anticommunist regimes and movements throughout the Third World. The president made explicit his commitment to undermining left-wing Third World regimes with the pronouncement of his Reagan Doctrine in 1985. This ideology was at the heart of the administration's most damaging scandal, the Iran-contra Affair of 1986–1987.

The Reagan administration during its first term viewed the Middle East primarily through the prism of the Cold War. In 1982 the United States gave Israel a tacit permission to invade Lebanon, where the PLO, the recipient of Soviet aid, had established a significant military presence. The Israelis became mired in fighting in Lebanon; they were aligned with Maronite Christian militias which, after the assasination of their leader Bashir Gemayel, perpetrated a massacre at two Palestinian refugee camps. Secretary of State Alexander M. Haig, Jr., had been the primary advocate of allowing the Israelis a free hand in Lebanon; the failure of this policy, and his continuing power struggle with White House staffers, led the president to request his resignation. Haig was replaced by a former Nixon cabinet member, George P. Shultz. An embarrassed Reagan administration pressured Israel into withdrawing its forces from most of Lebanon and sent in American troops to patrol the Lebanese capital, Beirut, and nearby areas. In October 1983 Shiite guerrillas drove a truck with high explosives into the U.S. Marine barracks in Beirut, killing 241 soldiers. Reagan ordered the withdrawal of the troops from Lebanon in January 1984 and directed the battleship New Jersey, stationed off the Lebanese coast, to shell Palestinian military positions. The Reagan administration was deeply embarrassed by the truck bombing. The United States would find itself repeatedly using military force against Islamic powers during the 1980s – U.S. fighters engaged in dogfights with Syrian jets over Lebanon in 1984; U.S. bombers attacked Lybia in 1986 in an attempt to punish Libyan dictator Mu'ammar al-Qaddafi, who vociferously denounced the United States and supported Arab terrorist factions operatiing against the West; U.S. naval vessels engaged Iranian gunboats in the Persian Gulf in 1987 while attempting to protect Kuwaiti oil tankers. These military engagements pointed the way to America's first post-Cold War conflict, the Persian Gulf War of 1990–1991.

Reagan quickly rebounded from the attack on the Marine barracks. Two days after the Shiite truck bombing, U.S. troops landed on the shores of the Caribbean island of Grenada, where a revolutionary government had declared a Marxist state and solicited Cuban – and by extension, Soviet – economic aid. The ostensible reason for the invasion was to rescue American medical students who attended a local university, but it was clear from the great size of the attacking force that the United States intended to topple the government. The length of time it would take to plan such an operation also made it unlikely, as some critics later charged, that Reagan had ordered the invasion to deflect criticism from the Beirut truck bombing. The amphibious assault, although faultily executed, was a success; at a cost of almost ninety American, Grenadan, and Cuban lives, the United States overthrew the communist government of the island nation.

The Reagan administration encountered more formidable difficulties in its attempts to beat back what it saw as the communist challenge elsewhere in Latin America. The United States was providing military and economic aid to El Salvador as the government attempted without success to defeat a resilient leftist revolutionary guerrilla faction; many domestic critics, including a growing student-protest movement, railed against Reagan for providing aid to El Salvador despite human-rights violations there that included the murder of at least thirty thousand peasants in the 1970s by the Salvadoran military, the rape and murder of four American nuns in 1980, and the assassination of San Salvador's Archbishop Romero in the same year by right-wing paramilitary extremists with ties to the Salvadoran ARENA political party.

The Reagan administration gave high priority to its program of providing military aid to the contra rebel movement, composed primarily of ex-members of the Somocista Guardia Nacional, in Sandinista-ruled Nicaragua. With American technical support, the contras mined Managua harbor in 1984. Congress, fearing another Vietnam, passed the Boland amendment later the same year, which banned American aid to the contras. The Reagan administration, unwilling to terminate the program, began looking for ways to fund the rebels secretly. They used several different schemes, including covert funding by the CIA and the solicitation of funds from Arab Gulf State rulers. They

finally hit upon what seemed a perfect idea to guarantee secrecy. Iran had been paying the United
States for American military equipment as part of
an unacknowledged arms-for-hostages deal which
the Reagan administration had initiated in an effort
to gain the release of Americans held captive by
Shiite guerrillas in Lebanon. Congress had no
knowledge of the arrangement or of the revenue
generated by the arms sales. Administration officials took the money paid by the Iranians and used
it to purchase arms for the contras. CIA director
William J. Casey and national security staffer Oliver North had also considered using proceeds from
the sales to Iran to create a secret fund for what
they called "off the shelf" covert operations not
monitored by Congress.

The Second Cold War

In 1983 the "second" Cold War appeared to
reach new heights. Reagan made his "Evil Empire"
speech to a group of Christian clerics. The Soviets
walked out of arms-control talks in protest against
the American deployment of cruise missiles in
Europe, which had been planned during the Carter
administration. The Soviet Union shot down a
Korean Airlines 747 passenger jet that had strayed
into Soviet airspace. In the United States, films and
television productions that depicted the waging
and aftermath of thermonuclear war, such as *Testa-
ment*, *The Day After*, and *Threads*, both fed and
reflected a growing anxiety among the American
public that the nation was on the verge of an apocalyptic nuclear encounter with the Soviet Union.

In the midst of this anxiety, President Reagan
proposed the creation of a shield designed to stop
incoming Soviet missiles from hitting their targets.
Reagan had been assured of the feasibility of the
idea by Edward Teller, a physicist popularly
known as the "father of the H-bomb." Critics of
the idea argued that it would undermine the concept of MAD, that had formed the basis of strategic planning and preserved a delicate "balance of
terror" between the two superpowers. Reagan suggested in response that the United States, after per-
fecting this missile shield, would provide its technology to the Soviet Union. The resulting program, referred to as the Strategic Defense Initiative
(SDI) and popularly known as "Star Wars," was
estimated to cost hundreds of billions of dollars to
develop and deploy. Critics in the scientific and
strategic-planning communities declared that the
program was technically unfeasible and practically
unworkable. Since the Soviet Union possessed
thousands of nuclear warheads, even if 90 percent

of all incoming Soviet missiles could be stopped
before striking the United States, which was a
generous estimate of the defensive system's effectiveness, an unacceptably large number of nuclear
missiles would still get through and destroy the
United States. While Reagan himself continued to
present SDI as a potential space shield to protect
the entire United States, others in the administration began to back off from this premise and looked to the program as a means of protecting American ICBMs.

The Soviets protested the entire program in any
form as a violation of the 1972 ABM Treaty.
Moreover, the war in Afghanistan had bogged
down – much as the Vietnam war had mired the
United States – and the Soviet economy worsened.
The Soviets became increasingly anxious that the
United States intended to defeat them economically by drastically increasing military expenditures and forcing the Soviet Union into a new arms
race that it could ill afford. Reagan had already
revived the B-1 bomber program and embarked on
the construction of a six-hundred-ship navy. The
Strategic Defense Initiative, if carried forward and
forcing a Soviet response, would accelerate the process of the Soviet Union's economic decline. Even
moderate U.S. expenditures on SDI might be
enough to push the Soviet Union over the brink.

In the 1984 presidential campaign Reagan easily
defeated challenger Walter Mondale, who had
been vice-president during the Carter administration. Reagan's campaign played up foreign-policy
issues. One of his most successful television advertisements depicted a bear lumbering through the
woods while a voice-over told the viewer that the
bear might be harmless or it might not, but one
should always carry a gun while walking in the
woods "in case there is a bear." At the same time
Reagan began speaking of the possibility of renewed dialogue between the United States and the
Soviet Union.

Voting Americans in large part agreed with
Reagan's depiction of the Soviet Union as potentially dangerous, an image which was buttressed by
the shooting down of a Korean passenger jet and
by news reports of Soviet brutality as it waged an
increasingly bloody battle against Afghan rebels.
Additionally, the Soviet government had stagnated
in the hands of an ossified gerontocracy. Brezhnev
died in 1982 and was replaced by KGB chief Yuri
Andropov, who in turn died in 1984 and was
replaced by Konstantin Chernenko. Chernenko
seemed to many observers to be near death as he
assumed the premiership. Andropov was ill for

most of his tenure as premier, but he saw the need for new blood in the government's ruling circle and positioned his young (by Soviet standards) protégé, Mikhail Gorbachev, to assume a top leadership post. Chernenko had been a feeble compromise choice for premier when Andropov died. But he too died within a year of assuming power, and Gorbachev was chosen, on 11 March 1985, as the leader of the Soviet Union. The greatest revolution in Soviet politics and society since the October 1917 Revolution was about to begin.

Soviet Reform Under Gorbachev

Mikhail Gorbachev was an intellectual child of the Khrushchev years. Gorbachev, like many idealistic and well-educated Russians in the 1950s, had been surprised by the revelations during the Twentieth Party Congress of 1956 of Stalin's tyranny. This group of Russians had been disappointed by Khrushchev's failure to reform and the Soviet Union's subsequent economic and political stagnation under Brezhnev and his successors. The new Soviet leader, in sharp contrast to his parochial and xenophobic predecessors (excepting his mentor Andropov), was highly educated and cosmopolitan in outlook. He held a law degree and his wife had a Ph.D. in psychology. Gorbachev realized that the Stalinist state had crippled the Soviet Union economically and socially and in its dealings with the West; he would undertake to dismantle the apparatus and provide a new "socialism with a human face" in order to save the Communist party. Gorbachev surrounded himself with reform-minded communists such as Eduard Amvrosiyevich Shevardnadze, who became the new Soviet foreign minister on 2 July, and Alexander Yakovlev, who had studied in the United States during the 1950s. He called for glasnost, or openness and perestroika, or restructuring, in the Soviet Union to achieve his goal of a revitalized Soviet state.

As part of his program of change, Gorbachev adopted a conciliatory tone toward the United States and the West. Early in 1985 he met with Conservative British prime minister Margaret Thatcher, an ardent anticommunist, who declared in turn that the West could do business with the Soviet leader. President Reagan, a close friend and ideological ally of Thatcher, took note of her pronouncement on Gorbachev. A summit between the heads of the two superpowers was scheduled to be held in Geneva 19–21 November 1985. Their meeting would be the beginning of the end of the Cold War. The Geneva summit produced no significant accords. Its value was in bringing Reagan

and Gorbachev together so they could take each others' measure. The result was that Reagan, like Thatcher, concluded that the Soviet leader was someone he could work with.

The tensions between the superpowers, however, did not disappear. One problem was that Gorbachev was trying to split the Western alliance, a strategy which aroused American suspicion. Gorbachev, addressing the Soviet Union's West European neighbors, spoke of a "common European home," implying that the United States was an interloper in Continental affairs. The Reagan administration moved ahead with the SDI program, which Gorbachev denounced as destabilizing. The Soviet Union declared a unilateral moratorium on nuclear testing that the United States refused to join. A Soviet nuclear reactor at Chernobyl, in the Ukraine, suffered a meltdown that released radiation into the atmosphere, causing a radioactive cloud to spread over Europe, affecting food supplies as far away as Sweden. The Soviet Union initially tried to cover up the accident, the worst in the history of nuclear power. But finally, the accident spurred greater Soviet openness, manifested in the Soviet Union sending out for Western help.

Tensions in the superpower relationship continued, however. In mid 1986, the United States arrested a Soviet diplomat in the United States and declared that he was a KGB agent engaged in espionage. The Soviets responded by arresting an American journalist, Nicholas Daniloff, charging him with espionage as well. At first the United States refused to swap detainees because, the president said, the Soviet was guilty and Daniloff was not, but ultimately a trade was arranged. Shortly after the resolution of the Daniloff affair, Reagan and Gorbachev met at Reykjavík, Iceland, for a hastily arranged summit. The two leaders came close to signing a treaty eliminating all nuclear weapons and delivery systems, but the deal failed when Reagan refused to bargain away SDI. Reagan, who had stated on a number of occasions that his dream was the elimination of all nuclear weapons on earth, expressed profound diappointment over the summit's failure, but Reykjavik convinced Reagan and Gorbachev that they should pursue more modest goals.

The United States and the Soviet Union agreed in fall 1987 to the elimination of short- and medium-range nuclear missiles in Europe. Although the two superpowers still possessed thousands of nuclear warheads that they continued to point at each other, the Intermediate Nuclear Forces (INF) Treaty, signed in December, was historic: it was the first time since the Washington Naval Conference of 1923 that major powers had agreed to the destruction of existing weapons. Just as important, the traditionally secretive Soviets agreed to intrusive on-site inspections of its nuclear facilities. Reagan was adamant on this issue during negotiations, reciting to Gorbachev the Russian proverb, "trust, but verify." The INF Treaty set a precedent for the negotiation of a START treaty that would be signed in July 1991, after the Cold War had ended.

In the midst of the thaw in U.S.-Soviet relations, the Iran-contra scandal, the result of revelations of the administration's covert attempts to fund the contras in Nicaragua, threatened to cripple the Reagan administration much as Watergate had damaged the Nixon presidency. But Reagan, nick-named the "teflon president" by admirers and crit-ics, was not Nixon, and the U.S. domestic political climate in 1986–1987 was different from that of 1973–1974. Few in Congress or in the public wanted to see Reagan end up disgraced; despite revelations of a secret White House group set up to funnel money to the contras, the president emerged from the scandal largely unharmed politi-cally.

The Soviet Union was changing at a quickening pace. Glasnost and perestroika brought in their wake demands for greater democratization in the Soviet Union. Criticism of the government was now being tolerated by the government. Gorbachev announced in mid 1988 that the Soviet Union would withdraw from Afghanistan. He also announced the unilateral withdrawal of five hun-dred thousand troops and ten thousand tanks from Eastern Europe. Reagan and Gorbachev reached agreement on the withdrawal of Cuban troops from Angola, which ended a civil war that had been raging there for over a decade. The Soviet Union was moving toward disengagement from its costly occupation of the Eastern European satellite states and its adventurism abroad. With the with-drawal of Soviet political and military support, the communist regimes of Central and Eastern fell within a year.

Ronald Reagan was succeeded by his vice-presi-dent, George Bush. Bush was a pragmatic Republi-can with extensive foreign policy experience, hav-ing served as U.S. ambassador to the United Na-tions, America's representative to the People's Re-public of China, and director of the CIA. The new president, distinguishing himself from his predeces-sor, announced that he would move cautiously in his dealings with Gorbachev. Bush's vice-president,

Dan Quayle, declared that he was still suspicious of the Soviet Union's motives. For all the talk of perestroika and glasnost, the Soviet Union still continued to modernize its nuclear arsenal, and so did the United States; the Cubans were still receiv-ing massive Soviet economic aid; the Communist party still held an official monopoly on political power in the Soviet Union. It seemed for a brief moment that the Bush administration might not share Reagan's enthusiasm for rapprochement with the Soviet Union. But the evidence that a new era in international relations was at hand was strong.

End of the Brezhnev Doctrine

Gorbachev announced that he was scrapping the Brezhnev Doctrine in favor of greater autonomy for the nations of the Eastern bloc. The Brezhnev Doctrine had codified what everyone in Eastern Europe and elsewhere always knew – that the So-viet Union reserved unto itself the right to invade its satellite states whenever it felt its security was threatened, which meant whenever orthodox com-munism was in danger of being reformed beyond Soviet tolerance. The Soviets had exercised their right in 1953 against East Germany, in 1956 against Hungary, and in 1968 against Czechoslova-kia; Poland narrowly avoided similar Soviet inter-vention in 1981 when the indigenous communist government suppressed the pro-democracy Solidar-ity union and imposed martial law. But the Soviet empire was expensive to maintain. Gorbachev was hoping for the "Finlandization" of Eastern Europe, that is, the maintenance of quiescent independent states that would pose no threat to the Soviet Union. Finland had long been left to its own de-vices by the Soviet Union on the understanding that the Finns would maintain a friendly neutral-ity; this arrangement had been agreeable to Fin-land and cheap for the Soviet Union, which did not have to pay for a costly occupation. Gorbachev expected the Eastern bloc states to follow the So-viet Union's lead and adopt the moderate reforms he was attempting to implement at home. The sat-ellites had different ideas.

The Revolutionary Year of 1989

The year 1989, like 1848, 1919, and 1945, would go down in history as one of modern Europe's watershed years. Reform movements sprang up in Eastern bloc nations as the Soviet Union withdrew its support from the communist dictatorships. A democracy movement developed in China as well, and more than a million mostly youthful protestors converged on Beijing's Tiananmen Square in May 1989, just as Gorbachev arrived for talks with Chinese leader Deng. The Chinese government responded to the protestors' demands for democratization by ordering the military to disperse the demonstrators, which the military did with brutality. The suppression of the pro democracy forces also included secret trials and summary executions of protest leaders. The Bush administration initially condemned the attack and cut off high level contacts with the Chinese government, but it secretly restored relations within a matter of weeks. When the resumption of contacts was leaked, Bush justified the move by claiming that the United States could better aid democratization in China by maintaining its dialogue with Deng and the other leaders.

The Soviet empire continued to crumble. In Poland, the Solidarity movement was legalized; soon the union's leaders were negotiating with the military rulers for an orderly transfer of power after the communists lost the general elections. Solidarity assumed control of most government functions in August 1989. Hungary's communist government was ousted by a reform-minded faction that pledged to hold free elections the following year. After futile attempts to suppress a popular democratic uprising, Czechoslovakia's hardliners relinquished power; Václav Havel, a writer who had spent several months in prison during 1989 for writing antigovernment works, was chosen president of the Czechoslovak federation by the end of the year. Even Bulgaria's Stalinist dictator, Todor Zhivkov, was toppled by a reform faction. Only in Romania was there significant bloodshed when reformist communists staged a coup and executed dictator Nicolae Ceausescu and his wife.

The most momentous upheaval took place in East Germany. The Stalinist regime there had declared that East Germany had no need for perestroika, but when the new reformist regime in Hungary opened its western borders, a flood of mostly young East Germans traveled to Hungary in order to escape. At the same time, protests against the government sent hundreds of thousands of East Germans into the streets. East German dictator Erich Hoenecker ordered army troops to fire on the protestors, but others within the government overrode Hoenecker's command and deposed him. The new government pledged itself to democratic reforms, but such promises did not stanch the flow of refugees from East Germany. Finally, the new leaders, left with no other

viable option, declared the right of free transit for East German ctizens. A large number of East Germans converged on the Berlin Wall, the symbol of communist denial of freedom to its subjects. On 9 November 1989 East Germany announced the opening of all its borders, including the Berlin Wall. The next day, 10 November, East and West Germans joined in dismantling the wall, with thousands dancing atop the concrete barrier as they wielded sledgehammers and picks and other tools. With the collapse of the wall, the creation of a true "common European home" could become a reality. Slightly more than a year later, on 31 March 1991, the Warsaw Pact, and with it the threat of the long-feared Soviet march west to the Atlantic, ceased to exist. The Cold War was finally over.

After the Cold War

In the new international system that emerged, events that would have been unthinkable only a short time before came to pass with numbing rapidity: on 13 March 1990 the Soviet Congress of the Peoples Deputies abolished the "leading role" of the Soviet Communist party, ending its historic monopoly on power in the Soviet Union; the Sandinistas peacefully transferred power to a democratically elected government in Nicaragua; on 3 October 1990 West and East Germany united as the Federal Republic of Germany; the Soviet Union agreed to a U.S.-led military alliance which, under the auspices of the United Nations, defeated Iraq in the 1991 Persian Gulf war; and the START treaty was signed.

The new danger to Europe's well-being, that of old ethnic rivalries coming to the fore as repressive communism was lifted, was demonstrated by a bloody civil war in ethnically torn Yugoslavia. Bitter ethnic strife in Soviet Georgia, Azerbaijan, and elsewhere in the Soviet Union, indicated the gravity of the danger. For all its instability and unpredictability, the post–Cold War order was a system in which the likelihood of nuclear armageddon, the greatest threat ever to mankind and the planet itself, had decreased. As Gorbachev declared on 31 July 1991, at the opening of the summit at which the START treaty was signed, "[t]he beginning of a new era in history has been a tough test indeed for the leaders of states, requiring enormous efforts, a sense of high responsibilities, strictest realism and vision.... We are beginning to realize that we need each other, that the security, internal stability and dynamic development of each of our two countries benefits both of them."

Notes

1. Roger E. Kanet and Edward A. Kolodziej, eds., *The Cold War as Cooperation: Superpower Cooperation in Regional Conflict Management* (Baltimore: Johns Hopkins University Press, 1991), xiii.

2. Quoted in Thomas G. Patterson, ed., *Major Problems in American Foreign Policy: Documents and Essays,* vol. 2 (Lexington, Mass.: D.C. Heath, 1978), 96–97.

3. See Betty Miller Unterberger, "President Wilson and the Decision to Send Troops to Siberia," *Pacific Historical Review,* 24 (February 1955): 63–74. See also the essays in Betty Miller Unterberger, ed., *American Intervention in the Russian Civil War* (Lexington, Mass.: D.C. Heath, 1969).

4. Linda Killen, "The Search for a Democratic Russia," *Diplomatic History* 2, no. 3 (Summer 1978): 241. There is a debate about whether Wilson meant the Siberian expedition to be instrumental in toppling the Bolshevik regime. Maddox argues this goal was central to Wilson thinking, while Kennan and Unterberger emphasize other reasons for the intervention. See Robert J. Maddox, *The Unknown War with Russia: Wilson's Siberian Intervention* (San Rafael, Calif.: Presidio Press, 1977); Maddox, *From War to Cold War: The Education of Harry S. Truman* (Boulder, Colo.: Westview, 1988), 1–2; George F. Kennan, *The Decision to Intervene* (Princeton: Princeton University Press, 1958), and Betty Miller Unterberger, *America's Siberian Intervention, 1918–1920* (Durham: Duke University Press, 1956).

5. John G. Stoessinger, *Nations in Darkness* (New York: Random House, 1971), 143.

6. See Thomas Maddux, *Years of Estrangement: American Relations with the Soviet Union, 1933–1941* (Tallahassee: University Presses of Florida, 1980), 14–15; John Lewis Gaddis, *Strategies of Containment: A Critical Appraisal of Postwar American National Security Policy* (New York: Oxford University Press, 1982), 6.

7. James A. Nathan and James K. Oliver, *United States Foreign Policy and World Order,* 3rd ed. (Boston: Little, Brown, 1985), 23, 48 (n. 35).

8. See Amos Perlmutter, *Not So Grand Alliance: FDR-Stalin War Relationship* (Columbia: University of Missouri Press, 1993). Cf. George F. Kennan, *Russia and the West under Lenin and Stalin* (Boston: Little, Brown, 1961), 350–51.

9. Herbert Feis, *Churchill, Roosevelt and Stalin* (Princeton: Princeton University Press, 1957), 584; Allen Dulles, *Secret Surrender* (New York: Harper & Row, 1966), 146–51; John Lewis Gaddis, *The United States and the Origins of the Cold War, 1941–1947* (New York: Columbia University Press, 1972), 93. For good discussions of the issue of separate peace, see Vojtech Mastny, *Russia's Road to the Cold War: Diplomacy, Warfare, and the Politics of Communism, 1941–1945* (New York: Columbia University Press, 1979), 73–85; Mastny, "Stalin and the Prospects of a Separate Peace in World War II," *American Historical Review* 77, no. 5 (December 1972): 1365–88; and Lynn Etheridge Davis, *The Cold War Begins: Soviet-American Conflict over Eastern Europe* (Princeton: Princeton University Press, 1974).

10. Nathan and Oliver, 30.

11. Harry S. Truman, *Memoirs,* vol. 1, *Year of Decision* (Garden City: Doubleday, 1955), 82; Robert J. Donovan, *Conflict and Crisis: The Presidency of Harry S. Truman, 1945–1948* (New York: Norton, 1977), 42, (n. 33). Sherwood also defines the Polish issue as a symbol of American foreign policy, in Sherwood, *Roosevelt and Hopkins,* 899.

12. Winston Churchill, *Triumph and Tragedy,* vol. 6 of *Second World War* (Boston: Houghton Mifflin, 1950), 639; Walter Millis, ed., *The Forrestal Diaries* (New York: Viking, 1951), 78; Truman, *Year of Decision,* 412; Daniel Yergin, *Shattered Peace: The Origins of the Cold War and the National Security State* (Boston: Houghton Mifflin, 1977), 101, 115, 120, 433 (n. 19).

13. Gaddis, *The United States and the Origins of the Cold War, 1941–1947,* 264. On the perception among American policy makers of the diplomatic benefits of the bomb, see Yergin, *Shattered Peace,* 120; Feis, *Churchill, Roosevelt and Stalin,* 194.

14. Nathan and Oliver, 53.

15. Walter LaFeber, *America, Russia, and the Cold War, 1945–1971* (New York: Wiley, 1972), 30.

16. See discussions of the speech and the reactions to it in Gaddis, *The United States and the Origins of the Cold War, 1941–1947,* 299–302; Walter LaFeber, *America, Russia, and the Cold War, 1945–1975,* 3rd ed. (New York: Wiley, 1976), 39; Lloyd Gardner, *Architects of Illusion: Men and Ideas in American Foreign Policy* (Chicago: Quadrangle Books, 1970), 315–16; C. Ben Wright, *George F. Kennan, Scholar-Diplomat: 1926–1945* (Ph.D. dissertation, University of Wisconsin, 1972), 392–93; and Marshall Schulman, *Stalin's Foreign Policy Reappraised* (New York: Atheneum, 1963), 13–21.

17. The text of the speech, under the title "The Sinews

of Peace," is reproduced in *Vital Speeches of the Day,* 15 March 1946, p. 332.

18. Gaddis, *Strategies of Containment,* 19. See discussions of Kennan and the origins of containment in David Mayers, *George Kennan and the Dilemmas of U.S. Foreign Policy* (New York: Oxford University Press, 1988), 105–31; Anders Stephanson, *Kennan and the Art of Foreign Policy* (Cambridge: Harvard University Press, 1989); Walter L. Hixson, *George F. Kennan, Cold War Iconoclast* (New York: Columbia University Press, 1989); Wilson Miscamble, *George F. Kennan, the Policy Planning Staff and American Foreign Policy, 1947–1950* (Ph.D. dissertation, University of Notre Dame, 1980); Wright, *George F. Kennan, Scholar-Diplomat: 1926–1946*; John Lewis Gaddis, "Containment: A Reassessment," *Foreign Affairs* (July 1977); Louis Halle, "George F. Kennan and the Common Mind," *Virginia Quarterly Review* (Winter 1969); Daniel P. Harrington, "Kennan, Bohlen, and the Riga Axioms," *Diplomatic History* (Fall 1978); and C. Ben Wright, "Mr. 'X' and Containment," *Slavic Review* 35 (March 1976): 1–36.

19. For the text of the Long Telegram, see Kennan, *Memoirs: 1925–1950,* pp. 547–65; and Thomas Etzold and John Lewis Gaddis, eds., *Containment: Documents on American Policy and Strategy, 1945–1950* (New York: Columbia University Press, 1978), 50–63. Isaacson and Thomas write that the telegram was in fact only 5,540-word long. See Walter Isaacson and Evan Thomas, *The Wise Men: Six Friends and the World They Made* (New York: Simon and Schuster, 1986), 352. On the origins and consequences of the Long Telegram, see Mayers, *George Kennan and the Dilemmas of U.S. Foreign Policy,* 97–102; Stephanson, *Kennan and the Art of Foreign Policy,* 45–53; Hixson, *George F. Kennan, Cold War Iconoclast,* 29–32; Louis Halle, *The Cold War as History* (New York: Harper & Row, 1967), 105; Wright, *George F. Kennan, Scholar-Diplomat: 1926–1946,* 411–21; Yergin, *Shattered Peace,* 168–71; Joseph M. Jones, *The Fifteen Weeks* (New York: Viking, 1955), 133; Deborah Larson, *Origins of Containment: A Psychological Explanation* (Princeton: Princeton University Press, 1985), 256; and Dean G. Acheson, *Present at the Creation: My Years at the State Department* (New York: Norton, 1969), 151.

20. Stephanson, *Kennan and the Art of Foreign Policy,* 45.

21. Mayers, *George Kennan and the Dilemmas of U.S. Foreign Policy,* 100

22. See account of the meeting in Jones, *The fifteen Weeks,* 138–41; and Acheson, *Present at the Creation,* 219.

23. Acheson, *Present at the Creation,* 219.

24. Nathan and Oliver, *United States Foreign Policy and World Order,* 3rd ed., 63. See discussions of the Truman Doctrine John Lewis Gaddis, "Was the Truman Doc-

trine a Real Turning Point?" *Foreign Affairs* 52 (January 1974): 386–402, "Epilogue," in David Mayers, *Cracking the Monolith: U.S. Policy against the Sino-Soviet Alliance, 1949–1955* (Baton Rouge: Louisiana State University Press, 1986). For good discussions of the domestic context and ramifications of the doctrine, see Richard M. Freeland, *The Truman Doctrine and the Origins of McCarthyism: Foreign Policy, Domestic Politics and Internal Security, 1946–1948* (New York: Knopf, 1972); the essays in Robert Griffith and Athan Theoharis, eds., *The Specter: Original Essays on the Cold War and the Origins of McCarthyism* (New York: New Viewpoints, 1974); and Thomas G. Paterson, "Presidential Foreign Policy, Public Opinion, and Congress: The Truman Years," *Diplomatic History* 3 (Winter 1979): 1–18.

25. Harry S Truman, "The Truman Doctrine: Special Message to Congress on Greece and Turkey, 12 March 1947," *Public Papers of the Presidents of the United States,* Harry S Truman, 1947 (Washington, D.C.: Government Printing Office, 1948), 178.

26. Hixson, *George F. Kennan,* 56–58; Wright, *George F. Kennan: Scholar-Diplomat,* 436; Etzold and Gaddis, eds., *Containment: Documents on American Policy and Strategy, 1945–1950,* 126–127.

27. George F. Kennan, "The Sources of Soviet Conduct," *Foreign Affairs* 25 (July 1947): 566–82.

28. For background of the "X" article, see Kennan, *Memoirs: 1925–1940,* 354–57; Hixson, *George F. Kennan,* 40–45; Mayers, *George Kennan and the Dilemmas of U.S. Foreign policy,* 112–14; Halle, *The Cold War as History,* 107. For analysis of the article, see John Lewis Gaddis, "Containment: A Reassessment," *Foreign Affairs* 55 (July 1977): 873–87; Gaddis, *Strategies of Containment,* 25–53; Eduard M. Mark, "The Question of Containment: A Reply to John Lewis Gaddis," *Foreign Affairs* 56 (January 1978): 430–41; Mark, "What Kind of Containment?" in Thomas G. Paterson, ed. *Containment and the Cold War* (Reading, Mass.: Adison-Wesley, 1973), 96–109; David Mayers, "Containment and the Primacy of Diplomacy: George Kennan's Views, 1947–1948," *International Security* 11, no. 1 (Summer 1986): 124–62; Wright, "Mr. 'X' and Containment"; Charles Gati, "What Containment Meant," *Foreign Policy,* no. 7 (Summer 1972): 22–40. An interesting "deconstructionist" analysis is offered by Stephanson, *Kennan and the Art of Foreign Policy,* 73–85, and passim.

29. Gaddis, *Strategies of Containment,* 60.

30. Gregg Herken, *The Winning Weapon: The Atomic Bomb in the Cold War, 1945–1950* (New York: Vintage Books, 1982), 257–69; Harry A. Borowski, *A Hollow Threat: Strategic Air Power and Containment before Korea* (Westport, Conn.: Greenwood, 1982), 125–28; Avi Shlaim, *The United States and the Berlin Blockade, 1948–*

1949: A Study in Crisis Decision-Making (Berkeley: University of California Press, 1983), 234–40; George H. Quester, *Nuclear Diplomacy: The First Twenty-Five Years* (New York: Dunellen, 1970), 48–49; John Lewis Gaddis, "The Origins of Self-Deterrence: The United States and the Non-Use of Nuclear Weapons, 1945–1958," ch. 5 in Gaddis, *The Long Peace: Inquiries into the History of the Cold War* (New York: Oxford University Press, 1987), 110; Daniel F. Harrington, "American Policy in the Berlin Crisis of 1948–1949" (Ph.D. Dissertation, Indiana University, 1979), 110–14.

31. Josef Joffe, *The Limited Partnership: Europe, the United States, and the Burdens of Alliance* (Cambridge: Ballinger, 1987), esp. ch. 5.

32. For an excellent study of these events see the Tang Tsou, *America's Failure in China, 1941–1950* (Chicago: University of Chicago Press, 1963).

33. See David Alan Rosenberg, "U.S. Nuclear Stockpile, 1945 to 1950," *Bulletin of the Atomic Scientists* (May 1982): 25–30; and Rosenberg, "The Origins of Overkill: Nuclear Weapons and American Strategy, 1945–1960," *International Security* 7, no. 4 (Spring 1983): 3–71.

34. Richard G. Hewlet and Francis Duncan, *Atomic Shield, 1947/1952*, vol. 2, *A History of the United States Atomic Energy Commission* (University Park, Pa.: Pennsylvania State University press, 1969), ch. 12; McGeorge Bundy, *Danger and Survival: Choice about the Bomb in the First Fifty Years* (New York: Random House, 1988), 199–214; David Alan Rosenberg, "American Atomic Strategy and the Hydrogen Bomb Decision," *Journal of American History* 66 (June 1979): 62–87; Lawrence Freedman, *The Evolution of Nuclear Strategy* (New York: St. Martin's, 1983), 65–68.

35. Walter Schneir and Miriam Schneir, *Invitation to an Inquest* (New York: Penguin Books, 1973), 59–89. For a thorough discussion of the Rosenberg case, see Ronald Radosh and Joyce Milton, *The Rosenberg File: A Search for the Truth* (New York: Holt, Reinhart and Winston, 1983).

36. Richard H. Rovere, *Seneator Joe McCarthy* (New York: Harcourt, Brace, 1959), 170–77.

37. For very good studies of McCarthy see Rovere, *Seneator Joe McCarthy*; and David Oshinsky, *A Conspiracy So Immense: The World of Joe McCarthy* (New York: Free Press, 1983).

38. The best book on the Hiss case is Allen Weinstein, *Perjury – the Hiss-Chambers Case* (New York: Knopf, 1978).

39. Donovan, *Conflict and Crisis*, 293–98; Truman, *Memoirs*, vol. 2, *Years of Trial and Hope*, 321–22; Latham, *The Communist Controversy in Washington*, 203–16; Kenneth O'Reilly, *Hoover and the Un-Americans: The FBI, HUAC, and the Red Menace* (Philadelphia: Temple University Press, 1983), 75–76, 102; Bennett, *The Party of Fear*, 286–92; and Richard M. Fried, *Men against McCarthy* (New York: Columbia University Press, 1976), 9; David Caute, *The Great Fear: The Anti-Communist Purge under Truman and Eisenhower* (New York: Simon & Schuster, 1978), 24–31; Alan D. Harper, *The Politics of Loyalty: The White House and the Communist Issue, 1946–1952* (Westport, Conn.: Greenwood, 1969), 20–59; Alonzo L. Hamby, *Beyond the New Deal: Harry S. Truman and American Liberalism* (New York: Columbia University Press, 1973), 170–72. For the stories of two of the "China Hands," see Gary May, *China Scapegoat: The Diplomatic Ordeal of John Carter Vincent* (Washington, D.C.: New Republic, 1978); and Robert P. Newman, *Owen Lattimore and the "Loss" of China* (Berkeley: University of California Press, 1992).

40. Freeland, *The Truman Doctrine and the Origins of McCarthyism*, 4–11, 87–100, 120–25.

41. Stoessinger, *Nations in Darkness*, 148.

42. Hammond, "NSC-68: Prologue to Rearmament," in Warner R. Schilling, Paul Y. Hammond, and Glenn H. Snyder, *Strategy, Politics, and Defense Budgets*, (New York: Columbia University Press, 1962), 340–41.

43. Robert W. Tucker, *Nation or Empire? The Debate over American Foreign Policy* (Baltimore: Johns Hopkins University Press, 1968), 28.

44. Acheson, *Present at the Creation*, 357; David S. McLellan, *Dean Acheson: The State Department Years* (New York: Dodd, Mead, 1977), 209–11; Merle Miller, *Plain Speaking: An Oral Biography of Harry Truman* (New York: Berkeley, Medallion, 1974), 286–87.

45. See discussions of the Soviet role in Allen S. Whiting, *China Crosses the Yalu: The Decision to Enter the Korean War* (Stanford: Stanford University Press, 1960), 42–43.

46. Adam Ulam, *The Rivals: America and Russia since World War II* (New York: Viking, 1971), 171.

47. Truman, *Memoirs*, vol. 2, *Years of Trial and Hope*, 333.

48. Truman, *Memoirs*, vol. 2, *Years of Trial and Hope*, 339. See the discussion of Truman's decision making in Glenn D. Paige, *The Korean Decision, June 24–30, 1950* (New York: Free Press, 1968). The best discussion of US policy in Korea is Rosemary Foot, *The Wrong War: American Policy and the Dimensions of the Korean Conflict, 1950–1953* (Ithaca: Cornell University Press, 1985).

49. For a good history of the war, see Clay Blair, *The Forgotten War: American in Korea, 1950–1953* (New York: Times Books, 1987).

50. Quoted in Nathan and Oliver, *United States Foreign Policy and World Order*, 141.

51. See discussion of nuclear weapons and the Korean war in Richard K. Betts, *Nuclear Blackmail and Nuclear Balance* (Washington, D.C.: Brookings Institution, 1987), 31–47; Bundy, *Danger and Survival*, 238–45.

52. Betts, *Nuclear Blackmail and Nuclear Balance*, 32. Fro discussion of the role of nuclear weapons.

53. Bundy, *Danger and Survival*, 231–32; Betts, *Nuclear Blackmail and Nuclear Balance*, 33–37.

54. Bundy, *Danger and Survival*, 231; Betts, *Nuclear Blackmail and Nuclear Balance*, 37; Foot, *The Wrong War*, 114–15, 155, 157; Gaddis, "The Origins of Self-Deterrence: The United States and the Non-Use of Nuclear Weapons, 1945–1958," 115–23; Maxwell D. Taylor, *Swords and Plowshares* (New York: Norton, 1972), 134.

55. Gaddis, "The Origins of Self-Deterrence: The United States and the Non-Use of Nuclear Weapons, 1945–1958," 123–25, 127; Gaddis, *Strategies of Containment*, 168–69. For a critique of revisionist views of Eisenhower as a "closet dove" who rattled the nuclear saber to keep hawks in check, see Betts, *Nuclear Blackmail and Nuclear Balance*, 76–79.

56. Betts, *Nuclear Blackmail and Nuclear Balance*, 38.

57. There are two debates here, not one: the first is whether the Eisenhower Administration was bluffing when it threatened to use nuclear weapons in Korea; the second is about the role the administration's threats, whether real or not, played in convincing the Chinese and North Korean to agree to a cease fire. Bundy tends to discount both the administration's readiness to act on its nuclear threats and the role those threats had in settling the war. See Bundy, *Danger and Survival*, 238–45, esp. 240–41. Gaddis, too, believes Eisenhower did not seriously contemplate the use of nuclear weapons: "What is clear is that the President was more eager to *talk* about the possibility of using nuclear weapons there than he was actually to do so." Gaddis, "The Origins of Self-Deterrence: The United States and the Non-Use of Nuclear Weapons, 1945–1958," p. 128. For discussions doubting the importance of nuclear threats in persuading the Chinese and the North Koreans, see Barry M. Blechman and Robert Powell, "What in the Name of God is Strategic Superiority?" *Political Science Quarterly* 97 (Winter 1982–82): 589–602. Foot, in her *The Wrong War*, believes the administration was serious in its threats, but doubts these threats were decisive in the calculations of the Chinese and the North Koreans. See also Rosemary Foot, *A Substitute for Victory: The Politics of Peace Making at the Korean Armistice Talks* (Ithaca: Cornell University Press, 1991). See also Edward C. Keefer, "President Dwight D. Eisenhower and the end of the Korean War," *Diplomatic History* 10 (Summer 1986).

58. See Dwight D. Eisenhower, *The White House Years*, vol. 1, *Mandate for Change, 1953–1956* (Garden City: Doubleday, 1963), 180–181; Sherman Adams, *Firsthand Report: The Story of the Eisenhower Administration* (New York: Harper and Bros, 1961), 48–49, Gaddis, "The Origins of Self-Deterrence: The United States and the

Non-Use of Nuclear Weapons, 1945–1958," 126; Samuel F. Wells, Jr., "The Origins of Massive Retaliation," *Political Science Quarterly* 96 (Spring 1981); Gaddis, *Strategies or Containment*, 169.

59. On Eisenhower's motives in seeking the Republican nomination, see Gaddis, *Strategies of Containment*, 119–20, 127, 129–30; Herbert S. Parmet, *Eisenhower and the American Crusade* (New York: Macmillan, 1972), 45–47; Peter Lyon, *Eisenhower: Portrait of the Hero*, (Boston: Little, Brown, 1974) 425–33; Eisenhower, *Mandate for Change*, 13–22.

60. Quoted in Steven Metz, "Eisenhower and the Planning of American Grand Strategy," *Journal of Strategic Studies* 14 (March 1991): 53.

61. The following discussion is based on Gaddis, *Strategies of Containment*, 146–63; and Glenn H. Snyder, "The 'New Look' of 1953," in Schilling, Hammond, and Snyder *Strategy, Politics, and Defense Budgets*, 386–456.

62. Metz, "Eisenhower and the Planning of American Grand Strategy," 60–61.

63. Gaddis, *Strategies of Containment*, 129–36.

64. Eisenhower, *Mandate for Change*, 535, 541. See also Metz, "Eisenhower and the Planning of American Grand Strategy," 51–53.

65. Gaddis, *Strategies of Containment*, 145–46; Metz, "Eisenhower and the Planning of American Grand Strategy," 54–55.

66. Gaddis writes that later a fourth option was added — negotiations with the Soviet Union within a two-year limit. the two year limit reflected the belief that within two years the USSR would gain the ability to balance the US nuclear forces. Gaddis, *Strategies of Containment*, 146.

67. Gaddis, *Strategies of Containment*, 146. Others argue that the administration's chosen strategic concept was closer to option 1, with some movement toward option 2. See Metz, "Eisenhower and the Planning of American Grand Strategy," 55; and Snyder, "The 'New Look' of 1953," 409.

68. For elaboration on asymmetrical strategies, see Gaddis, "Containment and the Logic of Strategy," *The National Interest* no. 10 (Winter 1987/88): 27–38; and Gaddis, *Strategies of Containment*, 352–53.

69. Eisenhower, *The White House Years*, vol. 2, *Waging Peace, 1956–1961* (Garden City: Doubleday, 1965), 627.

70. Gaddis, *Strategies of Containment*, 146–48.

71. Gaddis, *Strategies of Containment*, 151.

72. Gaddis, *Strategies of Containment*, 164, 171.

73. Gaddis, *Strategies of Containment*, 161.

74. Gaddis, *Strategies of Containment*, 146–52. For Analysis

of the role of nuclear weapons in the administration's strategy, see Bundy, *Danger and Survival,* ch. 6.

75. John Foster Dulles, "A Policy of Boldness," *Life,* 19 may 1952, p. 154. See discussion in Bundy, *Danger and Survival,* 236–60.

76. Metz, "Eisenhower and the Planning of American Grand Strategy," 56.

77. Gaddis, *Strategies of Containment,* 152–54.

78. Gaddis, *Strategies of Containment, 154–57.*

79. Kirk Porter and Donald Johnson, comps., *National Party Platforms, 1840–1964* (Urbana: University of Illinois Press, 1966).

80. Gaddis, *Strategies of Containment,* 157–59.

81. Gaddis, *Strategies of Containment,* 158–59.

82. See Betts, *Nuclear Blackmail and Nuclear Balance,* 48–54; and John Prados, *the Sky Would Fall: Operation Vulture: The U.S. Bombing Mission in Indochina, 1954* (New York: Dial Press, 1983).

83. Betts, *Nuclear Blackmail and Nuclear Balance,* 50–51, 53; George C. Herring and Richard H. Immerman, "Eisenhower, Dulles, and Dienbienphu: 'The Day We Didn't Go to War' Revisitied," *Journal of American History* 71 (September, 1984): 349.

84. Eisenhower made an early reference to the "domino theory" in April 1954. See "The President's News Conference," 7 April 1954, reprinted in Sam C. Sarkesian with Robert A. Vitas, eds., *U.S. National Security Policy and Strategy: Documents and Policy Proposals* (New York: Greenwood, 1988), 58.

85. Betts, *Nuclear Blackmail and Nuclear Balance,* 54–62. See also Leonard H. D. Gordon, "United States Opposition to Use of Force in the Taiwan Strait, 1954–1962," *Journal of American History* 72 (December 1985): 637–60.

86. See J. H. Kalicki, *The Pattern of Sino-American Crises: Political-Military Interactions in the 1950s* (New York: Cambridge University Press, 1975), 149–51.

87. During the height of the crisis, Eisenhower expressed confidence that there would be no war over the islands. See Eisenhower, *Mandate for Change,* 477–79; and Townsend Hoopes, *The Devil and John Foster Dulles,* (Boston: Little, Brown, 1973), 281.

88. Emmet John Hughes, *The Ordeal of Power,* (New York: Dell, 1964), 96; Bohlen, *Witness to History,* 356, 371; Hoopes, *The Devil and John Foster Dulles,* 173.

89. See Adam Ulam, *Expansion and Coexistence: Soviet Foreign Policy, 1917–1973,* rev. ed. (New York: Praeger, 1974), 534–71, Coral Bell, *Negotiations from Strength* (New York: Knopf, 1963), 100–136. Gaddis writes that the administration's willingness to negotiate with the communist powers was an important element in its strategy. The general relaxation in international relations that followed Stalin's death increased the weight of negotiations in the administration's approach. Gaddis, Strategies of Containment, 159–61.

90. Ulam, *Expansion and Coexistence, rev. ed.,* 560–62.

91. For a critical assessment of the Eisenhower administration's record in the Third World, see Gaddis, *Strategies of Containment,* 175–82.

92. Mario Zucconi, "The United States and Western Europe," in L. Carl Brown, ed., *Centerstage: American Diplomacy since World War II,* (New York: Holmes & Meier, 1990) 133.

93. There are many studies of the Suez affair. Among the best are Evelyn Shuckburgh, *Descent to Suez* (London: Weidenfeld & Nicolson, 1986); Hugh Thomas, *The Suez Affair* (London: Weidenfeld & Nicolson, 1987); and the essays in William Roger Louis and Roger Owen, eds., *Suez 1956: The Crisis and its Consequences* (New York: Oxford University Press, 1991).

94. Gaddis, *Strategies of Containment,* 183.

95. Freedman, *The Evolution of Nuclear Strategy,* 139.

96. Arnold L. Horelick and Myron Rush, *Strategic Power and Soviet Foreign Policy* (Chicago: University of Chicago Press, 1966), 110; Gaddis, *Strategies of Containment,* 183–84.

97. Freedman, *The Evolution of Nuclear Strategy,* 158–63; Bundy, *Danger and Survival,* 334–50. See also Morton H. Halperin, "The Gaither Committee and the Policy Process," *World Politics* 13, no. 3 (April 1961): 360–84.

98. Albert Wohlstetter, "The Delicate Balance of Terror," *Foreign Affairs* 37 (January 1959): 211–34.

99. Henry A. Kissinger, "Limited War: Conventional or Nuclear?" in Donald G. Brennan, ed., *Arms Control, Disarmament and National Security* (New York: Braziller, 1961), 146.

100. See discussion in Bundy, *Danger and Survival,* 347–48.

101. Hoopes, *The Devil and John Foster Dulles,* 436.

102. Betts, *Nuclear Blackmail and Nuclear Balance,* 66–67; Eisenhower, *Waging Peace* 276–78.

103. Betts, *Nuclear Blackmail and Nuclear Balance,* 68–75; Nathan and Oliver, *United States Foreign Policy and World Order, 211.*

104. See David Wise and Thomas R. Ross, *The U-2 Affair* (New York: Random House, 1962);

105. The classic treatment is David Halberstam, *The Best and the Brightest* (New York: Random House, 1969).

106. On the Kennedy administration's foreign policy, see Gaddis, *Strategies of Containment,* chaps. 7, 8; Seyom Brown, *The Faces of Power: Constancy and Change in United States Foreign Policy from Truman to Reagan* (New York:

Columbia University Press, 1983) 149–277; and the essays in Thomas G. Paterson, ed., *Kennedy's Quest for Victory; American Foreign Policy, 1961–1963* (New York: Oxford University Press 1991. For a recent study of the U.S.-Soviet relations during the Kennedy administration, see Michael R. Beschloss, *The Crisis Years: Kennedy and Khrushchev 1960–1963* (New York: HarperCollins, 1991).

107. See Peter S. Wyden, *Bay of Pigs: The Untold Story* (New York: Simon & Schuster, 1979).

108. Graham T. Allison, *Essence of Decision: Explaining the Cuban Missile Crisis* (Boston: Little, Brown, 1971); James G. Blight and David A. Welch, *On the Brink: American and Soviets Reexamine the Cuban Missile Crisis* (New York: Hill & Wang, 1989).

109. For a discussion of the U.S. involvement in Vietnam, see Leslie H. Gelb abd Richard K. Betts, *The Irony of Vietnam: The System Worked* (Washington, D.C.: Brookings, 1979).

110. For recent studies, see Robert Dallek, *Lone Star Rising: Lyndon Johnson and His Times, 1908–1960* (New York: Oxford University Press, 1991); and Robert Caro, *The Years of Lyndon Johnson,* vol. 1: *The Path to Power* (New York: Vintage, 1982); and vol. 2, *Means of Ascent* (New York: Vintage, 1990).

111. See Larry Berman, *Lyndon Johnson's War: The Road to Stalemate in Vietnam* (New York: Norton, 1989).

112. For a history of the war, see Eric Hammel, *Six Days in June* (New York: Scribners, 1992).

113. On Nixon's and Kissinger's foreign policy, see: Coral Bell, *The Diplomacy of Detente — The Kissinger Era* (New York: St. Martin's Press, 1977); Henry Brandon, *The Retreat of American Power* (New York: Norton, 1973); Seyom Brown, *The Crisis of Power: An Interpretation of United States Foreign Policy in the Kissinger Years* (New York: Columbia University Press, 1973); the relevant chapters in Brown, *The Faces of Power:* Alastair Buchan, *The End of the Postwar Era: A New Balance of World Power* (London: Weidenfeld and Nicolson, 1974); Dan Caldwell, *American-Soviet Relations: From 1947 to the Nixon-Kissinger Grand Design* (Westport, Conn.: Greenwood, 1981); James Chace, *A World Elsewhere: The New American Foreign Policy* (New York: Scribners, 1973); Raymond Garthoff, *Detente and Confrontation: American-Soviet Relations from Nixon to Reagan* (Washington, D.C.: Brookings, 1985); Anthony

Hartley, *American Foreign Policy in the Nixon Era,* Adelphi Papers no. 110 (London: International Institute for Strategic Studies, Winter 1974–75); Seymour Hersh, *The Price of Power: Kissinger in the Nixon White House* (New York: Summit, 1983); Alan M. Jones, Jr., ed. *U.S. Foreign Policy in a Changing World: The Nixon Administration, 1969–1973* (New York: David McKay, 1973); Henry Kissinger, *White House Years* (Boston: Little, Brown, 1979); Robert S. Litwak, *Detente and the Nixon Doctrine: American Foreign Policy, 1969–1976* (New York: Cambridge University Press, 1984); Robert Osgood et al., *Retreat from Empire? The First Nixon Administration* (Baltimore: Johns Hopkins University Press, 1973); Jonathan Schell, *Time of Illusion* (New York: Knopf, 1976); Gerard Smith, *Doubletalk: the Story of SALT I* (Garden City: Doubleday, 1980); Tad Szulc, *The Illusion of Peace: Foreign Policy in the Nixon-Kissinger Years : Reshaping America's Foreign Policy* (New York: Paragon, 1989); and the relevant chapters in Gaddis, *Strategies of Containment.*

114. See David Mayers, *Cracking the Monolith: U.S. Policy against the Sino-Soviet Alliance, 1949–1955* (Baton Rouge: Louisiana State University Press, 1986); Dorothy Borg and Waldo Heinrichs, eds., *Uncertain Years: Chinese-American Relations, 1947–1950* (New York: Columbia University Press, 1980); William Barnds, *China and America: The Search for a New Relationship* (New York: New York University Press, 1977); Arnold Xiangzev Jiang, *The United States and China* (Chicago: University of Chicago Press, 1988).

115. See William E. Griffith, *The Ostpolitik of the Federal Republic of Germany* (Cambridge: MIT Press, 1982).

116. See the relevant chapters in Gaddis, *Strategies of Containment;* and Brown, *The Faces of Power.*

117. See Strobe Talbot, *Endgame: The Inside Story of SALT II* (New York: Harper and Row, 1979); and Thomas W. Wolfe, *The SALT Experience* (Cambridge: Ballinger, 1979).

118. On the events leading to the fall of the Shah, see Gary Sick, *All Fall Down: America's Tragic Encounter with Iran* (New York: Penguin, 1986); and James Bill, *The Eagle and the Lion: The Tragedy of American-Iranian Relations* (New Haven: Yale University Press, 1988). For a more general discussion, see Richard W. Cottam, *Iran and the United States: A Cold War Case Study* (Pittsburgh: University of Pittsburgh Press, 1988).

Acheson-Lilienthal Report

On 23 January 1946 Secretary of State James F. Byrnes appointed a committee to fashion U.S. foreign policy to the international control of nuclear energy. Dean Acheson was chairman of the committee, whose members were Vannevar Bush, James B. Conant, Leslie Grove, and John J. McCloy. The committee had a board of consultants chaired by David Lilienthal, chairman of the Tennessee Valley Authority. The committee met to work on the report at Dumbarton Oaks on 7 March 1946. After several revisions and corrections, the committee came to an agreement on the wording of the report on 17 March. It was made public on 28 March.

The report proposed the establishment of an Atomic Development Authority that would have a global monopoly or control over the entire range of nuclear production, from mining to enrichment to manufacturing. The staff of the authority would be international. While closely monitoring nuclear activity to make sure it would not lead to the production of nuclear weapons, the Atomic Development Authority would also encourage research in and development of the peaceful use of the atom.

On the same day the committee agreed on the report, President Harry S Truman asked Bernard Baruch to be the chief U.S. negotiator at the United Nations. Baruch, seventy-five years old at the time, insisted on being allowed to change some elements of the report and its recommendations, especially in the area of enforcement. He proceeded on 14 June 1946 to present to the United Nations Atomic Energy Commission what came to be called the Baruch Plan. The Soviet refusal of the Baruch Plan, however, killed it after six months of negotiations.

Reference

McGeorge Bundy, *Danger and Survival: Choices about the Bomb in the First Fifty Years* (New York: Random House, 1988).

–B. F.

SEE ALSO THESE RELATED ENTRIES
Dean Acheson, 1; Atoms for Peace, 3; Bernard Baruch, 1; Baruch Plan, 3.

Agency for International Development

In his 1961 inaugural address, President John F. Kennedy pledged economic support to underdeveloped countries, declaring that U.S. aid was necessary "not because the Communists may be doing it, not because we seek their votes, but because it is right." In his March address to the nation Kennedy reemphasized his pledge to the Third World by calling on the United States to undertake a "Decade of Development" and asking Congress to create an organization that would direct existing aid efforts and refocus U.S. policies of economic assistance abroad. In response, Congress passed the Foreign Assistance Act in September of 1961, creating the Agency for International Development (AID) when the new legislation was activated in November. In accordance with the act, AID was to function as an arm of the State Department and be headed by an under secretary of state. The agency's funding was to be annually appropriated by Congress.

In keeping with its stated mission, AID was to direct economic assistance to those applicant countries that met criteria composed of five basic principles: an assisted nation must exhibit a willingness to help itself by assuming part of its economic burden; it should have specific economic goals and measures that will stimulate private enterprise; it should make long-range economic commitments; it should intend to make social progress in the areas of education, housing, social services, and land reform – guaranteeing that its citizens will directly benefit from economic assistance; and it should be aided by a cooperative effort shared by the countries of the free world. The AID program of assistance has worked closely with the Export-Import Bank – which finances the purchasing of matériel by assisted countries – and the Peace Corps, which provides U.S. manpower in assisting a country's economic, agricultural, educational, and social progress.

Although its ostensible reason in creating AID was humanitarian, the Kennedy administration tacitly sought to use the agency's mission of economic assistance in order to contain communist influence in the Third World. As such, AID focused its efforts on those regions that served as battlegrounds for competing East-West ideologies: Latin America, Africa, the Near East, South Asia, and the Far East. The value of waging the Cold War along economic fronts was first realized with the implementation of the Marshall Plan, which, by giving economic aid to European countries recovering from World War II, protected Western Europe from the perceived communist intention of taking advantage of the European postwar economic and social devastation. The 1950s saw a series of U.S. assistance programs aimed at the Third World, beginning with the 1950 Act for International Development that sent American technicians to selected countries. The "Food for Peace" program, activated in the mid 1950s, drew on the U.S. agricultural surplus in exporting food to less developed nations. The Development Loan Fund, created in 1957, guaranteed low-interest loans to Third World countries looking to bolster their economies.

With the end of the Cold War, the missions of economic assistance programs aimed at the Third World are being reevaluated. The administration

Part of a food shipment sent to Honduras by the Agency for International Development

of President Bill Clinton is considering cutbacks in the funding of programs such as AID.

Reference

Robert F. Zimmerman, *Dollars, Diplomacy, and Dependency: Dilemmas of U.S. Economic Aid* (Boulder, Colo.: L. Rienner, 1993).

– D. L.

SEE ALSO THESE RELATED ENTRIES
Containment, 3; John F. Kennedy, 1; Marshall Plan, 3.

Alliance for Progress

The Alliance for Progress was unveiled in a speech by President John F. Kennedy made to ambassadors from Latin America and the Caribbean on 13 March 1961. The alliance, formally created in August 1961 by the Inter-American Economic and Social Council in a meeting in Puenta del Este, Uruguay, combined economic, political, and security measures, to create, in Abraham F. Lowenthal's words, "the most ambitious U.S. approach to Latin America ever designed."

Having its origins in a 1958 plan devised by the Brazilian president Juscelino Kubitschek de Oliveira and called Operation Pan-America, the alliance sought to counter the growing appeal of communism in Latin America. The leftist regime of Jacobo Arbenz Guzmán in Guatemala, the anti-American riots Vice-president Richard M. Nixon encountered on his visit to several Latin American countries in 1958, and the growing influence of Fidel Castro Ruz and his revolution in Cuba convinced U.S. policymakers that the best way to fight the spread of communism in Latin America was to promote economic and social reform in tackling the conditions that made communism seem appealing by comparison: poverty and inequality.

The alliance's plan called for investing $20 billion of public and private funds during a ten-year period, an investment the alliance planners hoped would raise per capita income in Latin America by 2.5 percent annually. The alliance also called for Latin American countries to distribute wealth more equally, invest in education and health services, reform the political process, and train local forces to fight communist insurgencies.

U.S. Involvement in Latin America

One result of the creation of the alliance was greater U.S. involvement in the internal affairs of Latin American countries. It soon became clear, however, that the alliance's plan and its implementation were beset by tensions and contradictions. U.S. policymakers, though more intimately involved now in the domestic affairs of Latin American countries, discovered that they could not fine-tune the pace of economic and political reform in foreign countries. Moreover, the sometimes heavy-handed U.S. involvement in the domestic affairs of Latin American countries gave rise to nationalist resentment. In addition, the goal of economic reform and more-equal distribution of

wealth at times came into conflict with the interests of American businesses. The training of local militaries to fight communist insurgencies also made Latin American governments more adept at political repression of legitimate opposition groups, thus weakening the process of democratization.

Latin American countries began to demand a greater role in running the alliance within two years after its creation. The United States, however, preferring to deal with the Latin American countries on a bilateral basis, refused, and, under Lyndon B. Johnson, the United States began to provide less money to the alliance. The foreign-policy concerns of the Johnson administration were also being slowly absorbed by the Vietnam War. Another reason for the U.S. loss of interest was that, following the 1962 Cuban Missile Crisis, Castro's appeal in Latin America was beginning to wane. The administration's attention to Latin America was now directed at solving immediate crises, such as the 1965 uprising in the Dominican Republic, and long-term development and reform goals were deemphasized. Johnson combined the posts of assistant secretary of state for inter-American affairs and U.S. coordinator for the Alliance of Progress and appointed Thomas C. Mann to the new post. Mann immediately pronounced the Mann Doctrine, which stipulated that the United States would be neutral on questions of political and social reforms of Latin American countries.

The alliance fell short of its original goals. However, as Lowenthal writes, "The Alliance contributed significantly to Latin America's development. Despite the Alliance's flaws and disappointments, many Latin Americans still regard it as the most positive U.S. policy for the Hemisphere to date."

References

Jerome Levinson and Juan de Onis, *The Alliance that Lost Its Way* (Chicago: Quadrangle, 1970);

Abraham F. Lowenthal, *Partners in Conflict: The United States and Latin America* (Baltimore: Johns Hopkins University Press, 1987).

                                                                                                                                        – B. F.

SEE ALSO THESE RELATED ENTRIES
Jacobo Arbenz Guzmán 2; Fidel Castro Ruz, 2; John F. Kennedy, 1.

American Federation of Labor and Congress of Industrial Organizations

The American Federation of Labor and Congress of Industrial Organizations (AFL-CIO) is the largest and most powerful labor organization in the United States. It was formed in 1955 from a merger of two existing bodies: the AFL, which since its inception in 1886 consisted of workers in skilled trades and crafts; and the CIO, formed in 1935, which represented unskilled workers in mass-production industries such as steel, automobiles, textiles, and rubber.

For twenty years prior to the merger, the two groups had wasted much effort in jurisdictional disputes. The merger in 1955 resulted from the realization by both organizations that they could strengthen their political and economic clout by acting in concert. George Meany of the AFL became the first president. The new organization retained structural aspects of both the AFL and the CIO. There were separate departments for trades – such as for railway workers and maritime employees – but also an industrial department, headed by Walter Reuther of the CIO, that concerned itself with national unions of noncraft workers.

Involvement in U.S. Foreign Policy

Meany, a large, gregarious man, had formerly been a plumber. He proved an influential and controversial leader of the AFL-CIO and knew many world political and labor leaders. An unabashed hawk on foreign policy issues, he denounced communism in the strongest terms and allied himself solidly with firm policies toward the Soviet Union. During the U.S. defense cuts following the Korean War, he warned of "the deadly drift into defeatism that has swung the free world far off course." Throughout the Vietnam War, Meany never wavered in his support of U.S. involvement there and the policies of President Lyndon B. Johnson.

After World War II Meany supported rebuilding free labor movements in West Germany, France, and Italy as a buffer against communism. The AFL-CIO pursued an aggressive foreign aid program to achieve these ends. During the administration of Dwight D. Eisenhower it funded training courses for foreign labor leaders and escorted them on tours of the United States to show off working conditions and standards of living.

Meany also collaborated with the Central Intelligence Agency (CIA) against leftist regimes around the world. In 1954, for example, shortly before the AFL merged with the CIO, Meany helped the CIA topple the freely elected Guatemalan government of Jacobo Arbenz Guzmán. The Eisenhower administration considered Arbenz to be a communist threat and set out to overthrow him. The CIA financed a liberation army, headed by Carlos Castillo Armas, that ousted Arbenz later that year. To aid CIA efforts, the AFL funded the National Union of Free Workers of Guatemala, which endorsed Arbenz's ouster. Meany also helped the CIA by writing a public letter to the Guatemalan president denouncing the communist influence in his country.

Relations with Foreign Labor Movements

Meany's ardent anticommunism put the AFL-CIO at odds with international Marxist-Leninist labor movements, favored by the Soviets and their allies, which urged violent overthrow of the capitalist system. Historically the American labor movement had never been as radical or as revolutionary as its European counterparts. In the United States the emphasis of organized labor had been on im proving the workers' lot through direct economic pressure, such as strikes and boycotts. The idea was to work within the capitalist system to achieve "bread and butter goals," such as improved wages and working conditions. Collective bargaining, whereby unions and employers negotiate terms of employment, became the main function of the trade unions.

Unlike the British labor movement, the AFL-CIO had no political party, nor did it advocate socialism. After Meany died in 1979 and was succeeded by Lane Kirkland, however, the AFL-CIO allied itself more closely with the Democratic party. During the 1960s the organization adopted a liberal stance on civil rights and became integrated racially; it also advocated equal pay for women and was active in promoting trade unionism in less developed countries.

AFL-CIO

George Meany welcoming Aleksandr Solzhenitsyn to a 1975 meeting of the AFL-CIO

Union membership has been declining in the United States over the past few decades, as the service economy has taken precedence over the manufacturing sector. At its peak the AFL-CIO numbered 18 million members in 1955, or 24 percent of the labor force; by the late 1980s it had slipped to 17 million members, or 18 percent of the labor force.

References

Derek C. Bok and John T. Dunlop, *Labor and the American Community* (New York: Simon & Schuster, 1970);

George Morris, *CIA and American Labor: The Subversion of the AFL-CIO's Foreign Policy* (New York: International Publishers, 1967);

Joseph G. Rayback, *A History of American Labor,* revised and expanded edition (New York: Macmillan, 1966);

Archie Robinson, *George Meany and His Times* (New York: Simon & Schuster, 1981).

– M. G.

SEE ALSO THESE RELATED ENTRIES
Central Intelligence Agency, 3; Dwight D. Eisenhower, 1; George Meany, 1; Leon Trotsky, 2.

Americans For Democratic Action

The Americans for Democratic Action (ADA) was a coalition of liberals that, beginning in 1947, worked to oppose the inclusion of communists in progressive politics. Its members, in practicing a classic Cold War liberalism, supported a blend of free-market economics and social welfare programs at home and an interventionist, anti-Soviet foreign policy abroad. The ADA was a staunch supporter of President Harry S Truman's policy of containment. Its support of Adlai Stevenson was critical to his capturing the 1952 Democratic presidential nomination.

Despite its opposition to communism, the ADA, in its firm commitment to civil liberties, was a persistent and powerful opponent of attempts in the early 1950s to curtail the civil rights of communists when anticommunist hysteria was at its height. The ADA opposed many internal security measures, most of which were of dubious constitution-ality and sought to repeal those that did pass. The ADA also fought loyalty oaths, the censorship of textbooks, and the continued existence of the House Un-American Activities Committee.

The ADA was founded in 1947, and its membership through the mid 1960s included many of the most prominent figures in American liberalism. Arthur M. Schlesinger, Jr., Hubert H. Humphrey, and Reinhold Niebuhr played major roles. The ADA was a casualty of the Vietnam War. The failed American intervention discredited an activist foreign policy against communist regimes.

Reference

Steven M. Gillon, *Politics and Vision: the ADA and American Liberalism, 1947–1985* (New York: Oxford University Press, 1987).

– C. S. B.

SEE ALSO THESE RELATED ENTRIES
Containment, 3; Hubert H. Humphrey, 1; Reinhold Niebuhr, 1; Arthur M. Schlesinger, Jr., 1.

Arab-Israeli War, 1973

The 1973 Arab-Israeli war, known to the Israelis as the Yom Kippur War and to the Arabs as the Ramadan War, was the fourth to break out between Arabs and Israelis since the establishment of Israel in 1948. After the 1967 Six-Day War, intermittent fighting had continued between the Arab states and Israel. Finally, frustrated with Israel's refusal to negotiate the return of the occupied territories, the Arab states, led by Egypt, launched a surprise attack on Israel on 6 October 1973, the Jewish holy day of Yom Kippur, believing that the alertness of the Israeli forces would be reduced. The Egyptian army of President Anwar Sadat attacked from across the Suez Canal and broke into the Sinai, while Syrian forces moved into Israel from the Golan Heights in the north. Joined by Jordanian, Iraqi, and Libyan military units, the Egyptian and Syrian armies made substantial gains and inflicted heavier losses on Israel than in any previous Arab-Israeli war. The Israeli forces had driven back the Syrian forces and surrounded the Egyptian forces by crossing the Suez and installing troops on the west bank of the canal.

The significance of the 1973 war goes far beyond the actual fighting that took place. The war profoundly shook Israel, demonstrating that the military advantage it once held over its Arab foes had diminished. The war also resulted in a worldwide disruption of oil supplies when, during the final days of the fighting, the Arab oil states declared an oil embargo on the United States and the Netherlands, and reduced supplies to Western Europe. Finally, on an international level, Soviet support of the Arab states and U.S. support of Israel

Wide World/Bettmann Archives

Delegations from Israel (left) and Egypt (right) signing the cease-fire agreement after their October 1973 war

almost led to a nuclear confrontation between the two superpowers. The confrontation was averted when a worldwide U.S. strategic alert persuaded the Soviets to cancel plans to dispatch Soviet units to the Middle East.

The buildup to the war had been progressing since the end of the previous war in 1967. In 1969–1971 there was the costly war of attrition between Egypt and Israel, and in 1972 and 1973, as Arab-Israeli tensions mounted, a vicious cycle of Arab attacks on Israeli targets followed by Israeli raids into Lebanon and Syria developed. Sadat was steadily moving Egypt toward another war, in order to recover the territories lost in 1967. He received the support of his Arab neighbors and acquired arms from the Soviet Union. On 6 October the Egyptian and Syrian attacks were launched, and Egypt managed to break down the supposedly invulnerable Israeli Bar-Lev defense line along the Suez Canal and enter the Sinai. Almost simultaneously on the northern front, the Syrians broke through the Israeli lines on the Golan Heights. They inflicted heavy losses on the Israelis, who had been taken by surprise. By the end of that first day, the Egyptians had positioned five hundred tanks and missiles across the Canal and had destroyed one hundred Israeli tanks.

The tables soon turned, however. Israel began a rapid mobilization of its reserve forces, and by the third day of the war it was able to curtail the Syr-

ian advance into the Golan Heights. Israeli jets struck into Syria, bombing Damascus and Homs, and heavy civilian casualties were reported. In its highly successful counterattack, Israel drove the Syrians to within twenty miles of Damascus, far beyond the 1967 cease-fire lines, and Israeli artillery shelled the suburbs of Damascus.

U.S. Soviet Involvement

On the diplomatic front, there was a flurry of activity. But the early attempts by the UN Security Council to achieve a cease-fire amounted to nothing, since Israel – backed by the United States – refused to consider Egyptian demands – supported by the Soviet Union – that a cease-fire agreement include Israeli withdrawal to the pre-1967 borders. Meanwhile, the fighting continued, and the superpowers became more directly involved. The Soviets began an arms airlift to Syria and Egypt, asserting that the United States was supplying Israel with large quantities of weapons. The United States, in turn, announced that it had launched a "massive airlift" of arms to Israel in order to counter the military imbalance caused by the Soviet shipments. In addition, fleets from both superpowers were massing in the Mediterranean and eastern Atlantic.

On 22 October the UN Security Council was finally able to adopt a cease-fire resolution acceptable to both Israel and Egypt. Syria accepted UN

Resolution 338 the following day, but the cease-fire broke down when fighting continued around Suez. On 24 October the United Nations resolved to send a peacekeeping force to "supervise the observance of the 1973 ceasefire." Fighting continued until the UN force arrived in the war zone, and a cease-fire agreement was signed on November 11.

The shuttle diplomacy of U.S. secretary of state Henry Kissinger brought about a disengagement agreement between Israel and Egypt which was signed on 17 January 1974. Israel agreed to withdraw in the Sinai to a line twenty miles from the Suez Canal, while Egypt reduced its forces on the canal's east bank. In May 1974 Kissinger's diplomacy led Israel and Syria to withdraw their troops to lines on each side of the 1967 cease-fire line, and a UN buffer zone was established between the two nations.

An estimated eighty-five hundred Arabs and twenty-eight hundred Israelis were killed in the 1973 war; approximately twenty thousand Arabs and nine thousand Israelis were wounded. Although these numbers clearly tipped the balance of military success in Israel's favor, Israel's losses re-

mained the largest it had ever suffered in its wars with its Arab neighbors. The confrontation between the superpowers ended peacefully, though not before both nations had put their military forces on alert, coming precariously close to a nuclear clash. The war also demonstrated the overwhelming dependence of the industrialized nations on Arab oil when, for the first time, oil was used as a political weapon.

References

Trevor N. Dupuy, *Elusive Victory: The Arab-Israeli Wars, 1947–1974* (New York: Harper & Row, 1978);

Saad El-Shazly, *The Arab Military Option* (San Francisco: American Mideast Research, 1986);

Muhammad Haykal, *The Road to Ramadan* (London: Collins, 1975);

Nadav Safran, *Israel: The Embattled Ally* (Cambridge: Harvard University Press, 1981);

Lester A. Sobel, ed., *Israel and the Arabs: The October 1973 War* (New York: Facts on File, 1974).

– V. A.

SEE ALSO THESE RELATED ENTRIES
Leonid Brezhnev, 2; Henry Kissinger, 1; Golda Meir, 2; Organization of Petroleum Exporting Countries, 3.

Arms Control and Disarmament Agency

The Arms Control and Disarmament Agency (ACDA) was created on 26 September 1961 when President John F. Kennedy signed the Arms Control and Disarmament (ACD) Act. Despite his interest in general and complete disarmament, Kennedy did not lobby on behalf of the bill, because he did not wish to risk a major political defeat early in his administration. John J. McCloy, Kennedy's senior disarmament adviser, was the administration's moving force behind the new agency.

The ACD Act made the agency's director "the principal adviser to the Secretary of State and the President on arms control matters." As Duncan Clarke notes, ACDA thus became "a quasi-independent agency whose Director, in his capacity as

arms control adviser, could go directly to the President. But policy coordination was to be ensured, and suspected disarmers tethered, by linking ACDA closely to State."

Agency's Functions

In the legislation creating the agency, Congress assigned ACDA four "primary functions," the most important of which is the "preparation for and management of United States participation in international negotiations in the arms control and disarmament field." Although ACDA held a congressional mandate to play an instrumental role in international arms-control negotiations, there have been instances where the agency was ignored in arms talks – most notably by President Richard M.

3

Nixon and Henry Kissinger during the Strategic Arms Limitations Talks (SALT) negotiations.

ACDA is also required to oversee and implement American "participation in such control systems as may become part of United States arms control and disarmament activities." As a result of this statute, the chief U.S. representative to the Standing Consultative Committee, the verification body established by the two SALT agreements, was an ACDA official. Clarke notes, however, that "in reality, the CIA, because of its unique capabilities, has dominated the monitoring of arms control agreements."

The agency's two other functions are to conduct, support, and coordinate research in order to formulate arms-control and disarmament policies and to disseminate and coordinate "public information concerning arms control and disarmament." In compliance with the latter mandate, the agency issues numerous reports annually, including *Documents on Disarmament,* which publishes the basic documents relating to arms control and disarmament, and *World Military Expenditures and Arms Transfers.*

One of the more important organizations within ACDA is the General Advisory Committee (GAC). The GAC is required to meet twice annually so that it can "advise the Director on arms control and disarmament activities." The committee is best remembered for its 1968 recommendation that the United States suspend testing of the multiple independently targetable reentry vehicle (MIRV).

References

"Arms Control and Disarmament Act" (P.L. 87-297) in *United States Code: Congressional and Administrative News, 87th Congress, First Session, 1961* (Saint Paul, Minn.: Western Publishing, 1962);

Donald G. Brennan, ed., *Arms Control, Disarmament, and National Security* (New York: George Braziller, 1961);

Duncan Clarke, *Politics of Arms Control: The Role and Effectiveness of the U.S. Arms Control and Disarmament Agency* (New York: Free Press, 1979);

Seymour Melman, *Inspection for Disarmament* (New York: Columbia University Press, 1958);

Phillip Noel-Baker, *The Arms Race: A Programme for World Disarmament* (London: J. Calder, 1958);

Thomas Schelling and Morton Halperin, eds., *Strategy and Arms Control* (New York: Twentieth Century Fund, 1961).

—J. C. R.

SEE ALSO THESE RELATED ENTRIES
Henry Kissinger, 1; MRVs and MIRVs, 3; Richard M. Nixon, 1; Strategic Arms Limitation Talks, 3.

Atomic Energy Commission

A 1947 meeting of the Atomic Energy Commission: (clockwise from left) General Manager Carroll Wilson, Commissioners Sumner T. Pike and Robert F. Bacher, Chairman David E. Lilienthal, Commissioners Lewis L. Strauss and William W. Waymack

The Atomic Energy Commission (AEC) was established by the Atomic Energy Act of 1946. The act gave the AEC control over all aspects of nuclear energy, including the research, development, testing, and construction of nuclear warheads. The AEC consisted of five full-time civilian members appointed by the president. The act also set up the nine-member General Advisory Council (GAC) to advise members of the committee on scientific and technical questions.

On 30 August 1954 Congress passed a new Atomic Energy Act, which allowed the AEC to license private companies to build nuclear power reactors and regulate the nuclear industry. The fact that the AEC had to pursue two roles simultaneously – both promoting and regulating nuclear energy development – made lawmakers uneasy, and on 11 October 1974 Congress passed the Energy Reorganization Act, which took effect on 19 January 1975. The act abolished the AEC, transferring its regulatory functions to the new Nuclear Regulatory Commission (NRC). The weapon-related activities and nuclear research and development functions of the AEC were transferred to the new Energy Research and Development Administration (ERDA). On 4 August 1977 President Jimmy Carter created the Department of Energy (DOE) by signing the Department of Energy Organization Act. The weapon-related responsibilities of ERDA were transferred to the new department. The DOE continues today to be in charge of nuclear weapons activities.

References

McGeorge Bundy, *Danger and Survival: Choices about the Bomb in the First Fifty Years* (New York: Random House, 1988);

Peter Douglas Feaver, *Guarding the Guardians: Civilian Control of Nuclear Weapons in the United States* (Ithaca, N.Y.: Cornell University Press, 1992).

– B.F.

SEE ALSO THESE RELATED ENTRIES
Jimmy Carter, 1; Nuclear Proliferation, 3.

Atoms for Peace

In a speech to the General Assembly of the United Nations on 8 October 1953, President Dwight D. Eisenhower called on the nations of the world to turn away from the current focus in nuclear research on building atomic weapons and, instead, concentrate on the peaceful use of nuclear energy. He proposed that countries then engaged in nuclear research and development contribute uranium and fissionable material from their arsenals to an international agency that would encourage peaceful use of the atom, worldwide.

The speech prompted an examination of possible international cooperation in nuclear matters. It also led to the establishment of the International Atomic Energy Agency (IAEA), which globally monitored atomic activities. But it was not vigorously pursued by the Eisenhower administration, and the Soviet response was not helpful. The proposal did little, therefore, to constrain or slow down the arms race between the superpowers.

References

McGeorge Bundy, *Danger and Survival: Choices about the Bomb in the First Fifty Years* (New York: Random House, 1988);

Richard G. Hewlett and Jack M. Holl, *Atoms for Peace and War, 1953–1961: Eisenhower and the Atomic Energy Commission* (Berkeley: University of California Press, 1989).

– B.F.

SEE ALSO THESE RELATED ENTRIES
Atomic Energy Commission, 3; Dwight D. Eisenhower, 1.

Baghdad Pact

The Baghdad Pact was a 1955 Western-sponsored military alliance aimed at aligning Middle Eastern countries with Western interests. It was devised by the British and the Americans with different intentions in mind. For the United States, the Baghdad Pact represents one of the earliest instances of U.S. Cold War policy in its attempt to curb Soviet influence in the Middle East. For the British, it represents one of the disintegrating empire's last attempts to hold on to its position in the region. The pact failed to get off the ground because most Arab states saw it as a thinly veiled effort by the West to perpetuate its political and military domination of the area. Egyptian president

Gamal Abdul Nasser's efforts to rally the Arab masses against the pact succeeded, and the Baghdad Pact was abandoned.

The idea for the Baghdad Pact was developed after Egyptian opposition to the original 1953 Western plan to form a Middle East Defense Organization (MEDO) caused it to be dropped. This new plan was geared toward the "Northern Tier" countries – the countries between Turkey and Pakistan – which, because of their proximity to the Soviet Union, had more reason to enter into multilateral military alliances with the West. In 1954 a military assistance pact was concluded between Turkey and Pakistan. U.S. secretary of state John Foster Dulles decided that the Arab states were not ready to enter into an anticommunist pact because of their growing nationalism and because they were much more concerned with Israel than with the Soviet Union. Great Britain, on the other hand, wanted the Arab states to join, and it managed to interest its main ally in the region, Iraq, in a Western pact.

Opposition to Pact

In February 1955, notwithstanding fierce opposition from Egypt, Iraqi prime minister Nuri Said signed an agreement with Turkey which became the core of the Baghdad Pact. Great Britain, Pakistan, and Iran all joined the alliance later that year. The United States did not formally join, but it was a de facto member. Iraq wanted other Arab states to join the pact, but Egypt and Saudi Arabia prevented that from happening.

Both Egypt and Saudi Arabia feared an increase in Iraq's power in the region, and they endeavored to isolate Iraq from the other members of the Arab League by promoting a tripartite security pact (linking Cairo with Riyadh and Damascus) to counter the Northern Tier alliances. Cairo also launched a "Free Iraq" radio station in which the Baghdad Pact and Nuri Said were attacked virulently. These broadcasts found sympathetic ears throughout the Arab world.

In Jordan, where the monarchy was Hashemite, as in Iraq, and British-influenced, it was expected that the country would sign the pact. But the Egyptian broadcasts rallied the Jordanian populace against the alliance, and violent riots broke out in Jordan protesting against "foreign pacts." In December, King Hussein abandoned the idea of joining the Baghdad Pact. In Syria, despite Prime Minister Faris al-Khouri's attempt to portray the Baghdad Pact as an alliance directed against Israel, popular opposition prevailed and Syria gave up the idea. In Lebanon even the Western military and economic assistance that would follow if the country joined the pact was not tempting enough to risk incurring the wrath of the Egyptian-led Arab League.

The Baghdad Pact ultimately failed. It was meant to contain Soviet expansionism, but its focus on the Northern Tier was its downfall. Rather than attempt to dismantle the pact, the Soviets simply went straight to the Arab heartland and provided arms, aid, and technical assistance to Egypt, Syria, Yemen, and, after the 1958 revolution, Iraq. As a result, by the end of the 1950s, rather than being under Western influence to the exclusion of the Soviet Union, the Middle East had become deeply involved in the conflict between East and West.

References

George Lenczowski, *The Middle East in World Affairs* (Ithaca, N.Y.: Cornell University Press, 1980);

David E. Long and Bernard Reich, *The Government and Politics of the Middle East and North Africa*, revised edition (Boulder, Colo.: Westview, 1986);

Peter Mansfield, *The Arabs* (London: Lane, 1977);

Edith Penrose and E. F., *Iraq: International Relations and National Development* (London: Benn; Boulder, Colo.: Westview, 1978).

– V.A.

SEE ALSO THESE RELATED ENTRIES
Containment, 3; John Foster Dulles, 1; Gamal Abdul Nasser, 2; Suez Crisis, 3.

Baruch Plan

In 1946 Secretary of State James F. Byrnes appointed Bernard Baruch to be U.S. representative to the United Nations Atomic Energy Committee. The committee was examining ideas for international control over nuclear energy. The American position, which Baruch was supposed to represent, was embodied in the Acheson-Lilienthal report. Baruch insisted that the report was not strong enough on the issue of enforcement of any agreement reached by the United Nations on controlling atomic energy. As part of strengthening the enforcement mechanism, Baruch suggested that the United Nations be authorized to impose "swift and sure penalties" on violators and that the permanent members of the Security Council not be allowed to exercise their veto power to prevent such penalties from being imposed on them. Dean Acheson understood that the Soviet Union would never agree to relinquish its veto power; moreover, imposing penalties on a great power engaging in nuclear development meant going to war against it, and he doubted that there was support in the United States for this. Acheson and Lilienthal saw their plan less as a means to prevent the spread of nuclear weapons and more as a mechanism that would provide early warning of a large-scale violation, allowing different countries to choose a response to the violation.

Harry S Truman sided with Baruch on the issue of the veto. Baruch presented his plan to the committee on 14 June 1946. The discussions took six months, and, as expected, the Soviets rejected the plan. By December 1946 the Baruch Plan was dead.

References

McGeorge Bundy, *Danger and Survival: Choices about the Bomb in the First Fifty Years* (New York: Random House, 1988);

Gregg Herken, *The Winning Weapon: The Atomic Bomb in the Cold War, 1945–1950* (New York: Vintage, 1982).

– B. F.

SEE ALSO THESE RELATED ENTRIES
Dean Acheson, 1; Acheson-Lilienthal Plan, 3; Harry S Truman, 1; United Nations, 3.

Bay of Pigs Invasion

On 17 April 1961, shortly after President John F. Kennedy took office, close to fifteen hundred Central Intelligence Agency (CIA)–trained Cuban exiles landed in the Bay of Pigs, constituting the initial phase of what CIA planners hoped would be a campaign resulting in Cuban leader Fidel Castro's ouster. The invasion, planned during the last years of Dwight D. Eisenhower's administration, failed abysmally: it was not greeted by a popular uprising against the Castro regime, but rather by the Cuban military whose intelligence had learned of the invasion in advance. With the invaders pinned down on the beach, Kennedy decided to cut U.S. losses and refused to authorize the use of U.S. air cover on their behalf. Several hundred of the invaders were killed; the rest were taken prisoner. In December 1962, after protracted negotiations, the Cubans released the 1,113 prisoners in return for $53 million worth of food and medicine.

Reference

Peter Wyden, *Bay of Pigs: The Untold Story* (New York: Simon & Schuster, 1979).

– B. F.

SEE ALSO THESE RELATED ENTRIES
Fidel Castro Ruz, 2; Central Intelligence Agency, 3; John F. Kennedy, 1.

Berlin Crisis, 1948

In the late 1940s the United States and Great Britain, the major Western powers occupying the western part of Germany, began to take measures to consolidate their occupation zone into one German state. The Soviet Union, which had twice been invaded by a strong Germany, viewed these moves with apprehension and sought to use the fact that Berlin – itself divided into occupation sectors – was located deep within the Soviet occupation zone to try and slow the process. In April 1948 it halted Western military supplies to West Berlin. On 24 June, responding to the Western powers' policy of currency reform in the occupation zones, the Soviets imposed a blockade on West Berlin, cutting off all land and water routes to and from the Western sectors of Berlin, in the process creating one of the most serious crises of the early Cold War.

The United States considered a military challenge to the Soviet blockade, but the idea was rejected. To remind the Soviets of the risks they were taking, however, President Harry S Truman ordered two groups of B-29 bombers – the type that had dropped atom bombs on Japan – to fly to England, although the particular aircraft sent there had not been modified to carry A-bombs, of which the Soviets were probably aware. When that threat failed, the Truman administration chose instead to begin a massive airlift of supplies into West Berlin. The airlift was successful in delivering provisions to the Berliners and sustaining them. It also provided a psychological boost to the Western European nations by demonstrating U.S. resolve to stand by them in a crisis. On 4 May 1949 the Soviets called off the blockade. The blockade, intended to slow the creation of an independent West German state, in fact accelerated the process and also hastened the creation of the North Atlantic Treaty Organization (NATO).

Reference

Avi Shlaim, *The United States and the Berlin Blockade, 1948–1949: A Study in Crisis Decision-making* (Berkeley: University of California Press, 1983).

– C. S. B

> SEE ALSO THESE RELATED ENTRIES
> North Atlantic Treaty Org, 3; Harry S Truman, 1.

Berlin Wall

On 13 August 1961 East Germany began erecting around West Berlin a nine-foot wall – topped with barbed wire and guarded by soldiers – to keep East Germans from crossing into West Berlin and defecting to the West. The Soviet Union had long regarded the Western presence in Berlin as a direct affront to its hegemony in Eastern Europe. Many millions of people had defected via West Berlin, and the viability of East Germany was seriously in doubt.

Since 1958 the Soviets had demanded that the Western Allies abandon all their occupation rights to Berlin left over from World War II. When John F. Kennedy became president in 1961, Soviet leader Nikita S. Khrushchev stepped up his demands that the United States pull out. Through the spring and summer, Kennedy and Khrushchev had increasingly strained discussions on the matter, with the Soviet government making various threats to resolve the question unilaterally and Kennedy asserting the rights of the United States, Britain, and France to continue to keep troops in the Western sectors of the city on the grounds that World War II had not formally ended with a peace treaty. The Soviets promptly threatened to sign a separate peace with East Germany, thus in their eyes ending Allied occupation rights in Berlin. Sensing that the dispute was going to drag on, and

Warsaw Pact troops overseeing the building of the Berlin Wall, 13 August 1961

unwilling to risk a nuclear war over Berlin, Kennedy took steps to ensure that the United States had sufficient troops in the city so that the Soviets could drive them out only at great cost.

The building of the wall came as a surprise to the West. Though the Soviets had sporadically cut off East Berlin's access to West Berlin, no one expected that they would build a wall to isolate West Berlin permanently. For several days Allied troops faced off against Soviet tanks as the wall was erected. Short of war, there was little the United States could do. The Soviets were careful to continue to permit Allied troops to come into East Berlin, but no longer could East Germans enter West Berlin.

The crisis receded slowly. Khrushchev's deadline of December 1961 for all Allied troops to be out of the city passed without notice. In the 1970s, as part of West German chancellor Willy Brandt's Ostpolitik – the West German policy of détente with the Soviet Union – the four powers signed an agreement under which East Germany allowed its citizens to enter West Berlin under carefully spelled out conditions.

In 1989 Soviet president and general secretary Mikhail Gorbachev explicitly renounced the

Brezhnev Doctrine – the policy that had pledged the use of force in protecting Soviet interests and had retroactively validated the sealing off of East Berlin from West Berlin. In mid year Hungary took Gorbachev's cue and opened its borders to Austria, in effect giving East Germans an escape route to the West. On 9 November the East German government announced that its borders with West Germany – and the border between East and West Berlin – would be opened. On 3 October 1990 the two Germanies reunited, and by the end of the year the Berlin Wall – the most recognizable symbol of the Cold War – had been dismantled, in part by Berliners and tourists in search of a souvenir piece of the wall.

References

Doris M. Epler, *The Berlin Wall: How it Rose and Why it Fell* (Brookfield, Conn.: Millbrook, 1992);

Norman Gelb, *The Berlin Wall: Kennedy, Khrushchev, and a Showdown in the Heart of Europe* (New York: Times Books, 1986).

– C. S. B.

SEE ALSO THESE RELATED ENTRIES
Berlin Crisis, 1948, 3; Willy Brandt, 1; Brezhnev Doctrine, 3; John F. Kennedy, 1; Nikita S. Khrushchev, 2; Ostpolitik, 3.

Bomber Gap

In the mid 1950s the U.S. government became increasingly concerned with the growth of Soviet atomic capabilities. This concern was reflected in the emergence of the concept of the "bomber gap," the belief that the Soviet Union enjoyed a decisive numerical advantage in strategic bombers. Many analysts feared that the Soviets would try to use this advantage to extract concessions from the United States during an international crisis by threatening to eliminate American retaliatory forces.

In 1954 U.S. intelligence experts concluded that the Soviets were beginning to produce a new bomber, called the Bison, that had an intercontinental range. U.S. Air Force intelligence officials estimated that the Soviets had built between twenty-five and forty Bison bombers. These estimates were shattered on 13 July 1955, when American military attachés observed three formations of Bison bombers flying overhead during the Aviation Day parade in Moscow. Assuming the Soviets would display only half the bombers they had built, air force intelligence estimated that the Soviet Union had at least fifty-six intercontinental bombers. Using this new assessment, the 1956 National Intelligence Estimate (NIE) predicted that by as early as 1960 the Soviets would have five hundred Bisons.

Air force analysts relied heavily on deductive reasoning to arrive at these conclusions. Analysts used aerial photography to determine the size of the Fili manufacturing plant in Moscow, the only plant in the Soviet Union capable of producing strategic bombers. Knowing the size of the plant, they estimated the maximum number of Bisons the Soviets could produce. Their estimates were later confirmed by a head count of the bombers leaving the plant. The air force assessment gained additional credibility because it substantiated claims that the Soviet Union was trying to tilt the strategic balance in its favor.

The air force estimate, however, was not the government's only intelligence assessment. The economic intelligence division of the Central Intelligence Agency (CIA) made startling discoveries that undermined air force conclusions. From its extensive knowledge of Soviet production methods, which it had gained through studies on Soviet manufactured goods, CIA analysts knew that the Bisons bore serial numbers and production dates. By reading the numbers on the tails of the planes, CIA analysts concluded that the Soviets were producing about half as many Bisons as the NIE and the air force estimated.

The heated dispute between the CIA and the air force over the existence of the bomber gap continued until 4 October 1957, when the Soviet Union launched Sputnik. The Soviet demonstration of its superiority in intercontinental ballistic missiles enabled the air force to drop its objections to the CIA bomber estimates, but it continued to maintain its view of the Soviet threat. The National Intelligence Estimate was subsequently changed, ending the bomber-gap controversy.

— B. D. K.

SEE ALSO THESE RELATED ENTRIES
Central Intelligence Agency, 3; Allen Dulles, 1; Curtis LeMay, 1; Missile Gap, 3.

Bretton Woods Conference

A large Victorian hotel in Bretton Woods, New Hampshire – a rustic mountain resort – was the site of a major international conference that succeeded in shaping the course of world economic relations during the post-World War II era. Held for three weeks during July 1944, the conference represented a significant shift toward international cooperation among the participants, who were eager to create a new economic order that would avert both war and financial ruin. It also marked the first time that a group of nations attempted to solve their economic problems by setting up permanent international institutions.

At the conclusion of the conference, John Maynard Keynes, the distinguished economist who headed the British delegation, commented, "We have shown that a concourse of forty-four nations are actually able to work together at a constructive task in amity and unbroken accord. Few believed it possible." In twenty-two days delegates had drawn up documents which created two major global institutions: the International Monetary Fund (IMF) and the International Bank for Reconstruction and Development (IBRD).

IMF and IBRD

The IMF was designed to assure the stability of exchange rates and, when necessary, permit orderly adjustment of these rates. Its purpose was to eliminate the monetary crises that had paralyzed nations in the prewar period and that were still fresh in the minds of the participants.

The IBRD was set up to provide long-term credit to nations ravaged by war. It was aimed to help European nations rebuild peacefully and avoid debilitating effects arising from their deficits viewed against North American balance-of-payments surpluses.

GATT

At the conference, delegates also ratified the General Agreement on Tariffs and Trade (GATT). The GATT is a largely voluntary agreement among major trading nations to lower barriers to international trade. It includes schedules of tariff concessions, a code of rules governing exports and imports, and the establishment of periodic meetings among member nations to discuss trade prob-

Alfred Eisenstaedt
Henry J. Morganthau, Jr., and John Maynard Keynes conferring at the Bretton Woods Conference, 1944

lems. Currently there are over one hundred participating countries, including the United States, most countries of Western Europe, former Eastern-bloc states, and many Latin American, African, and Asian countries such as Japan, India, and Pakistan. Together, these nations account for more than 80 percent of world trade.

Seven hundred thirty persons – among them government officials, economists, observers, and technicians – took part in the conference, grappling over the shape of future economic relations. Since some of the participating countries were still at war, several were represented by governments-in-exile. Britain, the United States, and Canada became the dominant voices at the conference, while Germany, Japan, and Italy were still viewed as enemies.

Secretary of the Treasury Henry Morgenthau led the American delegation and thus was given a major role by President Franklin D. Roosevelt in designing the postwar financial order. The United States took the lead in advocating the gold standard and dollar convertibility. Morgenthau's close friendship with Roosevelt was in part responsible for his prominent position in the American delegation: Roosevelt tended to grant him greater responsibility than was given Cordell Hull, the secretary of state, who was responsible for trade negotiations.

The policies hammered out at Bretton Woods were largely successful over the next twenty-five years, a period that witnessed unprecedented world economic and trade growth.

References

A. L. K. Acheson, J. F. Chant, and M. F. J. Prachowny, eds., *Bretton Woods Revisited* (Toronto: University of Toronto Press, 1972);

Paul A. Samuelson, *Economics* (New York: McGraw-Hill, 1986);

Armand Van Dormael, *Bretton Woods: Birth of A Monetary System* (London: Macmillan, 1978).

– M. G.

SEE ALSO THESE RELATED ENTRIES
Henry Morgenthau, Jr., 1; Franklin D. Roosevelt, 1.

Brezhnev Doctrine

The Brezhnev Doctrine condoned armed intervention by one member of the "Socialist Commonwealth" – which consisted mainly of East European socialist states – in the internal affairs of another deemed to be departing from socialism. It was often called a doctrine of "limited sovereignty" in the West and "socialist internationalism," or "socialist sovereignty," in the East. Although the substance of the doctrine is as old as the Soviet sphere of influence, the doctrine was first explicitly enunciated by Soviet leader Leonid I. Brezhnev after the Warsaw Pact invasion of Czechoslovakia in 1968. The concept has been regarded as the guiding principle of Soviet–East European relations until the late 1980s. In October 1989 Soviet president and general secretary Mikhail S. Gorbachev declared that the Soviet Union had no moral or political right to interfere in the affairs of its East European neighbors. His spokesman, Gennadi I. Gerasimov, embroidered the theme jokingly, saying that Moscow had given up the "Brezhnev doctrine" for the "Sinatra doctrine" ("I Did It My Way").

Socialist Internationalism

The key concept of the Brezhnev Doctrine is the principle of socialist internationalism. It was developed under Nikita S. Khrushchev as a subcategory of proletarian internationalism. After World War II, proletarian internationalism referred to the relationships among ruling and nonruling communist parties around the world. When socialist states assisted communist parties in nonsocialist states, they did so in the name of proletarian internationalism. Socialist internationalism, on the other hand, referred to the relationships among socialist countries. The socialist states were claimed to share common goals, an ideology, and an enemy. Under Brezhnev the application of the principle of socialist internationalism came to be limited to the subset of socialist states that he called the Socialist Commonwealth. On 13 November 1968 Brezhnev explained the application of the theory of socialist internationalism to contemporary circumstances in Eastern Europe, noting that "when a threat arises to the cause of socialism in one country – a threat to the security of the Socialist Commonwealth as a whole – this is no longer a problem for that country's people, but a common problem, the concern of all socialist countries." As such, the doctrine of socialist internationalism was a theory of both collective responsibility and limited sovereignty. It also suggested that the use of military force is justified to save socialism as it is defined by the Communist party of the Soviet Union (CPSU).

The concept of socialist internationalism was enunciated most explicitly by the Soviets in the aftermath of the Warsaw Pact invasion of Czechoslovakia in 1968. In that year, Czechoslovaks became increasingly vocal in expressing their dissatisfaction with the authoritarian rule of First Secretary Antonín Novotny. The power conflict between the reformers and antireformers in the Czechoslovakian Communist party resulted in the replacement of Antonín Novotny by Aleksander Dubcek on 5 January 1968. On 16 April 1968 the central committee of the party adopted the so-called Action Program, which promoted greater intraparty democracy, restoration of civil rights, comprehensive economic reforms, and other political changes. The Soviet leaders became concerned over losing control of the Communist party of Czechoslovakia. During the night of 20–21 August 1968, Soviet, East German, Polish, Hungarian, and Bulgarian troops invaded Czechoslovakia.

After the invasion *Pravda,* the official organ of the Central Committee of the Soviet Communist party, on 26 September 1968, published an article in which the Czechoslovak progressives were accused of undermining the principles of Marxism-Leninism. The key argument of the article, entitled the "Sovereignty and the International Obligations of Socialist Countries," forms the heart of the Brezhnev Doctrine: "There is no doubt that the peoples of the socialist countries and the Communist Parties have and must have freedom to determine their country's path of development. However, any decision of theirs must damage neither socialism in their own country nor the fundamental interest of the other socialist countries nor the worldwide workers' movement, which is waging a struggle for socialism. This means that every Communist Party is responsible not only to its own people but also to all the socialist countries and to the entire communist movement. Whoever forgets this by placing sole emphasis on the autonomy and independence of Communist Parties lapses into onesidedness, shrinking his international obligations."

These words signify the two faces of socialist internationalism and, therefore, the Brezhnev Doctrine. On the one hand, socialist states were said to be sovereign; on the other hand, their political behavior was restricted to serve the "fundamental interests" of the other socialist states and the worldwide workers' movement. Nonruling communist parties were not, however, explicitly limited in their sovereignty. The ties between ruling and nonruling communist parties were covered by the concept of proletarian internationalism, which carried no threat of enforcement, the Brezhnev Doctrine, thus, was not meant to serve as a justification for the use of force against a nonsocialist government or against a nonruling communist party.

Socialist Commonwealth

The geographical boundaries of the Brezhnev Doctrine remained vague in spite of some Soviet attempts to define them. In his address to the Twenty-sixth Party Congress in 1981, Brezhnev implied that at the minimum the members of the commonwealth included Poland, East Germany, Czechoslovakia, Hungary, Romania, Vietnam, Cuba, Laos, Mongolia, and the Soviet Union as members of the Socialist Commonwealth, excluding from mention China, Albania, Yugoslavia, North Korea, and Cambodia.

The members of the commonwealth included mostly those socialist states that had close ties to the Soviet Union, often expressed in bilateral or multilateral treaties. China was excluded from the group because of the Sino-Soviet schism that had reached its climax between 1960 and 1964. Since that time China saw itself operating independently of the Soviet-led socialist camp. It rejected the principle of socialist internationalism, insisting on the right of national sovereignty as both a matter of principle and a matter of national self-interest. When the Warsaw Pact forces invaded Czechoslovakia, China denounced the action more harshly than any other socialist state. Along with the Sino-Soviet border clashes of 1969, the invasion of Czechoslovakia led to the Sino-American rapprochement of the early 1970s, when the Chinese leaders explicitly acknowledged that the Soviet Union, and not the United States, posed the greatest threat to their country's security. Given the strained relations between China and the Soviet Union, it was assumed that the Soviets would not intervene militarily either in North Korea or Cambodia, fearing that such an action would involve the Soviet Union in a war with China.

Yugoslavia's exclusion from Brezhnev's concept of the Socialist Commonwealth can be explained by a long history of ideological and political tensions between Belgrade and Moscow. By 1950 Yugoslav theorists had begun developing a principle of "different roads to communism," challenging the leading role of the Soviet Union within the communist camp. In the 1950s Yugoslavia became the first socialist country to challenge Soviet ideological and political hegemony — and the first one to get away with it. Ironically, at this time it was the Chinese rather than the Soviets who were demanding tough measures against Yugoslavia. The Chinese called the Yugoslav leader, Marshal Josip Broz Tito, "Judas and Renegade," and accused him of attempting to turn the communist camp into a loose confederation. During the de-Stalinization campaign initiated by Khrushchev in 1956, the Soviet leader, much to the disappointment of the Chinese, rehabilitated Tito and publicly recognized Yugoslavia as a member of the Socialist Commonwealth. In spite of mutual efforts to repair relations, the two countries remained distant. In 1968 Yugoslavia, together with Albania and Romania, publicly condemned Soviet interference in Czechoslovakia. In his report to the Twenty-fourth Congress of the CPSU, Soviet leader Brezhnev announced that the Soviet people wished that Yugoslavia's ties to the Socialist Commonwealth would become stronger, implying that he did not include Yugoslavia in the inner circle of the socialist states.

The principle of socialist internationalism, or the Brezhnev Doctrine, was embedded in Eastern European Communist party programs as well as in the treaties between the members of the Socialist Commonwealth. The Soviet-Czechoslovak Treaty of May 1970, for instance, affirmed the Brezhnev Doctrine, noting that the "support, strengthening, and defense of socialist achievements, gained at the price of heroic efforts and self-denying labor of each people, are the common international duty of socialist countries." There was one notable exception to this rule – Romania. The 1970 Soviet-Romanian treaty was careful not to commit Romania to joint defense of "gains of socialism," and limited Romanian obligations to consultation and the defense of state borders. On the basis of this treaty, some scholars pointed to Romania as a nonadherent to the Brezhnev Doctrine.

In trying to predict the circumstances under which the Soviets were likely to intervene militarily in the internal affairs of other socialist states, some analysts tried to define the geographical frontiers of the application of the Brezhnev Doctrine by looking not only at the membership of the Socialist Commonwealth or the pronounced support for the doctrine on the part of the socialist states, but also at the practical possibility of Soviet military action. Kulski, for instance, argued that the Soviets would not apply the Brezhnev Doctrine to Cuba and North Vietnam for the reason that they are beyond the reach of Soviet armed forces. It can also be argued that the Soviets refrained from using force in defense of socialism against a socialist country if the country in question was not perceived as important to Soviet security.

Soviet Intervention

After World War II, the Soviet Union took military action on the basis of socialist internationalism on two occasions: in Hungary in October–November 1956 and in Czechoslovakia in 1968. The Soviet invasion of Afghanistan in 1979 was not justified by the Soviets in terms of the Brezhnev Doctrine. The potential threat of Soviet intervention was apparent on two other occasions: in 1956, during the Polish crisis, and in the early 1980s, when the Soviet Union came close to using its military to suppress Solidarity, the independent trade union movement in Poland. As a result of these interventions and threats of intervention, the Soviets undermined the legitimacy of the regimes in question and encouraged the view in the West that the Eastern European states should be regarded as captive nations rather than an integral part of the Soviet empire.

Although the term *Brezhnev Doctrine* came into use after the Warsaw Pact invasion in Czechoslovakia, the Soviets justified their invasion of Hungary in 1956 in similar terms. The Hungarian revolution began on 23 October 1956 with a peaceful demonstration of students whose demands centered on the reinstatement of Imre Nagy, the prime minister who had been dismissed in March 1955, and ended with Soviet military intervention on 4 November 1956. The Hungarian revolution was largely a function of long-repressed popular opposition to the Soviet Union and to communism. The intervention is best explained by Soviet unwillingness to tolerate the political changes that the Hungarian revolution appeared to bring about.

Western observers regarded the Brezhnev Doctrine as an ideological justification for Soviet military intervention whenever Moscow felt its influence was being threatened by the independent policies of socialist states. The Soviets were vague in evoking the doctrine to justify their intervention in Afghanistan in December 1979. Afghanistan never belonged to the Socialist Commonwealth, as defined by Brezhnev, and the regime in power before the Soviet military intervention may have been pro-Soviet but hardly socialist. At one point during the intervention, Moscow justified Soviet military action with a claim that Hafizullah Amin, the man who became a prime minister of the pro-Soviet Afghan regime in March 1979, was a Central Intelligence Agency agent who intended to betray the revolution. In other words, the Soviets attempted to convey an image of "fraternal assistance" between two socialist states, one of which was in danger of being undermined from within. Later, however, the Soviets denied that they had anything to do with the removal of Amin and his accomplices, thus denying that the intervention could be justified with the Brezhnev Doctrine.

On the basis of the practical record concerning the application of the Brezhnev Doctrine, it can be argued that the doctrine does not provide adequate guidance to understanding Soviet foreign policy decisions in the post-Stalin era. It was of little use in predicting Soviet behavior in the Polish crises of 1956 and 1980, or the outcome of the schism between the Soviet Union and Yugoslavia. The 1956 Polish uprising began with workers' riots in Poznan on 28 June and ended with the election of Wladyslaw Gomulka as first secretary of the Communist party on 21 October. Gomulka's election was clearly against the will of the Soviet leadership, which accused him of promoting "national communism" and of showing inadequate understanding of the role of the Soviet Union in world communism. Despite the spread of unofficial discussion clubs in Poland, workers' protests against "the dictatorship of the proletariat," and the decision of the Polish Communist party to side with the workers and reject the Soviet line that "foreign agents" – not the workers – were behind the riots, the Soviets did not invade Poland. They instead backed down on the composition of the party leadership and tolerated Polish choices in their domestic affairs. They did not invoke the Brezhnev Doctrine.

The Brezhnev Doctrine served as a warning to the Eastern European socialist states not to ignore the ideological and political principles set by the Soviet Union, or damage Soviet security interests. Some of the most important of these principles were the maintenance of a Leninist one-party system, the demonstration of loyalty to the Soviet Union, and continued membership in the Warsaw Pact and Council for Mutual Economic Assistance (Comecon). The violation of these principles did not always lead to Soviet invasion, but the possibility of such an invasion served to check political initiative in Eastern Europe until 1989. The principle of socialist internationalism was also used to signal to Western powers the limits of Soviet tolerance of Western involvement in the affairs of Eastern Europe.

Distinguishing between proletarian and socialist internationalism made it possible for the Soviet Union to enlist support of both the nonruling and ruling communist parties. The support of nonruling communist parties was invited by the Soviets with assurances that these parties could retain the right to function as independent national forces within their respective countries and that the principle of socialist internationalism did not apply to them. The support of the ruling communist parties was obtained by the Soviets with insistence that socialism in any member country of the commonwealth could survive only with collective effort. The Brezhnev Doctrine thus created an ideological tie between European socialist states based on mutually perceived necessity to preserve socialism. This perception was an important component of the cohesion that the Soviets tried to forge within the Warsaw Pact and Comecon. The disintegration of the Socialist Commonwealth at the end of 1989 signified the inability of the Soviets to obtain the dual goals of stability and cohesion in Eastern Europe. By 1990, the Brezhnev Doctrine was dead.

References

Zbigniew K. Brzezinski, *The Soviet Bloc: Unity and Conflict,* revised and enlarged edition (New York: Harvard University Press, 1967);

Charles Gati, *The Bloc that Failed: Soviet-East European Relations in Transition* (Bloomington: Indiana University Press, 1990);

Gerard Holden, *The Warsaw Pact: Soviet Security and Bloc Politics* (New York: Blackwell, 1989);

Wladyslaw W. Kulski, *The Soviet Union in World Affairs: A Documented Analysis (1964–1972)* (Syracuse, N.Y.: Syracuse University Press, 1973).

                                                              – M. H.

SEE ALSO THESE RELATED ENTRIES
Leninism, 3; Josip Broz Tito, 2; Warsaw Pact, 3.

Brinksmanship

In a 16 January 1956 interview in *Life* magazine, Secretary of State John Foster Dulles, in summing up his foreign-policy stance, declared, "The ability to get to the verge without getting into the war is the necessary art. If you cannot master it, you inevitably get into war. If you try to run away from it, if you are scared to go to the brink, you are lost." After the interview, "brinksmanship" became a term used to describe the Dwight D. Eisenhower administration's willingness to assume more risks in defense of U.S. interests. The goal of the administration was to lower the cost of maintaining American defense institutions by relying on the threat to use U.S. nuclear weapons against even relatively modest Soviet transgressions. Policymakers in the administration believed that the effectiveness of such a threat would be enhanced if the United States developed a reputation for being willing to "go to the brink" of nuclear war if need be.

References

McGeorge Bundy, *Danger and Survival: Choices about the Bomb in the First Fifty Years* (New York: Random House, 1988);

Lawrence Freedman, *The Evolution of Nuclear Strategy* (New York: St. Martin's Press, 1981);

John Lewis Gaddis, *Strategies of Containment: A Critical Appraisal of Postwar American National Security Policy* (New York: Oxford University Press, 1982);

Thomas C. Schelling, *Arms and Influence* (New Haven: Yale University Press, 1966);

Thomas C. Schelling, *The Strategy of Conflict* (Cambridge, Mass.: Harvard University Press, 1960);

James Shepley, "How Dules Averted War," *Life*, 40 (16 January 1956): 71-80.

– B. F.

SEE ALSO THESE RELATED ENTRIES
Deterrence, 3; John Foster Dulles, 1; Dwight D. Eisenhower, 1.

Carter Doctrine

The Carter Doctrine was announced by U.S. president Jimmy Carter in response to the Soviet invasion of Afghanistan in December 1979. Coming near the end of President Carter's term, the doctrine marked a hardening of the Carter administration's foreign policy attitudes. According to this doctrine, "An attempt by any outside force to gain control of the Persian Gulf region will be regarded as an assault on the vital interests of the United States of America, and such an assault will be repelled by any means necessary, including military force."

This response to the Soviet invasion brought the containment strategy back to the forefront of U.S. foreign policy, directly applying it to southwest Asia and the Persian Gulf region.

Hardening of U.S. Foreign Policy

By 1980 the Carter administration had largely abandoned its earlier, optimistic conception of international relations. Three developments were posing increasingly taxing challenges to the United States and the West: the steady growth and increasing global reach of Soviet military power; the heavy dependence of the industrialized democracies on Middle Eastern oil; and the changes occurring in many areas of the developing world resulting in a redistribution of global power. Two events in particular prompted the administration to adopt a more hard-line view of international politics. The American hostage crisis in Iran and the Soviet invasion of Afghanistan had both shattered the administration's assumption that global politics were becoming less contentious and that more relaxed U.S. foreign and defense policies were appropriate. The Soviet invasion was particularly distressing to Carter because it was the first direct intervention by Soviet forces outside the boundaries of the Warsaw Pact countries. The administration felt that the U.S. foreign policy goals of promoting global community and maintaining global stability were jeopardized by this blatant manifestation of Soviet expansionism. There was a need to reaffirm the containment of the Soviet Union as a primary goal of U.S. policy. Only after achieving this goal and assuring the stability of the international system would the United States again pursue more cooperative policies toward the Soviet Union.

This latest example of Soviet expansion was occurring in the Persian Gulf and southwest Asia, and U.S. containment efforts accordingly were focused on these unstable regions. The Carter Doctrine was an integral part of this effort, for it directly confronted the attempt by the Soviet Union to move into the area. The doctrine drove U.S. policymakers to seek a modernization and innovation of military power, recalling attitudes from the post-World War II era. One of the immediate results of the doctrine was the creation of the Rapid Deployment Force (RDF), for the Carter Doctrine made it necessary for the United States to be able to project its military into the Middle East and southwest Asia.

The significance of the Carter Doctrine was described by Carter's National Security Adviser, Zbigniew Brzezinski: "It reflects the recognition that the central challenge of this decade is likely to be as massive and enduring as that confronted by American leadership in the first post-World War II decades." The doctrine, indeed, marked the beginning of a decade that would see a massive buildup of the American military and a rededication of the U.S. to the containment policy.

References

M. Glenn Abernathy, Dilys M. Hill, and Phill Williams, eds., *The Carter Years: The President and Policy Making* (New York: St. Martin's Press, 1984);

Zbigniew K. Brzezinski, *Power and Principle: Memoirs of the National Security Adviser* (New York: Farrar, Straus, Giroux, 1983);

Jimmy Carter, *Keeping Faith: Memoirs of a President* (Toronto: Bantam, 1982);

Hamilton Jordan, *Crisis: The Last Year of the Carter Presidency* (New York: Putnam, 1982);

Jerel A. Rosati, *The Carter Administration's Quest for Global Community: Beliefs and Their Impact on Behavior* (Columbia: University of South Carolina Press, 1987).

–J. H.

SEE ALSO THESE RELATED ENTRIES
Zbigniew K. Brzezinski, 1;   Jimmy Carter, 1;
Ruholla Musavi Khomeini, 2; Rapid Deployment
Force, 3; Cyrus R. Vance, 1.

Central Intelligence Agency

The Central Intelligence Agency (CIA) was established by the United States in 1947, in the beginnings of the Cold War to gather intelligence and analyze Soviet military capabilities and political intentions. The agency's scope of activities was later enlarged to include covert paramilitary operations, and it soon offered America's elite the chance to serve on the front lines in the war against communism. The agency's best-known covert operation is its failed invasion of Cuba in April 1961 at the Bay of Pigs.

As an executive agency of the government, the fortunes of the CIA were tied to the goodwill of the president. Beginning with Lyndon B. Johnson in the mid to late 1960s, the agency saw its influence on American foreign policy decline, largely because of its unwillingness to compromise its objectivity for the president's political benefit. In the 1970s the U.S. Congress assumed greater control over the agency, after an investigation by the Senate's Church Committee produced evidence of improprieties committed by the CIA both in the United States and abroad. By the end of the 1980s the CIA had become a Washington bureaucracy, less inclined toward risky overseas adventures and more concerned with defining its role in the post–Cold War world.

National Security Act

The National Security Act of 26 July 1947 established the CIA as an executive agency of the United States government, headed by the director of central intelligence (DCI), who already served as the president's chief intelligence adviser. The DCI was additionally expected to coordinate through the National Security Council the overall American intelligence effort, of which the CIA was only one part. In practice, however, no DCI has ever been able to perform all of these tasks equally well; other members of the intelligence community – for example, the Federal Bureau of Investigation (FBI), the State Department, and the military intelligence groups – have all successfully maintained their autonomy over the years. The CIA itself had difficulty preserving its own independence when it was first established. Only the skill and dedication of the first DCIs and the support of President Harry S Truman prevented the agency from falling under the control of the State Department or the Joint Chiefs of Staff.

National Intelligence Estimates

The CIA was an outgrowth of the Office of Strategic Services (OSS) – the U.S. intelligence organization during World War II – and it was imbued with the glamour and attitudes of its predecessor. Approximately a third of the CIA officers in 1947 were OSS veterans, as were three future DCIs: Allen Dulles, Richard M. Helms, and William J. Casey. In organization and methodology the CIA reflected OSS emphasis on research and analysis on the one hand, and covert paramilitary operations on the other. The gist of research in the early days was embodied in National Intelligence Estimates (NIEs), collaborative studies by the intelligence community to provide a consensus of opinion on specific issues of major importance to American foreign and defense concerns. The agency's Office of National Estimates was to a great extent responsible for the final shape of the NIEs, and, from 1947 on, NIEs set the tone for official U.S. thinking toward the Soviet Union. Collectively a "digest of the Cold War," they tended to approach their subjects in terms of the likelihood of armed conflict between the United States and the Soviet Union. Initially, heavy emphasis was placed on the military capabilities of the Soviet Union and its specific plans for projecting power abroad, particularly in Europe. On 19 December 1947, for example, an NIE was produced on the status of the Soviet atomic program. Later in the decade a dispute between the agency and the air force developed over the size and capability of the Soviet strategic bomber force. The air force argued that the Soviet Union by 1959 would have over a thousand bombers, placing the United States at an overwhelming disadvantage. CIA analysts argued otherwise, contending that the Soviets had neither the technology nor the resources to build such an armada. Only in 1956 with the use of aerial reconnaissance photography was the argument over the "bomber gap" settled conclusively, the verdict in favor of the CIA.

CIA analysis did suffer some failures in the early days, the most embarrassing of which was its inability to predict the beginning of the Korean

War in 1950 when communist forces from the North attacked the South on 25 June. The agency had also failed to foresee the Israeli victory over the Arab forces in Palestine in 1948, shortly before the declaration of the state of Israel.

On 19 December 1947 a secret annex to National Security Council (NSC) Directive 4 created the Office of Special Operations (OSO), giving the CIA authority to conduct espionage activities. A second department, the Office of Policy Coordination (OPC), funded by the CIA but run by the secretaries of defense and state, was established on 18 June 1948 specifically to engage in more-aggressive covert operations than those of the OSO. Soon after becoming DCI in October 1950, General Walter Bedell Smith took over the OPC, but the two offices continued to operate independently within the agency, competing for new recruits and occasionally duplicating each other's activities. But on 2 January 1951 the OSO and the OPC were merged into the newly created Directorate of Plans, which now took over all CIA covert operations. The first such operation had occurred before the Italian elections of May 1948, when CIA support was considered a decisive factor in the victory of Alcide De Gasperi and the Christian Democrats over their communist rivals. In 1949 the agency joined Great Britain's Secret Intelligence Service (SIS) in a failed paramilitary effort to bring down Enver Hoxha's communist government in Albania.

Central Intelligence Act of 1949

The CIA was unique among U.S. intelligence organizations in that it was an executive agency; its head, the DCI, had immediate access to the president. Furthermore, its activities and budget were largely exempt from congressional scrutiny and control. The Central Intelligence Act of 1949 did give Congress the authority to regulate the agency but not its clandestine activities, and for twenty-five years Congress chose not to exercise this power. This absence of formal congressional oversight was an advantage to the agency in the early days of the Cold War as it tried to establish itself as a distinct and influential player in American foreign policy. Also in the agency's favor was the strong support of Presidents Truman and Dwight D. Eisenhower.

In the 1950s, under the benevolent patronage of President Eisenhower, the CIA had some of its greatest successes and enjoyed its highest prestige. On 26 February 1953 Allen Dulles was sworn in as DCI. Dulles had been deputy director for plans in charge of the agency's covert activities, and as DCI

he gave preference to clandestine operations. In 1953 he approved a project to tunnel into East Berlin from the West in order to tap into the communications circuits of the Soviet air force. The tunneling was completed in February 1955, and the CIA immediately tapped into a rich yield of Soviet communications secrets. The Soviets discovered the tunnel in April 1956 and rendered it useless, but the backlog of communications intercepted took another two and a half years for the CIA to process.

Operation Ajax

In June 1953 the CIA contrived Operation Ajax to overthrow Iranian leader Mohammad Mossadegh, who had come to power in 1951 and nationalized British petroleum concerns in the country. After rumors of a possible Iranian-Soviet alliance, President Eisenhower agreed to a British proposal to remove Mossadegh. The operation, planned largely by former OSS operative Kermit Roosevelt (grandson of Theodore Roosevelt), was a complete success: in September 1953 Mossadegh was arrested and replaced by General Fazlollah Zahedi. Subsequently, American oil companies were able to secure a foothold in Iran on an equal basis with the restored British interests.

Operation Success

The CIA next went ahead with its plans to overthrow Jacobo Arbenz Guzmán of Guatemala, who had won the elections of March 1951 and, like Mossadegh, had nationalized his country's largest commercial concern – in the case of Guatemala, the United Fruit Company. The CIA had made plans in 1952 to train and equip Guatemalan exiles, who would invade the country from Nicaragua. Between January and June 1954 the agency spent about $20 million to build an army and an air force. On 18 June, Operation Success was launched, and the CIA army deposed Arbenz within a few days, replacing him with Colonel Carlos Castillo Armas.

U-2 Affair

In December 1954 the CIA was given the task of developing a new reconnaissance aircraft that could be used to monitor Soviet military capabilities. Richard Bissell, a brilliant economist, was placed in charge of the project. The CIA spent about $19 million to develop the plane, called the U-2, and its first test flight took place on 6 August 1955. Flying at seventy thousand feet, beyond the range of any existing antiaircraft missiles, the U-2 could take photographs of objects on the ground with spectacular clarity. The CIA began flying missions over the Soviet Union in June 1956. On 1 May 1960, however, a U-2 piloted by Francis Gary Powers was shot down over the Soviet Union, an incident which gave Soviet leader Nikita S. Khrushchev an excuse to cancel the planned Paris summit with the American, British, and French leaders.

Bay of Pigs Invasion

The best known CIA covert operation occurred in April 1961, when a force of agency-recruited exiles landed at the Bay of Pigs in Cuba in an unsuccessful attempt to depose Fidel Castro Ruz. Two years earlier Castro had seized power, and relations between Cuba and the United States soon deteriorated. In March 1960 the CIA began plans for a covert operation to oust him from power. By the time John F. Kennedy became president in 1961, Castro had signed a Cuban-Soviet trade agreement and was receiving military equipment from the Soviet Union. Under increasing domestic pressure to take firm action against Cuba, Kennedy approved the CIA plan, which by this point had evolved into a full-scale military operation. On 17 April 1961 a fifteen-hundred-man brigade organized and funded by the CIA landed at Zapata, Cuba, hoping to precipitate a popular rebellion against Castro. Within three days, however, the well-equipped Cuban army had destroyed the invasion force. Kennedy was largely blamed for the rout, having refused to allow any significant American military participation, and he in turn held Dulles and Bissell responsible for the failure. Dulles resigned seven months later, replaced by John A. McCone as DCI on 29 November 1961. Before Dulles left, he saw the agency move to its new headquarters in Langley, Virginia, on the Potomac River, eight miles from Washington, where it had previously been occupying an assortment of buildings downtown and along the Mall.

Directorate of Science and Technology

The ascension of McCone to DCI marked a major change in the operational mission of the CIA. McCone had little regard for covert operations and instead gave priority to technical collection methods. He set up the Directorate of Science and Technology (DS&T) in 1962 in order to keep the agency involved in satellite- and aircraft-surveillance programs. During the 1960s DS&T and the air force would feud over control of American reconnaissance efforts. Control of covert opera-

tions, on the other hand, was informally taken over by Kennedy and run by his brother Robert, the attorney general.

After Kennedy's assassination on 22 November 1963, the agency's relationship with the White House changed yet again. The new president, Johnson, had little patience with intelligence matters, and McCone was no longer even invited to the occasional meetings of the NSC. To protest his sharply diminished stature, McCone resigned as DCI, and was replaced on 28 April 1965 by Admiral William F. Raborn, Jr. Raborn, with no intelligence background, proved to be an inept, if amiable, DCI, lasting only a year in the job. (He was once overheard to ask, "Who's this fellow Oligarchy anyway?") Helms, the deputy director of plans, had been requested to accompany Raborn on his infrequent briefings of the president, and following Raborn's departure Helms took over as DCI on 30 June 1966.

Vietnam War

During the Vietnam War the operational activities of the CIA were generally limited to training and advising the South Vietnamese in counterinsurgency techniques to encourage rural resistance to the Vietcong. Since the early 1950s, with the exception of Guatemala and the Bay of Pigs, the agency had moved away from direct paramilitary operations. In Vietnam the most ambitious counterinsurgency program was Operation Phoenix, devised by former CIA analyst Robert W. Komer in 1967 to identify and eliminate Vietcong cadres living among the South Vietnamese. Although it was not officially a CIA program, it had full agency support: William E. Colby, for example, left the agency for a while to work as second in command on Komer's staff in Saigon. The effectiveness of Operation Phoenix was debatable. It provided a good source of intelligence about the Vietcong, but it was soon stigmatized by allegations of widespread assassination — Komer was to acquire the nickname "Blowtorch" — allegations which when revealed during the 1970s further damaged the CIA's image.

The CIA had been producing NIEs on Vietnam since 1953. As American involvement in the war grew, the agency's reports became steadily more pessimistic, and the CIA soon lost favor with Johnson for its attempt to remain neutral. In 1966 a dispute arose between the CIA and the military over estimates of Vietcong troop strength. The CIA credited the Vietcong with a far greater number of troops than the Military Assistance Command

Vietnam (MACV) was willing to concede, implying that the military campaign had been less successful than Johnson was trying to lead the American public to believe. The MACV, however, realized that a political backlash would occur should the agency's numbers be accepted: the U.S. troop levels in Vietnam would have to be increased and the war would continue for longer than had been predicted. Consequently, domestic support for the war, already tenuous, could be expected to lessen Johnson's chances for reelection in 1968. Ultimately, the CIA figures were borne out with the Tet offensive in January 1968, when the Vietcong launched a massive assault, using far more troops than the MACV had admitted they possessed. On 31 March 1968, three days after being advised to withdraw from the war by a group of senior advisers, Johnson announced that he would not run for reelection.

Under the Nixon Administration

When Richard M. Nixon became president, the CIA grew more isolated than ever from the White House. Nixon and National Security Adviser Henry Kissinger – later named secretary of state in Nixon's administration – acted to control foreign policy from the White House, and Kissinger was informally assigned control of intelligence matters through the NSC.

In 1970 the agency became involved in its first major covert operation in ten years, an attempt to depose Chilean president Salvador Allende Gossens, whose promises to nationalize industry worried several American multinational firms, including International Telephone and Telegraph (ITT) and Anaconda Copper. Initial efforts – allegedly involving plans of assassination – to remove Allende failed, but he was overthrown in a military coup in 1973. The CIA's image suffered grievously when its participation in the coup became known.

The agency's reputation hit a low point in the mid 1970s. The effectiveness of the CIA had been called into question by its failure to predict a series of significant world events: the Soviet invasion of Czechoslovakia in 1968, the Arab-Israeli war in 1973 and the subsequent Arab oil embargo, and several events in 1974 – India's first test of a nuclear device, the coup in Cyprus, and the Turkish invasion of that island. The agency was widely thought to be involved in the controversies surrounding the Nixon administration, such as the Watergate break-in of 1972. After Gerald R. Ford became president in August 1974, public opinion

forced the first large-scale congressional investigation of the CIA.

Church Committee

In January 1975 the U.S. Senate established the Church Committee, which for two years comprehensively investigated the agency's activities since its inception in 1947. On the subject of political assassination, Senator Frank Church of Idaho hypothesized that the CIA might be a "rogue elephant rampaging out of control, over which no effective direction was being given." The results of the study were published and seemed to confirm the public's worst suspicions of the CIA. Over the years, the agency had plotted to assassinate several foreign leaders: Patrice Lumumba of the Congo, Castro of Cuba, and Colonel Abdul Kassem of Iraq. Although the Church Committee determined that the CIA had not actually assassinated anyone, it concluded that the agency had encouraged or been aware of several other successful attempts – on the lives of Rafael Leónidas Trujillo Molina of the Dominican Republic, Ngo Dinh Diem of South Vietnam, and General René Schneider of Chile. David Atlee Phillips, a retired agent, concluded that ultimately the CIA had been a "rogue mouse."

More damaging to the CIA, however, were committee findings that implicated the CIA in a variety of domestic operations against American citizens, operations in direct contravention of the CIA charter: mail openings, surveillance of the antiwar movement, and perhaps most bizarre of all, the testing of psychedelic and mind-control drugs, sometimes on unwitting victims. Historian Henry Steele Commager said, "It is this indifference to constitutional restraints that is perhaps most threatening of all the evidence that emerges from the findings of the Church Committee."

As a result of these revelations, Congress passed the Hughes-Ryan Foreign Assistance Act in 1974, which severely circumscribed the agency's ability to engage in covert operations. Eight separate subcommittees now required advance notification of any proposed CIA operation apart from intelligence collection.

Colby was DCI during most of these public scrutinies of the agency, having replaced James R. Schlesinger in July 1973. Colby's willingness to go along with Congress during its investigation embittered many in the agency, who viewed this as a form of treachery, and morale plummeted. Colby's strategy of holding nothing back from the congressional investigators, however, probably saved the agency. Ford was finally forced to limit further revelations of CIA activities, realizing that at stake was ultimately America's reputation in the world. Colby said in February 1976 that the congressional inquiries had strengthened the agency, setting the boundaries "within which it should, and should not, operate."

Colby left the agency on 30 January 1976 and was replaced by George Bush, later dubbed an "efficient custodian" of the agency, who undertook no new operations but rather directed his efforts to improving morale in the agency.

Under the Carter Administration

When Jimmy Carter entered the White House in January 1977, he replaced Bush with Admiral Stansfield Turner, who made no secret of his disdain for the agency's covert operations. Turner soon became the most disliked and distrusted DCI in the agency's history. He fired most of the operatives in the Directorate of Operations, the renamed clandestine branch of the agency, and this purge effectively dismantled the CIA's ability to undertake large-scale covert activities.

Carter's neglect of and disregard for the agency came back to haunt him: the CIA was unable to predict the overthrow of the government of the shah of Iran in February 1979 and its replacement by Ayatollah Ruholla Musavi Khomeini's fervently anti-American Islamic state. The CIA further failed to predict the takeover of the United States embassy in Tehran on 4 November 1979 and the seizure of American hostages. The failure of the American military operation to rescue the hostages in April 1980 resulted in large part from the lack of adequate U.S. intelligence emanating from within Iran. In fact, the one operative in Iran during the crisis had been called out of retirement by the agency. During Carter's last year as president, he ordered an increase in covert operations, belatedly realizing the need for such activities.

Under the Reagan Administration

When Ronald Reagan became president in 1981, he replaced Turner with Casey, a former OSS agent. Reagan and Casey made rebuilding the agency's paramilitary operations a top priority, but congressional controls continued to limit the actual extent of their use. As a result, Reagan's practice was to conduct covert operations through third-part governments – for example, by asking Argentina to train the contra rebels fighting against the Sandinista regime in Nicaragua. The agency's largest covert action since Vietnam was to arm Afghan guerrillas to fight Soviet forces, which had invaded

the country in December 1979. Relatively few CIA people were involved in the operation, however, and most aid went through Pakistan and China. Reagan also saw less need to hide American intervention in the Third World. When the United States invaded the Caribbean island of Grenada, which had become politically close to Cuba, it was revealing to note that the CIA had no real involvement.

Casey resigned due to poor health in January 1987 and Reagan named Deputy Director Robert Gates to succeed him. Gates, a career agency official, had risen through the Directorate of Intelligence with little or no background in operations. The Senate, however, was reluctant to confirm an agency insider after its Tower Commission found evidence that CIA operatives had been involved in a scheme to sell arms to Iran and funnel the proceeds to the contras in Central America – the so-called Iran-contra scandal. Reagan then nominated William H. Webster, the head of the FBI, who was confirmed as DCI by the Senate on 29 May 1987.

When former CIA head Bush became president in January 1989, he retained Webster as his DCI in order to preserve continuity, feeling that the position should be nonpolitical. In the following two years the image and morale of the agency continued to improve, but it still had not regained its former position near the center of the national security apparatus.

At the start of the 1990s the future role of the CIA seemed uncertain. There were widespread calls for its dissolution, since the primary motive for the agency's existence – to counter the Soviet threat – had apparently receded with the end of the Cold War. Many Americans had already come to associate the agency with institutionalized encroachments on such constitutional rights as due process and freedom of speech. Under the pretext of national security, the agency still withheld vast amounts of information from the public, operated under a secret budget, and engaged in a wide variety of activities that raised questions of operational ethics – as the Church Committee revealed in the 1970s. These Americans saw the functions and methods of the CIA as inherently incompatible with the values of a democratic society. There have been suggestions that the operating mission of the CIA be altered in keeping with post–Cold War conditions.

References

Philip Agee, *Inside the Company: CIA Diary* (Harmondsworth, U.K.: Penguin, 1975);

Ray S. Cline, *Secrets, Spies and Scholars: Blueprint of the Essential CIA* (Washington, D.C.: Acropolis, 1976);

William Colby and Peter Forbath, *Honorable Men: My Life in the CIA* (New York: Simon & Schuster, 1978);

Orrin DeForest and David Chanoff, *Slow Burn: The Rise and Bitter Fall of American Intelligence in Vietnam* (New York: Simon & Schuster, 1990),

Trumbull Higgins, *The Perfect Failure: Kennedy, Eisenhower and the CIA at the Bay of Pigs* (New York: Norton, 1977);

James Hougan, *Secret Agenda: Watergate, Deep Throat and the CIA* (New York: Random House, 1984);

Richard H. Immerman, *The CIA in Guatemala: The Foreign Policy of Intervention* (Austin: University of Texas Press, 1982);

Loch K. Johnson, *America's Secret Power: The CIA in a Democratic Society* (New York: Oxford University Press, 1989);

Victor Marchetti, *The CIA and the Cult of Intelligence* (New York: Knopf, 1974);

John Prados, *President's Secret Wars: CIA and Pentagon Covert Operations since World War II* (New York: William Morrow, 1986);

John Ranelagh, *The Agency: The Rise and Decline of the CIA* (New York: Simon & Schuster, 1986).

– M. B.

SEE ALSO THESE RELATED ENTRIES

Bay of Pigs Invasion, 3; William J. Casey, 1; Frank Church, 1; William E. Colby, 1; Allen Dulles, 1; Richard M. Helms, 1; John A. McCone, 1; Francis Gary Powers, 1; Walter Bedell Smith, 1.

China Lobby

The China Lobby was the name given to an informal group of Americans working on behalf of Chiang Kai-shek's Chinese nationalist government. It exercised considerable influence over U.S. policy toward China through its ability to mobilize congressional support for its goals, marking a rare instance in the postwar period in which Congress dictated matters of foreign policy to the executive office.

By the late 1940s the China Lobby had begun to materialize as an amorphous group of organizations and individuals working to increase U.S. support given to Chiang in his fight against communist forces in the Chinese civil war. The communists, led by Mao Zedong, took over mainland China in 1949, but the Lobby continued to work on behalf of the nationalists by eliminating from positions of influence anyone in the U.S. government critical of Chiang's Kuomintang regime on Taiwan. The Lobby was highly effective in controlling the debate over Chiang's collapse. The failure was blamed on a supposed lack of American will caused by a conspiracy of procommunist officials in the State Department. These officials, so the Lobby charged, undermined intentions to aid the nationalists by spying against the United States and Chiang, promoting naive views of the communists, and spreading lies about Chiang. For a generation, these charges succeeded in crippling the State Department's ability to assess Mao and the communists.

Targets of the China Lobby

A particular target of the China Lobby was the group of American diplomats, collectively known as the China Hands, who had served in China since the late 1930s. Many were not only critical of the corruption and incompetence surrounding the Chinese nationalist government but had accurately forecast that the communists were a force to be reckoned with and would very likely win the war. The China Hands were eventually driven from the government, some on charges that amounted to disloyalty. On several occasions, even Secretaries of State Dean Acheson and George C. Marshall came under attack for arguing that increased U.S. aid to the nationalists was a waste.

The Lobby's charges, however, came at a time of growing tensions with the Soviets and general anticommunist sentiment, and found resonance with the American public. Chiang had been the beneficiary of considerable publicity during World War II as the leader of what was considered to be one of the world's great powers. Moreover, Chiang and his wife had had close ties to the American missionary community in China. Also in Chiang's favor was the particular influence of one of the Lobby's members, Henry R. Luce, born in China to Presbyterian missionary parents and founder and publisher of the *Time, Life,* and *Fortune* magazine empire. Luce used his magazine to attack anyone critical of Chiang.

The Lobby's institutional apparatus was the Committee of One Million Against the Admission of Communist China to the United Nations. It was founded in the spring of 1953 after reports that the People's Republic of China (PRC) would gain membership to the United Nations following the end of hostilities in Korea. The committee circulated petitions nationally, solicited funds for newspaper advertisements, and worked to pass congressional resolutions which called on the United States not to extend diplomatic recognition to the communists as the legitimate government of China, and to prevent the admission of China by threatening to withdraw if the communists were given membership. At other times the committee worked to maintain trade sanctions against China. In the late 1950s the committee sought to have the United States defend the islands of Quemoy and Matsu from communist attack. Occupied by the nationalists, the islands were used to shell the mainland, and tensions rose when communist China appeared ready to seize them.

Despite its grandiose name, the committee was composed of only a small handful of activists. It was, however, successful throughout the 1950s and into the 1960s because many members of Congress – Democrats and Republicans alike – allowed their names to be used in the committee's activities. Congressional resolutions on behalf of the committee's efforts usually passed by lopsided margins.

Loss of Support

The committee's grip on America's one-China policy – which recognized the nationalists on Taiwan as China's only legitimate government – held until the mid 1960s, and only began to weaken as the appearance of bipartisanship began to vanish. By 1960 many of the figures who contributed funds to the committee's efforts, its newspaper advertisements especially, were increasingly perceived as aligned with causes sympathetic with the hard-line anticommunist conservatism of Republican senator Barry Goldwater of Arizona. President John F. Kennedy is reported to have flirted with the idea of recognizing the communist government as part of a two-China policy. He wanted to wait until his second term out of fear for what Luce's criticisms in the pages of *Time* magazine would do to his reelection prospects. In his 1960 campaign debates against Vice-president Richard M. Nixon, Kennedy had aroused considerable alarm in conservative circles when he denied that the United States was obliged to defend the Quemoy and Matsu islands.

Although the China Lobby continued to lose support throughout the 1960s, U.S. policy toward China remained unchanged because President Lyndon B. Johnson was preoccupied with the Vietnam War and was not inclined to want to change policy to recognize a Chinese communist government that was supporting North Vietnam.

The Lobby effectively came to an end in July 1971 when President Richard M. Nixon announced that he would be traveling to China to meet with Mao. Nixon's grand strategy regarding the Soviet Union required some accommodation of China, and in agreeing to visit he was conceding that the China Lobby had worked for a generation to deny communists legitimacy. Nixon, moreover, reasserted presidential leadership of America's China policy for the first time in over twenty years. The United States did not extend full diplomatic recognition to China until 1979, but by then the Lobby was no longer a consideration.

References

Stanley D. Bachrack, *The Committee of One Million: "China Lobby" Politics, 1953–1971* (New York: Columbia University Press, 1976);

Ross Y. Koen, *The China Lobby in American Politics* (New York: Macmillan, 1960).

– C. S. B.

SEE ALSO THESE RELATED ENTRIES
Chiang Kai-shek, 2; Henry R. Luce, 1; Richard M. Nixon, 1.

Cominform

The International Bureau of Communist and Workers' Parties, designated by the abbreviation Cominform, was founded in September 1947 in Sklarska Poreba in the Silesia region of Poland and was dissolved in April 1956. It consisted of representatives from the communist governments of Bulgaria, Czechoslovakia, Hungary, Poland, Romania, the Soviet Union, and, until 1948, Yugoslavia, as well as representatives of the French and Italian Communist parties. While the official role of the organization was to exchange information, the Cominform's principal task was to allow the Soviet leader, Joseph Stalin, to coordinate the development of the Eastern European countries, especially their foreign policies. The creation of the Cominform marked a new stage in Soviet policy toward Eastern Europe that now required adherence by other Communist parties to Soviet standards. It also denoted a major turning point in U.S.-Soviet relations and was both a cause and consequence of the deepening Cold War.

The dissolution of the Comintern, or Third (Communist) International, in May 1943 had created an organizational void in relations among communist nations, a gap which the Cominform was created to fill. There were several key differences between the Comintern and the Information Bureau, however. The earlier organization was open to all Communist parties, whereas Stalin himself determined membership in the Cominform. The Comintern had formal decision-making powers, an executive committee, and a secretariat, but the newer Information Bureau did not. The Cominform had only its official weekly newspaper, *For a Lasting Peace, For a People's Democracy,* edited by the Soviet philosopher P. F. Yudin. Finally, the Comintern had openly encouraged worldwide revolution, while the Cominform existed, at least in theory, to exchange information and voluntarily coordinate policies.

The Cominform's headquarters were established in Belgrade, Yugoslavia, in 1947 and, following that country's expulsion from the organization in June 1948, transferred to Bucharest, Romania. During its almost nine years of existence the Information Bureau held few formal meetings; other than the founding meeting in September 1947 the Cominform met only four other times – in January and June 1948, November 1949, and sometime in 1950. Of the five gatherings, only three were reported in the communist press, and an aura of secrecy surrounded the organization until its dissolution by Nikita S. Khrushchev in the changed international environment of 1956.

Truman Doctrine and Marshall Plan

At the time of its formation the Cominform was generally viewed in the West as the opening round of a more militant and confrontational Soviet policy, and in retrospect it is clear that its creation signaled a deterioration in U.S.-Soviet relations. It is now generally assumed, however, that the birth of the Information Bureau was largely a defensive reaction to U.S. policy.

In March 1947, in response to situations in Greece and Turkey, President Harry S Truman announced a new U.S. policy of providing support for "free peoples who are resisting attempted subjugation by armed minorities or by outside pressures." The Truman Doctrine, as this policy came to be called, represented a commitment by the United States to provide military assistance to countries resisting communism. This was followed in June 1947 by Secretary of State George C. Marshall's announcement, in a commencement address at Harvard University, of the European Recovery Program or Marshall Plan. The Marshall Plan promised massive economic aid to war-torn Europe, including the Soviet Union, but required a formal European initiative for joint recovery.

Both the Truman Doctrine and the Marshall Plan were interpreted in Moscow as part of a U.S. attempt to roll back communism and Soviet influence in Europe, and the Soviets objected to what they considered the "extortionate terms" of the program. At the founding meeting of the Cominform, the Russians argued that the real aim of the Marshall Plan was not economic recovery but economic aggression against Eastern Europe. Two days after the Soviets rejected the plan on 2 July, the Czechoslovak government voted to accept it. Poland, Hungary, and Romania were preparing to follow suit when Stalin intervened and forced the Czechoslovaks to reverse their decision. In this sense the Cominform's creation, while itself a contributor to the worsening Cold War, was a defensive response to perceived U.S. aggression in the form of the Truman Doctrine and Marshall Plan.

Such U.S. policies only worsened the already dire internal needs of the communist world in 1947. The Cominform was established as an institutional framework for the accomplishment of two tasks: consolidating Soviet control over Eastern Europe and reorienting the Western European Communist parties. By 1947 Communist parties had come to power and were seeking to consolidate their control in Eastern Europe. The Information Bureau provided a means of directing development of the new "peoples' democracies" along Soviet lines and of reining in any deviant communists, especially Marshal Josip Broz Tito of Yugoslavia.

At the same time, the French, Italian, and Belgian Communist parties all had been expelled from coalition governments by 1947. The Cominform marked the end of the old strategy of seeking power by cooperating with noncommunist political parties in coalition governments and the birth of a new policy of struggle against the Marshall Plan and the pro-American regimes of Western Europe through strikes, riots, and sabotage. The first general strikes were launched in France and Italy in November 1947.

Founding Meeting

The secret meeting at which the Cominform was founded was attended by representatives of nine communist parties: E. Kardelj and Milovan Djilas from Yugoslavia; Vulko Chervenkov and V. Poptomov from Bulgaria; Gheorghe Gheorghiu-Dej and Anna Pauker from Romania; M. Farkas and Jozsef Revai from Hungary; M. Minc and Wladyslaw Gomulka from Poland; Rudolf Slánsky and St. Bastovansky from Czechoslovakia; Andrei Zhdanov and Georgi Malenkov from the Soviet Union; Jacques Duclos and Etienne Farjon from France; and Luigi Longo and Eugenio Reale from Italy.

Equally important as those attending the meeting were those who were not invited. First, none of the principals from the Cominform's predecessor, the Comintern, was present at the Cominform's birth – to prevent the appearance that the earlier organization was being resurrected. During the entire six days of the meeting the word *Comintern* was apparently never mentioned. Second, Germany was excluded since the Soviets thought an agreement with the West for a neutral demilitarized Germany was still possible. Albania was not present because it was designated for absorption by Yugoslavia, and the Asian Communist parties were

excluded to demonstrate that the Soviet Union did not support insurrectionary movements. Finally, the fact that the U.S. Communist party was not invited indicated Stalin's continued aspirations for cooperation with the West.

In his address to the founding meeting of the Cominform, Zhdanov outlined the doctrinal rivalry between communism and capitalism – an ideological legacy that remained a cornerstone of both communist and noncommunist thought throughout the Cold War. According to Zhdanov's appraisal, the world was divided into two opposing blocs: an imperialist, antidemocratic camp headed by the United States and an anti-imperialist, democratic one led by the Soviet Union.

Zhdanov's declaration was followed by a speech by another Soviet, Malenkov, on Soviet policies to purify the cultural and scientific spheres of "cosmopolitan" and "idealistic" influences. Malenkov's address suggested the proper model for the Eastern European parties to follow internally in order to build communist states.

The Western Communist parties also were seriously reprimanded at the initial meeting of the new organization. Both the French and the Italians were made to confess the errors of their earlier policy of seeking to share power with noncommunist parties as part of coalition governments. While both parties admitted to having prematurely laid down their arms and agreed to renew the struggle against their governments in the future, no one mentioned that the original postwar policy of cooperation also had been undertaken on Moscow's orders.

The criticism of the Western communists was loudly and vehemently led by the Yugoslavs, who were strongly encouraged by Zhdanov. None of the other participants supported the militant line, and the Soviets vetoed Yugoslavia's apparently harmless suggestion of tribute to the struggle of the Greek communists. Scholars disagree on whether this encouragement of a militant line at odds with Moscow's more moderate view was a deliberate trap set by the Soviets to gain more control over Tito and to widen the gulf between the Yugoslavs and other Communist parties.

Expulsion of Yugolsavia

The ideological conflict between the Soviet Union and Yugoslavia intensified during 1947 and 1948, and the Cominform was the weapon Stalin ultimately used to settle the dispute. Tito's vision of a communist bloc composed of equal partners proved to be incompatible with Stalin's view of the primary role of the Communist party of the Soviet Union (CPSU) in the world revolutionary process.

Although Marshal Tito accepted the leading role of the CPSU in communist movements, he also sought more autonomy for his own party through a closer association of the Eastern European nations. Tito objected to Soviet pressure exerted on many domestic and foreign-policy issues, pressure he thought violated the concepts of sovereignty and nationalism.

At a specially convened meeting in Bucharest, Romania, in June 1948, Yugoslavia was expelled from the Cominform for nationalistic and anti-Soviet behavior departing from the principles of Marxism-Leninism. Tito's policies were roundly condemned both at the meeting and in the Cominform newspaper, and the Yugoslav Communist party was encouraged to oust its leaders.

The effects of the Yugoslav expulsion were widespread. By early July the Polish and Bulgarian Communist parties were called upon to revise their doctrines and policies. Gomulka was accused of deviations and removed as Polish Communist secretary in August 1948 in an effort to prevent the emergence of another potential Tito. The CPSU emerged from the Soviet-Yugoslav conflict as the leading revolutionary party; the role of nationalism in the transformation of Eastern Europe was downplayed while that of the Red Army was emphasized; the Cominform was used as a means of creating discipline among Communist parties; and various "nationalistic elements," including the Social Democratic parties of Eastern Europe, where liquidated. A wave of arrests and executions followed in June 1949.

U.S. Response

Despite Stalin's efforts to prevent such an impression, the general inference drawn in the West from the formation of the Cominform was that it represented a revival of the Comintern and a political and ideological offensive by the Soviets against the West.

Although most were alarmed by the founding meeting, several U.S. policymakers viewed the Cominform as a response to Western policy and a signal of weakness in the communist bloc. The Soviet conflict with Yugoslavia, in particular, demonstrated weakness rather than the image of strength it was intended to project. Both George F. Kennan, director of the Policy Planning Staff at the State Department, and Charles E. Bohlen, an expert in the State Department on the Soviet Union, viewed the creation of the Cominform as a defensive reac-

tion to U.S. policy, and Bohlen even thought it would contribute to Western unity and encourage support for the Marshall Plan. Few Westerners noted the differences between the Cominform and the Comintern, however, and the new organization was generally perceived to represent a shift to a more provocative Soviet strategy.

The Cominform Disbanded

To the extent that the Cominform was designed to ensure coordination among the communist nations, the Soviet-Yugoslav conflict deprived the organization of its reason for existence. Although it continued to operate for several years, the Cominform's main effects on international relations were mapped out at its initial meeting, and its subsequent impact was slight.

Following Stalin's death in 1953 the organization lingered on if only as a source of embarrassment to the Soviets. The new Soviet leader, Khrushchev, dissolved the Cominform shortly after the Twentieth CPSU Congress in February 1956. The international situation facing the Soviets was dramatically different from that of 1947: Khrushchev was emphasizing a policy of peaceful coexistence with the West, allowing nations to follow different paths to socialism, encouraging overtures to noncommunists, and focusing on the Third World as the location of revolution.

On 18 April 1956 the Soviet newspaper *Pravda* published a communiqué announcing that the eight-member Communist parties of the Cominform had agreed to disband the organization. The official reason given was that the Information Bureau had fulfilled its functions: the nonruling Communist parties of Western Europe, according to the communiqué, were stronger than ever, and communism had generally succeeded in moving beyond the confines of a single country into Eastern Europe. No organizational framework was established to replace the Cominform.

References

Vojtech Mastny, "Stalin and the Militarization of the Cold War," *International Security*, 9 (Winter 1983–1984): 109–129;

William O. McCagg, Jr., "Domestic Politics and Soviet Foreign Policy at the Cominform Conference in 1947," *Slavic and Soviet Series*, 2 (Spring 1977): 3–30;

Eugenio Reale, "The Founding of the Cominform," in *The Comintern: Historical Highlights,* edited by Milorad M. Drachkovitch (Stanford, Cal.: Hoover Institution, 1966);

William Taubman, *Stalin's American Policy: From Entente to Detente to Cold War* (New York: Norton, 1982);

Heinz Timmermann, "The Cominform's Effects on Soviet Foreign Policy," *Studies in Contemporary Communism,* 18 (Spring 1985): 3–23;

Adam B. Ulam, *Expansion and Coexistence: The History of Soviet Foreign Policy, 1917–67* (New York: Praeger, 1968);

Ulam, *The Rivals: America and Russia since World War II* (New York: Viking, 1971);

Ulam, *Titoism and the Cominform* (Cambridge, Mass.: Harvard University Press, 1952);

United States Congress, House of Representatives, Committee on Foreign Affairs, *The Strategies and Tactics of World Communism,* Supplement No. 1, "One Hundred Years of Communism, 1848–1948" (Washington, D.C.: U.S. Government Printing Office, 1947).

– S. M. P.

SEE ALSO THESE RELATED ENTRIES
Georgi M. Malenkov, 2; Marshall Plan, 3. Joseph Stalin, 2; Josip Broz Tito, 2; Truman Doctrine, 3.

Committee on the Present Danger

The Committee on the Present Danger was founded in November 1976 as a nonpartisan, nonprofit organization dedicated to alerting the nation to what its members perceived as the danger of the continued growth of the Soviet nuclear arsenal. The origins of the committee lay in "Team B," an ad hoc advisory group formed in 1975 by George Bush, then director of the Central Intelligence Agency (CIA). Bush asked hard-line foreign-policy specialists to provide an independent assessment of Soviet military capabilities and intentions – a report that was to serve as an alternative to the CIA official estimate, which some conservatives criticized as too benign to serve as a basis for national security policy. As it turned out, the Team went far beyond its mandate in prescribing a crash military buildup. In November 1976 five Team B members – Paul H. Nitze, Eugene Victor Rostow, Elmo Zumwalt, Jr., Richard V. Allen, and Max M. Kampelman – decided to found the Committee on the Present Danger, borrowing the name from a 1950 group established by conservatives to publicize the threat of communist expansion. At its height, the committee included 150 leading private citizens, of which 60 percent were Democrats and 40 percent Republicans.

Like Team B, the Committee on the Present Danger offered an alarming analysis of Soviet military capabilities and intentions. Richard Pipes, a professor of Russian history at Harvard University who had chaired Team B, argued that the Soviets rejected the concept of nuclear deterrence that, in Pipes's view, was peculiarly American. Analyzing the public statements and writings of Russian civilian and military leaders, Pipes contended that they rejected the view that nuclear war was suicidal. Unlike Americans, who think nuclear weapons are useful only as a deterrent, Russian leaders, Pipes asserted, think nuclear war will have winners and losers, that there will be a meaningful difference between winning and losing, and that nuclear weapons have value as a compellant. In the July 1977 issue of *Commentary,* Pipes articulated his views in an article entitled "Why the Soviet Union Thinks It Could Fight and Win a Nuclear War," concluding that the differences between American and Soviet attitudes had a destabilizing effect. Pipes was particularly persuasive in enumerating Soviet military developments that, he argued, were incongruous with the American concept of mutual vulnerability, especially the continued growth of the Soviet nuclear arsenal and the massive Soviet civil defense program.

These developments were also monitored by other committee members. Paul H. Nitze, who served as the committee's chairman for policy studies, widely publicized his concerns in two 1976 articles. The first, "Assuring Strategic Stability in an Era of Détente," appeared in *Foreign Affairs,* and the second, "Deterring our Deterrent," in *Foreign Policy.* Nitze argued that the United States had permitted the Soviet Union to develop a decisive nu-

Some members of the Committee on the Present Danger: (clockwise from left) Max M. Kampelman, Charles Tyroler II, Richard V. Allen, Eugene V. Rostow, Henry H. Fowler, Charles Burton Marshall, Charles E. Walker, Edward Bennett Williams, and Paul H. Nitze

merical advantage in "heavy" intercontinental ballistic missiles (ICBMs), the strategic nuclear weapons most able to destroy nuclear missiles protected by hardened missile silos. Heavy ICBMs carry several powerful nuclear warheads, or multiple independently targeted reentry vehicles (MIRVs). With a numerical advantage in these accurate, multiwarhead missiles, the Soviet Union could destroy the entire American land-based system with a fraction of its own ICBM force. A Soviet strike of this magnitude against American ICBMs would reduce the residual American nuclear arsenal to a ragged collection of intercontinental bombers and submarine-launched ballistic missiles (SLBMs), neither of which would be accurate enough to destroy Soviet ICBMs.

Following a Soviet strike, Nitze reasoned, the president would be faced with a dilemma of having to choose between two equally bad options. He could either abstain from retaliating against Soviet cities – the only targets that the remaining American weapons could destroy – and accept Soviet demands in the hope of avoiding further damage to American society, or order an attack on Soviet cities and invite a devastating Soviet retaliation.

If the president chose to attack Soviet cities, the Soviets would escalate by attacking American cities, something they had refrained from doing in

their initial attack. Nitze, fearing that the Soviet threat to retaliate would deter an American attack against Soviet urban targets, concluded that the president would acquiesce to Soviet demands in the hope that they would refrain from further strikes. Nitze did not believe that this strategic imbalance would necessarily lead to war, but he was certain that the United States would have to bow to the Soviets during a crisis because of the Soviet numerical superiority in accurate, powerful, multiwarhead ICBMs.

Leading committee members, many of whom were Democrats, met with President Jimmy Carter in the early days of his administration, advising him to counter Soviet efforts. The administration, however, failed to respond enthusiastically to the committee's advice. By July 1977 the committee had turned its attention to the second set of Strategic Arms Limitation Talks (SALT II) and the emerging SALT II treaty. Meeting with newspaper boards around the nation, committee members argued that the treaty enabled the Soviets to achieve nuclear superiority. Committee efforts were instrumental in diminishing public support for the SALT II treaty, which eventually died in the Senate in 1979.

While its advice fell on deaf ears in the Carter administration, the committee's views significantly influenced the defense policies of Ronald Reagan, himself a committee member. Thirty-one other committee members went on to important positions in the Reagan administration, including Richard Perle, appointed assistant secretary of defense for international security policy; Paul H. Nitze, made chief negotiator for the intermediate nuclear forces (INF) talks; Eugene Victor Rostow, named head of the Arms Control and Disarmament Agency (ACDA); Jeane J. Kirkpatrick, appointed U.S. ambassador to the United Nations; William J. Casey, named director of the CIA; and George P. Shultz, appointed secretary of state in 1982.

References

Robert Conquest, *Present Danger* (Stanford, Cal.: Hoover Institution Press, 1979);

Paul H. Nitze, "Assuring Strategic Stability in an Era of Détente," *Foreign Affairs,* 54 (January 1976): 207–232;

Paul H. Nitze, "Deterring our Deterrent," *Foreign Policy,* no. 25 (Winter 1976–1977): 195–210;

Richard Pipes, "Team B: The Reality Behind the Myth," *Commentary,* 82 (October 1986): 25–40;

Richard Pipes, "Why the Soviet Union Thinks It Could Fight and Win a Nuclear War," *Commentary,* 64 (July 1977): 21–34;

Norman Podhoretz, *The Present Danger: "Do We Have the Will to Reverse the Decline of American Power?"* (New York: Simon & Schuster, 1980);

Strobe Talbott, *The Master of the Game* (New York: Knopf, 1988);

Charles Tyroler II, ed., *Alerting America: The Papers of the Committee on the Present Danger* (Washington, D.C.: Pergamon-Brassey's, 1984).

                  – B. D. K.

SEE ALSO THESE RELATED ENTRIES
Jimmy Carter, 1; MRVs and MIRVs, 3; Paul H. Nitze, 1; Richard Perle, 1; Ronald Reagan, 1; Strategic Arms Limitation Talks, 3.

Conference on Security and Cooperation in Europe

The Conference on Security and Cooperation in Europe (CSCE) is a forum created in the early 1970s by which thirty-five European and North American states meet periodically to discuss common security. Its original mission was to address pan-European concerns outside the military framework of a U.S.-Soviet Cold War rivalry. Even the neutral and nonaligned states sent representatives.

The CSCE grew out of the détente policies of President Richard M. Nixon, who reshaped U.S. foreign policy to reflect the belief that the United States and the Soviet Union had a common interest in a stable international system in which disputes did not have to lead to crises. The CSCE represented the routinization and institutionalization of détente. It hoped to achieve territorial stability for the post–World War II frontiers and establish greater economic ties between East and West.

The attempts made by the CSCE to move beyond Cold War assumptions about European stability have not fared well in post–Cold War Europe. A reunited Germany has revitalized the German problem long central to European security, while territorial disputes and economic nationalism, issues once thought resolved, have reemerged.

Reference

John Freeman, *Security and the CSCE Process: The Stockholm Conference and Beyond* (New York: St. Martin's Press, 1991).

                  – C. S. B.

SEE ALSO THESE RELATED ENTRIES
Détente, 3; Richard M. Nixon, 1.

Congress for Cultural Freedom

The Congress for Cultural Freedom (CCF) was an organization of anticommunist liberal intellectuals dedicated to fighting the spread and influence of communism. These intellectuals were inspired by the admonition of William Phillips, editor of *Partisan Review,* who said in 1946 that "the Left must not permit the struggle against Stalinism to be appropriated by the Right." The impetus for the creation of the CCF was the ongoing struggle in liberal circles between anti-Soviet and pro-Soviet (or "anti-anti-Soviet") intellectuals. Things came to a head when the Cultural and Scientific Conference for World Peace was held at the Waldorf-Astoria in New York in March 1949. Sidney Hook accused the conference of being "a perfect case study of ... Communist propaganda," and with others created the Americans for Intellectual Freedom (AIF). Two Americans living in Europe – Michael Josselson and Melvin Lasky – were instrumental in organizing the first meeting of the CCF in June 1950 in West Berlin. Among the American delegates were Hook and Arthur M. Schlesinger, Jr.

The congress, headquartered in Paris, sponsored the national affiliates and organized international conferences and publications, the most famous of which was *Encounter,* which began publication in England in October 1953. The U.S. affiliate of the congress was the American Committee for Cultural Freedom (ACCF), and among its members were liberals such as Hook and Schlesinger and conservatives such as Whittaker Chambers. The CCF and its activities prompted important debates among American and European intellectuals in the 1950s. In the United States liberal members of the ACCF were in conflict over issues raised by McCarthyism, the Rosenbergs, and the treatment of the "China Hands" – policy makers in the State Department accused of being pro-Chinese communist. With the appeal of communism waning in the 1960s, the CCF and its affiliates went into decline. Further tarnishing CCF reputations were revelations in the 1960s that the Central Intelligence Agency (CIA) had partially funded the CCF and *Encounter.* The demise of communism and the Soviet Union also brought about the closing of *Encounter.*

As historian Alexander Bloom has noted the importance of the CCF was considerable. It legitimized a principled liberal position during a period in which right-wing hysteria threatened to sweep moderates and liberals away with the communists. The creation of the CCF, for liberal anti-communists, occurred at a time when "the historical moment matched the intellectual effort, and they won the day. The achievement of liberal anti-communism extended far beyond the questions asked, and the success long outlived the resolution of the issues at hand."

References

Alexander Bloom, *Prodigal Sons: The New York Intellectuals and Their World* (New York: Oxford University Press, 1986);

Peter Coleman, *The Liberal Conspiracy: The Congress for Cultural Freedom and the Struggle for the Mind of Postwar Europe* (New York: Free Press, 1989);

Sidney Hook, *Out of Step: An Unquiet Life in the 20th Century* (New York: Harper & Row, 1987);

Melvin J. Lasky, *On the Barricades, and Off* (New Brunswick, N.J.: Transaction, 1989);

Alan M. Wald, *The New York Intellectuals: The Rise and Decline of the Anti-Stalinist Left from the 1930s to the 1980s* (Chapel Hill: University of North Carolina Press, 1987).

– B. F.

SEE ALSO THESE RELATED ENTRIES
China Lobby, 3; Melvin J. Lasky, 1; McCarthyism, 3; Ethel and Julius Rosenberg, 1; Arthur M. Schlesinger, Jr., 1.

Containment

Containment served as the basis of American strategic thinking toward the Soviet Union during the Cold War. Its principal architect was George F. Kennan, a career diplomat who felt that after World War II the United States required a new approach to the Soviet Union, its ally during the war but increasingly a powerful rival. To Kennan, the twin dictates of history and ideology had forced the Soviet Union upon a course of relentless expansion, making it a serious threat to vital American security interests, and containment was Kennan's prescribed response to counter the threat of Soviet hegemony around the world. In May 1947 he was named the first director of the State Department's Policy Planning Staff. Here he was ideally placed to present and argue his new strategy to America's leaders. In July 1947 his "X Article" eloquently, yet incompletely, presented his ideas on containment to the general public. In a series of official lectures and policy reports during the same period, however, Kennan developed his ideas more fully – ideas which served to motivate and justify American actions during the early days of the Cold War.

The Influence of George F. Kennan

The idea of containment arose from Kennan's feeling that the assumptions on which the United States had based its dealings with the Soviet Union during World War II were seriously flawed, and that a new strategy was necessary now that the Soviets appeared to threaten American interests in the postwar era. In Kennan's view, U.S. president Franklin D. Roosevelt had mistakenly thought that Soviet foreign policy was dictated by external threats, most recently in the form of Adolf Hitler and Germany. If this threat from the outside were removed, then the Soviet Union would behave like any normal state, with the same hopes, fears, and desires to which the United States could then appeal. Furthermore, Roosevelt thought that the Soviet Union could be integrated into a small group of world powers – the so-called Four Policemen – with the United States, China, and Great Britain as the other members. These four powers would not just maintain order in the rest of the world, but, perhaps as importantly, would also act to restrain each other. In essence, Roosevelt was proposing an old-fashioned balance-of-power arrangement among the victors of World War II. The four powers would deal among themselves to create mutually acceptable "spheres of influence" and maintain a tenuous harmony through the exploitation and balancing of each member's self-interest.

To Kennan's mind, however, the Soviet Union, ruled by Joseph Stalin, had proved impervious to attempts by the United States and the West to exert leverage over it. The Soviets seemed prepared to keep their occupational forces in Eastern Europe and the Balkans indefinitely – in many cases against the obvious desires of the native peoples. During and after the war, the United States had tantalizingly hinted at economic aid, in the form of lend-lease, reconstruction loans, and the promise of large reparations from defeated Germany. All of this was offered in the hopes of influencing Soviet behavior and enticing them to permit democratic governments in Eastern Europe. But Stalin was unmoved by these offerings. Similarly, the Soviets seemed oblivious to more-threatening gestures, such as the American decision to retain control of the atomic bomb and its technology.

In a remarkably influential telegram of eight thousand words sent from Moscow to the State Department on 22 February 1946, Kennan explained why American efforts to change Soviet behavior had failed. The "Long Telegram" claimed that Soviet leaders had historically needed the fiction of a "hostile international environment" in order to maintain the legitimacy of their dictatorship and the "sacrifices they felt bound to demand" from the people. With the defeat of Germany and Japan, Soviet leaders were building up the "U.S. and the United Kingdom to fill the gap."

In the July 1947 issue of *Foreign Affairs,* Kennan published "The Sources of Soviet Conduct" – an X appearing in the byline in keeping with the State Department policy of anonymity. What came to be known as the X Article further describes the imperatives of Soviet foreign policy: the Soviet need to excuse the domestic repression, combined with the dictates of Marxist ideology, meant "that there can never be on Moscow's side any sincere assumption of a community of aims between the Soviet Union and powers which are regarded as capitalist." The Soviet Union may indulge in "tactical manœuvers" that are "permissible in dealing with the enemy," but the basic antagonism remains. In the meanwhile, of vital interest to the Soviet Union is that the "'Socialist fatherland'" be "cherished and defended by all good Communists at home and abroad, its fortunes promoted, its enemies badgered and confounded."

Because the interpretation of Marxist ideology rests with the leaders in the Kremlin, "truth is not a constant. . . . It is only the most recent manifestation of the wisdom of those in whom the ultimate wisdom is supposed to reside." Soviet leaders, because of political and tactical expediency, could, therefore afford to take a flexible, long-term view in the "pursuit of Communist purposes," and "the Kremlin has no compunction about retreating in the face of superior force." Kennan saw Soviet foreign policy as a "fluid stream" that moves inexorably to fill "every nook and cranny available to it in the basin of world power." The implications for American foreign diplomacy were twofold: On the one hand [Soviet diplomacy] is more sensitive to contrary force, more ready to yield on individual sectors of the diplomatic front when that force is felt to be too strong, and thus more rational in the logic and rhetoric of power. On the other hand it cannot be easily defeated or discouraged by a single victory on the part of its opponents. Given this, Kennan asserted that American policy in regard to the Soviet Union "must be that of a long-term, patient but firm and vigilant containment of Russian expansive tendencies." Containment would be carried out by the "application of counter-force at a series of constantly shifting geographical and political points, corresponding to the shifts and manœuvres of Soviet policy."

Essential to understanding containment are several larger concepts that relate to Kennan's view on America's proper role in the world. He did not feel that the United States should attempt to remake the world in its image – that is, conduct foreign policy according to parliamentary rules in the arena of international organizations such as the United Nations. This approach, he believed, was essentially an illusion, and made little allowance for differences in the distribution of power and the willingness of other states to wield it, especially against American interests. He thought instead that the national interest would best be served through a "particularist" approach, to maintain equilibrium in the world through a balance of power so that no one country, or group of countries, could achieve undue dominance. The particularist approach allowed the United States to view other countries and regions in terms of their "true" capabilities and

intentions. Kennan listed five regions that he thought were of "importance to us from the standpoint of national security." Besides the United States, these "five centers of industrial and military power" were Great Britain, Germany and Central Europe, the Soviet Union, and Japan. All of them, singly or collectively, had – because of population, industrial strength, and tradition – the ability to endanger the United States. And at the time Kennan was writing, only one of the five – the Soviet Union – was in hostile hands. Elsewhere, Communist parties, presumably under Moscow's control, were gaining power especially in Western Europe. It was the purpose of containment to ensure that the other four "power centers" did not fall under Soviet control.

This did not mean that the United States did not have other interests elsewhere in the world. It did, but Kennan considered the peripheral areas bordering the "vital" Eurasian landmass to be almost by definition of lesser importance. (In Kennan's mind, South America, Africa, and Australia were under little danger from Soviet encroachment.) These areas served variously as sources of raw materials or as channels of transportation or access to and from the Eurasian center.

Kennan's thinking on the importance of defending the periphery changed dramatically during the mid 1940s. He originally thought that the United States should confront the Soviets "at every point where they show signs of encroaching upon the interest of a peaceful and stable world." Similarly, when President Harry S Truman offered in March 1947 to provide American aid to Greece and Turkey, he appeared simultaneously to be making a worldwide offer to "support free peoples who are resisting attempted subjugation by armed minorities or outside pressures." But by mid 1947, Kennan had come to believe that defense of the entire "perimeter" around Eurasia would inordinately strain America's limited resources. Instead, the United States should adopt a "strongpoint defense," which would permit the selective concentration of forces on those areas that were "vital." Greece and Turkey, although on the periphery, were thus necessary to American security because of their strategic location in the Eastern Mediterranean region. Other, less important regions could even be conceded to the Soviets if this did not unduly endanger American interests. The Truman administration, in fact, generally judged each request for foreign aid separately, basing its decision on American interests and the estimated effectiveness of the aid.

Kennan also felt that the Soviet Union would rely primarily on psychological means in its struggle for the other power centers, especially Western Europe and Japan. The Soviet Union itself had been devastated in the war and would be chary of risking a confrontation with the United States, at that time the only power in the world with nuclear weapons.

Last, Kennan recognized that the resources that America had to project its power abroad would be seriously reduced after the war. American defense expenditures, for example, had declined from $81.6 billion to $13.1 billion between 1945 and 1947, and the number of troops went from 12 million to 1.6 million in the same period. It was the peculiar genius of containment that took into account these new constraints on American foreign policy and yet offered the United States a strategy with which to counter the Soviet threat.

The Stages of Containment

By the end of 1948 Kennan saw the strategy of containment as unfolding in three distinct stages. First, the United States would act to restore the balance of power by encouraging self-confidence to grow in those countries that had been left vulnerable to Soviet power after the defeat of Germany and Japan. Second, American foreign policy would play on differences between the Soviet Union and the international communist movement so as to limit the Soviet ability to act beyond its borders. Third, the United States would attempt to alter, gradually, the Soviet concept of international relations, so as eventually to allow both sides to coexist harmoniously.

Because Europe and Japan contained so much of the world's potential industrial and military power, Kennan thought them essential to the maintenance of a balance of power. But they had been devastated during the war. Their populations were exhausted and demoralized, and seen as especially vulnerable to Soviet pressure. He thought it necessary that their self-confidence be bolstered in order to strengthen their "natural forces of resistance" against Soviet pressure. In Europe, this was accomplished primarily by means of the European Recovery Program (ERP), announced by Secretary of State George C. Marshall in June 1947. The Marshall Plan was an offer of economic assistance extended to Europe by the United States that the Europeans would be expected to carry out largely by themselves. In this way, American interference in European affairs would remain at a minimum — a sensitive issue for Kennan — and European self-confidence would be encouraged to grow. Kennan insisted that the Marshall Plan treat the region as a whole, because collectively, rather than singly, would the European countries be most successful in withstanding Soviet pressure. Furthermore, by acting in concert, Germany might be successfully incorporated back into the European community. Kennan viewed Germany as absolutely necessary to European federation, for without federation Kennan believed, "the other countries of Europe can have no protection against a new attempt at foreign domination." For Japan, Kennan favored rehabilitation over punishment and control of America's defeated enemies. He urged that the United States delay any peace treaty with the Japanese until a more stable society could take root.

Military force did not play a very great role in Kennan's conception of containment. To be sure, a military presence was necessary to secure the balance of power, if only to establish the credibility of American intentions. In Kennan's mind, however, the ultimate goal of containment was to alter the Soviet conception of international behavior, and military force was ill-suited to this end. The Soviet threat was political, rather than military in nature, Kennan said, and "if it is not entirely a military threat, I doubt that it can be effectively met entirely by military means."

Once the balance of power had been reestablished, the second step of containment would be to try to limit the ability of the Soviet Union to extend power and influence abroad. During and after World War II, the Soviets had begun to reach beyond their borders through the creation of puppet regimes, especially in Eastern Europe, and the manipulation of foreign Communist parties in Western Europe and elsewhere. Kennan was early in recognizing the tensions existing within international communism, and he thought that the United States should exploit these tensions in order to best deter Soviet hegemonic ambitions.

He saw that the iron discipline imposed by the Soviets was considered excessive by some of their followers — a situation which led to a steady stream of apostate communists, disillusioned with Moscow's strict demands. His suspicions were realized as relations between Yugoslavia and Moscow worsened after World War II. Yugoslavian leader Joseph Broz Tito — who, with Soviet help, had risen to prominence during the war — continued to pursue policies independent of Moscow's direction, ignoring the objections of Joseph Stalin. Tito persisted on this course until finally, in June 1948, Stalin expelled Yugoslavia from the Communist Information Bureau (Cominform). Stalin had created the Cominform primarily as a means to exert continued Soviet control over local communists once they had come to power in their own countries.

Kennan thought that the best place for the American strategy to work was in Western Europe, where Communist parties existed with some popular support but lacked support from a Soviet military presence. The United States, Kennan felt, should ensure the success of the Marshall Plan, which, by alleviating economic distress, would remove the conditions that allowed communism to thrive in the first place. In Eastern Europe, he thought the chances of removing Soviet-backed puppet regimes were slim, and that the United States should do nothing to encourage a Soviet military reaction.

The third step in the process of containment would be to effect a fundamental change in the Soviet concept of international relations and encourage Soviet leaders to accept a particularist approach to the world, in which they would be prepared to tolerate diversity. This was much the same approach that Kennan urged on American leaders. He proposed to alter Soviet behavior by a combination of deterrents and inducements that he termed "counter-pressure." In the X article he explained: "the United States has it in its power to increase enormously the strains under which Soviet policy must operate, to force upon the Kremlin a far greater degree of moderation and circumspection than it has had to observe in recent years, and in this way to promote tendencies which must eventually find their outlet in either the break-up or the gradual mellowing of Soviet power."

Kennan considered it important that the United States reward "good behavior" by the Soviets. It was in this third step that U.S. policy regarding the Soviets in the late 1940s diverged the most from Kennan's thinking. Kennan most particularly objected to the creation of the North Atlantic Treaty Organization (NATO), the establishment of an independent West Germany, and the decision to build the hydrogen bomb. With the creation of NATO in April 1949, Kennan felt that the European countries had mistaken a political threat for a military one. Furthermore, a military alliance among the countries would only set in place the political division between Eastern and Western Europe, making it that much more difficult to reconcile differences with the Soviet Union, of which a divided Europe was the most obvious symptom.

Kennan also thought that the creation of a West German state out of the three Western occupation zones was a mistake and that it would be the clearest sign of a divided Europe. He proposed that Germany instead should be disarmed and the four occupying powers withdraw, leaving the country demilitarized and neutral. Kennan's plan, however, was rejected, and an independent Federal Republic of Germany came into existence in May 1949.

After the Soviet Union detonated its first atomic device in August 1949, members of Congress and the military urged for the development of a yet more powerful weapon, the hydrogen bomb. Kennan argued strenuously against this, continuing to view the use of military force with misgivings. He thought rather that the United States should possess only that level of atomic weaponry necessary to provide a credible deterrent, and that in any case it should follow a policy of "no first use." But, again, his objections were overridden.

By the time Kennan left the Policy Planning Staff in late 1949, his views on the Soviet Union and containment had come to be heeded less and less in Washington. This was in part due to his continued insistence that the Soviet threat was political rather than military in nature. But Soviet actions at the time seemed to belie this: the blockade of Berlin, the ongoing purges of Eastern European political leaders, and several fiery speeches by Soviet representatives in the United Nations were delivered simultaneously with the Soviet test of its first atomic weapon in August 1949. The military threat had never appeared more ominous than now, and Kennan's approach was becoming too subtle and nuanced for the public and Congress. Kennan himself felt that the strategy of containment seemed to have become a goal in itself rather than as a way to end the Cold War.

References

John Lewis Gaddis, *Strategies of Containment* (New York: Oxford University Press, 1982);

George F. Kennan, *Memoirs: 1925–1950* (Boston: Little, Brown, 1967);

X[George F. Kennan], "The Sources of Soviet Conduct," *Foreign Affairs*, 25 (July 1947): 566–582.

– M. B.

SEE ALSO THESE RELATED ENTRIES
George F. Kennan, 1; The Long Telegram, 3; George C. Marshall, 1; Marshall Plan, 3; Joseph Stalin, 2; Harry S Truman, 1; Truman Doctrine, 3; X Article, 3.

Contras

The contras were counterrevolutionary guerrillas fighting to overthrow the left-wing Sandinista government of Nicaragua during most of the 1980s. In 1979 the Sandinistas succeeded in ousting the country's longtime dictator, General Anastasio Somoza Debayle. American policy tried to encourage the Sandinistas to keep their pledges of democracy and political pluralism. Instead, they became increasingly anti-American and autocratic. When Nicaragua turned to the Soviet Union and Cuba for military and economic aid and began to support a left-wing insurgency in neighboring El Salvador, President Ronald Reagan decided in 1981 that the United States should support the contras.

With their ties to Somoza, the contras never developed much of a following in Nicaragua. Their military victories were few and tended toward acts of terrorism. The Sandinistas' heavy-handed retaliation was all that permitted the contras what small measure of support they had.

Despite Reagan's efforts to portray them in the best possible light, the contras and their cause never mustered much enthusiasm in Congress. In 1983 and 1984 Congress passed the Boland Amendments designed to cut off U.S. aid to the contras. Efforts to circumvent the Boland Amendments led to scandal in the Reagan administration – the Iran-contra affair. Under the direction of officials in the White House, U.S. weapons were sold to Iran in exchange for the release of American hostages in Lebanon. Profits from the sales were then diverted to the contras.

Under international pressure, Nicaragua held free elections in 1988. The Sandinistas were decisively defeated and their leader stepped down. Few, if any, of the contras, had a role in the new government.

References

Leslie Cockburn, *Out of Control: The Story of the Reagan Administration's Secret War in Nicaragua, the Illegal Arms Pipeline, and the Contra Drug Connection* (New York: Atlantic Monthly Press, 1987);

Michael Arthur Ledeen, *Perilous Statecraft: An Insider's Account of the Iran-Contra Affair* (New York: Scribners, 1988).

– C. S. B.

SEE ALSO THESE RELATED ENTRIES
Anastasio Somoza Debayle, 2; Iran-Contra Affair, 3; Ronald Reagan, 1.

Convergence

The theory of convergence, advanced mostly by liberal economists and social scientists in the 1950s and 1960s, argued that the Soviet and American societies were growing socially and politically closer to each other, despite the heated rhetoric that characterized U.S.-Soviet public exchanges. The forces of industrialization and urbanization were making the Soviet society more plural and less centralized, it was argued, diminishing the influence of communist ideology. These forces would create a modern middle class unwilling to continue to live in a highly regimented society commanded from above. The decentralization of Soviet society and the lessening of communist orthodoxy would lead to a "mellowing" of the Soviet Union in other spheres as well, moderating its antagonism toward the West and its adventurist foreign policy. Convergence theorists implied that, until Soviet norms and practices began to converge with those of Western societies, there was little chance of close cooperation between East and West.

References

Frederick C. Barghoorn, *Politics USSR* (Boston: Little, Brown, 1972);

Zbigniew Brzezinski and Samuel P. Huntington, *Political Power: US/USSR* (New York: Viking, 1963).

                                                                                                                              – B. F.

SEE ALSO THESE RELATED ENTRIES
Détente, 3.

Council on Foreign Relations

The Council on Foreign Relations is the preeminent private institution to work on behalf of a moderate bipartisan interventionist American foreign policy. During its heyday between 1947 and 1968, the council's membership was drawn predominantly from the ranks of America's business and political elite. With its publications, conferences, and social gatherings, the council played a critical role in defining the range of politically acceptable opinion in the debate over the U.S. strategy in the Cold War.

The council originated with a group of internationally minded bankers and lawyers who had been advisers to the American delegation to the Versailles peace conference at the end of World War I. Concerned both about America's return to isolationism and that their expertise and opinions were insufficiently regarded in Washington, the group founded the council in New York in 1921. Bipartisan from the beginning, it was dedicated to advancing the cause of a conservative but activist American foreign policy that would be commensurate with America's growing economic power. The following year the council began publishing a quarterly journal, *Foreign Affairs,* with Hamilton Fish Armstrong as editor. Membership eventually numbered around two thousand.

Through the 1920s and 1930s the council had relatively little influence. Its centrist internationalism was given little regard by an apathetic American public. Reciprocating the sentiment, the council held in pronounced disdain the opinions of the general public, though it was never the secret society some alleged. Members were overwhelmingly drawn from the educated eastern upper class, with a heavy tilt toward Wall Street finance and corporate law. Other members included higher-level diplomats and noted journalists and professors. Relatively few elected politicians were invited to join, the council believing that they all too easily catered to an ill-informed public. Politicians, especially those from the Midwest and Far West, believed that association with the council members would not be favorably regarded by the electorate. The council saw itself as offering a private forum for its members and carefully chosen guests to discuss selected issues of international importance. In these interwar years, the range of competing views was so narrow that the most spirited discussions were on whether guest speakers should occasionally include isolationists. Armstrong later bragged that when *Foreign Affairs* published articles by someone he considered an opponent of the council he ran them as he received them, in all their unedited glory. By the mid 1930s, with the growing threat posed by Nazi Germany and Fascist Italy to Western democracies, and Britain in particular, the council began stepping up its case against the isolationist interwar American foreign policy. Despite its illustrious membership, however, the council continued to play only a marginal role in U.S. foreign policy before World War II.

The "X" Article

The council began to influence the course of American foreign policy with the rise of the Cold War in 1947. With the United States taking a leading political, economic, and military role in the world, the council helped provide the intellectual underpinnings to justify containment as the American Cold War strategy. In July 1947 *Foreign Affairs* carried one of its most influential articles, "The Sources of Soviet Conduct." Written by George F. Kennan, who used the pseudonym "X," the "X" Article traced the roots of Soviet expansionism back several centuries into Russian history. The article became the foundation for a containment strategy by which the United States would merely offer counterpressure to Soviet pressures. The American Right, however, preferred an aggressive rollback policy – the Left, accommodation and cooperation.

The council helped to ensure that both political parties stood almost eye-to-eye on foreign policy. Until the Vietnam War shattered the consensus, the foreign policies of the Republicans and Democrats differed hardly at all, the Republicans being perceived as marginally more anti-communist.

By the early 1950s the council enjoyed quasi-governmental status. Many of its members were, if not diplomats, high-ranking political appointees in foreign-policy and national-security posts. The social status of other members gave them entrée to virtually all policymakers. Foreigners regarded *Foreign Affairs* as the semiofficial house organ of the State Department. Changes in policy, American and foreign, were frequently announced in speeches at the council's townhouse on New York's Upper East Side. Foreign leaders in New York on business often met council members for more private talks.

Conventional Foreign Policy

The council's influence was such that it was seen as the repository of the conventional wisdom of American foreign policy. Despite the beliefs of conspiracy-theorists from the Left and the Right, the council never determined U.S. foreign policy. Rather, its members' opinions tended to represent the range of views considered politically acceptable. These ranged between the classic containment policies of Dean Acheson and the avowed

rollback policy of John Foster Dulles. Both were council members who were later to become secretaries of state. Of the militant isolationism of General Douglas MacArthur, the anti-communist hysteria of Senator Joseph R. McCarthy, and the radical conservatism of Senator Barry Goldwater – all political positions which for a time at least held credence with the public – none managed to find acceptance with the council.

By the mid 1960s the council's influence had crested. Changing sources of political power coming from America's western and southern regions diminished the council's influence, if only in relative terms. Goldwater's capture of the 1964 Republican presidential nomination – capping an ugly primary followed by his defeat by President Lyndon B. Johnson in the general election – marked the end of the Republican liberal wing. The Republican center held together long enough to deliver the 1968 nomination to Richard M. Nixon, but Nixon's lower-middle-class upbringing made him uncomfortable with the culture and style of the Eastern upper class.

The Vietnam War sparked acrimonious political unrest which in the end shattered the consensus over postwar American foreign policy. The American establishment, operating through the council, was perceived as endorsing a foreign policy at best self-interested and at worst criminal. The council responded by attempting to open up its membership to more liberals, minorities, and women. *Foreign Affairs* began to publish more divergent viewpoints though there was never any feeling of a genuine debate taking place within its pages. The bipartisan consensus shattered, Vietnam opened up the debate over U.S. foreign policy to viewpoints which were never before considered.

Reference

Robert Schulzinger, *The Wise Men of Foreign Affairs: The History of the Council on Foreign Relations* (New York: Columbia University Press, 1984).

– C. S. B.

> SEE ALSO THESE RELATED ENTRIES
> Dean Acheson, 1; Containment, 3; John Foster Dulles, 1; George F. Kennan, 1; "X" Article, 3.

Counterinsurgency

Counterinsurgency, the actions a country takes – whether military, political, economic, or psychological – to defeat domestic subversion, was regarded as the means by which the United States could help countries defeat communist insurgencies without a major American investment of resources. The doctrine of counterinsurgency was applied most frequently from the 1950s through the mid 1960s in the former European colonies, recently made independent, in Asia and Africa. The techniques of counterinsurgency were almost always surreptitious.

In its early application, in the suppression of the Huk Rebellion in the Philippines in the early 1950s, counterinsurgency was still benign, even admirable. Operatives of the Central Intelligence Agency, the most famous being Edward Lansdale, earned reputations for their sensitivity and subtlety in mixing military engagements against the guerrillas with efforts at identifying the United States with nationalist aspirations and democratic processes. Many of the early advocates of counterin-surgency were themselves quite sympathetic to the anticolonial sensibilities of the long suppressed peasants.

The high point of American counterinsurgency came in Vietnam during the early years of the administration of President John F. Kennedy. The United States sought to undermine and counteract the appeal of the procommunist Vietcong insurgency with a variety of economic-development schemes and nation-building programs. They were not successful, and by the late 1960s counterinsurgency came to be identified with the Phoenix Program, a brutal and bloody campaign of terror, torture, and assassination waged against suspected Vietcong members. With that, counterinsurgency lost whatever luster remained.

Reference

Douglas S. Blaufarb, *The Counterinsurgency Era* (New York: Free Press, 1977).

– C. S. B.

SEE ALSO THESE RELATED ENTRIES
Central Intelligence Agency, 3; John F. Kennedy, 1.

Cuban Missile Crisis

The Cuban Missile Crisis was a momentous event in modern history: for thirteen days in October 1962, the United States and the Soviet Union stood poised on the brink of nuclear war. At issue was the presence of Soviet strategic missiles in Cuba, a situation which the United States viewed as a threat to the nuclear balance between the superpowers and to its prestige in the hemisphere and credibility in the world. The removal of the missiles was probably President John F. Kennedy's most significant foreign policy success.

Bay of Pigs Invasion

In January 1959 Fidel Castro Ruz seized power in Cuba after waging a guerrilla war against American-supported dictator Fulgencio Bastista y Zaldívar. Thereafter Cuban relations with the United States rapidly deteriorated, and Castro sought closer ties with the Soviet Union. On 7 May 1960 Castro established diplomatic relations with Moscow, and a Cuban-Soviet trade agreement soon followed. By July 1960 Cuba was receiving Soviet military equipment, and on 16 April 1961 Castro announced that the Cuban revolution was socialist. This remains debatable, but at the time it seemed to confirm the worst fears of the United States concerning the nature of Fidel Castro. The next day a small exile army, organized and armed by the United States, landed at the Bay of Pigs in Cuba, intent on precipitating a popular rebellion against Castro. Within three days, however, the well-equipped Cuban army had destroyed the invasion force. The failure of the invasion did not deter American efforts to oust Castro. By early 1962 the United States had "embarked on a concerted campaign of overt and covert political, economic, psychological and clandestine operations" against Cuba.

The Bay of Pigs invasion had been prompted largely by American fears that the Soviets might try to establish a nuclear rocket base in Cuba. The Soviet Union already had missiles that could reach the United States, but their accuracy was doubtful, and American leaders were aware of the Soviet strategic inferiority – made public by Deputy Secretary of Defense Roswell Leavitt Gilpatric in a speech on 21 October 1961, much to Moscow's chagrin. On the other hand, missiles fired from Cuba, only ninety miles from the United States, had a much better chance of hitting their targets, and they would reduce America's warning and response time to only a few minutes. But perhaps most important, American leaders realized that the prestige of the United States was at stake, that a Soviet threat should not emanate from within the hemisphere.

Soviet leader Nikita S. Khrushchev, however, discounted these fears as baseless. On 2 January 1961, Khrushchev called rumors that the Soviet Union might establish missile bases in Cuba "foul slander." In a note to President Kennedy following the Bay of Pigs invasion, Khrushchev assured him that the Soviet Union had no intention of establishing bases in Cuba.

In July 1962 Castro sent his brother, Raúl, to Moscow on an unexplained mission. Later that July, U.S. Navy reconnaissance planes began to take notice of a steady stream of ships making for Cuba from Soviet-controlled ports on the Black and Baltic seas. The ships docked at the port of Mariel on Cuba's northern coast and unloaded various types of military equipment, including twenty-four surface-to-air missile (SAM) batteries, forty-two MiG-21 intercepter aircraft, antiship cruise missiles, missile-armed Komar patrol boats, and forty-two IL-28 light bombers. By late August American intelligence had confirmed these arms deliveries, if not all the details. What the intelligence reports failed to confirm, however, was the Soviet deployment of a Strategic Rocket Forces division to Cuba, with a total of eighty SS-4 (medium-range) and SS-4 (intermediate range) missiles and forty nuclear warheads. By mid October forty-two of the planned eighty missiles had arrived in Cuba, and construction of four launch sites was proceeding.

On 29 August photographs from a U-2 reconnaissance plane provided the first evidence of SAM sites. But a Soviet spokesman on 2 September merely said that the Soviet Union had agreed to provide armaments in response to a Cuban request for assistance, and he implied that the SAMs were for a defensive purpose only. On 4 September Soviet ambassador Anatoly Dobrynin called on President Kennedy's brother, Robert, the attorney general, and assured him that the Soviet Union would create no problems for the United States during the fall election campaign. That same day President Kennedy publicly announced that the introduction of Soviet missiles into Cuba would raise issues of the "gravest" kind. On 6 September Dobrynin met with presidential adviser Theodore Sorensen to repeat his earlier promise of no Soviet interference in American "internal affairs."

U-2 Photographs

Kennedy remained unmollified. On 7 September he was granted authority by Congress to call up 150,000 military reservists. On 13 September he stated publicly that, although Soviet arms shipments up to then did not "constitute a serious threat" to the United States, if the Soviet Union were to make Cuba an offensive military base, then the United States "will do whatever must be done to protect its own security." On 19 September the authoritative U.S. Intelligence Board concluded in a National Intelligence Estimate (NIE) that the Soviet emplacement of missiles in Cuba was "highly unlikely."

The United States continued to fly U-2 missions, with seven sorties taking place between 29 August and 7 October. The overflights brought back more photographs of SAM installations, but none of offensive missiles. On 21 September, however, the Central Intelligence Agency received a report from an eyewitness who claimed to have seen a missile larger than a SAM on a Cuban highway on 12 September. On 14 October a U-2 flew over western Cuba, an area that had not been photographed since 5 September. This flight brought back photographs of the area around San Cristobal showing trapezoidal-patterned SAM sites, the usual Soviet arrangement for protecting strategic missile installations. Within the trapezoids were missile erectors, launchers, and transporters. High-ranking officials were told about the photographs on Monday evening, 15 October.

Ex Comm

The next morning, McGeorge Bundy, the national security adviser, told Kennedy the news. Kennedy immediately called for a meeting later on that morning with a group of his most trusted advisers: Vice-president Lyndon B. Johnson, Secretary of State Dean Rusk, Secretary of Defense Robert S. McNamara, Robert F. Kennedy, General Maxwell D. Taylor, Deputy Secretary of Defense Roswell Gilpatric, Under Secretary of State George W. Ball, Bundy, Special Counsel Theodore Sorensen, Secretary of the Treasury Douglas Dillon, and Ambassador Charles E. Bohlen. This group, with a few later additions, would come to be known as the Executive Committee (Ex Comm) of the National Security Council. Meeting two or three times a day during its first week of existence, it served as President Kennedy's prime source of advice and inspiration as the missile crisis unfolded.

That morning Ex Comm discussed a broad range of possible American responses. From the be-

ginning the American position was certain: to see the missiles removed from Cuba. Kennedy announced that he wanted no public disclosure of the missiles until he had decided on a course of action: he wanted to control events rather than react to them. Accordingly, he would adhere to his scheduled appointments, giving no indication that anything was amiss.

The next day, while Kennedy was in Connecticut to make campaign appearances, Ex Comm discussed six possible American responses, laid out in Tracks A through F, and ranging from taking no immediate action to planning an invasion of Cuba. Discussion soon narrowed down to Track D – a naval blockade to prevent military equipment from reaching Cuba – and Track E, a surprise air strike to remove the bases. Robert Kennedy soon emerged as the informal chairman of the Ex Comm while the president was away. He vigorously opposed an air strike, arguing that it violated the best traditions of the United States. The chief proponent of an air strike was Dean Acheson, the veteran cold warrior who had been invited to join Ex Comm.

Ex Comm met next on the morning of 18 October. Its members were informed that the first Soviet missiles would be ready for launch within eighteen hours. Later that day Soviet foreign minister Andrei Gromyko met with Kennedy in the White House. The two first discussed the situation in Berlin and then talk turned to Cuba. Gromyko said in a general way that the only weapons on the island were SAMs, and Kennedy replied that the United States did not intend to invade Cuba.

At the second Ex Comm meeting that day, a consensus was slowly developing against an air strike. Ball headed the "blockade group," consisting of McNamara, Gilpatric, Robert Kennedy, Llewellyn E. Thompson, Dillon, and former secretary of defense Robert A. Lovett, a newcomer to Ex Comm. The "air strike" group was led by Bundy and comprised John A. McCone, Dillon, Taylor, Acheson, and another newcomer, Assistant Secretary for Defense Paul H. Nitze. It should be noted that many Ex Comm members changed their minds, some more than once, through the course of the deliberations.

Later that evening, the Ex Comm members trooped to the White House to meet with the president. Kennedy tentatively decided on a blockade, explaining that by keeping the American response at this level, he could take progressively more drastic action if the situation warranted. An initial air strike, on the other hand, would probably accomplish little and an invasion of Cuba would ultimately be required. Kennedy then ordered the

A Soviet missle installation under construction at San Cristóbal, Cuba, in 1962; this photograph was taken from an American U-2 spy plane

Joint Chiefs of Staff to develop a plan for a blockade.

On Friday, 19 October, U.S. military forces were put on alert. Kennedy continued his campaign appearances, going by train to Cleveland and Chicago. Ex Comm met most of the day. By now, most members felt that a blockade was inevitable, and they decided to secure a resolution from the Organization of American States (OAS) that would support the American action.

On 20 October, Kennedy cut short his campaign trip and returned to Washington. He met in the afternoon with Ex Comm and was shown the result of their deliberations. He endorsed the idea of seeking OAS approval and of calling an emergency meeting of the United Nations (UN) Security Council during his televised speech, now scheduled for 22 October. That day the first American ships moved out of port to assume blockade stations in the Caribbean.

On the morning of 21 October Kennedy heard last minute arguments from the Joint Chiefs in favor of an air strike, but after the air force admitted it could not promise to knock out all of the missiles, Kennedy confirmed his decision to institute a blockade.

The next day Acheson met with French president Charles de Gaulle in Paris, who promised his support to the United States. In Washington Ex Comm was formally established by National Security Council Action Memorandum 196. Later that day Kennedy informed five congressional leaders of the situation. Senators Richard Russell and J. William Fulbright immediately urged the president to invade Cuba, angering him with their lack of support for the proposed blockade.

Kennedy's Announcement

At seven o'clock that evening, Kennedy went on television to announce the discovery of the Soviet rockets, emphasizing the surreptitious nature of their deployment. He ignored the Cubans, instead directing his comments to Moscow: any missile fired from Cuba at a target in the Western hemisphere would be construed as an attack by the Soviet Union against the United States and "would require a full retaliatory response upon the Soviet Union." He announced the imposition of a naval "quarantine" and called on Khrushchev to remove the missiles. Shortly thereafter, U.S. Ambassador to the United Nations Adlai Stevenson repeated Kennedy's demand at a special meeting of the Security Council.

On Tuesday, 23 October, the OAS unanimously passed a declaration of support for Kennedy's decision. This, coupled with strong public support from the European allies, damaged Soviet hopes of effecting a split within the OAS and the North Atlantic Treaty Organization (NATO).

The quarantine was drawn by ten o'clock in the morning of 24 October. There were twenty five Soviet or Soviet-chartered ships spread across the Atlantic en route to Cuba. Late in the day it appeared as if some of the ships had altered course.

The next morning two of the ships were allowed through, after U.S. Navy ships had determined they contained no armaments. Later it was announced that twelve of the twenty-five ships had turned back. At the United Nations the Security Council adjourned after an acrimonious and inconclusive debate between Stevenson and his Soviet counterpart, Ambassador Valerian Zorin.

In the morning of 26 October the U.S. Navy boarded a Lebanese-registered freighter that was attempting to cross the blockade. Kennedy had ordered that the first Soviet-chartered ship to be boarded should be of neutral registry, both to signal his seriousness of purpose to Khrushchev as well as to avoid a direct confrontation between Americans and Soviets.

Later that day a member of the Soviet embassy in Washington, Alexander S. Fomin, met with an American television newsman, John Scali, and offered to withdraw the missiles if Kennedy would pledge not to invade Cuba. That evening a letter from Khrushchev addressed to Kennedy arrived via the American embassy in Moscow, which seemed to confirm part of Fomin's message.

Negotiations

Before the United States could respond, Radio Moscow broadcast the following morning a different offer: the Soviet Union would remove the missiles from Cuba provided that the United States remove its Jupiter missiles from Turkey, a demand Ex Comm had feared they would at some point make. The previous two messages from Moscow had omitted mention of Turkey. Robert Kennedy then came up with the idea that ended the crisis:

he proposed that the president agree to the offer made the day before by Fomin, and simply ignore the issue of Turkey. This Kennedy did; a message was sent to Moscow offering that if the Soviet Union removed its missiles from Cuba, the United States would pledge not to invade Cuba and would be prepared to discuss "other armaments." Many years later it was revealed by Bundy that after the Ex Comm meeting on 27 October several committee members went to the White House. Here Dean Rusk proposed that the United States offer to remove the Jupiter missiles from Turkey to help resolve the crisis, a highly secret quid pro quo. Robert Kennedy did, in fact, make the offer to Dobrynin in one of their few meetings, warning that it was a personal guarantee only and would be denied and withdrawn if the Soviets ever revealed it publicly.

On the morning of 28 October Radio Moscow broadcast its acceptance of the terms, and the Cuban Missile Crisis passed the critical stage. The naval quarantine continued for another twenty-three days, until the Soviets dismantled their bases and agreed to remove the IL-28 bombers.

President Kennedy was resolved to end the Cuban Missile Crisis through negotiation. By pledging not to attack Cuba, he allowed the Soviets a way out: if the missiles were seen as being for Cuba's defense, then they were no longer needed. Afterward, relations between the United States and the Soviet Union generally improved, and the following August the Limited Nuclear Test Ban Treaty was signed.

References

Raymond L. Gartoff, *Reflection on the Cuban Missile Crisis,* revised edition (Washington: Brookings Institution, 1989);

Robert F. Kennedy, *Thirteen Days: A Memoir of the Cuban Missile Crisis* (New York: Norton, 1971);

Robert Smith Thompson, *The Missiles of October: The Declassified Story of John F. Kennedy and the Cuban Missile Crisis* (New York: Simon & Schuster, 1992).

– M. B.

SEE ALSO THESE RELATED ENTRIES

Bay of Pigs Invasion, 3; McGeorge Bundy, 1; Fidel Castro Ruz 2; Raúl Castro Ruz, 2; John F. Kennedy, 1; Robert F. Kennedy, 1; Nikita S. Khrushchev, 2; Limited Nuclear Test Ban Treaty, 3; Organization of American States, 3.

Détente

Richard M. Nixon and Leonid Brezhnev toasting their agreement to the SALT I treaty at the May 1972 summit meeting

Détente was President Richard M. Nixon's attempt to move American foreign policy away from the classic Cold War strategy of containing Soviet advances to a more nuanced approach that better reflected contemporary global realities. Nixon, working with Henry Kissinger, his national security adviser later named secretary of state, sought to construct a new global order that treated the United States and the Soviet Union as conservative status quo powers, each with a vested interest in stability. The Soviet Union would be encouraged to participate responsibly in global politics through a combination of strategic and economic rewards. Soviet behavior was linked to promises of economic benefits, which the always-ailing Soviet economy required, and increased international prestige – something the Soviet leadership craved.

Reasons for Détente

Détente as a policy to change Soviet conduct abroad arose from American weakness and served as a response to persistent and deep, even structural, developments that by the late 1960s had eroded U.S. power abroad. The United States had long relied on its nuclear advantage to compensate for the Soviet advantage in conventional weapons. Since their humiliation in the Cuban Missile Crisis of 1962, however, the Soviets had embarked upon a massive buildup of their strategic arsenal and were close to achieving nuclear parity with the United States. What this meant was that the American security guarantees to Western Europe had been gradually neutralized. Furthermore, the rapidly growing economic power of West Germany and Japan had, in relative terms, resulted in a severely weakened American economic position. The post–World War II rebuilding of the Western European and Japanese economies had helped cement political and military ties with the United States, keeping them out of the Soviet orbit. By the mid 1960s, however, international economic disputes had begun to divide the West over balance-of-payments problems, energy policies, and import restriction, to name just a few.

The Vietnam War, from about 1965 on, had also enervated America, economically and politically. President Lyndon B. Johnson had pursued a full-scale though undeclared war while neglecting to meet the war's domestic and international costs. To fund the war without raising taxes, Johnson too often selected the low-cost option in meeting America's other international needs and commitments. By the time the Vietnam conflict had degenerated into a war of attrition with no end in sight, the will of the American public to tolerate containment's extensive and expensive commitments abroad had evaporated.

Application of Policy

Nixon took office in 1969 determined to rethink American post–World War II foreign policy. Nixon needed to normalize relations with the Soviet Union. Both superpowers, he felt, had an interest in confining their rivalry to mutually agreeable spheres. Accepting that the Soviets had reached nuclear parity, Nixon pursued the first arms-control agreements of the Cold War. By agreeing to limit both the numbers and kinds of weapons in their arsenals, both countries were helping guarantee nuclear stability. The Soviets were also permitted to buy American agricultural commodities at what turned out to be excellent prices, a move that generated considerable criticism at home. Needing to extricate the United States from Vietnam, Nixon hoped that pursuing a policy of détente toward the Soviets would also help provide the United States with an avenue for an honorable exit. Although Nixon did succeed in removing the U.S. presence from Vietnam, the Soviets' role in aiding Nixon's efforts is debatable.

Détente was best known for Nixon's rapprochement with China. By the late 1960s, it was clear that the Soviet Union and China regarded each other – and not the United States – as its principal enemy. The normalization of Sino-American relations would be a means for the United States to bring pressure on the Soviets. The United States would hold the balance of power between two implacable enemies.

As Kissinger conceived it, détente represented the philosophical deepening of American foreign policy. The United States needed to move away from the undifferentiated globalism characteristic of Cold War containment and toward a more nuanced understanding of its vital national interests. Advancing these interests could frequently be accomplished through relationships with regimes whose ideologies

and domestic policies were, by American standards, unsavory. In its implementation, the policy of détente tended to place more emphasis on a country's foreign policies rather than its domestic character.

The application of détente by Nixon and Kissinger aroused ever-growing opposition in Congress and in Republican ranks. Kissinger personally carried out foreign diplomacy in such secrecy that not only was the Congress not informed, but neither was the State Department. Congress responded with a series of laws limiting the freedom of action of the executive office in foreign policy. In both Democratic and Republican ranks, the administration's inattention to issues such as human rights and, more generally, the domestic character of regimes led to charges of cynicism. By 1976 Kissinger's role in American foreign policy had become a bitter political issue. In Reagan's unsuccessful bid for the 1976 Republican presidential nomination, he won the support of many conservatives for promising to reverse Kissinger's approach of being indifferent to anticommunist insurgencies.

The delicate maneuvering and balancing that the Nixon-Kissinger diplomacy of détente required were often thwarted by congressional action. Amendments limiting the administration's ability to help South Vietnam and, later, anticommunist forces in Angola and Mozambique prevented Kissinger from using American power as leverage in dealing with the Soviets. Congress also denied the Soviet Union the status of a most favored nation, limiting Kissinger's ability to offer the Soviets carrots in return for a more responsible Soviet foreign policy.

Despite these setbacks, détente was to remain at the core of American foreign policy through the end of the Cold War, largely because its geostrategic underpinnings remained valid.

References:
Coral Bell, *The Diplomacy of Détente: The Kissinger Era* (London: Robertson, 1977);

Michael B. Froman, *The Development of the Idea of Détente: Coming to Terms* (New York: St. Martin's Press, 1991);

John G. Stoessinger, *Crusaders and Pragmatists: Movers of Modern American Foreign Policy* (New York: Norton, 1979).
                                                                – C. S. B.

> SEE ALSO THESE RELATED ENTRIES
> Henry Kissinger, 1; Richard M. Nixon, 1; Vietnam War, 3.

Deterrence

In the context of international politics, policies of deterrence predate the nuclear age. The British deployment of a dominant navy in the nineteenth century and the French cultivation of alliances in the eighteenth century, for example, were ways in which these nations attempted to discourage possible enemies from committing acts of aggression. Deterrence was an essential aspect of the balance of power – a theory based on the political relationships between the European countries of pre–World War I – which held that one country, or alliance, could be politically checked by the show of military strength of another country, or alliance. The goals of the deterring nation are to preserve the peace and maintain political status quo, yet the means to these ends involve preparation for war.

This relationship between political goals and the means by which these goals could be achieved was evident in the Cold War. Both superpowers, the United States and the Soviet Union, aimed their arsenals of nuclear and conventional weapons at the other, preparing to use them if war came about. Each was interested in perpetuating the status quo by maintaining the sovereignty of its postwar sphere of influence, and neither side wished a military confrontation.

The novel destructiveness of nuclear weapons added a new dimension to the traditional concept of deterrence, however. Because both sides understood the dramatic costs of a nuclear war, and because neither side could defend itself against a nuclear attack, nuclear deterrence became as much a deterrence against global war as it was against an act of aggression by either side. Of course, in such an arrangement a side willing to risk nuclear war has a diplomatic advantage over the side unwilling to risk it, as was demonstrated during the confrontation between the United States and the Soviet Union in the Cuban Missile Crisis. After the Cuban Missile Crisis, however, neither side exploited this potential advantage or even approached actively threatening the other. This system of mutual restraint became an important element of nuclear deterrence.

Balance of Terror

The central component of nuclear deterrence since the mid 1960s has been the "balance of terror." Both superpowers were deterred from committing an act of aggression against the other less by the possibility of military, and therefore political, defeat and more by the terror of global nuclear war. As a nuclear strategy, the balance of terror is based on the ability – or "second-strike capability" – of either side to destroy the other's population centers and economic resources, even after being hit with a massive first strike. The balance of terror, however, did not apply to the first two decades of the Cold War. For the first four years after the American atomic bombardment of Japan, there was no balance whatsoever, for the Soviets were unable to test successfully their own atomic bomb until October 1949. To the extent that the United States envisioned active use of its atomic monopoly, American policymakers were deterred by their tiny arsenal of atomic weapons and inadequate means of delivering them in any quantity, and they were further restrained by world opinion.

Shortly after the Soviet test, the United States developed the hydrogen bomb (H-bomb), a weapon with many times the explosive power of the original atomic bomb (A-bomb). By 1953 the Soviets had manufactured their own H-bomb, and by the mid 1950s both sides had deployed hundreds of these immense weapons and had greatly expanded their air forces in order to deliver them.

In the latter part of that decade, the intercontinental ballistic missile (ICBM) began to replace the long-range bomber as the primary means of delivering a nuclear device. The Soviet launch of Sputnik, the first man-made satellite, in October 1957 sparked American fears that Soviet superiority in missile technology could provide the Soviets with a crucial edge in the arms race. U.S. president John F. Kennedy, in his 1960 campaign against Richard M. Nixon, warned Americans of an impending "missile gap" – a lag in one country's missile production relative to that of another country – with which the Soviets could coerce the Western world.

The Cuban Missile Crisis, which took place 16–28 October 1962, was a central event in the genesis of the balance of terror. Kennedy's showdown with Soviet premier Nikita Khrushchev, concluding with the Soviets backing down and removing their missiles from Cuba, illustrated the fallacy of the missile gap: the United States, with superior technology and economic capacity, held a significant nuclear lead over the Soviets. Khrushchev – who would be deposed less than two years later – and the Soviet leadership vowed after the crisis never to be in an inferior nuclear position again. After 1962 the Soviet Union embarked on a massive buildup of nuclear weapons, and by the mid 1960s both sides had the capability of destroying the other. This parity, called mutual assured destruction (MAD), meant that by 1990 each side had deployed some ten thousand nuclear warheads, fitted to land- and sea-based ballistic missiles, cruise missiles, battlefield rockets, and many other weapons.

A unique relationship between the two nuclear superpowers emerged as a result of this balance, affecting all nations. For the first time in the history of international relations, every nation, including the "great powers" themselves, was at the mercy of either of the nuclear giants. If the United States or the Soviet Union wished to destroy a nation completely, it was capable of doing so easily. The concept of sovereign defense – that a nation, by either effectively arming itself or cultivating reliable alliances, can withstand the attack of any other power – therefore was no longer a viable part of defense policy. Offense, in the nuclear age, qualitatively overwhelms defense. Also, the existence of second-strike capability, guaranteed by the deployment of ballistic missiles in elusive submarines and hardened land-based silos, made an attack on either of the two superpowers suicidal. Regardless of how many warheads one side had, it was unable to attack the other without risking the destruction of most of its population. The concept of armed conquest – attacking another nation for rational political and economic gain – therefore no longer threatened the two superpowers, nor indeed any nation that maintained an invulnerable second-strike deterrent and was publicly willing to use it.

Political scientists referred to this relationship between the Soviet Union and the United States as a "stable regime" of mutual deterrence. As long as the two nations were willing to maintain their second-strike capability, war between the two became a highly irrational prospect.

Opposition to this concept of stable regime developed, particularly in the 1980s. Many in the West questioned the morality of threatening mass destruction in order to ensure political stability. In the early 1980s a growing "freeze" movement in the United States and Western Europe, citing the thousands of already-existing warheads, argued for the cessation, or freezing, of the production of new nuclear weapons. Radicals and pacifists argued for unilateral nuclear disarmament, denouncing the deployment of nuclear weapons as immoral.

Vulnerability to nuclear attack within the framework of a stable regime troubled others on the right wing of the political spectrum. It was in order to solve this problem that many Western strategists developed plans for preemptive attacks on Soviet second-strike facilities and created scenarios of winnable nuclear war. Similarly, many argued for a system that would defend against nuclear attack; this concept caught the imagination of President Ronald Reagan, who in 1983 proposed his Strategic Defense Initiative (SDI), also known as "Star Wars."

Counterforce and Countervalue

Within the broader stable regime of nuclear deterrence exist two basic nuclear strategies, generally referred to as "counterforce" and "countervalue." Adherents to counterforce deterrence believe that a nuclear war can remain limited, and thus propose policies that foresee various levels of nuclear conflict. Adherents to countervalue deterrence, on the other hand, doubt that nuclear escalation can be contained, and so propose policies that reject the use of nuclear weapons in limited conflict.

Counterforce nuclear strategy is related to traditional military strategy in two fundamental ways. First, the scale of an attack is proportionate to a rational military objective. The option of using nuclear weapons therefore applies to all sorts of military challenges, and to these challenges different types of nuclear attack are envisioned. The response to a terrorist bombing might be the destruction of a small embankment with one battlefield nuclear weapon; the response to a Soviet invasion of Austria might be a launch of intermediate-range missiles at military targets in Eastern Europe; the response to an all-out nuclear attack on the United States might be a launch of hundreds of submarine-launched ballistic missiles toward Soviet cities. As was the case in prenuclear military strategy – particularly that of military theorist Carl von Clausewitz – a resort to arms is to respond to a particular political or military situation. Second, counterforce strategy focuses on military targets over civilian ones. Once again, this focus is based on the prenuclear conviction that the ultimate objective in a war is to destroy the military capability of one's adversary. Moreover, counterforce strategists also point out that a strategy that emphasizes attacking military targets – such as bases, forts, maritime ships, and industry – has a distinct moral advantage over a strategy of targeting large urban populations. This latter issue reflects an aspect of a military tradition, *jus in bello* (just conduct during war), which condemns the killing of civilians.

The concept of counterforce came to characterize American nuclear strategy in the early 1960s. President Kennedy, along with Secretary of Defense Robert S. McNamara, among others, introduced a nuclear strategy called "flexible response." In contrast to the "massive retaliation" policy of President Dwight D. Eisenhower's secretary of state John Foster Dulles, which threatened nuclear attack over even small offenses, flexible response offered a series of nuclear contingencies for various situations. Inherent to this strategy was the concept of escalation: a nuclear war would escalate gradually and could be stopped short of all-out war. The flexible response was thus considered to be an intrinsically defensive strategy. Some counterforce strategists in the late 1970s moved toward a "countervailing" strategy in which the emphasis shifted from denying one's opponent victory to seeking victory. Countervailing was based on the presumption that a strategy that does not anticipate victory is not credible.

Countervalue deterrence stresses the avoidance of nuclear war rather than its limitations or conformity to traditional elements of rational military strategy. In contrast to counterforce deterrence, countervalue breaks in two decisive ways from traditional strategy. First, countervalue targeting policy is not designed to accomplish rational military objectives. Nuclear weapons are pointed at cities, economic resources, and other targets of "value" to the adversary. The sole objective of these weapons is to deter the adversary from launching a nuclear attack by presenting the adversary with the mere possibility of nuclear retaliation, a new sort of diplomacy that presidential adviser McGeorge Bundy had called "existential deterrence."

Second, an actual countervalue attack – the sudden extermination of millions of civilians – does not conform to any conceivable moral standard. Countervalue deterrence does owe its origins to the no-longer-applicable policy of "strategic bombing," which dictates that, in a modern war waged between industrial nations, bombing cities effectively devastates civilian morale and thus the industry necessary to continue fighting. During World War II, Germany, Great Britain, and the United States all engaged in this form of warfare. A countervalue nuclear attack, however, is not designed to destroy the will of the adversary to continue; rather, it is a reaction to a first nuclear aggression that is not designed to have any moral value, achieve any rational objective, or conform to just-war standards.

Many of the arms-control initiatives between the Soviet Union and the United States in the last three decades were based on the logic of countervalue deterrence. Most prominent of these are the Anti-Ballistic Missile (ABM) Treaty, signed in 1972, which outlawed comprehensive defense systems designed to shoot down incoming missiles, and the Intermediate-range Nuclear Forces (INF) Treaty, signed in 1987, which removed medium-range missiles from Europe. Both treaties, as well as other less successful ones (such as the Strategic Arms Limitations Talks [SALT]), removed incentives for fighting a nuclear war, while leaving the second-strike capabilities that make up countervalue strategy intact.

Some countervalue strategists, most notably McNamara, have argued for a policy of minimum deterrence. Typical countervalue strategy entails deployment of extensive missile systems and a modest range of attack options. Under minimum deterrence, only a relatively small number of missiles are deployed, and their mission is to deter only a direct nuclear attack.

Problem of Credibility

An important, underlying matter that nuclear strategists consider when analyzing deterrence is the problem of credibility. Indeed, whether one's nuclear strategy is believed by the other side is fundamental to the concept of deterrence.

This dilemma has intrigued students of modern strategy, and a "deterrence theory" has emerged in order to deal with both the traditional and unique problems of war in the nuclear age. These theorists argue that American policymakers must convey irrational, immoral tendencies, because a rational, moral actor cannot credibly threaten nuclear war. The necessity to act this way is based upon two fundamental assumptions: the lesson of appeasement and the anarchic nature of international politics.

The lesson of appeasement, which is based most notably on the capitulation of Western leaders to the demands of Adolf Hitler prior to World War II, suggests that peace is threatened when an aggressive nation is allowed to capitalize on its actions. In an era, therefore, when territorial integrity is defended with nuclear weapons – as had been the case with the North Atlantic Treaty Organization (NATO) defense of Western Europe – a deterring nation must convince a potential aggressor that nuclear war will follow an act of aggression, even if such a threat is not politically credible.

The anarchic nature of international politics – based on the general observation that nations value their own sovereignty much more than they value international law and order and that they will not put the former at appreciable risk in order to preserve the latter – suggests that peace is threatened when a nation even suspects that its existence is in jeopardy. In the nuclear era, basic sovereignty is protected, at root, by the threat of nuclear retaliation. A deterring nation thus must convince a potential conqueror that wholesale devastation – in effect, national suicide – will precede surrender, even if such a threat does not appear to be morally credible.

Advocates of counterforce policy point out that countervalue policy is simply a plan for irretrievable suicide; countervalue advocates reply that a belief that a nuclear war can be fought rationally and won is a reckless and incredible policy.

The assumptions that have developed from the experience of bipolar nuclear deterrence between the United States and the Soviet Union are now no longer necessarily relevant. In an increasingly multipolar world the familiar and stable regime of nuclear deterrence gives way to something unforeseen.

References

David Gates, *Non-offensive Defence: An Alternative Strategy for NATO?* (New York: St. Martin's Press, 1991);

Dean Wilkening, *Strategic Defenses and First-strike Stability* (Santa Monica, Cal.: Rand, 1986).

– C. C.

SEE ALSO THESE RELATED ENTRIES

McGeorge Bundy, 1; Cuban Missile Crisis, 3; John Foster Dulles, 1; Flexible Response, 3; Intermediate-range Nuclear Forces Treaty, 3; John F. Kennedy, 1; Massive Retaliation, 3; Robert S. McNamara, 1; Missile Gap, 3; Mutual Assured Destruction, 3; Sputnik, 3.

Dien Bien Phu

From March to May 1954 Dien Bien Phu, a French garrison in Vietnam, was besieged by communist Vietminh forces under the command of General Vo Nguyen Giap. When the French surrendered on 7 May they had been effectively driven from all of French Indochina. France agreed to give its colonies independence. Indochina was divided into Laos, Cambodia, and Vietnam, with Vietnam further partitioned into a communist-dominated North and a Western-oriented South.

The siege of Dien Bien Phu also marked a turning point in the role of the U.S. military in Vietnam. President Dwight D. Eisenhower resisted the urgings of his military advisers to intervene to save the French. Even so, after the surrender of Dien Bien Phu the United States would assume sole responsibility for maintaining the political and military viability of South Vietnam against the efforts of the North to unify the country under communist domination.

References

Vo Nguyen Giap, *Dien Bien Phu* (Hanoi: Foreign Languages Publishing House, 1984);

Peter Macdonald, *Giap: The Victory in Vietnam* (New York and London: Norton, 1993);

Edgar O'Ballance, *The Indochina War, 1945–1954* (London: Faber, 1964).

C. S. B.

SEE ALSO THESE RELATED ENTRIES
Dwight D. Eisenhower, 1; Vo Nguyen Giap, 2.

Domino Theory

Applied mostly to Asia and Latin America, the domino theory was an important concept in post–World War II U.S. foreign policy, influencing foreign-policy thinking from the late 1940s to the late 1960s. The theory's name served as a metaphoric description of the spread of communism around the world; believers in the domino theory likened nations to a row of dominoes: if the first domino toppled – becoming communist controlled – the fall of the other dominoes – neighboring countries – became inevitable. The task of U.S. policy, then, was to prevent the fall of the first domino. The domino theory was used to explain the sense of alarm with which successive administrations viewed the coming to power of communist leaders in countries in which the United States had no vital interests, the most striking example being U.S. involvement in the Vietnam War. It was argued that the importance of such countries was not intrinsic; rather, they were important in that they were the "first domino" in their region, and in that their fall to communism would soon be followed by the fall of their neighbors.

Reference

John Lewis Gaddis, *Strategies of Containment: A Critical Appraisal of Postwar American National Security Policy* (New York: Oxford University Press, 1982).

SEE ALSO THESE RELATED ENTRIES
Vietnam War, 3.

Eisenhower Doctrine

The Eisenhower Doctrine, announced by U.S. president Dwight D. Eisenhower on 5 January 1957, pledged military and economic aid to any Middle Eastern country needing help in resisting communist aggression. Marking another escalation in the Cold War, the doctrine was intended to check the increase of Soviet influence in the Middle East – the supply of arms to Egypt by communist countries, primarily the Soviet Union, and the increasingly strong Soviet support given the Arab states.

The doctrine also partially served as a response to the 1956 Suez Canal crisis, in which French, British, and Israeli forces launched an attack on Egypt. The British and the French had hoped to reclaim the Suez Canal from Egypt, and the Israelis sought to reopen the Straits of Tiran. Eisenhower and U.S. secretary of state John Foster Dulles angrily condemned the aggression as a violation of the United Nations charter. Internationally humiliated and pressured by both the United States and the Soviet Union to withdraw, the British and French forces left the canal zone, the Israelis removed their land forces from Egypt's Sinai peninsula, and a United Nations peacekeeping force was placed between the Israeli and Egyptian armies. Hoping to counter the impression that the United States and the Soviet Union acted in collusion in denouncing the attack, Eisenhower proclaimed that the United States would use armed forces to protect the independence of any Middle Eastern country seeking American help. The United States gained considerable influence in the Middle East by lessening European presence in the region, offering help to beleaguered Middle East states, and confronting the advance of Soviet influence in the region.

The Eisenhower Doctrine did not effect radical change in U.S. foreign policy, however, for the Truman Doctrine had pledged similar support to

Greece and Turkey ten years earlier. The doctrine was simply an outgrowth or continuation of the U.S. policy of containment, which called for resistance around the globe to any extension of the Soviet sphere of influence. The Eisenhower Doctrine was an important step in developing the policy of containment and direct intervention, and it was invoked less than two years after its conception when, in July of 1958, U.S. troops were sent to protect the Lebanese government from attack by leftist rebels. The doctrine helped lay the foundation for policies that would lead to increased American military intervention in "hot spots" around the world and culminate in American involvement in Vietnam.

References

Dwight D. Eisenhower, *The Papers of Dwight David Eisenhower* (Baltimore: Johns Hopkins University Press, 1970);

William Bragg Ewald, *Eisenhower the President: Crucial Days, 1951–1960* (Englewood Cliffs, N.J.: Prentice-Hall, 1981);

Richard A. Melanson, ed., *Reevaluating Eisenhower: American Foreign Policy in the 1950s* (Urbana: University of Illinois Press, 1987);

Donald Neff, *Warriors at Suez: Eisenhower Takes America into the Middle East* (New York: Linden/Simon & Schuster, 1981).

–J. H.

SEE ALSO THESE RELATED ENTRIES
Containment, 3; John Foster Dulles, 1; Dwight D. Eisenhower, 1; Gamal Abdul Nasser, 2; Suez Crisis, 3.

Escalation

In his book *On Escalation: Metaphors and Scenarios* (1965), escalation was defined by Herman Kahn as "an increase in the level of conflict in international crisis situations." The expansion may be gradual or sudden, qualitative or quantitative, or both. Kahn described the increasing levels of violence in war as "rungs" on an "escalation ladder." Kahn's scenario posited forty-four such rungs, with nuclear weapons being introduced on the fifteenth rung and "spasm war" being the forty-fourth, and most destructive, level.

The concept of escalation gave rise to a derivative concept, that of "escalation dominance." The burden of decision making during a nuclear exchange is always found on the side contemplating escalation to the next level of violence. It was theorized that the country enjoying a favorable balance of nuclear capabilities relative to its adversary would be more willing to escalate. For example, a country with a robust civil defense system to protect its citizens from nuclear devastation – assuming such defense were at all possible – would be less hesitant to escalate the nuclear exchange to a level on which both sides would target each other's cities.

References

Lawrence Freedman, *The Evolution of Nuclear Strategy* (New York: St. Martin's Press, 1981);

John Lewis Gaddis, *Strategies of Containment: A Critical Appraisal of Postwar American National Security Policy* (New York: Oxford University Press, 1982);

Herman Kahn, *On Escalation: Metaphors and Scenarios* (Baltimore: Penguin, 1965);

Thomas C. Schelling, *Arms and Influence* (New Haven: Yale University Press, 1966);

Thomas C. Schelling, *The Strategy of Conflict* (New York: Oxford University Press, 1960).

–B. F.

SEE ALSO THESE RELATED ENTRIES
Deterrence, 3; Strategic Defense Initiative, 3.

European Economic Community

The European Economic Community (EEC) was established by the March 1957 Treaty of Rome which came into force on 1 January 1958. The organization's name was shortened to the European Community (EC) ten years later. The community's central decision-making bodies are the European Commission, council of ministers, the European Council, and the European Parliament. Until June 1979 members to the European Parliament were appointed by the parliaments of the member states. Since then members are elected in direct elections in each country. The original treaty gave the council of ministers the authority to make binding decisions by a majority vote. When Charles de Gaulle came to power in France, he objected to this surrender of sovereignty, and in January 1966 the decision-making mechanism was changed: if a member country deemed a certain decision by the council to be of "fundamental importance," that decision had to pass by a unanimous vote.

Member states of the EC committed themselves to abolish tariffs and other obstacles to free trade in order to create an integrated market. In 1979 the EC adopted a new currency, the European Currency Unit (ECU), to make trading and exchange of services among member states easier to calculate and administer. Although the EC made impressive progress toward economic integration, there is still considerable resistance in European countries to give up control over their economic life to the EC institutions in Brussels. The latest example is Britain's decision in the fall of 1992 to withdraw from the Exchange Rate Mechanism (ERM).

The EC envisioned itself not only as a framework for economic integration, but also as a vehicle for greater political cooperation among the Western European nations. In 1981 the German foreign minister Hans-Dietrich Genscher and his Italian counterpart Emilio Colombo presented a plan for a greater political integration of the Western European nations. Although the EC never formally adopted the Genscher-Colombo plan, the organization took steps to increase political cooperation among its members. The move toward greater political integration has been even slower than the move toward economic integration, and opposition to it even stiffer. In Denmark voters rejected a proposal European leaders agreed upon at the Maastricht summit, while in France supporters of the treaty barely eked out a slim victory over opponents.

The process of European economic and political integration was helped by the presence of a common adversary, the Soviet Union. It is unclear how the end of the Cold War will affect this process.

References

Merry Bromberger, *Jean Monnet and the United States of Europe* (New York: Coward-McCann, 1969);

Douglas Brinkley and Clifford P. Hackett, eds., *Jean Monnet: The Path to European Unity* (New York: St. Martin's Press, 1991).

– B. F.

SEE ALSO THESE RELATED ENTRIES
Charles de Gaulle, 1; Edward Heath, 1; Jean Monnet, 1.

Federal Republic of Germany

The Federal Republic of Germany (FRG) was originally the state comprising the American, British, and French occupation zones of defeated Nazi Germany. These western zones – the communists being in control of eastern Germany and East Berlin – adopted a constitution in May 1949, establishing the FRG under a multiparty system. Free elections were held in August, and Konrad Adenauer was elected chancellor.

Until the early 1970s, West Germany regarded itself as a temporary measure: when the Cold War resolved itself, it would reabsorb the territories held by Germany in 1938. Until then, West Germany was to be considered the only German state to speak legitimately on behalf of all Germans. Following the opening of the Berlin Wall in November 1989, the East German state collapsed and in October 1990 was absorbed into the Federal Republic.

The Federal Republic today comprises the territory of the old East and West Germanies. It has renounced any claim to territory once held by Germany that is today part of Poland and the Czech Republic.

References

Willy Brandt, *My Life in Politics* (New York: Viking, 1992);

Lawrence L. Whetten, *Germany's Ostpolitik: Relations Between the Federal Republic and the Warsaw Pact Countries* (New York: Oxford University Press, 1971).

– C. S. B.

SEE ALSO THESE RELATED ENTRIES
Konrad Adenauer, 1; Berlin Crisis, 3; Berlin Wall, 3; Willy Brandt, 1; Ostpolitik, 3.

Finlandization

Finlandization is a term used to describe the phenomenon whereby one nation dominates and neutralizes another without overt military conquest. The pressure may be imposed through a variety of means, such as the implicit threat of force from the proximity of shared boundaries, attempts to influence the politicians and the public-policy debates in a country, and the manipulation of the press. This process may be slow and insidious, but over time it can fundamentally shift the balance of power.

Coined by policy adviser Richard Lowenthal during the Richard M. Nixon administration – which sought to defeat the Mansfield Resolution, a proposal to withdraw American troops from Western Europe – the term "Finlandization" expressed the fear of Western European countries that they too would fall prey to the steady increase in power that the Soviet Union had exerted over Finland after the end of World War II. The Mansfield Resolution stirred profound fears among the member countries in the North Atlantic Treaty Organization (NATO) over what would happen if America were to withdraw its military protection, and after 1969 the phrase was widely used in debates on international affairs.

Finlandization sought to describe Finnish post–World War II foreign-policy conduct. After the war the Soviet Union had begun to exert increasing influence in that country. Finland had followed what political scientist James Rosenau called "adaptive politics" toward the Soviet Union. This notion of adaptation is derived from biology, where organisms faced with a change in their environment either adapt or die.

In adapting, Finland voluntarily extended deference to the Soviet Union and did not enter alliances with any state without Soviet permission.

Thus, in 1947, Finland had to refuse the American offer of assistance through the Marshall Plan because the Soviet Union would not permit it. Finland also balanced its trade between East and West, even though trade with the West was more lucrative. In exchange for membership in the European Economic Community (EEC), Finland was required by the Soviets to establish a formal relationship with the COMECON countries. The Soviets also preferred to control Finland's most critical import – oil. The Finns received two-thirds of their energy supplies from the Eastern-bloc nations.

The Soviet Union retained the right to grant approval or disapproval of certain political leaders in Finland. The Finnish press rarely criticized the Soviet Union, instead usually accepting and promoting the Soviet position on most issues. Finland was committed to side with the Soviet Union if war were to break out in Scandinavia or in all of Europe. Finland maintained only a small, mostly Soviet-equipped army inadequate for border defense.

As the 1970s progressed, the popularity of Finlandization as a concept grew, especially among European commentators. Critics charged that it was no more than repackaged Cold War rhetoric, used by hawks to promote a military buildup. Those who propounded it used their arguments to justify the arms race. Unless the West kept up militarily with the Warsaw Pact nations, the reasoning went, Europe risked falling under Soviet influence.

These fears were fed by several parallel developments: the increasing military strength and political clout of the Soviet Union; the growing militancy of the Third World; and the collapse of the Bretton Woods system, which had governed postwar economic relations successfully from 1944 to about 1969. Europe also felt vulnerable because the previous twenty-five years had witnessed Europe's role on the world stage eclipsed by two superpowers – the United States and the Soviet Union. Prior to World War II, Europe had been the focal point of world politics. For the nations of Western Europe the war was followed by the loss of colonial possessions and by economic exhaustion.

Western Europe was forced to turn to the United States for protection. The Marshall Plan – underwritten by the United States – had been instrumental in rebuilding the continent. The economic prosperity that followed, however, was not accompanied by a European assumption of a greater political and military role in world affairs. A sense of dependency on the United States developed among many Western European nations. Crises in the postwar period were viewed as problems for the Americans and the Soviets to iron out.

Europe had also witnessed the rise of the welfare state and the diminishing importance of class structure during the postwar period. Political power had passed from the aristocrats to the lower and middle classes. The democratization and materialization of European society made the idea of war increasingly unacceptable.

During the 1970s, however, Europeans began to doubt the United States' resolve to protect them. The Soviet Union had achieved nuclear parity with the United States, while retaining its military nonnuclear superiority. The United States had lost the Vietnam War, and American politicians called for "retrenchment." European fears of Finlandization were fueled against this backdrop. Members of NATO doubted they could face the Soviet challenge without U.S. support and were afraid they would be transformed into neutralized states in the shadow of Soviet might.

Political scientists who believed in the threat of Finlandization argued that what happened in Finland could happen to the rest of Western Europe. They, however, had their critics who claimed that that was an impossibility, that what happened in Finland was a unique case because of shared borders and a history of former dominion over Finland by the Soviets.

References

Adam Garfinkle, *"Finlandization": A Map to A Metaphor* Monograph, number 24 (Philadelphia: Foreign Policy Research Institute, 1978);

Hans Mouritzen, *Finlandization: Towards a General Theory of Adaptive Politics* (Aldershot, U.K.: Avebury, 1988);

Fred W. Riggs, ed., *International Studies: Present Status and Future Prospects* (Philadelphia: American Academy of Political and Social Science, 1971);

James N. Rosenau, *The Study of Political Adaptation* (London: F. Pinter / New York: Nichols, 1981).

– M. G.

SEE ALSO THESE RELATED ENTRIES
Bretton Woods Conference, 3; Domino Theory, 3; Linkage, 3.

Flexible Response

In rejecting the nuclear-weapons-oriented New Look policy and massive retaliation strategy of the administration of President Dwight D. Eisenhower, the administration of President John F. Kennedy chose a strategy of flexible response in countering the Soviet threat. The term was borrowed from General Maxwell D. Taylor's *The Uncertain Trumpet* (1960).

The main purpose of the New Look policy was to lower the cost of protecting U.S. interests by decreasing conventional military spending and increasing American reliance on nuclear weapons, even if that reliance entailed the risk of either doing nothing to counter Soviet transgressions or responding disproportionately to the threat. The main purpose of flexible response, therefore, was to minimize the risks of doing nothing or doing too much, even at a higher financial cost. In articulating the importance of the new deterrence policy, Secretary of Defense Robert S. McNamara de-clared, "We must be in a position to confront [the Russians] at any level of provocation with an appropriate military response."

The main elements of flexible response were characterized by decreasing reliance on nuclear weapons — while modernizing the U.S. missile fleet — increasing conventional capabilities, creating and strengthening counterinsurgency capabilities, solidifying alliances, and giving new importance to non-military elements of foreign policy, such as economic aid.

References

Lawrence Freedman, *The Evolution of Nuclear Strategy* (New York: St. Martin's Press, 1981);

John Lewis Gaddis, *Strategies of Containment: A Critical Appraisal of Postwar American National Security Policy* (New York: Oxford University Press, 1982).

— B. F.

SEE ALSO THESE RELATED ENTRIES
Deterrence, 3; Massive Retaliation, 3; New Look Policy, 3.

Gaither Committee

In April 1957 President Dwight D. Eisenhower heeded the advice of the National Security Council (NSC) and commissioned a study by the Science Advisory Commission of the Office of Defense Mobilization to determine the value of various measures to protect the United States against nuclear attack. Eisenhower's decision came in response to growing concern about the possibility of a surprise Soviet nuclear attack. Known as the Gaither Committee for its chairman, H. Rowan Gaither, the group completed its report, entitled "Deterrence and Survival in the Nuclear Age," in November 1957.

Citing evidence that Soviet defense spending might double that of the United States by the end of the 1960s, the committee found that America risked becoming vulnerable to a Soviet nuclear first-strike if it failed to adopt three measures. First, the United States needed to enhance its own offensive missile capability by accelerating the production of intercontinental ballistic missiles (ICBMs) and submarine-launched ballistic missiles (SLBMs), and by deploying intermediate range ballistic missiles (IRBMs) in Europe. Second, the committee recommended that the United States protect its own retaliatory forces through a variety of methods, including deploying antiballistic missiles (ABMs), hardening missile silos, dispersing air force bases, and improving warning systems. Finally, the report called for the adoption of extensive civil defense measures. The committee, estimating that these measures would cost $55 million over a five-year period, saw no other way to protect the nation.

One month before the completion of the report, on 4 October 1957, the Soviet Union launched Sputnik, the first man-made satellite. The dramatic event, which suggested that the Soviet Union had achieved a decisive advantage in ballistic missile technology, seemed to confirm the validity and urgency of the Gaither Committee report.

President Eisenhower adopted some of the committee's less costly measures but refused to implement all of its recommendations. He reconfigured the deployment of Strategic Air Command bases across the continental United States, began deploying IRBMs in Europe, and accelerated the development of the American ICBM.

H. Rowan Gaither, chairman of a special committee created by President Dwight D. Eisenhower to study American readiness for nuclear attack

Eisenhower disagreed with much of the report's analysis. He felt that the committee underestimated the political and military significance of American missile deployments in Europe, which posed an offensive threat to the Soviet Union and increased the number and variety of targets the Soviets needed to attack to execute a disarming first strike. Secretary of State John Foster Dulles convinced the president to reject the proposed civil defense measures, arguing that such measures would send a message to America's allies that the United States was adopting a "Fortress America" strategy, leaving Europe to defend itself. Finally, Eisenhower rejected the committee's assessment of the Soviet ballistic missile program. The U-2, a high altitude American reconnaisance jet, had begun conducting secret flights over the Soviet Union, revealing that the

Soviet missile program was less developed than previously thought.

References

Lawrence Freedman, *The Evolution of Nuclear Strategy* (New York: St. Martin's Press, 1981);

John Lewis Gaddis, *Strategies of Containment: A Critical Appraisal of Postwar American National Security Policy* (New York: Oxford University Press, 1982);

Morton H. Halperin, "The Gaither Committee and the Policy Process," *World Politics,* 13 (April 1961).

– B. D. K.

SEE ALSO THESE RELATED ENTRIES
Dwight D. Eisenhower, 1; Herman Kahn, 1; Sputnik, 3; Albert J. Wohlstetter, 1.

Geneva Summit

The Geneva summit was the first meeting between the leaders of the United States and the Soviet Union since the Potsdam Conference ten years earlier. In early 1955 Nikita S. Khrushchev, solidifying his position of leadership in the Soviet Union during the two years after Joseph Stalin's death in March 1953, moved to make a summit meeting with U.S. president Dwight D. Eisenhower possible. He called for a foreign-ministers meeting to discuss an end to the Soviet occupation of Austria, and accepted some of the U.S. disarmament proposals without the usual Soviet preconditions, such as the abolition of nuclear weapons.

The two leaders met in Geneva, Switzerland, at the beginning of summer. The new Soviet flexibility regarding Austria and certain arms-control ideas, and Eisenhower's Open Skies proposals, engendered what journalists were quick to call the "spirit of Geneva," meaning a relaxation of the Cold War tensions between the superpowers. Although the summit did not achieve agreements between the two sides on substantive issues, the two nations – for a while, at least – appeared to be withdrawing from the brink of war.

Reference

McGeorge Bundy, *Danger and Survival: Choices about the Bomb in the First Fifty Years* (New York: Random House, 1988).

– B. F.

SEE ALSO THESE RELATED ENTRIES
Dwight D. Eisenhower, 1; Nikita S. Khrushchev, 2; Open Skies Policy, 3; Potsdam Conference, 3.

Glassboro Summit

From 23 to 25 June 1967, U.S. president Lyndon B. Johnson and Soviet premier Alexsei Nikolaevich Kosygin held a summit meeting in Glassboro, New Jersey. During their two days of talks, the two leaders discussed the Arab-Israeli conflict, the Vietnam War, and the superpowers' efforts at reaching arms-control agreements.

The Middle East Crisis

The ostensible reason for Kosygin's trip to the United States was to lead a special Soviet delegation to the United Nations at a time when that international organization was searching for a permanent settlement to the Arab-Israeli conflict. The UN had turned its attention to the Middle East following the Six Day War fought between the Arabs and Israelis earlier that month. According to Johnson, after his administration became aware of Kosygin's impending visit, the Soviets began hinting "that Kosygin would welcome a meeting" between the two powers, "preferably in New York." Glassboro was selected as the meeting site because of its proximity to New York and Washington.

The two leaders failed to reach a consensus on how to work for peace in the Middle East. During the final press conference Kosygin called for the Israelis to withdraw to their prewar boundaries. Johnson indicated that he and Kosygin were "a long way from total difference" on the conflict because the Soviets had acknowledged, unlike several Arab states, that each nation in the region had a right to exist. But the two leaders displayed important differences over Vietnam.

Arms Control

Although they remained far apart on regional matters, Johnson and Kosygin did make limited progress on arms-control issues. At the meeting Kosygin did not seem impressed by U.S. defense secretary Robert S. McNamara's argument that an extensive Soviet antiballistic missile (AMB) system would force the United States to build additional intercontinental ballistic missiles (ICBMs). Instead, the premier reasserted the long-standing Soviet position that ABMs were "defensive" weapons and that any effort to limit them would have to be dealt with as part of a comprehensive accord covering "offensive" weapons − meaning ICBMs − as well.

Lisa Steiner / Pix

Soviet Premier Alexsei Kosygin and President Lyndon B. Johnson briefing the press on the outcome of the Glassboro summit

According to John Newhouse, the "Glassboro experience may have moved Kosygin and some of his Kremlin colleagues to do what Washington thought they had already been doing − looking hard at the problems of stable deterrence. Glassboro, as [former Secretary of State Dean] Rusk suggests, may have been the start of SALT for the Russians."

In addition to serving as a precursor to the SALT negotiations, the Glassboro summit also enabled the two superpowers to register their progress toward negotiating the worldwide Nuclear Non-Proliferation Treaty (NPT). As a result of a decision made at the summit, the superpowers tabled a draft accord in Geneva later that summer. Their efforts ultimately produced the NPT in 1970. Today, 140 countries adhere to the accord, which is designed to slow the spread of nuclear weapons.

Although no formal agreements were reached during the Glassboro summit, the superpowers made progress on arms-control matters, giving the summit its historical importance.

References
Raymond L. Garthoff, *Detente and Confrontation* (Washington, D.C.: Brookings Institution, 1985);

Andrei Gromyko, *Memoirs* (London: Hutchinson, 1989);

Seymour H. Hersh, *The Price of Power* (New York: Summit, 1983);

Lyndon B. Johnson, *The Vantage Point* (New York: Holt, Rinehart & Winston, 1971);

Henry Kissinger, *White House Years* (New York: Little, Brown, 1979);

John Newhouse, *Cold Dawn: The Story of SALT* (New York: Holt, Rinehart & Winston, 1973);

Richard M. Nixon, *R N: The Memoirs of Richard Nixon* (New York: Grosset & Dunlap, 1978);

Gerard C. Smith, *Doubletalk* (New York: Doubleday, 1980).

–J. C. R.

SEE ALSO THESE RELATED ENTRIES
Lyndon B. Johnson, 1; Alexsei Nikolaevich Kosygin, 2; Robert S. McNamara, 1. Nuclear Proliferation, 3.

Group of 77

The Group of 77 (G-77) is a formal coalition of Third World states that was created to represent and articulate Third World interests regarding trade and development. Active mainly in multilateral forums and negotiations between the advanced industrial countries and the less developed countries, the G-77 operates within the framework of the United Nations and has been closely identified with the UN Conference on Trade and Development (UNCTAD). The G-77 was largely responsible for formulating and advocating the New International Economic Order (NIEO).

Founded in 1965 by seventy-seven Third World countries, the G-77 has its origins in the first UN Conference on Trade and Development in 1964, referred to as UNCTAD-I. The idea of the conference was to use the numerical advantage of the less developed countries (LDCs) and multilateral forums, such as the United Nations, to push through proposals beneficial to LDCs in the areas of international trade and economic development.

Constituted as a permanent coalition, the G-77 is made up of regional groupings, or blocs, such as the Africa bloc, to which member countries first belong. The supreme organ of the G-77 is the ministerial meeting, which outlines strategies and policies. The ministerial meeting also elects a president for the group, who is usually a foreign minister from the host country. Membership in the G-77 overlaps substantially with that of the Non-Aligned Movement (NAM) – some of the founding members of the group include Algeria, Argentina, Egypt, Mexico, and Iraq. By 1982 the G-77 consisted of 125 member states. A division of labor exists between the G-77 and the NAM, whereby the former addresses itself to transnational economic and social issues and the latter to security and political issues.

The objectives of the G-77 can be divided into two categories. First and foremost, it seeks changes in the international trading system and economic relations which the group believes will result in a more just and less exploitative international economic system and one which significantly narrows the gap between the rich advanced industrial countries (AICs), the so-called North, and the poor LDCs, or South. The group also focuses its efforts on reforming international organizations, such as the United Nations, as well as international financial institutions, such as the International Bank for Reconstruction and Development (IBRD, or World Bank) and the International Monetary Fund (IMF).

The group has argued that the existing international economic system works to the detriment of the less developed countries. It has criticized the international trading system – which is governed by the General Agreement on Tariffs and Trade (GATT) – for not having special provisions for trade in primary (agricultural and mineral) products, which, the G-77 argues, suffer from deteriorating terms of trade relative to manufactured products. The G-77 has called for an international agreement that would govern primary products and grant discriminatory preference for such products. In order to redress international inequality and reform what was considered to be an unjust and exploitative international economic system, a collection of proposals – that came to be known as the NIEO – was adopted at the Sixth Special Session of the UN General Assembly. A key element in the NIEO was a call to create an integrated commodity program; its purpose was to prevent primary products' price fluctuations and finance commodity agreements. The NIEO also contained proposals made to improve access into AIC markets as well as proposals that would allow greater LDC control over multinational corporations. Some scholars assert that the G-77 has sought nothing short of the radical transformation of the existing market-oriented international economic system, interpreting its proposals as an attack on the liberal international order.

In seeking reforms in international organizations and financial institutions, the G-77 did not simply confine itself to redressing what it viewed as international inequality and exploitation; it also sought a larger role in international economic affairs and their management. The group sought greater decision-making powers in institutions whose decisions and actions generally affected the entire global economy. The G-77 succeeded in having the UNCTAD established as a permanent agency of the United Nations. It also successfully proposed the Generalized System of Preferences, a trading agreement whereby LDC products are imported into AIC markets with minimal or no duties. The group has called for greater Third World representation in the World Bank and the IMF, proposing that the IMF adopt the UN General Assembly (UNGA) voting system of one nation, one vote.

The G-77 has been an advocacy forum for the Third World, and it was formed in order to strengthen the collective-bargaining capacity of the LDCs. It has represented the LDCs in nearly all international economic negotiations and has preferred multilateral negotiations under the direction of the UNGA. Its proposals have ranged from increased economic aid for LDCs to collective debt relief. The G-77 proposals, however, have been opposed and rejected by the leading AICs, such as the United States and Japan, and because of its size and heterogeneity the group itself has lacked a consensus in forging policy. As a collection of countries with different ideological, political, and economic makeup and interests, the G-77 has been prone to divergence of interests and policies among the members themselves, and not just with respect to the AICs. Despite these shortcomings the G-77 has been relatively successful in its advocacy of reforms in the international economic system.

References

Jagdish Bhagwati and John Gerard Ruggie, eds., *Power, Passions, and Purpose: Prospects for North-South Negotiations* (Cambridge: Massachusetts Institute of Technology Press, 1984);

Willy Brandt and others, eds., *North-South: A Programme for Survival* (London: Pan Books, 1980);

Karl Sauvant, *The Group of 77: Evolution, Structure, Organization* (Dobbs Ferry, N.Y.: Occana, 1981).

–J. R.-S.

SEE ALSO THESE RELATED ENTRIES
Non-Aligned Movement, 3.

Intermediate Nuclear Forces Treaty

The Intermediate Nuclear Forces (INF) Treaty was signed by U.S. president Ronald Reagan and Soviet general secretary Mikhail Gorbachev on 8 December 1987 and entered into force some six months later, following U.S. Senate ratification on 27 May 1988. The treaty banned the production and flight testing of all ground-launched, intermediate- and short-range missiles and called for the dismantling of the 1,752 existing Soviet missiles and 859 American missiles.

Origins of INF

The North Atlantic Treaty Organization (NATO), founded in 1949, has relied since the mid 1950s on the use of nuclear forces to protect Western Europe against Soviet attack. The members of NATO, still recovering from World War II and unable to match Soviet conventional manpower levels, decided in December 1954 to adopt a strategy calling for first use of nuclear weapons in the event of a Soviet conventional attack. The United States enjoyed a considerable nuclear advantage over the Soviet Union, and nuclear weapons were much cheaper than conventional forces. These considerations contributed to the decision in the late 1950s to deploy intermediate-range ballistic missiles (IRBMs) in Europe. The Thor and Jupiter IRBMs deployed in Italy, Turkey, and Great Britain were capable of hitting targets in the Soviet Union. These missiles, viewed as a temporary measure, were dismantled in the early 1960s once the United States had begun to deploy intercontinental ballistic missiles (ICBMs).

The Soviets responded to the American IRBMs with their own missiles, placing as many as 709 SS-3, SS-4, and SS-5 missiles in the territory of Warsaw Pact countries by the mid 1960s. The Soviet IRBM buildup and the overall development of the Soviet nuclear program undermined the credibility of the American strategy of massive retaliation, which called for the United States to respond to a Soviet attack in Europe with a massive nuclear strike against Soviet cities. To offset Soviet nuclear-force gains and to enhance the credibility of NATO's nuclear threat by ensuring a measured re-

action to any type of Soviet aggression, in 1967 NATO adopted the strategy of flexible response.

In the mid 1960s the Soviet Union began to build intercontinental ballistic missiles at a furious pace. In 1964 the American ICBM arsenal of 980 missiles was roughly five times larger than the Soviet force, but by 1971 the land-based Soviet arsenal had grown by a factor of eight and was now more than 50 percent larger than the American ICBM force. But the size of the Soviet arsenal was still offset by the qualitative superiority of the American weapons. Recognizing the existence of rough strategic parity and interested in avoiding a costly and potentially destabilizing arms race, the United States and the Soviet Union concluded the Strategic Arms Limitation Treaty (SALT I) in 1972.

While European leaders were generally pleased to see superpower relations improve, the West Germans, among others, worried that the United States had not done enough in SALT I to limit the threat posed to Europe by Soviet IRBMs, which they believed had become more important as a result of strategic parity. The Soviets had wanted SALT I to limit such American "forward-based systems" (FBS) as the intermediate range submarine-launched ballistic missiles assigned to NATO and the nuclear-capable aircraft stationed in Europe. The United States, however, insisted on focusing SALT I exclusively on intercontinental missile systems. The conflict subsided temporarily when the United States and the Soviet Union agreed to defer debate on FBS to the next round of strategic arms limitation talks, scheduled to begin after the completion of SALT I.

But European insecurity continued to grow in the mid 1970s, as the Soviet Union, largely in response to SALT I, began deploying SS-20 missiles. The Soviet Union also replaced several hundred aging and unsafe SS-4s and SS-5s with SS-11 ICBMs, but the SALT I ceilings, which counted SS-11s as ICBMs, soon discouraged this practice. In 1976 the Soviet Union started to field the intermediate-range SS-20, an accurate, multiwarhead, mobile missile that appeared to enable the Soviets to negate flexible response. The credibility of

NATO strategy, it was argued, hinged on the existence of viable military options at each level of escalation, but the SS-20, which erased whatever advantage NATO had in medium-range forces, seemed to make a wartime NATO escalation impractical.

The United States failed to address European concerns during the SALT II negotiations, further undermining European confidence. The November 1974 Vladivostok summit, which produced a tentative agreement that became the basis for the SALT II accords, again deferred consideration of medium-range systems to the next scheduled set of negotiations, SALT III. Meanwhile the Soviet Union continued to improve the quality of its ICBMs, an effort not restricted by SALT I. Soviet qualitative gains were so considerable that by the mid 1970s a growing number of American conservatives were asserting that the Soviets, not satisfied with parity, were on the verge of achieving nuclear superiority.

Thus, by 1977 European leaders were worrying that the Soviet Union had achieved parity, if not superiority, in the strategic realm and escalation dominance in the European theater, and would successfully decouple Europe from the U.S. strategic nuclear guarantee. The American threat to resort to nuclear force in the event of a Soviet attack in Europe was no longer credible. On 28 October 1977, in a speech before the International Institute of Strategic Studies in London, West German chancellor Helmut Schmidt drew public attention to European worries. British and German members of the NATO nuclear planning group subsequently began to press for an "evolutionary upward of adjustment" in NATO's nuclear forces to recouple Europe to the U.S. strategic arsenal.

European doubts about U.S. reliability were further heightened by President Jimmy Carter's mismanagement of alliance relations during his first years in office. Determined to avoid past mistakes, Carter began to work closely with European heads of state to reach agreement on new U.S. INF deployments. In January 1979 NATO leaders had decided to install 572 medium-range missiles in Europe by 1983. The systems consisted of 108 Pershing IIs to replace the existing 108 Pershing Is in West Germany, and 464 ground-launched cruise missiles (GLCMs) to be placed in Great Britain, Italy, Belgium, the Netherlands, and West Germany. The number was somewhat arbitrary, but NATO members did not want to exceed 600. Several hundred land-based missiles, it was felt, would recouple the U.S. strategic arsenal to Europe but avoid a second arms race with the So-

viet Union, which had deployed roughly 700 intermediate-range missiles in Europe.

In the spring of 1979 German and Dutch officials, concerned with political opposition to the new nuclear deployments, requested that the alliance develop arms control guidelines for the SALT III talks on intermediate-range forces. Responding to the request, NATO leaders agreed that the SALT III negotiations should try to reduce but not eliminate the planned deployments. On 12 December 1979 NATO defense and foreign ministers announced the Dual-Track decision. The first track called for the deployment of the Pershing IIs and GLCMs, and the second affirmed the alliance's willingness to work for a negotiated settlement.

INF Negotiations

The failure of the SALT II accords to win ratification in the U.S. Senate created concern among Europeans that SALT III and the negotiations over intermediate-range forces would never take place. In October 1980 the Carter administration, under pressure from European governments, initiated separate negotiations on intermediate-range forces, but these brief negotiations were suspended for the November 1980 elections. When the Ronald Reagan administration took office in January 1981, it undertook a thorough examination of American arms-control policy, further delaying the resumption of the talks, which finally convened at the end of November 1981. This first set of negotiations proved highly contentious. Neither the United States nor the Soviet Union was terribly interested in reaching agreement. The Americans put forward negotiating positions designed to ensure the introduction of the missiles, while the Soviets took measures to halt the U.S. deployments.

In the early years of the Reagan administration Richard Perle, the assistant secretary of defense for international security policy and the administration's point man on arms-control, played a dominant role in shaping the American INF negotiating position. Doubtful of the utility of arms control agreements with the Soviet Union, Perle convinced President Reagan to adopt the Zero Option, which called for a total ban on all European intermediate-range nuclear forces. This meant that the United States would forgo its deployments and that the Soviet Union would dismantle its SS-20s and remaining SS-4s and SS-5s. Perle did not believe that the Soviets would accept the proposal's unprecedented asymmetrical cuts in forces, but reaching an agreement was a low priority. He also recognized the rhetorical value of the Zero Option, an idea created by the West German peace movement and adopted by the German Social Democratic party. In a way typical of the public diplomacy that marked the first set of INF negotiations, Reagan announced the Zero Option in a speech to the National Press Club simulcast live to Europe.

Soviet general secretary Leonid Brezhnev promptly responded with his own public proposal for a moratorium on all INF deployments in Europe, freezing British, French, and Soviet forces and precluding the introduction of new American systems. The Soviets had long contended that negotiations on European missiles had to include British and French weapons, a condition the British, French, and Americans all rejected. Not to be outdone rhetorically, Brezhnev also indicated that once interim reductions had taken place he was prepared to accept the Zero Option for intermediate-range missiles and tactical nuclear weapons. In addition to efforts at the negotiating table, the Soviet government provided considerable funds through the East German Communist party to several Communist-front "peace" organizations in West Germany. These efforts intensified the public outcry in the West against deployment and produced considerable consternation among West German politicians.

Once the negotiations were under way, Paul H. Nitze, the chief American negotiator, and Yuli Kvitsinsky, his Soviet counterpart, worked out a tentative arrangement for cuts in INF systems that became known as the "Walk in the Woods" agreement. The deal permitted the United States to deploy seventy-five cruise missile launchers and the Soviets to maintain seventy-five SS-20s in Europe and freeze SS-20 deployments in Asia. The arrangement was eventually rejected by both President Reagan and the Soviet leadership. Perle was instrumental in convincing Reagan to reject the offer, even though the president had been receptive to it initially.

As the deployment date for the Pershing IIs neared, both countries began to increase the flexibility of their negotiating positions. State Department officials led by Richard R. Burt, assistant secretary of state for European and Canadian affairs, and European governments recognized that the Zero Option was viewed by the European public as a mechanism to ensure the Pershing deployment and worked to alter the American position. They put considerable pressure on the president to accept equal limits for Soviet and U.S. missiles above zero but below NATO's planned level of 572 missiles. This proposal, known as the Interim Solu-

tion, originated in Germany during the 1983 general election and won the support of West German chancellor Helmut Kohl and British prime minister Margaret Thatcher, who was also facing the possibility of a general election in 1983. Both Kohl and Thatcher feared that their strong support for the deployment of the NATO missiles would cost them votes. In a show of support, President Reagan formally put forward the Interim Solution at a press conference on 30 March 1983.

The Soviets rejected the American offer, which permitted deployment of U.S. missiles and did not take British and French systems into consideration. The Soviets, however, had also become more flexible. New Soviet leader Yuri Andropov made one concession after another in 1983 but stopped short of accepting the deployment of American missiles. In October, one month before the collapse of the talks, he announced he was prepared to reduce Soviet INF warheads to 420, bringing them down to the combined British and French level.

On 22 November 1983 the West German parliament narrowly approved the stationing of the Pershing IIs; one day later the Soviet Union withdrew from the INF talks in protest, threatening never to return. NATO governments claimed victory in successfully carrying out the introduction of the missiles, but the failure to produce a negotiated settlement damaged the broad European defense consensus that had supported the NATO nuclear deterrent for thirty years. Soviet propaganda successfully exploited the common European perception of President Reagan as a trigger-happy Hollywood cowboy itching for a nuclear showdown in Europe. Communist front organizations helped spawn the most massive demonstrations in Europe since World War II. Between 1981 and 1983 protests across Europe attracted hundreds of thousands of participants. One victim of the divisive debate over NATO's nuclear strategy was Chancellor Schmidt's Center-Left coalition government, which fell in October 1982 when the centrist Free Democrats formed a new government with Helmut Kohl's Christian Democrats.

On 12 March 1985 Mikhail Gorbachev, a reform-minded leader from the Sevastopol region of the Soviet Union, became the Communist party's general secretary. With a flair for the dramatic and an ability to capture the imagination of the Western public, Gorbachev helped transform Cold War superpower relations. His negotiating techniques were as successful as they were unorthodox. During the INF negotiations, for instance, he dropped every major Soviet demand, an unprecedented move in the annals of U.S.-Soviet relations. In the end he accepted a treaty that was more demanding than the initial Reagan Zero Option. It is unlikely the superpowers would have agreed to eliminate all medium- and short-range nuclear systems without Gorbachev's presence at the negotiations.

The INF talks reconvened in Geneva in March 1985, along with two other sets of talks, the Strategic Arms Reduction Talks (START) and the Nuclear and Space Talks. Gorbachev's first dramatic proposal came ten months later, on 15 January 1986. He agreed to accept the Zero Option, proposing to eliminate all U.S. and Soviet medium-range missiles in Europe over a period of five to seven years. It was not clear that these cuts were linked to the other parts of his proposal, which called for strategic-arms reductions and limits on President Reagan's Strategic Defense Initiative (SDI), a space-based ballistic-missile defense program. Gorbachev made his most concerted effort to gain concessions on SDI at the Reykjavik Summit in October 1986, offering an agreement along the lines of the Zero Option but also including limits on shorter-range systems. But Reagan refused to link cuts in any missile systems to limits on SDI.

Gorbachev decided to delink an INF agreement from SDI once he became convinced that Reagan would not agree to limitations on SDI. On 28 February 1987 Gorbachev announced he was prepared to sign "without delay" a separate INF agreement to eliminate all Soviet and American medium-range missiles in Europe within five years. Gorbachev was motivated by three goals. The removal of the Pershing IIs from Europe had long been a Soviet aim. The fast-flying, highly accurate Pershing IIs would have played an important role in any NATO attempt to eliminate, or "decapitate," Soviet leadership by threatening to hit Soviet command centers. The elimination of medium-range systems also coincided with the Soviet military's desire to confine any conflict in Europe to conventional weapons, in which the Soviets enjoyed considerable numerical advantages. And Gorbachev recognized that his acceptance of the Zero Option would create considerable debate within the NATO alliance, distancing the United States from its NATO allies.

The timing of Gorbachev's announcement, coming just two days after the release of the Tower Commission report on the Iran-contra scandal, was not insignificant. The report criticized the president for his failure to manage his National Security Council staff, which had engaged in illegal activities diverting profits from Iranian arms sales to the

contras, a U.S.-backed Nicaraguan guerrilla force. With his popularity at an all-time low, President Reagan keenly eyed progress in the INF negotiations as a way to restore public confidence in his presidency.

Recognizing that Gorbachev was finally willing to negotiate on favorable terms, the Reagan administration sought to draft an agreement that would gain the support of two-thirds of the U.S. senators needed for ratification. This meant that the treaty had to contain stringent verification procedures, including provisions for on-site inspections. On 4 March, less than one week after delinking the INF talks from SDI, Gorbachev agreed in principle to on-site verification, paving the way for the most comprehensive arms control verification package ever formulated by the superpowers.

Among other compliance provisions, the INF Treaty provided for preliminary inspection of designated sites to verify the number of missiles to be destroyed and "close-out" inspections to ensure that the missiles had been removed and the facilities razed. Another provision permitted on-site observation during the destruction of missiles and allowed for continued inspections over a thirteen-year period of all shipments leaving designated missile facilities in each country. The treaty also called for "short-notice inspections" at designated sites during the same thirteen-year period. Like the SALT agreements, the INF Treaty prohibits interference with "national technical means," the satellite and electronic signal reconnaissance used to verify arms-control agreements.

In addition to the verification procedures, the Reagan administration designed the general provisions of the treaty to discourage cheating. The Zero Option was expanded to the so-called "global double," which made the ban on medium-range missiles global and extended it to short-range missiles. The administration believed that the global double ban, the complete elimination of medium- and short-range missiles, would discourage any Soviet plan to conceal medium-range missiles illegally. If the Soviets were permitted to maintain INF forces in Asia or similar short-range missiles in Europe, they could continue flight-testing these systems. The testing of these systems would give the Soviets confidence in the operational reliability of its concealed medium-range systems. As Max M. Kampelman, chief U.S. negotiator in Geneva, commented, "A big concern of the Senators will be verification. It will be far easier to verify a treaty that achieves a global zero outcome than one that leaves some shorter-range missiles in Europe and SS-20s in Asia."

While the global zero idea received support from American allies, especially in Asia, the global double proved as divisive as the initial 1979 Dual-Track decision. Following Gorbachev's acceptance of the Zero Option in late February, West German chancellor Kohl joined French prime minister Jacques Chirac and British prime minister Margaret Thatcher in calling for President Reagan to negotiate reductions in Soviet short-range forces but to maintain NATO's short-range deployments.

When Reagan overruled the European request, accepting the double, Kohl's Center-Right coalition government nearly collapsed. Foreign minister and coalition partner Hans-Dietrich Genscher, hoping to win votes in the upcoming 17 May state elections, was prepared to accept the double. But Defense Minister Manfred Woerner rejected the proposal, arguing that the elimination of all short-range systems would leave Europe vulnerable to Soviet conventional forces. He wanted instead to convert the medium-range Pershing IIs to short-range Pershing IBs and replace Germany's seventy-two Pershing IAs with the IBs. Woerner was not alone in his views; at the first sign of serious American interest in the double, Alfred Dregger, a conservative member of the German parliament, proposed that the government seek Soviet support for a plan to reunify and neutralize Germany. After nearly six weeks of deliberations, Kohl reluctantly decided on 23 May to support the double, and after bringing disgruntled conservatives on board, he announced his coalition's acceptance on 2 June.

Ratification of the INF Treaty

After gaining allied consent, the Reagan administration put the final touches on the INF Treaty before the scheduled signing at a Washington summit meeting on 8 December 1987. Although ratification took five months, Senate passage of the treaty was never seriously in doubt. The delay was partly the work of hard-line conservative senators opposed in principle to arms control with the Soviet Union. Chief in this group was Republican senator Jesse Helms of North Carolina, who offered a series of amendments to alter the treaty. Helms and his supporters claimed that the Soviet Union had violated arms-control agreements frequently in the past and that it was naive to assume that it would comply with the INF Treaty. In addition they complained that the treaty was marred by countless drafting errors. This group of senators eventually recognized that they could not defeat

the treaty, but they hoped their arguments would persuade the administration to move more cautiously in the START negotiations. Others who entertained doubts on ratification were not prepared to speak out against a popular treaty and an equally popular president with impeccable anticommunist credentials.

More moderate legislators had other reasons for delaying treaty ratification. Several senators, including Democrat Sam Nunn of Georgia, the leading authority in the Senate on defense matters, were concerned with the military implications of the agreement. They feared that a total ban on medium- and short-range nuclear systems would leave Western Europe vulnerable to Soviet conventional attack. But these senators worried even more that failure to ratify the popular treaty would create a major crisis in NATO.

Senator Nunn also played a role in formulating the one substantive amendment to the treaty, pushed by Democrat Joseph R. Biden, Jr., of Delaware and Senate majority leader Robert C. Byrd, Democrat from West Virginia. The amendment, known as the "Biden condition," dealt with congressional treaty-interpretation powers and the Reagan administration's attempt to reinterpret the 1972 Anti-Ballistic Missile (ABM) Treaty. In 1985 the administration began to assert that the ABM Treaty did not limit SDI, although many senators felt it did. To support its claim, the administration argued that it was the president's prerogative to revise the interpretation given Congress by members of President Richard M. Nixon's administration during the ABM Treaty ratification hearings in 1972. The Democratic Senate leadership, fearing that the president was attempting to usurp the Senate's constitutional power to interpret treaties, offered an amendment to the INF Treaty stating that no president could later depart from the meaning of the INF Treaty as presented by the administration during ratification. The amendment was adopted by a vote of seventy-two to twenty-seven, receiving a significant number of Republican votes.

The final INF Treaty, which set two arms-control precedents – asymmetrical reductions in forces and extensive on-site verification procedures – was ratified by a ninety-three to five vote.

References

Jonathan Dean, *Watershed in Europe: Dismantling the East-West Military Confrontation* (Lexington, Ky.: Lexington Books, 1987);

Michael R. Gordon, "INF: A Hollow Victory?," *Foreign Policy* (Fall 1987): 159–179;

Richard A. Melanson, *Reconstructing Consensus: American Foreign Policy since the Vietnam War* (New York: St. Martin's Press, 1991);

David N. Schwartz, *NATO's Nuclear Dilemmas* (Washington, D.C.: Brookings Institution, 1984);

Strobe Talbott, *Deadly Gambits: The Reagan Administration and the Stalemate in Nuclear Arms Control* (New York: Knopf, 1988);

Pat Towell, "INF Treaty: Star Vehicle for Political Agendas," *Congressional Quarterly Weekly Report,* 30 January 1988, pp. 192–197;

Towell, "Panel Weighs INF Politics, Payoffs for NATO," *Congressional Quarterly Weekly Report,* 6 February 1988, pp. 259–264.

– B. D. K.

SEE ALSO THESE RELATED ENTRIES

Flexible Response, 3; Gaither Committee, 3; Mikhail Gorbachev, 2; Massive Retaliation, 3; Paul H. Nitze, 1; North Atlantic Treaty Organization, 3; Richard Perle, 1; Ronald Reagan, 1; Reykjavík Summit, 3; Eduard Amvrosiyevich Shevardnadze, 2; Strategic Arms Limitation Talks, 3.

Iran-Contra Affair

The Iran-contra affair was the effort by officials in the administration of President Ronald Reagan to evade congressional restrictions on aiding the contras in their guerrilla war against Nicaragua's Marxist Sandinista government. The scheme, which called for U.S. weapons to be secretly sold to Iran with the proceeds funneled to the contras, became the most embarrassing setback to the Reagan presidency. Details continue to emerge, years after the plan became public.

In 1983 and 1984 Congress passed several Boland amendments prohibiting Reagan from aiding the contras for the purpose of overthrowing the Sandinistas, who, with Cuba's backing, had wrested control of Nicaragua from Anastasio Somoza Debayle in July 1979. Reagan authorized his National Security Council (NSC) to find ways to continue to channel funds to the guerrillas. Oliver North, a Marine colonel, was placed in charge.

Beginning in June 1984 North and the NSC staff secretly raised $34 million for the contras from other countries. Another $2.7 million was contributed by American donors. North concealed his work from other government officials who then testified before Congress that the White House was obeying the Boland amendments. When word

leaked out in 1985 about the scheme, North and his superiors testified before Congress that the NSC was obeying both the letter and spirit of the law.

Arms Sales

In the summer of 1985 Israeli officials proposed that American missiles be sold to Iran in exchange for the release of seven American hostages held in Lebanon by groups friendly to Iran. The plan was also pitched as a potential gesture of goodwill toward allegedly pro-Western Iranian moderates. Despite that the plan violated laws governing the export of arms and contradicted U.S. policy regarding Iran, Reagan approved it over the objection of the State and Defense Departments.

Again, North and his NSC staff took over operational control. In August and September 1985 Israel sold 504 American antitank missiles to Iran. The Iranians released one American hostage. In November Iran bought 80 antiaircraft missiles; no hostages were released, however.

The sales did generate considerable profit, as the Israelis were charging the Iranians top dollar. North realized that he could divert the proceeds to the contras instead of turning them over to the

U.S. government as the law required. North pushed ahead with more sales, and, by May 1986, he and his various associates had generated some $8 million in profits. When no more hostages were released, however, Reagan's former national security adviser, Robert McFarlane, made a secret trip to Tehran to complain that Iran was not living up to its end of the deal. He was told that the Iranian government had never guaranteed the hostages' freedom, that it had only promised to attempt to arrange it.

The sales continued into November 1986 with only two more hostages being freed. On 3 November 1986 a Lebanese newspaper broke the story about the arms-for-hostages swap, and Congress convened a committee to investigate. Congress found it could never know all the facts, since so many documents had been destroyed. An accounting revealed that the deals generated nearly $48 million. Some $17 million went to the contras, the rest to a variety of uses including commissions and personal profits and expenses. In early 1993 a special prosecutor, Lawrence Walsh, is still investigating the deals and the later cover-up.

References:
Michael A. Ledeen, *Perilous Statecraft: An Insider's Account of the Iran-Contra Affair* (New York: Scribners, 1988);

Ann Wroe, *Lives, Lies, and the Iran-Contra Affair* (London & New York: Tauris, 1991).

– C. S. B.

SEE ALSO THESE RELATED ENTRIES
George Bush, 1; Ronald Reagan, 1; George Shultz, 1.

Iron Curtain Speech

The "iron curtain" speech, given by former British prime minister Winston Churchill on 5 March 1946 in Fulton, Missouri, while on a goodwill tour of the United States with President Harry S Truman, played an important role in persuading the American public of the need for a firm stance toward the Soviet Union. The speech served to highlight the differences between those in the West who believed cooperation with the Soviets was possible and those who did not. From 1945 to 1947 many Americans tended to support continued cooperation between the Allies; Churchill's speech was an attempt to counter these sentiments.

His speech created a sensation around the world. Communist publications everywhere denounced it, and on 13 March Soviet leader Joseph Stalin contemptuously likened Churchill to the Nazis. But the speech accomplished what Churchill intended: it succeeded in convincing the bulk of the American public that the postwar Soviet menace could only be countered by a strong Anglo-American alliance.

The speech was imbued with Churchill's purple rhetoric. Using vivid imagery to describe the communist menace in Europe, Churchill declared that "From Stettin in the Baltic to Trieste in the Adriatic an iron curtain has descended across the continent." From then on, the phrase *iron curtain* became widely used to describe the barriers erected by the Soviet Union after World War II to seal itself and Eastern Europe from contact with the West.

The speech was delivered only seven months after the conclusion of World War II. Memories of the war were still fresh in everyone's minds. Capitalizing on this, Churchill told the Missouri audience that the Soviet Union presented a dangerous threat to peace, which could only be resisted by a highly armed Anglo-American "fraternal association." He dwelled on the twofold menace of Soviet expansionism and communist "fifth columns," and he warned his audience of the dangers of drift and inaction: "Do not let us take the course of letting events drift along until it is too late."

For Churchill, these themes were not new. He had been advocating the ideas of steadfastness and resolve in the face of aggression for over two decades in a prolific output of books, articles, and speeches. The target of the iron curtain speech – the Soviet Union, rather than Germany – was also not new, as Churchill had been suspicious of Soviet intentions before and during the war. Churchill's speech carried a great deal of credibil-

Terry Savage

President Harry S. Truman and former prime minister Winston Churchill with Franc L. McCluer, president of Westminster College in Fulton, Missouri, where Churchill delivered his "iron curtain" speech on 5 March 1946

ity in America given his personal popularity and leadership during World War II, his long career on the international scene, and his early concern with Hitler's threat.

Until his retirement in 1955 Churchill was to continue to expound on the themes of his iron curtain speech. He maintained his view that the United States was the natural and invaluable ally of Great Britain, while the Soviet Union remained their natural enemy. He felt that meaningful negotiations with Moscow could only be conducted from the position of superior Anglo-American strength.

References

Charles E. Bohlen, *The Transformation of American Foreign Policy* (New York: Norton, 1969);

Fraser J. Harbutt, *The Iron Curtain: Churchill, America, and the Origins of the Cold War* (New York: Oxford University Press, 1986);

Joseph P. Lash, *Roosevelt and Churchill, 1939–1941: The Partnership that Saved the West* (New York: Norton, 1976).

– M. G.

SEE ALSO THESE RELATED ENTRIES
Winston Churchill, 1; Containment, 3; Truman Doctrine, 3.

Jackson-Vanik Amendment

The Jackson-Vanik amendment became a divisive issue in American politics in the early 1970s. Written by Democratic senator Henry M. Jackson of Washington and sponsored in the House of Representatives by Democratic congressman Charles A. Vanik of Ohio, the amendment linked granting most-favored-nation (MFN) trading status to the loosening of emigration policies in countries with nonmarket economies. The amendment undermined Secretary of State Henry A. Kissinger's policy of détente and severely strained U.S.-Soviet relations.

Linkage

The 1968 presidential election, which brought Richard M. Nixon to power, produced a shift in U.S. policy toward the Soviet Union. Nixon and his then national security adviser, Henry A. Kissinger, attempted through the policy of détente – or reduced tensions – to transform the Soviet Union's understanding of international relations, creating a new global order in which the Soviets played a stabilizing role. In implementing détente Kissinger adopted the tactic of "linkage," tying negotiations on particular issues to the successful resolution of other problems. The Soviets, for instance, had long sought access to Western credit and the relaxation of American trade barriers to bolster their sagging economy. Kissinger, believing that increasing Soviet economic dependency on the West would decrease Soviet incentive to destabilize the balance of power, was ready to offer the Soviet Union economic concessions in exchange for Soviet foreign-policy concessions. Kissinger was particularly interested in exploiting the Soviet desire for a trade agreement to gain more favorable conditions for the withdrawal of American forces from Vietnam.

On 18 October 1972 the two nations concluded a broad trade agreement, addressing difficulties that had hindered U.S.-Soviet trade relations since World War II. The Soviets agreed to pay off $722 million in lend-lease debts by 1 July 2001; the United States offered the Soviets subsidized grain sales, MFN trading status, and Export-Import Bank credits. MFN status gave Soviet exports the same tariff status as goods from friendly countries by reducing high tariffs imposed after World War II. Export-Import Bank credits increased the flow of American loans to finance the Soviet import of American goods. The agreement was expected to triple U.S.-Soviet trade during its three year duration but would not significantly affect overall U.S. commerce since trade between the two countries amounted to less than 1 percent of total American trade.

In response to the trade agreement, Senator Jackson, an outspoken critic of détente policies, proposed his own form of linkage. He offered an amendment to a trade reform bill linking the granting of MFN status and credits to communist nations to a Soviet lifting of restrictions and taxes on emigration. In effect, the amendment required the Soviet Union to increase the emigration of Soviet Jews. In January 1973 Congressman Vanik introduced a similar amendment in the House of Representatives.

Support for Amendment

The Jackson-Vanik amendment was supported by a diverse and unusual coalition of conservatives, liberals, and special interest groups. The liberal human-rights lobby supported the amendment because it would improve human-rights conditions for Soviet Jews. George Meany, head of the American Federation of Labor and Congress of Industrial Organizations, threw the support of organized labor behind the amendment, arguing that once the Soviet Union used American technology, gained through the proposed economic concessions, to increase the efficiency of the Soviet economy, Soviet leaders would not keep their side of the agreement on emigration. Conservatives also supported the amendment, believing that Jackson-Vanik had the potential to undo détente, which they rejected as wishful thinking that might unintentionally aid the Soviets. A totalitarian society such as the Soviet Union, they argued, was incapable of transformation. The amendment also drew strong support from the Jewish-Israeli lobby, interested in alleviating the plight of Soviet Jews and increasing the Jewish population of Israel. As a sponsor of the amendment, Jackson sided both with conservatives and the Jewish lobby, but he also hoped to use the publicity generated by the amendment to promote his campaign for the 1976 democratic nomination for the presidency.

Trade Reform Act

On 10 April 1973 the Nixon administration sent Congress a formal, comprehensive trade bill, called the Trade Reform Act of 1973. The act, which gave unprecedented authority to the president to alter U.S. tariffs and trade barriers, did not contain provisions regarding Soviet emigration policy. Nixon and Kissinger hoped that Soviet leader Leonid Brezhnev's recent lifting of the education tax that had been levied against Jewish applicants for emigration would appease supporters of the Jackson-Vanik legislation. Despite the administration's hopes the House of Representatives adopted the amendment by a vote of 272 to 140 in December 1973, incorporating Jackson-Vanik into the Trade Reform Act.

Kissinger, whom Nixon had appointed secretary of state in August 1973, began a complex set of trilateral negotiations among the administration, the supporters of the amendment, and the Soviets. He met with Senators Jackson, Abraham A. Ribicoff, Democrat from Connecticut, and Jacob K. Javits, Republican from New York, who demanded that the Soviets raise annual emigration totals to sixty thousand. On 8 August 1974 the Soviet ambassador in Washington, Anatoly Dobrynin, gave assurances that the Soviet government was prepared to allow fifty-five thousand Jews to emigrate annually. Ribicoff and Javits were prepared to accept this offer, but Senator Jackson, still hoping to use the issue to help his presidential campaign, refused to agree, until pressure from his supporters convinced him to accept the Soviet offer.

Having resolved the substantive issue, Kissinger next sought a means to convey Soviet assurances to Congress. His problem was that the Soviets would not agree to declare publicly their willingness to accede to American demands in altering Soviet domestic policy. Nor would Jackson agree to tacit Soviet assurances that would deny him the publicity that he sought. Kissinger finally arranged an exchange of public letters. President Gerald R. Ford had a letter drafted, stating that he had received Soviet assurances – not commitments – to the effect that the Soviet Union would place no obstacles on Jewish emigration except in cases of national security. Jackson, for his part, prepared a letter which stipulated that the number of Jewish emigrants should correspond to the number of applicants but that sixty thousand annually should serve as a minimum. On 18 October 1974 Ford, Kissinger, Vanik, Jackson, and Javits met for a televised letter-signing ceremony on the south lawn of the White House. Jackson had indicated earlier that he understood the need not to embarrass the Soviets, but during the ceremony he chose to exploit the television coverage, all but declaring the Soviet leaders had capitulated to him.

During Kissinger's next visit to Moscow, Brezhnev conveyed his anger at Jackson's performance. To calm Moscow, Kissinger argued that he had no prior knowledge of the content of Jackson's letter. Soviet foreign minister Andrei Gromyko nonetheless presented Kissinger a letter that explicitly rejected Jackson's interpretation of Soviet assurances. Believing that the Soviets were still prepared to allow a sixty-thousand emigration limit, Kissinger kept Gromyko's letter secret. Testifying to Congress in early December to allay congressional fears, Kissinger stated that if he asserted that a formal agreement on Jewish emigration existed between the Soviet and U.S. governments, the Soviets would repudiate his statement immediately. Kissinger intended to imply there was an informal agreement, although Gromyko's secret letter was proof to the contrary.

Kissinger's strategy worked initially, and Jackson supporters closed ranks behind the Trade Reform Act. On 18 December 1974, however, House-Senate conferees began deliberations on the Trade Reform Act and on another bill, dealing with the Export-Import Bank. The latter contained an amendment sponsored by Democratic senator Adlai Stevenson III of Illinois, and supported by Jackson, setting a four-year ceiling of $300 million on Export-Import Bank credits to the Soviet Union and an additional $40 million subceiling on loans that the Soviets could use for energy exploration. The Stevenson restrictions significantly limited Export-Import Bank loans to the Soviet Union, which had amounted to $469 million during the previous fifteen months. The amendment included a provision enabling Congress to increase Export-Import Bank credit levels. Stevenson's and Jackson's aim was to ensure that Congress, and not Henry Kissinger, in whom they had lost confidence, would have effective veto power over U.S.-Soviet trade relations.

Failure of Diplomacy

On the same day TASS, the Soviet News agency, reported that "leading circles ... categorically reject as inadmissible any attempts from whomever they come, to interfere in affairs which are entirely within the internal competence of the Soviet State." The Soviets also released the previously secret 26 October letter from Gromyko to Kissinger, in which the Soviet foreign minister explicitly stated that the Soviet government rejected Jackson's interpretation of Soviet policy regarding emigration. Soviet leaders were unwilling to be party to Kissinger's secret diplomacy, fearing that they would be expected to fulfill obligations that they had never agreed to in the first place.

The Trade Reform Act with the Jackson-Vanik amendment passed on 20 December by a vote of 72 to 4 in the Senate and by 343 to 36 in the House of Representatives, and the Export-Import Act was signed on 21 December. On 1 January 1975, however, the Soviet Union notified the United States that it would not honor the provisions of the 1972 trade agreement, an announcement that had been foreshadowed by the earlier TASS report and the release of the Gromyko letter.

Overall, Henry Kissinger's attempt to extract political concessions from the Soviet Union for American economic concessions failed. Following the Soviet withdrawal from the trade agreement, Soviet-American trade declined measurably. On 30 January 1975 the Soviets canceled their wheat purchases, and on 17 February they concluded a $2-billion five-year agreement with the United Kingdom to purchase British technology using British credits. The Soviets also received $10 billion in additional credits from other Western nations.

Almost all of the parties involved in the Jackson-Vanik amendment lost in some measure. The Jewish lobby, Israel, and Soviet Jews helplessly watched on as emigration figures fell from thirty-five thousand in 1973 to thirteen thousand in 1975. The Ford administration, and particularly Kissinger, lost significant credibility in the eyes of the Soviet Union because it had been unable to convince Congress to support its policies. The only winners were conservatives who never liked the Nixon-Ford-Kissinger policy of détente.

References

Dan Caldwell, *American Soviet Relations* (Westport, Conn.: Greenwood, 1981);

Raymond Garthoff, *Detente and Confrontation* (Washington, D.C.: Brookings Institution, 1985);

Henry A. Kissinger, *White House Years* (Boston: Little, Brown, 1979);

Henry A. Kissinger, *Years of Upheaval* (Boston: Little, Brown, 1982)

Paula Stern, *Water's Edge: Domestic Politics and the Making of American Foreign Policy* (Westport, Conn.: Greenwood, 1979).

– B. D. K.

KGB

The KGB (*Komitet gosudarstvennoy bezopasnosti* – Committee for State Security) is the civilian arm of Russian intelligence responsible, before the demise of the Soviet Union in December 1991, for domestic security and foreign intelligence gathering. It was also actively engaged in propaganda and subversion outside the Soviet Union to further the interests of the Soviet state.

From its inception in 1917, the Soviet Union emphasized tight control over its citizens through pervasive intelligence gathering. Before 1954 intelligence, counterintelligence, and domestic security functions were carried out by different organizations, the most famous of which were the *Cheka,* which became the GPU in 1922, and the NKVD,

which succeeded the GPU in July 1934, its responsibilities absorbed later by the MGB. The MGB was replaced by the KGB.

The chairman of the KGB was a member of the Politburo and reported directly to the general secretary of the Communist party of the Soviet Union. The organization consisted of four chief directorates, seven independent Directorates, and six independent departments, each of which was further divided into suborganizations and departments. The most important elements of the KGB were the first chief directorate, which was responsible for all foreign operations, including electronic intelligence gathering and human espionage, propaganda, subversion, and counterespionage; the Bor-

177

der Guards Chief Directorate, responsible for patrolling the borders of the Soviet Union; and the Armed Forces Independent Directorate, which was responsible for the political loyalty of the armed forces – including the nuclear rockets forces – and the GRU. The Armed Forces Independent Directorate was responsible for the safety of the Soviet leadership.

KGB personnel, including its director, took part in the failed August 1991 coup against Soviet president and general secretary Mikhail Gorbachev. Since the demise of the Soviet Union, Russian president Boris Yeltsin has moved to place reform-minded civilians at the head of the organization, whose future in Russia is far from clear.

References:

John J. Dziak, *Chekisty: A History of the KGB* (Lexington, Mass.: Lexington Books, 1988);

Peter Deriabin, *KGB: Masters of the Soviet Union* (New York: Hippocrene, 1990).

            – B. F.

> **SEE ALSO THESE RELATED ENTRIES**
> Mikhail Gorbachev, 2; Joseph Stalin, 2.

Korean War

The Korean War is the forgotten fight of the Cold War. It settled nothing. After inflicting millions in casualties, the fighting ended in 1953 with an armistice that left both sides about where they were when the war began three years before.

The Dividing of Korea

Korea began to take shape as an early Cold War battleground for the Soviet Union and the United States in the weeks following the end of World War II. Following an agreement reached by President Harry S Truman and Soviet leader Joseph Stalin at the Potsdam Conference in Germany in July 1945, Japanese troops in Korea south of the 38th parallel were to surrender to the Americans. Japanese troops to the north were to surrender to the Soviets.

The 38th parallel quickly became the de facto boundary between an American-dominated South Korea and a communist-dominated North Korea. Though both the United States and the Soviet Union had pledged themselves to support a united and independent Korea, neither was prepared to see the other power dominate the Korean peninsula. The United Nations (UN) sought to resolve matters by calling for general elections to establish a single national government. The Soviets refused to permit the elections in the North if certain pro-American parties were allowed to participate. The elections went ahead in the South in 1948, and a new government under Syngman Rhee was duly declared by the UN as the only lawful government in Korea. The Soviets responded by having Kim Il-Sung, leader of the Korean Communist party, appointed premier and declared his government as the only lawful one.

Over the next two years the two Koreas built up their militaries and began cross-border attacks. Though the United States considered Korea to have an increasingly important role in the emerging Cold War rivalry with the Soviets, Truman nevertheless withdrew all American combat troops, giving Korea military and economic aid in their stead. The South was thus unprepared for the full-scale invasion launched by the North on 25 June 1950.

UN Intervention

The following day the United Nations intervened. It branded North Korea an aggressor and called on its members to help South Korea. On 27 June Truman ordered U.S. forces in the region into combat. Ground forces under the supreme command of General Douglas MacArthur arrived on 4 July.

The North Korean advance continued unchecked for the next few weeks. By the time UN forces had arrived in strength, North Korea had

Lt. Gen. William K. Harrison, Jr. (seated at left), and Gen. Nam Il (seated at right) signing the armistice agreement that ended the Korean War, 27 July 1953

overrun almost all of the South. MacArthur's forces were reduced to occupying a small perimeter around the southeastern port of Pusan. On 15 September 1950 MacArthur made a daring amphibious landing at Inchon, in the far north of South Korea. It was far behind North Korean lines, and the landing took the North by surprise. Communist troops retreated or surrendered by the thousands as MacArthur began a rapid advance up the Korean peninsula. By 1 October he was in control of all of South Korea and his UN troops began to cross the 38th parallel to take the war to the North. Their advance continued almost unchecked. By the end of October, the first of MacArthur's largely American army was approaching the Yalu River, North Korea's border with China.

The war now took on an added dimension. To allay Chinese suspicions that the UN coalition was nothing more than an American effort to impose a U.S.-backed government on North Korea, Truman ordered MacArthur not to deploy American troops along the Yalu. Truman's relations with MacArthur were rocky at their best, and MacArthur did little to hide his contempt for the president. Nor did Truman allow him to bomb targets in China, a restriction which enraged MacArthur. On 26 November, shortly after MacArthur started his final offensive to crush the North Koreans, China entered the war on a grand scale. Chinese troops,

eventually numbering 1.2 million, quickly forced the outnumbered forces under MacArthur into a retreat that soon became a rout before MacArthur managed to regain control. By the end of January 1951 the fighting slowed down to a war of attrition. It was now a strategic stalemate, each side just about where they were when the war started.

MacArthur soon found himself in the middle of an increasingly bitter dispute with Truman regarding military operations and U.S. foreign policy in general. The United States was simply unwilling to commit its resources to a major war in Asia, most likely including war with China, to win in Korea. MacArthur was unwilling to accept this, and throughout the winter of 1951 he agitated in the press and among his supporters in Congress for a stepped-up U.S. commitment, including extending the war into China. In late March the United States proposed a truce that MacArthur quickly denounced, and the proposal collapsed. MacArthur seemed oblivious to reprimands and admonitions, and finally, on 11 April 1951, Truman sacked him for insubordination.

Cease-fire Talks

With neither side willing to launch any new offenses, each was ready to start talks leading to a cease-fire. On 10 July both sides sat down at Kaesong and later at P'anmunjon to work out an armistice. With neither side having gained much on the battlefield, the important issues on the table were how to restore Korean status quo. The United States refused Chinese demands that all foreign troops be withdrawn from Korea. The United States also refused to restore the 38th parallel as the border, holding out in favor of existing battle lines. The issue which caused the talks to break down entirely was the American refusal to repatriate North Korean and Chinese prisoners of war against their will.

Talks resumed in 1953. Stalin had died in March 1953, and the Soviets were eager to end the war. In the United States, Dwight D. Eisenhower had won the presidency on a promise to "go to Korea." Most Americans understood this to mean that he was also ready to make peace, though Eisenhower seems to have been willing to force a peace by threatening to use American atomic bombs.

In this atmosphere the talks began to show progress. The new obstacle was the South Korean government. It was clear that the United States and the Soviets were moving toward a permanent armistice despite South Korean demands that the fighting resume. When the Soviets agreed to permit the United Nations to take all prisoners of war who did not wish to go home, South Korea unilaterally released almost thirty thousand North Koreans it said had become anticommunist. It was a defiant act that drove the Soviets from the bargaining table for a month.

By the time talks resumed in late July, the United States had convinced the South Korean government to accept an armistice that left Korea divided, in return for American commitments of economic aid to rebuild and a promise of American troops if the North invaded again.

An armistice was concluded on 27 July 1953 on terms that indicated neither side had gained or lost much after three years of fighting. Until the Gulf War of 1991, Korea was the outstanding example of collective security in which the United Nations was able to mobilize a military response to an attack on one of its members.

References

Bruce Cummings, *The Origins of the Korean War: Liberation and the Emergence of Separate Regimes, 1945–1947* (Princeton, N.J.: Princeton University Press, 1981);

Bruce Cummings, ed., *Child of Conflict: The Korean American Relationship, 1943–1953* (Seattle: University of Washington, 1983).

                                                      – C. S. B.

SEE ALSO THESE RELATED ENTRIES
Dwight D. Eisenhower, 1; Kim Il-Sung, 2; Douglas MacArthur, 1; Syngman Rhee, 2; Harry S Truman, 1.

Leninism

Leninism refers to the theoretical interpretations and practical applications of Marxism by Vladimir Ilyich Ulyanov (1870–1924), a Russian Marxist who adopted the pseudonym of Lenin in 1897. Vladimir Ulyanov was born in the Volga town of Simbirsk (renamed Ulyanovsk). His father died when Vladimir was fifteen, and when he was seventeen his elder brother, Alexander, became involved in a plot to assassinate the czar, was caught, and executed. Radicalized by the death of his brother, Lenin began to read the works of Karl Marx, a German social scientist and revolutionary who founded the movement bearing his name. By the time of his death, Lenin had founded a Marxist party in Russia, called the Bolshevik party, guided that party to the successful seizure of power in October 1917, established the Communist International in 1919, led the Bolsheviks to victory in the Russian civil war (1918–1921), and consolidated the position of a new regime.

The main contributions of Leninism to the ideology of communism include Lenin's theories of party, revolution, imperialism, and socialist construction. While Western scholars have regarded Leninism as a distinctive version of Marxism, Soviet scholars have maintained that Lenin made no fundamental changes in Marxism but merely extended its scope. Lenin himself never used the term "Leninism," which was coined by rivals for vying for power in the Soviet Union after his death in January 1924. Joseph Stalin (1879–1953) popularized the term in April 1924 when he delivered a series of lectures at the Communist University in Moscow. In these lectures Stalin defined Leninism as "Marxism in the epoch of imperialism and proletarian revolution." He also emphasized that Leninism meant, above all, the need for unity and discipline in the Communist party, the role of the party as leader of the masses, and the vital need to preserve the support of the peasants for the proletarian dictatorship. The dictatorship of the proletariat was, according to Marxist thought, the authoritarian rule of the majority over the minority, consisting of the middle class, or the "bourgeoisie." Stalin, as all the Soviet leaders after him, took Leninism as the ideological touchstone and the source of legitimacy for the role of the Communist party of the Soviet Union (CPSU) in Soviet society.

Stalin's interpretation of Leninism is, however, only one way of understanding Leninism. Lenin passed through many stages in his intellectual development and, like other major thinkers, was not always consistent with the positions he took. Consequently, one can talk about not one but two Lenins: the Lenin who was an internationalist, a gradualist, and democratic; and the Lenin who instituted centralism, advocated revolutionary violence and terror, and who was a Soviet patriot. These two contradictory sides of Lenin's intellect and character are partly explained by the dual influences of Marxism and the non-Marxist Russian revolutionary and political traditions on Lenin. The lack of individual freedoms, widespread repression of dissent, and lack of free elections in Russia convinced Lenin that the evolutionary socialism of Eduard Bernstein (1850–1932), with its emphasis on the formation of socialist mass parties that would try to achieve socialism through reforms rather than a revolution, was not applicable to Russian conditions.

Lenin developed his theory of party systematically in the pamphlet entitled *What Is To Be Done?* (1902). The pamphlet can be regarded as the most influential document of the communist movement to date. Instead of advocating the establishment of mass working-class parties, as did Western socialists, Lenin called for the formation of a highly centralized party composed of dedicated, tested, and professional revolutionaries organized along clandestine and highly centralized lines. Without the leadership of such a revolutionary party, Lenin insisted, Russian workers could not arrive at more than "trade-union consciousness," contenting themselves with piecemeal reforms and ignoring calls for a fundamental change in their life conditions. Unlike Marx, Lenin did not believe that the workers could spontaneously create a revolution. Such activity in Russia was precluded not only by the backwardness of working-class consciousness but also by the autocratic nature of the Russian state.

Democratic Socialism

The notion of a centralized and disciplined party as the instrument of revolution was significant to Lenin's thought. Lenin first referred to the system of party discipline, which he advocated as "democratic centralism," in 1906. Democratic centralism purported to combine free intraparty discussion with absolute unity of action. The term was better defined in the party statutes in 1919 where it was stated that the decisions of the higher organs are absolutely binding on lower organs of the party. Decisions would be resolved according to the majority vote of the central committee of the party, but once general policy was agreed upon, the day-to-day operation of the party had to be decided centrally.

Lenin's theory of party with its emphasis on the principle of democratic centralism became the most identifiable feature of communist systems as diverse as those of the Soviet Union, the People's Republic of China, and Yugoslavia. The dissemination of Lenin's theory of party was carried out through the Communist International (Comintern), founded by Lenin in 1919. The central mission of the Communist International was to unite the proletariat of all countries under the leadership of communists, as opposed to social democrats, for the purpose of establishing socialism worldwide. Lenin's theory of party and the principle of democratic centralism were the two cornerstones on which the Communist party of the Soviet Union and, eventually, communist parties of all member countries of the Comintern were founded. The principle of democratic centralism was included in the Twenty-One Conditions of Admission to the Comintern conceived at the Second Congress in August 1920. The justification for the discipline and hierarchy was found in the experience of Russian Bolsheviks in their revolution of 1917 and was articulated by Lenin in his "Left-Wing Communism: An Infantile Disorder" (1920), in which Lenin proclaimed that "the experience of the victorious dictatorship of the proletariat in Russia has clearly shown ... that absolute centralization and rigorous discipline in the proletariat" are essential to the "victory over bourgeoisie."

Spreading the Revolution

Although Stalin dissolved the Comintern in May 1943, the pattern of subordination of foreign communist parties to the Soviet party-state remained almost unchanged until the late 1960s, when Eurocommunism rose to challenge Moscow's right to define communism. Within the communist bloc, the role of the Soviet Union as the incarnation of proletarian power and the vanguard of the international revolutionary movement was directly challenged only by Josip Broz Tito of Yugoslavia and Mao Zedong of China. Other communist leaders, such as Imre Nagy of Hungary and Aleksander Dubcek of Czechoslovakia, who attempted to establish "national roads to socialism," were promptly silenced by the Kremlin. On 22 September 1947 nine European communist parties under Soviet leadership established the Communist Information Bureau (Cominform) as a modified version of the Comintern. Its formation was justified by the intensification of the East-West conflict and U.S. attempts to roll back socialism with the policy of containment. Together with the Warsaw Pact and the Council of Mutual Economic Assistance (CEMA), Cominform served the Soviet interests by strengthening the commitment to socialism within the bloc and providing diplomatic and political support to the Soviet foreign policy.

Widespread revolutionary activity in the less developed countries was never expected by Karl Marx, who had insisted that the socialist revolution could take place only after capitalism had created material abundance. Initially, Lenin had accepted the Marxist theory of revolution, arguing for the necessity of passing through the stage of bourgeois democracy on the way to socialism. Later, however, Lenin made the Marxist theory of revolution relevant to the situations in the underdeveloped countries by arguing that the Russian bourgeoisie was too weak and unwilling to complete the bourgeois-democratic revolution by itself. The proletariat, therefore, should take upon itself the task of completing the bourgeois revolution. In order to do so, Lenin proposed in his *Two Tactics of Social-Democracy in the Democratic Revolution* (1905), an alliance should be formed between the proletariat and the peasantry. This alliance would overthrow the autocracy and complete the bourgeois-democratic revolution. The result of the revolution would be not a socialist dictatorship of the proletariat, as Marx had predicted, but a "revolutionary-democratic dictatorship of the proletariat and the peasantry." Once the democratic revolution in Russia had taken place, Lenin argued, its example would carry the revolution into Europe. This revolution would, in turn, help the Bolsheviks to complete the socialist revolution in Russia. The socialist revolutions in Europe, however, failed to materialize. In his *Imperialism, the Highest Stage of Capitalism* (1917) Lenin explained the failure of European socialist revolutions in terms of imperialism, claiming that capitalists in the developed areas of Europe and North America had helped to alleviate the misery and exploitation of the industrial worker in the West by transferring the exploitation to the underdeveloped countries. By doing so, the capitalists had turned the proletariat in the West into an "aristocracy" of the working class, too well-off to desire a socialist revolution. Lenin predicted that the exploited working class of the Third World would further the cause of world revolution by providing a spark which would ignite socialist revolutions in more industrialized countries.

Lenin's argument that proletarian revolutions could take place in underdeveloped societies as well as highly developed capitalist states had far-reaching implications. By giving an ideological blessing to revolutionary activity in underdeveloped countries, Lenin provided a justification for socialist revolutions not only in Russia but also in many Third World countries. Committed to the Leninist worldview, the Soviet leaderships at times adopted the furtherance of the world revolutionary process as a matter of their highest priority. They viewed the Chinese, Cuban, Vietnamese, and Angolan revolutions as part of the continuing anti-imperialist struggle and committed socialist states worldwide to providing them with military and financial support. The Soviet policy of supporting revolutionary movements in the Third World countries combined with combative Soviet rhetoric in defense of world revolution, in turn, served to increase the insecurity of nonsocialist nations. During the Cold War, the United States became obsessed with the communist menace, and as Marshall D. Shulman asserts, "anticommunism became a central dogma of American purpose abroad."

Imperialism

Lenin's theory of imperialism has also had a lasting impact on the traditional Soviet theory of international relations which, according to Allen Lynch, includes: the primacy of objective, economic factors; the law of uneven capitalist development as the generator of the driving tensions of international relations; the classification of states into oppressors and oppressed; the inevitability of war in a class-driven international society; and the inseparability of the survival of socialism from the successful advent of the world revolution. The primacy of economic factors in human history was taken as a given by Lenin, who insisted that imperialism was not only a particular kind of power relationship but an essentially economic condition created on the basis of economic rather than political considerations. Once all the colonies had been divided among the imperialist states, Lenin predicted, the only possibility for continued economic growth of advanced capitalist states would lie in the redivision of the colonies. In their search for

new sources of raw materials and new possibilities for the investment of surplus capital, the imperialist states would find themselves in conflict with one another. According to Lenin, imperialism would inevitably result in a war among the capitalist states.

Lenin's theory of war was later to include the notion that a war was also unavoidable between socialist and capitalist countries. "As long as capitalism and socialism exist," Lenin wrote, "we cannot live in peace; in the end one or the other will triumph." It can be argued that Lenin's theory of war formed the foundation for the immediate postwar Soviet view of the world as divided between two hostile politico-military camps: the imperialist and antidemocratic camp led by the United States and the anti-imperialist and democratic camp led by the Soviet Union. This view was somewhat modified by Stalin in 1952 when he implied in his short essay, "Economic Problems of Socialism in the U.S.S.R." that Lenin's prediction concerning the ultimate clash between the two camps was no longer valid. In 1956 Soviet leader Nikita S. Khrushchev officially revised the Leninist theory of war by proclaiming at the Twentieth Congress of the CPSU that wars between capitalist and socialist states were possible but not inevitable. This theory of "peaceful coexistence" formed the officially accepted basis for Soviet foreign policy after 1956.

State and Revolution

Carrying out a successful socialist revolution, whether in industrialized or underdeveloped countries, was only a beginning for what was to become communism in its mature stage, characterized by democracy and material abundance. As the first country where socialist revolution – as defined by Lenin, not by Marx – had taken place, the Soviet Union would serve as an example to other underdeveloped countries aspiring to socialism. But it was not clear to Lenin, or any other Bolshevik for that matter, how one should construct a socialist state. In his *State and Revolution* (1917), Lenin described the character of state power in the transitional period between capitalism and communism on the basis of Marx's conception of the dictatorship of the proletariat. In accordance with Marxist lines, Lenin insisted that the bourgeois state was an instrument of class domination and that the immediate goal should be its destruction and replacement by a dictatorship of the proletariat. The new dictatorship, while restricting the freedom of capitalists, would at the same time mean an immense expansion of democracy: the majority of the population would rise to take an independent part, not only in voting and elections, but also in the everyday administration of the state. It should be noted, however, that this view of a transitional society had little chance to materialize in Russia. The socialist revolution in that country had been conducted by a minority composed of peasants, workers, and intellectuals, not by the majority of the population, which belonged to the working class. The dictatorship of the Russian proletariat was by definition a minority dictatorship.

What is interesting about Lenin's *State and Revolution* is that its emphasis on direct democracy, spontaneous mass initiative, and genuine freedom is incongruous with the elitism, realism, and authoritarianism that permeated his other works. In addition, the new Soviet state that began to develop under Lenin's leadership was bureaucratized and devoid of individual freedoms, and, as such, far from the ideal state Lenin depicted in 1917. Some scholars have argued that *State and Revolution* was written by a Lenin who was intoxicated with the optimism of 1917, and thus the work should be considered as a fundamental deviation from the general line of Lenin's thought. Others have maintained that *State and Revolution* was a theoretical work looking into the future, depicting a model of future society. The debate over the interpretation of *State and Revolution* is closely intertwined with the debate concerning the so-called continuity thesis. The advocates of this thesis claim that Stalinism, defined as communism characterized by excess bureaucratization, nationalism, mass terror, absence of democracy, censorship, police repression, and cult of personality, was a direct continuation of Leninism. The opponents of the continuity theses would be inclined to see *State and Revolution* as a theoretical work looking into the future and find fault with the Soviet state, as it emerged under Stalin, for failing to live up to Lenin's expectations.

Impact of Leninism

The impact of Leninism has been great in the twentieth century. The Leninist parties in Russia, China, Yugoslavia, and Vietnam have been able to lead a socialist revolution to victory in armed conflict and establish effective control of government. In some communist systems, especially in the Soviet Union and China, the Leninist parties have furthermore been able to direct the "take-off" phase of industrialization and mobilization with impressive results, but at a tremendous human cost. After World War II Leninism as interpreted by Stalin, rather than Marxism, became the ideological basis for communism practically defined as collective ownership of the means of production, central economic planning, and rule by a single political party.

The post-World War II ideological division of the world had its roots in the Leninist black-and-white view of international relations. Along Leninist lines, the Soviet leaders – with the exception of Mikhail Gorbachev – regarded the United States as the leading capitalist and imperialist power unappeasably hostile to the Soviet Union. In the Soviet view, there was no place for ideological neutrality in a world divided between the camps of communism and capitalism. Both the East and West, therefore, were anxious to draw as many nations as possible into their own sphere of influence. Within ten years after World War II communist parties professing Leninist principles came to power in Poland, Romania, Bulgaria, Hungary, Yugoslavia, Albania, Czechoslovakia, East Germany, North Korea, China, and North Vietnam (though not recognized until 1954).

In some of these countries the local communist parties were able to develop a mass popular following of their own. In Europe this was the case with Yugoslavia and Albania, where the communists came to power after fighting a successful struggle for national liberation from German occupation. In other countries, most notably in China and Vietnam, the communists were able to assume control of the government in a protracted revolutionary war. In China, Mao Zedong's People's Liberation Army defeated Chiang Kai-shek's U.S.-backed nationalist armies in 1949, and in North Vietnam, Ho Chi Minh's Vietminh were able to overcome what they saw as French attempts to recolonialize Indochina.

Most of the countries that became communist after World War II were directly or indirectly helped by the Soviet Union. In Poland, Romania, East Germany, and North Korea, the local communist parties came to power largely through the aid of an occupational force – the Soviet Red Army. In Czechoslovakia, Hungary, and Bulgaria, Soviet involvement was less pronounced. In these countries local communist parties had widespread popular support mostly due to their resistance to both reactionary aristocracies and fascism. The strategy often used by the Soviet-backed communist parties in Eastern Europe was the so-called salami tactic: the communist parties "sliced off," one piece at a time, the noncommunist power positions within the coalition governments of national unity.

After 1960 several communist systems emerged in Latin America, Asia, and Africa, expanding the geographical scope of communism. In the early 1960s Cuba declared itself communist, and indigenous communist movements were later able to gain control in Vietnam, Cambodia, and Laos. In Africa, communist influence was most substantial in Mozambique, Ethiopia, and Angola. Although it would be a mistake to claim that all communist parties in the world have been Leninist, or those that have succeeded in gaining power have done so by relying on Lenin's theory of revolution, nearly all communist parties have derived much of their revolutionary energy and theoretical guidance from Leninism. Once in power, these parties have usually adopted socialism in its Leninist form as their official ideology, proclaiming the superiority of the socialist over the capitalist system. More often than not this stance automatically entailed a hostile attitude toward the "camp of capitalism" led by the United States.

Since the death of Lenin, both communist and noncommunist theoreticians have been able to distill conflicting versions of "Leninism" from his writings and political decisions. In the Soviet Union, Stalin founded a totalitarian state justifying it with the writings of Lenin. In doing so, Stalin emphasized the Lenin who was centralist and a Soviet patriot rather than the one who was democratic and an internationalist. As a result, the Communist party of the Soviet Union confiscated state power instead of relinquishing it, closing to individuals and groups outside the party any meaningful participation in politics.

After World War II, Eastern European communist regimes adopted Leninism as interpreted by Stalin. The recent breakdown of communist systems around the world seems to indicate that Leninism is no longer valid. At most, Leninism has been effective in some selective countries as a strategy of revolu-

tion. The Stalinist version of Leninism as a strategy of economic development, however, was somewhat successful during the initial "take-off" phase of modernization in some underdeveloped countries, such as Russia and China. But it has not been able to meet the challenges of the third industrial revolution with its emphasis on high technology. At the beginning of this century Lenin wrote, "In the final analysis the competition and struggle between capitalism and socialism will be resolved in favor of the system that attains a higher level of economic productivity." Some seventy-five years later capitalism rather than socialism appears to have emerged as a victor in this competition.

References

Edward Hallett Carr, *The Bolshevik Revolution 1917–1923,* volume 1 (Baltimore: Penguin, 1950);

Stephen F. Cohen, "Bolshevism and Stalinism," in *Stalinism: Essays in Historical Interpretation,* edited by Robert C. Tucker (New York: Norton, 1977);

David Lane, *Leninism: A Sociological Interpretation* (Cambridge, U.K.: Cambridge University Press, 1981);

Allen Lynch, *The Soviet Study of International Relations* (New York: Cambridge University Press, 1987);

Alfred G. Meyer, *Leninism* (Cambridge, Mass.: Harvard University Press, 1957);

Marshall D. Shulman, "Relations with the Soviet Union," in *Agenda for the Nation,* edited by Kermit Gordon (Washington, D.C.: Brookings Institute, 1968);

Joseph Stalin, "Economic Problems of Socialism in the U.S.S.R.," in *The Essential Stalin: Major Theoretical Writings, 1905–1952,* edited by Bruce Franklin (New York: Anchor, 1972);

Robert C. Tucker, ed., *The Lenin Anthology* (New York: Norton, 1975).

– M. H.

SEE ALSO THESE RELATED ENTRIES
Containment, 3; Mao Zedong, 2; Josip Broz Tito, 2; Truman Doctrine, 3; Warsaw Pact, 3.

Limited Nuclear Options

On 10 January 1974 Secretary of Defense James R. Schlesinger announced at a press conference before the Overseas Writers Association that he was implementing a new nuclear targeting strategy for the United States called Limited Nuclear Options (LNO).

According to Schlesinger, the policy of assured destruction, instituted by Secretary of Defense Robert S. McNamara on 6 December 1963, was no longer sufficient for deterrence. Emphasizing the American ability to target Soviet population centers in the event of war, the strategy of assured destruction was to serve as an effective deterrent against a Soviet nuclear attack. There was doubt, however, that a U.S. nuclear threat aimed at Soviet cities was credible. No president, Schlesinger believed, would initiate the use of nuclear force against population centers, knowing that such an attack would invite the Soviets to retaliate against American cities.

Schlesinger adopted the strategy of Limited Nuclear Options to try to avoid the uncontrolled escalation inherent in the strategy of assured destruction. Limited Nuclear Options presented the president with a menu of attack plans, varying from the use of one or two nuclear devices against Soviet military targets to the launch of a massive nuclear retaliatory attack. Each option was tailored to a specific contingency: if the Soviet Union were to gain an advantage in a conventional conflict in Western Europe, Limited Nuclear Options might call for the use of one or two nuclear devices to demonstrate American resolve and to convince the Soviets to halt their attack. Schlesinger did not believe that the superpowers could fight a controlled nuclear war, but he did believe that the controlled use of a few nuclear weapons would strengthen the North Atlantic Treaty Organization's (NATO) nuclear deterrent.

The press and public perceived Schlesinger's announcement as a dramatic change in nuclear targeting policy; however, it was primarily articulating a shift in American nuclear declaratory policy. Since the early 1960s the American nuclear targeting plan – the Single Integrated Operational Plan (SIOP) – had offered the president a variety of options. In fact, Schlesinger's interest in Limited Nuclear Options grew out of the initial implementation of selective nuclear attacks under McNamara. In the early 1960s McNamara envisaged a limited nuclear attack against Soviet nuclear forces, but the growth of the Soviet nuclear arsenal during the decade meant that even the most limited American nuclear attack would involve thousands of nuclear weapons. In the mid 1960s Schlesinger worked on a program, called Nuclear Options and Nuclear Operations (NU-OPTS), intended to create plans for limited nuclear strikes. By 1974 the NU-OPTS plan had been incorporated into the National Security Decision Memorandum, NSDM-242. Schlesinger's 10 January 1974 press conference was intended to announce publicly this modification of U.S. nuclear policy.

References
Lawrence Freedman, *The Evolution of Nuclear Strategy* (New York: St. Martin's Press, 1981);

Colin S. Gray, "Nuclear Strategy: The Case for a Theory of Victory," *International Security,* 4 (Summer 1979): 54–87;

Colin S. Gray and Keith Payne, "Victory Is Possible," *Foreign Policy,* no. 39 (Summer 1980): 14–27;

Fred Kaplan, *The Wizards of Armageddon* (New York: Simon & Schuster, 1983);

Robert Scheer, *With Enough Shovels: Reagan, Bush, and Nuclear War* (New York: Random House, 1983).

                                                  – B. D. K.

SEE ALSO THESE RELATED ENTRIES
Deterrence, 3; Robert S. McNamara, 1; James R. Schlesinger, 1.

Limited Test Ban Treaty

The treaty banning nuclear weapon tests in the atmosphere, in outer space, and under water, known as the Limited Test Ban Treaty (LTB), signed in Moscow on 5 August 1963, was intended to "put an end to the contamination of man's environment by radioactive substances." President John F. Kennedy considered the treaty a triumph not only for his presidency and the nation, but for the whole world. In a nationally televised address, the president summarized the importance of the treaty: "For the first time agreement has been reached on bringing the forces of nuclear destruction under international control."

Limits on nuclear testing had been debated for many years before the signing of the LTB. The United States and the Soviet Union – the two major nuclear powers – and Great Britain had tried to negotiate a total ban on nuclear testing. But the attempt failed because of disagreement between the Soviets and the Western powers over measures to verify treaty compliance. Recognizing that techniques for monitoring underground tests from a distance were not sufficient, all three powers agreed that on-site inspections were necessary to verify the ban, but disputes arose over the number of inspections to be permitted by the treaty. A compromise was finally struck during trilateral meetings in Moscow in the summer of 1963, when W. Averell Harriman, the U.S. negotiator, and his British and Soviet counterparts agreed to limit the ban to tests in the atmosphere, outer space, and under water, all of which could be monitored without recourse to on-site inspection. A similar limited ban on nuclear testing had been proposed by thirty-four U.S. senators the previous May.

A key to the successful negotiation of the limited test ban was the improvement in relations between the Soviet Union and the United States after the October 1962 Cuban Missile Crisis. Testifying before the Senate Foreign Relations Committee in March 1963, Secretary of State Dean Rusk commented, "During the past year, for the first time nuclear powers had to look at nuclear exchange as an operational matter. Men had a chance to peer into the pit of the inferno." Eager to avoid a similar encounter, both nations sought improved relations. It was in this context that the treaty was finally completed in August 1963.

The treaty appealed to the Kennedy administration for reasons beyond the need to protect the environment from radioactive contamination. Rusk, who felt that the test ban discouraged both superpowers from deploying untested weapons, argued that the treaty was militarily sound. In addition, Rusk suggested during congressional hearings that the treaty was important as a breakthrough in superpower relations. He believed that it would have a salutary effect on Soviet behavior, encouraging the Soviet Union to cooperate with the United States and the West in other areas.

More than one hundred countries have signed the treaty. France and China are the only major nuclear powers to have refused to do so.

References

Coit Blacker and Gloria Duffy, eds., *International Arms Control* (Stanford, Cal.: Stanford University Press, 1985);

Glenn T. Seaborg, *Kennedy, Khruschev, and the Test Ban* (Berkeley: University of California Press, 1981).

Ronald J. Terchek, *The Making of The Test Ban Treaty* (The Hague: M. Nijhoff, 1970);

– B. D. K.

SEE ALSO THESE RELATED ENTRIES
W. Averell Harriman, 1; John F. Kennedy, 1; Dean Rusk, 1.

Linkage

A central concept of U.S. détente policies pursued by President Richard M. Nixon and National Security Adviser Henry Kissinger – later named secretary of state – "linkage," in Kissinger's words, provided the Soviet leaders with "incentives for moderation and penalties for intransigence." To produce such incentives and penalties, Kissinger insisted on linking different policies to each other in order to gain leverage, in effect telling the Soviets: if you want an agreement on A, you must also agree on B.

Linkage was an active instrument of policy used by Nixon and Kissinger to exploit the Soviet desire for Western credits and technology in order to moderate their conduct in foreign policy and curb their military buildup. Critics of linkage argued that Nixon and Kissinger did not have the degree of control over positive inducements (such as economic aid to the Soviets) or negative sanctions (such as intervening economically or militarily in regions contested by the Soviets) to make the policy work. Kissinger's practice of linking Western economic aid with Soviet foreign-policy – and especially military – concessions, for instance, were hampered by Congress, which at times sought a linkage of its own, which was incongruous with the administration's foreign-policy pursuits. In 1974 Congress passed the Jackson-Vanick amendment to the Trade Reform Act of 1973, linking the granting of most-favored-nation status to the Soviet Union to Soviet emigration policies regarding Jews. The amendment undercut Kissinger's negotiations with the Soviets, severely straining U.S.-Soviet relations. In December 1975 Congress passed the Clark amendment, preventing the administration of President Gerald R. Ford from aiding pro-Western forces in Angola and further curbing Kissinger's ability to use military intervention to extract Soviet concessions.

References

McGeorge Bundy, *Danger and Survival: Choices about the Bomb in the First Fifty Years* (New York: Random House, 1988);

John Lewis Gaddis, *Strategies of Containment: A Critical Appraisal of Postwar American National Security Policy* (New York: Oxford University Press, 1982);

Raymond L. Garthoff, *Detente and Confrontation: American-Soviet Relations from Nixon to Reagan* (Washington, D.C.: Brookings Institution, 1985);

Robert S. Litwak, *Detente and the Nixon Doctrine: American Foreign Policy and the Pursuit of Stability, 1969–1976* (New York: Cambridge, 1984).

– B. F.

SEE ALSO THESE RELATED ENTRIES
Jackson-Vanick Amendment, 3; Henry Kissinger, 1.

Long Telegram

The Long Telegram was George F. Kennan's eight-thousand-word message of 22 February 1946, which described Soviet attitudes toward the outside world and Soviet leader Joseph Stalin's foreign policy objectives. A little-known Foreign Service diplomat stationed in Moscow in late 1945 during the early stages of the Cold War, Kennan was frustrated with his lack of influence on Washington policymakers and struggled to be heard. When the Treasury Department, in February 1946, cabled the American embassy in Moscow for information and analysis of Soviet reasons for recently refusing to join the International Monetary Fund and the World Bank, Kennan had his chance. His reply, which came to be known as the Long Telegram, gained him recognition in Washington as an expert on Soviet affairs.

When Kennan arrived in Moscow in late 1945, U.S.–Soviet relations were beginning to deteriorate rapidly. A broad set of problems was tearing the wartime alliance apart: the Soviets had not been invited to share in the defeat and occupation of Japan; were not budging from the sector they occupied in northern Iran; were exerting pressure on Turkey for easy access through the Black Sea Straits; and had begun the imposition process in Eastern Europe that resulted in Soviet-aligned communist regimes. In addition, on 9 February 1946, shortly before Kennan wrote his telegram, Stalin delivered a speech in which he stressed the incompatibility of communism and capitalism.

Despite the mounting tensions, there was in Washington little knowledge concerning the goals of Soviet policy, and there was no consensus on the best method for managing relations with Moscow. Some officials thought the Soviet demand for secure, friendly borders should be accommodated, while others were more critical and urged taking a hard line toward the Soviet Union. Kennan's critical views were well received by the latter group, for his telegram cogently and persuasively argued that behind the ideological posturing and rhetoric, the Soviets viewed the world suspiciously in a traditionally Russian manner, driven by an instinctive sense of insecurity and inferiority in its relations with the West. According to Kennan, Marxism was merely a moral front behind which the Soviet rulers justified oppression at home and sought political expansion abroad. His

telegram also warned that the Soviets would endeavor to weaken the West and hamstring its recovery from the war by employing any means available to them, such as international labor organizations, pan-Slavism in Eastern Europe, and even the Orthodox church. Kennan concluded his message by pleading with Washington to deal with the Soviets in a realistic and no-nonsense manner, expressing the hope that the United States would mature and be strengthened as a result of its contest with the Soviet Union.

The Long Telegram had a substantial impact on U.S. foreign policy because it was highly regarded by several of President Harry S Truman's close advisers. Secretary of the Navy James V. Forrestal was so impressed with the telegram that he ordered copies distributed to members of Truman's cabinet, most of whom reviewed the telegram favorably. In effect, the telegram filled a conceptual gap by answering the question of why the Soviet Union did not embrace America's international agenda and appeared unlikely to cooperate with it. By the end of 1946 the cumulative impact of Kennan's telegram, British prime minister Winston Churchill's warnings that the iron curtain would divide the continent, and the report by George Elsey and Clark Clifford about an alleged Soviet military threat, solidified a growing consensus in Washington for the adoption of a hard-line policy toward the Soviet Union.

References

George F. Kennan, *American Diplomacy: 1900–1950* (Chicago: University of Chicago Press, 1951 and 1984);

George F. Kennan, *Memoirs, 1925–1950,* 2 volumes (Boston: Little, Brown, 1967–1972);

George F. Kennan, *Realities of American Foreign Policy* (Princeton: Princeton University Press, 1954);

Walter L. Hixson, *George F. Kennan: Cold War Iconoclast* (New York: Columbia University Press, 1989);

David Meyers, *George Kennan and the Dilemmas of U.S. Foreign Policy* (New York: Oxford University Press, 1988);

Anders Stephanson, *Kennan and the Art of Foreign Policy* (Cambridge, Mass.: Harvard University Press, 1989).

                                                        –J. H.

> **SEE ALSO THESE RELATED ENTRIES**
> James V. Forrestal, 1; Iron Curtain Speech, 3; George F. Kennan, 1; Joseph Stalin, 2; Harry S Truman, 1; The X Article, 3.

Manhattan Project

Scientist creating the first nuclear reaction, under the west stands of Stagg Field at the University of Chicago, 2 December 1942 (painting by Gary Sheehan)

The Manhattan Project was the name given to the intense, concerted U.S. effort to develop nuclear weapons.

On 9 October 1941 Vannevar Bush reported to President Franklin Delano Roosevelt and Vice-president Henry A. Wallace the latest achievements of the British in nuclear research. The British were optimistic that they were on the verge of discovering a war-ending atomic weapon. Impressed with Bush's report, Roosevelt told Bush to expedite nuclear research in the United States "in every possible way."

With the Japanese attack on Pearl Harbor in December 1941 and the subsequent U.S. entry into the war, Roosevelt gave Bush the green light to proceed with building the atomic bomb in June 1942. Bush and James B. Conant assigned the Manhattan district army engineers the task of locating the sites, procuring the materials necessary, and developing the procedures for the bomb project. On 17 September, General Leslie Groves was named commander of the Manhattan Project.

The first steps toward developing the bomb were taken by physicist Enrico Fermi at the University of Chicago. On 2 December 1942, under the bleachers of Stagg Field, the university's football stadium, Fermi generated the first controlled nuclear chain reaction. Later that month, Roosevelt authorized \$400 million for uranium separation and plutonium production plants. Work on different aspects of nuclear reaction continued at various laboratories around the country. In March 1943 Groves decided to open a nuclear weapons laboratory in Los Alamos, New Mexico, under the directorship of J. Robert Oppenheimer. By the spring of 1945 more than two thousand scientists and engineers had come to work at Los Alamos.

On 16 July 1945, in the desert near Alamogordo, the first atomic bomb was tested successfully. Three weeks later, a bomb was dropped on Hiroshima. The nuclear age had begun.

References

McGeorge Bundy, *Danger and Survival: Choices about the Bomb in the First Fifty Years* (New York: Random House, 1988);

Daniel J. Kevles, *The Physicists: The History of a Scientific Community in Modern America* (Cambridge, Mass.: Harvard University Press, 1987);

William Lawren, *The General and the Bomb: A Biography of General Leslie R. Groves, Director of the Manhattan Project* (New York: Dodd, Mead, 1988);

Richard Rhodes, *The Making of the Atomic Bomb* (New York: Simon & Schuster, 1988).

– B. F.

SEE ALSO THESE RELATED ENTRIES
James B. Conant, 1; J. Robert Oppenheimer, 1; Franklin D. Roosevelt, 1; Edward Teller, 1; Harry S Truman, 1.

Marshall Plan

The Marshall Plan was the American offer of economic assistance made to Europe and the Soviet Union in June 1947 to repair the destruction wrought by World War II. Almost immediately rejected by the Soviet Union and its satellites, the Marshall Plan served to hasten and define the postwar division of Europe into two competing blocs. As such, it was the most successful implementation of the new American policy of containing the expansion of Soviet power.

American designs for the Marshall Plan were greatly inspired by the success of President Franklin Delano Roosevelt's New Deal in transforming the economy and society of the United States into a neocapitalist Keynesian model with central institutions of planning and administration. To a large extent, the Marshall Plan intended to re-create this same model for Europe in order to enable the region to reap the benefits of free trade and multilateralism. But the loss of national sovereignty that this overarching transformation implied met with strong objections by European countries, which had so recently been at war with one another. At the end of the Marshall Plan in 1950, Europe was economically back on its feet again, but it had failed to develop into the grand design originally envisioned by the New Dealers who implemented it.

Postwar European Devastation

The origins of the Marshall Plan must be viewed against the larger backdrop of economic and political conditions in postwar Europe, the growing tensions between the United States and the Soviet Union, and the question of Germany's future relations with its neighbors, especially France. Europe had been plagued by shortages of food and raw materials since the end of the war. The summers of 1946 and 1947 witnessed severe droughts and the intervening winter had been one of the worst of the century. In early 1946 the average European was surviving on barely two thousand calories per day in contrast to more than thirty-three hundred in the United States. The chances for imminent recovery appeared slim – traditional transportation links between Europe and the rest of the world had been largely severed during the war, a situation which left Europeans unable to sell their products overseas. This inability to export, combined with the general economic slowdown caused by the widespread destruction of industrial plants and equipment, meant that Europe had little foreign exchange with which to buy goods from the United States – the one country that still had a large and functioning economy. The consequent "dollar gap" threatened to impede the rebuilding of Europe's productive capacity unless the United States provided financial assistance to correct the balance-of-payments crisis and enable Europe to feed itself and buy the capital goods on which its recovery hinged. By the beginning of 1947 the United States had, in fact, given over $9 billion of aid to Europe – but in such a haphazard fashion that European recovery lagged far behind expectations.

American leaders became fully aware of European penury in March 1947 when Great Britain informed them that it no longer had the economic means to continue military and economic aid to anticommunist forces in Greece. President Harry S Truman addressed Congress on 12 March 1947 to urge American assumption of aid to Greece. But, perhaps more importantly, Truman had come to recognize the need for a more comprehensive and sustained program of economic assistance to the countries of Western Europe – both to prevent wholesale famine in the short term and to encourage Europe's economic recovery in the long term. U.S. economists concluded that, without this recovery, continued American assistance would be necessary for an indeterminate period – a disheartening prospect to many U.S. officials.

Simultaneously, there was a growing anticommunist consensus within the U.S. government that reacted with alarm to the continuing Soviet consolidation of power in Central Europe. American officials feared that the Soviet Union would exploit the economic crisis to extend its political control over Western Europe, as well. Italy and France, they thought, with large and growing Communist parties capable of electoral victory, appeared to be in the most danger of falling under Soviet hegemony. Soon George F. Kennan, director of the State Department's new policy planning staff, emerged as America's leading expositor of the nature of the Soviet threat. Uniquely authoritative by virtue of his knowledge of Soviet affairs and his experience in Moscow during the war, Kennan provided the intellectual underpinnings for the American response to the threat of Soviet expansion – a response known as containment.

The Long Telegram

In February 1946 Kennan, while serving in Moscow as a Foreign Service diplomat, had analyzed the motivations behind Soviet foreign policy and sent his findings to Washington in a remarkably influential essay called the Long Telegram. Soviet behavior toward the rest of the world, according to Kennan, was driven by its leaders' necessity to justify the ruthless methods by which they kept themselves in power. Only by portraying the outside world as inherently hostile could the Soviet Union ask its people to accept the deprivation and suffering that they had endured since the Bolshevik revolution in 1917. More to the point of Soviet-American relations, the unremitting hostility with which the Soviets faced the world forced them into a course of relentless expansion, an expansion which in the immediate postwar period directly threatened Western Europe.

Kennan viewed this threat with the utmost seriousness: Great Britain and Central Europe were two of the five "centers of military and industrial power" in the world that had the capacity to threaten the United States, and thus it was essential to keep them out of Soviet control. The Soviet threat, he thought, was more psychological than military, made all the more severe by widespread demoralization in Europe in the aftermath of the war. As long as the United States was committed to defend Europe, the Soviets would not use force to gain control, rather they would play on the fears and hunger of the people to seize power by political means.

Kennan thought that the best way to counter such Soviet actions was through economic assistance, offered by the United States to Europe as a whole. Economic aid meshed neatly with Kennan's larger ideas of contain-

ment. The revival of the European economy would remove the conditions under which he felt that communism took root and thrived – hunger, poverty, desperation, and fear. An economic recovery, furthermore, would act to restore European "self-confidence," especially if Europeans were to have the major share in its planning and implementation. By offering assistance to Europe as a single entity, it would force the separate countries to work collectively, allowing them to present a united front against the threat of Soviet hegemony.

Kennan thought that the treatment of Western Europe as one unit would solve the particular problem of what to do with defeated Germany, which sat as a vacuum of power in Central Europe, enticing the Soviet Union closer with promises of huge war reparations and great industrial potential. To keep this vast industrial power out of Soviet hands, either the allied occupation forces would have to remain in Germany or Germany would have to be reconstituted as a sovereign state, able to withstand pressures from the Soviet Union. There were problems with both of these choices: either the allies would have to bear the cost of continued occupation or Germany's neighbors would be faced with the specter of an old enemy returned to power just a few short years after the war. Kennan thought that if the controlled reconstruction of Germany took place within an integrated Europe, Germany could serve as a locomotive to pull the rest of Europe behind it, without generating excessive fears of renewed aggression.

The arguments of Kennan and a few other key government officials quickly convinced Truman of the need for a comprehensive offer of aid to Europe – an offer made by Secretary of State George C. Marshall in a commencement speech at Harvard University on 5 June 1947. The address, drafted by his assistant – Soviet expert Charles E. Bohlen – gave few specifics for European recovery because none had been drawn up yet. Rather, it contained an amalgam of ideas taken from Kennan's most recent report and a memorandum by Undersecretary of State William L. Clayton. Marshall said that American assistance should "not be on a piece-meal basis as various crises develop," an implicit limit on the extent of the Truman Doctrine aid, enunciated earlier in March. "The initiative," Marshall said, "must come from Europe."

The high-level American officials who devised the plan invited Soviet and East European participation, but with some reluctance. Marshall, for example, had met privately with Soviet leader Joseph Stalin at the Moscow Council of Foreign Ministers meeting in April 1947 and came away convinced that the Soviets wanted to block the recovery of Europe, hoping to turn the political and economic turmoil to their advantage. Kennan doubted that the Soviets would accept any aid that was conditioned on close cooperation with Western Europe, but he thought it wise in any case to make the offer: if the Soviets rejected it, they would be held responsible for the inevitable division of Europe. In the unlikely case of Soviet acceptance, the United States could then use it to force the Eastern European states away from the "near-exclusive Soviet orientation of their economies," thereby breaking the Soviet hegemony.

Soviet Rejection of the Plan

As expected, the Soviet Union, unwilling to cede management of its economy to outsiders, rejected Marshall Plan assistance at a conference in Paris called to discuss it in late June of 1947. Soviet foreign minister Vyacheslav Michailovich Molotov said that the plan would violate the sovereignty of the countries involved, opening them up to undue American influence. He also objected to the inclusion of Germany in the plan until a peace treaty had been decided upon by the four allied powers. Molotov, suspicious that the Marshall Plan was essentially a political program aimed against the Soviet Union, walked out of the Paris conference on 3 July 1947, much to the relief of the other participants. Soon after, the foreign ministers of Poland and Czechoslovakia were summoned to Moscow and pressured by Stalin into declining Marshall Plan aid.

The split between the countries that accepted American economic assistance and those that rejected it isolated the communists and hardened, if not set, the growing division of Europe into rival blocs. Western leaders now expected the Soviet Union to do everything possible to spoil the chances for success of European recovery – a fear which gave the planners in Washington a heightened sense of urgency. Truman had already created three separate government committees to study the problems of European recovery. On 12 July 1947 representatives of sixteen countries gathered in Paris to discuss plans for recovery in light of the available resources. Establishing the Committee on European Economic Cooperation (CEEC), they agreed to draft a comprehensive plan outlining European requirements and intentions – a plan that they were to present to the United States by 1 September.

Although the United States considered itself more an initiator than an architect of European recovery and was inclined to leave the planning and implementation of assistance to its beneficiaries, the Americans insisted on certain basic principles on which Marshall Plan aid was contingent. These principles of self-help, mutual aid, and joint programming, it was hoped, would lead to the economic – and even political – unification of Europe, a unification that would strengthen what Kennan called the "natural forces of resistance" and restore the balance of power against communism. The United

Workers rebuilding Berlin as part of a project funded by the Marshall Plan

States would benefit not only in terms of security by keeping this vital area out of Soviet control, but also in economic terms, for a successful and prosperous American economy required trade and investment abroad. The recovery of Europe was required for a multilateral system of world trade.

Marshall Plan Guidelines

The guidelines that the United States set for the Marshall Plan evolved directly from the philosophy and methods of the New Deal, the extensive reconstruction of the American economy launched by Roosevelt in the aftermath of the Great Depression of the 1930s. The strength of the American economy, thought the shapers of the Marshall Plan, could be credited to the success of the New Deal in creating a mixed capitalist economy that relied heavily on national institutions of planning and administration set within a framework of Keynesian monetary and fiscal policies. To a large degree, the Marshall Plan was an attempt by the United States to re-create a similar arrangement for Europe, one that would fuse the separate economies of the sovereign nations together under the direction of supranational planning agencies to allow for the most rational allocation of production and distribution by taking advantage of economies of scale and comparative advantage.

On 30 August 1947 American officials met with the CEEC in Paris to present proposals to the Europeans to increase production, stabilize finances, reduce monetary barriers and liberalize trade. The CEEC had already estimated that Europe might need $29 billion in aid, and even this might not make the region self-supporting at the end of the Marshall Plan period. They were, however, unwilling to take measures that meant transcending national sovereignties or reducing living standards. Only with the imminent threat of congressional disapproval did the CEEC bow to U.S. demands.

In spring of 1948 Congress passed the Economic Cooperation Act, authorizing almost $5 billion to finance the first year of the expected four-year European Recovery Program (ERP) and establishing the Economic Cooperation Administration to oversee the disbursement of this money, which took the form of both grants and loans. Only in the summer of 1948 did the Marshall Plan begin to emphasize reconstruction over relief, but by 1949 both industrial output and volume of trade had regained their prewar levels. Much of this increase can be attributed to the fact that European countries were devoting one-fifth of their national output to capital expenditures. American assistance during this period provided the critical margin that enabled the participants to import essential goods and cover the ensuing trade deficits. More important than money, perhaps, was the American emphasis on production and marketing skills, and the importance of forming partnerships among government, labor, and management.

U.S.-British-French Relations

During the first two years of the Marshall Plan, disputes and compromises over the degree of cooperation thought necessary for economic recovery defined relations among the Americans, British, and French. The disputes reflected underlying political differences among the countries. Great Britain, for instance, was acutely aware after the war that it was no longer a great power, and it was torn by conflicting demands placed upon it by the United States, Western Europe, and the British Commonwealth. Ernest Bevin, the British foreign minister, initially pressed for closer cooperation with continental Europe, one that would include the Commonwealth. Addressing the House of Commons on 22 January 1948, Bevin even called for a "consolidation of Western Europe . . . as a unit." But Great Britain soon discovered that it would be difficult to reconcile political leadership of the Commonwealth with closer economic ties to Europe. The Commonwealth and Britain were linked by the pound sterling,

at the time a "soft" and overvalued currency. Closer financial ties with Europe – in the form of a payments union – would require Great Britain to devalue the pound to bring it into line with other European currencies, an action that would financially hurt the Commonwealth, whose members held large reserves of sterling for trade with Britain. When forced to define British interests, Bevin retreated from his earlier calls for consolidation with Europe, instead supplying vague promises of cooperation. Great Britain would not sacrifice its several strategic interests for closer ties with Europe, wanting ultimately to preserve some semblance of a world power by becoming the linchpin holding together three overlapping blocs – serving as undisputed leader of the Commonwealth, leader of Western Europe, and partner in the "special relationship" with the United States. As part of its emphasis on greater European integration, but more specifically to balance the expected resurgence of German industrial power, the United States urged Great Britain to forge closer ties with the Continent, however. Since the onset of the Cold War, the United States never questioned the necessity of keeping Germany – or at least the western zones of occupation – out of Soviet control and allowing for the eventual reconstruction of the German economy to serve as the foundation of European economic power. But a strong British role in Europe would mean easing French worries of a rehabilitated Germany, whose productive output traditionally surpassed that of its neighbor. The United States hoped that Britain could play the pivotal role in overcoming these French security concerns by acting as a counterweight to German economic hegemony.

The French, for their part, saw German rehabilitation as a threat to the French desire to serve as the economic and political leader of Europe. Immediately after the war France had launched the Monnet Plan to rebuild its economy and assume economic preeminence on the Continent, and German recovery directly threatened this.

By the summer of 1949 the worsening dollar gap – epitomized by the sterling crisis in Great Britain – threatened to derail the entire recovery program. Much of the Marshall Plan money was being spent to cover the trade deficits between the United States and Europe. To end the sterling crisis and solve the dollar gap, the United States would have to reconcile Britain's dual commitment to the Commonwealth and to a welfare state with larger plans for European integrations and multilateralism. For this grand design to work, however, Britain would have to devalue the pound. As the crisis deepened in 1949, the British, Americans, and Canadians agreed at a tripartite conference in September that, in return for devaluing its currency, Britain would be allowed to maintain itself apart from the

Continent, its economy sheltered from the competitive dangers of a free-market system. In two papers approved by the Cabinet on 27 October 1949, the British rejected supranationalism in favor of its commitments to the Commonwealth and its unique position within the North Atlantic system of overlapping blocs.

Schuman Plan and Treaty of Paris

By distancing themselves from Europe, the British implicitly left the French to deal with the problem of a renascent West Germany. From this abandonment came the Schuman Plan, devised by Jean Monnet and approved by the French parliament on 9 May 1950, whereby France and Germany agreed to combine their coal and steel resources under a single authority. The Schuman Plan evolved into the Treaty of Paris, signed on 18 April 1951, which established the European Coal and Steel Community (ECSC) with six members: France, Germany, Italy, and the Benelux countries – Belgium, Holland, and Luxembourg. By laying the foundation for a settlement between the Germans and their Western adversaries in World War II, the community served as the first supranational body of the type originally envisioned by the planners of European recovery.

By the middle of 1950 the Marshall Plan had produced mixed results. It had been successful in reducing government controls on trade restrictions and other barriers to free trade. Similarly, it had seen the creation of the European Payments Union that tied Great Britain, however tenuously, to a continental settlements scheme. But with the exception of the Schuman Plan, the European Recovery Program still had failed to establish any truly supranational institutions of planning and administration that the United States felt were necessary to put Western Europe on an economic and political course fully competitive in a world of free trade. The countries of Western Europe would not make the necessary sacrifices of their national sovereignty.

The Korean War

The outbreak of the Korean War on 25 June 1950 threatened to slow recovery as Congress diverted Marshall Plan funds from economic to military purposes. Even before the war, it was expected that recovery would enable governments to devote more to the common defense of Europe against the forces of communism. But Korea accelerated the growing demands on military-related expenditures. Within three days of the outbreak of war, Congress slashed $208 million from the budget of the European Cooperation Administration. European economies initially benefitted from the increases in output demanded for war production, but soon the attendant shortages of raw materials led to price increases that en-

dangered Europe's balance of trade with the rest of the world.

The entry of China into the Korean War in November 1950 gave an even greater sense of urgency to the American commitment to military defense of Europe. The communists were now perceived to be stronger and more determined than ever, requiring still greater sacrifices for rearmament by the United States and its allies. Accordingly, Marshall aid was redirected into military channels. In the congressional elections of November 1950, conservative Republicans scored respectable victories, successes that endangered the high degree of bipartisanship that had been essential for the previous support of the Marshall Plan. The growing strength of the isolationists – who denounced the Europeans for not contributing enough to the war effort in Korea – put the supporters of European recovery on the defensive. In the 1951 foreign-aid bill, Congress included only a little more than one billion dollars for European economic assistance. But to signify the end of the European Recovery Program, these funds would be administered from a new office in the State Department. The European Cooperation Administration officially shut down in late December 1951, six months before the Marshall Plan's original deadline in mid 1952.

During the life of the Marshall Plan, Western Europe's total national product increased by more than 32 percent and industrial production increased by 40 percent above its prewar level. Although the American contribution was quite small in quantitative terms, serving mostly to shore up the deteriorating payments crisis, it enabled Europe to remain afloat during the harsh and chaotic period that characterized the first days of the Cold War. The Marshall Plan can be credited for many postwar successes in U.S. foreign policy: the reintegration of Germany into Europe, the containment of the Soviet Union, and the revival of large-scale production. The Marshall Plan also served as a model for the North Atlantic Treaty Organization, which more than anything else kept the peace in postwar Europe. Much of the wider political and economic integration which the plan failed to achieve during its short life is expected to happen with the inception of the Single European Act at the end of 1992.

References

John Gimbel, *The Origins of the Marshall Plan* (Stanford, Cal.: Stanford University Press, 1976);

Michael J. Hogan, *The Marshall Plan: America, Britain, and the Reconstruction of Western Europe, 1947–1952* (New York: Cambridge University Press, 1987);

Charles S. Maier and Günter Bischof, eds., *The Marshall Plan and Germany: West German Development within the Framework of the European Recovery Program* (New York: Berg, 1991);

Imanuel Wexler, *The Marshall Plan Revisited: The European Recovery Program in Economic Perspective* (Westport, Conn.: Greenwood Press, 1983).

– M. B.

SEE ALSO THESE RELATED ENTRIES

Ernest Bevin, 1; Containment, 3; George F. Kennan, 1; Korean War, 3; Long Telegram, 2; George C. Marshall, 1; Vyacheslav Molotov, 2; North Atlantic Treaty Organization, 3; Franklin D. Roosevelt, 1; Harry S Truman, 1.

Massive Retaliation

One of the main tenets of President Dwight D. Eisenhower's New Look policy, Massive Retaliation exemplified the administration's willingness to use nuclear weapons to achieve, in John Foster Dulles's words, "maximum protection at bearable cost." In a speech to the Council on Foreign Relations on 12 January 1954, Dulles said that American security could be achieved at lower cost by relying on a "deterrent of massive retaliatory power." The thinking behind Massive Retaliation was that by relying on its technological edge, the United States could regain the initiative in its competition with the Soviet Union. Critics of Massive Retaliation argued that the destructive power of nuclear weapons would make American policymakers reluctant to use these weapons except to counter the most extreme threats to the most vital of U.S. interests. This reluctance would leave the Soviet Union free to undermine American interests below the level that would trigger an American nuclear response. Criticism of Massive Retaliation gave rise to the Kennedy administration's Flexible Response strategy.

References

McGeorge Bundy, *Danger and Survival: Choices about the Bomb in the First Fifty Years* (New York: Random House, 1988);

Lawrence Freedman, *The Evolution of Nuclear Strategy* (New York: St. Martin's Press, 1981);

John Lewis Gaddis, *Strategies of Containment: A Critical Appraisal of Postwar American National Security Policy* (New York: Oxford University Press, 1982).

– B. F.

SEE ALSO THESE RELATED ENTRIES

Dwight D. Eisenhower, 1; Flexible Response, 3; New Look Policy, 3.

Mayaguez Crisis

On 12 May 1975 an American container ship, the SS *Mayaguez*, was seized by troops of Cambodia's Khmer Rouge government. The *Mayaguez* had sailed from Hong Kong on 8 May and was destined for Sattahip, Thailand. The ship was sixty miles from the Cambodian coast in the Gulf of Siam when it was seized near Koh Tang, a small island claimed by both Vietnam and Cambodia. The crew of the *Mayaguez*, thirty-nine merchant seamen, was taken to Sihanoukville on the Cambodian mainland and detained there for three days.

The administration of President Gerald R. Ford, trying to have the crew released as quickly as possible, airlifted eleven hundred Marines to Utapao Air Base in Thailand and made diplomatic overtures to the Peoples' Republic of China, the only nation with established diplomatic ties with the Khmer Rouge government, but the Chinese were unable and unwilling to exert any influence over Phnom Penh. Reports of Khmer Rouge atrocities, which later became widespread, were already beginning to be heard in the West.

On 14 May 1975, having received no Cambodian response to U.S. demands to free the crew, President Gerald R. Ford ordered the use of force. The Marines stormed Koh Tang on 14 May after having attacked and sunk three Cambodian gunboats in the vicinity. The Cambodians offered to release the ship and its crew and placed the crew aboard a Thai fishing boat to return to the *Mayaguez*. A U.S. destroyer intercepted the fishing boat and picked up the crew. Fifteen U.S. military personnel were killed in the rescue.

The timing of this incident was significant. The Khmer Rouge had taken power in Cambodia only weeks before the *Mayaguez* incident. Western security analysts had speculated that the seizure was a result of Khmer Rouge bravado in the aftermath of their victory over the U.S.-backed Cambodian government of Lon Nol. The *Mayaguez* Crisis was also the first test of the War Powers Act, which was passed in 1973 as a means to increase the role of Congress in deciding the use of American military power.

U.S. Navy

U. S. Marines recapturing the SS Mayaguez *from Cambodian troops, 14 May 1975*

The *Mayaguez* incident was an important test of American power in the immediate post-Vietnam era. Many foreign-policy analysts believed that, having recently suffered embarrassing foreign-policy setbacks in the fall of South Vietnam, it was important for the United States to demonstrate its ability and resolve to protect its interests. The *Mayaguez* incident provided the Ford administration the opportunity to demonstrate just that.

References

Gerald R. Ford, *A Time to Heal: The Autobiography of Gerald Ford* (New York: Harper & Row, 1979);

Henry A. Kissinger, *White House Years* (Boston: Little, Brown, 1979);

Roy Rowan, *The Four Days of Mayaguez* (New York: Norton, 1975).

– M. F.

SEE ALSO THESE RELATED ENTRIES
Gerald R. Ford, 1; Henry Kissinger, 1; Post-Vietnam Syndrome, 3

McCarthyism

Robert Phillips

A meeting of the Senate Internal Security Subcommittee. Sen. Joseph R. McCarthy is seated at left, facing the camera.

First published in the *Washington Post* in March 1950, Block's cartoon showed an elephant being prodded toward a platform supported by a teetering stack of buckets filled with mud. "McCARTHYISM" was written across the top bucket, and the caption read, "You Mean I'm Supposed To Stand On That?"

The term *McCarthyism* was coined by political cartoonist Herbert Block. The cartoon meant to illustrate the Republican party's reluctant endorsement Senator Joseph R. McCarthy's smear-campaign tactics used in his efforts to expose communists in the U.S. government. In 1950 McCarthy accused the Truman administration of harboring communists, and over the next four years McCarthyism took hold of the American public. McCarthy had acquired a large following by playing on fears of communist infiltration – fears which were in part inspired by Soviet aggression abroad.

From 1950 to 1954, partly out of agreement with McCarthy's stated goals if not his methods, partly out of fear of the consequences of public disagreement, few senators dared to criticize McCarthy. His popularity declined drastically, however, when he slandered the army in 1954, and most Americans came to perceive him as a demagogue during the nationally televised "Army-McCarthy" hearings of 1954. His censure by the Senate at the end of 1954 signaled a major erosion of

McCarthy's political support, and by 1957, the year of his death, he had been rendered an insignificant player in American politics. The ism, however, has outlived him.

Born 14 November 1908 in Outagamie County, near Grand Chute, Wisconsin, McCarthy grew up on his parents' 142-acre farm, known locally as "the Irish settlement." He attended Underhill Country School, Little Wolf High School, and Marquette University in Milwaukee, where he studied law. From 1935 to 1941 McCarthy served as a lawyer and a circuit judge in Wisconsin's tenth district. He joined the Marine Corps in 1941 and resigned in 1944 to return to Wisconsin to settle on a career in politics.

Elected senator as a Republican in 1946, he was unknown until 9 February 1950, when he delivered a speech to the Ohio County Women's Republican Club in Wheeling, West Virginia, charging the State Department with knowingly employing communists and thus contributing to the spread of communism in Eastern Europe and mainland China. A Senate commission was then formed to investigate the allegations, and McCarthyism was born.

Victims of McCarthyism

McCarthy's activities did not lead to the conviction of a single U.S. government official on charges of subversion. McCarthy's influence, however, was such that victims of his smears were often fired, demoted, or blacklisted; and two presidents – Harry S Truman and Dwight D. Eisenhower – considered the possible reaction of McCarthy in formulating their policies. It is likely, for example, that Truman decided to send the Seventh Fleet to "guard" Taiwan after the outbreak of the Korean War in order to combat perceptions that the Democrats had contributed to the 1949 victory of communist leader Mao Zedong in China. And during the 1952 campaign Eisenhower toured Wisconsin with McCarthy and failed to disassociate himself from McCarthy's scurrilous attacks on General George C. Marshall, to whom Eisenhower owed his promotion to commander of the European theater of operations during World War II.

Among the primary victims of McCarthy's red-baiting were China specialists in the State Department whom the senator associated with the "loss of China" to the communists in 1949. Of those officials John S. Service and John P. Davies were fired, and John C. Vincent and Oliver E. Clubb were forced to retire. Also prominent among McCarthy's targets were members of the cultural and journalistic worlds, especially the "Hollywood 10," which included Ring Lardner, Jr. – who was indicted – and radio personality Drew Pearson, who lost his radio-program sponsorship.

McCarthy's Appeal

McCarthy gained international notoriety and seemed to many foreigners to personify an ugly side of America. To the senator's diehard followers, McCarthyism was militant patriotism – "Americanism with the sleeves rolled," as McCarthy himself defined the term. To most Americans, however, McCarthyism became a synonym for baseless defamation.

Two reasons have often been given to explain the anticommunist fever that gripped the nation in the early post–World War II era. The first explanation cites overreaction to the profound psychological shock of events, such as the fall of Eastern Europe and China to communism and Soviet detonation of an atomic bomb in 1949. The second explanation finds in McCarthyism an expression of the latent xenophobia of some Americans, a resurgence of an American isolationist impulse which was evident following World War I. In sum McCarthyism has been explained as both a by-product of the Cold War and the expression of forces antedating the Cold War. McCarthyism was perhaps most of all a flight from the reality of a great external danger to the illusion of a great but more easily manageable internal conspiracy. Though communists penetrated American government in the 1930s and 1940s, their influence was largely eliminated by the 1950s, the decade which saw the trial of Alger Hiss, an adviser to President Franklin D. Roosevelt, on espionage charges. By the advent of McCarthyism an extensive system of security clearance checks was instituted in order to screen out unreliable candidates for sensitive federal positions.

However, at the same time that the internal communist threat was diminishing, Americans appeared to become vulnerable as never before to an international communist conspiracy. One third of mankind was living under communist rule by the time of Soviet leader Joseph Stalin's death in 1953. Moreover, for the first time, U.S. natural defense barriers, the two great oceans, offered scant protection from foreign military threats. Soviet nuclear power created a more dangerous international environment for the United States. McCarthyism was thus partly a response to real danger, though its identification of the source of danger as primarily internal was skewed.

References

Jack Anderson and Ronald W. May, *McCarthy the Man, the Senator, the -Ism* (Boston: Beacon, 1952);

Fred J. Cook, *The Nightmare Decade* (New York: Random House, 1971);

Mark Hollingsworth and Richard Norton-Taylor, *Blacklist* (London: Hogarth, 1988);

E. J. Kahn, Jr., *The China Hands* (New York: Viking, 1975);

Gordon Kahn, *Hollywood on Trial* (New York: Boni & Gaer, 1948);

Joe McCarthy, *McCarthyism, the Fight for America* (New York: Devin Adair, 1952);

Joe McCarthy, *The Story of General George C. Marshall* (New York: Devin Adair, 1952);

Michael P. Rogin, *The Intellectuals and McCarthy* (Cambridge: Massachusetts Institute of Technology Press, 1967);

Richard Rovere, *Senator Joe McCarthy* (New York: Meridian, 1962).

–J. W.

SEE ALSO THESE RELATED ENTRIES
Dwight D. Eisenhower, 1; Alger Hiss, 1; Harry S Truman, 1.

Missile Gap

The "Missile Gap," the belief that the Soviet Union was developing a decisive advantage in intercontinental ballistic missiles (ICBMs), emerged as a contentious issue in American politics in 1957. The Soviet launch of Sputnik, the first artificial satellite, on 4 October 1957 sent shock waves through the American body politic. Suggesting Soviet missile superiority, Sputnik made the fear of a Soviet missile attack a major political issue in the United States. The November 1957 National Intelligence Estimate (NIE), generated by the Central Intelligence Agency (CIA), reflected this concern in its conclusion that the Soviets could have five hundred ICBMs as early as 1961, giving the Soviets a decisive strategic advantage.

Bomber Gap

The missile gap controversy followed on the heels of another alleged strategic gap between the superpowers. In the mid 1950s air force intelligence persuaded Allen Dulles, the director of the CIA and the official responsible for the NIE, that there was a "Bomber Gap." According to air force intelligence, the Soviet Union was producing the Bison intercontinental bomber at a rate far faster than American bomber production. As late as 1957 air force intelligence estimated that the Soviets would have five hundred Bison bombers by the early 1960s – an estimate disputed by the CIA. Following the launch of Sputnik, however, the air force shifted its attention from Soviet bomber production to Soviet missiles.

As word spread within the government of the air force's classified estimates of Soviet missile capabilities, President Dwight D. Eisenhower faced increasing pressure to counter the presumed Soviet buildup. Senator Stuart Symington, a Democrat from Montana who had presidential aspirations for the 1960 campaign, became the most vocal congressional critic of the administration. In July 1958 Symington began to pressure CIA director Dulles to accept the air force findings.

Within the administration there were conflicting views about the missile gap. Monitoring Soviet missile test flights, CIA specialists were able to reconstruct the size, weight, accuracy, explosive power, fuel-loading mechanism, and capacity of the new Soviet ICBM. They concluded that the number of Soviet ICBM tests had decreased significantly by the summer of 1958, suggesting that the Soviet program was still in early development. Dulles remained ambivalent about his agency's findings. In the February 1960 NIE he cited the various intelligence positions on the missile gap without supporting any of them.

Missile Gap Politics

Eisenhower took a much stronger stance. Photographs from the U-2, a new American high-altitude reconnaissance jet, indicated that the Soviet Union had built only a handful of ICBMs. So sensitive was the U-2 program that no member of Congress, including Senator Symington, was aware of its existence. Ignorant of the intelligence gathered through the U-2, the Democrats became increasingly critical of Eisenhower's apparent lack of action or concern. Congressional criticism in turn drew increasing public attention to the issue. While Symington failed in his presidential bid in the 1960 Democratic primaries, Senator John F. Kennedy of Massachusetts, exploited the missile gap in his campaign, charging that the Eisenhower administration and Vice-president Richard M. Nixon, Kennedy's opponent, had allowed America to fall dangerously behind the Soviet Union in nuclear missiles.

Following his victory, President Kennedy learned the truth about the missile gap. It existed but favored the United States. The United States was building hundreds of missiles, while the Soviets had but a handful. The Department of Defense, however, continued to use the alleged "Gap" to justify a crash ICBM procurement program. By 1964 the United States had deployed 834 ICBMs, while the Soviet Union had 120 missiles.

Reference

Edgar M. Bottome, *The Missile Gap: A Study of the Formulation of Military and Political Policy* (Rutherford, N.J.: Fairleigh Dickinson University Press, 1971).

– B. D. K.

MRVs and MIRVs

Multiple reentry vehicles (MRVs) were first deployed in 1961 on the Polaris A-3, a submarine-launched ballistic missile (SLBM). The A-3 used an MRV delivery system called Claw that enabled the United States Navy to load three warheads onto one SLBM. The warheads separated from the missile in flight but traveled toward the same target.

The reasons for deploying the MRV system were defensive and fiscal. In 1964 the Soviet Union began deploying a ballistic missile defense called Galosh. The army initially urged Secretary of Defense Robert S. McNamara to build a missile defense to counter the Soviet deployment, but McNamara, who rejected the army's recommendation, chose instead to support the MRV project as a less expensive way to counter Soviet defenses. MRV technology increased threefold the number of American warheads, tripling the number of targets Soviet missile defenses had to defend against.

By 1964 the American space program had refined MRV guidance, developing a post-boost control system. Unlike the Claw, which merely propelled the three warheads toward a given target, the post-boost control system, consisting of a maneuvering "bus" within the nose cone of the missile, allowed each warhead to be aimed at a different target. This system became known as a multiple independently targeted reentry vehicle, or MIRV.

MIRV technology dramatically increased the number of warheads in the American nuclear arsenal. In 1970 Strategic Air Command (SAC), the branch of the air force responsible for strategic bombers and missiles, began deploying a MIRVed intercontinental ballistic missile (ICBM), the Minuteman III; one year later the navy deployed a MIRVed SLBM on the Polaris submarine. Before introducing MIRV technology in 1970, the United States had 1,710 ballistic missiles and 1,710 warheads. Fifteen years later, in 1985, the U.S. arsenal had decreased by 42 missiles, to 1,668, but the total number of warheads had increased nearly fivefold to 7,932.

Whereas MRV was deployed primarily in response to Soviet ballistic missile defenses, MIRVs were deployed primarily to counter the growth of the Soviet rocket forces, which had grown by more than one thousand missiles in the 1960s. To target Soviet missiles and military installations, SAC pressed Secretary McNamara to expand U.S. ICBM forces to ten thousand missiles. Concerned with the budgetary implications of the air force proposal, McNamara imposed a one-thousand-missile ceiling, but agreed to adopt MIRV technology to enable SAC to target the entire Soviet arsenal.

The Soviet Union lagged five to ten years behind the Americans in multiple warhead technology, deploying their first MIRVed missile, the SS-11, in 1975 and their first MIRVed SLBM in 1979.

Many experts believe that the emergence of MIRV technology destabilized the strategic balance. With MIRVed nuclear arsenals, each superpower had an incentive to strike first in a crisis because a relatively small number of MIRVed missiles can destroy a large number of the adversary's warheads. The disparity between the number of warheads and missiles was especially great in the case of the Soviet Union, which could load as many as thirty warheads onto its powerful ICBMs.

Reference

Ted Greenwood, *Making the MIRV: A Study of Defense Decision-Making* (Cambridge, Mass.: Ballinger, 1975).

– B. D. K.

SEE ALSO THESE RELATED ENTRIES
Curtis LeMay, 1; Strategic Air Command, 3.

Multilateral Force Proposal

The Multilateral Force (MLF) proposal, put forth by the United States in the early 1960s, called for a strategic missile force that would be jointly owned, operated, and controlled by both the nuclear and nonnuclear countries in the North Atlantic Treaty Organization (NATO).

The concept of an MLF first evolved out of a series of NATO studies undertaken in 1957 to produce a credible response to what appeared to be a Soviet lead in intercontinental ballistic missiles (ICBMs). One of the conclusions stated that a force of mobile, medium-range ballistic missiles (MRBMs), manned by multinational NATO units, would be a viable deterrent against the evolving Soviet missile force. This proposal, however, was shelved for years as it became apparent that the United States had the technology necessary to build its own ICBM force.

In 1960 a group of State Department officials renewed the call for the MLF, which, according to their plan, would be constituted of several hundred Polaris missiles based in submarines. The reasons behind the American resurrection of the MLF and its continued prominence in international affairs are many. First, State Department officials were very concerned about nuclear proliferation and the possibility that Germany would want to follow the British and the French in developing an independent nuclear deterrent. Second, the supposed "linkage" between NATO's conventional and nuclear deterrents and the U.S. strategic nuclear force was viewed with increasing incredulity by many Europeans. Third, the NATO allies had to fill a gap in NATO's force structure to match the high number of Soviet MRBMs recently deployed against Western Europe. Finally, the State Department thought that the deployment of the MLF would relieve some of NATO's political problems regarding diplomatic negotiations and ease the political and financial burdens carried by the United States in maintaining NATO's nuclear deterrent.

Diplomatic Negotiations

An inability to develop a broad European constituency for the proposal was the largest problem facing proponents of the MLF. While Germany and Italy eventually gave their support to the MLF, France under Charles de Gaulle tried to avoid any form of military integration whenever possible, and Britain wanted to continue to maintain its independent nuclear force. Smaller countries did not want to sacrifice other military programs in order to pay for the force.

Nevertheless, the problems which continued to plague NATO concerning nuclear matters and the possibility that Germany might drift away from its Atlantic ties in favor of stronger Franco-German cooperation propelled State Department officials to press for the ratification of an MLF treaty. The final MLF proposal, put forth in 1963, called for a fleet of twenty-five surface ships each carrying eight Polaris A3 missiles. Diplomatic pressure in favor of the MLF was exerted by the United States on its allies, and eventually the British Foreign Office countered with a proposal of its own. Called the Atlantic Nuclear Force (ANF), the British proposal called for the combining of already existing nuclear forces – such as the British V-bomber, the American and British Polaris submarines, and perhaps certain French forces – into one multinational force.

In 1965 British prime minister Harold Wilson brought the ANF proposal to his Washington meeting with President Lyndon B. Johnson. To the relief of the British, Johnson stated that he would take the British proposal under serious consideration. He confessed that his strong support for the MLF was put upon him by his key adviser at the State Department. Lacking congressional and allied support and a consensus within his own administration, and facing opposition from Moscow which was threatening the proposed Non-Proliferation Treaty, Johnson believed that a continued American insistence on the program would be too costly. After this setback, the MLF (as well as the ANF) quickly faded away as a serious military option, and NATO continued to rely on U.S. nuclear weapons as its deterrent.

Reference

John Baylis, *Anglo-American Defense Relations, 1939–1980* (New York: St. Martin's Press, 1981).

– P.M.

SEE ALSO THESE RELATED ENTRIES
Deterrence, 3; Flexible Response, 3; Linkage, 3.

Munich Analogy

The Munich analogy uses the Munich agreement of 1938 to exemplify the consequences of failing to resist aggression at the right time. The analogy has been used by Western diplomats and policymakers in arguing that the search for peace at any price only emboldens the aggressor; in the end, appeasement not only fails to prevent war, but it ensures that when war comes, it is under the least auspicious circumstances for the peace party.

Munich Agreement of 1938

On 27 September 1938, after weeks of bluster and threats, Adolf Hitler sent seven German divisions to the Czech frontier and issued an ultimatum to the Prague government to hand over a portion of its territory, the Sudetenland. Three million ethnic Germans lived in the region, and Hitler had coveted its rich resources. A new European war appeared certain. France had a treaty obligation to defend Czechoslovakia, and Britain was expected to follow France.

Desperate to avoid bloodshed in "a faraway country" populated by people "of whom we know nothing," British prime minister Neville Chamberlain flew to Munich to talk the terms of a settlement. On 29 and 30 September Chamberlain and French prime minister Edouard Daladier met with Hitler and Italian dictator Benito Mussolini in the Bavarian city and accepted Hitler's demands for an immediate occupation of the Sudetenland by the German troops. Czech representatives were not allowed to participate in the meeting, and when it was over they were asked in and told to accept the decision of the four-power conference. Neville Chamberlain returned to Britain with an agreement that he said would quench Hitler's thirst for territory and pull Europe back from the brink of war. It was to be a "peace in our time," in the prime minister's words.

On 1–7 October Nazi troops invaded the Sudetenland without firing a shot, but that did not satisfy Hitler. Six months later the Wehrmacht marched into Prague, to be followed in September 1939 by the invasion of Poland. Chamberlain's capitulation did not forestall the European war, which the prime minister had sought frantically to prevent.

Lessons of Munich Agreement

In the decades after Munich, recognition of these lessons conditioned the Western response to the Soviet Union, the start of the Cold War, and the Korean and Vietnam conflicts. In 1972, for example, U.S. vice-president Spiro T. Agnew assailed the Democratic presidential candidate George McGovern by saying that "even Chamberlain did not carry a beggar's cup to Munich – as McGovern proposes to carry to Hanoi." In 1977 an article by Bayard Rustin and Carl Gershman in *Commentary* magazine called the U.S. failure to counter the Soviets in Angola the clearest demonstration "since Munich [of] impotence of the democratic world in the face of totalitarian aggression." This analogy was pursued further in 1985 by Jeane Kirkpatrick, U.S. ambassador to the United Nations, who attacked critics of American help to Nicaraguan contras by saying, "it is not Vietnam that's the appropriate analogy – it's Munich." The Munich agreement became an all-encompassing symbol of appeasement and a conspicuous absence of political and moral backbone in foreign policy.

References

Donald Lammers, *Explaining Munich: The Search for Motive in British Policy* (Stanford, Cal.: Hoover Institute, 1966);

Henri Nogueres, *Munich: Peace for Our Time* (New York, McGraw, 1965);

Telford Taylor, *Munich: The Price of Peace* (Garden City, N.Y., Doubleday, 1979).

                                             –J. M.

SEE ALSO THESE RELATED ENTRIES
Jeane J. Kirkpatrick, 1; Korean War, 3; George S. McGovern, 1; Vietnam War, 3.

Mutual and Balanced Force Reductions Talks

From the mid 1950s until the early 1990s the North Atlantic Treaty Organization (NATO) and the Warsaw Pact stationed large armies facing one another in Central Europe, preparing for the possibility of war. By the end of the 1980s about 2 million soldiers were deployed along the western boundaries of the Iron Curtain, a development which, as one author noted, was "the largest peacetime military confrontation in history." In 1973 NATO and the Warsaw Pact began the Mutual and Balanced Force Reductions (MBFR) talks, which attempted to add some measure of stability to the Cold War and begin to dismantle the massive military buildup. While the talks ultimately proved unsuccessful, they nevertheless began the important process of working out the specifics of troop cuts and verification and stabilization measures. This experience would prove useful in the Conventional Forces Europe (CFE) talks, which began in 1987.

The MBFR talks were born out of political considerations in the late 1960s and early 1970s. Few observers actually believed that the talks would soon produce an agreement on rapid military reductions in Europe. Rather, MBFR talks were seen as a means of testing Soviet dedication to détente and staving off potentially risky unilateral reductions being proposed by politicians in the NATO countries.

NATO proposed the MBFR talks as a response to Soviet calls for a European Security Conference, which the Soviets hoped would provide a treaty with the West that would legitimize the post–World War II Eastern European borders as Stalin had drawn them. Since there existed no formal treaty ending that war, the Soviets feared that questions regarding borders could eventually spark another war and force the Soviets to give up the land that they had annexed after the Third Reich's defeat. The Kremlin also sought to contain the possible expansion of the West German army, limit U.S. forces in Central Europe, and, in so doing, lower its own military – and financial – commitment to the confrontation.

Goals of Western Alliance

For the Western Alliance, the MBFR talks presented a means to accomplish several goals. Soviet entry into the talks was widely seen as a response to NATO's agreement to enter into the Conference on Security and Cooperation in Europe (CSCE) and eventually ratify Europe's new borders. The MBFR talks were also a means to focus attention on what NATO regarded as the most pressing problem facing the two alliances: the massive military buildup. The Warsaw Pact's sizable tank, artillery, and ground troop deployments – and nearby reserve forces – had long worried the Western allies and a consensus had emerged in the mid 1960s that NATO should seek disarmament talks aimed at reducing the two alliances' forces to a common, lower level.

Another and perhaps more important reason why Western countries wanted to engage the Warsaw Pact in conventional disarmament talks was that their budgets were straining under the weight of what some considered high defense-spending levels. Thus MBFR could be used by Western governments to halt calls – such as the Mansfield amendments in the United States – for unilateral cutbacks from NATO since such reductions would hurt NATO's negotiating position.

The Western Alliance's initial proposal was to call for a reduction of ground-force levels to 700,000 men on both sides. According to NATO numbers, the Eastern-bloc countries would have to make greater cuts since they had some 200,000 more soldiers in the region. The first phase would involve the withdrawal of 29,000 U.S. soldiers (but not their equipment) and a Soviet tank army (68,000 soldiers and 1,700 tanks). The NATO proposal also called for a series of confidence-building measures that included advanced notification of maneuvers in the treaty-limited region and on-site inspections to verify compliance with the accord.

Warsaw Pact Proposals

The East's proposals differed widely from what the West put on the negotiating table. The Soviet Union disputed NATO's numbers on the Warsaw Pact's forces and insisted that military parity already existed in Central Europe. An exchange of data, according to the Soviets, was not needed, and the cuts could be taken from current levels. The East proposed instead to have each nation cut 17 percent of its contribution to its respective alliance, with the totals for both sides balancing out because of the existing "parity" between NATO and the Warsaw Pact. Phase I would entail the withdrawal of 20,000 Soviet troops in exchange for 13,000 U.S. troops. NATO refused to accept the East's approach to the talks since it would codify what it thought to be a Warsaw Pact advantage in weapons that would keep certain countries – such as the United States, Great Britain, Belgium, and the Netherlands – from reducing their contributions to the alliance if NATO wanted to maintain an overall balance of forces.

The fact that the two sides disagreed on whether or not a military balance existed stymied the negotiations from their beginning in 1973 until their end in 1987. One of the most significant advances in the talks, however, came in 1978 when NATO and the Warsaw Pact came to an agreement that the alliances should cut their forces to a total of 900,000 ground and air personnel and a subtotal of 700,000 ground troops. The inability to find a mutually acceptable set of data on the forces, however, stalled this proposal, and the talks continued to stagnate. Finally, in 1985, NATO proposed to postpone the establishment of a data base and cut 5,000 U.S. troops and 11,500 Soviet troops as a means to breathe new life into MBFR. While the Warsaw Pact's initial response seemed positive, NATO found the East's counterproposal to be significantly less forthcoming than expected, especially concerning verification and confidence-building measures.

After the failure of the 1985 NATO proposal, most observers considered the MBFR talks to be dead in the water. When newly appointed Soviet general secretary Mikhail Gorbachev presented his "Budapest Appeal" for a new "comprehensive approach" to the disarmament talks, however, the NATO countries proposed to conclude the MBFR negotiations and establish a fresh mandate for a new set of Central Forces in Europe (CFE) negotiations.

While the MBFR talks ultimately were unsuccessful, they nevertheless played an important role in NATO and Warsaw Pact efforts to reduce the conventional forces deployed against each other. First, the MBFR negotiations began a dialogue that would later continue in the much more successful CFE talks. Second, and perhaps more importantly, MBFR revealed the key issues on which NATO and the Warsaw Pact differed, and it thus presented future negotiators with a set of problems to work out. This fact was clearly in evidence in Gorbachev's Budapest appeal, which included the possibility of on-site inspections – something NATO considered vital to an agreement in spite of Soviet refusals from 1973 onward.

References

John Borawski, "Mutual Force Reductions in Europe from a Soviet Perspective," *Orbis*, 22 (Winter 1979): 845–873;

Abbott Brayton, "MBFR and Conventional Forces in Europe," *World Today*, 40 (December 1984): 497–507;

Sam Nunn, "Mutual and Balanced Force Reductions – A Need to Shift Our Focus," *Atlantic Community Quarterly*, 16 (Spring 1978): 18–21;

Richard F. Staar, "The MBFR Process and Its Prospects," *Orbis*, 27 (Winter 1984): 999–1009;

David S. Yost, "Beyond MBFR: The Atlantic to the Urals Gambit," *Orbis,* 31 (Spring 1987): 99–134.

– P.M.

SEE ALSO THESE RELATED ENTRIES
Détente, 3.

Mutual Assured Destruction

Mutual assured destruction (MAD) is a strategy for the employment of nuclear weapons that grew out of the nuclear deterrence strategy of the administrations of John F. Kennedy and Lyndon B. Johnson. Initially known as assured destruction, the policy was formulated in order to provide an answer to the question that was often asked of American defense planners about nuclear weapons: "How much is enough?" The question was asked with increasing urgency as the United States was moving away from targeting cities to targeting military installations. Whereas the number of population centers was limited and fixed, the number of military targets was large and growing.

The need to devise a new nuclear strategy was recognized early by the Dwight D. Eisenhower administration. The Killian Report, presented to the National Security Council (NSC) in 1955, acknowledged shortcomings in the strategy of massive retaliation and its reliance on the then-overwhelming American nuclear superiority. That superiority was being eroded by the buildup of the Soviet nuclear arsenal, confirmed by intelligence reports. Without nuclear superiority, threats by the United States to use its nuclear weapons against Soviet cities on behalf of its European allies were no longer credible.

Assured Destruction

The doctrine of assured destruction was formulated to set a quantitative limit on the new nuclear arsenal the United States was building in response to this problem of credibility. Devised early in Kennedy's tenure, the term was first used in 1964. Assured destruction rested on the assumption that the threat of a nuclear strike launched against the enemy's population and industrial centers with atomic weapons would deter the enemy from launching a first-strike attack. Kennedy's secretary of defense, Robert S. McNamara, believing that the targeting of cities created a stable "balance of terror" between the United States and the Soviet Union, stipulated that the success of assured destruction as a deterrent could be guaranteed by the ability to destroy from 20 to 30 percent of the enemy's population, and 50 to 75 percent of the enemy's industrial capacity.

While McNamara publicly adopted assured destruction, the actual plans being developed by the United States for fighting a nuclear war were of a different kind. The nuclear doctrine known as "counterforce" sought to deter attack through the ability to fight a limited, protracted nuclear war while avoiding, to the extent possible, damage to the civilian population. Since the targeting of Soviet nuclear weapons and other military assets may have meant that the United States would have been the first to resort to nuclear attack in seeking to disarm the Soviets, some force planners viewed the mutual targeting of nuclear arsenals as destabilizing. Counterforce nuclear targeting strategy was also criticized as infeasible during this period for technical reasons, as the early intercontinental ballistic missiles (ICBMs) were not accurate enough to strike Soviet missile silos.

The acquisition by the Soviets of an assured destruction capability in the 1960s led to the emergence of mutual assured destruction, or MAD. The MAD posture was criticized for a variety of reasons. Many opposed MAD on moral grounds, objecting to what was perceived as holding the populations of the two countries hostage and purposefully threatening the lives of noncombatants. In 1984 a pastoral letter issued by a group of Roman Catholic bishops denounced nuclear deterrence based on this argument.

MAD Criticized

Some critics of MAD offered alternatives to the balance of terror. The belief that defense is moral while deterrence is immoral provided the impetus for the Strategic Defense Initiative (SDI). Proposed by President Ronald Reagan in a 1983 speech, the SDI program was to "make nuclear weapons impotent and obsolete."

Others opposed MAD for strategic reasons. These critics asserted that the purpose of Soviet nuclear strategy was not to deter a nuclear war, but to fight and win a nuclear war. These critics say that concepts such as "unacceptable damage" are peculiarly Western and are not necessarily shared by the Soviets, and that the MAD threat to destroy cities might not deter the Soviets from launching a first strike.

The balance of terror was the linchpin of the superpower-deterrent relationship, although MAD was modified to meet changing strategic realities. In 1967 the doctrine of flexible response was adopted by the North Atlantic Treaty Organization (NATO) as its grand strategy, providing for a broader range of targeting options, including counterforce targeting. During the 1970s and 1980s, as Soviet nuclear capabilities increased and as technological advancements made high-accuracy strikes possible, more and more counterforce targeting options were included in U.S. strategy.

References

Lawrence Freedman, *The Evolution of Nuclear Strategy* (New York: St. Martin's Press, 1981);

Colin S. Gray, "Nuclear Strategy: The Case for a Theory of Victory," *International Security,* 4 (Summer 1979): 54–87;

Robert Jervis, "Why Nuclear Superiority Doesn't Matter," *Political Science Quarterly,* no. 94 (Winter 1979/1980): 617–633.

– M. F.

SEE ALSO THESE RELATED ENTRIES
Deterrence, 3; Flexible Response, 3; Limited Nuclear Options, 3; Robert S. McNamara, 1; North Atlantic Treaty Organization, 3; Strategic Defense Initiative, 3.

National Security Act

The National Security Act of 1947 created the National Security Council (NSC), the Central Intelligence Agency (CIA), the United States Air Force, and the post of secretary of defense, all symbols of the first permanent, peacetime defense establishment in the United States. In expectation of America's sustained and comprehensive engagement in world affairs, the National Security Act sought to integrate economic, military, and intelligence resources with foreign policy objectives in order to ensure the most effective projection of U.S. power abroad.

The National Security Act had its genesis in the contentious issue of the unification of the armed forces, fought out between the army and the navy and their adherents since 1943. The military services had been forced by wartime exigency and circumstance into unprecedented cooperation, making decisions in a variety of ad hoc arrangements. The army soon began to urge that these arrangements be permanently maintained after the war. Citing the expected reduction in military expenditures, the army argued that unification at the highest level of the armed services was necessary to avoid needless and costly duplication of effort, thereby ensuring the most efficient distribution of limited defense dollars. But the navy, also mindful of the expected struggle over the military budget, worried that the army would come to dominate any unified structure to the navy's detriment, and it lobbied vociferously against unification. By the end of the war, the dispute had assumed a high degree of vehemence. Assistant Secretary of War John McCloy derided the "peculiar psychology of the Navy Department, which frequently seemed to retire from the realm of logic into the dim religious world in which Neptune was God, Mahan his prophet, and the United States Navy the only true Church."

Eberstadt Report

In 1945 Secretary of the Navy James Forrestal decided to take the offensive and commissioned his friend Ferdinand Eberstadt to study the subject and propose changes that the navy could support. Forrestal wrote to Eberstadt on 19 June 1945 and pointedly asked, "Would unification of the War and Navy Departments under a single head improve our national security?" and "What form of postwar organization should be established and maintained to enable the military services and other Government departments and agencies most effectively to provide for the protection of our national security?"

The Eberstadt Report of 22 October 1945 rejected the idea of a single unified department, suggesting instead a "federal" arrangement of three services — war, navy, and a newly independent air force — headed by a civilian secretary. This arrangement was largely in accord with prevailing navy thinking, but Eberstadt went beyond the idea of mere military reorganization. The situation, he reported, "calls for action far more drastic and far-reaching than simply unification of the military services. It calls for a complete realignment of our governmental organizations to serve our national security in the light of our new world power and position, our new international commitments and risks and the epochal new scientific discoveries."

Almost all of the new agencies that Eberstadt recommended found their way into the National Security Act. The NSC, which Forrestal called "perhaps the most important feature" of the unification bill, was created, as was the CIA. A National Security Resources Board was necessary "to implement military plans in the industrial and civilian fields." Eberstadt's report also proposed that the Joint Chiefs of Staff be retained on a permanent basis to advise the president and the secretary of defense.

Between 22 October 1945, when the Eberstadt Report was released, and 26 July 1947, when the National Security Act was passed, debate raged in Congress over the proposed unification. The struggle centered on army proposals for a department of defense, a secretary of defense, and a chief of staff — all of which President Harry S Truman favored. The navy, however, continued to voice its opposition. During the debate Forrestal was critical in reaching a compromise.

The National Security Act of 1947 ultimately created a national military establishment headed by a secretary of defense, who would be expected to act as a coordinator of the three separate military departments. The day that President Truman signed the act he offered Forrestal the position of first secretary of defense. Forrestal assumed the post on 17 September 1947.

Two years later, under the National Security Act Amendments of 1949, the national military establishment was converted to the status of executive department and renamed the Department of Defense. The military services were stripped of their executive status and more firmly subordinated under the secretary of defense.

Reference

Robert G. Albion and Robert H. Connery, *Forrestal and the Navy* (New York: Columbia University Press, 1962).

                                                                                    – M. B.

SEE ALSO THESE RELATED ENTRIES

James V. Forrestal, 1; National Security Council, 3.

National Security Council

The National Security Council (NSC) came into existence on 26 July 1947 under the provisions of the National Security Act of 1947, which was designed to create a more unified defense establishment. The NSC was largely the brainchild of U.S. secretary of the navy James Forrestal, who in 1945 predicted that the United States would assume the leading postwar role in world affairs – a role that would require the close integration of American economic and military resources in order to achieve U.S. objectives. Forrestal thought that this coordinated foreign policy should logically flow from the White House, given the president's dual role as head of government and head of the military. Forrestal, however, was aware of the political vagaries inherent to the executive office. So he proposed that the NSC, composed of the president and a handful of cabinet-level officials, would review issues, develop policies, and advise the president on the most critical issues of national security facing the United States. These NSC principals would be supported by a full-time staff under the direction of an executive secretary. In practice, the organizational structure of the staff and the actual composition of the council itself would vary with each presidential administration.

Under Truman

The influence of the NSC on U.S. foreign policy has waxed and waned over the years, dependent mostly on the working style of each president and the degree of importance he has granted the NSC. From its inception until the present, the NSC has gone through three distinct phases of development. The first phase occurred from 1947 until 1960, when the NSC became institutionalized in the executive office. Originally, President Harry S Truman viewed the council with some misgivings, suspecting

that it might be a congressional attempt to limit presidential authority. Additionally, Truman very much wanted a strong secretary of state with whom he could share the decision-making process in shaping foreign policy. In a letter to the NSC on 26 July 1948, Truman defended his "complete freedom to accept, reject and amend the Council's advice and to consult with other members of his official family." He appointed fellow Missouri businessman and reserve admiral Sidney Souers to be executive secretary, and until the outbreak of the Korean War in June 1950 Truman attended only twelve of the fifty-seven scheduled sessions of the NSC. Even so, the NSC recommended many courses of action that Truman ultimately followed in the early days of the Cold War – aid to the Greek government during that country's civil war, covert involvement in the Italian elections of May 1948, and aid to Berlin during the blockade of 1948–1949. These policies were contained in papers prepared by NSC staff members, who were situated across the street from the White House in the executive office building.

With time NSC principals began to assign the production of policy papers to the staffs of their own agencies. Perhaps the most influential American policy statement during Truman's term was NSC-68, drafted between March and April of 1950 by officials at the State and Defense Departments. An analysis of Soviet intentions and capabilities, NSC-68 served as a blueprint for American policy in the early days of the Cold War and justified a rapid increase in American military spending – up to 20 percent of the gross national product – so as not to fall behind the Soviet Union. The NSC approved the document in April 1950, and it thereafter served to galvanize United States policy regarding the Soviet Union.

When North Korea invaded South Korea in 1950, Truman's attitude toward the council quickly changed, and the NSC finally attained a certain legitimacy. Truman consulted with the NSC on almost a daily basis, relying on it for much of the advice he received during the war. He attended sixty-two of the seventy-one formal sessions of the council, at whose meetings the director of Central Intelligence (DCI), the chairman of the Joint Chiefs of Staff, and other officials were increasingly seen.

Under Eisenhower

Under President Dwight D. Eisenhower the NSC became a fully institutionalized part of the U.S. foreign policy establishment. Eisenhower streamlined the organizational structure of the NSC to give it clear lines of authority and responsibility. He also created the much-publicized position of special assistant to the president for national security affairs. Robert Cutler, a Boston banker, first held this post, and chaired an intra-agency committee, the NSC Planning Board, to prepare policy papers for the formal sessions. A second group within the NSC, the Operations Coordinating Board, was created to oversee the actual implementation of presidential decisions. Although Eisenhower publicly gave the impression that the NSC was at the center of his foreign policy decision making, in truth he relied as much if not more on his secretary of state, John Foster Dulles, and his office of the staff secretary. Eisenhower was never able to rid the NSC of bureaucratic rivalries, and so he increasingly came to use NSC meetings as a formal stage upon which his cabinet officials would unwittingly air their differences before a watchful president.

In 1953 Eisenhower did attempt to derive a comprehensive national security strategy toward the Soviet Union from a series of NSC meetings, called the Solarium exercise. From these came NSC 162/2, which contained the notion of massive retaliation. The paper also recommended a greater American emphasis on regional security alliances, and this led directly to the formation of the Southeast Asia Treaty Organization (SEATO) and the Central Treaty Organization (CENTO).

Toward the end of Eisenhower's presidency, the NSC came under increasing criticism for having become too rigid and stultified. Critics said that council meetings had begun to resemble legislative sessions, with the members negotiating among themselves on behalf of their narrow departmental interests rather than in a rational and deliberative manner designed to provide the president with the best advice with which to serve the country. In mid 1959 a congressional subcommittee under Democratic senator Henry M. Jackson responded to these criticisms with a study designed to provide the incoming administration with suggestions on how to reform the NSC.

Under Kennedy

The second distinct phase in the history of the NSC began in 1961 when John F. Kennedy became president, and lasted until 1980. According to Zbigniew Brzezinski, the NSC during this phase was marked by a "higher degree of personalization, which in time also became excessive." Kennedy and his advisers agreed with the Jackson subcommittee that the NSC had become too bureaucratized. In keeping with his deliberately disorganized style, Kennedy set about to transform policy making into a looser and more open system, in the process dismantling much of the elaborate apparatus of the NSC under Eisenhower and abolishing the Planning Board and the Operations Coordinating Board. Kennedy named McGeorge Bundy as his special assistant for national security affairs, the first public figure to hold the position. Bundy was a brilliant, highly outspoken figure – a former dean of Harvard College who viewed the apparatus of government more as an obstacle to circumvent than as a system to learn and master. Bundy was instructed to present his own views on policy to the president as part of the broader operating style Kennedy favored. Power accrued to Bundy in no small part because of awkward relations between Kennedy and his secretary of state, Dean Rusk. From this point on, the special assistant for national security affairs became an important figure in the cycle of foreign policy decision making. He was no longer merely a neutral coordinator of other people's views, but a major initiator of policy in his own right.

If Kennedy and Bundy brought a fresh approach to organizing the NSC, then they also sacrificed much of the council's former thoroughness and coherence. Decisions were increasingly made on an ad hoc basis as Kennedy would assign a cabinet official from the relevant department to study a particular problem and present proposals for action to him. Eventually this manner of policy formation caused Kennedy's foreign policy to assume a reactive tone. Issues of major importance would be addressed after they had come to warrant presidential attention. The deficiencies of this system became apparent in April 1961 during the Bay of Pigs invasion of Cuba, an operation supervised largely by the Central Intelligence Agency but characterized by little overall coordination or implementation of plans.

In the aftermath of the fiasco, Bundy acted in such a way as to strengthen the future role of the head of the NSC staff in the decision-making process of U.S. foreign policy. He moved the office of the national security adviser into the White House to ensure immediate access to the president. Bundy dealt with the established agencies in a highly selective fashion, drawing on the expertise of those officials whom he considered to be most able to serve the president. The most important decisions were made after Kennedy had consulted with an "inner group" of four to six advisers. The formal processes of the NSC, however, continued to suffer from official disregard and presidential neglect.

Under Johnson

In the Johnson White House the NSC continued to play the same marginal role that it had under Kennedy. Like Kennedy, Lyndon B. Johnson liked to conduct affairs through direct operational control. For advice, Johnson usually relied on senior officials such as Rusk or Defense Secretary Robert McNamara, both of whom had remained in the cabinet following Kennedy's assassination. Bundy remained as special assistant for national security affairs until 1966, when he was replaced by Walt W. Rostow, who was given the title of special assistant to the president.

Under Nixon and Ford

Richard M. Nixon was elected president in 1968, promising to "restore the National Security Council to its preeminent role in national security planning." He began by appointing Harvard professor Henry A. Kissinger to be his assistant for national security affairs, a title which placed him in the ranks of the most senior presidential aides. Nixon and Kissinger immediately brought foreign policy into the White House to an extent never seen before. Most of Nixon's substantive accomplishments in foreign affairs were the work of Nixon as the chief strategist and Kissinger as his master tactician. They contrived to exclude Secretary of State William P. Rogers and other cabinet officers from participation in the larger foreign policy issues facing the Nixon administration — the normalization of relations with the People's Republic of China, the prosecution of the war in Vietnam, and the pursuit of détente with the Soviet Union. During his tenure as national security adviser, Kissinger greatly increased the size of the NSC staff, enlarging it so as to form a small-scale state department to maintain tight control over an organization that Kissinger viewed as a dangerous rival. The formal National Security Council, however, declined in importance as Nixon paid less and less heed to the advice of its principals. But, in time, even many NSC staffers were increasingly left in the dark as the Nixon-Kissinger team created their own "back channel" in order to carry out diplomacy in secret. The most well known back channel linked Kissinger with Soviet ambassador Anatoli Dobrynin. First meeting at Dobrynin's apartment on 14 February 1969, the two began discussions on a wide variety of issues, the most crucial paralleling the highly public Strategic Arms Limitation Talks (SALT). Kissinger also began secret negotiations with Hanoi on 4 August 1969 on ending the Vietnam War.

By the time Nixon's second term began, Kissinger had become his premier foreign policy adviser, eclipsing the rest of the cabinet — and almost overshadowing the president. On 22 August 1973 Nixon named Kissinger secretary of state, a position he would hold concurrent with that of national security adviser. Kissinger remained in both positions after Gerald Ford became president in 1974. But in Ford's "Halloween Massacre" of November 1975, Kissinger lost his job as head of the NSC and was replaced by Admiral Brent Scowcroft, who had served as Kissinger's deputy.

With Scowcroft's ascension, the NSC principals regained some of their former primacy and the full council met regularly to consider policy. The NSC staff was streamlined and generally functioned without discord for the remainder of Ford's term.

Under Carter

Jimmy Carter became president in January 1977, promising to end Kissinger-style "Lone Ranger" diplomacy and to rely on his secretary of state, Cyrus Vance. Carter wanted the formal NSC to have a much greater role in the making of U.S. foreign policy, and he increased the number of its statutory members to include such officials as the attorney general and the secretary of the treasury. Carter appointed Zbigniew Brzezinski, a Columbia professor, to serve as his national security adviser. Brzezinski had previously advised politicians and had actively tutored Carter in foreign affairs throughout the presidential race. Soon after his appointment, however, Brzezinski decided to be a "strong" national security adviser. He convinced Carter to create two interagency bodies, the cabinet-level Special Coordination Committee (SCC), which he chaired, and the Policy Review Committee (PRC), which would run the day-to-day affairs of the NSC. The SCC had responsibility for arms control, crisis management, and covert operations. The full council would only meet when necessary.

Tensions between Brzezinski and Vance soon became apparent over such issues as the Soviet presence in Africa. Brzezinski essentially sought to link Soviet behavior that the United States found objectionable to the more basic tenor of Soviet-American relations, while Vance preferred to resolve differences with the Soviet Union through quiet diplomacy, one issue at a time. Brzezinski, with both cabinet-level status and close access to the president, generally had the upper hand in the struggle for influence and power. By 1979 Brzezinski had emerged as the administration's foreign policy spokesman. But tensions between Brzezinski and Vance continued to surface, making the formation of American foreign policy appear haphazard and erratic and crippling Carter's relations with U.S. allies.

Under Reagan and Bush

Ronald Reagan become president in 1981 and was convinced that Jimmy Carter had failed to maintain America's rightful position in the world. Reagan especially wanted to strengthen American military power, and to this end he decided to elevate the role of the secretary of defense to a more prominent position in the creation of foreign policy. His principal adviser in this area, however, would be his secretary of state. Much of the conflict over foreign policy during Reagan's tenure was caused by tensions between Defense Secretary Caspar Weinberger and Secretary of State George Shultz, and none of Reagan's national security advisers had the influence of these two men. According to Brzezinski, Reagan began the third distinct phase in the evolution of the NSC, which "involved its degradation."

Like many of his predecessors, Reagan promised to reform the NSC staff, to make it less influential. The head of the NSC was to serve more as a coordinator than as an initiator of foreign policy. Richard Allen, Reagan's first national security adviser, did function largely according to this scheme. He and his staff were isolated from the mainstream and, as a result, were an almost invisible part of the administration. Allen only lasted a year, during which time Reagan still had not formally defined the role the NSC was to play in his administration, relying for advice on his National Security Planning Group, chaired by his vice-president, George Bush.

Allen was succeeded by William Clark, and the NSC immediately began to take a more active role in the operational side of foreign policy, a process which culminated under John Poindexter. As Reagan's fourth national security adviser, Poindexter advised the president to sell arms secretly to Iran, in direct contrast to Reagan's publicly stated aversion to such a policy. Under the direction of marine colonel Oliver L. North – a member of the NSC staff – some of the money from these sales went to finance antigovernment guerrillas in Nicaragua. Poindexter resigned when revelations of the Iran-contra scandal broke in 1986. The operation became the worst scandal in the Reagan administration. That North was able to conduct such an operation bears testimony to the institutional power that the NSC had accumulated over the years.

After the Iran-contra affair Reagan promised to reform the NSC, adopting in part recommendations from the report issued by Republican senator John Tower's board of inquiry into the arms deals. Frank Carlucci, Poindexter's successor, abolished the NSC's political-military staff and replaced about half the staff in his first three months. When Carlucci was named secretary of defense in 1987, General Colin Powell became Reagan's sixth and last national security adviser. Powell's greatest achievement in that post was in his work planning Reagan's summit meetings with Soviet leader Mikhail Gorbachev in December 1987 and May 1988. At their second meeting the two signed the Intermediate Nuclear Forces Treaty on intermediate-range nuclear weapons. Powell and the NSC staff received much of the credit for the smooth ratification of the treaty.

President George Bush changed little in the organization of the NSC staff that he inherited from Reagan in 1989. Brent Scowcroft was named national security adviser, a position he had briefly held under Gerald Ford. Under Ford, Scowcroft had been considered one of the best managers ever to head the NSC.

The NSC apparatus is but one part of the foreign policy process in the United States. As such, its influence in decision making has varied in the more than forty years since its creation in 1947 — largely because of its status as part of the executive branch. The role and prestige of each NSC is a reflection of the operating style of the president it has served.

References

Constantine C. Menges, *Inside the National Security Council: The True Story of the Making and Unmaking of Reagan's Foreign Policy* (New York: Simon & Schuster, 1988);

John Prados, *Keepers of the Keys: A History of the National Security Council From Truman to Bush* (New York: Morrow, 1991).

— M. B.

SEE ALSO THESE RELATED ENTRIES
Zbigniew Brzezinski, 1; McGeorge Bundy, 1; Frank Carlucci, 1; Henry Kissinger, 1; National Security Act, 3; National Security Council Memorandum–68, 3; Colin Powell, 1; Walt W. Rostow, 1; Brent Scowcroft, 1.

National Security Council Memorandum–68

In 1949 President Harry S Truman directed Secretary of State Dean G. Acheson and Secretary of Defense James V. Forrestal to conduct a study of American foreign policy. Two events in 1949, the victory of Mao Zedong's communist forces in the Chinese civil war and the Soviet explosion of an atomic bomb, convinced the president that his administration had failed to formulate a global policy to stop the spread of communism, to which he had dedicated his foreign policy in his March 1947 announcement of the Truman Doctrine.

Paul H. Nitze, director of Policy Planning in the State Department, assumed much of the responsibility for this study. By April 1950 he and his staff had completed the report, which became known as National Security Council memorandum–68 (NSC-68). At first glance NSC-68 appears quite similar to George F. Kennan's strategy of containment, but their approaches differed both in their understanding of the Soviet threat and in the means they advocated to counter it. The view of containment offered in NSC-68 served as the basis for U.S. national security policy for more than three decades.

The memorandum rested on an unremittingly dark view of the Soviet Union. It argued that the Soviet Union was a totalitarian menace constitutionally incapable of tolerating diversity: "The existence and persistence of the idea of freedom is a permanent and continuous threat to the foundation of the slave society; and it therefore regards as intolerable the long continued existence of freedom in the world."

The memorandum stressed military means in containing communism. Nitze rejected Kennan's idea that the United States needed only to defend key global areas of military-industrial might to ensure American security. If Western European countries thought that the United States could not come to their defense, they would begin of their own accord to accommodate the Soviet Union. Nitze argued that the United States needed to create a perimeter defense around the Soviet Union that would counter any form of Soviet expansion. If the United States failed to demonstrate its will through military preparedness, Nitze feared that the United States would lose credibility as a world power.

NSC-68 accordingly called for a system of military alliances that would fence in the Soviet empire even in geopolitically less significant areas such as South Asia. While the memorandum endorsed the decision to build the hydrogen bomb, it questioned the utility of nuclear threats in light of the successful Soviet atomic test. Instead, NSC-68 reasserted the importance of conventional military might and called for a massive conventional buildup.

Defense Spending

This recommendation had a significant impact on Western Europe. In September 1950 the United States decided to deploy four to six army divisions on the European continent and to participate militarily in the North Atlantic Treaty Organization (NATO). The Joint Chiefs of Staff, reluctant to increase U.S. military obligations before the administration had increased defense spending, initially opposed this decision. To gain the Chiefs' support, the Truman administration agreed to the rearmament of West Germany and its membership in NATO.

Mounting a global military response to the Soviet threat dramatically increased U.S. military expenditures. In April 1950, before approving NSC-68, Truman set a $13.5 billion ceiling on defense spending for fiscal year 1951. On 19 July he requested an additional $10 billion. On 1 August he asked Congress for $4 billion more; three days later he requested another $1.6 billion. Finally, on 1 December, Truman submitted requests for $16.8 billion. Despite his commitment to a ceiling on defense spending, the president raised his initial $13.5 billion defense-authorization request to $48.2 billion, an increase of 257 percent.

Republicans, led by former president Herbert Hoover, Senator Robert A. Taft of Ohio, Governor Thomas E. Dewey of New York, Senator Arthur H. Vandenberg of Michigan, and John Foster Dulles, criticized the administration's defense policies. They argued that Truman's expenditures would create massive debt, sap the strength of the dollar, and discourage incentives for national economic growth. In response, the proponents of NSC-68 argued that increases in defense spending would actually spur economic growth by augmenting federal investment in the economy. Drawing on the American economic experience during World War II, Nitze argued that the federal government could simultaneously raise the American standard of living and increase defense spending by operating the economy closer to its capacity.

Requirements of Containment

Because the authors of NSC-68 considered the Soviet threat to be immediate, they tended to focus on the shortterm military requirements of containment, paying little attention to long-term goals or strategy. The document mentioned the possibility of exploiting nationalist or other contradictory sentiments within the international communist movement but made no practical suggestions as to how the United States would accomplish this. Similarly, while NSC-68 recognized the desirability of changing the Soviet understanding of international conventions and norms, it failed to explain how this would be done, rejecting the use of negotiations and suggesting that internal changes in the Soviet Union would only occur when the Soviets became convinced of the superiority of Western political and economic institutions.

President Truman did not immediately approve NSC-68, and he might never have done so if it were not for the Korean War. Nitze submitted the report in April 1950, but administration leaders resisted its prescriptions until communist North Korea invaded South Korea on 23 June 1950. North Korean aggression seemed to confirm Nitze's view of totalitarianism and suggested that the United States had failed once again to deter communist expansion.

References

John Lewis Gaddis, *Strategies of Containment: A Critical Appraisal of Postwar American National Security Policy* (New York: Oxford University Press, 1982);

Paul H. Nitze and John Lewis Gaddis, "NSC-68 and the Soviet Threat Reconsidered," *International Security,* 4 (Spring 1980): 164–176;

Sam Postbrief, "Departure from Incrementalism in U.S. Strategic Planning: The Origins of NSC-68," *Naval War College Review,* 33 (March–April 1980): 34–57;

Steven L. Rearden, *The Evolution of American Strategic Doctrine: Paul H. Nitze and the Soviet Challenge* (Boulder, Colo.: Westview, 1984);

Strobe Talbott, *The Master of the Game: Paul Nitze and the Nuclear Peace* (New York: Knopf, 1988);

Samuel F. Wells, Jr., "Sounding the Tocsin: NSC-68 and the Soviet Threat," *International Security,* 4 (Fall 1979): 116–158.

                                                                                        – B. D. K.

SEE ALSO THESE RELATED ENTRIES
Containment, 3; George F. Kennan, 1; Paul H. Nitze, 1; North Atlantic Treaty Organization, 3; Harry S Truman, 1.

New Look Policy

The New Look policy was a strategic doctrine adopted by the administration of Dwight D. Eisenhower to maintain U.S. military commitments at a lower cost. Promulgated in a 30 October 1953 National Security Council paper, NSC 162/2, titled *Basic National Security Policy,* the New Look policy stipulated that U.S. military strategy must meet the Soviet threat without, at the same time, "seriously weakening the U.S. economy or undermining our fundamental values and institutions." The administration pointed to World War II and the Korean War as examples of the prohibitive costs associated with preparing for and fighting large-scale conventional wars. The new policy was based on the conviction that in order to thwart Soviet designs U.S. strategy must be asymmetrical – that is, it must rely on American strengths to counter Soviet weaknesses rather than emulate the other side's strategy. Asymmetrical strategy meant that the United States, if attacked, would choose the means, location, and intensity of response in order to maximize its advantages over the aggressor: Secretary of State John Foster Dulles stated that a potential enemy must know "that he cannot always prescribe battle conditions that suit him." Specifically, the doctrine stressed that the new nuclear technology allowed the United States to shrink its forces while increasing their firepower.

The doctrine called for close cooperation between the United States and its allies, reliance on U.S. superiority in nuclear weapons to deter a Soviet attack, and – if deterrence failed – massive retaliation. New Look led to a reliance by the North Atlantic Treaty Organization (NATO) on nuclear forces, in the process changing the role of U.S. ground troops in Europe from blocking a Soviet invasion of Western Europe to serving as a "trip wire" that would trigger a U.S. nuclear retaliation against the Soviet Union if the Western alliance were attacked.

References

McGeorge Bundy, *Danger and Survival: Choices about the Bomb in the First Fifty Years* (New York: Random House, 1988);

Lawrence Freedman, *The Evolution of Nuclear Strategy* (New York: St. Martin's Press, 1981);

John Lewis Gaddis, *Strategies of Containment: A Critical Appraisal of Postwar American National Security Policy* (New York: Oxford University Press, 1982).

                                                                                          – B. F.

SEE ALSO THESE RELATED ENTRIES

Deterrence, 3; Dwight D. Eisenhower, 1; Massive Retaliation, 3.

Non-Aligned Movement

Third World leaders meeting at the Bandung Conference, April 1955

The Non-Aligned Movement (NAM) is a loose coalition of Third World countries that adopted a nonaligned foreign policy in their relations with Eastern and Western powers during the Cold War.

The Non-Aligned Movement began during the height of the Cold War, when several independent states from Asia, Africa, and the Middle East gathered in Bandung, Indonesia, in April 1955 for a conference hosted by Indonesian president Bung Sukarno. Attended by twenty-nine countries, the conference was the first major gathering of Third World countries and had the aim of fostering solidarity among the newly independent states and advancing common principles to avoid entanglement in the East-West rivalry. Among the participants in the conference were Josip Broz Tito of Yugoslavia, Gamal Abdul Nasser of Egypt, Jawaharlal Nehru of India, Kwame Nkrumah of Ghana, and Zhou Enlai, the foreign minister of the People's Republic of China. Sukarno, Tito, Nasser, and Nehru would come to dominate the movement as well as international diplomacy regarding the Third World. These leaders individually came to play prominent roles in the Cold War period, as a result of both the strategic and political importance of their re-

spective countries and the force of their personalities.

The business of the Bandung Conference centered around denouncing colonialism and adopting the "Five Principles of Coexistence," a resolution sponsored by Zhou. Containing the general aims of the movement, these principles called for mutual respect for territorial integrity and sovereignty; nonaggression; noninterference in the internal affairs of others; equality and mutual benefit; and peaceful coexistence. The summit meetings of the movement rotate among the member states every five years, with the first summit conference held in Belgrade, Yugoslavia, in 1961. The host country for the summit assumes the chairmanship of the NAM until the next summit. The NAM is distinct from most other Third World groupings and forums, such as the Group of 77, in that it operates largely outside of the United Nations and focuses more on political and security issues than on economic and developmental issues.

Role in East-West Rivalry

By the late 1980s NAM had come to include nearly every country in the Third World. Its members, however, played different, and often opposing, roles in the rivalry between the Eastern- and Western-bloc countries. While there are NAM countries that pursued what most scholars consider to be authentic nonaligned foreign policies, many displayed either a marked and consistent pro-Soviet policy or a pro-Western stance. Countries such as Afghanistan, Angola, Cuba, and Ethiopia had formal treaties of military and economic cooperation with the Soviet Union. Others, such as the Philippines, Thailand, and Zaire, had formal treaties with the United States. In both its official declarations and policy stance, NAM generally displayed a more anti-Western orientation, partly as a result of crosscutting north-south issues and the decolonization process. American officials often criticized the movement as a disguised forum for advocating pro-Soviet policies.

By and large, the members of this formal grouping of Third World states became the targets of either (or both) amity or hostility from the two superpowers, especially in the high points of the Cold War when both sought to capitalize on the decolonization process. Many of the member countries became political battlegrounds on which the superpowers played out their rivalry and challenged the influence and position of the other. On the other hand, the superpowers themselves often became the targets of skillful manipulation by these same states, which sought their own internal and external economic, political, and security objectives – objectives which ranged from economic development assistance to the projection of power beyond their own borders.

Relations within the NAM

The diversity of membership in the NAM was a persistent source of strain, normally preventing agreement on anything other than general statements of principles. A long-standing debate in the NAM had been over the question of how far the movement should lean to one side or the other in the East-West conflict. Early in the movement's development Nehru and Tito attempted to guide it under a policy of taking a foreign policy stance equidistant from the two competing blocs. The movement nearly split during its September 1979 summit conference in Havana, Cuba, where the summit chairman, Fidel Castro Ruz, advocated that NAM adopt an unambiguous pro-Soviet policy. Cuba, however, was among the handful of NAM members that supported the Soviet invasion of Afghanistan, which was widely condemned in the Third World.

Despite its limited successes and effectiveness, the Non-Aligned Movement was a forum from which Third World states sought to assert influence in international relations and achieve collective protection from what many of its members viewed as the hazards of the East-West global rivalry. Although the movement was frequently used by some members to push through their own individual alignment and policy preferences, many others sought to make it a forum for a truly nonaligned foreign policy. With the passing of the Cold War, the fate of the Non-Aligned Movement is problematic.

References

A. W. Singham, ed., *The Nonaligned Movement in World Politics* (Westport, Conn.: Lawrence Hill, 1977);

A. W. Singham and Shirley Hune, *Non-alignment in an Age of Alignments* (Westport, Conn.: Lawrence Hill, 1986).
                                                                 –J. R.-S.

North Atlantic Treaty Organization

An instrument of Cold War diplomacy, the North Atlantic Treaty Organization (NATO) was established to maintain the peace in postwar Europe. The United States, a founding member of NATO, committed itself for the first time in its history to a major peacetime alliance.

Since its creation in April 1949, the alliance has been singularly successful in its original aim of containing Soviet aggression against Western Europe. But, perhaps equally as important, it has given Europe over forty uninterrupted years of peace, as the United States stood ready to defuse tensions within the alliance. The existence of NATO made possible the sovereignty and rearmament of the Federal Republic of Germany (FRG) within a decade after World War II and allowed Germany's neighbors to overcome fears of an old enemy.

But the history of NATO has been a history of tensions and disputes between the United States and its allies. In the late 1950s some Europeans began to question the sincerity of American nuclear guarantees. In 1966 France withdrew its forces from NATO military command in assertion of a more independent course, free of perceived American hegemony. The early 1980s saw unprecedented popular discord in Europe in response to the American deployment there of new intermediate-range missiles.

The predecessor to NATO was the Western Union, a limited political and defensive community first proposed by British foreign secretary Ernest Bevin in a speech to the House of Commons on 22 January 1948. Bevin saw Europe as tottering on the edge of political catastrophe in the aftermath of World War II: Communist parties in France and Italy – with substantial popular support – were gaining political ground, Soviet-backed puppet governments appeared to be springing up in one Eastern European country after another, and the Soviet Union was making threatening gestures over occupied Berlin. Bevin's fears were shared by other European statesmen, most notably French foreign minister Georges Bidault. Within two months of Bevin's speech the Brussels Pact was signed, on 17 March, linking Britain, France, and the Benelux countries – Belgium, the Netherlands, and Luxembourg – in a fifty-year treaty. The members of the pact not only promised to support one another in the event of an armed attack on one or more of their members, but also agreed to "coordinate their economic activities as to produce . . . the elimination of conflict in their economic policies."

Bevin and Bidault wanted the United States to participate in the Western Union, seeing American involvement as vital to the survival and ultimate success of the pact. The emphasis that they placed on economic coordination was, indeed, designed to mesh with America's recently announced Marshall Plan, which provided economic assistance to Europe.

But the idea of a formal pact between the United States and Europe, military or otherwise, did not figure prominently in American public thinking at the time. As late as June 1950, when the Korean War broke out, the United States intended to disengage from Europe and bring its occupational troops home. The Marshall Plan had been seen originally as a way to ensure European recovery and self-reliance so that continued American intervention in European affairs would become unnecessary. Isolationism, especially as expressed by a powerful group of midwestern Republican senators, remained a strong force with which Washington still had to contend.

But American support for a common defensive arrangement with Europe grew in 1948 as political instability threatened the subcontinent. In February a Soviet-backed Communist regime came to power in Czechoslovakia, and April elections in Italy were menaced by the well-organized Italian Communist party. An alliance with Western Europe increasingly was seen by American leaders as one way to implement the new doctrine of containment, most cogently expressed by George Kennan. Kennan, however, did not consider NATO to be an accurate manifestation of his thinking – Europeans, he feared, had mistaken a political for a military threat.

North Atlantic Treaty

On 1 July 1948 initial talks for the proposed North Atlantic Treaty began in Washington among representatives of the United States, Canada, and the members of the Brussels Pact. A large question facing the American representatives, who already favored U.S. participation in a European military alliance, was how to overcome domestic objections. The Joint Chiefs of Staff were wary of greater European demands on their limited stockpiles of military equipment. Some American politicians, such as Republican senator Arthur Vandenberg, a recent convert to internationalism on the basis of the United Nations, felt that the proposed alliance would contravene both the spirit and the letter of the UN charter, which was meant to ensure peace through collective security for all, and not through military alliances beyond its jurisdiction. When the treaty was finally signed in Washington nine months later on 4 April 1949, American negotiators had ensured the inclusion of provisions that would make the treaty palatable to its domestic critics. There were numerous references to the primacy of the United Nations, especially in Article 1, which disavowed the "use of force in any manner inconsistent with the purposes of the United Nations." Article 7 similarly bowed to the "responsibility of the Security Council for the maintenance of international peace and security." The Joint Chiefs of Staff were partially mollified when the treaty made provision for the defense of Europe to the Rhine River only and put off any more comprehensive plan for all of Europe.

The North Atlantic Treaty was finally ratified by the United States on 21 July 1949 and entered into force on 24 August. The heart of the agreement was stated in Article 5, which pledged that in the case of an "armed attack against one or more of [its members] in Europe or North America, [this] shall be considered an attack against them all, and consequently . . . each of them . . . will assist the Party or Parties so attacked by taking . . . such action as it deems necessary, including the use of armed force, to restore and maintain the security of the North Atlantic area."

The efforts of the alliance in its first year were directed at drafting plans for the defense of Europe. On 27 January 1950 the "strategic concept" was approved, whereby each member would assume those duties it could best perform for the alliance as a whole. Under this concept the United States assumed sole responsibility for strategic bombing but shared NATO duties with the British in regard to the open seas. In May 1950 the governing council of NATO approved an ambitious plan to defend Europe from a Soviet attack at least to the Rhine and preferably as far as the Oder River. This plan was to be operationally effective in 1954. The previous American plan had essentially provided for the evacuation of U.S. troops

and the establishment of a line of defense along the Pyrenees.

With the outbreak of the Korean War on 25 June 1950, the United States suddenly raised its estimation of the value of NATO. Sharing the Truman ad-ministration's view that the communist attack on South Korea presaged a similar Soviet plan for Germany, Congress in August 1950 approved an additional $4 billion of aid to strengthen European military forces. American occupational troops in Europe quickly assumed the role of combat forces ready to counter a Soviet attack. Moreover, the United States decided to send additional soldiers to Europe solely as a counter to any Soviet moves.

German Rearmament

The Korean War also underscored the question of the relationship of Germany to the alliance. Control of Germany had, since the beginning of the Cold War, been regarded as the key prize by both the United States and the Soviet Union. In 1949, within a month after the creation of NATO, the Federal Republic of Germany had been established as a semi-independent state, bringing at least the western half of the country further into the Western camp. With greater military spending caused by the Korean War, the United States increasingly saw the necessity of West German representation, however limited, within NATO. And because the planned line of defense against a Soviet attack was to be along the Rhine, there were also calls for West Germany to bear some of the burden for its own defense.

But most Europeans, especially the French, recoiled at the idea of a rearmed Germany, even one under the control of NATO. By selecting the former wartime commander of the Allied armies in Europe, Dwight D. Eisenhower, as the supreme commander of NATO's forces, the United States thought it would overcome European resistance to German entry into the alliance. When this appeared not to work, U.S. secretary of state Dean Acheson linked further American aid to NATO to the inclusion of German troops in the alliance, a demand which angered the French.

It was left to Jean Monnet, a brilliant French economist, to come up with an idea that would allow German rearmament. Monnet had shortly before conceived the Schuman Plan, under which France and Germany combined their coal and steel resources under a common authority, in effect allowing the renascent German economy entry into postwar Europe, but in such a way as to discour-

National Archives

Vice-president Alben W. Barkley and President Harry S Truman watching Secretary of State Dean Acheson sign the North Atlantic Treaty on 4 April 1949

age German domination. In October 1950 Monnet applied this concept to NATO. His plan, named after French prime minister Rene Plevan, would provide for a one-hundred-thousand-member European military force that would eventually include battalion-sized German units under a central European command. The Plevan Plan ultimately led to an American-supported treaty in May 1952 creating the European Defense Community (EDC). But the United States had not reckoned on the enduring French fear of a rearmed Germany. France signed the EDC agreement on 27 May but, before ratifying the treaty, insisted on explicit Anglo-American guarantees directed against Germany. When these guarantees were not provided, the French parliament allowed the treaty to expire.

British foreign secretary Anthony Eden neatly resolved the dilemma. Sitting in his bath in September 1954, he came up with the idea of the Federal Republic's simultaneous entry into both NATO and the Western Union. In the minds of the French, the Western Union had been directed more at the potential threat of a revived, remilitarized Germany than at the possibility of an invasion by the Soviet Union. The preamble to the Brussels Pact in fact enjoined its members to "take such

steps as may be held to be necessary in the event of a renewal by Germany of a policy of aggression." And because Great Britain was a member of the Western Union, but would not have been part of the purely continental EDC, France would now have British guarantees against Germany. Implicit American guarantees against German aggression would be provided by West German entry into NATO. Eden's arrangement was worked out at the London Conference of September 1954, where Great Britain assuaged French fears of Germany by agreeing to maintain four divisions on the continent at all times. The way had been paved for West Germany to enter the now-renamed Western European Union (WEU) with an army entirely under NATO control and with no right to manufacture atomic, biological, or chemical weapons.

Third World

In the 1950s relations between the United States and its principal NATO allies were strained by conflicts that took place "out-of-area" – a NATO euphemism for what would later come to be called the Third World. Following the defeat of its forces at Dien Bien Phu in June 1954, the French government of Pierre Mendes-France secured a complete withdrawal from Indochina at the Geneva Conference in July 1954. But the French, already embittered by the refusal of the United States to assist its garrison at Dien Bien Phu, viewed American intervention in Indochina to fight against communist forces as especially duplicitous.

Similarly, during the Suez crisis of 1956, when British, French, and Israeli forces jointly invaded Egypt after President Abdul Nasser nationalized the canal, President Eisenhower refused to provide American aid, instead echoing the Soviet demand for withdrawal from Egypt. That the United States also failed to support the British currency as it verged on collapse during the crisis badly shook British confidence and underscored British reliance on the United States. American failure to support its allies in Indochina and Egypt drove home the point that the United States intended to remain the undisputed leader of NATO but would not underwrite the imperial ambitions of its allies.

NATO Military Doctrine

NATO military doctrine began to undergo a profound change within a year after the Suez Crisis. Hitherto security in Western Europe had rested on the American promise of "massive retaliation," whereby, according to John Foster Dulles, any Soviet aggression would be met by a "great capacity to retaliate, instantly, by means and at places of our own choosing." This thinly veiled threat of nuclear response meant that for most of the 1950s relatively few conventional forces were seen as necessary to defend Europe from the numerically superior Eastern-bloc armies. It was even thought that if NATO deployed too many men the Soviet Union might believe that NATO would not automatically respond to a Soviet attack with nuclear weapons. The United States, for its part, guaranteed the defense of Europe with its nuclear umbrella, knowing that it lay safely beyond the reach of Soviet retaliation.

But with the launch of Sputnik, the first earth satellite, in October 1957, the Soviet Union demonstrated that it now had the means to launch intercontinental ballistic missiles against the United States, against which there was no defense. This fact dramatically changed strategic thinking in the West. NATO's European members began to question American willingness and resolve to use nuclear weapons to defend them if this now meant that the Soviet Union might retaliate directly against the United States. From this point on, the alliance has been sorely tested by disputes over nuclear strategy.

As if to confirm the worst fears of its allies, the United States gradually began to abandon massive retaliation in the last years of the Eisenhower administration, in favor of a new strategy called flexible response, which gave the United States the means to match, step-by-step, any act of Soviet aggression. Flexible response consisted of a triad of conventional forces and tactical and strategic nuclear weapons, a combination that placed the conventional defense of Europe at the forefront of American military doctrine, serving to postpone an escalation to nuclear warfare. Although NATO would not officially adopt flexible response until December 1967, it effectively became the prevailing American doctrine under President John F. Kennedy.

French Rejection of NATO

In December 1958 Charles de Gaulle became the first president of the Fifth Republic of France. He immediately acted to reassert French military and political independence in European affairs and to end what he perceived to be the "Anglo-Saxon hegemony" over France and Europe. What he was ultimately striving for was to make Europe a loose confederation under French leadership.

De Gaulle initially directed his efforts to removing France from NATO. In a memorandum to Brit-

ish prime minister Harold Macmillan and President Eisenhower, dated 17 September 1958, de Gaulle proposed that NATO be replaced by an Atlantic Directorate, a tripartite arrangement whereby the United States, Great Britain, and France would be equal partners over all "political and strategic questions of world importance." De Gaulle probably realized the impracticable nature of his request and was therefore not surprised at British and American reluctance to endorse it. His next step, in March 1959, was to withdraw the French fleet in the Mediterranean from NATO control. This began a slow but steady disengagement of France from the alliance – an alliance which de Gaulle felt was too dependent on the United States. In particular, he resented the "special relationship" between the British and the Americans, and viewed Britain more or less as an extension of American foreign policy. On 22 February 1966 de Gaulle announced that France would officially withdraw from NATO military command. He gave his former allies a year to move NATO headquarters from France.

French rejection of NATO was probably the most traumatic and divisive event in the history of the alliance. But in large part it was made possible by the success of the alliance over the years in deterring an attack from the Soviet Union. By the mid 1960s many Europeans had come to view the Soviet Union with less fear, believing that they could arrive at some sort of understanding with their large neighbor. The West Germans in particular were eager to pursue *Ostpolitik* – their own form of détente toward the Soviet Union – in the hopes of securing closer economic and political ties with East Germany. The Harmel Report, calling for the encouragement of détente, was approved by NATO at the same meeting of the governing council in December 1967 that adopted flexible response as the official Western military answer to a Soviet attack. Even the Soviet invasion of Czechoslovakia in 1968 to crush the reform movement known as the Prague Spring only deterred for a short while the growing assumption of normal relations between the Soviet Union and Western Europe.

Dissatisfaction with NATO

European members of NATO were also increasingly dissatisfied with the United States over its involvement in Vietnam during the 1960s and its simultaneous neglect of NATO. NATO's smaller members, in particular, increasingly voiced their discontent with American policy. Turkey, for example, resented President Lyndon B. Johnson's refusal to allow the use of American military equipment in its struggle with Greece over the Mediterranean island of Cyprus.

American disenchantment with NATO mirrored that of the Europeans. The Europeans were especially perceived as unwilling to bear a fair burden of NATO's costs. In 1966 Mike Mansfield, Democratic senator from Montana, introduced the first in a series of congressional resolutions to cut the number of American troops committed to NATO. Although the resolutions were never passed by Congress, they served to put the nations of Western Europe on notice to contribute more to their own defense. In 1971, for example, the West Germans agreed to provide over $2 billion to the United States.

President Richard M. Nixon entered the White House in January 1969 determined to devote more attention to NATO in an effort to improve relations with the European allies. He vigorously resisted calls in the United States for troop reductions in Europe, arguing that American ability to counter Soviet aggression would suffer. But Nixon was viewed with some suspicion by the allies. The Nixon Doctrine, articulated in large part by National Security Adviser Henry Kissinger, announced new limitations on the use of American power to fight communism around the world. It has been argued this was merely a device that allowed Nixon a graceful way to end American involvement in the Vietnam War, but in Europe it was widely felt that this new display of modesty by the United States might signal a disengagement from its responsibilities to the alliance. These fears were fueled by Nixon's rapprochement with Red China in 1972, which indicated to the Europeans a new flexibility in U.S. foreign policy and a possible refocusing of American strategic interests at the expense of NATO.

The Europeans had similar reservations about the Strategic Arms Limitations Talks (SALT) treaty, signed by Nixon in Moscow in May 1972. The negotiations essentially sought to reduce the numbers of nuclear weapons that could be used to strike directly against the superpowers. The Soviets, however, insisted on including NATO's European-based nuclear bombers – the forward-based systems that could reach the Soviet Union – in the American figures and were equally insistent on excluding their own medium-range missiles that could target Europe. The United States was seen by some as making a bilateral agreement to protect

itself against the Soviet Union while ignoring the security concerns of its allies.

Buildup of NATO Forces

By the time President Jimmy Carter entered office in January 1977, détente with the Soviet Union was no longer politically fashionable in the United States. In Europe, as well, there were resurgent fears of growing Soviet military power directed at European targets. Of particular concern was the new Soviet intermediate-range missile, the SS-20, deployed first in 1977 and capable of reaching Western Europe – but not the United States – from bases in Central Europe and the western part of the Soviet Union. Carter's first response to these fears was to urge the NATO allies to strengthen their conventional capabilities through an increase in defense spending. But many European leaders, especially West German chancellor Helmut Schmidt, preferred an alternative – the cruise missile, a small, low-flying, and extremely accurate means of delivering nuclear warheads to Soviet targets.

Carter, however, as part of the ongoing SALT II negotiations, had offered in his "Protocol" of 1977 to ban the cruise missile but to allow the Soviets to keep their advanced Backfire bomber in exchange for certain other concessions, an offer which astounded NATO's European members. On 28 October 1977 Schmidt spoke in London and, in effect, accused the United States of ignoring European security demands and requesting new long-range weapons with which to counter Soviet ones. The dispute, ostensibly dealing with military affairs, was essentially a political one and turned on the issue of whether the United States was willing to risk its own arms-control agreements with the Soviet Union in order to guarantee European security.

Over the next two years Schmidt campaigned for the introduction of more-advanced intermediate-range weapons into Europe. At a meeting on the Caribbean islands of Guadeloupe in January 1979 with Schmidt, British prime minister James Callahan, and French president Valéry Giscard d'Estaing, President Carter announced what would become the "dual-track" decision: the United States would deploy the new missiles in Europe within four years if arms-control negotiations with the Soviet Union failed to reduce the number of intermediate-range delivery systems. Later, at the December 1979 special meeting of NATO's foreign and defense ministries in Brussels, the decision was made public: 572 missiles – 464 cruise and 108

Pershing IIs — would be placed in five European countries, the first to arrive in the winter of 1983–1984. Simultaneously, NATO would reduce the number of other nuclear warheads as this deployment proceeded and would seek to "further the course of arms control and détente in the 1980s ... through a broad set of initiatives."

The issue came to a head in late 1983 when the first missiles were to arrive in Germany. Millions of demonstrators had protested in Europe, especially in Great Britain and West Germany, against the missile deployments. Schmidt lost a vote of no confidence on 1 October 1982, and his party lost the national elections in March 1983 to Helmut Kohl's Christian Democrats, largely because of the proposed deployment. On 23 November 1983, the day that the first Pershing arrived in Europe, Soviet negotiators walked out of the Geneva intermediate nuclear force talks. The furor over the missiles seemed to risk tearing the entire alliance apart.

Official Soviet policy since the deployments were announced had been that no American missiles could be placed in Europe. It was the latest attempt by the Soviet Union to "decouple" Europe, and especially Germany, from the protection offered by the United States. The risk to the United States was that West Germany would become neutral, upsetting the basis of the entire postwar order. Even President François Mitterand of France recognized the danger of German pacifism: as early as 1979 he supported the deployment of the missiles to Europe.

Tensions within NATO worsened after Ronald Reagan became president in 1981. Reagan's commitment to a major arms buildup and his pronouncements against the Soviet Union worried many Europeans who were nervous at being caught once again in a cross fire between the Soviet Union and the United States. After the Polish government declared martial law in 1981, Reagan tried to block European efforts to build a natural gas pipeline which would supply Poland with Soviet gas, demanding that American equipment not be exported to the Eastern bloc for this purpose. The Europeans rebelled and ultimately ignored American demands.

The struggle over the pipeline was part of a much larger dispute over economic policies. European leaders criticized American fiscal laxity which had caused high interest rates and an overvalued dollar; the United States in turn accused its allies of dumping subsidized products onto the American market.

INF Treaty

At their December 1987 meeting in Washington, Soviet leader Mikhail Gorbachev and Reagan reached agreement on the Intermediate Nuclear Forces (INF) Treaty to remove all medium-range missiles from Europe, including Soviet SS-20s and American cruise and Pershing missiles. The agreement was made possible largely because of Gorbachev's concern over Reagan's ambitious plan to develop an antiballistic missile defense system that would sit in outer space – the Strategic Defense Initiative (SDI), or "Star Wars." Gorbachev dropped a long-standing Soviet objection to allowing British and French nuclear forces to exist beyond the scope of any agreement with the United States, which had been Reagan's "zero-option."

SDI unnerved Europeans as well as Soviets, because, if successful and if matched by the Soviet Union, it implied an arrangement by which the superpowers could sit safely ensconced behind impenetrable barriers, leaving Europe vulnerable. The INF treaty in 1987 had similarly unnerved European leaders, who felt that the superpower arrangement provided by the treaty would leave Europe out in the cold.

NATO, unlike many other alliances in history, has served its purposes well, for not only has it deterred an attack by the Soviet Union against Western Europe, it has allowed its European members to coexist peacefully with one another. With the end of the Cold War and the ostensible purpose for the existence of the alliance, the future of NATO remains uncertain.

References

Lawrence Freedman, ed., *The Troubled Alliance: Atlantic Relations in the 1980s* (New York: St. Martin's Press, 1983);

Robert J. Jackson, ed., *Continuity of Discord: Crises and Responses in the Atlantic Community* (New York: Praeger, 1985);

Josef Joffe, *The Limited Partnership: Europe, the United States, and the Burdens of Alliance* (Cambridge, Mass.: Ballinger, 1987).

– M. B.

SEE ALSO THESE RELATED ENTRIES

Ernest Bevin, 1; Jimmy Carter, 1; Containment, 3; Charles de Gaulle, 1; Détente, 3; John Foster Dulles, 1; Dwight D. Eisenhower, 1; Flexible Response, 3; Mikhail Gorbachev, 2; INF Treaty, 3; Lyndon B. Johnson, 1; Korean War, 3; Mike Mansfield, 1; Marshall Plan, 3; Jean Monnet, 1; Multilateral Force Proposal, 3; Ostpolitik, 3; SALT, 3; Helmut Schmidt, 1; Sputnik, 3; Suez Crisis, 3;

Nuclear Freeze Movement

In the early 1980s, in reaction to pronouncements by officials in the administration of President Ronald Reagan concerning the possibility of fighting and "prevailing" in a nuclear war, antinuclear activists created the nuclear freeze movement. In 1984 the Democratic candidate for the presidency, Walter Mondale, endorsed the movement's goals of freezing the production of nuclear weapons. The movement never gained wide public support, and the reductions in U.S.-Soviet tensions that resulted from Soviet president and general secretary Mikhail Gorbachev's social and political reforms in the Soviet Union — and the subsequent end to the Cold War — brought about its demise in the second half of the 1980s.

References

McGeorge Bundy, *Danger and Survival: Choices about the Bomb in the First Fifty Years* (New York: Random House, 1988);

Douglas C. Waller, *Congress and the Nuclear Freeze* (Amherst: University of Massachusetts Press, 1987).

– B. F.

SEE ALSO THESE RELATED ENTRIES
Mikhail Gorbachev, 2; Nuclear Proliferation, 3; Ronald Reagan, 1.

Nuclear Proliferation

Nuclear-weapons proliferation – the spread of atomic and thermonuclear weapons among nations – has been an enduring aspect of world politics since World War II. During the Cold War, nuclear analysts tended to treat nuclear proliferation as an issue of secondary importance, as questions about nuclear strategy and the arms race were much more pressing. However, the dismantling of the Soviet Union and the reemergence of ethnic and nationalistic tensions around the globe have added to the potential for nuclear proliferation.

Political scientists have distinguished between two generations of nuclear powers. The first generation includes five states – the United States, the Soviet Union, Great Britain, France, and China – all of whom created large nuclear arsenals and integrated them into their armed forces with explicit nuclear strategies. The second-generation states – Israel, India, South Africa, and Pakistan – on the other hand, secretly developed small nuclear arsenals, sometimes in violation of the international Nuclear Nonproliferation Treaty.

First Generation

The United States was the first nation to develop atomic weapons. In 1939 President Franklin D. Roosevelt commissioned the research and development of a super weapon based on atomic fission. He accelerated the program in the winter of 1942 by creating the Manhattan Project, which brought leading U.S. scientists and engineers together in Los Alamos, New Mexico, to concentrate on the development of the weapon.

U.S. interest in the atomic bomb was fueled by the fear that Nazi Germany would build it first. Following the German surrender on 7 May 1945, the United States continued its atomic program, hoping to use the atomic bomb in the war against Japan. Scientists conducted the first successful atomic test fifty miles northwest of Alamogordo, New Mexico, on 16 July 1945. Within one month the United States had dropped two atomic bombs on Japan – on Hiroshima, on 6 August 1945, and on Nagasaki, on 9 August 1945. Days later Japan surrendered, ending World War II.

The Soviet Union took the first steps toward developing an atomic bomb in 1939, when Soviet scientists began working on a controlled, explosive uranium chain reaction. Research was suspended from 1941 to 1943 during the German invasion but then resumed. In July 1946 the Soviet Union rejected the U.S.-sponsored Baruch Plan proposing international control of all atomic material to prevent nuclear proliferation. Soviet leader Joseph Stalin, who believed that atomic weapons would become an essential military and political element of national power in the postwar world, did not trust the United States to comply with the provisions of the plan. The Soviets detonated their first atomic bomb in August 1949.

Great Britain and France were the next two nations to acquire atomic weapons. Both were motivated almost exclusively by political considerations, as neither faced a pressing military need to build the atomic bomb. Britain played a leading role in conducting atomic feasibility studies in 1939, and during World War II British scientists collaborated with their American counterparts in the Manhattan Project. The success of the U.S. atomic project contributed to the British decision in 1945 to construct atomic facilities to produce the plutonium necessary to build atomic weapons. Britain conducted a successful atomic test in October 1952, becoming the third nuclear power.

A secret French nuclear weapons program began in 1956, the result of an assertive atomic energy commission and defense ministry. The French government during the Fourth Republic was so weak institutionally that the program proceeded without its explicit consent. A cabinet-level decision to build atomic weapons came in April 1958, but the program was so far along that cabinet approval had become a formality. General Charles de Gaulle, who returned to power in May 1958, used nuclear weapons to restore French national prestige. He wanted France to regain superpower status and felt that the possession of nuclear weapons would make her the leader of a Europe independent of the Soviet Union and the United States. Nuclear weapons were also psychologically important to the French military, which had had successive defeats in World War II, French Indochina, and North Africa.

The Peoples Republic of China detonated an atomic bomb in 1964. China's decision to build the atomic bomb was spurred largely by fear of the United States. After President Dwight D. Eisenhower made vague threats to use nuclear force against it toward the end of the Korean War, China wanted to build atomic weapons to avoid U.S. nuclear coercion. China began an atomic weapons production program in the mid 1950s, receiving help from the Soviet Union in producing weapons-grade uranium.

Nuclear Proliferation

Concern over the spread of nuclear weapons emerged after World War II. American statesmen, including Dean Acheson, secretary of state from 1949 to 1953, began working for the international control of atomic energy in 1945. The United States submitted the Baruch Plan to the United Nations in February 1946, but the plan, which called for the placing of all nuclear material under international control, was promptly rejected by the Soviet Union. In the absence of an international regime to control nuclear proliferation, Congress passed the McMahon Act of 1946, banning all nuclear exports.

Nations pursued atomic energy for civilian as well as military purposes. As an inexpensive source for electricity, nuclear power was particularly attractive. Recognizing the importance of the civilian uses of atomic energy, President Eisenhower proposed the Atoms for Peace program at the United Nations in December 1953. The program was designed to prevent a global nuclear arms race by encouraging nations to dedicate their nuclear materials to peaceful uses. Atoms for Peace offered nonnuclear states the technical assistance necessary to develop nuclear power facilities, provided that the recipients agreed not to divert plutonium to military purposes. Electricity-generating nuclear power plants produce plutonium as a by-product, which, like enriched uranium, can be used to build nuclear weapons.

Atoms for Peace also called for the creation of the International Atomic Energy Agency (IAEA) that was designed to supply nuclear material for peaceful uses. The IAEA used safeguards to protect against the diversion of nuclear material for military ends. The most stringent provisions consisted of periodic inspections of member nuclear facilities, but even these measures were limited, since nations were given six months notice before an inspection. Military facilities in the United States and the Soviet Union were exempt from inspection. Nor did the IAEA have the right to inspect all nuclear material received by other states.

The most comprehensive attempt to confine the spread of nuclear weapons was the Nuclear Nonproliferation Treaty (NPT). This stipulated that none of the five nuclear powers should transfer nuclear weapons to nonnuclear states or in any way assist them in their attempts to develop nuclear munitions. It also called for nonnuclear states to refrain from developing nuclear arms. One hundred thirty-six nations signed the NPT, which entered into force on 5 March 1970. France and China are the only two major nuclear powers that have not signed the treaty, although France has publicly declared its adherence to NPT provisions. Israel, Libya, Pakistan, Argentina, Brazil and other nations have refused to sign the agreement. Two countries that initially refused to sign

the NPT, North Korea and South Africa, have recently subscribed to the treaty.

Although the Senate ratified the NPT in 1970, Congress did not take an active interest in nuclear proliferation until India detonated an atomic device in 1974. The Indian test and subsequent Pakistani efforts prompted major congressional efforts to slow the spread of nuclear weapons. In 1976 legislators passed the Symington amendment to the Foreign Assistance Act of 1961. Sponsored by Democratic senator Stuart Symington of Montana, the amendment prohibited American aid to countries dealing in unsafeguarded nuclear technology. A second amendment to the 1961 act, sponsored by Democratic senator John Glenn of Ohio in 1977, stipulated that the detonation of an atomic device would result in suspension of American aid. These measures led the United States to cut off aid to Pakistan in September 1977.

After the Soviet Union invaded Afghanistan in December 1979, neighboring Pakistan became increasingly important to the United States as a channel for aid to the Afghan rebels. In February 1982 President Ronald Reagan restored and increased aid to Pakistan under a Foreign Assistance Act provision that permitted the president to waive certain restrictions deemed injurious to U.S. national interest. In August 1985, as Pakistan continued its efforts to build an atomic bomb, Congress passed another amendment to the 1961 Foreign Assistance Act, sponsored by Democratic senator Alan Cranston of California. The amendment sought to discourage Pakistani nuclear efforts by instructing the president to certify in a letter to Congress that Pakistan does not possess nuclear weapons and that American aid would diminish Pakistani interest in building a bomb. The certification has to be submitted each year during which Pakistan receives U.S. aid. The amendment also mandated the cutting of aid to countries illegally exporting material that would significantly enhance another country's nuclear capabilities. Like the other two congressional efforts, the Cranston amendment had little effect as the successive administration continued to exempt Pakistan from congressional restrictions for strategic reasons.

Second Generation

Israel was the first nuclear power of the second generation and is in possession of an impressive nuclear arsenal. The Israelis, who built the atomic bomb to protect themselves from hostile Arab states, completed construction of an atomic weapon by the late 1960s and later produced a thermonuclear device, making Israel the only second-generation state to do so. To deliver the weapon, Israel, like the other second-generation states, can adapt high-performance fighters to carry nuclear missiles or arm its arsenal of surface-to-air ballistic missiles with nuclear warheads. Its longest range missile, the Jericho II, has a range of up to twenty-two hundred miles with a five-hundred-kilogram warhead.

Three other nations – India, South Africa, and Pakistan – have acquired atomic weapons. India completed construction of an atomic device by the early 1970s and conducted an atomic test, which it termed "a peaceful nuclear explosion," in May 1974. India introduced the weapon primarily for reasons of prestige, although there was also some concern on its part about Chinese nuclear capabilities. India has amassed large quantities of plutonium, but it continues to deny building nuclear weapons. It could deliver its explosives with jet aircraft or the Agni ballistic missile, which has a range of fifteen-hundred miles. India remains the last country openly to explode a nuclear bomb.

A rival to India since birth, Pakistan feared that India might use atomic force in the next Indo-Pakistani war and did not want to be subject to nuclear blackmail. Pakistan succeeded in building an atomic device sometime between 1986 and 1988. For delivery, Pakistan could adapt a jet fighter or use the King Hawk ballistic missile with a range of 180 miles. South Africa, which is surrounded by black African states hostile to its white-minority government, developed atomic weapons in 1980 or 1981 with the help of Israel, with whom it is suspected to have conducted a nuclear test over the South Atlantic in the fall of 1979. It is also thought that South Africa has a ballistic missile with a range of at least twelve-hundred miles.

Some scholars characterize the differences between first- and second-generation nuclear proliferation as differences between "visible" and "opaque" proliferation. They term the five major nuclear powers as visible because these states openly developed and tested and publicly announced their nuclear capabilities, displaying their weapons and elaborating strategic doctrines for their use. In contrast, the second-generation countries, or opaque nuclear states, have constructed nuclear weapons in secrecy, avoiding testing, denying their existence, and refusing to explain how they plan to use them. Scholars note that international nonproliferation efforts, such as the NPT, have failed to prevent opaque nuclear proliferation because NPT safeguards were designed to deal with the visible acquisition of nuclear weapons.

Discussion of nuclear proliferation tends to obscure the prevalence of nonproliferation. The majority of states that possess the technological capability to develop nuclear weapons have chosen not to do so. More than forty nations can build an atomic bomb, but only nine have. There are many reasons for this, but the most important is that most nuclear-capable nations have satisfied their security needs by other means. Western European states and Japan, for instance, provided for their security by collective defense – the North Atlantic Treaty Organization (NATO) – and the U.S. nuclear guarantee. There is little reason for them to seek an independent nuclear deterrent.

Another obstacle to nuclear buildup is the political cost that a state must be prepared to pay if it is viewed by the other nations as a maverick nuclear power. The military risks involved in acquiring nuclear weapons also discourage some states. In the early 1980s, for instance, Israel bombed the Iraqi nuclear reactor at Osiraq, fearing that Iraq was using plutonium from the reactor to build its own atomic bomb. Rather than run the risk of encouraging neighbors to develop their nuclear potential many nations have decided to pursue ballistic missile technology and chemical and biological weapons as substitutes for nuclear weapons. Iraq employed chemical weapons during its eight-year conventional war with Iran (1980–1988). Syria and Libya have also developed large stockpiles of chemical weapons.

Significance of Nuclear Proliferation

There has been considerable scholarly debate in recent decades over whether nuclear proliferation would increase or decrease the probability of war. Some scholars, focusing on the stabilizing effects that nuclear weapons had on the U.S.-Soviet relationship, argue that nuclear proliferation would bring stability to volatile regions, further claiming that even a small arsenal of nuclear weapons would create a powerful deterrent given the high costs associated with nuclear war.

Other scholars reject the notion that the fear of nuclear war is the only basis of deterrence, and they are less sanguine about the effects of nuclear proliferation. They argue that the nuclear arsenals of second-generation countries would be smaller and more vulnerable than the superpowers' arsenals, and that the absence of sophisticated fail-safe technology would increase the probability of accidental or unauthorized use of atomic weapons. Other destabilizing factors in post–Cold War relations are political institutions in the developing world and the presence of religious fundamentalism, ethnic strife, tribal rivalry, and subnational groupings, which may make Third World leaders less reluctant to resort to nuclear force. Finally, some scholars argue that the geographic proximity of many adversaries in unstable regions would create an incentive for leaders to launch preemptive strikes. In sum, these scholars argue that the net effect of the spread of nuclear weapons would be to destabilize already volatile regions.

References

Coit Blacker and Gloria Duffy, eds., *International Arms Control* (Palo Alto, Cal.: Stanford University Press, 1984);

Lewis A. Dunn, *Controlling The Bomb* (New Haven, Conn.: Yale University Press, 1982);

Leonard S. Spector, *The Undeclared Bomb* (Cambridge: Ballinger, 1988).

– B. D. K.

SEE ALSO THESE RELATED ENTRIES
Acheson-Lilienthal Plan, 3; Atoms for Peace, 3; Deterrence, 3.

Open Skies

Open Skies was an arms-control arrangement proposed by President Dwight D. Eisenhower on 21 July 1955, during his summit meeting with Soviet leader Nikita S. Khrushchev in Geneva, Switzerland. Eisenhower proposed that each country give the other a "complete blueprint" of its "military establishments, from beginning to end," and that the United States and the Soviet Union be allowed to fly unlimited reconnaissance missions over each other's territory so that arms-control agreements could be verified. The Soviet Union rejected the proposal and nothing came of it, although it provided the Eisenhower administration with a public-relations victory.

Reference

McGeorge Bundy, *Danger and Survival: Choices about the Bomb in the First Fifty Years* (New York: Random House, 1988).

– B. F.

SEE ALSO THESE RELATED ENTRIES
Dwight D. Eisenhower, 1; Nikita S. Khrushchev, 2.

Organization of American States

The Organization of American States (OAS) is comprised of most of the independent states in the Western Hemisphere. The two most notable non-members are Canada and Cuba. Canada never joined the community because of her ties to Europe, and Cuba was ejected from the organization in 1962.

The OAS charter was signed on 30 April 1948, at the conclusion of the Ninth Pan-American Conference held in Bogotá, Colombia. Evolving out of the Union of American Republics and the International Union of American Republics – formed in 1910 and 1890, respectively – the OAS was designed to strengthen the peace and security of the Western Hemisphere, promote the peaceful settlement of disputes between member states, provide for collective security, and encourage cooperation in social, cultural, and economic matters. The orientation of the OAS has been largely anticommunist.

Regional Security

The OAS was founded on the principles of the Monroe Doctrine. The organization attempted to "continentalize" the Monroe Doctrine by creating collective defense obligations for member states without restricting the right of the United States to take action in self-defense. The member states viewed the principle that an attack upon one American state would be considered as an attack upon all as an especially integral part of the OAS Charter.

The most important organ of the organization is the General Assembly, which meets annually. The Meeting of Consultation of Foreign Ministers supplements the assembly by serving as the executive body in the event of hostilities between member states. The Permanent Council is the third organ of the OAS. It operates in permanent session, is composed of an ambassador from each member state, and acts as the organization's executive committee. The General Secretariat of the OAS is located in Washington, D.C.

The OAS has made several important decisions on regional security. For example, in 1962, during what was to become known as the Cuban Missile Crisis, the OAS extended support to U.S. president John F. Kennedy in the quarantine against the shipment of Soviet missiles to Cuba. The OAS also supported the 1965 intervention of the United States in the Dominican Republic.

The OAS has also made significant achievements in the economic and social fields, the most notable of these being the establishment of the Alliance for Progress through the OAS adoption of the Charter of Puenta del Este in 1961. Although the Alliance for Progress was ultimately regarded as a failure, it was a program designed to aid in the economic and social development of Third World Latin American countries, with the additional objective of promoting democracy in the region. In 1979 the OAS created the Inter-American Court of Human Rights at San Jose, Costa Rica.

The OAS is viewed by many as an ineffective body greatly influenced by its strongest member, the United States. Although the organization adopts anti-American rhetoric on occasion, it rarely makes decisions contrary to U.S. desires.

References

Inis L. Claude, *The OAS, the UN, and the United States* (New York: Carnegie Endowment for International Peace, 1964);

John C. Dreier, *The Organization of American States and the Hemisphere Crisis* (New York: Harper & Row, 1962);

Abraham F. Lowenthal, *Partners in Conflict: The United States and Latin America* (Baltimore: Johns Hopkins University Press, 1987);

William Manger, *Pan America in Crisis* (Washington, D.C.: Public Affairs Press, 1961);

Bruce Palmer, *Intervention in the Caribbean* (Lexington: University Press of Kentucky, 1989);

Lars Schoultz, *National Security and United States Policy toward Latin America* (Princeton: Princeton University Press, 1987);

Jerome Slater, *The OAS and United States Foreign Policy* (Columbus: Ohio State University Press, 1967).

– J. H.

SEE ALSO THESE RELATED ENTRIES
Fidel Castro Ruz, 2; Lyndon Johnson, 1; John F. Kennedy, 1; Daniel Ortega Saavedra, 2.

Organization of Petroleum Exporting Countries

The Organization of Petroleum Exporting Countries (OPEC) was formed in 1960 as a way for oil-producing countries to gain control over their natural resource. During its thirty-year history, OPEC has set price restrictions on and determined output levels of its members' oil.

In the 1960s OPEC moved to insulate its members' revenue from drops in crude market prices. In the 1970s it attempted to increase significantly oil prices and to confront political crises as a group. In the 1980s OPEC sought to counter increased competition from non- OPEC oil exporters by setting production quotas and investing in refining and marketing operations. In the early 1990s OPEC has confronted dissension within its ranks over oil policy.

Founding of OPEC

The founding of OPEC was due to the changing relationships between the oil-rich countries and the major European and American oil companies that had controlled the market through concessionary agreements since the early 1900s. As the countries gradually gained control over their natural resource through profit-sharing agreements, a clash between the two sides became inevitable.

In February 1959 the major oil companies unilaterally reduced posted prices by 10 percent, leading to an informal agreement among the producing countries at the First Arab Petroleum Congress. In August 1960, after U.S. import-control legislation had reduced demand and pushed prices down, the major oil companies again cut posted prices without consulting the producing countries. Representatives of Iraq, Iran, Saudi Arabia, Kuwait, and Venezuela – which produced nearly 90 percent of all world petroleum – met in Baghdad on 14 September 1960 and formed OPEC. The new organization adopted two resolutions: one directly addressed the issue of price fluctuations, and the other stated the group's principal aim as the unification of petroleum policies among member countries.

With the exception of having addressed issues regarding member governments' share of the profit earned by foreign oil companies, OPEC did not operate as a united front against the large oil companies until more than a decade later. One of

OPEC's first significant actions, however, came in 1969. Libya, following the overthrow of King Idris by Colonel Mu'ammar al-Qaddafi, forced Occidental Petroleum Corporation – the largest independent oil company in Libya – to renegotiate its contract by cutting output and threatening a production stoppage. As a result, OPEC negotiated a new pricing system in the Tehran and Tripoli agreements of 1971 that included posted price increases of 30 percent, income tax raises of 55 percent, and the abolishing of special allowances on crude oil sales. Although it was Libya and not OPEC as a group that originally brought about the price increase, the event proved a watershed in bringing OPEC closer to its goal of participation in the industry's operations. In most cases, member countries gained 25 percent participation at first, achieved 60 percent within two years, and held almost full control by the 1980s.

The 1970s

The 1970s were the height of OPEC's power. Worldwide demand for oil had pushed prices up and OPEC dominated the oil-export market. Its member countries, of which there were thirteen by the mid 1970s, produced half the world's oil and held two-thirds of the global reserves. Following the Arab-Israeli war of October 1973, OPEC used its strength to raise the posted price by 70 percent, and the Organization of Arab Petroleum Exporting Countries (OAPEC) announced an embargo on countries friendly to Israel, and world oil prices quadrupled. During the next two years, as fears of an energy crisis spread, price hikes occurred in rapid succession.

As high oil prices and an increased global focus on energy conservation led to an oversupply in the late 1970s, OPEC's cohesion as a price setter broke down. Because of disagreements between Saudi Arabia and Iran, OPEC established a two-tier system in 1977. Saudi Arabia and the United Arab Emirates (UAE) raised their prices by 5 percent, while the other eleven members raised them by 10 percent. As a result, Saudi Arabia and the UAE pumped more oil than OPEC's other members. In June 1977 Saudi Arabia restored normal market share by matching the higher price level.

In late 1978, as Iranian revolutionary forces were undermining the country's monarchy, Iranian oil exports were suspended. Saudi Arabia filled the gap by increasing output and then dropped back to allow Iran to readjust, but Iran's pumping levels remained low. At the same time buyers flooded the spot market, raising prices there and setting the stage for further price hikes. As the oil companies discovered that contracts held only for as long as circumstances did not change, long-term contracts were replaced with short-term ones and spot sales. Through 1980 and into 1981, while Saudi Arabia prescribed to quarterly price increases, Libya, Algeria, and other price hawks set prices higher than did the Saudis, forcing Saudi Arabia to restore pricing unity by pushing the benchmark price toward the assumed level. Those OPEC price hikes, totaling 150 percent, contributed to later problems by reducing economic growth and encouraging development of non-OPEC oil reserves.

The 1980s

In the 1980s OPEC's role changed as it countered alternatives to OPEC oil and tried to strengthen its own structure. In 1982, when a softening oil market and a price erosion demanded a response, OPEC established prorationing. Some countries, however, attempted to beat the sustained drop in demand for OPEC oil by cheating on both output and price. After stormy negotiations in 1983, OPEC reduced the selling price for the first time in its history and set quotas for individual member countries and a lower quota for total production. Saudi Arabia took the role of swing producer, agreeing to raise or lower its own output to meet overall levels. Two years later, Saudi Arabia used its role to discipline cheating OPEC members and free-riding non-OPEC producers.

As demand continues to shift away from OPEC oil, however, member countries are moving outside the OPEC framework and downstreaming their operations to include petrochemicals, refining, and distribution. During the late 1980s, for example, the national oil companies of Saudi Arabia, Kuwait, Venezuela, and Abu Dhabi (UAE) bought distribution subsidiaries from Gulf and Texaco among others. The downstreaming reflects both the scarcity of development opportunities for these oil-rich countries and their desire to decrease their economic dependence on one raw material. Downstream operations also enable OPEC countries to discount their oil, which some analysts have argued undermines OPEC's future strength.

Disunity

Recent OPEC meetings have been marked by internal disunity and bickering, first between Saudi Arabia and Kuwait and, more recently, between Iraq and Kuwait. In August 1990 Iraq invaded Kuwait after accusing it of overproducing oil in order to depress prices. As OPEC leaders met in Geneva in the summer of 1990, Iraq had threatened Kuwait with military force for cheating on its production quotas.

Other developing countries with a variety of natural resources had once looked to OPEC as a model of gaining control over natural resources. Today's OPEC, however, is weaker than it had been, and its member countries are in control of a lower percentage of world oil production; other raw-material groups have not yet been set up effectively.

References

Albert L. Danielson, *The Evolution of OPEC* (New York: Harcourt Brace Jovanovich, 1982);

Fereidun Fesharaki and David T. Isaak, *OPEC, the Gulf and the World Petroleum Market: A Study in Government Policy and Downstream Operations* (Boulder, Colo.: Westview, 1983);

Arabinda Ghosh, *OPEC, the Petroleum Industry, and United States Energy Policy* (Westport, Conn.: Quorum Books, 1983);

David Hawdon, ed., *The Changing Structure of the World Oil Industry* (London: Croom Helm, 1985);

Kenneth R. Odell, *Oil and World Power* (New York: Penguin, 1985);

J. E. Peterson, *The Politics of Middle Eastern Oil* (Washington, D.C.: Middle East Institute, 1983).

                                                                              – A. F.

SEE ALSO THESE RELATED ENTRIES
Jimmy Carter, 1; Ronald Reagan, 1.

Ostpolitik

The signing of the Russo-German nonaggression pact in Moscow, 1970; seated at the table are West German foreign minister Walter Scheel, West German chancellor Willy Brandt, Soviet prime minister Alexsei Kosygin, and Soviet foreign minister Andrei Gromyko

Ostpolitik (east politics) was West German chancellor Willy Brandt's policy of no longer calling into question the legitimacy of those Soviet bloc states partially carved out of the territory of the defeated Nazi Germany. Since its inception in 1949, West Germany had always regarded itself as the one true Germany, the only German state with a legitimate claim to the lands of the 1938 pre–World War II Germany. Implicit in this belief was that the Cold War political and territorial divisions were only temporary and would someday be resolved in the West's favor. Ostpolitik, which won Brandt a Nobel Peace Prize in 1971, was an important step in resolving lingering European East-West tensions in that it accepted the Cold War as the status quo – rather than an aberration – for the forseeable future.

Under the Hallstein Doctrine, West Germany had refused to recognize the legitimacy of East Germany. It withheld diplomatic recognition to any country which had diplomatic relations with East Germany. To the Soviet bloc, West Germany's claim to East Germany and to territory in Poland and Czechoslovakia under the guise of reunification was evidence that American-dominated Western Europe did not regard Soviet domination of Eastern Europe as legitimate. In August 1970, however, Brandt signed a treaty with the Soviets to affirm the permanence of the existing boundaries of the two Germanies, the Soviet Union, and Czechoslovakia. West Germany, moreover, agreed to renounce the use of force to achieve its aims in Eastern Europe.

This treaty led to additional talks in 1971 among Britain, France, the Soviet Union, and the United States to address lingering questions regarding the continuing Western occupation of West Berlin. The success of the talks led to direct negotiations between East and West Germany. In 1972 West Germany finally agreed to extend diplomatic recognition to East Germany. Brandt signed similar treaties with Poland in 1970 and Czechoslovakia in 1973.

References

Marion Gräfin Dönhoff, *Foe Into Friend: The Makers of the New Germany from Konrad Adenauer to Helmut Schmidt* (London: Weidenfeld & Nicolson, 1982);

William E. Griffith, *The Ostpolitik of the Federal Republic of Germany* (Cambridge, Mass.: Massachusetts Institute of Technology Press, 1982);

Henry Ashby Turner, Jr., *The Two Germanies Since 1945* (New Haven: Yale University Press, 1987).

– C. S. B.

SEE ALSO THESE RELATED ENTRIES
Willy Brandt, 1; Federal Republic of Germany, 3.

Perestroika

Although previous leaders of the Soviet Union sometimes discussed "restructuring" the economy, the Russian term *perestroika* is most frequently associated with the sweeping economic reforms of General Secretary and President Mikhail S. Gorbachev. After becoming Communist party leader in March 1985, Gorbachev initiated an extensive reform program identified by the overarching slogan "new thinking" or simply by the term *perestroika*.

Perestroika, the restructuring of the stagnant Soviet economy, was accompanied by, and its success necessitated, policies of glasnost (openness) and demokratizatsiia (democratization), as well as new thinking in foreign policy. Gorbachev's policy of glasnost was an attempt to open Soviet society by providing increased opportunities for freedom of speech, association, and the press, and by giving more power to consumers, employees, and managers. The second element of new thinking, democratization, mandated freer elections and a more just and evenly applied legal system. In the realm of foreign policy Gorbachev's new thinking manifested itself in a relaxation of the U.S.-Soviet rivalry and a withdrawal from national liberation struggles in the Third World.

Although sometimes used to refer to the overall program of reform, perestroika most appropriately refers to Gorbachev's "revolution from above" in the economic sphere. Many of the economic reforms had been attempted before; what was unique and radical about perestroika is the depth and scope of the changes envisioned. These economic reforms represented significant changes in the administration of planning, production, and distribution of goods within the Soviet Union. Specifically, Gorbachev's reforms were an effort to introduce work incentives for employees and managers, improve the quality of goods, achieve technological modernization, increase production and efficiency, replace the hierarchical command system with market relationships, and bring the Soviet Union into the world economy. Together with glasnost, and new thinking in foreign policy, perestroika signaled a major turning point in Soviet history and the waning of the Cold War.

Origins and Objectives

By 1985 economic growth rates in the Soviet Union had fallen to less than half their 1970 levels. Under the leadership of Leonid I. Brezhnev the average annual growth in the gross national product (GNP) fell from 3 percent for the 1971–1975 period to 1.9 percent for 1976–1980, while growth in material production fell from 3.2 percent to 1 percent. At his death in 1982, Brezhnev was succeeded by Yuri V. Andropov, whose own death and succession by Konstantin U. Chernenko in 1984 left too little time to implement the economic reforms he sought. In 1981–1985 the GNP grew an average of only 1.8 percent a year, while the change in material production averaged a scant .6 percent. The Soviet economy had reached a stage of virtual stagnation marked by declines in growth rates, labor productivity, and return on capital investment.

Gorbachev arrived in Moscow in 1978 and became the Communist party official in charge of agriculture. By 1982 he was beginning to form his views on perestroika and, under Andropov's patronage, quickly became a leading decision maker on economic issues. According to Gorbachev, by the time he became general secretary in 1985, he had already begun to plot the details of perestroika.

In planning his reforms Gorbachev was heavily influenced by many economic advisers, most notably Abel Aganbegyan, rector of the Academy of the National Economy under the U.S.S.R. Council of Ministers; Leonid Albalkin, director of the Soviet Academy of Sciences' Economic Institute; and sociologist Tatiana Zaslavskaia. In 1983 Gorbachev commissioned a study by Zaslavskaia known as the Novosibirsk Report, a critique of the structural problems of the Soviet economy that influenced both Andropov's and Gorbachev's reform projects.

The ongoing series of reforms grouped under the umbrella of perestroika was a response to the economic stagnation of the 1970s and early 1980s and was conceived as a means of improving the aggregate economic performance of the economy and of satisfying the material needs of the population. Three distinct phases of reform may be discerned within the 1985–1990 period.

Uskoreniye

For two years after his election as general secretary, Gorbachev emphasized the "human factor" and making existing economic institutions work better. From March 1985 to June 1987 he employed a strategy of *uskoreniye* (acceleration) of social and economic development, emphasizing modernization and discipline. These reforms were conventional relative to those which were to follow and represented an effort to increase growth rates for all major sectors of the economy. Gorbachev's early policy goal was to achieve a transition from "extensive" economic development based on a growth of resources to "intensive" development based on increased efficiency in resource use.

Gorbachev attempted to squeeze more out of existing economic structures by introducing new technologies, increasing labor discipline and productivity, and allowing economics, not ideology, to dictate investment. In May 1985 the Soviet government announced a major antialcohol campaign to improve worker discipline. The production of inexpensive wines was ordered halted by 1988, production of vodka was curtailed, its price was increased significantly, liquor-store hours were shortened,

and retail outlets for alcohol were ordered moved geographically farther from workplaces. The program was far from successful – people resented it, home production of moonshine led to a sugar shortage, and government revenues fell sharply while a black market in alcohol sales flourished.

As general secretary, Gorbachev first voiced his ideas of acceleration and the need for economic reform at the April 1985 Plenary Meeting of the Central Committee. On 11 June Gorbachev announced his plan for "radical changes" to another plenary session of the Central Committee, although the only specific proposal was for a significant decrease in construction of new factories and a focus on modernizing existing plants.

Although there was talk of radical reforms, the first year of Gorbachev's leadership was marked by an emphasis on modernization, discipline, personnel changes, and the fight against corruption and bribery. The Twenty-Seventh Congress of the Communist party in February 1986 documented the broad ideas of perestroika in "Main Directions of the Economic and Social Development of the USSR in the Period 1986–90 and the Prospects up to the year 2000," but again few specifics were added.

Problems soon arose with the new reforms. In May 1986 a new state quality-control agency, Gospriomka, was formed. The plan backfired, however, when the agency began rejecting as much as 80 percent of a factory's output, resulting in a significant decline in production, and the program was halted within the year. Similarly, the May 1986 limits on unearned income, intended to curb bribery, had the result of hindering private enterprise.

By early 1987 Gorbachev apparently concluded that the problem was not merely one of discipline but a more fundamental one of the centralized nature of the Soviet economy. The beginning of this change can be seen in the May 1987 decree authorizing moonlighting in various jobs. As of 1 May private enterprises were allowed, although the hiring of employees remained forbidden.

Restructuring

The second major period of Gorbachev's economic reforms, from June 1987 to June 1989, was marked by a more radical restructuring of the economy, greater privatization, increased decentralization, a shift from administrative management to economic management, and a transition to self-financed and self-managed enterprises. This phase itself can be thought of as encompassing two distinct stages.

The first began in June 1987 with Gorbachev's presentation of his first comprehensive reform to the Central Committee, and the shift to more-radical reforms was embodied in two documents approved by the Central Committee at the June Plenum. The "Basic Provisions for Fundamentally Reorganizing Economic Management" outlined the creation of a new economic system in which state planning was balanced by market forces. While the state would continue to guide production through target figures, state orders, and economic normatives (taxes, financial allocations, and pricing parameters), the Basic Provisions provided greater independence and accountability for individual enterprises. It also included a decree that prices increasingly be set by market forces, not by the state.

The second document, the "State Law on the Socialist Enterprise," focused entirely on the greater independence and responsibility of enterprises. The new law, which went into effect 1 January 1988, introduced the possibility of bankruptcy for enterprises unable to maintain themselves financially. It provided for the autonomy of enterprises through self-planning, -management, and -financing and made that independence possible through the introduction of contractual pricing and wholesale trade. Most important, the Law on State Enterprises introduced the concept of *khozraschet* (cost accounting), which required enterprises to meet all expenses, including wages and salaries, through profits from the sale of products. While in theory this law meant that factories were to be responsible for profits and losses and dependent upon consumer demand, in reality the state still controlled the supply of raw materials, and state orders could and did take as much as 100 percent of a plant's production.

A more radical wave of reform marked by increased privatization of enterprises began in May 1988 with the Law on Cooperatives and was continued at the Nineteenth Party Conference in June. Cooperatives, or small group businesses having at least three members, were permitted and encouraged by the law but were limited to such areas as recycling of industrial by-products, production of consumer goods, and services such as car repair, cleaning, and the "public provision of meals." The Law on Cooperatives has been the only major success of perestroika to date; in the first half of 1989 the total number of new cooperatives in the Soviet Union rose from 78,000 to 133,000. The total number of people working at least part-time in co-

operatives climbed from about 70,000 in 1988 to 4.5 million in 1990, and after two years of operation cooperatives accounted for approximately 5 percent of the Soviet GNP.

Toward a Market Economy

During mid 1989 Gorbachev entered a new stage and hesitantly began advocating a market economy for the Soviet Union. In July Parliament approved economic autonomy for the Baltic republics, and in August the government began offering foreign currency to grain farmers who increased production. Prime Minister Nikolai I. Ryzhkov's "economic recovery plan," which called for a near market system by 1993, was approved by the Congress of People's Deputies in December 1989. In January 1990 the ruble, the Soviet currency, was devalued by 90 percent for tourist exchanges, in principle an early step toward a wider devaluation. The following month the government permitted lifetime leasing of land with the right to inherit, although it stopped short of allowing purchasing and selling of property. A March 1990 law on ownership paved the way for limited ownership of business and farms and the creation of stock markets. That same month Gorbachev stated his intention to use the powers of his new office as president of the Soviet Union to develop a market economy. The devaluation of the ruble and the subsequent announcement in May 1990 of limited price reforms prompted fears of a further devaluation and a shortage of consumer goods, both of which spurred panic buying.

Opposition

Perestroika was plagued by internal contradictions, obstacles to implementation, and outright opposition. Economic reform was opposed from the Right and Left, by those who thought it went too far as well as those who felt it did not go nearly far enough in changing the Soviet economic system. Hard-liners, such as Politburo member Yegor Ligachev, objected to many of the proposed reforms on the grounds that they moved too far from a centralized system. While agreeing in principle with the need for economic change, such opponents argued for a large role for a centralized party bureaucracy. Ligachev also protested Gorbachev's new thinking in foreign policy as a premature relaxation of relations with the West. On the other side, Gorbachev was roundly and repeatedly criticized by the more radical reformer Boris Yeltsin, former Moscow party chief and president of the Russian Republic.

In addition to direct political opposition, the Soviet economic, social, and political systems presented structural impediments to reform. The entrenched power of the political and administrative bureaucracy was threatened by such reforms, and many of the planning organs and ministries therefore rejected them. Even more important was the opposition of many Soviet citizens who feared shortages of consumer goods and whose work habits were slow to change. It is difficult to increase labor productivity in a country in which the work ethic and the historical relationship between workers and managers can both be aptly summed up by the old saying: "We pretend to work and they pretend to pay us."

Finally, perestroika was haunted by internal contradictions. The notions of a revolution from above conceived and implemented by the government was at odds with the ideas of democratization and openness that were encouraged by the authorities and necessary in order to carry out the reforms. There was also a more fundamental contradiction between the short-term economic growth hoped for and the long-term reform and restructuring of the Soviet economy also sought. This is apparent in the differences between acceleration and perestroika; it is difficult if not impossible to increase the growth rate and the standard of living while radically restructuring capital and the underlying nature of the economic system.

While new thinking in foreign policy heralded the end of the Cold War, and glasnost and democratization brought significant changes to the lives of Soviet citizens, 1990 saw little success in the area of domestic economic reform. The growth in the GNP, which climbed from a 1.8 percent annual average in 1981–1985 to 4.5 percent in 1986, fell again to 1.3 percent in 1987, 2.2 percent in 1988, and 1.4 percent in 1989. The change in material production, which had fallen to a pitiful .6 percent average for 1981–1985, rose briefly to 3 percent in 1986 before plummeting. The growth in production was 1 percent in 1987, –1 percent in 1988, and –4.5 percent in 1989. Since the collapse of the Soviet Union, many economists fear that the 1990s will be a period of hyperinflation for the Russian economy.

References

Abel G. Aganbegyan, *The Economic Challenge of Perestroika*, edited by Michael Barratt Brown (Bloomington: Indiana University Press, 1988);

Abel G. Aganbegyan, ed., *Perestroika Annual*, volume 2 (Washington, D.C.: Brassey's, 1989);

Anders Asland, *Gorbachev's Struggle for Economic Reform: The Soviet Reform Process, 1985–88* (Ithaca, N.Y.: Cornell University Press, 1989);

Seweryn Bialer and Michael Mandelbaum, eds., *Gorbachev's Russia and American Foreign Policy* (Boulder, Colo.: Westview, 1988);

Mikhail S. Gorbachev, *Perestroika: New Thinking for Our Country and the World* (New York: Harper & Row, 1987);

Gorbachev's Era of New Thinking, special edition of *Journal of International Affairs*, 42 (Spring 1989);

Ronald J. Hill and Jan Ake Dellenbrandt, eds., *Gorbachev and Perestroika: Towards a New Socialism?* (Hants, U.K.: Edward Elgar, 1989);

Jerry F. Hough, *Opening Up the Soviet Economy* (Washington, D.C.: Brookings Institution, 1988);

Anthony Jones and William Moskoff, eds., *Perestroika and the Economy: New Thinking in Soviet Economics* (Armonk, N.Y.: M. E. Sharpe, 1989);

Gertrude E. Liebowitz, ed., *Beyond Perestroika: The Future of Gorbachev's USSR*, translated by Gus Fagan (London: Verso, 1989);

William Green Miller, ed., *Toward a More Civil Society? The USSR Under Mikhail Sergeevich Gorbachev* (New York: Harper & Row, 1989).

– S. M. P.

SEE ALSO THESE RELATED ENTRIES

Yuri Andropov, 2; George Bush, 1; Geneva Summit, 3; Intermediate Nuclear Forces Treaty, 3; North Atlantic Treaty Organization, 3; Ronald Reagan, 1; Reykjavík Summit, 3; Eduard Shevardnadze, 2; Strategic Arms Reductions Talks, 3; Warsaw Pact, 3.

Post-Vietnam Syndrome

Post-Vietnam syndrome was the belief that in the wake of America's disastrous experience in Vietnam, the United States no longer had the will to intervene militarily in the affairs of another country to protect its vital national interests. Another analysis of U.S. foreign policy in the post-Vietnam era argues that military force no longer played a dominant role in power politics; instead, economic power or moral persuasion was used for leverage in international politics.

Whether U.S. policymakers believed in a post-Vietnam syndrome or not, it is clear that from 1968 on, U.S. foreign policy suffered a crisis of confidence that made undeclared military interventions, as in Vietnam, impossible. The war was purported to have taught America lessons about intervening militarily in the Third World, though everyone disagreed on what those lessons were. Conservatives and members of the military establishment argue that President Lyndon B. Johnson tied the hands of the military by fighting only a limited war in Vietnam and, therefore, not permitting the United States to win. The lesson of Vietnam, so this argument concludes, is that the United States should commit troops abroad only if it intends a complete victory, and should avoid limited wars with purely political goals.

Post-Vietnam syndrome has been partly offered as an explanation for Jimmy Carter's dovish and successful campaign in which he all but boasted that he would never want to see an American killed in combat while he was president. Such attitudes, however, helped doom his foreign policy. Whatever his other successes, Carter handicapped U.S. foreign policy because adversaries understood that the United States would not resort to force. In 1980 Ronald Reagan staged a landslide victory over Carter, in part due to Reagan's promise of a return to hawkish foreign policy. Reagan proved to be a president with few hesitations over using military force in the name of U.S. interests.

References

Francis Fitzgerald, *Fire in the Lake: The Vietnamese and Americans in Vietnam* (New York: Vintage, 1973);

Leslie Gelb and Richard K. Betts: *The Irony of Vietnam: The System Worked* (Washington, D.C.: The Brookings Institution, 1979);

David Halberstam, *The Best and the Brightest* (New York: Random House, 1969);

Arnold R. Isaacs, *Without Honor: Defeat in Vietnam and Cambodia* (Baltimore: Johns Hopkins University Press, 1983);

– C. S. B.

SEE ALSO THESE RELATED ENTRIES
Jimmy Carter, 1; Lyndon B. Johnson, 1; Ronald Reagan, 1.

Potsdam Conference

Between 17 July and 2 August 1945 Soviet, British, and American leaders met in the German city of Potsdam to discuss Allied aims. In the five months since the Yalta Conference – held on 4–11 February 1945 – the alliance between the Soviet Union, Great Britain, and the United States had begun to deteriorate. In an atmosphere of suspicion and distrust, the meetings at Potsdam failed to resolve the major issues facing the Allies. In the final communiqué they did little more than agree to disagree.

The Potsdam meeting took place after months of mounting distrust between the Western powers and the Soviet Union – tensions that had become apparent during World War II. The German defeat had stirred Russian suspicions of the West. Soviet leader Joseph Stalin's cautious battle tactics and fierce German resistance along the eastern front stalled the advance of the Red Army fifty miles outside of Berlin. On the western front, once the Allies captured the Remagen Bridge on 7 March 1945 and crossed the Rhine River, German defenses collapsed. American and British forces advanced so swiftly into the heart of Germany that the Russians began to fear that the German army had concluded a secret agreement with the Anglo-Americans, opening the western front in exchange for lenient treatment. These suspicions were fueled by the disclosure of negotiations on the surrender of German forces in Italy in March 1945.

East-West Distrust

The British and the Americans, for their part, no longer viewed the Soviets simply as wartime partners. President Franklin D. Roosevelt, who had been the Soviets' staunchest Allied supporter during the war, died on 12 March 1945. His successor, President Harry S Truman, had no personal rapport with Stalin. More importantly, the United States no longer felt that Russian troop support was essential in the war against Japan. The need for military cooperation, the reason for the alliance in the first place, was evaporating.

The West also began to suspect that Stalin had violated the Yalta Conference's Declaration on Liberated Europe, which called for support for the principle of self-determination for nations liberated from German occupation. On 6 March the Soviets had executed a bloodless coup in Bucharest, the capital of Romania, installing Petru Groza, the Romanian communist leader. In Poland, Stalin adopted repressive tactics, imprisoning members of the underground who had fought against Nazi Germany. With the Polish underground eliminated, the Russian-backed communist regime solidified its position of authority in Warsaw.

The conference opened on 17 July. Addressing the issue of Germany first, the Allies decided to divide the issue into political and economic questions. On the political side, Truman, Churchill, and Stalin were able to agree in principle to a uniform system of administration in the German occupation zones. The task was handed to the Allied foreign ministers, who promptly approved a four-point plan calling for the demoralization, denazification, demilitarization, and democratization of Germany.

Disagreements, particularly between Stalin and Churchill, became increasingly frequent and caustic. By the seventh day the talks had ground to a halt. The three leaders had discussed Romania, Italy, Yugoslavia, Hungary, Greece, Spain, Austria,

Prime Minister Winston Churchill, President Harry S Truman, and Soviet leader Joseph Stalin at the Potsdam Conference

Turkey, and Korea, as well as Germany, without reaching a single additional agreement. They managed to proceed to new issues only by tabling disputes for the foreign ministers to discuss. The foreign ministers, who were effective in elaborating the details of plans for their respective leaders, could not resolve fundamental conflicts, however.

Economic and Political Issues

The most significant issues that separated the Anglo-Americans from the Russians were economic policy toward Germany and Soviet actions in Eastern Europe. Churchill had convinced Truman that it would be imprudent to set a fixed sum of reparations for Germany, arguing that this would depress the German economy, require Allied subsidies, and, in the end, cause economic turmoil and social unrest. Allied economic policy toward Germany was further complicated by the new Polish-German border, which the Russians had established along the Oder and Neisse rivers, approximately one hundred miles west of the old border. Churchill worried that the new border would inspire German resentment and that the loss of rich farmland to Poland and subsequent influx of refugees from the East would leave Germany dependent upon the Allies for its subsistence.

Stalin was unmoved by Churchill's arguments. He was not interested in an enlightened peace. He argued bluntly that the Allies had agreed to $20 billion in reparations from Germany which included at least $10 billion for the Soviet Union.

The second disagreement concerned the unilateral steps taken by the Soviets to establish communist regimes in Romania, Poland, and Bulgaria. The complaints, however, were rebuffed by Stalin. When the subject arose, he frequently turned the conversation to American activities in Italy and British moves in Greece to bolster prodemocratic groups.

On 25 July the talks were suspended for the British general elections. When the Labour party surprisingly defeated the Conservative party, the new British prime minister, Clement Attlee, traveled immediately to Potsdam, replacing Winston Churchill. The change of British leadership did not affect the conference, as Attlee had served in the wartime coalition government as deputy prime minister and had been attending the meetings at Potsdam with Churchill, but the intermission allowed U.S. secretary of state James F. Byrnes to begin formulating a series of proposals to resolve the stalemates.

On 30 July Byrnes presented three proposals to the foreign ministers. The first dealt with German reparations, the second addressed the Polish border issue, and the third pertained to questions relating to Italy, Bulgaria, Finland, Hungary, and Romania, whose regimes had collaborated with the Germans. The last two proposals had little effect, but they were useful in that they facilitated an agreement on German reparations. Byrnes suggested that the Polish frontiers be finalized later at the proposed German peace conference. For the interim, he suggested that the existing boundaries that the Russians had drawn serve as the temporary border. As for Italy and the Balkans, Byrnes suggested that the Council of Foreign Ministers address the peace treaty with Italy as their first priority and that treaties with the other Central and Eastern European states be their secondary concern.

Byrnes's most meaningful proposal dealt with German reparations. He suggested that each Ally determine reparations in its own zone of occupation and proposed that the Western Allies ship one-eighth of surplus German capital equipment in their zones without charge to the Soviet zone, and send another eighth in return for food and coal from the East. Byrnes's proposals met with initial resistance from Stalin, but an agreement was finally reached by increasing the Soviet share of gratis reparations from 12.5 percent to 15 percent.

The Western press portrayed the Potsdam accords as a moderate success. The agreements, however, were agreements in name only – little more than recognition of the existence of Western and Soviet spheres of influence. The lack of agreement at Potsdam signaled growing friction between the East and West. Within a year, in a speech at Fulton, Missouri, Winston Churchill was able to declare that an "iron curtain" had fallen over Eastern Europe.

References

Robert J. Donovan, *Conflict and Crisis* (New York: Norton, 1977);

John Lewis Gaddis, *The United States and the Origins of the Cold War* (New York: Columbia University Press, 1982);

William H. McNeill, *America, Britain, and Russia: Their Cooperation and Conflict, 1941–1946* (New York: Johnson Reprint Corporation, 1970).

– B. D. K.

SEE ALSO THESE RELATED ENTRIES
Joseph Stalin, 2; Harry S Truman, 1; Yalta Conference, 3.

Presidential Directive–59

On 20 July 1980 President Jimmy Carter signed Presidential Directive–59 (PD-59). The directive was intended to enhance the American nuclear deterrent by improving U.S. ability to wage a protracted, limited nuclear war.

The authors of PD-59 sought to improve the U.S. nuclear deterrent by threatening the targets that the Soviet leadership valued most, the command, control, communications, and intelligence (C^3I) structure that the Soviet leadership needed to control Soviet nuclear forces during war. The directive also ordered the targeting of the hardened bunkers that protected the Soviet leadership during a nuclear crisis. Another goal of PD-59 was the destruction of the powerful Soviet arsenal of large intercontinental ballistic missiles (ICBMs), which the Soviets might have used to extract concessions from the United States during an international crisis. The directive also ordered the targeting of Soviet industry to impair its ability to recover from nuclear war.

The directive required the United States to enhance the precision of its nuclear weapons and the ability to re-aim its remaining nuclear forces following a Soviet nuclear strike. The retargeted missiles could then threaten mobile Soviet targets that had relocated during the initial Soviet attack. To accomplish this mission, the United States needed to enhance its C^3I capabilities and maintain a "secure strategic reserve," an invulnerable missile arsenal that could be held in reserve during early nuclear exchanges.

Response to Soviet Buildup

PD-59 was drawn up in response to the continued growth of the Soviet nuclear arsenal in the 1970s. In 1967 the United States froze its ICBM arsenal at 1,054 missiles. The Soviet Union reached that level in 1969 but continued to build missiles, deploying as many as 1,587 by 1973. The United States also halted its deployment of ICBM nuclear warheads at 2,144 in 1975. The Soviet Union achieved approximate numerical parity in warheads in 1976, but it continued to build warheads, deploying as many as 6,426 by 1987. During the 1970s the Soviets added approximately 4,000 warheads to their arsenal, generating considerable concern among American officials, who began to fear that the Soviet Union would try to exploit the size of its land-based nuclear arsenal. PD-59 was designed to deal with this problem, making it impossible for the Soviets to coerce the U.S. government during a nuclear crisis.

PD-59 has often been misconstrued as a dramatic shift in American nuclear strategy from civilian population centers to military targets. Press reports of the day suggested that before PD-59, U.S. nuclear targeting policy assumed that nuclear war would consist of brief, spasmodic exchanges, culminating in global holocaust. Since its inception, however, U.S. nuclear targeting policy has provided for Soviet military targets. By the early 1950s American officials had created nuclear attack plans for three sets of targets named after the first initial of the missions their destruction was intended to achieve: Retardation, Deterrence, and Blunting. The first group were conventional military assets, known as "Romeo" targets, the destruction of which would retard a Soviet attack in Western Europe. Another set of targets, called "Delta" targets, were centers of population that the U.S. would threaten to attack as a punitive measure to deter Soviet aggression. The final group of targets, referred to as "Bravo" targets by American nuclear planners, focused on Soviet nuclear forces in the hope of limiting damage to the United States in the event of war.

References

Zbigniew K. Brzezinski, *Power and Principle: Memoirs of the National Security Advisor, 1977–1981* (New York: Farrar, Straus, Giroux, 1983);

Jimmy Carter, *Keeping Faith: Memoirs of a President* (New York: Bantam, 1982);

Lawrence Freedman, *The Evolution of Nuclear Strategy* (New York: St. Martin's Press, 1981);

Fred Kaplan, *The Wizards of Armageddon* (New York: Simon & Schuster, 1983).

– B. D. K.

SEE ALSO THESE RELATED ENTRIES
Harold Brown, 1; Zbigniew Brzezinski, 1; Jimmy Carter, 1; Committee on the Present Danger, 3; Deterrence, 3.

Radio Free Europe

Polish-language flyer for Radio Free Europe and Radio Liberty

Radio Free Europe, along with Radio Liberty, is a nonprofit corporation headquartered in Munich, Germany. The objective of these two radio stations during the Cold War was to provide the populations of communist Eastern-bloc countries with news, opinions, music, and religious programs from democracies in the West, especially the United States.

The United States created Radio Free Europe (RFE) and Radio Liberty (RL) in 1950 and 1951, respectively. The idea for the radio stations came about because radio broadcasting had proved such a powerful weapon during World War II. As the Nazis and their Italian allies conquered most of Europe, the spirits of the British were bolstered by hearing the inspiring words of leaders such as Prime Minister Winston S. Churchill over the airwaves.

During the war Churchill and the other Allied leaders used radio broadcasting to rally the people of the besieged democracies. President Frank-

lin D. Roosevelt had reassured Americans with his "fireside chats." News broadcasts into occupied Europe helped keep hope alive, while Adolf Hitler and Benito Mussolini responded with harsh condemnations of the Allies and used radio to consolidate their own power.

In an era before television, radio was particularly vital in quickly communicating news to large masses of people. During World War II Allied soldiers and sailors around the world tuned in for news and entertainment on the Armed Forces Radio Service (AFRS). It was the first worldwide radio network and had some eight hundred stations by May 1945, when Nazi Germany collapsed.

In 1948 American scientists invented the transistor, which revolutionized radio technology and ushered in a new era of solid-state radios. New, battery-operated "transistor" radios could be carried anywhere. This gave radio broadcasting a huge boost during the 1950s and vastly improved the technological know-how necessary to create RFE and RL.

The programming of RFE and RL was controversial. The Soviet government, fearing that the news broadcast over the stations would stir political dissent among their satellite countries, tried to jam the airwaves so that broadcasts could not be heard. Nonetheless, listeners of RFE and RL remained loyal; more than half of the those surveyed during the 1980s in Eastern European countries listed the stations as their preferred source for news. Furthermore, RFE and RL was used as a vehicle to advance American political interests. During the administration of President Richard M. Nixon, for example, Secretary of State Henry Kissinger tried to tone down criticisms of the Soviet government on RFE and RL as part of an effort to achieve détente.

Until 1971 the U.S. government financed RFE and RL through funds covertly channeled through the Central Intelligence Agency. In 1973 a semiautonomous agency, the Board for International Broadcasting, was set up to run the two stations and oversee their finances. The two stations were merged in 1976 into one corporation, Radio Free Europe/Radio Liberty, Incorporated.

RFE continues to broadcast into former Eastern-bloc countries in six languages. The mission of RFE/RL, however, has changed somewhat since the end of the Cold War. It has undertaken the task of helping these countries to cope with democratization, including training former Eastern-bloc reporters in how a free press operates.

References

Erik Barnouw, *The Golden Web: A History of Broadcasting in the United States, 1933–1953* (New York: Oxford University Press, 1968);

Alden R. Carter, *Radio: From Marconi to the Space Age* (New York: Franklin Watts, 1987).

SEE ALSO THESE RELATED ENTRIES
Winston S. Churchill, 1; Henry Kissinger, 1; Franklin D. Roosevelt, 1.

Rapid Deployment Force

The Rapid Deployment Force (RDF), established during the Carter administration, is a military force designed for quick reaction to crises emerging in the Middle East/Persian Gulf region. Designated as the U.S. Central Command (USCENTCOM) on 1 January 1983, the RDF is the major U.S. military force for operations in the Middle East, Southwest Asia, and northeastern Africa.

When U.S. president Jimmy Carter entered office, he initiated planning for the use of rapid deployment forces throughout the world. By 1979, following the Iranian revolution and fighting between North and South Yemen in 1978, planners began to emphasize the use of these forces in the Middle East. In response to the Soviet invasion of Afghanistan in December 1979, President Carter announced the Carter Doctrine, pushing RDF planning toward implementation.

The RDF was officially established on 1 March 1980 as the Rapid Deployment Joint Task Force (RDJTF), with headquarters at MacDill AFB in Tampa, Florida. Although based in the United States, the RDF was designed as a multiservice quick-strike force that could be swiftly deployed in regions of conflict and used in a wide range of situations, from employment of a few small units to use of the entire RDF itself. It was also envisioned that the RDF would respond to a variety of threats, including external aggression from the Soviet Union or threats from regional actors such as Iran or South Yemen.

At the time of its establishment, critics questioned the multiple missions of the RDF as well as its ability to counter a Soviet attack in the Persian Gulf. These questions sparked a heated debate in the early 1980s over the role of the RDF.

In an effort to upgrade the RDF, the Ronald Reagan administration decided in January 1983 to convert the RDJTF into USCENTCOM, a unified multiservice command that oversees planning and operations for the Southwest Asia region. This move signaled the administration's growing recognition of the volatility and strategic importance of the region. Military planners also hoped that USCENTCOM would enhance the range of options available to the United States in the event of a crisis.

USCENTCOM is composed of units from the army, navy, air force, and marines. Designed for response to a variety of contingencies, its primary purpose was to deter a Soviet attack in the Persian Gulf region and defend Western access to oil resources in the Gulf. USCENTCOM also seeks to promote security in the region by counterbalancing the regional threat posed by states such as Iran and Iraq. This latter task is pursued through security assistance programs and joint military training and exercise programs with friendly states.

In comparison to the other six unified U.S. commands, USCENTCOM is unique because it has no forces permanently based in its area of operations. All of the forces assigned to USCENTCOM have other missions outside of the Middle East. As a result, the primary day-to-day emphasis of USCENTCOM is on the planning and administration of security assistance programs.

Because its forces are not based in the region, USCENTCOM has undertaken several measures to improve the speed with which its forces can be deployed. It relies heavily on limited access to re-gional facilities in Kenya, Oman, Somalia, and other friendly states. The need to transport troops and equipment over long distances has led USCENTCOM to improve its airlift and sealift capabilities and to rely on prepositioned supplies.

The focus of USCENTCOM on the Middle East region also makes it unique in comparison to the rapid deployment forces of other nations. For example, the French Forces d'Action Rapide train for a variety of contingencies, ranging from war in Europe to conflicts within former French colonies. Although foreign RDF forces also stress army and marine operations, they rarely include air force and naval units within their RDF command structure, unlike USCENTCOM. In this sense, the RDF forces of other nations tend to be more similar to the U.S. Special Operations Command, with its emphasis on combating insurgencies and other low-intensity threats.

References

Sherwood S. Cordier, *U.S. Military Power and Rapid Deployment Requirements in the 1980s* (Boulder, Colo.: Westview, 1983);

Maxwell Orme Johnson, *The Military as an Instrument of U.S. Policy in Southwest Asia: The Rapid Deployment Joint Task Force, 1979–1982* (Boulder, Colo.: Westview, 1983).

– E. P.

SEE ALSO THESE RELATED ENTRIES
Zbigniew Brzezinski, 1; Jimmy Carter, 1; Carter Doctrine, 3. Deterrence, 3.

243

Reagan Doctrine

The Reagan Doctrine declared that the United States would oppose any perceived Soviet advances in the Third World by offering military aid and counterinsurgency training to anticommunist governments. At the same time the United States was prepared to support guerrilla movements attempting to overthrow governments considered Marxist or pro-Soviet.

The Reagan Doctrine, consequently, viewed conflict in the Third World through the prism of a U.S.-Soviet Cold War rivalry. But mindful of the experience in Vietnam, the United States was not prepared to risk its power and prestige to aid anti-communist movements. All the United States was willing to do was raise the cost of Soviet military and economic aid to client states. At one point in the 1980s the United States was supporting anticommunist insurgencies in Angola, Cambodia, Afghanistan, and Nicaragua. In Afghanistan, American interest waned almost immediately following the Soviet decision to pull its troops out.

References:
Christopher C. DeMuth, *The Reagan Doctrine and Beyond* (Washington, D.C.: American Enterprise Institute For Public Policy Research, 1987).

– C. S. B.

SEE ALSO THESE RELATED ENTRIES
Ronald Reagan, 1.

Red Army

The armed forces of the Soviet Union, known simply as the Red Army, was one of the most influential institutions of the Soviet state, and one of the most important institutional players in twentieth-century international affairs. From Moscow's vantage point, the Red Army saved communism from capitalist assault on four occasions: the Bolshevik revolution, the Russian civil war, World War II, and the Cold War. From a Western perspective, the Red Army was successful not only in saving the Soviet Union from external threats, but also in perpetuating a brutal totalitarian system at home and in Eastern Europe, exporting communist revolution abroad, and ultimately spending the Soviet economy into bankruptcy.

1917-1928: The Birth of the Red Army

The Red Army was formed out of two diametrically opposed forces: the Russian Imperial Army and the Bolshevik forces which crippled the Imperial Army and swept the revolutionaries into power. The Bolsheviks had long worked to weaken the Imperial Army from within and create their own armed forces. Called the Red Guards, the Bolshevik army was composed of armed factory workers who were led by Bolshevik agents. When V. I. Lenin and his comrades finally gave the order to overthrow the provisional government, they could rely on over 250,000 Red Guards, soldiers, and sailors to help them storm the Winter Palace. One of Lenin's first moves after seizing control of the government was to dismantle the Imperial Army — which he saw as the greatest threat to the revolution — replacing thousands of old imperial officers with members of the Red Guards or with revolutionary soldiers. When the Germans attacked in mid February and began to route the enthusiastic but untrained Red Guard units, however, Bolshevik dreams of quick peace and demobilization vanished.

The official birthdate of the Red Army of Workers and Peasants is 23 February 1918, when Lenin rallied thousands of volunteers to join the new army in Petrograd and marched them off to nearby

Pskov to battle the advancing Germans. Despite some initial Soviet successes, the professional German army was more than a match for the communist volunteers, and the Bolshevik government was forced to accept the previously unpalatable German demands at the Brest Litovsk peace talks.

The true founding of the Red Army was on 22 April 1918, when the Bolsheviks ordered the conscription of workers and peasants – other classes were not trusted by the Bolsheviks – and began to reconstruct a large standing army despite Marxist tenets against such a force. A month after the signing of the Brest Litovsk Treaty, the Russian civil war began and foreign troops intervened. British, French, and American troops entered the north and south of Russia, and Japanese and American troops entered Siberia. The Allies had quickly turned against the Bolshevik government when it withdrew Russia from the war, and they began to aid the White anti-Bolshevik forces in the hope of toppling the communist government and reestablishing an eastern front in the war.

Leon Trotsky, who had been appointed commissar for war in March 1918, realized that the young Soviet state would need a large, professional army if it was going to survive. Against the wishes of Red Guard commanders and other Bolshevik military leaders, Trotsky reversed earlier Bolshevik orders and formed a traditional land army with a strong chain of command and strict discipline. Over twenty-two thousand officers of the now defunct Imperial Army joined the new Red Army, and many ex-czarist officers served in high positions. In order to ensure the loyalty of these officers, Trotsky created a system composed of political officers, or commissars, who permeated all levels of the armed forces and had the authority to overrule the orders of regular military officers.

As the threat to the Soviet state became more critical and the Bolsheviks further consolidated power over the territory which they controlled, the Red Army burgeoned in size from three hundred thousand in May 1918 to over three million by the end of 1919. Command over these forces was reinforced by the "Red Terror," carried out by the Cheka, or secret police. The Cheka disposed of civilian counterrevolutionaries, shot troops who retreated against orders, and either executed or threatened to execute officers who failed in battle.

The forces facing the Bolsheviks were impressive. The White armies were led by ex-czarist officers such as Aleksander Kolchak, Anton Denikin, and Nikolai Yudenich and manned by Cossacks and other peasant soldiers. By the end of the summer of 1918 White forces held 75 percent of the territory formerly controlled by the Russian Empire. On 2 September 1918 the Kremlin declared their territory to be an armed camp and desperately began to rally the people to the defense of the socialist state. Nationalization of industry, or war communism, was introduced to provide the Soviet military with needed material. To cope with the massive influx of soldiers into the army, Trotsky drafted more ex-czarist officers and over two hundred thousand of the old Imperial Army's warrant and noncommissioned officers.

In 1919 White armies advanced toward Moscow on three fronts and came within 150 miles of the city. Kazan, Kiev, Odessa, and Tsaritsyn were all captured, and White forces came within 20 miles of Petrograd before sailors from the Kronstadt naval base arrived and finally stymied the offensive. Soon the massive size of the Red Army combined with increasingly effective leadership began to have an effect on the war. The White forces, which failed to attract broad support among the populace and were losing the aid given to them by the war-weary Allies, began to lose ground. White armies were forced south to Crimea and east past the Urals, while the Allies began to withdraw their forces in the spring of 1920.

Poland's attack on the Soviet Union brought another threat to the communist government. The Polish army occupied Kiev in May 1920, and demanded that its borders with the Soviet Union be moved eastward from the Curzon Line to the states' previous 1772 borders. Mikhail Tukhachevsky marched the Red Army back to the gates of Warsaw, where a counterattack prevented the Soviets from capturing the city. An armistice was signed in October 1920.

Although the civil war would continue through 1922, the Bolshiviks were at last not threatened with imminent defeat. As the civil war drew to an end, the Soviets used the Red Army to consolidate their control over the lands previously held by the Russian Empire. The Red Army was used to crush revolts by peasants, Cossacks, and the inhabitants of the southern regions, such as Georgia and Central Asia.

The best known revolt of the time, however, was staged by the very men who helped the Bolsheviks seize power in 1917 – the sailors at Kronstadt. The Kronstadt Uprising began on 7 March 1921 in response to the devastating economic conditions brought about by Lenin's policy of war communism. The Kremlin, aware of the economic hardships, nevertheless ordered the army to quell the rebellion instead of negotiating with the sailors. The first assault on the base failed as many members of the Red Army refused to fight their fellow Russians. After one out of every five soldiers was shot, however, the remaining Red Army dutifully attacked the base under Tukhachevsky's leadership and succeeded in subduing the sailors. The fourteen thousand sailors who did not die repelling the assault were later shot or imprisoned.

The Red Army, triumphant in the revolution and the civil war, nevertheless revealed its weaknesses during the first May Day parade. It was poorly disciplined in spite of Trotsky's harsh measures and equipped with only a few modern weapons, most of which were produced abroad. While the devastated economy did not allow the Soviets to modernize fully the Red Army in the early 1920s, it did undergo considerable transformations. In a compromise between Trotsky and Tukhachevsky on one side and Mikhail Frunze, Klement Efremovich Voroshilov, and Vasilii Blyukher on the other, the peacetime Red Army was established with both professional and regional militia units. Trotsky set conscription at the age of twenty-one, divided the country into nine military districts, reorganized the field staff comprised of mostly czarist officers, and focused on political indoctrination as a key in military education.

In order to help modernize the Soviet forces and train its officers, the Kremlin signed the secret Rapallo Treaty in 1922, which allowed Germany to circumvent the Treaty of Versailles by using Soviet territory to produce weapons and conduct exercises. The treaty provided the Red Army with the chance to send its most able officers to German staff courses, and much of what Russian officers learned there was later incorporated into Soviet military doctrine. Although Joseph Stalin removed Trotsky from his position as commissar of the army and navy in 1924, Trotsky's policies remained mostly intact during the tenure of Frunze (1925) and Voroshilov (1925–1941). When the Soviet economy finally began to recover in the late 1920s, Moscow was able to strengthen its armed forces.

1924–1941: Industrialization to World War II

With the rise of Stalin and the beginning of the first Five Year Plan in late 1928, the Kremlin began its program of massive industrialization and, once a heavy industrial base was in place, military modernization. In 1929 the "State of Defense of the USSR" committed the country to equal the number of soldiers that would be fielded by the probable enemies of the Soviet Union and surpass their ene-

mies in the number of tanks, aircraft, and artillery. Soviet results were very impressive. By 1932 the Soviet Union had a tank force equal to that of France, the strongest military power in Europe at the time. The strength of the Red Army was increased from 885,000 men in 1933 to 1,513,400 men in 1938 and the air force was more than tripled in size between 1930 and 1936, when over three thousand aircraft reportedly took part in the May Day parade.

Tukhachevsky, who had returned from studying in Germany, helped Voroshilov plan the mechanization of the Soviet armed forces and tried to prepare the Soviet army for combined arms warfare and massive tank strikes. Between 1935 and 1938 all territorial units were converted into professional cadre mechanized divisions. The participation of Soviet volunteer units in the Spanish civil war demonstrated that Soviet weaponry was still somewhat behind that of Germany, but Moscow quickly strove to correct these deficiencies. More important, the war led the Soviet military to conclude wrongly that its doctrine of mechanization was improper, and in 1939 the Soviet general staff disbanded the mechanized divisions.

Concurrent with the Soviet military buildup, however, was Stalin's attempt to gain complete control over the military. Stalin ordered all officers to join the Communist party, and those who did not were relieved of their commands. In 1931 officers who had either supported Stalin's rivals or were of questionable loyalty were also fired. Stalin clearly wanted all officers to have their careers dependent upon him. Adolf Hitler's ascension to power and the consequent rearmament of Germany brought Stalin's paranoia about the military to a peak in the late 1930s, and beginning in 1937 the military was devastated by his purges. Three out of the five Soviet marshals – Tukhachevsky, Egorov, and Blyukher – were killed, as were all of the troop commanders of the military districts. All corps commanders, along with almost all division and brigade commanders, were removed from the army. Although one-fourth of the repressed officers were rehabilitated for World War II, the purges killed over one-half of the senior Soviet officers. After the purges, the military leadership was left with inexperienced and confused personnel who were quickly promoted to high posts and often were unable to carry out their duties.

The Great Patriotic War

Referred to by the Soviets as the Great Patriotic War, World War II caused great suffering in the

Soviet Union, a state which had lost millions over the previous twenty years to revolution, civil war, famine, collectivization, and the purges. World War II, however, served to legitimize the Soviet state in the eyes of its people. For the forty-five years after the war, the Red Army used the victory over Nazi Germany to increase its prestige and demand inordinate funds for its programs.

While Stalin had succeeded in building formidable armed forces, Germany's path toward war and Japan's expansion in Asia threatened the Soviet Union with a two-front war. This threat coupled with the Soviet inability to reach a collective security agreement with the Western powers, propelled the paranoid Stalin to sign the Molotov-Ribbentrop Non-Aggression Pact with Germany in August of 1939. On 1 September 1939 Hitler, in accordance with the secret provisions of the treaty, invaded Poland, and the Soviets moved in from the east on 17 September, annexing the Baltic states along with eastern Poland later in 1939 and 1940.

Stalin also launched the Winter War against Finland during the winter of 1939 to 1940. When Finland refused to cede territory to Moscow to appease Soviet concern over the security of the Kronstadt naval base, the Kremlin abrogated the nonaggression treaty between the two countries and invaded. While Voroshilov planned to steamroll over the Finns' Mannerheim line, the Finnish army thwarted the advances of the larger Soviet force and inflicted heavy casualties on the Soviets. It was only when massive reinforcements were brought in that the Soviets were able to accomplish their objectives. The impression that the Soviet invasion of Poland and the Russo-Finnish War left on the rest of the world was that the purges had decimated the Red Army, rendering it a large, inefficient force. Hitler, who supported Finland, certainly drew these conclusions.

On 22 June 1941 Hitler invaded the Soviet Union and the "Great Patriotic War" began. Stalin had repeatedly refused to heed the warnings of the West and his own diplomats that Nazi Germany was planning an attack on the Soviet Union, and he instead believed that war could be averted until 1942, when Red Army reforms would be completed. Soviet units were not even on alert when the Wehrmacht attacked and were taken completely by surprise. Stalin was so shocked by Hitler's attack that he went into seclusion for eleven days.

Hitler committed 152 German divisions and 29 divisions from other Eastern European allies to the attack along with some 5,000 aircraft. Soviet forces numbered 4,207,000 men in 303 divisions – what amounted to a small numerical advantage. Many of the Soviet divisions, however, were not up to full strength and were equipped with obsolete weapons. Stalin's lack of preparation for the attack proved devastating as 2,000 aircraft were destroyed on the ground and 90 percent of the front line tanks were eliminated in the early days of the war. On all three axes of the Nazi attack – toward Leningrad, Moscow, and the Ukraine – the Red Army suffered tremendous losses in both personnel and matériel and was forced to retreat. The Wehrmacht quickly advanced to within fifty miles of Leningrad and began its nine-hundred-day siege of the city. Moscow might have fallen in the early days of the war had Hitler not diverted some of his central forces to the south to assist in the capture of Kiev. During this time Dmitry Fedorovich Ustinov, the future Soviet defense minister, oversaw the massive transfer of war industry from the threatened regions of the country to east of the Urals. Some fifteen thousand enterprises and as many as ten million people were moved beyond the Nazis' reach in order to help build the armaments that the Red Army would use to defeat the Germans.

In September 1941 Hitler concentrated his forces for a final assault on Moscow. The Germans deployed over 1 million men, 1,700 tanks, 950 aircraft, and 14,000 guns and mortars against a combined Soviet force of 800,000 men, 780 tanks, 545 aircraft, and 6,800 guns and mortars. As the Nazis advanced to within twenty miles of the city, Stalin transferred the government from Moscow to Kuybyshev. On 7 December the Soviets began their counterattack and were eventually successful in pushing the German forces back to a couple hundred miles outside of Moscow. After this battle and the U.S. entry into World War II, the lend-lease matériel provided by the United States, along with the matériel provided by the British, began to arrive en masse at Soviet ports. Some 16,400 aircraft, 10,000 tanks, and 450,000 vehicles were sent to the Soviet Union between 1941 and 1945.

For the Red Army, 1944 was a year of resounding successes. Leningrad's siege was lifted in January and the eastern and southern Ukraine were liberated that spring. After the summer-fall campaign of 1942, the Soviets were successful in expelling the Germans from all Soviet territory, except for a portion of Latvia. The Red Army also moved into Poland, Czechoslovakia, Hungary, Romania, Bulgaria, and Yugoslavia. As the Soviets swept through Eastern Europe, Voroshilov's reparations committee confiscated and moved much of the economically useful machinery to the Soviet Union. Losses continued to be high for both sides throughout the year as the Soviets had drafted both the young and the old to increase the army's size to 12.4 million men.

Facing the Allied advance in the West and the massive Red Army in the East, the Wehrmach was simply outnumbered and outgunned. The Red Army captured Warsaw on 17 January, after the Nazis brutally quelled the Warsaw Uprising a few days before, and liberated Vienna on 7 April. In Germany, Soviet troops met up with U.S. forces on 25 April, captured the Reichstag on 30 April, and finally achieved victory on 8 May when the Nazis surrendered.

The victory over Germany, however, did not conclude Soviet participation in World War II since Stalin had agreed at the Yalta Conference to commit Soviet forces against the Japanese. Soviet entry into the war with Japan was originally planned to begin in late August. On 6 August, however, the United States dropped the atomic bomb on Hiroshima and Stalin declared war on 8 August in order to participate in the battle and demand concessions from Japan. The Red Army was successful in defeating Japanese forces in the Far East by 20 August, and on 2 September Emperor Hirohito unconditionally surrendered to Allied forces.

The price which the Soviet Union payed for its survival in World War II was enormous. Over thirty million people, a majority of whom were civilians, died from starvation, hypothermia, German bullets, or the horrors of the Nazi concentration camps. The Soviet peoples fought for their own survival, with Stalin having to rely on nationalist and religious sentiments to rally his population. Nonetheless, it was communism, and for a time Stalin himself, that could take credit for defending and protecting the people, and the Red Army had gained a new credibility as an effective military force.

Beginning of the Cold War

World War II left the Soviet armed forces in control of Eastern and large parts of Central Europe. The Kremlin used its power to ensure that its new allies would be ruled by satellite communist governments which would subordinate their interests to those of the Soviet Union. Northern Korea, which the Soviets had occupied after the Japanese surrender, also was ruled by a communist dictatorship. In the late 1940s Stalin stationed some of his

more loyal military leaders in the east to assist and plan the invasion of South Korea. North Korean divisions were rotated into Siberia where they were trained by Soviet officers then sent back to their homeland. Although Stalin did not commit ground troops to the war as had Mao Zedong, Soviet aviation units were covertly transferred to North Korea and fought against American forces during the war. As a result of heightened international tensions and U.S. military expansion during the Korean War, the Soviet army grew from 2,800,000 to 5,700,000 men.

In Europe, the Soviets were faced by a fearful and newly united West which had founded the North Atlantic Treaty Organization (NATO) in 1949 as an attempt to protect itself from the Soviet divisions still occupying Eastern Europe. In the same year Stalin succeeded in making the Soviet Union the world's second nuclear power, a development which American experts did not expect to take place for another four years. The Cold War was on, and in the eyes of the Soviet Union "capitalist encirclement" – a doctrine which Stalin first proclaimed in 1931 – again seemed to be building around the Soviet Union.

Stalin's death in March of 1953 brought about profound changes in the Soviet armed forces (officially, the Red Army ceased to exist after the end of World War II). In February 1942 Stalin had announced his five "permanently operating factors" which, according to himself and his historians, were responsible for the Soviet victory over fascism. Any analysis of the war or discussion of Soviet military doctrine was forbidden during Stalin's reign since it might contradict what the "military genius" had stated. After his death in 1953, however, this began to change.

In 1955 Marshal Georgi K. Zhukov became the minister of defense and called for a reassessment of World War II, a fresh look at Soviet military doctrine, and an analysis of recent developments in military affairs. This reevaluation became particularly important since in 1955 West Germany created its new army and joined NATO, and the Eastern bloc nations created the Warsaw Pact in response. In 1956, at the Twentieth Party Congress, Nikita S. Khrushchev delivered his secret speech in which he revealed Stalin's mistakes in preparing for and conducting the war and also declared that a new look should be taken at developments in military science. With the development of thermonuclear weapons in both the United States and the Soviet Union and the introduction of ballistic missiles, nuclear weapons suddenly became much easier to deliver to targets and thus a more important weapon. What emerged from the studies that followed Khrushchev's speech was a general consensus that nuclear weapons and their new delivery systems had produced dramatic changes in warfare and would be decisive factors in the future conduct of war.

On 14 January 1960 Khrushchev formally recognized this revolutionary development in Soviet military doctrine. While war was no longer "fatalistically inevitable" – a revision of Soviet military doctrine made by Khrushchev at the Twentieth Party Congress – it would necessarily be nuclear. Khrushchev believed that the Soviet Union's strategic rocket forces, formed in December 1959, would represent the "main means of achieving final war aims, and the main means of deterrence." Since U.S. policy still adhered to the doctrine of massive retaliation, the Soviets believed that a nuclear preemptive strike in the face of an impending attack was the preferable and perhaps only viable way to conduct war. As Soviet defector Colonel Oleg Penkovsky wrote in his report to Western intelligence services, "A future war will begin with a sudden nuclear strike against the enemy. There will be no declaration of war. Quite to the contrary, an effort will be made to avoid a declaration of war." According to the new doctrine, the Soviet Union might suffer massive losses in such a war, but "the socialist camp will win and capitalism will be destroyed forever." The Soviets planned for both a massive initial strike and a prolonged nuclear war, and they therefore equipped their missile launchers with reloads, something which American planners did not do.

The primary aim of the Kremlin thus was to prepare the armed forces and the entire country for such a war. The production and development of nuclear warheads and missiles was increased dramatically in the early 1960s as the Soviet Union had over six hundred intermediate- and medium-range ballistic missile launchers by 1964–1965 and continued to deploy the SS-7 and SS-8. The Soviets also began the development of the SS-9 and SS-11 missiles in 1960 and began their deployment in 1966. The SS-9 was the first Soviet intercontinental ballistic missile (ICBM) capable of damage limitation (counterforce strikes that could destroy hardened American nuclear targets), while the SS-11 was deployed against soft targets such as airfields or urban/industrial targets.

At about this time the Soviet Union also began to develop MIRVed (multiple independently targeted reentry vehicle) ICBMs capable of delivering more than one warhead from a single rocket. Both hard-target capable missiles (SS-18s and SS-19s) and soft-target missiles (SS-16s and SS-17s) were developed. The other two legs of the Soviet strategic triad, the submarine and bomber elements, were also modernized during this period. Soviet strategic defenses were deployed as well in the 1960s. Air defense missiles and interceptors were produced and modernized, the Moscow antiballistic missile (ABM) system was constructed, and, toward the end of the decade, strategic antisubmarine capabilities were enhanced.

While NATO's adoption of the policy of flexible response in 1967 led Soviet military planners to give more attention to the conventional forces which faced Western armies, the expansion of Soviet nuclear forces proceeded apace in the 1970s. In 1970 the Soviet Union had some 2,400 warheads on ready-to-launch ballistic missiles and perhaps another 1,600 to 3,600 on reloads. By the end of 1980, however, the Soviets had deployed 9,000 warheads on ready missiles and perhaps had up to another 11,000 on refires. In the 1980s Soviet missiles became more accurate and, with the deployment of the SS-24 and SS-25, more mobile. The deployment of these forces, and especially of the highly accurate MIRVed SS-18 mod-5, raised questions in the West about whether the Soviets were seeking nuclear parity or nuclear superiority with a viable first strike capability.

The Correlation of Forces

As the Cold War proceeded and the Soviet Union continued to enhance its armed forces, the political and military leadership believed that the "correlation of forces" was moving in favor of the socialist camp. With the establishment of approximate nuclear parity in the early 1970s and the apparent decline in American political and military influence, Soviet foreign and military policy became more focused on projecting its power and influence abroad.

After the inception of the Warsaw Pact in 1953, the Soviet ground forces deployed in Eastern Europe and the Soviet Union outnumbered NATO forces in both men and matériel. When the Sino-Soviet split escalated into hostilities in the early 1960s, military deployments in the Far Eastern Military District were similarly expanded. Thus, while the Soviets dedicated a great deal of attention and resources to nuclear weapons, conventional weapons were far from ignored and actually saw action along the Soviet Union's western, southern, and eastern borders.

When the Soviets' Eastern European allies approached or went beyond the limits of what the Soviets considered acceptable behavior, the Soviet armed forces were always present to enforce the primacy of Soviet strategic concerns. In 1953 riots in East Germany were quelled by Soviet army units stationed there to protect the people from the nearby imperialist forces. In 1956, when Hungarian political and economic reforms veered into "counterrevolution" and the government declared that it sought to remove itself from the Warsaw Pact, Soviet forces, along with other Eastern European armies, marched into Hungary to offer what was termed "fraternal assistance." Twelve years later, when the government in Prague appeared to be following a similar path, Warsaw Pact forces again were used to quell internal dissent within the East bloc.

Hostilities between the Soviet Union and China erupted in the late 1960s over border disputes along the Amur and Ussuri rivers. This conflict, along with the Czechoslovakian invasion in 1968, was used by Defense Minister Andrei Antonovich Grechko to point out the need for a large land army, something which had been questioned by the Soviet leadership since Khrushchev enacted serious cuts in conventional forces in the early 1960s.

During the 1970s the growth in the power of the Soviet armed forces, the apparent decline of American power after Vietnam, and the increasing influence of developing countries and national liberation movements convinced Moscow that it should make better use of its military might to pursue Soviet goals throughout the world. Under Sergei Gorshkov, the Soviet navy underwent a dramatic expansion that allowed it to project significant power for the first time in its history. Military aid to Third World radical elements became the norm in Soviet foreign policy as Moscow supported sympathetic regimes in Ethiopia, Angola, Mozambique, and Nicaragua. The culmination of Soviet "expansionism" came in 1979, when the Soviet Union invaded Afghanistan after its ruler, who had been moving away from his previously close ties with Moscow, was deposed and assassinated.

Decline of Soviet Military Power

The Soviet move into Afghanistan immediately raised fears in the West that Russia was again trying expand into the Middle East, putting at risk Western oil supplies. The Soviet invasion of Afghanistan, along with the modernization of Soviet strategic and conventional forces, resulted in the American military buildup of the 1980s. By the end of President Ronald Reagan's second term, the Soviet military found itself confronted with a newly reinvigorated opponent that was deploying advanced weaponry unmatched by the Soviet military-industrial complex. Because of U.S. support of the *Mujahadeen* – the rebel force fighting the Soviet-backed government in Afghanistan – Soviet forces became mired in a guerrilla war in Afghanistan which they could not seem to win, and casualties soon began to mount. The Soviet economy was also faltering under heavy military spending (approximately 15 percent of the Soviet gross national product) and an incredibly inefficient command-administrative system.

When Mikhail Gorbachev became general secretary in 1985, it was obvious that some major changes in Soviet military policy had to take place. Gorbachev and his advisers, in believing that Soviet security could not be guaranteed by more armaments, sought to use political solutions and reach arms reductions that would introduce a more stable era of mutual security. Beginning in 1985 the Soviet Union's positions on various arms control issues became noticeably more flexible and drew nearer to the West's positions. New energy was injected into the intermediate-range nuclear forces (INF) and strategic arms reduction talks (START) negotiations, and conventional forces in Europe (CFE) talks began in 1987. In December 1987 the United States and the Soviet Union signed the INF Treaty which eliminated the American Pershing II and cruise missiles and Soviet SS-20, SS-4, and SS-5 missiles which had been initially deployed in the 1970s.

In 1987 the Soviet Union and the Warsaw Pact declared that their military doctrine was based on "defensive defense" and "reasonable sufficiency," indicating that Warsaw Pact forces would be altered in strength and type deployed so as to not pose an offensive threat to the West. While Western analysts were justifiably skeptical of this proclamation, later developments showed that this revision of military doctrine had wide-ranging effects on the Soviet armed forces and the Warsaw Pact. In an address to the United Nations in December of 1988, Gorbachev announced massive unilateral cuts in Soviet conventional forces, the withdrawal of six tank divisions from East Germany, and a steep reduction in Soviet military spending. Soviet divisions were also reconfigured to have fewer tanks and, as the Soviets claimed, less offensive firepower.

tanks and, as the Soviets claimed, less offensive firepower.

By November of 1990 NATO and the Warsaw Pact were close to a CFE agreement that would entail drastic reductions in the armaments of the Soviet Union and the Warsaw Pact and establish a wide range of confidence-building measures. With the de facto disintegration of the Warsaw Pact and end of the Cold War, a CFE accord would be the first major element in the establishment of a new security structure in Europe. The Soviet Union and the United States were also on the verge of a START agreement which would significantly reduce the number of strategic nuclear launchers and nuclear warheads held by both sides and limit "heavy" ballistic missiles which were deemed to be particularly destabilizing.

In 1990 the military and the civilian government fought over military policy and the defense budget, leaving the Soviet armed forces in a state of confusion and disarray. The use of the army to quell domestic ethnic unrest and the recognition of widespread brutality toward recruits exacerbated draft problems in the republics. The collapse of the Warsaw Pact and resulting withdrawal of forces from Eastern Europe was also extremely painful for the Soviet military. The Soviet army was humiliated and stung by accusations in Eastern Europe and the Soviet republics that it was an occupation force; and it was demoralized by the inability of the Soviet economy to build new facilities for units withdrawn from abroad and absorb the men released from military service. This, along with declining defense budgets and the debate on whether to transform the army into a professional or territorially based force, left the Soviet armed forces in an especially weak position just as the country seemed to verge on collapse.

References

Robert P. Berman and John C. Baker, *Soviet Strategic Forces: Requirements and Responses* (Washington, D.C.: The Brookings Institution, 1982);

Seweryn Bialer, ed., *Stalin and His Generals: Soviet Military Memoirs of World War II* (New York: Pegasus, 1969);

John Erickson, *The Soviet High Command* (New York: St. Martin's Press, 1962);

John Erickson and E. J. Feuchtwanger, *Soviet Military Power and Performance* (London: Macmillan, 1979);

David Holloway, *The Soviet Union and the Arms Race* (New Haven: Yale University Press, 1983);

William Lee and Richard Staar, *Soviet Military Policy Since World War II* (Stanford, Cal.: Hoover Institution Press, 1986);

Edgar O'Ballance, *The Red Army* (London: Faber & Faber, 1964);

V. Rapoport and Y. Alexeev, *High Treason: Essays on the History of the Red Army, 1918–1938* (Durham, N.C.: Duke University Press, 1985);

H. F. and W. F. Scott, *The Armed Forces of the USSR,* revised edition (Boulder, Colo.: Westview, 1984);

H. F. and W. F. Scott, *The Soviet Art of War* (Boulder, Colo.: Westview, 1982);

H. F. and W. F. Scott, *Soviet Military Doctrine: Continuity, Formulation, and Dissemination* (Boulder, Colo.: Westview, 1988).

– P. M.

SEE ALSO THESE RELATED ENTRIES
Deterrence, 3; Intermediate Range Nuclear Forces Treaty, 3; Joseph Stalin, 2; Leon Trotsky, 2.

Refuseniks

"Refuseniks" were Jews living in the Soviet Union who had applied for but were denied permission to emigrate. Although from 1968 until near the end of the Cold War nearly half a million Jews were allowed to leave the Soviet Union—making the Jewish emigration campaign the most successful dissident movement in Soviet history—a gap existed between the numbers of individuals who sought to leave and those who were granted permission. From the mid 1960s to the dissolution of the Soviet Union, the barriers to Jewish emigration rose and fell with the domestic political climate and the state of U.S.-Soviet relations.

The basic document required by an individual seeking to leave was the *vyzov*, a formal invitation from a relative in Israel. Once this invitation arrived, a person requested "references" from his or her workplace and applied to the *OVIR* (Soviet Emigration Office) for an exit visa. Soviet Jews who applied for visas often faced the loss of their jobs and homes, as well as harassment and arrest for their desire to emigrate. During the 1970s the term *refuseniks* came into common usage to describe the group of persons who were denied official permission to leave the Soviet Union and were persecuted for expressing the desire to do so.

Origins of the Emigration Movement

The birth of the Jewish emigration movement in the Soviet Union may be attributed to disparate causes: rampant anti-Semitism; the growth of other dissident movements in the 1960s; and the Six Day War and the subsequent breaking of Soviet-Israeli diplomatic relations.

There was a long history of anti-Semitism in Czarist Russia. Following the Bolshevik revolution of October 1917 all discriminatory laws were erased, but most of the synagogues were closed down and Jewish education for children was prohibited. At the same time that they were denied the right of religious expression and the opportunity to teach or learn the Hebrew language, Soviet Jews were identified as one of the country's "nationalities" and were "guaranteed" the right to cultural and national expression under Soviet law. Official Soviet policy heightened individuals' awareness of themselves as Jews and simultaneously discrimi-

nated against and denied them the right to practice their religion.

In the aftermath of World War II, with Soviet recognition of the new Israeli state in 1948 and the rise of anti-Semitism in the Soviet Union, many Soviet Jews became highly nationalistic toward Israel. Many began to express the desire to leave for Israel especially, at that time, to help the new state in its war for independence. In 1950 Vitaly Svechinsky, a leader of the Jewish movement in the Soviet Union, was arrested along with two friends, charged with treason, and sentenced to ten years in prison for a plot to cross the southern border into Turkey and escape to Israel.

By the early 1960s small groups of young people, mostly students, were gathering informally in different cities to learn Hebrew, listen to foreign news broadcasts, and celebrate Jewish holidays. Beginning in the mid to late 1960s, increasing numbers of Jews petitioned the Soviet government for permission to immigrate to Israel.

At the same time, other dissident movements were also evolving. Following the 1966 trial of Yuli Daniel and Andrei Sinyavsky, usually cited as the beginning of the democratic movement in the Soviet Union, many Jewish writers and intellectuals became involved and together made up a very high percentage of that movement's most active members. The relationship between the emigration movement and other dissident movements in the Soviet Union was not close, however. Especially in the early years, many Jews thought that common action with the dissidents would hinder their chances for leaving. The Jewish emigration movement centered around the narrow issue of obtaining the right for Jews to leave the Soviet Union for Israel, and many refuseniks thought that connecting this issue to the internal reforms and the broader aims of the burgeoning human-rights movement would only hurt the Jewish cause.

By early 1967 Soviet authorities were granting an increasing number of exit visas. In the first five months of that year there was relatively heavy emigration to Israel, primarily in response to Premier Alexei Nikolaevich Kosygin's Paris Declaration of December 1966 in which he stated to the world that any Jew who wanted to leave the Soviet Union could do so.

Refuseniks demonstrating outside the ministry of external affairs

This practice was abruptly halted by the outbreak of the Six Day War between Israel and Egypt in 1967. In the aftermath of the stunning Israeli victory the Soviets, who were allied with the Arabs, severed diplomatic relations with the state of Israel. The Soviet press severely criticized Israel, with commentary and cartoons comparing the Jewish state with Nazi Germany and Moshe Dayan, the Israeli defense minister, with Adolf Hitler. Following the war the Soviet Government instituted an official policy of anti-Zionism that labeled support for the Jewish national state as a form of racism. On 22 September 1970 the government formalized the preexisting practice of compelling anyone over sixteen years of age who received an exit visa to Israel to pay five hundred rubles for compulsory renunciation of his or her Soviet citizenship.

The Leningrad Trials

No other single event had as dramatic an impact on the Jewish emigration movement as the Six Day War and its aftermath. It aroused feelings of national pride and helped transform what had previously been an emerging sense of national identification into a full-fledged movement to emigrate to Israel. Increasing numbers of Jews began to apply for visas, and the refuseniks appeared for the first time as a recognized group in the major cities. In February 1969 the dissident publication, *Chronicle of Current Events,* began reporting the persecution of a Jew who had requested a visa to Israel. By 1970 the emigration movement had started publishing its own journal, *Iskhod* (Exodus), which contained records of house searches, arrests, and trials, as well as collective appeals and petitions on behalf of Jews seeking to leave the Soviet Union. At the same time, however, the number of visas being granted was diminishing. Between late 1968 and 1970 only 4,235 Jews were allowed to leave.

In 1970 a series of events was set into motion which was to mobilize the emigration movement and lead to an enormous increase in the number of Jews exiting the Soviet Union. That year, out of

253

desperation, a small group of Jewish activists based primarily in Riga, the capital of Latvia, planned to hijack a small plane to Sweden. Their plan was thwarted when the KGB was informed of the plot, and on 15 June 1970 twelve people were arrested at Leningrad's Smolny airport. A series of simultaneous raids in Riga, Leningrad, Moscow, Kiev, Odessa, and Kharkov resulted in many arrests and the confiscation of material on Israeli and Jewish history.

Although hijacking itself was not a crime under Soviet law, the defendants were charged with treason, and on Christmas Eve 1970 Edward Kuznetsov and Mark Dymshits were sentenced to death for their role in the planned hijacking. The international outcry was immediate; twenty-four governments, the Vatican, and even some Western Communist parties protested. Although an appeal could not legally be heard until 5 January 1971, in a move unprecedented in Soviet legal practice the Supreme Court convened six days after the verdict to hear an appeal. In response to world opinion the sentences were commuted to fifteen years in labor camps. What had begun as an attempt by the Soviet government to crush the Jewish emigration movement ended by heightening world opinion and mobilizing the movement within the Soviet Union.

A Decade of Emigration

In March 1971 there began a dramatic increase in Soviet emigration that was to last until 1981. During those ten years over 250,000 Soviet Jews were allowed to leave, and the world became increasingly aware of the plight of Jews and especially refuseniks in the Soviet Union. More than 300,000 others requested invitations to Israel but were denied permission by the Soviet authorities. Throughout the decade the level of emigration and the restrictions placed on those seeking to emigrate frequently were dependent upon the state of relations between the United States and the Soviet Union.

In the aftermath of the Leningrad trials and with the new détente in U.S.-Soviet relations, emigration reached a peak in 1972, when 31,681 Jews emigrated, and 1973, when 34,733 left. At the same time, however, the number of refuseniks also grew as many Jews, especially those engaged in scientific work who might possess "state secrets," were refused permission to emigrate. These individuals frequently were also denied employment in their field. In August 1972 the government formally required specialists leaving for Israel to pay a large

education tax varying according to the individual's educational level. The tax provided a means of obtaining foreign currency for the state but was a serious burden on individuals seeking to leave. For an engineer, the tax – which had to be paid before leaving – could equal as much as five to seven years' salary.

The period from 1974 to 1977 witnessed a downturn in Jewish emigration as U.S.-Soviet relations cooled in the aftermath of the October 1973 Arab-Israeli War. Less than 21,000 Jews were allowed to emigrate in 1974, 13,221 in 1975, and 16,736 in 1977. Still these figures were substantially higher than any year in the previous decade. The U.S. Congress responded in 1974–1975 to the declining number of Jewish émigrés and the rising awareness of the plight of the refuseniks with the Jackson-Vanik amendment, which tied lower tariff rates and increased trade through most-favored-nation status for the Soviets to freer Jewish emigration, and the Stevenson amendment, which sharply restricted U.S. loans to the Soviet Union.

Beginning in 1974 Soviet Jewish émigrés, motivated more by harsh conditions in the Soviet Union than by Zionism and inspired by the improving U.S.-Soviet relationship in the late 1970s, began listing the United States as their destination. By 1978 these individuals, who were called *noshrim* in Israel, made up more than half of the Soviet Jewish émigrés.

The Jimmy Carter administration oversaw an upswing in relations between the superpowers, which was also reflected in Soviet emigration policies. In 1978 Jewish emigration jumped to 28,864 and in 1979 to a decade high of 51,320. During the following year, 21,471 Jews left the Soviet Union.

At the same time, however, persecution of refuseniks continued. One of the more internationally renowned refuseniks, Anatoly Shcharansky, was arrested in 1977 and sentenced the next year to thirteen years in prison. Shcharansky had been a refusenik since 1973 and had been seeking permission since 1974 to join his wife, Avital, in Israel. He had been active in an unofficial group established in Moscow to monitor Soviet observance of the human-rights provisions of the 1975 Helsinki accords.

The Gates Close

In the early 1980s the fate of Soviet refuseniks was once again closely intertwined with the state of superpower relations. The renewal of the Cold War in the aftermath of the 1979 Soviet invasion of Afghanistan and the 1980 U.S. presidential elections won by Ronald Reagan foreshadowed a dip in Soviet Jewish emigration. In 1981, 9,447 Jews were allowed to leave, but less than 2,700 were granted permission in 1982. By 1984 Jewish emigration dropped to its lowest point in the past twenty-five years with only 896 persons allowed to leave during the entire year.

Significant new barriers to emigration were also added in the 1980s. Working hours of many visa offices were shortened, and invitations sent from Israel by registered mail frequently disappeared in the Soviet postal system. Throughout the previous decade the requirement that an individual obtain a formal invitation from a relative in Israel had been liberally interpreted. In early 1980 a restriction was introduced that allowed only parents or children already residing in Israel to issue invitations. This new restriction created – in addition to the refuseniks – a whole new group of Soviet Jews who were refused even the opportunity to emigrate. Finally, in 1982 the Soviet authorities decreed that an application ceased to be valid after six months. This meant that, if a request was denied, a new application required a new *vyzov* from Israel.

Glasnost and Jewish Emigration

Another wave of Jewish emigration from the Soviet Union began in March 1987. Soviet leader Mikhail Gorbachev's economic policy of perestroika (restructuring) and his political and cultural policy of glasnost (openness) were accompanied by an improvement in Soviet-Israeli relations, the release of many of the most well-known refuseniks, and the easing of restrictions on teaching Hebrew and practicing Judaism.

Over 71,000 Jews were allowed to leave the Soviet Union in 1989, and 10,500 left in the month of April 1990 alone. Beginning in December 1989 an increasing number of these émigrés once again headed to Israel. Although less than 18 percent of the Jews leaving the Soviet Union with Israeli visas from 1987 to 1989 actually went to Israel, over 97 percent did so in early 1990. This increase was largely a result of a change in U.S. immigration policies which made it more difficult for Soviet Jews to enter the United States.

References

Mark Abzel, *Refusenik,* edited by Grace Pierce Forbes (Boston: Houghton Mifflin, 1981);

Albert Axelrad, *Refusenik: Voices of Struggle and Hope* (Bristol, Ind.: Wyndham Hall, 1987);

Robert O. Freedman, ed., *Soviet Jewry in the Decisive Decade* (Durham, N.C.: Duke University Press, 1984);

Martin Gilbert, *The Jews of Hope* (London: Macmillan, 1984);

Joshua Rubenstein, *Soviet Dissidents: Their Struggle for Human Rights* (Boston: Beacon Press, 1985);

Thomas E. Sawyer, *The Jewish Minority in the Soviet Union* (Boulder, Colo.: Westview, 1979);

Leonard Schroeter, *The Last Exodus* (Seattle: University of Washington Press, 1979);

Harry G. Shaffer, *The Soviet Treatment of Jews* (New York: Praeger, 1974);

Marshall S. Shatz, *Soviet Dissent in Historical Perspective* (Cambridge: Cambridge University Press, 1980).

– S. M. P.

SEE ALSO THESE RELATED ENTRIES
Jimmy Carter, 1; Mikhail Gorbachev, 2; Jackson-Vanik Amendment, 3.

Reykjavík Summit

White House Photo

Soviet leader Mikhail Gorbachev and President Ronald Reagan at the Reykjavík Summit, 11 October 1986

The Reykjavík summit between President Ronald Reagan and Soviet president and general secretary Mikhail Gorbachev took place in Reykjavík, Iceland, on the weekend of 11 October 1986. The summit saw several important breakthroughs in arms control, although it failed to produce a comprehensive agreement on strategic-arms reductions.

Gorbachev proposed the meeting in a 19 September letter to President Reagan, hand-delivered by Soviet foreign minister Eduard Amvrosiyevich Shevardnadze. He proposed the Reykjavík meeting to lay the groundwork for a summit to be held in Washington, D.C., the following year and to spark the stalled Geneva arms-control talks. In 1986 Geneva was the site of three sets of arms-control negotiations: the Intermediate-Range Nuclear Forces (INF) talks, the Strategic Arms Reduction Talks (START), and the Space and Defense talks. Gorbachev's letter led Reagan to believe that a Reykjavík summit would be a success because the Soviet leader was willing to drop his insistence on linking an INF agreement to restrictions on the ballistic-missile-defense program, known as the Strategic Defense Initiative (SDI, or "Star Wars"). The Soviets had long sought to limit testing and deployment of ballistic-missile defenses, which they and

many American experts considered destabilizing. They believed that ballistic-missile defenses would undermine the existing condition of deterrence based on vulnerability, in which neither superpower dares harm the other's vital interests for fear of provoking nuclear retaliation.

Surprise Proposals

Gorbachev dominated the talks at Reykjavík from the outset. In the opening round he unveiled a surprise proposal that contained an unprecedented Soviet call for a 50 percent reduction in strategic nuclear forces and promised additional cuts in the most powerful Soviet missiles. His dramatic proposal hinged on one condition, that the United States continue to comply for ten years with the 1972 Antiballistic Missile Treaty (ABM) that outlawed the testing in space and deployment of antimissile defenses. Gorbachev had lured Reagan to Reykjavík with the hope of an INF treaty, but his real aim was a comprehensive strategic-arms-reduction agreement that would include a moratorium on the deployment of SDI.

The talks, scheduled for two days, proceeded at an exhausting pace. On 12 October both sides agreed to extend the negotiations and added one final meeting, during which Gorbachev unveiled yet another surprise proposal, calling for the elimination of all nuclear weapons within ten years. In the end the talks failed to produce an agreement for comprehensive reductions in strategic or intermediate nuclear forces. President Reagan flatly refused to place restrictions on SDI, which he believed offered both countries the best hope for survival in a nuclear world.

Despite the ultimate failure of Gorbachev's plan, its sweeping character enabled the negotiations to progress on several arms-control issues. Working groups led by the Reagan administration's chief arms negotiator, Paul H. Nitze, and Soviet marshal Sergei Akhromeyev were able to develop the negotiating framework for sizable and stabilizing cuts in strategic forces, calling for both sides to reduce their forces to sixty thousand nuclear warheads and sixteen hundred launchers (missiles). The groups also made headway on the INF question, agreeing to eliminate all land-based intermediate-range nuclear forces. In addition, they worked out a provisional solution to the strategic-defense problem by proposing that neither side withdraw from the ABM treaty or deploy strategic defenses within a given time period.

References

Paul H. Nitze, *From Hiroshima to Glasnost* (New York: Weidenfeld & Nicolson, 1989);

Strobe Talbott, *The Master of the Game* (New York: Knopf, 1988).

– B. D. K.

SEE ALSO THESE RELATED ENTRIES
Mikhail Gorbachev, 2; Intermediate Nuclear Forces Treaty, 3; Paul H. Nitze, 1; Richard Perle, 1; Ronald Reagan, 1; Strategic Defense Initiative, 3.

Sputnik

Sputnik, built by the Soviet Union, was the first successful man-made satellite ever sent into space. It was launched on 4 October 1957 as part of a cooperative effort of world scientists to learn more about the earth, sun, and solar-terrestrial relationships. This effort, of which the United States was a member, was under the auspices of a program called the International Geophysical Year (IGY), and Sputnik I was the first satellite in the program. Its scientific mission for IGY was to measure and send back information from space about temperature, cosmic rays, and meteoroids.

Sputnik, which means "fellow traveler" in Russian, weighed only 184 pounds, and thus was miniscule compared to modern satellites which sometimes weigh 12 tons. It had a three-stage rocket, or modified ballistic missile, which propelled it into space. The twenty-three-inch spherical satellite was sealed behind a protective cone on top of the last stage and spun off from the burned-out booster rocket once it was in orbit.

The rocket technology behind Sputnik originated largely from the work of the Soviet scientist Konstantin Tsiolkovsky (1857–1935), who worked on mathematical relationships between rocket mass and fuel mass. He figured out that rocket velocity depends on the relative weight of the rocket. His 1903 work, entitled *Investigation of Cosmic Space by Reactive Machines,* talked of earth satellites and interplanetary rockets, and was considered the world's first valid description of ways in which human beings could fly beyond earth's atmosphere.

Sputnik carried two radios, and while it circled the earth it emitted a distinctive beep signal which could be heard on shortwave radio receivers all over the world. The satellite could also be seen by people as it sped through the heavens. At its perigee it was 142 miles away; at its apogee, 588 miles. Thus it created a sensation, as people from different nations could see it or tune into its signal as it orbited the planet once every hour and a half at a speed of 18,000 miles per hour.

The *New York Times* wrote of Sputnik's flight: "It is clear that 4 October 1957 will go down in the annals of history as the day of one of the greatest achievements of man." The satellite's successful orbit startled many in the West who believed that the Soviet Union was technologically backward.

Beginnings of the Space Race

Not to be outdone by the Soviet Union, the United States sent its own unmanned satellite, Explorer I, into space on 31 January 1958. Among other findings, it confirmed the existence of a zone of dangerous radiation surrounding the earth. A succession of other Soviet and American satellites followed during the late 1950s and early 1960s. Some of these carried animal passengers. Sputnik II, for example, launched on 3 November 1957, carried a black and white dog called Laika ("Barker"). She died during the first week in orbit. The Soviet Union went on to send up mice, rats, and rabbits successfully into space, and the United States orbited a chimpanzee named Ham in 1961.

These pioneering artificial satellites provided the first accurate scientific data about space. They were also test vehicles for designing spacecraft in which people could be sent into orbit.

Although Sputnik did not have an avowedly military purpose, it nonetheless exacerbated Cold War tensions, for the technology it employed could be used for war. Sputnik showed that the Soviet Union could send a rocket at a very high altitude to any part of the earth; it thus paved the way for intercontinental ballistic missiles (ICBMs). In the wake of Sputnik's successful flight, American military leaders, such as General Curtis LeMay of the air force, called for enhanced U.S. efforts in strategic air power. There were also public discussions about the United States falling behind the Russians in science and the need for crash scientific programs in schools.

Soviet technicians examining a model of Sputnik

References

Erik Bergaust, ed., *Illustrated Space Encyclopedia* (New York: Putnam, 1965);

John Ege, *Sputnik* (Oslo: Gyldendal, 1983);

Firmin J. Kreiger, *The Space Programs of the Soviet Union* (Santa Monica, Cal.: RAND, 1967);

E. I. Riabchikov, *Russians In Space* (Garden City, N.Y.: Doubleday, 1971).

– M. G.

SEE ALSO THESE RELATED ENTRIES
Dwight D. Eisenhower, 1; Intercontinental Ballistic Missile, 3; Curtis LeMay, 1.

Strategic Air Command

At the end of World War II, the United States decided to make strategic air power a vital element of its military forces. The bombing of Nazi Germany and Imperial Japan was believed to have played an important role in the Allied victory, and the advent of the air-deliverable atomic bomb at Hiroshima and Nagasaki made the bomber "the greatest offensive weapon of all times." For these reasons the United States made a special effort to maintain its long-range bomber forces in the midst of demobilization, and the Strategic Air Command (SAC) was created on 21 March 1946. According to its mission statement, SAC must be able to conduct long-range operations in any part of the world at any time, an ability that was tested early in the Cold War.

Many air-power advocates have maintained that the United States should rely on its air forces to enforce the postwar *Pax Americana* and close the gap between American commitments and the country's military capabilities. When tensions with the Soviet Union escalated after World War II, SAC rapidly expanded its forces under the leadership of General Curtis LeMay. During the Berlin blockade of 1948, two B-29 groups were sent to England and two other groups were sent to Germany while other SAC forces were placed on alert. SAC forces also participated in the Korean War, dropping some 167,000 tons of conventional bombs from 1950 to 1953. This bombardment, along with naval firepower, proved to be of great assistance in helping UN forces repel numerically superior North Korean and Chinese forces.

With the explosion of the first Soviet hydrogen bomb in 1953 and John Foster Dulles's announcement of the new policy of massive retaliation in 1954, SAC nuclear forces acquired added importance and funding. As the United States and Soviet Union entered the nuclear arms race, it became clear that the number of nuclear warheads deployed and their means of delivery would be key determinants in nuclear power and deterrence. In the mid 1950s SAC began to deploy the B-52 bomber and KC-135 tanker, and the United States enjoyed a clear advantage over the Soviet Union in numbers of nuclear warheads and delivery vehicles. The launch of Sputnik in 1957 and the test of the first Soviet ICBM which followed led to the

much heralded "missile gap" of the late 1950s. In 1959 the United States replied by deploying its first ICBM, the Atlas D, with a SAC unit, and since that time SAC has remained in charge of both strategic bombers and ICBMs. Under SAC, American missile forces were expanded dramatically in the 1960s as Titan and Minuteman ICBMs became operational. Beginning in 1967 these forces were modernized and the United States deployed the Minuteman III, the first ICBM to be a multiple independently targeted reentry vehicle (MIRV).

In 1962 SAC long-range reconnaissance aircraft played an integral role in the Cuban Missile Crisis. A SAC U-2 plane photographed the deployment of Soviet intermediate-range ballistic missiles on Cuba, and soon President John F. Kennedy was determined to demonstrate U.S. resolve and have the Soviets remove the missiles. He thus placed SAC on full-alert status, and B-52s were ordered to maintain a constant airborne alert to protect against Soviet attack and send a strong signal to Moscow. Beginning in 1965 conventionally armed SAC B-52s began bombing targets in Vietnam. The "Rolling Thunder" bombing campaign conducted under the Johnson administration and the "Linebacker" campaigns ordered by President Nixon were used for both military and political purposes. Militarily, the bombing campaigns were used to help stop North Vietnamese forces from moving south, and, politically, they were employed to bring the North to the negotiating table and accept American terms for peace. Linebacker II, otherwise known as the "Christmas bombings," was successful in helping to force the negotiations that secured U.S. withdrawal from the war.

During the 1970s and 1980s, SAC continued to modernize its forces, albeit at a somewhat slower pace when compared to the first decades of the Cold War. The Short Range Attack Missile (SRAM), which was deployed on strategic bombers, was introduced in the early 1970s. In the 1980s the air force deployed the Air Launched Cruise Missile (ALCM), which allowed bombers to launch their weapons in a "stand-off mode" – the ability to fire weapons at targets from distant launch areas. SAC also began to deploy the first units of the B-1B bomber and KC-10 tanker aircraft, along with the highly MIRVed and very accurate Peacekeeper missile.

Reference

Robert F. Futrell, *Ideas, Concepts, Doctrine: A History of Basic Thinking in the United States Air Force, 1907–1964* (Maxwell Air Force Base, Ala.: Air University, 1971).

– P. M.

Strategic Arms Limitation Talks

On 26 May 1972 President Richard M. Nixon signed the Anti-Ballistic Missile (ABM) Treaty and the Interim Offensive Forces Agreement. The signing of these agreements marked the culmination of the Strategic Arms Limitations Talks (SALT) that had begun three years earlier.

Throughout the 1960s the United States sought to persuade the Soviet Union to negotiate an agreement to limit both offensive and defensive strategic forces. The U.S. interest in arms control stemmed largely from American concern over the development of the Soviet ABM system. The Soviets had been working on an ABM system throughout the decade and began deploying one, called Galosh, around Moscow in late 1964. In arguing that ballistic-missile defenses were destabilizing, experts reasoned that if the Soviet Union believed that an ABM system would protect it against an American retaliatory strike, it might be tempted to launch a nuclear first strike to weaken American nuclear forces. An ABM treaty also offered both nations an opportunity to avoid a costly arms race. Without a treaty both nations would be forced to adopt costly countermeasures – such as deploying missile defenses or increasing intercontinental ballistic missile (ICBM) deployments – to render ineffective the ballistic-missile defenses of the other side.

The Soviets initially resisted American proposals to negotiate limits on the deployment of offensive and defensive strategic systems. Their hesitancy stemmed largely from the inferiority of their strategic nuclear arsenal. In 1964, when President Lyndon B. Johnson initially offered to freeze systems, the United States had deployed 834 ICBMs, 416 submarine-launched ballistic missiles (SLBMs),

and 630 intercontinental bombers. The Soviet Union had deployed only 200 ICBMs, 120 SLBMs, and 190 bombers at that time. In 1969, when the SALT talks began, the Soviet Union had achieved rough parity in ICBMs; the United States had deployed 1,054, compared to 1,050 Soviet missiles.

In addition to American nuclear superiority, the Soviets were concerned with the potential proliferation of nuclear weapons, especially in Germany and Japan. Only after the completion of the July 1968 Nuclear Nonproliferation Treaty (NPT), designed to halt the spread of nuclear weapons, did the Soviet Union officially announce its intention to begin negotiations on strategic systems. Finally, the development of satellite reconnaissance offered both superpowers an acceptable method of verifying arms-control agreements.

SALT Negotiations

The SALT talks were scheduled to start on 30 September 1968, but the 20 August Soviet invasion of Czechoslovakia caused the United States to delay the negotiations in protest. The talks finally began in Helsinki, Finland, on 17 November 1969. The U.S. negotiating team was led by Gerard C. Smith, director of the Arms Control and Disarmament Agency (ACDA). The Soviets were led by Deputy Foreign Minister Vladimir Semenov.

The SALT talks resulted in four agreements: the Accident Measures Agreement, the Revised "Hot Line" Agreement, the ABM Treaty, and the Interim Offensive Forces Agreement. The first two accords, each an executive agreement, became effective the day they were signed, 30 September 1971, and were intended to increase the superpowers' confidence in each other. The ABM treaty and the Interim Offensive Forces Agreement, which constituted the core of the SALT process, were signed in Moscow on 26 May 1972, but did not enter into force until ratified by the Senate on 3 August.

The ABM treaty defines an ABM defense as "a system to counter strategic ballistic missiles or their elements in flight trajectory." The treaty permitted each nation to deploy a ballistic-missile defense of no more than one hundred ABM launchers and interceptor missiles at two sites. The treaty was later amended to limit deployment to one site – the Soviets choosing to deploy their system around Moscow, and the United States choosing not to deploy. The treaty prohibited the testing or building of mobile land-based, space-based, air-based, or sea-based missile defenses. It also restricted the construction of radars to prevent the rapid deployment of an ABM system. There was no limitation on the duration of the treaty, but either party could withdraw at will.

Another key part of the SALT accords, the Interim Offensive Forces Agreement, required both nations to freeze the deployment of fixed ICBM launchers as of 1 July 1972. The freeze focused on launchers, or silos, because the satellite techniques used to verify the agreement were incapable of counting missiles. This freeze permitted the United States to maintain 1,054 launchers and the Soviet Union, 1,618 launchers. In addition, the agreement prohibited further deployment of heavy ICBMs whose superior throw weight – or nuclear tonnage – many experts found destabilizing. The United States was eager to limit the Soviets to the 313 heavy missiles they had already deployed.

The agreement allowed the United States to deploy 710 SLBMs on 44 modern ballistic-missile submarines, while permitting the Soviet Union 950 missiles on 62 submarines. As neither had built up to its limit, the agreement permitted both to do so provided that they eliminate an ICBM launcher for every submarine launcher deployed. The agreement did not address intercontinental bombers, of which, in 1972, the United States had 455 and the Soviet Union 140. Finally, the Interim Offensive Forces Agreement placed no qualitative restrictions on either nation's nuclear arsenal, allowing both to improve missile accuracy and continue to MIRV (multiple warhead missiles) their arsenals, that is, increase the number of warheads each missile could deliver. The agreement was to last five

years, during which time both sides agreed to negotiate a more permanent set of limitations.

Disputes vexed the negotiations over the Interim Offensive Agreement. Initially, the Soviets and the Americans were unable to define the word *strategic*. The Soviet Union argued that a strategic weapon was one capable of reaching the other superpower's homeland, a definition that enabled it to include American short-range nuclear systems based in Europe. The United States countered that these weapons were designed for the defense of Europe and that including them and their Soviet countersystems would complicate the talks immeasurably. Instead, the Americans wanted to use missile range to define which systems were strategic. The Soviets eventually agreed to postpone discussion of short-range systems to the follow-on talks to SALT, sensing that this issue would pose an insurmountable obstacle to an ABM treaty.

The next major dispute concerned numerical limits on missiles. The Americans sought to reduce heavy missiles; the Soviets, however, rejected the American position, arguing that throw-weight restrictions would have a disproportionate effect on their arsenal. Unable to resolve this difference, both sides agreed to freeze the number of ICBMs and heavy ICBMs. The source of this dispute lay largely in the differing ways the two countries configured their arsenals. The United States placed a greater emphasis on maintaining a "triad" – a balanced force composed of bombers, submarines, and land-based missiles. The Soviets, on the other hand, relied heavily on land-based systems and as a result resisted such stringent restrictions on such systems.

While the ABM Treaty was ratified by the Senate by a vote of 88 to 2, the Interim Offensive Forces Agreement sparked contentious debate. Democratic senator Henry M. Jackson of Washington led a group of conservative legislators argued that the agreement was destabilizing because it permitted the Soviet Union a decisive numerical advantage in heavy missiles. The agreement eventually passed by a wide margin – 88 to 2 in the Senate, 307 to 4 in the House of Representatives – but only after Jackson won approval for an amendment prohibiting future administrations from negotiating limits that permitted the Soviets a numerical advantage in warheads, launchers, or missiles.

SALT II

With SALT I ratified, the Strategic Arms Limitation Talks resumed in November 1972 to replace the five-year Interim Offensive Forces Agreement with a permanent treaty. Because the Salt I negotiations set some of the more complex issues aside for later talks, the SALT II negotiations encountered added difficulties.

Apart from the inherent technical complexities, American political developments also posed serious problems. The Watergate scandal undermined the authority of the Nixon administration. Henry Kissinger, the administration's SALT architect, was reluctant to press for accords with the Soviets, fearing that critics of the administration would characterize any agreement as an attempt by President Nixon to rescue his political position. The administration was further hurt by bureaucratic infighting. Conservatives in the Department of Defense, adopting Jackson's position, opposed any new agreement that was not premised on numerical equality of forces. The Soviets, for their part, did not seem eager to deal with Nixon. With negotiations lagging, both sides began testing new weapons systems in 1973. The Soviets began testing MIRVs, while Kissinger encouraged the air force to develop long-range cruise missiles to enhance the American bargaining position.

Following Nixon's resignation in August 1974, the talks gained momentum. In November, President Gerald R. Ford met with Soviet general secretary Leonid Brezhnev in Vladivostok, where the two leaders were able to agree on a framework for the eventual SALT II agreement. Disputes over two weapon systems, the Soviet Backfire bomber and the U.S. cruise missile, developed while the SALT negotiations were stalled and became contentious issues. When President Ford began his election campaign in 1976, the negotiations ground to a halt.

In March 1977 new president Jimmy Carter unilaterally abandoned the Vladivostok understanding and surprised the Soviets by proposing substantially lower limits in some areas. The Carter proposal became a diplomatic fiasco, promoting a public rebuke by Soviet foreign minister Andrei Gromyko. Carter eventually returned to the Vladivostok framework, and the SALT II agreement was signed by Carter and Brezhnev on 18 June 1979.

Carter and Brezhnev signed four documents, the most important being the treaty stipulating numerical limits and sublimits on launchers, qualitative weapon constraints, and measures to improve methods of verification. The agreement set an overall ceiling of 2,400 on strategic missile launchers – ICBMs, SLBMs, and bombers – which would be reduced to 2,250 by 1 January 1981. The treaty also established a series of sublimits on strategic

launchers including a subceiling of 1,320 on all MIRVed systems. A further sublimit of 1,200 was applied to MIRVed ICBMs and SLBMs, and a third subceiling of 820 was placed MIRVed ICBMs.

In addition to these quantitative limits, the SALT II accords placed qualitative restrictions on missile systems. Each nation was permitted to deploy one new type of ICBM and one new SLBM, but neither could be a heavy missile. Another provision froze the number of warheads on current launchers to the maximum number already tested for that launcher. This meant that the heavy Soviet SS-18, which could deliver as many as thirty warheads, would carry no more than ten, while the SS-19 would carry no more than six. MIRVs had been set aside during SALT I partly because of the difficulty in verifying adherence to limits. To solve this problem, both nations agreed to count the maximum number of warheads a missile could carry instead of the actual number that it carried at any given time.

Carter sent the treaty to the Senate for ratification on 22 June 1979, but his administration misjudged congressional reaction. Many conservatives criticized both the treaty and President Carter's arms-control policy. In addition, a massive direct-mail campaign conducted by several conservative political action committees attacked the SALT II accords in the hope of making them a major issue in the upcoming 1980 presidential election. Then, in August 1979, word of a Soviet combat brigade in Cuba was leaked to the press, appearing to confirm the aggressive character of Soviet foreign policy about which the conservatives were warning. Fearing the political consequences of ratifying the treaty, Democratic senator Frank Church of Idaho – chairman of the Senate Foreign Relations Committee – announced that the Senate would not consider the treaty until the Soviets removed the brigade from Cuba. The SALT II treaty finally died in December 1979 when the Soviet Union invaded Afghanistan. Recognizing that the Senate would not ratify it, Carter decided to table the treaty in the Senate. Although the treaty was never ratified by the Senate, both nations have largely adhered to its provisions.

References

Coit Blacker and Gloria Duffy, eds., *International Arms Control* (Stanford, Cal.: Stanford University Press, 1985);

John Newhouse, *Cold Dawn: The Story of SALT* (New York: Holt, Reinhart, and Winston, 1973);

Gerard Smith, *Double Talk: The Story of The First Strategic Arms Limitations Talks* (Garden City, N.Y.: Doubleday, 1980);

Strobe Talbott, *End Game* (New York: Harper & Row, 1980).

– B. D. K.

SEE ALSO THESE RELATED ENTRIES

Jimmy Carter, 1; Committee on the Present Danger, 3; Henry M. Jackson, 1; Henry Kissinger, 1; Richard Perle, 1.

Strategic Defense Initiative

In a televised address on 23 March 1983, President Ronald Reagan urged the American scientific community to develop the means to create a ballistic missile defense to render nuclear weapons "impotent and obsolete." The Strategic Defense Initiative (SDI) was born. The speech signified a shift in the American strategic orientation and a break with policies followed by Democratic and Republican administrations in the past. The underlying theme of the speech was the assertion that the policies of nuclear deterrence that had governed the strategic relationship between the United States and the Soviet Union had outlived their usefulness – and that the existing lines of Cold War defense, which assured nuclear destruction in retaliation to a nuclear attack, were no longer acceptable. In the eyes of Soviet policymakers SDI presented a destabilizing element in the Cold War balance.

History of Nuclear Defense

The debate over the feasibility of a defense against nuclear attack was not new. During the first fifteen years of the nuclear age, when nuclear gravity bombs were carried aboard bombers, defense against nuclear attack was almost synonymous with air defense. There was a difference, however: the destructiveness of nuclear weapons required an almost leak-proof defense, because even a small number of bombs would inflict serious damage on the society subject to attack.

The development of the intercontinental ballistic missile (ICBM) in the late 1950s and early 1960s complicated matters for defense strategists. Although scientists and engineers attempted to meet

Associated Press

Dr. Edward Teller and President Ronald Reagan at a 1988 conference on the Strategic Defense Initiative

this new offensive challenge and several antimissile systems were designed and deployed, it soon became apparent that, short of major scientific and engineering breakthroughs, the offense had come to dominate the strategic relationship.

The 1972 Antiballistic Missile (ABM) Treaty, proscribing the testing and deployment of ballistic missile defenses, reflected and codified this recognition of offensive supremacy. The absence of reliable defenses against incoming missiles was not perceived as something wholly negative. The ascendancy of the offense was accompanied by the development of theories extolling the virtues of utter vulnerability to nuclear attack. The argument was advanced that the best insurance against nuclear adventurism and the temptation to use nuclear weapons in a crisis was the vulnerability of the attacking country to retaliation. Furthermore, since antimissile defenses would, in any case, do little against a massive attack, defense deployments would have the pernicious effect of lulling leaders into complacency in the mistaken belief that their societies were now defended by a shield. This kind of trust placed in defensive deployments, so the argument went, could lead to a cavalier attitude taken by leaders in examining their offensive nuclear options.

The belief in the impracticality and folly of defensive efforts in the nuclear age was central to the deterrence strategies of mutual assured destruction (MAD) – promises of retaliatory nuclear strikes – that came to dominate American military and political thinking since the early 1960s. There were attempts in the late 1960s and early 1970s to develop defensive systems, notably Sentinel and Safeguard, comprised of high- and low-altitude intercepting missiles. These defensive efforts, however, went against the grain of the new strategic culture that welcomed the dominance of the offense and posited mutual vulnerability as mankind's last, best hope in the face of the nuclear menace.

Shift in U.S. Defense Policy

The radical shift in U.S. nuclear-deterrence policy began at a December 1982 meeting between Reagan and his Joint Chiefs of Staff. Reagan queried the Joint Chiefs on the possibility of deemphasizing offensive capability as a nuclear deterrent and, instead, placing a greater reliance on defense. In another meeting held with the Joint Chiefs of Staff on 11 February 1983, the chief of naval operations, Admiral James D. Watkins, argued for a forward strategic defense. Two weeks prior to the meeting, Watkins had been in contact with American physicist Edward Teller, who had been a key participant in the Manhattan Project and an influential proponent of nuclear-deterrence policies. Since the early days of the Reagan administration, Teller had been pressing the White House to explore the possibilities of a missile-defense system that relied on X-ray laser technology. Watkins's arguments, which were based on Teller's vision of a defense system, captured Reagan's imagination.

During the 23 March 1983 televised address Reagan conceded to the American public that a shield composed of either land- or space-based weapons defending against a nuclear attack was a dream, but he nevertheless characterized SDI as the centerpiece of his administration's defense policy. Dubbed "Star Wars" by the American media, the Reagan proposal served as a challenge to the scientific-military community and captured the public's attention as had no other presidential declaration of peacetime defense policy.

The U.S. military establishment, however, placed little credence in Star Wars, claiming that such a defense system would do little to thwart a massive nuclear attack. The proposal was also met with skepticism by the U.S. Office of Technological Assessment (OTA) and the Federation of American Scientists (FAS), both organizations questioning the plausibility of developing the kind of weapons Reagan envisioned – and further doubting the reliability of SDI in the event of nuclear attack. SDI was also hampered by the Antiballistic Missile (ABM) Treaty signed by the United States and the Soviet Union in 1972. The Soviets objected to SDI on the grounds that it would violate the treaty and severely upset the strategic balance between the two superpowers. In reviewing the ABM Treaty, however, Pentagon lawyers determined that a Star Wars defense system would fall under the classification of "exotic" weapons – an additional classification that the United States had attempted to ban during ABM Treaty negotiations, but the ban had been met by Soviet objections. This gave rise to the Reagan administration's position that SDI development was not limited by the ABM Treaty.

Beginning in 1983 Congress began appropriating billions of dollars for SDI development. Although many experts in the Reagan administration and in the scientific community agreed that SDI was at least a decade away from deployment, the concept of Star Wars helped serve notice to the Soviet Union during the mid and late 1980s that the existing balance of power was about to experience a significant shift. SDI became an important chip in further arms negotiations with the Soviets and was a major irritant to Soviet negotiators when the ABM Treaty was addressed at the Reykjavík summit, despite public understanding that the viability of SDI was suspect.

References
William J. Broad, *Star Warriors* (New York: Simon & Schuster, 1985);

William J. Broad, *Teller's War: The Top-Secret Story behind the Star Wars Deception* (New York: Simon & Schuster, 1992);

Harold Brown, ed., *Strategic Defense Initiative: Shield or Snare?* (Boulder, Colo.: Westview, 1987);

John Prados, *Keepers of the Keys: A History of the National Security Council from Truman to Bush* (New York: Morrow, 1991).

– B. F. and D. L.

SEE ALSO THESE RELATED ENTRIES
Deterrence, 3; Nuclear Proliferation, 3; Ronald Reagan, 1; Reykjavík Summit, 3.

Suez Crisis

The Suez Crisis was a product of rising tensions in the Middle East as several Arab nations slowly regained strength in the aftermath of the 1948 creation and international recognition of the state of Israel. In Egypt, Syria, and Iraq, new political forces emerged that used military defeat in the war against Israel as political ammunition against traditional leaderships. In Egypt, a military coup threw out the regime of King Farouk in 1952, paving the way for the 1954 ascent of Colonel Gamal Abdul Nasser as the leader of Egypt and the first populist leader of the Arab world. Because of European and American reluctance to take anti-Israeli positions, and mindful of the West's colonial heritage, Nasser and other Arab leaders took a decidedly anti-Western stance. The Soviet Union accordingly saw Nasser's Egypt as the place to begin its penetration into the Middle East. The first shipments of arms from the Eastern bloc to Egypt began in the mid 1950s via Czechoslovakia.

Nasser completed the removal of the last vestiges of the colonial European presence in Egypt by nationalizing the Suez Canal Company on 26 July 1956. This move was prompted by Nasser's wish to retaliate for the recent British and American withdrawal of their offer to help finance his coveted Aswan High Dam project. It was also inspired by Nasser's wish to demonstrate Egypt's independence and exploit Arab nationalism and xenophobia to further his claim for Pan-Arab leadership.

In the ensuing international uproar over the canal's nationalization, Nasser claimed that under international law Egypt was entitled to nationalize the canal. He promised Egypt would conform to the terms for the operation of the canal stipulated in the Convention of 1888 written when the canal

Egyptian president Gamal Abdul Nasser announcing the nationalization of the Suez Canal, 26 July 1956

was built. True to his word, Nasser did not interfere with traffic in the canal after the takeover. In further guarantees, Nasser stated on 12 August and again on 9 September that he was willing to convene with the other signatories of the Convention of 1888 to review and reaffirm his guarantee of passage through the canal. But he also announced that an international agency's control of the canal would constitute "collective colonialism," create friction within Egypt, and impede close cooperation between Egypt and the canal's users. Finally, Nasser wielded the UN Charter as an additional defense of his position, insisting the charter's call for peaceful resolution of the conflict be recognized and that Western measures to exert economic and military pressure on Egypt be condemned.

British Response

British prime minister Anthony Eden and his cabinet were shocked by Nasser's action, which they viewed as a grave threat to vital British interests. The nationalization of the canal was of major concern to the British, for their ships were the most frequent users of the canal, with 60 to 70 percent of the oil required for the British economy relying on the canal for passage from the Middle East. The canal's takeover was not foremost among British concerns; they feared for the future position of Great Britain in the Middle East. If Nasser could exploit rising Arab nationalism and dominate the region, Britain's sources of Middle East oil would be threatened, and its control of the gulf undermined. British distrust of Nasser and fear of his Pan-Arabic designs prompted Prime Minister Eden – who compared him to Hitler – to seek Nasser's removal and the destruction of his regime. In coordination with the French, the British began to draw up military contingency plans designed to retake the canal by force if negotiations did not result in a "denationalization" of the canal and the consequent humiliation of Nasser.

French Response

Like the British, the French feared that the nationalization of the canal jeopardized substantial French economic interests; 48 percent of the French oil supply came through the Canal. Antagonism between the French government and Nasser, an antagonism that was the driving force governing French policy in the crisis, stemmed from Nasser's support for the rebels struggling to end French colonial rule in Algeria. Convinced that Nasser's elimination would greatly facilitate a French victory over the Algerian rebels, and propelled by the desire to reassert themselves as a world power after a succession of embarrassing failures in Indochina and Morocco, the French arrived at the same conclusions as the British: Nasser could not be appeased and had to be discredited, either through diplomatic means or, failing that, by military force.

Outcome and U.S. Response

On 16 October 1956, after Nasser had rejected Western proposals for a resolution of the conflict, and after the United Nations (UN) Security Council failed to resolve the conflict, the British, French,

and Israeli leaders secretly signed an accord for collusion in a military assault on Egypt. The Israelis were motivated to join the British and French because of the growing Egyptian menace to Israeli security. Egyptian-inspired Palestinian fedayeen attacks on Israel were becoming more frequent, and Egypt had denied Israel the use of the canal and blocked the Straits of Tiran to Israeli shipping. Israel also feared that Soviet military aid to Egypt and Nasser's growing influence in the Arab world threatened to upset the balance of power in the Middle East. On 29 October 1956 Israel attacked the Egyptian army in the Sinai peninsula, and two days later an Anglo-French air force attacked Egyptian airfields. By 2 November the Israeli forces occupied the Gaza Strip and Sinai, and on 6 November an Anglo-French seaborne force swept into the canal zone to claim control of the canal under the pretext of protecting it from warring Israeli and Egyptian forces.

Since the outset of the Suez Crisis, the United States had resisted calls by its European allies to resolve the crisis through forceful means. The Eisenhower administration was concerned about the nationalization of the canal, but viewed the crisis in terms of the U.S. policy of containment, fearing that direct Western military action in the Middle East might prompt further Soviet penetration into the region. The United States, therefore, chose to seek peaceful solutions to the Suez Crisis. When Britain, France, and Israel attacked Egypt, the United States angrily condemned the aggression as a violation of the UN Charter, causing severe tensions within the Western Alliance.

Without the support of the United States, the Anglo-French effort suffered. With the canal blocked with wreckage, vital oil supplies could not reach Europe, and U.S. aid aimed at easing the consequent oil shortage was conditional on a cease-fire and removal of the European forces from the canal zone. On 22 December the British and French, humiliated, withdrew from the canal. On 8 March 1957, under heavy diplomatic pressure from the United States and open threats by the Soviet Union, Israeli troops also withdrew from their advance positions and were separated from the Egyptian army by a UN peacekeeping force.

The Suez Crisis was important in three respects. It signified one of the last major efforts by Britain and France to slow down the process of their decline from the position of world leadership. After the failure of the Suez venture, the two appeared reconciled to the notion that new forces in their former colonies would from now on have to be accommodated rather than fought. The crisis also demonstrated U.S. unwillingness to support the British and the French in what appeared to be a desperate effort to cling to their past practices. It is important to note that the United States cooperated tacitly with the Soviet Union against the two members of the Western Alliance. Finally, the Suez Crisis marked a shift in Israeli military strategy. Israel conducted a lightning attack on Egyptian positions in the Sinai, using combined forces, deep armored penetrations, and surprise. Its tactics of mobility were to become the central elements of the Israeli military doctrine.

On 8 April, with the salvage and cleanup operation complete, the Suez Canal reopened under Egyptian control. By May 1957 all states except Israel were again using the canal.

References

Chester L. Cooper, *The Lion's Last Roar: Suez, 1956* (New York: Harper & Row, 1978);

Moshe Dayan, *Diary of the Sinai Campaign* (New York: Harper & Row, 1965);

Moshe Dayan, *Story of My Life* (London: Weidenfeld and Nicolson, 1976);

Dwight D. Eisenhower, *Waging Peace: 1956–1961: The White House Years* (New York: Doubleday, 1965);

Herman Finer, *Dulles Over Suez: The Theory and Practice of His Diplomacy* (Chicago: Quadrangle Books, 1964);

Muhammad Hasanayn Haykal, *Cutting the Lion's Tail: Suez through Egyptian Eyes* (New York: Arbor House, 1987);

Robert David Quixano Henriques, *One Hundred Hours to Suez: An Account of Israel's Campaign in the Sinai Peninsula* (London: Collins, 1957);

Selwyn Lloyd, *Suez 1956: A Personal Account* (London: Cape, 1978);

Roger Louis and Roger Owen, eds., *Suez 1956: The Crisis and Its Consequences* (Oxford, U.K.: Clarendon, 1989);

Donald Neff, *Warriors at Suez: Eisenhower Takes America into the Middle East* (New York: Linden Press, 1981);

Anthony Nutting, *No End of a Lesson: The Story of Suez* (London: Constable, 1967).

−J. H.

SEE ALSO THESE RELATED ENTRIES
John Foster Dulles, 1; Anthony Eden, 1; Dwight D. Eisenhower, 1; Eisenhower Doctrine, 3; Gamal Abdul Nasser, 2.

Tonkin Gulf Resolution

UPI/Bettman Archives

President Lyndon B. Johnson (second from right) meeting with the National Security Council—George W. Bell, Dean Rusk, and Robert S. McNamara—to discuss the Tonkin Gulf incident, 4 August 1964

The Tonkin Gulf resolution – enabling legislation passed by Congress in August 1964 – ceded to President Lyndon B. Johnson virtually unlimited authority in conducting military action in Vietnam. On the nights of 2 and 4 August North Vietnamese torpedo boats attacked the USS *Maddox* and *C. Turner Joy,* two American destroyers operating off the coast of North Vietnam. The circumstances of the attack are murky. The North Vietnamese may have confused the American warships with South Vietnamese patrol boats that operated in the area and frequently fired upon North Vietnamese positions. Other evidence suggests that the American presence was a deliberate provocation designed to give Johnson pretext to escalate the U.S. role in Vietnam, which at the time did not include direct combat.

The next day the State Department prepared the Gulf of Tonkin resolution (formally called the Southeast Asia resolution) asking Congress to grant the president the authority not merely to reply to attacks on U.S. forces in Vietnam but to have the power to do what had to be done to fulfill what the president considered American responsibilities in all of Southeast Asia.

Despite his misgivings that the passage of the resolution might result in unchecked presidential authority over Vietnam policy, Senator J. William Fulbright, at Johnson's request, used his position as chairman of the Senate Foreign Relations Committee to cut off meaningful debate likely to raise questions Johnson did not want raised. The resolution passed in the Senate by a vote of 88 to 2 and in the House by 416 to 0. Johnson signed the resolution on 10 August 1964. It was not repealed until 1970, after President Richard M. Nixon invoked it to justify his ordering troops into Cambodia and Laos.

References

David Halberstam, *The Best and the Brightest* (New York: Random House, 1969);

George C. Herring, *America's Longest War: The United States and Vietnam, 1950–1975* (New York: Knopf, 1985);

George Kahin, *Intervention: How America Became Involved in Vietnam* (New York: Knopf, 1986).

– C. S. B.

SEE ALSO THESE RELATED ENTRIES
J. William Fulbright, 1; Lyndon B. Johnson, 1; Vietnam War, 3.

Triad

Triad – the Latin word for a group of three – is a term used by the Pentagon in referring to the three principal means of U.S. nuclear weapons delivery: long-range manned bombers, intercontinental ballistic missiles (ICBMs), and submarine-launched ballistic missiles (SLBMs). Each "leg" of the triad has advantages and disadvantages. ICBMs are the most accurate and may be used against hardened targets, such as missile silos. They may also be retargeted. They enjoy secure communication with command authorities and are relatively inexpensive to maintain. The increasing accuracy of ballistic missiles, however, makes ICBMs in fixed silos theoretically vulnerable to an enemy attack. The SLBMs enjoy a high degree of invulnerability when deployed on "quiet" submarines – submarines undetectable by sonar. Their accuracy, however, is not yet as high as that of ICBMs, and communication with submarines is problematic. Manned bombers provide the highest degree of accuracy, may attack several targets distant from each other, and may be retargeted. Bombers may also be recalled after takeoff. Bombers, however, are slow and are vulnerable to air defenses. The United States decided to spread its nuclear warheads among the three means of delivery. Using only one means of delivery would risk a Soviet technological breakthrough that would render U.S. nuclear forces unusable.

References

McGeorge Bundy, *Danger and Survival: Choices about the Bomb in the First Fifty Years* (New York: Random House, 1988);

Thomas B. Cochran, William M. Arkin, and Milton M. Hoenig, *Nuclear Weapons Data Book,* volume 1 of *U.S. Nuclear Forces and Capabilities* (Cambridge, Mass.: Ballinger, 1984);

Lawrence Freedman, *The Evolution of Nuclear Strategy* (New York: St. Martin's Press, 1981).

– B. F.

Trilateralism

Trilateralism is the desire by the world's major capitalist states to promote a stable international order congenial to their economic and political interests. The term comes from the Trilateral Commission, a group of elite Western businessmen, bankers, politicians, and academics who convene periodically. About the only adherents to the power of trilateralism are conspiracy theorists, most from the further reaches of the Left, who see the Trilateral Commission as a plot to run the world.

The commission was founded by David Rockefeller in 1973, and he remains its key figure. Some five hundred people have been members, and over the years it has produced otherwise obscure studies on the West's prospects. Others see these studies as blueprints for worldwide American hegemony.

The aims of the commission are to foster an international order conducive to the world's most powerful multinational corporations. The commission favors free trade and closer economic ties among the West, the former Soviet-bloc countries, and the newly industrializing world. It has also sought to generate support for its views among the world's governments. The commission's membership included Jimmy Carter before he became president. The Carter administration appointed several members to high government posts, giving some publicity to what had been an obscure organization.

– C. S. B.

Truman Doctrine

On 12 March 1947, in a speech before a joint session of Congress, President Harry S Truman dedicated the foreign policy of his administration to the support of "free peoples who are resisting attempted subjugation by armed minorities or by outside pressures." This declaration of policy, which became known as the Truman Doctrine, was an explicit response to the spread of Soviet-style communism.

Following the end of World War II, the Soviets imposed repressive measures in Eastern Europe, installing communist regimes in Poland, Romania, Bulgaria, and Hungary. To the south, they supported communist guerrillas in Greece, made threats against Turkey, and only evacuated northern Iran in March 1946, after the United States had exerted great pressure. These actions convinced high-level American government officials, such as Under Secretary of State Dean Acheson, that the Soviet Union was bent on expansion.

On 21 February 1947 the British government informed the State Department that due to financial problems England was planning to halt economic and military aid to Greece and Turkey on 31 March. In the absence of British support, American officials feared that communist insurgents in Greece would take power. The State Department viewed the insurgents, who were supplied from Yugoslavia, Bulgaria, and Albania, as instruments of Soviet power. American authorities feared that the fall of Greece might trigger a chain reaction, bringing communist governments to power in Turkey, Iran, and perhaps even Italy and France, both of whose economies remained unstable. Given the geographic location, demographic strength, and industrial potential of these countries, State Department officials argued that it was essential for the United States to prevent further deterioration of the pro-Western position in the Mediterranean. President Truman accepted these recommendations, and within five days of the British notification the Truman administration had resolved to come to the aid of Greece and Turkey.

Congressional Support

The administration, needing to win the strong support of congressional leaders who were unaware of the crisis caused by the British decision to

UPI/Bettman Archives
President Harry S Truman presenting the foreign policy that became known as the Truman doctrine to a joint session of Congress, 12 March 1947

withdraw aid from Greece, invited leaders from both parties to a White House briefing on the crisis on 27 February. Secretary of State George C. Marshall spoke first, but his dry account of the State Department's rationale left the legislators unmoved. Sensing Marshall's failure to convince the congressmen, Under Secretary Acheson took the floor to make an emotional appeal for support. Not since ancient times, he argued, had the world been so divided between great powers. Not since the days of Athens and Sparta, Rome and Carthage, had the world been so polarized by "an unbridgeable ideological chasm" with "democracy and individual liberty" on one side and "dictatorship and absolute conformity" on the other. The United States needed to act in Greece to prevent the Soviet Union from dominating the globe.

Acheson's words left the congressional delegation stunned. Finally, Republican senator Arthur

Vandenberg of Michigan broke the silence, indicating that he would support the administration's request for aid, if President Truman and the administration explained to the American people, just as Acheson had explained to them, the importance of U.S. assistance. The administration understood Vandenberg's request: tightfisted conservative Republicans in Congress, who were unlikely to support U.S. economic and military aid out of charity, would provide assistance to Greece and Turkey to contain the spread of communism if pressed by their constituency.

The president went before Congress and the American people on 12 March to announce the Truman Doctrine. Written in part by Acheson and his staff at the State Department, the speech followed Vandenberg's recommendation, emphasizing the international division between democracy and communism and the threat the latter posed to the former: "At the present moment in world history nearly every nation must choose between alternative ways of life.... One way of life is based upon the will of the majority, and is distinguished by free institutions, representative government, free elections, guarantees of individual liberty, freedom of speech and religion, and freedom from political oppression. The second way of life is based upon the will of a minority forcibly imposed upon the majority. It relies upon terror and oppression, a controlled press and radio, fixed elections, and the suppression of personal freedoms."

Impact of Doctrine

Although Truman intended the speech to win support for American aid to Greece, it had a much greater impact. By justifying assistance to Greece on sweeping ideological grounds, the administration contributed to a "black and white" approach to American foreign policy, regarding U.S.-Soviet relations as a struggle between the forces of good and evil. Communism in any form anywhere came to be seen as a threat to American interests and security, requiring a response by the United States. Truman and his advisers did not want aid to Greece to set a precedent for American intervention everywhere. In other regions, such as China, where communists took power in 1949, the administration had no intention to bring force to bear on behalf of the Chinese nationalists, opponents of the communist takeover. Although the Truman Doctrine was not intended to commit the United States to the defense of noncommunists everywhere, its practical effect was to do just that.

References

Robert J. Donovan, *Conflict and Crisis* (New York: Norton, 1977);

John Lewis Gaddis, *The United States and the Origins of the Cold War, 1941–47* (New York: Columbia University Press, 1982);

Walter Isaacson and Evan Thomas, *The Wise Men* (New York: Simon & Schuster, 1986);

Harry S Truman, *Memoirs* (Garden City, N.Y.: Doubleday, 1955);

Daniel Yergin, *Shattered Peace: The Origins of the Cold War and The National Security State* (Boston: Houghton Mifflin, 1977).

          – B. D. K.

SEE ALSO THESE RELATED ENTRIES
Dean Acheson, 1; Containment, 3; Harry S Truman, 1.

Twentieth Party Congress of the Communist Party of the Soviet Union

The Twentieth Party Congress of the Communist party of the Soviet Union (CPSU) was a turning point in Soviet domestic and foreign policies. It was the first meeting of the party congress since the death of Joseph Stalin, and Nikita S. Khrushchev used the occasion to launch his new policies and, in the process, purge his rivals within the Politburo. The party congress lasted eleven days – 14–25 February 1956 – and included reports on every facet of the Soviet Union; however, it is best noted for Khrushchev's "secret speech," in which he launched his wide-ranging de-Stalinization campaign, and for his proclamation of peaceful coexistence with noncommunist states. Krushchev had three broad goals behind his speeches at the Twentieth Party Congress: to become the recognized leader in the Kremlin oligarchy and thus permit his domestic reforms to be enacted; to open communication between the East and West now that the Soviet Union was encircled by military alliances led by the United States and boasting a predominantly American nuclear arsenal; and to remove the rigid Stalinist doctrines which hampered Soviet relations with its socialist allies and the newly emerging Third World states.

De-Stalinization

De-Stalinization actually began in the Soviet Union soon after Stalin's death in 1953, with thousands of gulag prisoners beginning to return to Soviet society. The pace of de-Stalinization, however, remained a key issue in the Politburo as its more conservative members – such as Georgi Malenkov, Vyacheslav Molotov, and Lazar Kaganovich – wanted a slower, more gradual process that would protect the ideology and policies that they had helped Stalin build. In contrast, the reformers, led by Khrushchev, wanted a more complete break with the past to disassociate the new regime from the atrocities committed by Stalin. Both conservatives and reformers realized that exposing Stalin's crimes would also indict the people who were Stalin's close advisers. The revelations would thus weaken the conservatives and allow the reformers

to gain more power as the leaders of the new Soviet state.

Khrushchev began to lay the groundwork for a radical change in policy in the years prior to the Twentieth Party Congress. In May of 1955 Khrushchev visited Marshal Josip Broz Tito in Yugoslavia and began his effort to woo him back into the Soviet-led international communist movement. Two months later, in July, he met with President Dwight D. Eisenhower at the Geneva Summit and returned to Moscow lauding "the spirit of Geneva," which, he claimed, showed that the two superpowers could have normal relations. These two meetings, both of which were notable developments in themselves, foreshadowed Khrushchev's new foreign-policy tenets of "many roads to socialism" and "peaceful coexistence" which he announced in his Report of the Central Committee to the Congress on 14 February 1956.

In his Report to the Congress and in his famous secret speech of 24–25 February, Khrushchev attempted to de-Stalinize Soviet policy in three general areas: relations with other communist states and parties, relations with the West, and Soviet domestic politics. Tito's break with the Soviets, the 1953 riots in East Germany, and problems in Poland led Khrushchev and his fellow reformers to believe that the rigid Stalinist doctrine imposed upon Soviet satellites had to be changed if the Kremlin wanted to maintain dominion peacefully over worldwide communism. Similarly, Stalin's dogmatic views on socialist development had previously hindered Soviet relations with the newly liberated colonial states and the countries associated with the emerging Non-Aligned Movement. These countries were quickly becoming arenas for superpower competition, and Stalin's foreign-policy legacy was an impediment to current leaders. Khrushchev therefore broke with Stalin's views on socialist development by stating that "The conditions of Socialist development are different in different countries" and that each state should be able to follow a somewhat different road to its socialist development.

Delegates to the Twentieth Party Congress listening to Chairman Nikita S. Krushchev's denunciation of Joseph Stalin, February 1956

Seeking Improved East-West Relations

Khrushchev also used the congress to introduce his doctrinal basis for improving relations with the West. In the age of massive stockpiles of atomic weapons, a war with the United States would be devastating to both sides. Khrushchev was well aware of this and stated that since the "balance of forces" was currently in socialism's favor, war was not "fatalistically inevitable" and socialist states could live in peaceful coexistence with the imperialist forces.

While Stalin had previously declared that war between socialist and capitalist states was not inevitable, Khrushchev's statement that wars between capitalist countries were also avoidable was an obvious revision of Leninism. He further tried to decrease tensions between East and West by proclaiming that Communist parties did not necessarily have to attain power through violent means, but could rather seek peaceful transitions to socialism through parliamentary means. Economic, political, and ideological competition all became forms of class struggle. By making such statements, Khrushchev attempted to convince others that both he and his fellow communists at home and abroad were humanitarian reformers who were not girding themselves for certain war with the capitalists.

It was Khrushchev's long and detailed criticism of Stalin, however, that made the Twentieth Party Congress a watershed event in Soviet politics.

Khrushchev spoke for hours in front of the closed session about the extent of Stalin's purges, the execution of faithful party functionaries, and the suffering of the populace. Stalin, not simply Lavrenty Beria, the head of state security, as officials had previously claimed, was responsible for these atrocities. Khrushchev also criticized Stalin for not preparing the Red Army for the certain Nazi attack, for ordering the forced migration and deportation of the country's minorities, for ignoring the state of the nation, and for indulging in self-glorification in creating a cult of personality that surpassed that of V. I. Lenin. Stalin was also blamed for falsifying military history, treating the Chinese as colonial subjects, and causing the split with Tito's Yugoslavian government. Khrushchev, however, did praise Stalin's pre-1934 efforts at collectivization and eliminating "people's enemies."

Reactions to Speech

The repercussions of the speech varied greatly. In the Soviet Union the reaction was not overwhelming as Russians seemed to take it with characteristic stoicism   and complacency. For the communist governments in Eastern Europe, however, the speech was in many cases a crushing blow. These leaders were recently installed by Stalin and had been busy imitating his model of governance with repressions, purges, and dogmatism. Unlike the Soviet Union, however, these governments did not have historical legitimacy and had not had enough time to indoctrinate their societies. Collectivization and Stalinization had pushed the societies to their limits, and thus when Eastern European leaders admitted that false imprisonment, torture, and execution had occurred under their rule, people took to the streets.

In Poland strikes in Poznan led to a nationwide revolt that was put down by the military. Wladyslaw Gomulka, recently deposed, was brought back into the leadership to satisfy the demands of the reformers. In Hungary, where the repressed had been executed, the people rose up and held the government responsible. When Imre Nagy later rose to lead a new Hungarian government away from the Soviet Union and the Warsaw Pact, Khrushchev ordered Soviet troops into the country to extinguish the revolution. The speech was published by the U.S. State Department and reaction from the Communist parties of Western Europe were varied as some leaders were embarrassed by the revelations while others were relieved that the weight of past injustices had been lifted off the party.

In China, Mao Zedong and his fellow leaders initially accepted Khrushchev's speech with little criticism. They believed that the revelations would weaken the Soviet Union as the undisputed leader of world communism and that China would thus become a more valuable ally. Soviet aid to China indeed rose over the next two years, and Moscow even helped Beijing develop a nuclear-weapons programs. When relations later became sour between the two communist powers, however, Mao criticized Khrushchev's secret speech and the policy of peaceful coexistence as revisionist.

For Khrushchev, the Twentieth Congress and the secret speech had the desired effect on his career, solidifying his position as the Soviet leader. Molotov, Kaganovich, and Malenkov all lost the level of influence which they had enjoyed prior to the congress, and Khrushchev had a freer hand to implement his policies of decentralization and new agricultural initiatives – reforms that he hoped would rejuvenate the Soviet economy. His leadership of the party, however, continued to be questioned. Khrushchev would have been deposed a year later by the Anti-Party Group had he not been able to call an emergency session of the Central Committee, 40 percent of which had been elected at the Khrushchev-dominated Twentieth Congress. His opponents nevertheless finally succeeded in ousting him seven years later, and many of his de-Stalinization policies were reversed once Leonid I. Brezhnev assumed control of the Communist party in 1964.

References

Frederic S. Burin, "The Communist Doctrine of the Inevitability of War," *American Political Science Review,* 57 (June 1963);

Nikita S. Khrushchev, *Khrushchev Remembers* (Boston: Little, Brown, 1974);

Carl A. Linden, *Khrushchev and the Soviet Leadership 1957–1964* (Baltimore: Johns Hopkins University Press, 1966);

Adam B. Ulam, *Expansion and Coexistence: The History of Soviet Foreign Policy, 1917–1967* (New York: Praeger, 1968);

Alexander Werth, "Khrushchev's Secret Speech," *New Statesman,* 51 (14 April 1956).

– P. M.

SEE ALSO THESE RELATED ENTRIES
Nikita S. Khrushchev, 2; Joseph Stalin, 2.

U–2 Affair

Francis Gary Powers, American pilot of the U-2 spy plane shot down over Soviet territory in May 1960, testifying at his espionage trial in Moscow, August 1960

The U-2 is a single-seat, high-altitude reconnaissance and research jet aircraft. The U-2 has a top speed of 494 miles (795 kilometers) per hour and an altitude ceiling of approximately eighty thousand feet (twenty-four thousand meters). The first prototype of the U-2 flew in 1955, and it was soon put into service in intelligence gathering, for which it gained international attention.

The U-2 was designed to be small, relatively fast, and capable of record-setting altitudes in order to escape radar and air defense detection. Utilizing high-powered camera equipment, it was capable of flying freely over hostile countries and photographing military installations for intelligence purposes. The most important task of the U-2 was its intelligence-gathering missions over the Soviet Union. Built in an era in which Cold War tensions were steadily increasing as the Soviet Union sealed off its frontiers, the U-2 became an important part of the U.S. intelligence arsenal.

Known as the U-2 Affair, the confrontation between the United States and the Soviet Union in 1960 began with the shooting down of a U-2 over the Soviet Union. On 1 May 1960 a U-2 piloted by Francis Gary Powers began a routine reconnaissance mission over the Soviet Union. The Soviets managed to shoot down Powers's U-2 and capture the American pilot. When Soviet leader Nikita S. Khrushchev announced on 5 May that a U-2 had been shot down over the Soviet Union and that its pilot was an American – Powers, defying orders, had carried some identification with him on the flight – the United States National Aeronautics and Space Administration (NASA) immediately claimed the plane was lost gathering weather information. Khrushchev then claimed Powers had admitted working for the Central Intelligence Agency (CIA) and had revealed that the flight was indeed an intelligence-gathering mission. In the ensuing uproar Khrushchev demanded that the U.S. government immediately stop the flights over Soviet territory, apologize for those already made, and punish the persons responsible. The Soviet prime minister also threatened retaliation against any nation allowing its airstrip facilities to be used by American U-2 aircraft. U.S. president Dwight D. Eisenhower's response that the flights were to be suspended for the remainder of his presidency did not satisfy the Soviet Union, and as a result the scheduled 16 May 1960 Paris summit meeting involving France, Britain, the Soviet Union, and the United States collapsed in confusion. Khrushchev also canceled President Eisenhower's planned June visit to Moscow.

The U-2 also played an important role in the 1962 Cuban Missile Crisis by confirming the presence of Soviet missiles in Cuba. The development of surface-to-air missiles and other advances in anti-aircraft technology, however, rendered the U-2 obsolete as a military reconnaissance aircraft. The United States eventually replaced the U-2 with the SR-71, a supersonic, high-flying aircraft, and later with satellites.

References

Michael R. Beschloss, *MAYDAY: The U-2 Affair* (New York: Harper & Row, 1987);

William M. Leary, *Perilous Missions: Civil Air Transport and CIA Covert Operations in Asia* (Tuscaloosa: University of Alabama Press, 1984);

John Prados, *President's Secret Wars: CIA and Pentagon Covert Operations from World War II through Iranscam* (New York: Morrow, 1986);

Paul B. Stares, *Space Weapons and U.S. Strategy: Origins and Development* (London: Croom Helm, 1985);

David Wise and Thomas B. Ross, *The U-2 Affair* (New York: Random House, 1962).

                                                                    – J. H.

SEE ALSO THESE RELATED ENTRIES
Central Intelligence Agency, 3. Dwight D. Eisenhower, 1; Nikita S. Khrushchev, 2; Francis Gary Powers, 1; Cuban Missile Crisis, 3.

United Nations Organization

The United Nations Organization (UN) was planned at the 1944 Dumbarton Oaks Conference and established at the 1945 San Francisco Conference. It was hoped that the United Nations would serve as something close to a world government, negotiating settlements and regulating conflicts among nations. The onset of the Cold War, however, prevented the organization from assuming such a role, and it became largely a vehicle which nations used to advance their foreign-policy goals. The United States, for instance, in exploiting Soviet nonparticipation in the Security Council deliberations, managed to have the UN give its blessing to the U.S. policy of resisting the North Korean invasion of South Korea in 1950. While its agencies were doing valuable if limited humanitarian and relief work, the UN managed to engage in its primary mission – peacekeeping – only in those areas where the United States and the Soviet Union were already in agreement about what was to be done. The two superpowers used their veto power to prevent UN intervention in other areas. The Soviet Union prevented UN intervention in Hungary in 1956 and Czechoslovakia in 1968. The United States prevented UN intervention in Guatemala in 1954, Lebanon in 1958, and the Vietnam War. UN peacekeeping forces were sent to the Israeli-Egyptian border in 1957, the Congo in 1960–1961, and to Cyprus in 1964.

The end of the Cold War once again raised hopes that the organization would assume its original mission. Agreement between the United States and the Soviet Union allowed strong UN support for the American-led coalition that in 1992 defeated Iraqi forces following the Iraqi invasion of Kuwait, and UN peacekeeping forces are now supervising cease-fire efforts in the former Yugoslavia.

American delegate Hamilton Fish Armstrong (standing) proposing an amendment at the conference that established the United Nations, 15 June 1945

References

Robert C. Hilderbrand, *Dumbarton Oaks: The Origins of the United Nations and the Search for Postwar Security* (Chapel Hill: University of North Carolina, 1990);

Mark W. Zacher, *Dag Hammarskjold's United Nations* (New York: Columbia University Press, 1970).

– B. F.

SEE ALSO THESE RELATED ENTRIES
Dag Hammarskjöld, 1; Korean War, 3; U Thant, 2; Vietnam War, 3.

Vietnam War

The American presence in the Vietnam War fueled social and political debate in the United States that tested the validity of U.S. policies of containment. As such, U.S. strategies used in waging the Cold War were, for the first time, publicly questioned.

In the first years after World War II, Vietnam was still part of French Indochina. Ho Chi Minh, the communist leader of the Vietnamese anticolonial forces, began a fight for independence in the late 1940s. Indochina was a backwater, but it was close enough to China and Korea for the United States to consider it as a security interest, fearing it might fall prey to another communist takeover in region. In early 1950 President Harry S Truman agreed to provide the French forces with economic and military aid. This commitment took on an added urgency in June 1950 when North Korea invaded South Korea.

Partitioning of Vietnam

In May 1954 French forces at Dien Bien Phu lost a decisive battle to Ho's communists. The United States considered direct military action, but backed off only because President Dwight D. Eisenhower feared becoming mired in a protracted land war similar to Korea. At the Geneva Conference in 1954, France agreed to grant independence to its former colonies in Indochina. Cambodia and Laos were to be neutral while Vietnam was partitioned. Internationally supervised elections to unite the country under a single government were scheduled for July 1956.

Over the next two years Ho consolidated his power by suppressing his enemies and installing a Marxist-Leninist regime. In the South, Ngo Dinh Diem, a genuine nationalist, emerged as the head of a government that resembled a Western constitutional republic but required continued American support for its survival. Diem's government — though legitimate — lacked authority and was thus vulnerable to procommunist insurgencies. With the United States turning a blind eye, Diem sabotaged the scheduled 1956 elections, and the temporary division hardened into two distinct regimes, with the North portraying itself as the only legitimate government to speak for all Vietnamese.

Ho began to aid the Vietcong, the procommunist insurgents in the South who sought to oust Diem and unite with the North. Though short of full-scale war, fighting escalated as the decade wore on. By 1960 the Vietcong was so active in the countryside that the Diem government had only the most tenuous control.

Asian Policy under Kennedy

Fearing that another Asian country was about to fall to Soviet- and Chinese-dominated communism, President John F. Kennedy significantly increased U.S. support to South Vietnam. The decisions directing the growing American military role in the war remained vague, however. Kennedy always resisted advice that the United States take a direct role in the fighting even as he acceded to calls for some kind of American military involvement. A few weeks after taking office, Kennedy directed that the military advise South Vietnamese troops without actively taking part in combat. By 1963 the U.S. had some sixteen thousand troops in South Vietnam. The United States also conducted covert operations in Laos and North Vietnam and launched sporadic bombing raids against the North. The U.S. goals, as defined by Kennedy and accepted by his successors, were limited to supporting an independent, noncommunist South Vietnamese state, to be accomplished by defeating or otherwise suppressing the North Vietnamese-aided Vietcong insurgency in the South. They were, given the temper of the time, goals very much in accord with what most Americans believed to be a reasonable policy.

Escalation under Johnson

In March 1964 the new president, Lyndon B. Johnson, ordered the secret bombing of military targets in North Vietnam. Johnson began to plan for a major escalation of the U.S. role in the war, though he worried that Congress would not support him. On the nights of 2 and 4 August 1964, North Vietnamese torpedo boats attacked two U.S. warships off the coast of North Vietnam. The attack provided Johnson with the pretext for requesting that Congress approve the Gulf of Tonkin resolution, granting the president the authority to take whatever measures he deemed necessary to

U. S. Secretary of State Henry Kissinger and North Vietnamese delegation head Le Duc Tho initialing the agreement that officially ended the Vietnam War, 27 January 1973

repel North Vietnamese attacks and prevent further aggression.

Through the fall of 1964 Johnson deliberated the extent of the new U.S. role. His options ranged from bombing raids in the North – as reprisal for Vietcong attacks in the South – to a full-scale air war in the North to the direct use of U.S. combat troops in the South. In February 1965 the Vietcong launched a major attack against an American advisers compound at Pleiku. Johnson responded by ordering the sustained bombing of the North. By late April Johnson approved sending up to 82,000 ground troops to defend U.S. airbases and engage in limited combat. After the first combat troops were in place, the U.S. military role continued to grow incrementally. At year's end the number was 184,000 and rising, the military always demanding more and Johnson reluctantly acceding. It was clear by the end of 1965 that the Johnson administration felt that the U.S. presence in Vietnam was now so great that any withdrawal short of victory would be a political defeat. By the end of 1967 U.S. troop strength hit 500,000 men.

By mid 1966 opposition to the war had begun to build. Americans had grown skeptical of Johnson's claims to be making progress. While Johnson still had support for his goals, support was never very deep. Middle America, if never truly antiwar, was growing disillusioned and had begun to believe that however admirable and limited America's intentions were, they were not worth the sacrifice and investment of American lives: the United States needed either to seek military victory or to abandon the field. The American public no longer tolerated an indefinite commitment. By early 1968 high government officials, including Robert S. McNamara – secretary of defense since 1961 – turned against the war.

The telling blow came at the end of January 1968, when the North Vietnamese and Vietcong began the Tet offensive, launching simultaneous attacks against virtually every city in the South. Although Tet failed militarily, it was for the North a political victory of magnificent proportions. The North was attempting nothing less than to spark a popular uprising to win the war once and for all. Despite the appalling casualties it suffered, the

North had stunningly repudiated Johnson's long-standing claim that the United States had brought the North to its knees and that final victory was imminent. In early February the military declared it needed two hundred thousand more troops to win. Johnson rejected their claim. From then on, until the final troop pullout in 1973, American policy attempted to salvage a bad investment, seeking to maintain the South Vietnamese regime without a U.S. military role.

Vietnamization

Vietnam cost Johnson his presidency, and in 1969 Richard M. Nixon took office. He had promised to end the war without specifying how. He did have a grand strategy for rethinking U.S. relations with the Soviet Union, relations largely frozen into place in 1947 when the Cold War began. Nixon felt he needed to downgrade the importance of Vietnam vis-à-vis the Soviet Union. This would, in turn, pave the way for some sort of face-saving peace agreement that would permit the United States to withdraw. He announced a policy of "Vietnamization": the United States would continue to supply arms and matériel to South Vietnam, but American troops would be gradually withdrawn. As peace talks in Paris dragged on, Nixon ordered a secret large-scale bombing campaign that particularly targeted neutral Cambodia, through which the Vietcong were moving supplies from the North to the South along the Ho Chi Minh Trail.

The peace talks dragged on through 1972. Shortly before the presidential election Nixon's national security adviser, Henry Kissinger, announced that "peace is at hand." His assessment was premature. The North Vietnamese had arrived at an agreement with the United States, but South Vietnam rejected terms that included the continued presence of communist troops in the south. With the deal foundering, the North modified its position before breaking off talks. After the elections Nixon responded in December 1972 with the "Christmas bombing" of Hanoi and Haiphong. The North came back to the table in January 1973, and within a month a cease-fire was concluded. The United States withdrew its forces and received in turn American POWs, although many soldiers missing in action remained unaccounted for. Communist troops remained in South Vietnam. The South Vietnamese government, which had been increasingly plagued by corruption and incompetence, was effectively doomed. Its end came on 27 January 1975, but not before the United States had a "decent interval" between the withdrawal of American troops and the South Vietamese government's collapse.

The Legacy of Vietnam

Vietnam sparked a virulent debate over U.S. foreign policy that has continued into the present, as Americans of every political stripe seem to have an opinion on why the U.S. failed. Clearly, though, Vietnam stands as an example of political realities simply overwhelming military strategy. An insurmountable obstacle facing the United States was that South Vietnam lacked a capable government that enjoyed public support, without which the U.S. military role could never be more than a series of tactical victories against a politically motivated enemy. The North could be damaged but not beaten.

The U.S. goal was never more than ending North Vietnam's support of the Vietcong guerrilla insurgency in the South. It was never to defeat the North, as is mistakenly believed. Conservatives and members of the military have argued that Johnson and Nixon tied the hands of the military by fighting only a limited war, one that somehow did not permit the United States to win. The lesson of Vietnam, this argument runs, is that the United States should commit troops abroad only if it intends a complete victory. A knockout blow against North Vietnam – such as direct U.S. invasion, use of tactical nuclear weapons, or the bombing of the North's system of flood control dikes – was never an option, however. Such a strategy raised the possibility of Soviet or Chinese intervention and a superpower confrontation. Nor were policymakers certain that American military occupation of the North would be any more successful than the French.

Other critics find fault with Johnson for not having requested a congressional declaration of war, believing that such a move would have focused attention on the war and rallied the public behind him. But Johnson understood that the American people would not entertain a full-scale declared war. Vietnam did not loom large enough in the American consciousness, there were no vital national interests at stake, and the war lacked galvanizing incidents to arouse the public in its favor.

The United States was doomed to fail. The North Vietnamese and Vietcong were more deeply committed to their cause than the United States. From Kennedy on, the United States could never explain in any convincing fashion why U.S. interests were so great that the United States required five hundred thousand troops in Vietnam, yet not so great as to risk a war with the Soviets or Chinese.

References

Larry Berman, *Planning a Tragedy: The Americanization of the War in Vietnam* (New York: Norton, 1982);

William Colby, *Honorable Men: My Life in the CIA* (New York: Simon & Schuster, 1978);

Francis Fitzgerald, *Fire in the Lake: The Vietnamese and Americans in Vietnam* (New York: Vintage, 1973);

Leslie Gelb, and Richard K. Betts, *The Irony of Vietnam: The System Worked* (Washington, D.C.: The Brookings Institution, 1979);

David Halberstam, *The Best and the Brightest* (New York: Random House, 1969);

Thomas Havens, *Fire Across the Sea: The Vietnam War and Japan* (Princeton, N.J.: Princeton University Press, 1987);

George C. Herring, *America's Longest War: The United States and Vietnam, 1950–1975* (New York: Knopf, 1985);

Arnold R. Isaacs, *Without Honor: Defeat in Vietnam and Cambodia* (Baltimore: Johns Hopkins University Press, 1983);

George Kahin, *Intervention: How America Became Involved in Vietnam* (New York: Knopf, 1986);

F. Charles Parker, *Vietnam, Strategy for a Stalemate* (New York: Paragon, 1989);

Gareth Porter, *A Peace Denied: The United States, Vietnam and the Paris Agreements* (Bloomington: Indiana University Press, 1975);

Herbert Schandler, *The Unmaking of a President: Lyndon Johnson and Vietnam* (Princeton: Princeton University Press, 1977);

Franz Schurmann, *The Logic of World Power: An Inquiry Into the Origins, Currents, and Contradictions of World Politics* (New York: Pantheon, 1974);

William Shawcross, *Sideshow: Kissinger, Nixon and the Destruction of Cambodia* (New York: Simon & Schuster, 1979).

– C. S. B.

SEE ALSO THESE RELATED ENTRIES

Containment, 3; Dien Bien Phu, 3; Dwight D. Eisenhower, 1; Gulf of Tonkin Resolution, 3; Ho Chi Minh, 2; Lyndon B. Johnson, 1; John F. Kennedy, 1; Henry Kissinger, 1; Ngo Dinh Diem, 3; Richard M. Nixon, 1.

Warsaw Treaty Organization

The Warsaw Treaty Organization (WTO), also known as the Warsaw Pact, was established in Warsaw on 14 May 1955 by Albania, Bulgaria, Hungary, the German Democratic Republic (GDR), Poland, Romania, the Soviet Union, and Czechoslovakia. It was to last for twenty years, and its existence was assured for another ten if no moves were made to dissolve it at least one year before the expiration date. Between 1955 and 1990 only one country, Albania, in 1968, withdrew from the pact. In 1956 the revolutionary government in Hungary tried to leave the pact but was prevented from doing so by the Soviet invasion.

Three reasons have been offered to explain the Soviet decision to form the Warsaw Pact. First, the Soviet Union formed the organization to counter the entry of the Federal Republic of Germany (FRG) into the North Atlantic Treaty Organization (NATO) on 5 May 1955. Second, WTO was established to provide for a legitimate Soviet military presence in Hungary and Romania after the Austrian State Treaty was signed on 15 May 1955. Since the treaty provided for the withdrawal of all occupying forces from Austria, the Soviets could no longer justify the stationing of their troops in these countries by referring to a need to protect communication lines between the Soviet occupation zone in Austria and the Soviet Union. Finally, some Soviet commentators have referred to the creation of Western-backed alliances outside Europe as a reason for establishing the pact. The alliances particularly mentioned are ANZUS – including Australia, New Zealand, and the United States – formed in 1951; the Southeast Asia Treaty Organization (SEATO), formed in 1954; and the Baghdad Pact (later CENTO, or the Central Treaty Organization), formed in 1955.

The establishment of the Warsaw Pact should be seen not only in the context of East-West conflict, but also in the context of the post-Stalin Soviet effort to develop a new relationship with the socialist states of Eastern Europe. It marked a shift away from Stalin's Moscow-centered satellite system, which ignored national needs and conditions and undermined the legitimacy of Eastern Europe's leaderships. In forming the Warsaw Pact, Nikita S. Khrushchev chose a new arrangement that recognized a degree of equality among the so-cialist-bloc countries while guaranteeing Soviet control of the alliance – an alliance which implied partnership based on common interest and mutual benefit.

The Warsaw Treaty committed its signatories to settle international disputes by peaceful means; work toward the prohibition of weapons of mass destruction; consult in the event of a threat to the signatories' security and render assistance as considered necessary in the event of an armed attack in Europe on any one of them; establish a joint command for their armed forces and a political consultative committee with the power to create auxiliary organs; shun any alliances with conflicting aims; cooperate in economic and cultural relations while not interfering in each other's internal affairs; allow other states to accede irrespective of their social and state system; and seek a general European treaty of collective security in which event the present treaty would become ineffective.

Despite the emphasis on cooperation and equality among pact members, the Soviet Union was clearly the dominating member of the organization and used the Warsaw Pact to preserve its own political and military hegemony over Eastern Europe. From the beginning the three northern states of Eastern Europe – Poland, Czechoslovakia, and the GDR – were the most important pact members. The GDR developed the closest relationship with the Soviet Union, proclaiming in its 1974 revised constitution that it would be "forever and irreversibly allied with the Soviet Union."

Although the Warsaw Pact charter describes the organization as a defensive alliance against external threats, without specifying any ideological basis for the alliance, the Warsaw Pact has spent much of its resources to ensure the internal ideological and political unity of the Soviet bloc. In 1976 the Warsaw Pact nations claimed that the treaty had been formed "with the aim of defending the gains of socialism." Similar commitments to a shared social system were made in many of the bilateral treaties concluded between the Soviet Union and Eastern European nations, with Romania the only exception. For most of its existence, therefore, the Warsaw Pact operated not only as a military alliance protecting itself against an armed attack, but also as a political enforcement agency designed to strengthen the commitment to socialism within the bloc itself.

Early Years of the Pact

The evolution of the pact can be divided into four major periods: the early years, from 1955 to 1964; the years of revitalization, from 1965 to 1968; the mature years, from 1969 to 1985; and the period of decreasing unity, which began in 1986. During the early years the pact served a global-political and diplomatic, rather than military, purpose. Its major function was to signal Soviet displeasure with the integration of the Federal Republic of Germany into NATO. During this period the pact also became an instrument for rallying East European support for Soviet positions in the steadily escalating Sino-Soviet dispute. It also functioned as a means to demonstrate Soviet ability to form its own alliance.

The organizational structure during the early period was simple. At the top of the hierarchy was the Political Consultative Committee (PCC), composed of representatives of the signatory states. The first meeting of the PCC took place in Prague in January 1956, when it set up the Permanent Commission (PC) and the Joint Secretariat (JS). The communiqué of the January meeting specified that the PCC should meet "when necessary, but no less than twice a year," but the PCC met only six times in the first ten years of its existence, and there was no meeting at all in the period between January 1956 and May 1958.

The early years witnessed very little effort to weld the Warsaw Pact into an integrated military alliance. This can be explained in part by Soviet military doctrine which at the time assumed that war in Europe would be nuclear from the outset, or would very rapidly become nuclear, and that nuclear war can be won by the side that has strategic superiority and strikes first. Under this doctrine the Soviet Union was to rely on the use of nuclear weapons in the earliest stages of a conflict in order to inflict massive damage to U.S. military capabilities. Since the utility of conventional forces seemed marginal in the event of a European war, Khrushchev ordered a dramatic shift away from conventional arms toward strategic nuclear forces. By 1960 the Soviet Union had 150 intercontinental bombers and about 10 intercontinental ballistic missiles (ICBMs). By 1966 it had 270 long-range bombers and 300 ICBMs.

Around 1961 the Soviet leadership came to believe that they had exaggerated the extent to which nuclear missiles could replace, rather than supple-

ment, traditional weapons systems. Accordingly, Khrushchev instituted a new policy of closer military cooperation with the East European members of the pact, aimed at improving the collective military efficiency of the alliance. A concept of "coalition warfare" was put forward with the goal of expanding the role of East European national forces in Soviet military planning. Coalition warfare called for the participation of the East European armed forces, in conjunction with Soviet forces, in rapid offensive mobile military operations against NATO. In order to achieve this kind of military cooperation, the non-Soviet members of the pact needed sophisticated equipment. In the mid 1960s the Soviet Union supplied the East European armed forces with modern T-54 and T-55 tanks, MIG-21 and SU-7 aircraft, and other new weapons. Some East European armed forces were also being supplied with nuclear-capable weapons systems (SU-7s, SCUD and FROG missiles) and trained for warfare in nuclear conditions. By the end of the mid 1960s the Soviets had come to view the East European armed forces as a significant contribution to Soviet military power.

Invasion of Hungary

The major crisis that erupted during the early period took place in Hungary in October–November 1956. Taking power amid growing popular unrest, Hungarian premier Imre Nagy announced Hungary's withdrawal from the Warsaw Pact, the abolition of the one-party system, and neutrality. He was overthrown by Soviet military invasion and replaced by János Kádár. Although Moscow rationalized the Hungarian intervention by reference to the Warsaw Treaty, there seemed to have been no consultations among WTO members. The Warsaw Treaty did not specify a Soviet right to intervene. In fact, the intervention was a breach of Article 1 of the treaty on the nonuse of force and Article 8 on noninterference in internal affairs. No PCC meeting discussed the Hungarian crisis. In the end it was not the Warsaw Pact but the Soviet Union that used its forces to restore its authority, though it more than likely had Romanian and Polish cooperation since some of the troops involved in the invasion were stationed in those countries.

Warsaw Pact under Brezhnev

The second period of the evolution of the Warsaw Pact began after Leonid Brezhnev and Alexsei Nikolaevich Kosygin gained control in the Soviet Union in October 1964. At the Twenty-third Party Congress of the Communist party of the Soviet

Union (CPSU) in March 1966, Brezhnev emphasized Soviet determination to improve the Warsaw Pact. The pact's defense organs began to meet on an annual basis, equipment was upgraded, and further education of cadres emphasized. In addition, increased emphasis was placed on joint pact military exercises.

The change in the Soviet attitudes toward the Warsaw Pact reflected a shift taking place in Soviet military doctrine. The new Soviet leadership not only acknowledged that the use of nuclear weapons might be limited in scale and geographic scope and that war might start with a conventional phase, they also reversed their earlier position on the inevitability of escalation to nuclear war and declared that it might be possible to avoid nuclear war in an East-West conflict, especially one that broke out in Europe. Soviet thinking on this issue was shaped by NATO's adoption of a "flexible response" strategy in Europe. Flexible response refers to the capability to react to a broad spectrum of threats, ranging from infiltration and conventional threats to response to a nuclear initiative by the adversary. As a result of a new doctrine, the role of Soviet strategic forces focused on nuclear deterrence rather than preemptive destruction. The adoption of a "limited war" doctrine also meant increased emphasis on conventional operations in the Soviet military planning. Basic Soviet military strategy assumed that war should be fought on Western territory and called for the defeat of NATO and the occupation of West Germany, France, and the Benelux in three weeks. This necessitated the substantial superiority of Warsaw Pact forces over NATO in virtually all categories of weapons systems.

Revitalization of the Pact

The main challenge to Warsaw Pact unity during the period of revitalization came from Czechoslovakia, until then a rather docile member of the bloc. The authoritarian rule of Antonín Novotny and economic problems caused profound dissatisfaction among the people. The first step in the revolution was taken on 5 January 1968, when Novotny was pressured to resign as first secretary of the Communist party and was replaced by Aleksander Dubcek. On 16 April the Central Committee of the party adopted the so-called Action Program. Although it reaffirmed the leading role of the Communist party, it also accepted other political parties. In foreign affairs the Action Program pledged to pursue increasingly autonomous policies but did not advocate policies that would threaten Soviet security interests. In May 1968 the Czechoslovak Gottwald Academy publicized some possibilities for an alternative Czechoslovak security policy, including a Central European security system without the Soviet Union and with outright neutrality.

From the Soviet point of view the liberalization movement in Czechoslovakia created a dangerous political precedent. The East German and Polish party leaders, in agreement with the Soviets, pressed for intervention. During the night of 20–21 August 1968, twenty-three Soviet divisions, together with two divisions from the Polish and East German armies, one division from Hungary, and a token brigade from Bulgaria, took Prague and other Czechoslovak cities. Romania refused to participate in the invasion. The military invasion of Czechoslovakia, a surprise action, was rapid and overwhelming. In twenty-four hours Czechoslovakia was an occupied country. Czechoslovakia offered no military resistance to the invasion.

The intervention led to the renunciation of the Warsaw Treaty by Albania and the refusal by Romania to accept that the Warsaw Treaty provided grounds for similar interventions. It also resulted in Soviet recognition of the dangers of lack of consultation within the bloc and, consequently, in the Soviet willingness to create new institutions in which the non-Soviet members of the Warsaw Pact would have a greater sense of participation in Warsaw Pact policy and action.

Period of Pact Unification

During the third period of the evolution of the Warsaw Pact, between 1969 and 1985, the pact matured into a relatively unified organization in which internal problems were settled without the use of force. At the organizational level reforms were carried out to enhance pact unity. The Budapest meeting of March 1969 added three new bodies to the pact's military structure: the Committee of Defense Ministers (CDM), the Military Council, and the Technical Council. The formation of the CDM was clearly a Soviet concession to the East Europeans, whose defense ministers had previously been subordinated to the Soviet commander in chief of the pact's joint command. In spite of the effort, the organizational changes fell short of hiding Soviet dominance in the pact. The Soviet officers occupied the key positions at the highest organizational levels. And even in peacetime non-Soviet WTO forces were not given independent access to nuclear weapons or provided with the most-advanced weapons systems available, suggesting that the Soviet Union did not trust its allies.

At the end of the 1960s and during the 1970s the Soviet leadership ascribed to East European military forces an important role in the supplementing of Soviet military capabilities for use in a European war. Defense spending increased significantly in Eastern Europe, especially in the GDR, where the defense budget increased by nearly 74 percent between 1969 and 1977.

During the period between 1969 and 1985 the Soviets attempted to broaden their influence in the Third World with increasing reliance on their East European allies. The non-Soviet members of the Warsaw Pact were not, however, made to serve in surrogate combat roles in Third World conflicts involving the Soviet Union; they merely rendered support to Soviet political and military objectives in the forms of arms supply, training, transport, and internal security. The most active pact members in the Third World were East Germany, Czechoslovakia, Hungary, Poland, and Bulgaria. From 1955 to 1980 the value of the Soviet bloc military aid was slightly more than $51 billion, of which $4.3 billion were furnished by non-Soviet bloc countries. The Middle East – followed by North Africa, South Asia, sub-Saharan Africa, Latin America, and East Asia – was the focus of Soviet bloc aid. Over the twenty-five year period beginning in 1955, some forty-five Third World countries received military aid from the Soviet bloc.

East Germany made a particularly strong contribution in rendering support to the Third World countries. Among the countries in which East Germans were active as police and security advisers were South Yemen, Angola, Ethiopia, Mozambique, and Libya. During the Angolan conflict (1975–1976) the East Germans provided arms, medical supplies, and training to the Soviet-backed forces of the Popular Movement of the Liberation of Angola (MPLA). They also allowed MPLA wounded to recuperate in East German hospitals. In addition, East German advisers helped in training guerrillas and planning guerrilla operations against Zimbabwe-Rhodesia and South-West Africa.

Other East European nations have also involved themselves in Soviet Third World activities. The Soviets used the Czechoslovakians as a nominal supplier of arms to Egypt during the Suez crisis of 1956. Czechoslovak military advisers and technicians were also present in Egypt at the time. In the Brezhnev period Eastern European countries pro-

vided military assistance to North Vietnam between 1965 and 1975 and to revolutionary movements fighting in so-called wars of liberation. During the Ethiopia-Somalia conflict in 1977–1978 the Soviets brought in East European military advisers and technicians to help the Ethiopians. After South Yemen attacked North Yemen in late February 1979, the number of Soviet and Eastern European military and security advisers in South Yemen doubled. In addition, several Eastern European states sent matériel and rendered military training and logistic support to the Salvadoran guerrillas in 1980.

In the 1970s the Soviet Union entered into a series of arms control agreements with the United States. The American military doctrine was based on the principle of "mutual assured destruction" (MAD), which held that only certainty of total destruction could deter the use of nuclear weapons. The Soviet willingness to enter into MAD-based agreements, such as the 1972 Antiballistic Missile (ABM) and Strategic Arms Limitation (SALT) treaties, was difficult to reconcile with their prevailing military doctrine. In January 1977 Brezhnev gave in the Soviet city of Tula a speech repudiating for the first time the notion that victory in nuclear war was possible.

Polish Crisis

During the period of mature years the forged cohesion within the pact was most directly threatened by the Polish crisis that erupted following the emergence of the independent Solidarity trade union movement in 1980. Although the Polish crisis did not end in Soviet intervention, as had the Czechoslovak crisis, it did lead to a declaration of martial law in December 1980 and an extensive militarization of Polish politics under General Wojciech Jaruzelski. According to Ryszard Kuklinski, a defector from the Polish general staff, a decision-in-principle was made in late 1980 to crush Solidarity either by external invasion with Soviet, Czechoslovak, and GDR forces or through internal action. Whatever the precise details of the imposition of martial law, the Soviet handling of the crisis suggested greater reluctance to intervene than in 1968. Martial law was lifted in July 1982.

Warsaw Pact under Gorbachev

The final period of the Warsaw Pact began with a change of the leadership in the Soviet Union. When Mikhail Gorbachev assumed power in the Kremlin in March 1985, the non-Soviet members of the pact had already become increasingly vocal, demanding more equitable participation in the pact activities. In 1983 the leaderships of both the GDR and Czechoslovakia openly displayed their lack of enthusiasm for Moscow's decision to deploy SS-22 missiles in their countries. Strain in the alliance became particularly pronounced after Gorbachev launched perestroika – a program of social and political reforms – in the Soviet Union. As the communist regimes fell in the GDR, Czechoslovakia, Bulgaria, and Romania in 1989, the new governments in these countries began to call for a transformation of the Warsaw Pact from a military to a political alliance. In June 1990 Gorbachev joined the East European leaders in calling for the transformation of the Warsaw Pact into a democratic grouping of independent sovereign states, ending forty-five years of Soviet military domination over Eastern Europe. With the unification of the two Germanys, the GDR membership in the Warsaw Pact ended.

Gorbachev's understanding of Soviet national security in the nuclear era was based on the concept of "nuclear sufficiency," defined as that level of military forces sufficient to repel aggression but insufficient to conduct offensive operations. According to Seweryn Bialer, the idea of nuclear sufficiency subsumes three related concepts: that a buildup of nuclear strategic weapons beyond the level of MAD is militarily meaningless; that the security that MAD provides will be as effective at lower force levels; and that a lower level of strategic deployment increases the security of both superpowers and of the world by making accidental war less likely and by easing psychological tensions. Reflecting Gorbachev's new security concepts, the PCC meeting in Berlin at the end of May 1987 produced a document in which it was proposed that conventional armaments should be reduced "down to the level at which neither side, in ensuring its defense, would have means for a sudden attack on the other side or for starting offensive operations in general."

In the military sphere three important developments took place in 1989 and 1990. First, the So-

viet Union accepted German unification and the membership of the unified Germany in NATO. Second, the Soviets agreed to remove Soviet troops from Hungary, Czechoslovakia, Poland, and the GDR. Third, the individual Warsaw Pact armies took decisive steps toward increasing their independence from Moscow's control. Hungary was first to cut down the size of its army and develop a new national defense doctrine. It redeployed some of its national troops from the western to the eastern part of the country, emphasizing that the Hungarian army was a national defensive army rather than an attack force aimed at Europe. Poland followed the Hungarian example, publicizing a new defense doctrine stating that it will "maintain only armed forces necessary for the defence of the country." The new governments of other Eastern European countries also made decisions to cut the size of their armed forces, in part due to the economic pressures, in part to their independent assessments concerning their own defense requirements.

References

Jonathan R. Adelman and Deborah Anne Palmieri, *The Dynamics of Soviet Foreign Policy* (New York: Harper & Row, 1989);

Seweryn Bialer, *Gorbachev's Russia and American Foreign Policy* (Boulder, Colo.: Westview, 1988);

Gerald Holden, *The Warsaw Pact: Soviet Security and Bloc Politics* (New York: Blackwell, 1989);

Stephen T. Hosmer and Thomas W. Wolfe, *Soviet Policy and Practice Toward Third World Conflicts* (Lexington, Mass.: Lexington Books, 1983);

Robin Alison Remington, *The Warsaw Pact: Case Studies in Communist Conflict Resolution* (Cambridge, Mass.: Massachusetts Institute of Technology Press, 1971);

Thomas W. Wolfe, "Evolution of Soviet Military Policy," in *The Soviet Union under Brezhnev and Kosygin: The Transition Years,* edited by John W. Strong (New York: Reinhold, 1971), pp. 75–92.

                                                                    –M.H.

SEE ALSO THESE RELATED ENTRIES

Brezhnev Doctrine, 3; Deterrence, 3; Flexible Response, 3; Intercontinental Ballistic Missile, 3; Intermediate Nuclear Forces Treaty, 3; Massive Retaliation, 3; Mutual Assured Destruction, 3; North Atlantic Treaty Organization, 3; Strategic Defense Initiative, 3; Star Wars, 3.

X Article

The X Article, published in the periodical *Foreign Affairs* in July 1947, was one of the first expressions of, and certainly the most cogent and influential early elaboration on, the need of the United States to contain the expansionist tendencies of the Soviet Union. It was written by George F. Kennan in January of that year, shortly before he was named director of policy planning at the State Department. The article, titled "The Sources of Soviet Conduct," concealed the identity of its author behind the byline "X" – because of State Department restrictions.

Kennan's article was based on a paper titled "Psychological Background of Soviet Foreign Policy," written in response to Secretary of the Navy James Vincent Forrestal's request for an analysis of the Soviet Union. Forrestal also demanded that the essay be "academically sound," implying that it should be tailored to support Forrestal's notions about the Soviet Union. Forrestal rejected Kennan's first version, forcing him to write a tougher sounding draft.

Kennan begins his paper with a lengthy discussion of Marxism and then moves to illustrate how Soviet ideology meshed with historically conditioned Russian attitudes and fears concerning the outside world. In examining Soviet foreign-policy objectives, the paper concludes that, because of the economic turmoil and disruption with which the Soviet Union was saddled as a result of World War II and its regime's oppressive domestic practices, there were limits to the degree to which the Soviets could embrace a foreign policy of restraint toward cooperation with the West. The paper urged the United States to adopt a policy that would "confront the Russians with unalterable counter-force at every point where they show signs of encroaching upon the interests of a peaceful and stable world."

The occasion for the X Article was a well-received lecture Kennan delivered to the Russian Study Group of the Council on Foreign Relations, after which the editor of *Foreign Affairs*, Hamilton Fish Armstrong, asked him for an article based on his talk. When Kennan submitted the essay he had written for Forrestal for publication, it was the idea of containment of the Soviet Union as a U.S. policy which came through. As *Foreign Affairs* was a periodical commonly regarded as an organ of the foreign-policy establishment, many took Kennan's article to be an articulation of the administration's doctrine and the principles underlying its foreign policy. This impression was strengthened by President Harry S Truman's recent Truman Doctrine speech, delivered in March 1947, and by the revelation that Kennan had authored the essay.

Kennan's idea of containment was generally embraced by Truman's and successive administrations, but to what degree Kennan's version of containment called for military, political-diplomatic, or economic means against the Soviet Union has been a point of serious contention. Kennan himself, in recent writings, has asserted that his idea of containment was primarily political and economic and that U.S. reliance on military means to contain the Soviet Union was a result of what he called "the militarization of U.S. foreign policy," which he never advocated.

References:

Walter L. Hixson, *George F. Kennan: Cold War Iconoclast* (New York: Columbia University Press, 1989);

George F. Kennan, *American Diplomacy: 1900–1950* (Chicago: University of Chicago Press, 1951; revised, 1984);

George F. Kennan, *Memoirs, 1925–1950* (Boston: Little, Brown, 1967);

George F. Kennan, *Memoirs, 1950–1963* (Boston: Little, Brown, 1972);

George F. Kennan, *Realities of American Foreign Policy* (Princeton: Princeton University Press, 1954);

David Mayers, *George Kennan and the Dilemmas of U.S. Foreign Policy* (New York: Oxford University Press, 1988);

Anders Stephanson, *Kennan and the Art of Foreign Policy* (Cambridge, Mass.: Harvard University Press, 1989);

X [George F. Kennan], "The Sources of Soviet Conduct," *Foreign Affairs*, 25 (July 1947): 566–582.

–J. H.

SEE ALSO THESE RELATED ENTRIES
Containment, 3; James V. Forrestal, 1; George F. Kennan, 1; Long Telegram, 3; Harry S Truman, 1.

Yalta Conference

On 2 February 1945 U.S. president Franklin Delano Roosevelt, British prime minister Winston S. Churchill, and Soviet leader Joseph Stalin met in the Crimean city of Yalta to discuss Allied war aims. During the week-long conference, the Big Three, as the leaders were known, reached several agreements, but the conference failed to resolve the significant conflicts between Stalin, on the one side, and Roosevelt and Churchill, on the other.

Roosevelt, who made the long journey to the Crimea despite his poor health, had two major objectives at Yalta. He first sought agreement on the new United Nations Organization, believing that the United Nations would facilitate the resolution of conflicts among the Allies and provide the cornerstone for a peaceful postwar world. Roosevelt's second concern was to reach agreement on basic Allied military strategy for the remainder of World War II. Roosevelt was particularly interested in gaining Russian troop support in the war effort in the Far East. Because the war in the Pacific appeared far from over at the time, the United States wanted the Red Army to help in the American invasion of Japan.

Churchill was concerned primarily with the postwar structure of Europe. While he supported the establishment of the United Nations, he felt that the future of Europe was more important. The United Nations could help maintain an existing peaceful order, he argued, but it could never create political stability. Churchill concentrated on a series of European problems: the status of Germany, the future role of liberated France, and the status of Poland. Churchill also wanted to clarify Britain's position in Iran and the Balkans. Unlike Roosevelt and Stalin, Churchill had little interest in the war effort against Japan.

Stalin had three principal aims at Yalta. First, he needed massive economic aid for his devastated nation. He wanted secondly to regain rights and territory lost during the Russo-Japanese War of 1904–1905. His third and most important goal was British and American agreement to a Russian sphere of influence in Eastern Europe to ensure Russian security.

Roosevelt and Stalin privately reached accord on the Far East. Stalin agreed to have the Red Army invade Manchuria and Japan within two or three months after the defeat of Germany. In return, Roosevelt agreed that Russia would receive the Kuril Islands, lower Sakhalin, access to Port Arthur and Dairen, control of the Chinese eastern and southern Manchurian railroads, and recognition of Outer Mongolia's independence from China. These measures effectively restored all the rights and land that Czar Nicholas II had lost to the Japanese in the 1904–1905 war.

The Big Three also reached agreement on the United Nations. Representatives of the Allied powers had met earlier from 21 August to 7 October 1944 at the Dumbarton Oaks estate to lay the groundwork for the United Nations in Washington, D.C. The negotiators at Dumbarton Oaks had left questions unresolved that the Big Three addressed at Yalta. Stalin dropped his initial demand for sixteen votes in the General Assembly, one for each Soviet republic, accepting three votes instead (one for the Soviet Union as a whole, and one each for the Ukrainian Republic and Belorussia). Stalin also accepted an American voting formula for the Security Council, the most important body within the international organization. The U.S. formula called for each of the five permanent members – the United States, the Soviet Union, Great Britain, France, and China – to retain the right to veto Security Council measures.

European Issues

There was less agreement on European issues. Stalin wanted Germany to pay $20 billion in reparations, half of which would go to the Soviet Union. Churchill refused to fix a reparations sum until the Allies had determined precisely what Germany could afford. He feared that Draconian reparations would destroy German society, causing starvation and social unrest. Unable to resolve the reparations question, the Big Three established a commission in Moscow to examine this question further. They also deferred decision on the issue of German territorial dismemberment, the prosecution of war criminals, and the Polish-German border. They did, however, agree to give France control of an occupational zone and a seat on the Allied Control Commission.

Prime Minister Winston Churchill, President Franklin D. Roosevelt, and Soviet leader Joseph Stalin at the Yalta Conference, February 1945

On the question of Poland, Stalin dealt from a position of strength, as the Red Army had consolidated physical control of Polish territory. Stalin threw his support behind the communist regime established in Lublin, while Churchill passionately defended the London-based Polish government-in-exile. Roosevelt was torn on the issue, siding with Churchill to the extent that he wanted a government representative of the Polish people, but agreeing at the same time that the Polish government should be acceptable to Moscow. A compromise was finally reached on the basis of an American proposal under which the Lublin regime would be recognized as the provisional government to consist of the Lublin government and "democratic leaders from Poland itself and from Poles abroad." It was pledged that the Polish government would hold elections "on the basis of universal suffrage and secret ballots as soon as possible." The Big Three decided to consult the Polish government before fixing the country's frontiers.

Discussion on Poland dominated the Yalta conference, leaving little time for consideration of the Balkans. In the end, neither Roosevelt nor Churchill was satisfied by the agreement on Poland, but since Russian troops had by this time pushed to the Oder River in eastern Germany, the Soviet promise to hold elections was the best they could hope for. They were also able to get Stalin's consent to a declaration on liberated europe, calling for the Big Three to support the principle of self-determination in Eastern Europe.

The disagreement over the future of Poland reflected a more profound conflict between Stalin and the Anglo-Americans. For Stalin, Russian security meant that the Eastern European states should remain under Soviet control. His designs on Eastern Europe were unacceptable to Great Britain and the United States. Both Churchill and Roosevelt believed firmly in the principle of self-determination, the exercise of which they did not believe conflicted with Russian security.

The conference closed on 11 February 1945. The Western press greeted it as a success. Although a few editorials noted the Allied disputes over Poland and Germany, none understood how profound the disagreements between the Anglo-Americans and the Soviets were.

References:

Pierre de Senarclens, *Yalta* (New Brunswick, N.J.: Transaction, 1988);

C. J. Sulzberger, *Such a Peace: The Roots and Ashes of Yalta* (New York: Continuum, 1982).

– B. D. K.

SEE ALSO THESE RELATED ENTRIES

Winston S. Churchill, 1; Potsdam Conference, 3; Franklin Delano Roosevelt, 1; Joseph Stalin, 2.

Selected Bibliography

The Cold War: Selected Bibliography

1.   History: Origins and Evolution

Ambrose, Stephen E. *Rise to Globalism: American Foreign Policy Since 1938*, rev. ed. New York: Penguin, 1976.

Aron, Raymond. *The Imperial Republic: The United States and the World, 1945–1963*. Englewood Cliffs, N. J.: Prentice-Hall, 1974.

Aronsen, Lawrence, and Martin Kitchen. *The Origins of the Cold War in Comparative Perspective: American, British, and Canadian Relations with the Soviet Union, 1941–1948*. New York: St. Martin's Press, 1988.

Davis, Lynn Etheridge. *The Cold War Begins: Soviet-American Conflict over Eastern Europe*. Princeton: Princeton University Press, 1974.

Deighton, Anne. *The Impossible Peace: Britain, the Division of Germany, and the Origins of the Cold War*. New York: Oxford University Press, 1990.

Deighton, Anne, ed. *Britain and the First Cold War*. New York: St. Martin's Press, 1990.

Donnelly, Desmond. *Struggle for the World: The Cold War, 1917–1965*. New York: St. Martin's Press, 1965.

Douglas, Roy. *From War to Cold War, 1942–1948*. New York: St. Martin's Press, 1981.

Feis, Herbert. *Churchill, Roosevelt, Stalin: The War They Waged and the Peace They Sought*. Princeton: Princeton University Press, 1957.

Feis, Herbert. *From Trust to Terror: The Onset of the Cold War, 1945–1950*. New York: Norton, 1970.

Fontaine, André. *History of the Cold War: From the October Revolution to the Korean War*. New York: Vintage, 1969.

Gaddis, John Lewis. *The Long Peace: Inquiries into the History of the Cold War*. New York: Oxford University Press, 1987.

Gaddis, John Lewis. *Russia, the Soviet Union, and the United States: An Interpretive History*. New York: Wiley, 1978.

Gaddis, John Lewis. *The United States and the Origins of the Cold War, 1941–1947*. New York: Columbia University Press, 1972.

Goldman, Eric F. *The Crucial Decade – and After: America, 1945–1960*. New York: Vintage, 1960.

Graebner, Norman A. *Cold War Diplomacy: American Foreign Policy, 1945–1960*. Princeton: Van Nostrand, 1962.

Halle, Louis J. *The Cold War as History*. New York: Harper & Row, 1967.

Herz, Martin F. *Beginnings of the Cold War*. Bloomington: Indiana University Press, 1966.

Jones, Joseph M. *The Fifteen Weeks (February 21–June 5, 1947)*. New York: Viking, 1955.

Kennan, George F. *Russia and the West under Lenin and Stalin*. Boston: Little, Brown, 1961.

Kim, Young Hum, ed. *Twenty Years of Crises: The Cold War Era*. Englewood Cliffs, N. J.: Prentice-Hall, 1968.

LaFeber, Walter. *America, Russia, and the Cold War, 1945–1975*. 3d ed. New York: Wiley, 1976.

LaFeber, Walter, comp. *America in the Cold War: Twenty Years of Revolutions and Response, 1947–1967*. New York: Wiley, 1969.

Lukacs, John A. *The Great Powers and Eastern Europe*. New York: American Book, 1953.

Messer, Robert. *The End of an Alliance: James F. Byrnes, Roosevelt, Truman, and the Origins of the Cold War*. Chapel Hill: University of North Carolina Press, 1982.

Paterson, Thomas. *Meeting the Communist Threat: Truman to Reagan*. New York: Oxford University Press, 1988.

Paterson, Thomas. *Soviet-American Confrontation: Postwar Reconstruction and the Origins of the Cold War*. Baltimore: Johns Hopkins University Press, 1973.

Paterson, Thomas, ed. *Containment and the Cold War*. Reading, Mass.: Addison, 1973.

Paterson, Thomas, ed. *On Every Front: The Making of the Cold War*. New York: Norton, 1979.

Pollard, Robert A. *Economic Security and the Origins of the Cold War, 1945–1950*. New York: Columbia University Press, 1985.

Quester, George H. *Nuclear Diplomacy: The First Twenty-five Years*. New York: Dunellen, 1970.

Rearden, Steven L. *The Evolution of American Strategic Doctrine: Paul H. Nitze and the Soviet Challenge*. SAIS Papers in International Affairs, No. 4. Boulder, Colo.: Westview, 1984.

Rees, David. *The Age of Containment: The Cold War, 1945–1965*. New York: St. Martin's Press, 1967.

Rothwell, Victor. *Britain and the Cold War, 1941–1947*. London: Cape, 1982.

Thomas, Hugh. *Armed Truce: The Beginnings of the Cold War, 1945–1946*. New York: Atheneum, 1987.

Ulam, Adam B. *The Rivals: America and Russia Since World War II*. New York: Viking, 1971.

Yergin, Daniel. *Shattered Peace: The Origins of the Cold War and the National Security State*. Boston: Houghton Mifflin, 1977.

1.1 Topics and Issues

The Cuban Missile Crisis

Allison, Graham T. *Essence of Decision: Explaining the Cuban Missile Crisis*. Boston: Little, Brown, 1971.

Blight, James G. and David A. Welch. *On the Brink: Americans and Soviets Reexamine the Cuban Missile Crisis*. New York: Hill & Wang, 1989.

Wyden, Peter S. *Bay of Pigs: The Untold Story*. New York: Simon & Schuster, 1979.

Espionage

Andrew, Christopher. *Secret Service: The Making of the British Intelligence Community*. London: Heinemann, 1985.

Boyle, Andrew. *The Climate of Treason: Five Who Spied for Russia*. London: Hutchinson, 1979.

Cecil, Robert. *A Divided Life: A Personal Portrait of The Spy Donald Maclean*. New York: Morrow, 1989.

Costello, John. *Mask of Treachery*. New York: Morrow, 1988.

Glees, Anthony. *The Secrets of the Service*. London: Cape, 1987; New York: Carroll & Graf, 1987.

Page, Bruce, David Leitch, and Phillip Knightly. *Philby: The Spy Who Betrayed a Generation*. London: Deutsch, 1968. Republished as *The Philby Conspiracy*. Garden City, N.Y.: Doubleday, 1968.

Seale, Patrick, and Maureen McConville. *Philby: The Long Road to Moscow*. London: Hamish Hamilton, 1973.

Weinstein, Allen. *Perjury – the Hiss-Chambers Case*. New York: Knopf, 1978.

The Marshall Plan

Arkes, Hadley. *Bureaucracy, the Marshall Plan, and the National Interest*. Princeton: Princeton University Press, 1972.

Gimbel, John. *The Origins of the Marshall Plan*. Stanford: Stanford University Press, 1976.

Hoffmann, Stanley, and Charles S. Maier, eds. *The Marshall Plan: A Retrospective*. Boulder, Colo.: Westview, 1984.

Hogan, Michael J. *The Marshall Plan: America, Britain and the Reconstruction of Western Europe, 1947–1952*. New York: Cambridge University Press, 1987.

NATO

Henderson, Nicholas. *The Birth of NATO*. London: Wiedenfeld & Nicholson, 1982.

Ireland, Timothy P. *Creating the Entangling Alliance: The Origins of the North Atlantic Treaty Organization*. Westport, Conn.: Greenwood Press, 1981.

Joffe, Josef. *The Limited Partnership: Europe, the United States, and the Burdens of Alliance*. Cambridge: Ballinger, 1987.

Kaplan, Lawrence S. *A Community of Interests: NATO and the Military Assistance Program, 1948–1951*. Washington, D.C.: Office of the Secretary of Defense, Historical Office, 1980.

Kaplan, Lawrence S. *The United States and NATO: The Formative Years*. Lexington: University of Kentucky, 1984.

Suez

Lloyd, Selwyn. *Suez 1956: A Personal Account*. London: Cape, 1978.

Shuckburgh, Evelyn. *Descent to Suez*. London: Weidenfeld & Nicolson, 1986.

Thomas, Hugh. *The Suez Affair*. London: Weidenfeld & Nicolson, 1967.

2. Interpretive Analysis

DePorte, Anton W. *Europe between the Superpowers: The Enduring Balance*. New Haven: Yale University Press, 1979.

Gaddis, John Lewis. *The Long Peace: Inquiries into the History of the Cold War*. New York: Oxford University Press, 1987.

Gaddis, John Lewis. *Strategies of Containment: A Critical Appraisal of Postwar American National Security Policy*. New York: Oxford University Press, 1982.

Melanson, Richard. *Writing History and Making Policy: The Cold War, Vietnam, and Revisionism*. Lanham, Md.: University Press of America, 1983.

Paterson, Thomas G., ed. *Cold War Critics: Alternatives to American Foreign Policy in the Truman Years*. Chicago: Quadrangle Books, 1971.

Ruff, R. M. *Orthodox, Realist, and Revisionist Interpretations of the Origins of the Cold War, 1962-1972*. PhD. dissertation, University of Georgia, 1973.

Tucker, Robert W. *Nation or Empire? The Debate over American Foreign Policy*. Baltimore: Johns Hopkins University Press, 1968.

2.1 Revisionist Interpretation

Alperovitz, Gar. *Atomic Diplomacy: Hiroshima and Potsdam; The Use of the Atomic Bomb and the American Confrontation with Soviet Power*. New York: Simon & Schuster, 1965.

Barnet, Richard J., and Marcus G. Raskin. *After Twenty Years: Alternatives to the Cold War in Europe*. New York: Random House, 1965.

Fleming, Denna Frank. *The Cold War and Its Origins, 1917–1960*. Garden City, N.Y.: Doubleday, 1961.

Horowitz, David. *Containment and Revolution*. Boston: Beacon, 1967.

Horowitz, David. *The Free World Colossus: A Critique of American Foreign Policy in the Cold War*. New York: Hill & Wang, 1965.

Kolko, Joyce, and Gabriel Kolko. *The Limits of Power: The World and the United States Foreign Policy, 1945–1954.* New York: Harper & Row, 1972.

Ruff, R. M. *Orthodox, Realist, and Revisionist Interpretations of the Origins of the Cold War.* PhD. dissertation, University of Georgia, 1973.

Williams, William Appleman. *The Tragedy of American Diplomacy.* Cleveland: World, 1959.

3. U.S. Policies by Region and Country

Asia

Baldwin, Frank, ed. *Without Parallel: The American-Korean Relationship Since 1945.* New York: Pantheon, 1974.

Barnds, William. *China and America: The Search for a New Relationship.* New York: New York University Press, 1977.

Borg, Dorothy, and Waldo Heinrichs, eds. *Uncertain Years: Chinese-American Relations, 1947–1950.* New York: Columbia University Press, 1980.

Buhite, Russell D. *Soviet-American Relations in Asia, 1945–1954.* Norman, Okla.: University of Oklahoma Press, 1981.

Dobbs, Charles M. *American Foreign Policy, the Cold War, and Korea, 1945–1950.* Kent, Ohio: Kent State University Press, 1981.

Donovan, Robert J. *The Devastating Times: The Hydrogen Bomb, China, and Korea.* Working Papers No. 6, Wilson Center, International Security Studies Program, Washington, D.C., 19 April 1979.

Fairbank, John K. *The United States and China,* 4th ed. Cambridge: Harvard University Press, 1979.

Hess, Gary R. *The United States' Emergence as a Southeast Asian Power, 1940–1950.* New York: Columbia University Press, 1987.

Jiang, Arnold Xiangze. *The United States and China.* Chicago: University of Chicago Press, 1988.

Matray, James. *The Reluctant Crusade: American Foreign Policy in Korea, 1941–1950.* Honolulu: University of Hawaii Press, 1985.

Tucker, Nancy Bernkopf. *Patterns in the Dust: Chinese-American Relations and the Recognition Controversy, 1949–1950.* New York: Columbia University Press, 1983.

The Korean War

Appleman, Roy E. *South to the Naktong, North to the Yalu: June–November 1950.* Washington, D.C.: Office of the Chief of Military History, 1960.

Blair, Clay. *The Forgotten War: America in Korea, 1950–1953.* New York: Times books, 1987.

Cumings, Bruce. *The Origins of the Korean War: Liberation and the Emergence of Separate Regimes, 1945–1947.* Princeton: Princeton University Press, 1981.

Cumings, Bruce, ed. *Child of Conflict: The Korean-American Relationship, 1943–1953.* Seattle: University of Washington Press, 1983.

Foot, Rosemary. *A Substitute for Victory: The Politics of Peacemaking at the Korean Armistice Talks.* Ithaca, N.Y.: Cornell University Press, 1990.

Foot, Rosemary. *The Wrong War: American Policy and the Dimensions of the Korean Conflict, 1950–1953.* Ithaca, N.Y.: Cornell University Press, 1985.

Kaufman, Burton I. *The Korean War: Challenges in Crisis, Credibility, and Command.* Philadelphia: Temple University Press, 1986.

MacDonald, Callum A. *Korea: The War Before Vietnam.* New York: Free Press/Macmillan, 1986.

Paige, Glenn D. *The Korean Decision, June 24–30, 1950.* New York: Free Press, 1968.

Simmons, Robert R. *The Strained Alliance: Peking, P'yongyang, Moscow, and the Politics of the Korean War.* New York: Free Press, 1975.

Germany

Backer, John H. *The Decision to Divide Germany: American Foreign Policy in Transition.* Durham: Duke University Press, 1978.

Backer, John H. *Priming the German Economy: American Occupational Policies, 1945–1948.* Durham: Duke University Press, 1971.

Backer, John H. *Winds of History: The German Years of Lucius DuBignon Clay.* New York: Van Nostrand Reinhold, 1983.

Bark, Dennis L., and David R. Gress. *A History of West Germany; 1: From Shadow to Substance, 1945–1963; 2: Democracy and Its Discontents, 1963–1988.* Oxford & New York: Blackwell, 1989.

Deighton, Anne. *The Impossible Peace: Britain, the Division of Germany, and the Origins of the Cold War.* New York: Oxford University Press, 1990.

Gimbel, John. *The American Occupation of Germany: Politics and the Military, 1945–1949.* Stanford: Stanford University Press, 1968.

Kuklick, Bruce. *American Policy and the Division of Germany: The Clash with Russia over Reparations.* Ithaca, N.Y.: Cornell University Press, 1972.

McGeehan, Robert. *The German Rearmament Question: American Diplomacy and European Defense after World War II.* Urbana: University of Illinois Press, 1971.

Schwartz, Thomas A. *From Occupation to Alliance: John J. McCloy and the Allied High Commission in the Federal Republic of Germany, 1949–1952.* PhD. dissertation, Harvard University, 1985.

Shlaim, Avi. *The United States and the Berlin Blockade, 1948–1949: A Study in Crisis Decision-making.* Berkeley: University of California Press, 1983.

Eastern Europe
Cronin, Audrey. *Great Power Politics and the Struggle over Austria, 1945–1955.* Ithaca, N.Y.: Cornell University Press, 1986.

Davis, Lynn Etheridge. *The Cold War Begins: Soviet-American Conflict over Eastern Europe.* Princeton: Princeton University Press, 1974.

Middle and Near East
Alroy, Gil Carl. *The Kissinger Experience: American Policy in the Middle East.* New York: Horizon, 1975.

Bill, James. *The Eagle and the Lion: The Tragedy of American-Iranian Relations.* New Haven: Yale University Press, 1988.

Cottam, Richard W. *Iran and the United States: A Cold War Case Study.* Pittsburgh: University of Pittsburgh Press, 1988.

Dowty, Alan. *Middle East Crisis: U.S. Decision-making in 1958, 1970, and 1973.* Berkeley: University of California Press, 1984.

Kelly, John B. *Arabia, the Gulf and the West.* New York: Basic Books, 1980.

Kuniholm, Bruce. *The Origins of the Cold War in the Near East: Great Power Conflict and Diplomacy in Iran, Turkey, and Greece.* Princeton: Princeton University Press, 1980.

Louis, William Roger. *The British Empire in the Middle East, 1945–1951: Arab Nationalism, the United States, and Postwar Imperialism.* New York: Oxford University Press, 1984.

Quandt, William B. *Decade of Decisions: American Policy toward the Arab-Israeli Conflict, 1967–1976.* Berkeley: University of California Press, 1977.

Sheehan, Edward. *The Arabs, Israelis and Kissinger: A Secret History of American Diplomacy in the Middle East.* New York: Reader's Digest Press, 1976.

Sick, Gary. *All Fall Down: America's Tragic Encounter with Iran.* New York: Random House, 1985.

Spiegel, Steven. *The Other Arab-Israeli Conflict: Making America's Middle East Policy from Truman to Reagan.* Chicago: University of Chicago Press, 1985.

Tillman, Seth. *The United States in the Middle East, Interests and Obstacles.* Bloomington: Indiana University Press, 1982.

Whetten, Lawrence L. *The Canal War: Four-Power Conflict in the Middle-East.* Cambridge: MIT Press, 1974.

U.S.-British Relations
Clarke, Sir Richard William Barnes. *Anglo-American Economic Collaboration in War and Peace, 1942–1949.* Edited by Sir Alec Cairncross. Oxford: Clarendon Press, 1982; New York: Oxford University Press, 1982.

Hathaway, Robert M. *Ambiguous Partnership: Britain and America, 1944–1947.* New York: Columbia University Press, 1981.

Louis, William Roger. *Imperialism at Bay 1941–1945: The United States and the Decolonization of the British Empire.* Oxford: Clarendon Press, 1977; New York: Oxford University Press, 1978.

McDonald, Ian S., ed. *Anglo-American Relations Since the Second World War.* New York: St. Martin's Press, 1974.

Ovendale, Ritchie. *The English-Speaking Alliance: Britain, the United States, the Dominions and the Cold War, 1945–1951.* London & Boston: Allen & Unwin, 1985.

U.S.-Soviet Relations
Blight, James G., and David A. Welch. *On the Brink: Americans and Soviets Reexamine the Cuban Missile Crisis.* New York: Hill & Wang, 1989.

Hyland, William. *Mortal Rivals: Superpower Relations from Nixon to Reagan.* New York: Random House, 1987.

4. The Vietnam War
Berman, Larry. *Planning a Tragedy: The Americanization of the War in Vietnam.* New York: Norton, 1982.

Colby, William. *Honorable Men: My Life in the CIA.* New York: Simon & Schuster, 1978.

Fitzgerald, Francis. *Fire in the Lake: The Vietnamese and the Americans in Vietnam.* Boston: Little, Brown, 1972.

Gelb, Leslie H., and Richard K. Betts. *The Irony of Vietnam: The System Worked.* Washington, D.C.: Brookings Institution, 1979.

Halberstam, David. *The Best and the Brightest.* New York: Random House, 1972

Havens, Thomas. *Fire across the Sea: The Vietnam War and Japan.* Princeton: Princeton University Press, 1987.

Herring, George C. *America's Longest War: The United States and Vietnam, 1950–1975.* New York: Wiley, 1979.

Herring, George C., ed. *The Secret Diplomacy of the Vietnam War: The Negotiating Volumes of the Pentagon Papers.* Austin: University of Texas Press, 1983.

Isaacs, Arnold R. *Without Honor: Defeat in Vietnam and Cambodia.* Baltimore: Johns Hopkins University Press, 1983.

Kahin, George. *Intervention: How America Became Involved in Vietnam.* New York: Knopf, 1986.

Parker, F. Charles. *Vietnam, Strategy for a Stalemate.* New York: Paragon House, 1989.

The Pentagon Papers: As Published by the New York Times. New York: Quadrangle Books, 1971.

Porter, Gareth. *A Peace Denied: The United States, Vietnam and the Paris Agreements.* Bloomington: Indiana University Press, 1975.

Schandler, Herbert. *The Unmaking of a President: Lyndon Johnson and Vietnam.* Princeton: Princeton University Press, 1977.

Schurmann, Franz. *The Logic of World Power: An Inquiry into the Origins, Currents, and Contradictions of World Politics.* New York: Pantheon, 1974.

Shawcross, William. *Sideshow: Kissinger, Nixon and the Destruction of Cambodia.* New York: Simon & Schuster, 1979.

Small, Melvin. *Johnson, Nixon, and the Doves.* New Brunswick: Rutgers University Press, 1988.

Snepp, Frank. *Decent Interval: An Insider's Account of Saigon's Indecent End.* New York: Random House, 1977.

5. Post-Vietnam U.S. Foreign Policy

Barber, Stephen. *America in Retreat.* Galeshead, U.K.: Northumberland Press, 1970.

Bell, Coral. *The Diplomacy of Detente: The Kissinger Era.* New York: St. Martin's Press, 1977.

Brandon, Henry. *The Retreat of American Power.* Garden City, N.Y.: Doubleday, 1973.

Buchan, Alastair. *The End of the Postwar Era: A New Balance of World Power.* London: Weidenfeld & Nicolson, 1974.

Buchan, Alastair. *Power and Equilibrium in the 1970s.* New York. Praeger, 1973.

Caldwell, Dan. *American-Soviet Relations: From 1947 to the Nixon-Kissinger Grand Design.* Westport, Conn.: Greenwood Press, 1981.

Chace, James. *A World Elsewhere: The New American Foreign Policy.* New York: Scribners, 1973.

Cox, Arthur. *The Dynamics of Detente.* New York: Norton, 1976.

Gardner, Lloyd C. *The Great Nixon Turn-around: America's New Foreign Policy in the Post-Liberal Era (How a Cold Warrior Climbed Clean Out of His Skin); Essays and Articles with an Introductory Statement.* New York: New Viewpoints, 1973.

Garthoff, Raymond. *Detente and Confrontation: American-Soviet Relations from Nixon to Reagan.* Washington, D.C.: Brookings Institution, 1985.

Hartley, Anthony. *American Foreign Policy in the Nixon Era.* Adelphi Papers no. 110. London: International Institute for Strategic Studies, Winter 1974–1975.

Hoffmann, Stanley. *Primacy or World Order: American Foreign Policy Since The Cold War.* New York: McGraw-Hill, 1978.

Hood, Donald. *"Lessons" of the Vietnam War: Henry Kissinger, George F. Kennan, Richard Falk and the Debate over Containment, 1965–1980.* PhD. dissertation, University of Washington, 1982.

Hyland, William. *Mortal Rivals: Superpower Relations from Nixon to Reagan.* New York: Random House, 1987.

Jones, Alan M., Jr., ed. *U.S. Foreign Policy in a Changing World: The Nixon Administration, 1969–1973.* New York: McKay, 1973.

Kattenburg, Paul. *The Vietnam Trauma in American Foreign Policy, 1945–75.* New Brunswick: Transaction Books, 1980.

Litwak, Robert S. *Detente and the Nixon Doctrine: American Foreign Policy and the Pursuit of Stability, 1969–1976.* New York: Cambridge University Press, 1984.

Morris, Roger. *Uncertain Greatness: Henry Kissinger and American Foreign Policy.* New York: Harper & Row, 1977.

Newhouse, John. *Cold Dawn: The Story of SALT.* New York: Holt, Rinehart & Winston, 1973.

Osgood, Robert, et al. *Retreat from Empire? the First Nixon Administration.* Baltimore: Johns Hopkins University Press, 1973.

Rosecrance, Richard, ed. *America as an Ordinary Country: U.S. Foreign Policy and the Future.* Ithaca, N.Y.: Cornell University Press, 1976.

Smith, Gerard. *Doubletalk: The Story of the First Strategic Arms Limitation Talks.* Garden City, N.Y.: Doubleday, 1980.

Sobel, Lester, ed. *Kissinger & Detente.* New York: Facts on File, 1975.

Stevenson, Richard. *The Rise and Fall of Detente: Relaxations of Tension in US-Soviet Relations, 1953–84.* Urbana: University of Illinois Press, 1985.

Sulzberger, C. L. *The World and Richard Nixon.* New York: Prentice-Hall, 1987.

Szulc, Tad. *The Illusion of Peace: Foreign Policy in the Nixon Years.* New York: Viking, 1978.

6. Memoirs of Participants

Acheson, Dean G. *Power and Diplomacy.* Cambridge: Harvard University Press, 1958.

Acheson, Dean G. *Present at the Creation: My Years in the State Department.* New York: Norton, 1969.

Acheson, Dean G. *Sketches from Life of Men I Have Known.* New York: Harper & Row, 1961.

Adenauer, Konrad. *Memoirs, 1945–1953.* Translated by Beate Ruhm von Oppen. Chicago: Regnery, 1966.

Attlee, Clement R. *As It Happened.* New York: Viking, 1954.

Attlee, Clement R. *Twilight of Empire: Memoirs of Prime Minister Clement Attlee.* New York: Barnes, 1962.

Ball, George. *The Discipline of Power: Essentials of a Modern World Structure.* Boston: Little, Brown, 1968.

Bidault, Georges. *Resistance: The Political Autobiography of Georges Bidault.* Translated by Marianne Sinclair. New York: Praeger, 1967.

Bohlen, Charles E. *The Transformation of American Foreign Policy.* New York: Norton, 1969.

Bohlen, Charles E. *Witness to History, 1929–1969.* New York: Norton, 1973.

Brandt, Willy. *People and Politics: The Years 1960–1975.* Boston: Little, Brown, 1978.

Clay, Lucius D. *The Papers of General Lucius D. Clay. Vol. I: Germany, 1945–1949,* edited by Jean E. Smith. Bloomington: Indiana University Press, 1974.

Colby, William. *Honorable Men: My Life in the CIA.* New York: Simon & Schuster, 1978.

Crossman, Richard. *The Diaries of a Cabinet Minister,* 3 vols. London: Hamilton & Cape, 1975–1977.

Dalton, Hugh. *High Tide and After: Memoirs, 1945–1960.* London: Muller, 1962.

Dobney, Frederick J., Jr., ed. *Selected Papers of Will Clayton.* Baltimore: Johns Hopkins University Press, 1971.

Eden, Anthony. *Full Circle.* Boston: Houghton Mifflin, 1960.

Eisenhower, Dwight D. *The White House Years,* 2 vols. Garden City, N.Y.: Doubleday, 1963.

Ferrell, Robert H., ed. *The Autobiography of Harry S. Truman.* Boulder, Colo.: Associated University Press, 1980.

Ferrell, Robert H., ed. *Off the Record: The Private Papers of Harry S. Truman.* New York: Harper & Row, 1980.

Forrestal, James. *The Forrestal Diaries: The Inner History of the Cold War,* edited by Walter Millis and E. S. Duffield. New York: Viking, 1951.

Gaitskell, Hugh. *The Diary of Hugh Gaitskell, 1945–1956,* edited by Philip M. Williams. London: Cape, 1983.

Haig, Alexander M. *Caveat: Realism, Reagan, and Foreign Policy.* New York: Macmillan, 1984.

Harriman, W. Averell. *America and Russia in a Changing World: A Half Century of Personal Observation.* Garden City, N.Y.: Doubleday, 1971.

Hoffmann, Paul G. *Peace Can Be Won.* Garden City, N.Y.: Doubleday, 1951.

Jenkins, Roy. *Partnership of Principle.* London: Secker & Warburg, 1985.

Kennan, George Frost. *Memoirs: 1925–1950.* Boston: Little, Brown, 1967.

Kennan, George Frost. *Memoirs, 1950–1963.* Boston: Little, Brown, 1972.

Kissinger, Henry. *White House Years.* Boston: Little, Brown, 1979.

Kissinger, Henry. *Years of Upheaval.* Boston: Little, Brown, 1982.

Lloyd, Selwyn. *Suez 1956: A Personal Account.* London: Cape, 1978.

Macmillan, Harold. *Pointing the Way.* London: Macmillan, 1972; New York: Harper & Row, 1972.

Macmillan, Harold. *Riding the Storm, 1956-1959.* London: Macmillan, 1971; New York: Harper & Row, 1971.

Macmillan, Harold. *Tides of Fortune, 1945–1955.* London: Macmillan, 1969; New York: Harper & Row, 1969.

Monnet, Jean. *Memoirs.* Translated by Richard Mayne. Garden City, N.Y.: Doubleday, 1978.

Morrison, Herbert. *Herbert Morrison: An Autobiography.* London: Odhams, 1960.

Nixon, Richard M. *In the Arena: A Memoir of Victory, Defeat and Renewal.* New York: Simon & Schuster, 1990.

Nixon, Richard M. *R N: The Memoirs of Richard Nixon.* New York: Grosset & Dunlap, 1978.

Nixon, Richard M. *Six Crises.* Garden City, N.Y.: Doubleday, 1962.

Owen, David. *Face the Future.* London: Cape, 1981.

Owen, David. *David Owen: Personally Speaking to Kenneth Harris.* London: Weidenfeld & Nicolson, 1987.

Spaak, Paul Henri Charles. *The Continuing Battle: Memoirs of a European, 1936–1966.* Translated by Henry Fox. Boston: Little, Brown, 1971.

Stettinius, Edward R. *Roosevelt and the Russians: The Yalta Conference.* Garden City, N.Y.: Doubleday, 1949.

Taylor, Maxwell D. *Swords and Plowshares.* New York: Norton, 1972.

Thatcher, Margaret. *In Defence of Freedom: Speeches on Britain's Relations with the World 1976–1986.* London: Aurum Press, 1986; Buffalo, N.Y.: Prometheus, 1987.

Truman, Harry S. *Memoirs, Vol. I: Year of Decisions.* Garden City, N.Y.: Doubleday, 1955.

Truman, Harry S. *Memoirs, Vol. II: Years of Trial and Hope.* Garden City, N.Y.: Doubleday, 1956.

Vandenberg, Arthur H. *The Private Papers of Senator Vandenberg.* Boston: Houghton Mifflin, 1952.

Walters, Vernon. *Silent Missions.* Garden City, N.Y.: Doubleday, 1978.

Williams, Edward Francis. *A Prime Minister Remembers: The War and Post-war Memoirs of the Rt. Hon. Earl Attlee Based on His Private Papers and on a Series of Recorded Conversations.* London: Heinemann, 1961.

6.1 Evaluation of Individual Policymakers, Including Biographical and Cognitive Analysis

Abrahamsen, David. *Nixon Vs. Nixon: An Emotional Tragedy.* New York: Farrar, Straus & Giroux, 1977.

Adams, Sherman. *Firsthand Report: The Story of the Eisenhower Administration.* New York: Harper & Row, 1961.

Ambrose, Stephen E. *Eisenhower, Vol. II, the President.* New York: Simon & Schuster, 1984.

Ambrose, Stephen E. *Nixon: The Education of a Politician, 1913–1962.* New York: Simon & Schuster, 1987.

Ambrose, Stephen E. *Nixon: The Triumph of a Politician, 1962-1972.* New York: Simon and Schuster, 1989.

Bernstein, Barton, ed. *Politics and Policies of the Truman Administration.* Chicago: Quadrangle Books, 1970.

Bernstein, Barton, and Allen Matusow, eds. *The Truman Administration: A Documentary History.* New York: Harper & Row, 1966.

Beschloss, Michael R. *The Crisis Years: Kennedy and Khrushchev, 1960–1963.* New York: Burlingame, 1991.

Brendon, Piers. *Ike: His Life and Times.* New York: Harper & Row, 1986.

Brodie, Fawn. *Richard Nixon: The Shaping of His Character.* New York: Norton, 1981.

Caldwell, Dan, ed. *Henry Kissinger: His Personality and Policies.* Durham: Duke University Press, 1983.

Callahan, David. *Dangerous Capabilities: Paul Nitze and the Cold War.* New York: HarperCollins, 1990.

Costello, William. *The Facts about Nixon: An Unauthorized Biography.* New York: Viking, 1960.

Dickson, Peter. *Kissinger and the Meaning of History.* New York: Cambridge University Press, 1978.

Donovan, Robert J. *Conflict and Crisis: The Presidency of Harry S. Truman, 1945–1948.* New York: Norton, 1977.

Donovan, Robert J. *Tumultuous Years: The Presidency of Harry S. Truman, 1949–1953.* New York: Norton, 1982.

Gardner, Lloyd. *Architects of Illusion: Men and Ideas in American Foreign Policy, 1941–1949.* Chicago: Quadrangle Books, 1970.

Gellman, Barton. *Contending with Kennan: Toward a Philosophy of American Power.* New York: Praeger, 1984.

Graubard, Stephen. *Kissinger: Portrait of a Mind.* New York: Norton, 1973.

Guhin, Michael A. *John Foster Dulles: A Statesman and His Times.* New York: Columbia University Press, 1972.

Hamby, Alonzo L. *Beyond the New Deal: Harry S. Truman and American Liberalism.* New York: Columbia University Press, 1973.

Hersh, Seymour. *The Price of Power: Kissinger in the Nixon White House.* New York: Summit Books, 1983.

Hixson, Walter L. *George F. Kennan, Cold War Iconoclast.* New York: Columbia University Press, 1989.

Hoopes, Townsend. *The Devil and John Foster Dulles.* Boston: Little, Brown, 1973.

Hughes, Emmet John. *The Ordeal of Power.* New York: Atheneum, 1963.

Immerman, Richard H., ed. *John Foster Dulles and the Diplomacy of the Cold War: A Reappraisal.* Princeton: Princeton University Press, 1989.

Isaacson, Walter, and Evan Thomas. *The Wise Men: Six Friends and the World They Made: Acheson, Bohlen, Harriman, Kennan, Lovett, McCloy.* New York: Simon & Schuster, 1986.

Kalb, Marvin, and Bernard Kalb. *Kissinger.* Boston: Little, Brown, 1974.

Kearns, Doris. *Lyndon Johnson and the American Dream.* New York: Harper & Row, 1976.

Kornitzer, Bela. *The Real Nixon: An Intimate Biography.* New York: Rand McNally, 1960.

Landau, David. *Kissinger: The Uses of Power.* Boston: Houghton Mifflin, 1972.

Larson, Deborah. *Origins of Containment: A Psychological Explanation.* Princeton: Princeton University Press, 1985.

Lyon, Peter. *Eisenhower: Portrait of the Hero.* Boston: Little, Brown, 1974.

McLellan, David S. *Dean Acheson: The State Department Years.* New York: Dodd, Mead, 1976.

Maddox, Robert J. *From War to Cold War: The Education of Harry S. Truman.* Boulder, Colo.: Westview, 1988.

Manchester, William. *American Caesar: Douglas MacArthur, 1880–1964.* Boston: Little, Brown, 1978.

Mankiewicz, Frank. *Perfectly Clear: Nixon from Whittier to Watergate.* New York: Quadrangle Books, 1973.

Markowitz, Norman. *The Rise and Fall of the People's Century: Henry A. Wallace and American Liberalism, 1941–1948.* New York: Free Press, 1973.

Martin, John Bartlow. *Adlai Stevenson and the World: The Life of Adlai E. Stevenson.* Garden City, N.Y.: Doubleday, 1977.

Martin, John Bartlow. *Adlai Stevenson of Illinois: The Life of Adlai E. Stevenson.* Garden City, N.Y.: Doubleday, 1976.

Mayers, David. *George Kennan and the Dilemmas of US Foreign Policy.* New York: Oxford University Press, 1988.

Mazlish, Bruce. *Kissinger: The European Mind in American Policy.* New York: Basic Books, 1976.

Mazlish, Bruce. *In Search of Nixon: A Psychohistorical Inquiry.* New York: Basic Books, 1972.

Mazo, Earl. *Richard Nixon: A Political and Personal Portrait.* New York: Harper, 1959.

Mazo, Earl, and Stephen Hess. *Nixon: A Political Portrait.* New York: Harper & Row, 1968.

Melanson, Richard, and David Mayers, eds. *Reevaluating Eisenhower: American Foreign Policy in the 1950s.* Urbana: University of Illinois Press, 1986.

Miller, Merle. *Plain Speaking: An Oral Biography of Harry S. Truman.* New York: Berkeley, 1974.

Morris, Roger. *Haig: The General's Progress.* New York: Playboy Press, 1982.

Morris, Roger. *Richard Milhouse Nixon: The Rise of an American Politician.* New York: Holt, 1990.

Nitze, Paul H., Ann M. Smith, and Steven L. Rearden. *From Hiroshima to Glasnost: At the Center of Decision — a Memoir.* New York: Grove Weidenfeld, 1989.

O'Brien, Michael. *McCarthy and McCarthyism in Wisconsin.* Columbia: University of Missouri Press, 1980.

Oshinsky, David. *A Conspiracy So Immense: The World of Joe McCarthy.* New York: Free Press, 1983.

Parmet, Herbert S. *Eisenhower and the American Crusades.* New York: Macmillan, 1972.

Parmet, Herbert S. *Richard Nixon and His America.* Boston: Little, Brown, 1990.

Patterson, James T. *Mr. Republican: A Biography of Robert A. Taft.* Boston: Houghton Mifflin, 1972.

Powers, Thomas. *The Man Who Kept the Secrets: Richard Helms and the CIA.* New York: Knopf, 1979.

Pruessen, Ronald W. *John Foster Dulles: The Road to Power.* New York: Free Press, 1982.

Raucher, Alan R. *Paul G. Hoffman: Architect of Foreign Aid.* Lexington: University Press of Kentucky, 1986.

Rearden, Steven L. *The Evolution of American Strategic Doctrine: Paul H. Nitze and the Soviet Challenge.* SAIS Papers in International Affairs, No. 4. Boulder, Colo.: Westview, 1984; Washington, D.C.: Foreign Policy Institute, School of Advanced International Studies, Johns Hopkins University, 1984.

Reeves, Thomas C. *The Life and Times of Joe McCarthy.* New York: Stein & Day, 1982.

Reeves, Thomas C. *A Question of Character: JFK, Image and Reality.* New York: Free Press, 1991.

Rovere, Richard H. *Senator Joe McCarthy.* New York: Harcourt, Brace, 1959.

Schandler, Herbert. *The Unmaking of a President: Lyndon Johnson and Vietnam.* Princeton: Princeton University Press, 1977.

Smith, Michael Joseph. *Realist Thought from Weber to Kissinger.* Baton Rouge: Louisiana State University Press, 1986.

Spanier, John. *The Truman-MacArthur Controversy and the Korean War.* Cambridge, Mass: Belknap Press at Harvard University, 1959.

Starr, Harvey. *Henry Kissinger: Perceptions of International Politics.* Lexington: University Press of Kentucky, 1984.

Steel, Ronald. *Walter Lippmann and the American Century.* Boston: Little, Brown, 1980.

Stephanson, Anders. *Kennan and the Art of Foreign Policy.* Cambridge: Harvard University Press, 1989.

Stoessinger, John G. *Crusaders and Pragmatists: Movers of Modern American Foreign Policy.* New York: Norton, 1979.

Stoessinger, John G. *Henry Kissinger: The Anguish of Power.* New York: Norton, 1976.

Talbott, Strobe. *The Master of the Game: Paul Nitze and the Nuclear Peace.* New York: Knopf, 1988.

Wicker, Tom. *One of Us: Richard Nixon and the American Dream.* New York: Random House, 1991.

Wills, Garry. *Nixon Agonistes: The Crisis of the Self-made Man.* Boston: Houghton Mifflin, 1970.

Witcover, Jules. *The Resurrection of Richard Nixon.* New York: Putnam's, 1970.

European Politicians

Barclay, Sir Roderick. *Ernest Bevin and the Foreign Office, 1932–1969.* London: Latimer, 1975.

Binder, David. *The Other German: Willy Brandt's Life and Times.* Washington, D.C.: New Republic, 1975.

Blake, Robert. *The Conservative Party from Peel to Thatcher.* London: Methuen, 1985.

Bruce-Gardyne, Jock. *Mrs. Thatcher's First Administration: The Prophets Confounded.* New York: St. Martin's Press, 1984.

Bullock, Alan. *Ernest Bevin: Foreign Secretary, 1945–1951.* New York: Norton, 1983.

Burridge, Trevor. *Clement Attlee, a Political Biography.* London: Cape, 1985.

Butler, David, and Dennis Kavanagh. *The British General Election of 1979.* London: Macmillan, 1980.

Carlton, David. *Anthony Eden: A Biography.* London: Lane, 1981.

Carr, Jonathan. *Helmut Schmidt: Helmsman of Germany.* London: Weidenfeld & Nicolson, 1985; New York: St. Martin's Press, 1985.

Churchill, Randolph S. *The Fight for the Tory Leadership: A Contemporary Chronicle.* London: Heinemann, 1964; Boston: Houghton Mifflin, 1964.

Churchill, Randolph. *The Rise and Fall of Sir Anthony Eden.* London: MacGibbon & Kee, 1959; New York: Putnam's, 1959.

Cooke, Colin. *The Life of Richard Stafford Cripps.* London: Hodder & Stoughton, 1957.

Donoughue, Bernard. *Prime Minister: The Conduct of Policy under Harold Wilson and James Callaghan, 1974–1979.* London: Cape, 1987.

Donoughue, Bernard, and G. W. Jones. *Herbert Morrison: Portrait of a Politician.* London: Weidenfeld & Nicolson, 1973.

Edinger, Lewis J. *Kurt Schumacher: A Study in Personality and Political Behavior.* Stanford: Stanford University Press, 1965.

Evans, Harold. *Downing Street Diary: The Macmillan Years, 1957–63.* London: Hodder & Stoughton, 1981.

Fisher, Sir Nigel. *Harold Macmillan: A Biography.* London: Weidenfeld & Nicolson, 1982; New York: St. Martin's Press, 1982.

Fisher, Nigel. *Ian Macleod.* London: Deutsch, 1973.

Foot, Michael. *Aneurin Bevan: A Biography.* New York: Atheneum, 1974.

Gardiner, George. *Margaret Thatcher: From Childhood to Leadership.* London: Kimber, 1975.

Hall, Stuart, and Martin Jacques, eds. *The Politics of Thatcherism.* London: Lawrence & Wishart, 1983.

Harris, Kenneth. *Attlee.* London: Weidenfeld & Nicolson, 1982.

Holmes, Martin. *The First Thatcher Government, 1979–1983.* London: Wheatsheaf Books, 1985.

Howard, Anthony. *RAB: The Life of R. A. Butler.* London: Cape, 1987.

Kavanagh, Dennis, ed. *Thatcherism and British Politics: The End of Consensus?.* Oxford & New York: Oxford University Press, 1987.

Keegan, William. *Mrs. Thatcher's Economic Experiment.* London: Lane, 1984.

Laqueur, Walter. *Stalin: The Glasnost Revelations.* New York: Scribners, 1990.

Minogue, Kenneth, and Michael Biddis, eds. *Thatcherism: Personality and Politics.* London: Macmillan, 1987; New York: St. Martin's Press, 1987.

Pimlott, Ben. *Hugh Dalton.* London: Cape, 1985.

Prittie, Terrence. *Willy Brandt: Portrait of a Statesman.* New York: Schocken, 1974.

Rhodes James, Robert. *Anthony Eden.* New York: McGraw-Hill, 1987.

Riddell, Peter. *The Thatcher Government.* Oxford: Robertson, 1983.

Sampson, Anthony. *Macmillan: A Study in Ambiguity.* London: Allen Lane, 1967; New York: Simon & Schuster, 1967.

Tucker, Robert C. *Stalin in Power: The Revolution from Above, 1928–1941.* New York: Norton, 1990.

Walters, Alan Arthur. *Britain's Economic Renaissance: Margaret Thatcher's Reforms, 1979–1984.* New York: Oxford University Press, 1986; Oxford: Oxford University Press, 1987.

Williams, Francis. *A Prime Minister Remembers: The War and Post-war Memoirs of the Rt. Hon. Earl Attlee.* London: Heinemann, 1961.

Williams, Philip M. *Hugh Gaitskell: A Political Biography.* London: Cape, 1979.

Young, Kenneth. *Sir Alec Douglas-Home.* London: Dent, 1970.

7. Policy-making, Political Institutions and Culture, Public Opinion

Bayley, Edwin R. *Joe McCarthy and the Press.* Madison: University of Wisconsin Press, 1981.

Bell, Daniel, ed. *The Radical Right: The New American Right, Expanded and Updated.* Garden City, N.Y.: Doubleday, 1963.

Bennett, David H. *The Party of Fear: From Nativist Movements to the New Right in American History.* Chapel Hill: University of North Carolina Press, 1988.

Biddle, Francis. *Fear of Freedom: A Discussion of the Contemporary Obsession of Anxiety and Fear in the United States, Its Historical Background and Present Expression, and Its Effect on National Security and on Free American Institutions.* Garden City, N.Y.: Doubleday, 1951.

Boyer, Paul S. *By the Bomb's Early Light: American Thought and Culture at the Dawn of the Atomic Age.* New York: Pantheon, 1985.

Caridi, Ronald J. *The Korean War and American Politics: The Republican Party as a Case Study.* 2d ed. Philadelphia: University of Pennsylvania Press, 1969.

Caute, David. *The Great Fear: The Anti-Communist Purge under Truman and Eisenhower.* New York: Simon & Schuster, 1977.

Divine, Robert A. *Foreign Policy and U.S. Presidential Elections, 1952–1960.* New York: Franklin Watts, 1974.

Freeland, Richard M. *The Truman Doctrine and the Origins of McCarthyism: Foreign Policy, Domestic Politics and Internal Security 1946–1948.* New York: Knopf, 1972.

Fried, Richard M. *Men Against McCarthy.* New York: Columbia University Press, 1976.

Griffith, Robert, and Athan G. Theoharis, eds. *The Specter: Original Essays on the Cold War and the Origins of McCarthyism.* New York: New Viewpoints, 1974.

Harper, Alan D. *The Politics of Loyalty: The White House and the Communist Issue, 1946–1952.* Westport, Conn.: Greenwood, 1969.

Heale, M. J. *American Anticommunism: Combating the Enemy Within, 1830–1970.* Baltimore: Johns Hopkins University Press, 1990.

Hofstadter, Richard. *The Paranoid Style in American Politics, and Other Essays.* New York: Knopf, 1965.

Hunt, Michael. *Ideology and U.S. Foreign Policy.* New Haven: Yale University Press, 1987.

Kutler, Stanley I. *The American Inquisition: Justice and Injustice in the Cold War.* New York: Hill & Wang, 1982.

Latham, Earl. *The Communist Controversy in Washington: From the New Deal to McCarthy.* Cambridge: Harvard University Press, 1966.

May, Gary. *China Scapegoat: The Diplomatic Ordeal of John Carter Vincent.* Washington, D.C.: New Republic, 1979.

O'Brien, Michael. *McCarthy and McCarthyism in Wisconsin.* Columbia: University of Missouri Press, 1980.

O'Reilly, Kenneth. *Hoover and the Un-Americans: The FBI, HUAC, and the Red Menace.* Philadelphia: Temple University Press, 1983.

Oshinsky, David. *A Conspiracy So Immense: The World of Joe McCarthy.* New York: Free Press, 1983.

Pells, Richard H. *The Liberal Mind in a Conservative Age: American Intellectuals in the 1940s and 1950s.* New York: Harper & Row, 1985.

Radosh, Ronald, and Joyce Milton. *The Rosenberg File: A Search for the Truth.* New York: Holt, Rinehart & Winston, 1983.

Reeves, Thomas C. *The Life and Times of Joe McCarthy.* New York: Stein & Day, 1982.

Rogin, Michael Paul. *The Intellectuals and McCarthy: The Radical Specter.* Cambridge: MIT Press, 1967.

Rovere, Richard H. *Senator Joe McCarthy.* New York: Harcourt, Brace, 1959.

Schneir, Walter, and Miriam Schneir. *Invitation to an Inquest.* Garden City, N.Y.: Doubleday, 1965.

Small, Melvin. *Johnson, Nixon, and the Doves.* New Brunswick: Rutgers University Press, 1988.

Stern, Paula. *Water's Edge: Domestic Politics and the Making of American Foreign Policy.* Westport, Conn.: Greenwood, 1979.

Whitfield, Stephen J. *The Culture of the Cold War.* Baltimore: Johns Hopkins University Press, 1991.

Yergin, Daniel. *Shattered Peace: The Origins of the Cold War and the National Security State.* Boston: Houghton Mifflin, 1977.

Bureaucracy

De Santis, Hugh. *The Diplomacy of Silence: The American Foreign Service, the Soviet Union and the Cold War, 1933–1947.* Chicago: University of Chicago Press, 1980.

Destler, I. M. *Presidents, Bureaucrats, and Foreign Policy: The Politics of Organizational Reform.* Princeton: Princeton University Press, 1972.

Jeffreys-Jones, Rhodri. *The C. I. A. and American Democracy.* New Haven: Yale University Press, 1989.

Kahler, Miles. *Decolonization in Britain and France: The Domestic Consequences of International Relations.* Princeton: Princeton University Press, 1984.

Miscamble, Wilson. *George F. Kennan and the Making of American Foreign Policy, 1947–1950.* Princeton: Princeton University Press, 1992.

Nye, Joseph S., Jr., ed. *The Making of America's Soviet Policy.* New Haven: Yale University Press, 1984.

Rearden, Steven L. *History of the Office of the Secretary of Defense, Vol. I: The Formative Years, 1947–1950.* Washington, D.C.: Government Printing Office, 1984.

Schulzinger, Robert D. *The Wise Men of Foreign Affairs: The History of the Council on Foreign Relations.* New York: Columbia University Press, 1984.

8. Military Aspects

Betts, Richard K. *Nuclear Blackmail and Nuclear Balance.* Washington, D.C.: Brookings Institution, 1987.

Borowski, Harry R. *A Hollow Threat: Strategic Air Power and Containment before Korea.* Westport, Conn.: Greenwood, 1982.

Brodie, Bernard, ed. *Absolute Weapon: Atomic Power and World Order.* New York: Harcourt, Brace, 1946.

Gowing, Margaret M. *Britain and Atomic Energy, 1939–1945.* New York: St. Martin's Press, 1964.

Gowing, Margaret M., and Lorna Arnold. *Independence and Deterrence: Britain and Atomic Energy, 1945–1952, Vol. I, Policy Making, Vol. II, Policy Execution.* New York: St. Martin's Press, 1974.

Herken, Gregg. *Counsels of War.* New York: Knopf, 1985.

Herken, Gregg. *The Winning Weapon: The Atomic Bomb in the Cold War, 1945–1950.* New York: Knopf, 1980.

Jervis, Robert. *The Illogic of American Nuclear Strategy.* Ithaca, N.Y.: Cornell University Press, 1984.

Kissinger, Henry A. *Nuclear Weapons and Foreign Policy.* New York: Harper & Row, 1957.

Sherwin, Martin. *A World Destroyed: The Atomic Bomb and the Grand Alliance.* New York: Knopf, 1975.

Taylor, Maxwell D. *Swords and Plowshares.* New York: Norton, 1972.

Weigley, Russell F. *The American Way of War: A History of United States Military Strategy and Policy.* New York: Macmillan, 1973.

9. Soviet Perspective

Bialer, Seweryn. *The Soviet Paradox: External Expansion, Internal Decline*. New York: Knopf, 1986.

Fischer, Louis. *Russia's Road from Peace to War: Soviet Foreign Relations, 1917–1941*. New York: Harper & Row, 1969.

Gati, Charles. *The Bloc That Failed: Soviet-East European Relations in Transition*. Bloomington: Indiana University Press, 1990.

Gelman, Harry. *The Brezhnev Politburo and the Decline of Detente*. Ithaca, N.Y.: Cornell University Press, 1984.

Glassman, Jon D. *Arms for the Arabs: The Soviet Union and War in the Middle East*. Baltimore: Johns Hopkins University Press, 1975.

Golan, Galia. *Yom Kippur and After: The Soviet Union and the Middle East Crisis*. Cambridge & New York: Cambridge University Press, 1977.

Hahn, Werner G. *Postwar Soviet Politics: The Fall of Zhdanov and the Defeat of Moderation, 1946–1953*. Ithaca, N.Y.: Cornell University Press, 1982.

Ra'anan, Gavriel D. *International Policy Formation in the USSR: Factional "Debates" During the Zhdanovschina*. Hamden: Archon Books, 1983.

Rubinstein, Alvin Z. *Red Star on the Nile*. Princeton: Princeton University Press, 1977.

Shulman, Marshall. *Stalin's Foreign Policy Reappraised*. Cambridge: Harvard University Press, 1963.

Snyder, Jack. *Myths of Empire: Domestic Politics and International Ambition*. Ithaca, N.Y.: Cornell University Press, 1991.

Ulam, Adam B. *Dangerous Relations: The Soviet Union in World Politics, 1970–1982*. New York: Oxford University Press, 1983.

Ulam, Adam B. *Expansion and Coexistence: The History of Soviet Foreign Policy, 1917–1967*. New York: Praeger, 1968.

Ulam, Adam B. *Expansion and Coexistence: Soviet Foreign Policy, 1917–1973*, 2d ed. New York: Praeger, 1974.

Uldrick, Teddy. *Diplomacy and Ideology: The Origins of Soviet Foreign Relations: 1917–1930*. London & Beverly Hills: Sage, 1979.

Wolfe, Thomas W. *Soviet Power and Europe, 1945–1970*. Baltimore: Johns Hopkins University Press, 1970.

10. European Perspective

Aronsen, Lawrence, and Martin Kitchen. *The Origins of the Cold War in Comparative Perspective: American, British, and Canadian Relations with the Soviet Union, 1941–1948*. New York: St. Martin's Press, 1988.

Buchan, Alastair. *Europe's Futures, Europe's Choices: Models of Western Europe in the 1970s*. New York: Columbia University Press, 1969.

Cairncross, Alec. *Years of Recovery: British Economic Policy, 1945–1951*. London: Methuen, 1985.

Cioc, Mark. *Pax Atomica: The Nuclear Defense Debate in West Germany During the Adenauer Era*. New York: Columbia University Press, 1988.

Deighton, Anne. *The Impossible Peace: Britain, the Division of Germany, and the Origins of the Cold War*. New York: Oxford University Press, 1990.

Deighton, Anne ed. *Britain and the First Cold War*. London: Macmillan, 1990; New York: St. Martin's Press, 1990.

Dockrill, Michael L. *British Defence Since 1945*. Oxford & New York: Blackwell, 1989.

Dockrill, Michael L. and John W. Young, eds. *British Foreign Policy, 1945–56*. London: Macmillan, 1989; New York: St. Martin's Press, 1989.

Drummond, Gordon D. *The German Social Democrats in Opposition, 1949–1960: The Case Against Rearmament*. Norman: University of Oklahoma Press, 1982.

Fitzsimons, Matthew A. *The Foreign Policy of the British Labour Government, 1945–1951*. Notre Dame: University of Notre Dame Press, 1953.

Frankel, Joseph. *British Foreign Policy, 1945–1973*. New York: Oxford University Press, 1975.

Hathaway, Robert M. *Ambiguous Partnership: Britain and America, 1944–1947*. New York: Columbia University Press, 1981.

Joffe, Josef. *The Limited Partnership: Europe, the United States, and the Burdens of Alliance*. Cambridge: Ballinger, 1987.

Kahler, Miles. *Decolonization in Britain and France: The Domestic Consequences of International Relations*. Princeton: Princeton University Press, 1984.

Louis, William Roger. *The British Empire in the Middle East, 1945–1951: Arab Nationalism, the United States, and Postwar Imperialism*. New York: Oxford University Press, 1984.

Ovendale, Ritchie. *The English-Speaking Alliance: Britain, the United States, the Dominions and the Cold War, 1945–1951*. London & Boston: Allen & Unwin, 1985.

Ovendale, Ritchie., ed. *The Foreign Policy of the British Labour Governments, 1945–1951*. Leicestershire: Leicester University Press, 1984.

Rothwell, Victor. *Britain and the Cold War, 1941–1947*. London: Cape, 1982.

Stent, Angela. *From Embargo to Ostpolitik: The Political Economy of West German–Soviet Relations, 1955–1980*. Cambridge & New York: Cambridge University Press, 1981.

Willis, Frank Roy. *France, Germany and the New Europe, 1945–1963*. London: Oxford University Press, 1968.

Wolffsohn, Michael. *West Germany's Foreign Policy in the Era of Brandt and Schmidt, 1969–1982: An Introduction.* Frankfurt am Main: Lang, 1986.

Young, John W. *Britain, France and the Unity of Europe, 1945–1951.* Leicester: Leicester University Press, 1984.

Young, John W., ed. *The Foreign Policy of Churchill's Peacetime Administration, 1951–1955.* Leicester: Leicester University Press, 1988.

Zametica, John, ed. *British Officials and British Foreign Policy, 1945–1950.* Leicester: Leicester University Press, 1990.

11. Document Collections

Deibel, Terry, and John Lewis Gaddis, eds. *Containment: Concept and Policy.* Washington, D.C.: National Defense University Press, 1986.

Etzold, Thomas H., and John Lewis Gaddis, eds. *Containment: Documents on American Policy and Strategy, 1945–1950.* New York: Columbia University Press, 1978.

Foreign Relations of the United States [1933–1957]. Washington, D.C.: Government Printing Office, 1952–1986.

Nelson, Anna. ed. *The State Department Policy Planning Staff Papers, 1947–1949.* New York: Garland Publishing, 1983.

Patterson, Thomas G., ed. *Major Problems in American Foreign Policy: Documents and Essays, Vol. 2 (since 1914).* Lexington, Mass.: Heath, 1978.

The Pentagon Papers: As Published by the New York Times. New York: Quadrangle Books, 1971.

The Secret Diplomacy of the Vietnam War: The Negotiating Volumes of the Pentagon Papers. Austin: University of Texas Press, 1983.

The State Department Policy Planning Staff Papers, 1947–1949. New York: Garland Publishing, 1983.

Archives

The following inventory lists institutional collections containing papers and oral histories of principal figures and agencies. Capsule career summaries are provided to indicate the focus of the collection.

Library Key

Note: All presidential libraries are administered by the National Archives and Records Administration (NARA). For regulations governing the use by researchers of historical materials in presidential libraries, see Regulations for the Public Use of Records in the National Archives, a NARA publication. University libraries are independently administered. Users should check with individual institutions for policies governing access to archives.

Clemson University (ClU)
Robert Muldrow Cooper Library
Clemson, SC 29634-3001
Tel.: (803)656-3026

Columbia University (CU)
Butler Library
535 W 114th Street
New York, NY 10027
Tel.:(212)854-2247

Dwight D. Eisenhower Library (DDE)
Abilene, KS 67410
Tel.:(913)263-4751
Hours: 9:00am-4:45pm, Mon.-Fri., Sat. by advance arrangement
ILL: finding aids and most oral history interviews

Gerald R. Ford Library (GRF)
1000 Beal Avenue
Ann Arbor, MI 48109
Tel.: (313)668-2218
8Fax: (313)668-2341
Hours: 8:45am-4:45pm, Mon.-Fri., Sat. morning by advance arrangement
ILL: Gerald R. Ford Scrapbooks and Grand Rapids Oral Histories

Lyndon Baines Johnson Library (LBJ)
2313 Red River Street
Austin, TX 78705
Tel.: (512)482-5137
Hours: 9:00am-5:00pm, Mon.-Fri.
ILL: oral history transcripts, finding aids, duplicates of task force reports, and additional items as possible

John Fitzgerald Kennedy Library (JFK)
Columbia Point
Boston, MA 02125
Tel.: (617)929-4500
Hours: 8:30am-4:30pm, Mon.-Fri., 9:00am-3:00pm, Sat.
ILL: oral history transcripts, cassette tapes and transcripts of presidential recordings, the Taylor Report on the Bay of Pigs Invasion, and at the discretion of the librarian, duplicate copies of books

Library of Congress (LoC)
Independent Ave at First Street SE,
Washington, DC 20540
Tel.: (202)707-5000

Richard M. Nixon Library (RMN)
18001 Yorba Linda Blvd
Yorba Linda, CA 92686
Tel.: (714)993-5075

Princeton University Library (PU)
One Washington Rd
Princeton, NJ 08544-2089
Tel.: (609)258-3180

Franklin D Roosevelt Library (FDR)
511 Albany Post Rd
Hyde Park, NY 12538
Tel.: (914)229-8114

Harry S Truman Library (HST)
Independence, MO 64050
Tel.: (816)833-1400
Hours: 8:45am-4:45 pm, Mon.-Fri., Sat. by advance arrangement
Inter-Library Loan (ILL): Finding aids and oral history interviews can be obtained by
ILL.

University of Kent at Canterbury Library (UKent)
Canterbury CT2 7NU
ENGLAND
Tel.:(0227)764000

University of Virginia (UVa)
Alderman Library
Charlottesville, VA 22903-2498
Tel.:(804)924-3026

Western Reserve Historical Society (WRHS)
10825 East Boulevard
Cleveland, OH 44106
Tel.: (216)721-5722

Yale University Library (YU)
Sterling Memorial Library
120 High Street
New Haven, CT 06520
Tel.: (203)432-1775

ACHESON, DEAN G.
Asst Sec of State, 1941–45
Under Sec of State, 1945–47
Sec of State, 1949–53
Papers, 1931–71   HST
Oral History   HST

ACHILLES, THEODORE C.
1st Sec, US Embassy, London, 1945;
    Brussels, 1946
Dir, Office of West European Affairs,
    Dept of State, 1947
US Vice Deputy, North Atlantic
    Council, 1950
Minister, US Embassy, Paris, 1952
Oral History   HST
                                   PU

ADAMS, SHERMAN
Asst to the President, 1953–58
Records, 1952–59   DDE
Oral History   DDE
(permission req)   PU

ADENAUER, KONRAD
Chancellor, Fed Rep of Germany
Oral History   HST

ALDRICH, WINTHROP
Amb to the UK, 1953–57
Oral History   DDE

ALLEN, GEORGE V.
Amb to Iran, 1946–48
Amb to Yugo, 1950–53
Amb to India and Nepal, 1953
Amb to Greece, 1956–57
Dir US Information Agency, 1957–
    60
Papers, 1944–69   HST
Oral History   DDE
(permission req)   PU
                                   CU

ALLIED COMMISSION FOR AUSTRIA
Selected Records, 1946, 1949–50 HST

ALPHAND, E. HERVE
French Amb to the US, 1956–65
Oral History (permission req) JFK

AMORY, ROBERT
Member, Nat Security Council Plan-
    ning Board, 1953–61
Deputy Dir, CIA, 1952–62

Papers, 1808–1980   JFK
Oral History   JFK

ANDERSON, CLINTON P.
Sec of Agriculture, 1945–48
Papers, 1942–46   HST

ANDERSON, EUGENE M.
Amb to Bulgaria, 1962–65
Oral History (portions closed) JFK

ANDERSON, GEORGE W.
Chief of Naval Operations, Joint
    Chiefs of Staff, 1961–63
Oral History (permission req) JFK

ANTHONY, ROBERT N.
Asst Sec, Dept of Defense
Files, 1967–68 (microfilm)   LBJ

ARNOLD, EDWIN G.
Dir, Far East Program Division, Eco-
    nomic Cooperation Admin and
    Mutual Security Agency, 1951–52
Papers, 1933–52   HST

AURAND, EVAN P.
Naval Aide to the President, 1957–61
Papers, 1934–72   DDE

AYERS, EBEN A.
Asst Press Sec to the President, 1945–
    50
Special Asst in White House Office,
    1951–53
Papers, 1908–53   HST
Oral History   HST

BADEAU, JOHN S.
Amb to the United Arab Republic
    (Egypt), 1961–64
Oral History   JFK

BAIRD, CHARLES F.
Asst and Under Sec of the Navy
Speeches, 1966–68   LBJ

BALL, GEORGE W.
Under Sec of State for Economic Af-
    fairs, 1961
Under Sec of State, 1961–66
US Amb to the UN, 1968
Papers, 1961–63   JFK
Notes, 1963–66   LBJ
Oral History   LBJ

BANCROFT, HARDING F.
Chief, Div of UN Political Affairs, Dept of State, 1945
US Deputy Rep, UN Collective Measures Committee, 1950–53
Oral History   HST

BARKER, RAY W.
Asst Chief of Staff, G–1, SHAEF, 1944–45
Papers, 1943–45   DDE
Oral History   DDE

BARKLEY, ALBEN W.
Vice President of the US, 1949–53
Correspondence with Truman, 1944–45 (microfilm)   UKent

BARNES, DONALD F.
President interp, Dept of State, 1956–66
Oral History   JFK

BARNETT, ROBERT W.
US Member of the Economic and Reparations Committee, 1945–49
Officer in Charge of Economic Affairs, Office of Chinese Affairs, Dept of State, 1949–51
Officer in Charge of Economic Affairs, Office of Western European Affairs, 1951–54
Oral History   HST

BARRETT, EDWARD W.
Asst Sec of State for Public Affairs, 1950–52
Oral History   HST

BARROWS, LELAND
Executive Asst to the US Special Representative in Europe, Economic Cooperation Admin, 1949–53
Dir, Mission to Greece, FAO, 1952–54
Oral History   HST

BARUCH, BERNARD M.
Presidential adv, 1930s, 1940s
Papers   PU

BATT, WILLIAM L.
Chief, Economic Cooperation Admin Mission to the UK, 1950–52
Papers, 1940–64   HST

BATTLE, LUCIUS
Foreign Affairs Specialist, Dept of State, 1946–49
Spec Asst to the Sec of State, 1949–53
US Amb to the United Arab Republic (Egypt), 1964–67
Asst Sec of State for Near Eastern and South Asian Affairs, 1967–68
Oral History   HST
Oral History   LBJ

BEACH, EDWARD L.
Chief of Naval Operations, 1947–48
Papers, 1935–62   DDE
Oral History   DDE

BEACH, EDWARD L. AND EVAN P. AURAND
Naval Aides to the President
Records, 1953–67   DDE

BECKER, NATHAN M.
Economic Adviser, Board of Economic Warfare
and Dept of State, 1941–47
Economic Adviser, Gen Staff, US–UN Forces, Korea, 1952–53
Oral History   HST

BELK, SAMUEL E.
Member, National Security Council Staff, 1959–65
Staff Member, Bureau of Internal Affairs, Dept of State, 1965–66
Papers, 1959–66   JFK

BELL, DAVID E.
Admin Asst to the President, 1951–53
Papers, 1946–53   HST
Files, 1949–53   HST
Oral History   HST

BELLOWS, EVERETT H.
Dir, Productivity and Special Assistance Division, US Special Representative in Europe, Mutual Security Agency, 1951–53
Papers, 1951–60   HST

BEN-GURION, DAVID
 Prime Minister, Israel, 1948–1953, 1955–63
 Oral History   JFK

BENDETSEN, KARL R.
 Gen Counselor, Dept of the Army, 1949
 Asst Sec of the Army, 1950–52
 Oral History   HST

BETHE, HANS
 Dir, Theoretical Physics Div, Los Alamos Lab, 1943–46
 Head of the President's Study of Disarmament, 1958
 Member of the Presidential Scientific Advisory Committee, 1956–60
 Oral History   DDE

BISSELL, RICHARD M., JR.
 Deputy Dir and Exec Sec, President's Committee on Foreign Aid (Harriman Committee), 1947–48
 Asst Administrator for Programs, Economic Cooperation Admin, 1948–51
 Acting Aministrator, Economic Cooperation Admin, 1951
 Consultant to the Administrator, Mutual Security Agency, 1953
 Spec Assistant to the Dir, 1954–59
 Deputy Dir of Plans, CIA, 1959–62
 Papers, 1907–80   LoC
 Oral History   HST
 Oral History   DDE
 (permission req)   JFK
 (permission req)   PU

BLAIR, WILLIAM
 Amb to Denmark, 1961–64
 Oral History (permission req)   JFK

BLAISDELL, THOMAS C., JR.
 Chief, Mission for Economic Affairs, London, 1945–46
 Dir, Office of International Trade, Dept of Commerce, 1947–49
 Asst Sec of Commerce, 1949–51
 Papers, 1933–51   HST
 Oral History   HST

BOHLEN, CHARLES E.
 Amb to USSR, 1953–57

Amb to the Philippines, 1957–59
 Spec Asst to the Sec of State for Soviet Affairs, 1959–61
 Amb to France, 1962–67
 Deputy Under Sec of State for Political Affairs, 1968–69
 Papers, 1969–70   LoC
 Oral History   DDE
                                                                    JFK
                                                                    LBJ
                                                                    CU

BOURGUBA, HABIB BEN ALI
 President of Tunis, 1957–88
 Oral History   JFK

BOURGUBA, HABIB, JR.
 Tunis Amb to the US, 1961–63
 Oral History   JFK

BOWIE, ROBERT R.
 Dir, Policy Planning Staff, Dept of State, 1953–55
 Asst Sec of State for Policy Planning, 1955–57
 Oral History   DDE

BOWLES, CHESTER
 US Amb to India, 1963–69
 Oral History   LBJ
                                                                    CU

BOWLES, EDWARD L.
 Consultant to the Sec of War and Spec Consultant to the Command Gen, Army Air Force, 1942–47
 Papers, 1945–50   HST

BOWSHER, CHARLES A.
 Asst Sec of the Navy
 Papers, 1967–68   LBJ

BRERETON, LEWIS H.
 Chairman, Military Liaison Committee to the Atomic Energy Commission, 1945–58
 Papers, 1918–67   DDE

BRIGGS, ELLIS
 Amb to Dominican Repub, 1944–45
 Amb to Uruguay, 1947–49
 Amb to Czechoslovakia, 1949–52
 Amb to Korea, 1952–55
 Amb to Peru, 1955–56
 Amb to Brazil, 1956–59

Amb to Greece, 1959–61
Oral History   DDE

BRIGGS, RUTH M.
Sec to Gen Walter Bedell Smith,
  1942–54
Manuscripts   DDE

BROOKS, ROBERT A.
Asst Sec of the Army
Papers, 1965–68   LBJ

BROWN, HAROLD
Dir, Defense Research and Engineer-
  ing, Dept of Defense, 1961–65
Sec of the Air Force
Sec of Defense, 1977–81
Scrapbooks, 1963–69   LBJ
Oral History (closed)   JFK
                                                                  LBJ

BROWN, WINTHROP
Chief, Div of Commercial Policy,
  Dept of State, 1945–48
Acting Dir, 1947–48, and Dir, 1948–
  50, Office of Intl Trade Policy,
  Dept of State
Dir, Office of Intl Materials Policy,
  Dept of State, 1950–52
Deputy to Min for Economic Affairs,
  US Embassy, London, 1952–55
Oral History   HST

BROWNELL, HERBERT
US Att Gen, 1953–61
Oral History (permission req)   PU

BRUCE, DAVID K. E.
Asst Sec of Commerce, 1947–48
Chief Admin Mission to France,
  1948–49
Amb to France, 1949–52
Under Sec of State, 1952–53
Amb to UK, 1961–69
Oral History   HST
(permission req)   PU
                                                                  JFK
                                                                  LBJ

BRZEZINSKI, ZBIGNIEW
Member, Policy Planning Council,
  Dept of State, 1966–68
Spec Asst for National Security Af-
  fairs, 1977–81
Oral History   LBJ

BULL, HAROLD R.
Chief of Staff, US Forces, European
  Theater, 1945–46
Papers, 1943–68   DDE

BUNDY, MCGEORGE
Spec Asst to the President for Na-
  tional Security Affairs, 1961–66
Papers, 1963–65   JFK
Files, 1961–63   JFK
Files, 1963–66   LBJ
Notes, 1963–66   LBJ
Oral History   JFK

BUNDY, WILLIAM P.
Deputy Asst Sec of Defense; Asst Sec
  of State for East Asian and Pacific
  Affairs
**Unpub Manuscript on
  US Policy in Vietnam**   LBJ
Oral History   LBJ

BURGESS, W. RANDOLPH
Deputy to the Sec of the Treasury,
  1953–54
Under Sec of the Treasury, 1955–57
US Perm Rep to NATO, 1957–61
Papers, 1951–62   DDE
Oral History   DDE

BURKE, ARLEIGH A.
Chief of Naval Operations, Joint
  Chiefs of
  Staff, 1955–61
Oral History   DDE
(permission req)   JFK

BURNS, ARTHUR F.
Chairman, Council of Economic Ad-
  visers, 1953–56
Chairman, Advisers Board on
  Growth and Stability, 1953–56
Chairman, Cabinet Committee on
  Small Business, 1956
Member, Presidential Adv Commit-
  tee on Labor–Management Policy,
  1961–66
Pres, National Board of Economic
  Research, 1957–67
Counsellor to the President, 1969–70
Chairman, Fed. Reserve System Bd
  of Governors, 1970–78
Amb to Fed Republic of Germany,
  1981–85
Papers, 1930–69   DDE

Papers, 1969–87	GRF	**CAMPBELL, JOHN C.**	
Oral History	CU	Officer in Charge, Balkan Affairs, Office of East European Affairs, 1949–55	
		Oral History	HST
BUTCHER, HARRY C.			
Naval Aide to Dwight D. Eisenhower		**CANNON, C. CRAIG**	
Papers, 1910–59	DDE	Aide to Dwight D. Eisenhower, 1946–48 and 1950–52	
		Papers, 1955–60	DDE
BUTTERWORTH, W. WALTON			
Counsel of Embassy, Madrid, 1944–46		**CARROLL, PAUL T.**	
Counsel of Embassy, Nanking, China, 1946–47		Military Assoc of Dwight D. Eisenhower, 1945–52	
Dir of Far Eastern Affairs, Dept of State, 1947–49		Staff Sec and Defense Liaison Official in the White House, 1953–54	
Asst Sec of State, 1949–50		Papers, 1941–68	DDE
Amb to Sweden, 1950–53			
Oral History	HST	**CEA, OFFICE OF THE CHAIRMAN**	
		Records, 1953–60	DDE
BYRNES, JAMES F.		**CENTRAL INTELLIGENCE AGENCY**	
US Sec of State, 1945–47		Records, 1963–69	LBJ
Papers	ClU	(microfilm)	LBJ
CABOT, JOHN M.		**CHASE, GORDON**	
Consul Gen, Shanghai, 1948–49		Member, National Security Council Staff, 1962–66	
Min to Finland, 1950–52		Papers, 1960–66	JFK
Amb to Pakistan, 1952–53			
Amb to Colombia, 1957–59		**CHAYES, ABRAM**	
Amb to Brazil, 1959–61		Legal Adv, Dept of State, 1961–64	
Amb to Poland, 1962–65		Papers, 1961–72	JFK
Papers, 1929–78		(microfilm)	JFK
(microfilm)	JFK	Oral History	
Oral History	HST	(portions closed)	JFK
	JFK		
	LBJ	**CHENEY, RICHARD B.**	
(permission req)	PU	Deputy Asst and Asst to the President, 1974–77;	
		Sec of Defense, 1989–	
CABOT, THOMAS D.		Files, 1974–77	GRF
Dir of Intl Security Affairs, Dept of State, 1951			
Oral History	HST	**CHERNE, LEO**	
		Member, 1973–76, Chair, 1976–77, President's Foreign Intelligence Adv Board	
CADY, JOHN F.		Member, Intelligence Oversight Board, 1976–77	
Chief, South Asian Branch, Div of Research for the Near East and Africa, Office of Intelligence Research, Dept of State, 1945–49		Papers, 1973–77 (1986)	GRF
Oral History	HST		
		Chiang Kai–shek	
CALLAWAY, HOWARD H.		Oral History	PU
Sec of the Army, 1973–75			
Papers, 1972–76	GRF		

CHIANG, CHING–KUO
Min without Portfolio, Representative
of China, 1958–69
Oral History   JFK

CLARKE, SIR ASHLEY
Min, UK Embassy, Paris, 1946–49
Deputy Under Sec of State for For-
eign Affairs, UK, 1950–53
Oral History   HST

CLAY, GEN. LUCIUS D., SR.
Commander in Chief, US Forces in
Europe and Military Governor,
US Zone, Fed Republic of Ger-
many, 1947–49
Oral History   HST
                                                          DDE
                                                          JFK
                                                          PU
                                                          CU

CLAYTON, WILL L.
Under Sec of State for Economic Af-
fairs, 1946–47
Papers, 1926–66   HST

CLEVELAND, HARLAN
Asst Sec of State for Intl Organiza-
tions Affairs, 1961–65
Amb to NATO, 1965–69
Papers, 1961–69   JFK
Oral History   JFK
                                                          LBJ

CLIFFORD, CLARK M.
Spec Counselor to the President,
1946–50
Papers, 1946–52   HST
Papers, 1957–61
(permission req)   JFK
(microfilm)   JFK
Files, 1946–50   HST
Papers, 1968–69   LBJ
Oral History   HST
                                                          LBJ

CLIFTON, GEN. CHESTER V.
Military Aide to the President, 1961–
65
Files, 1963–65   LBJ
Files, 1961–63   JFK

CLINE, RAY S.
CIA Chief of Strategy, Taiwan,
1958–62
Deputy Dir for Intelligence, CIA,
1962–66
Oral History   LBJ

CLUBB, O. EDMUND
US Foreign Serv Officer, 1928–52
Consul Gen, Vladivostok, USSR,
1944–46, Mukden, Manchuria,
1946, Harbin, Manchuria, 1946,
Changchun, Manchuria, 1946–47,
Beijing, 1947–50
Dir, Office of Chinese Affairs, Dept
of State, 1950–51
Oral History   HST

COLBY, WILLIAM E.
1st Sec, US Embassy, Saigon, 1959–
62
Chief, Far East Div, CIA, 1962–67
Dir Civil Operations and Revolu-
tionary Development Support, S
Vietnam, 1968–71
Exec Dir, CIA, 1971–72
Deputy Dir of Operations, CIA, 1973
Director of Central Intelligence,
1973–76
Oral History   LBJ

COLLINS, J. LAWTON
Commander, VII Corps, 1944–45
Chief of Staff of the Army, 1949–53
Papers, 1896–75   DDE

COMMITTEE FILE
Committee on Nuclear Proliferation,
President's Committee on the War-
ren Report,
Spec Committee on US Trade Rela-
tions with Eastern European
Countries and the Soviet Union
National Security File,
1963–69   LBJ

COMMITTEE FOR THE MARSHALL PLAN
Records, 1947–51   HST

CONNELLY, MATTHEW J.
Appointments Sec to the President,
1945–53
Notes, 1945–53   HST
Files, 1945–53   HST

CONWAY, ROSE A.
  Personal Sec to the President, 1945–
    72
  Papers, 1945–59   HST
  Files, 1945–53   HST

COOPER, CHESTER L.
  Staff, National Security Council,
    1964–66
  Asst to W. A. Harriman on Vietnam,
    1966–67
  Oral History   LBJ

COUNCIL OF ECONOMIC ADVISORS
  Records, 1953–61   DDE

COUNTRY FILE
  Dept of State and Dept of Defense
    cables, White House memoranda,
    CIA intelligence reports, ar-
    ranged by region and country
  National Security File,
    1963–69   LBJ

COUNTRY FILE, VIETNAM
  National Security File,
    1963–69   LBJ

COUVE DE MURVILLE, MAURICE
  Min of Foreign Affairs, France,
    1958–68
  Oral History   JFK
  (permission req)   PU

COWEN, MYRON M.
  Amb to Australia, 1948–49
  Amb to the Philippines, 1949–51
  Amb to Belgium, 1952–53
  Papers, 1948–65   HST

CUSHMAN, ROBERT E.
  Exec Asst to Vice President Nixon,
    1957–61
  Oral History   DDE

DANIELS, JONATHAN
  Press Sec to the President, 1945
  Papers   HST
  Oral History   HST

DAVIES, JOSEPH E.
  Amb to USSR, 1936–38
  Amb to Belgium and Luxembourg,
    1938–39
  Papers, 1860–1957   LoC

DAVIS, JOHN J.
  Dir, Foreign Intelligence Office
  Asst Chief of Staff for Intelligence,
    1957–61, 1963–66
  Asst Dir of Productivity, National Se-
    curity Agency, 1961–63;
  Asst Dir (Weapons Evaluation and
    Control) Arms Control and Disar-
    mament Agency, 1966–70
  Oral History   LBJ

DAVIS, NATHANIEL P.
  Minister–Counsel, US Embassy, Ma-
    nila, 1946–47
  Amb to Costa Rica, 1947–49
  Min to Hung, 1949–51
  Papers, 1916–57   HST

DEIMEL, HENRY L.
  Spec Asst to the Dir for Near Eastern
    and African Affairs, Dept of State,
    1945–49
  Counselor for Economic Affairs, US
    Embassy, New Dehli, 1949–52
  Oral History   HST

DENNISON, ROBERT L.
  Naval Aide to the President, 1948–53
  Papers, 1946–72   HST
  Files, 1946–53   HST
  Oral History   HST

DEPARTMENT OF DEFENSE
  Records, 1963–69   LBJ
  (microfilm, not open)   LBJ
  Department of State
  Records, 1946–69   LBJ
  (microfilm)   LBJ

DILLON, Clarence DOUGLAS
  Amb to France, 1953–57
  Deputy Under Sec of State for Eco-
    nomic Affairs, 1957–58;
  Under Sec of State, 1959–61
  Sec of the Treasury, 1961–65
  Papers, 1957–65   JFK
  Oral History (written permission)   DDE
                                                                LBJ
                                                                CU
  Oral History (portions closed,
    permission req.)   JFK
  (closed)   JFK
  (and Roosa, Robert V., Under Sec
    of Treasury for Monetary Affairs,
    permission req.)   JFK

DOUGLAS, JAMES H.
Under Sec, 1953–57, Sec, 1957–59, of
the Air Force
Deputy Sec of Defense, 1959–61
Oral History   DDE

DOUGLAS–HOME, SIR ALEC
Sec of State for Foreign Affairs, UK,
1960–63
Prime Minister, UK, 1963–64
Oral History   JFK
(closed)   JFK

DRAPER, WILLIAM H.
Under Sec of War, 1947
Under Sec of the Army, 1947–49
US Spec Rep in Europe, 1952–53
Oral History   HST

DRAPER, WILLIAM H., JR.
US Spec Rep to Europe, 1951–53
Chairman, US Presidential Commit-
tee to Study the US Military As-
sistance Program, 1958–59
Oral History   DDE

DULLES, ALLEN W.
Dir CIA, 1953–61
Papers   PU

DULLES, ELEANOR LANSING
Economic Office, Dept of State,
1942–45
US Rep, Bretton Woods Conf on Intl
Monetary Fund, 1944
Financial Attache, Vienna, 1945–49
Western European Div, Dept of State,
1949–51
Spec Asst, Office of German Affairs,
Dept of State, 1952–62
Papers, 1880–1973   DDE
Oral History   PU

DULLES, JOHN FOSTER
Sec of State, 1953–59
Papers, 1951–59   DDE
Papers   PU
Oral History   PU

DURBROW, ELBRIDGE
US Foreign Service Officer, 1930–68
Chief, Eastern European Div, Dept
of State, 1944–46
Counsel of Embassy, Moscow, 1946–
48

Min Counsel, US Embassy, Rome,
1952–54
US Amb to South Vietnam, 1957–61
Oral History   HST
                                                               LBJ

DUTTON, FREDERICK G.
Spec Asst to the President, 1961
Asst Sec of State for Congressional
Relations, 1961–64
Oral History   JFK
                                                               LBJ

EISENHOWER, DWIGHT D.
President of the US, 1953–61
Papers, 1953–61
   (part on microfilm)   DDE
Records, 1953–61
   (part on microfilm)   DDE
Oral History   DDE
                                                               PU

ELSEY, GEORGE M.
Admin Asst to the President, 1949–
51
Asst to Dir for Mutual Security,
1951–53
Papers, 1941–53   HST
Files, 1945–49   HST
Oral History   HST

ENTHOVEN, ALAIN C.
Deputy Asst Sec of Defense, 1962
Asst Sec of Defense for Systems
Analysis, 1965–68
Papers, 1960–69   LBJ
Oral History   LBJ

FARLEY, PHILIP J.
Spec Asst to the Sec of State for
Atomic Energy and Outer Space,
1961–62
Chief, Political Section, US Mission
to NATO, 1962
Oral History   JFK

FAY, PAUL B.
Under Sec of the Navy, 1961–63
Papers   JFK
Oral History (closed)   JFK

**FILES OF THE SPECIAL COMMITTEE OF THE
NATIONAL SECURITY COUNCIL**
National Security File, 1963–69   LBJ

FINLETTER, THOMAS K.
Sec of the Air Force, 1950–53
Amb to NATO, 1961–65
Papers, 1943–78 HST
Oral History HST
Oral History JFK
(portions closed) JFK

FINUCANE, CHARLES C.
Asst Sec of the Office for Financial Management, 1954–55
Under Sec of the Army, 1955–58
Asst Sec of Defense, 1958–61
Papers, 1945–69 DDE

FISHER, ADRIAN S.
Deputy Dir, Arms Control and Disarmament Agency, 1961–69
Oral History JFK

FLAX, ALEXANDER H.
Asst Sec for Research and Development, Dept of the Air Force
Papers, 1963–68 LBJ

FORRESTAL, JAMES
US Sec of Def, 1947–49
Diaries PU
Papers PU

FORRESTAL, MICHAEL V.
Asst to the President for Far East Affairs, 1962–64
Spec Asst to the Sec of State, 1964–65
Sr Staff Member, National Security Council, 1962–67
Oral History LBJ
(permission req) JFK

FOSKETT, JAMES H.
Naval Aide to the President, 1946–48
Papers, 1919–54 HST

FOSTER, WILLIAM C.
Dir, Arms Control and Disarmament Agency, 1961–69
Oral History
(portions closed) JFK

FRANKE, WILLIAM B.
Asst Sec of the Navy, 1954–57
Under Sec of the Navy, 1957–59
Sec of the Navy, 1959–61
Oral History DDE

FRANKS, LORD OLIVER
UK Amb to the US, 1948–52
Oral History HST

FREDERICKS, J. WAYNE
Deputy Asst Sec of State for African Affairs, 1961–67
Papers, 1957–73 JFK

FROST, LAURENCE H.
Dir, National Security Agency, 1960–62
Oral History
(portions closed) JFK

FULBRIGHT, J. WILLIAM
US Sen (D, Ark), 1945–75
Chairman, Senate Foreign Relations Committee, 1959–75
Oral History (permission req) JFK
(permission req) PU
CU

GAITHER, JAMES C.
Spec Asst to the President
Oral History LBJ

GALBRAITH, JOHN KENNETH
Amb to India, 1961–63
Papers, 1930–75 JFK

GALE, OLIVER M.
Spec Asst to the Sec of Defense, 1957–60
Memorandum re Sec of Defense, 1971 DDE

GARDINER, ARTHUR Z.
Spec Asst, Bureau of Near East, South Asian and African Affairs, Dept of State, 1954
Economic Counsel, US Embassy and Dir, Vietnam, 1958–62
Economic Mission, US Embassy, Tokyo, 1962–75
Papers, 1941–71 HST

GARNER, ROBERT L.
VP, World Bank, 1947–56
Papers, 1947–66 HST

GARWOOD, ELLEN CLAYTON
Daughter and Biographer of Will L. Clayton
Papers, 1958–60 HST

GATES, THOMAS S., JR.
Commander, US Naval Reserves, 1942–45
Under Sec of the Navy, 1953–57
Sec of the Navy, 1957–59
Deputy Sec of Defense, 1959–61
Oral History   DDE

GAVIN, JAMES M.
Deputy Chief of Staff for Plans and Research, 1955
Chief of Research and Development, 1956–57, Dept of the Army
Oral History
(permission req)   DDE

GELB, LESLIE H.
Coordinator of the Pentagon Papers Project under Sec of Defense Mc-Namara
Oral History   LBJ

GILPATRIC, ROSWELL L.
Asst Sec of the Air Force, 1951
Under Sec of the Air Force, 1951–53
Deputy Sec of Defense, 1961–64
Papers, 1956–67   JFK
Oral History   HST
(portions closed)   JFK

GINSBURGH, A. ROBERT
Staff Member to Sec of Defense, 1949–53
Papers, 1944–53   HST

GLEASON, S. EVERETT
Deputy Exec Sec, National Security Council, 1950–59
Historian, Dept of State, 1962–72
Papers, 1925–72   HST

GOODPASTER, ANDREW J.
Defense Liaison Office and Staff Sec to the President, 1954–61
Asst Div Commander, 3rd Infantry Div, 1961
Supreme Allied Commander, Europe, 1969–1974
Oral History   DDE
                                     LBJ
                                     PU

GOODWIN, RICHARD N.
Asst Spec Counselor to the President, 1961

Deputy Asst Sec of State for Inter-American Affairs, 1961–62
Dir, Intl Peace Corps Section, 1962–64
Papers, 1961–63   JFK

GOODWIN, ROBERT L.
Administrator, Defense Manpower Admin, 1950–53
Papers, 1943–61   HST

GORDON, LINCOLN
Dir, Programs Div, Office of the Economic Cooperation Admin Spec Rep in Europe, 1949–50
Economic Adviser to the Spec Asst to the President, 1950–51
Asst Dir for Mutual Security, 1951–52
Oral History   HST

GRADY, HENRY F.
Amb to India, 1947–48
Amb to Greece, 1948–50
Amb to Iran, 1950–51
Papers, 1932–57   HST

GRAHAM, DANIEL O.
Chief of Current Intelligence and Est, Military Assistance Committee, Vietnam, 1961–68
Oral History   LBJ

GRAY, GORDON
Asst Sec of the Army, 1947–49
Sec of the Army, 1949–50
Spec Asst to the President, 1950
Dir, Psychological Strategy Board, 1951
Chairman, Atomic Ebergy Commission Personal Security Board, which investigated J. Robert Oppenheimer, 1954
Asst Sec of Defense for Intl Security, 1955–57
Dir, Office of Defense Mobilization, 1957–58
Spec Asst to the President for National Security Affairs, 1958–61
Member, Foreign Intelligence Advisory Board, 1961–62
Scrapbook Copies, 1947–58   HST

Papers, 1956–76
  (part on microfilm)   DDE
Oral History   HST
                             DDE

GRAY, ROBERT K.
Spec Asst for Manpower, Navy Dept,
  1955–56
Spec Asst to the President, 1958–61
Papers, 1954–60   DDE

GREW, JOSEPH C.
Amb to Japan, 1932–41
Under Sec of State, 1945
Sec of State ad interim, 1945
Manuscripts   FDR

GREWE, WILHELM
Fed Rep of Germany Amb to the
  US, 1957–62
Fed Rep of Germany Amb to
  NATO, 1962–71
Oral History   JFK

GRIFFIN, R. ALLEN
Deputy Chief, China Aid Mission, Eco-
  nomic Cooperation Admin, 1948–49
Dir Far East Program Div, Economic
  Cooperation Admin, 1950
Spec Rep to the Far East, Economic
  Cooperation Admin and Mutual
  Security Agency, 1951–52
Oral History   HST

GRIFFIS, STANTON
Amb to Poland, 1947
Amb to Egypt, 1948
Amb to Argentina, 1949
Amb to Spain, 1951–52
Scrapbook Files, 1931–67   HST

GRIFFITH, PAUL H.
National Commander, American Le-
  gion, 1946–47
Asst Sec of Defense, 1949–50
Papers, 1946–66   HST

GRUENTHER, ALFRED M.
Supreme Allied Commander in Europe, NATO Forces, 1953–56
Oral History
  (written permission)   DDE

HAFSTAD, LAWRENCE R.

Exec Sec, Research and Development
  Board, Office of the Sec of Defense,
  1947–49
Papers, 1940–63   HST

HAGERTY, JAMES C.
Press Sec to the President, 1953–61
Papers, 1953–61   DDE
Oral History   DDE
                             PU

HAIG, ALEXANDER M.
Asst to the President, 1973–74
Sec of State, 1981–82
Files, 1973–74   GRF
Special Files   RMN

HALABY, NAJEEB E.
Govt Official involved in establ of
  CIA, Dept of Defense, and NATO
Foreign Affairs Adviser to Sec of De-
  fense, 1948–54
Oral History   DDE

HALPERIN, MORTON H.
Deputy Asst Sec of Defense for Intl
  Security Affairs
Staff Member, National Security Council
Papers, 1968–69   LBJ

HANES, JOHN W., JR.
Spec Asst to the Sec of State, 1953–
  57
Deputy Asst for Intl Organizations,
  1957–58
Admin, Bureau of Security and Con-
  sular Affairs, 1958–61
Manuscripts   DDE
Oral History   DDE

HARE, RAYMOND A.
Amb to Saudi Arabia, 1950–53
Amb to Lebanon, 1953–54
Dir Gen, US Foreign Service, 1954–
  56
Amb to Egypt, 1956–58
Amb to United Arab Rep (Egypt),
  1958–60
Deputy Under Sec of State for Polit-
  ical Affairs, 1960–61
Oral History   DDE

HARE, RAYMOND A.
Amb to Turkey, 1961–65
Oral History   JFK

HARKINS, PAUL D.
  Deputy Commander, US Army, Pacific
  Commander, US Military Assistance and Advisory Group, Vietnam
  Oral History   LBJ

HARLECH, LORD
  Min of State for Foreign Affairs, UK, 1957–61
  UK Amb to US, 1961–65
  Oral History (closed)   JFK

HARR, KARL G. JR.
  Spec Asst to the Under Sec of State, 1954–56
  Deputy Asst Sec of Defense for Intl Security Affairs, 1956–58
  Spec Asst to the President and V Chairman of the Operations Coordinating Board, 1958–61
  Oral History   DDE

HARRIMAN, W. AVERELL
  Amb to Russia, 1943–46
  Amb to UK, 1946
  Sec of Commerce, 1946–48
  US Spec Rep in Europe, Economic Cooperation Admin, 1948–50
  Dir for Mutual Security, 1951–53
  Amb at Large, 1961
  Sec of State for Far East Affairs, 1961–63
  Under Sec of State for Political Affairs, 1963–65
  Chief Negotiator at Paris Peace Talks on Vietnam, 1968–69
  Oral History   HST
                     JFK
                     LBJ
                     CU

HART, PARKER T.
  Min to Yemen, 1961–63
  Amb to Kuwait, 1962–63
  Amb to Saudi Arabia, 1961–65
  Oral History   JFK

HAYES, SAMUEL P.
  Chief, Spec Economic and Technical Mission to Indochina, 1951–52
  Asst Dir of the Mutual Security Agency for the Far East, 1952–53
  Oral History   HST

HEINZ, LUTHER C.
  Regional Dir for the Far East, Office of Internal Security Affairs, Dept of Defense, 1960–63
  Staff, Commander In Chief Pacific fleet
  Oral History   JFK

HELLER, WALTER W.
  Chairman, Council of Economic Advisers, 1961–64
  Papers, 1940–82   JFK
  (microfilm)   JFK

HELMS, RICHARD M.
  Deputy Dir of Operations, CIA, 1965–66
  Dir of Central Intelligence, 1966–73
  Oral History   JFK
                     LBJ

HENDERSON, LOY W.
  Dir, Office of Near East and African Affairs, Dept of State, 1945–48
  Amb to India, 1948–51
  Amb to Iran, 1951–55
  Papers   LoC
  Oral History   HST
                     DDE
                     CU
                     PU

HENDRICK, JAMES P.
  US Rep to the UN Commission on Human Rights, 1946–48
  Asst to the Administrator of the Economic Cooperation Admin, 1948–53
  Papers, 1941–84   HST

HERTER, CHRISTIAN A.
  Under Sec of State, 1957–59
  Sec of State, 1959–61
  Spec Rep for Trade Negotiations, 1963–67
  Papers, 1957–61   DDE
  Files, 1962–67   JFK
  Oral History   PU

HICKERSON, JOHN D.
  Dir, Office of European Affairs, Dept of State, 1947–49
  Asst Sec of State for UN Affairs, 1949–53
  Oral History   HST

HILL, JAMES T., JR.
General Counsel, Deputy of the Air
Force, 1950–52
Asst Sec of the Air Force, 1952–53
Papers, 1944–53   HST

HILSMAN, ROGER
Dir of Intelligence and Research,
Dept of State, 1961–63
Asst Sec of State for Far East Affairs,
1963–64
Papers, 1961–65   JFK
Oral History   JFK
                                       LBJ

HITLER, ADOLF
German Führer 1933-45
Collection   PU
Documents Collection   PU

HOFFMAN, LUTHER T.
Regional Dir in Charge of Family
Relations, UN Relief and Rehabil-
itation Admin, Changsha, China,
1946–47
Papers, 1946–65   HST

HOFFMAN, PAUL G.
Administrator, Economic Coopera-
tion Admin, 1948–50
Member, US Delagation to the UN,
1956–57
Managing Dir, UN Spec Fund, 1959–
66
Papers, 1928–72   HST
Oral History   HST
(retains copyright)   LBJ

HORSEY, OUTERBRIDGE
Min and Deputy Chief of Mission,
US Embassy, Rome, 1959–62
Amb to Czechoslovakia, 1963–66
Oral History   JFK

HOUGHTON, AMORY
Amb to France, 1957–61
Oral History
(written permission)   DDE
                                       CU

HOWARD, HARRY N.
Adviser, Div of Greek, Turkish, and
Iranian Affairs, Dept of State,
1947–49

UN Adviser, Bureau of Near
Eastern, S Asian and African Af-
fairs, Dept of State, 1949–56
Papers, 1944–55   HST

HULL, CORDELL
US Sec of State, 1933-44
Papers, 1908–56   LoC

HULTEN, CHARLES M.
Deputy Dir, Office of War Informa-
tion, 1944–55
Deputy Asst Sec of State, 1946–51
Papers, 1942–63   HST

HUMPHREY, GEORGE M.
Sec of the Treasury, 1953–57
Papers, 1912–70   WRHS
Oral History   PU

HURWITCH, ROBERT A.
Spec Asst for Cuban Affairs, Dept of
State, 1962–63
Oral History   JFK

IGNATIUS, PAUL R.
Asst Sec of the Army for Installation
and Logistics, 1961–63
Under Sec of the Army, 1964
Asst Sec of Defense, 1964–67
Sec of the Navy, 1967–69
Oral History (permission
req during his lifetime)   LBJ

INTELLIGENCE BRIEFINGS
President's daily intelligence briefings
National Security File,
1963–69   LBJ

INTELLIGENCE FILE
National Security File,
1963–69   LBJ

INTELLIGENCE REPORTS
Weekly briefings of Fmr
President Johnson, 1969–73   LBJ

IVERSON, KENNETH R.
Deputy Chief for Operations, Spec
Mission, Economic Cooperation
Admin, Greece, 1948–50
Papers, 1942–54   HST

JAVITS, JACOB K.
US Sen 1957–81
Oral History
(permission req)   PU

JERNEGAN, JOHN
Amb to Iraq, 1958–62
Oral History   JFK

JESSUP, FREDERICK PETER
CIA Employee, 1949–63
Member of the US Delegation to the
European Office of the UN,
1957–61
Staff Member, National Security
Council, 1963–72
Papers   LoC
Oral History   DDE

JESSUP, PHILIP C.
Oral History   CU

JOHNSON, EDGAR A. J.
Civil Administrator, S Korean In-
terim Govt, 1946–47
Chief Adviser to the Govt of Korea,
1947–48
Div Dir, Korean Program, Economic
Cooperation Admin, 1948–51
Economic Adviser, Economic Coop-
eration Admin Mission to Greece,
1951–52
Papers, 1946–65   HST

JOHNSON, JOSEPH E.
Official, Dept of State, 1945–47
Chief, Div of Intl Security Affairs,
1945–47
Policy Planning Staff, Dept of State,
1947
Deputy US Rep, Interim Committee,
UN Gen Assembly, 1948
Oral History   HST

JOHNSON, LYNDON BAINES
President of the US, 1963–69
Oral History

(CBS News interviews)   LBJ
(other interviews)   LBJ
(portions restricted)   LBJ

JOHNSON, U. ALEXIS
US Foreign Service Officer, 1935–77
Consul, Manila, 1945

Consul, Yokohama, Japan, 1946
Consul Gen, 1947–49
Deputy Dir, Office of Northeast
Asian Affairs, Dept of State, 1949–
51
Deputy Asst Sec of State for Far East
Affairs, 1951–53
Deputy Under Sec of State and
Under Sec of State for Political
Affairs, 1961–64, 1965–66
Deputy Amb to S Vietnam, 1964–65
Amb to Japan, 1966–69
Chief, US Delegation, Strategic Arms
Limitation Talks, 1973–77
Papers, 1963–85   LBJ
Diary Transcript, 1974–77   GRF
Oral History   HST
                                           LBJ

JONES, JOHN WESLEY
US Foreign Service Officer, 1930–71
1st Sec, US Embassy, Rome, 1945–48,
and Madrid, 1949–53
Oral History   HST

JONES, JOSEPH M.
Spec Asst to the Asst Sec of State for
Public Affairs, 1946–48
Papers, 1947–48   HST

KAISER, PHILIP M.
Asst Sec of Labor in Charge of Intl
Affairs, 1949–52
Amb to Senegal and Mauritania,
1961–64
Min at the US Embassy, London,
1964–69
Amb to Hung, 1977–80
Amb to Austria, 1980–81
**Papers, 1948–69,
1977–81**   HST

KATZ, MILTON
US Spec Rep in Europe, Economic
Cooperation Admin, 1950–51
Papers, 1932–52   HST
Oral History   HST

KAUFMANN, WILLIAM W.
Member, Dep of the Air Force Sci-
ence Advisory Board, 1961–63
Consultant, Dept of Defense, 1961–
Papers, 1953–83   JFK

KAYSEN, CARL
  Deputy Spec Asst to the President for
    National Security Affairs, 1961–63
  Papers, 1948–76   JFK

KEATING, KENNETH B.
  US Sen, 1958–64
  Oral History   CU

KELLER, K. T.
  Dir of Guided Missiles, Office of Sec
    of Defense, 1950–53
  Papers, 1947–54   HST

KENNAN, GEORGE F.
  Amb to Yugo, 1961–63
  Papers   PU
  Oral History
    (portions closed)   JFK
  (may not be reproduced)   PU

KENNEDY, JOHN FITZGERALD
  President of the US, 1961–63
  **National Security Files,
    1961–63**   JFK
  Security Classified Files   JFK

KENNEDY, ROBERT FRANCIS
  Attorney Gen, 1961–64
  US Sen, 1965–68
  Papers   JFK

KENNEDY, W. JOHN
  Under Sec of the Navy, 1947–49
  Chief of Mission, Economic Cooper-
    ation Admin, UK, 1949–50
  Deputy Dir for Mutual Security, 1952
  Papers, 1946–49   HST
  Oral History   HST

KEYSERLING, LEON H.
  V Chairman, 1946–50, and Chair-
    man, 1950–53, Council of Eco-
    nomic Advisers
  Oral History   HST

KHRUSHCHEV, NIKITA S.
  Chairman, Council of Ministers,
    USSR, 1958–64
  Oral History   JFK

KILLIAN, JAMES R., JR.
  Member, Scientific Advisory Com-
    mittee, Office of Defense Mobili-
    zation, 1951–57

Chairman, Army Scientific Advisory
    Panel, 1951–56
  Spec Asst to the President for Sci-
    ence and Technology, 1957–59
  Member, 1957–61, and Chairman,
    1957–59, Presidential Scientific
    Advisory Committee
  Oral History   DDE

KIMBALL, DAN A.
  Asst Sec of the Navy for Air, 1949
  Under Sec of the Navy, 1949–51
  Sec of the Navy, 1951–53
  Papers, 1949–53   HST

KINDLEBERGER, CHARLES P.
  Chief, Div of German and Austrian
    Affairs, Dept of State, 1947–50
  Papers, 1942–48   HST
  Oral History   HST

KIRK, ALAN G.
  Amb to USSR, 1948–52
  Papers, 1919–61   LoC

KIRKPATRICK, LYMAN B.
  Inspector Gen, CIA, 1953–61
  Oral History
    (permission req)   JFK

KISSINGER, HENRY A.
  Spec Asst to the President for Na-
    tional Security Affairs, 1969–73
  Sec of State, 1973–77
  **Photocopies of selected files
    from the Kissinger Papers
    at the Lib of Congress, 1974–77**   GRF
  **Papers (available 24 Dec 2001,
    or 5 yrs after death)**   LoC

KISTIAKOWSKY, GEORGE B.
  Spec Asst to the President for Sci-
    ence and Technology, 1959–61
  **Transcript of Diary,
    1959–60**   DDE
  Oral History   DDE

KOEHLER, JOHN T.
  Asst Sec of the Navy, 1949–51
  Papers, 1949–51   HST

KOHLER, FOY D.
Asst Sec of State for European Affairs, 1959–62
Amb to USSR, 1962–66
Oral History   JFK

KOMER, ROBERT W.
Interim Spec Asst for National Security Affairs, 1966
Spec Asst in Charge of Pacific and other Nonmilitary Programs in Vietnam, 1966–67
Files, 1966–67   LBJ

KOMER–LEONHART FILE
Maintained by the White House Office which directed nonmilitary programs in Vietnam, 1966–68
Subject File, 1966–68   LBJ

KONTOS, C. WILLIAM
Dir and Spec Rep of the President, Sinai Support Mission
Papers, 1976–82   GRF

KOREAN WAR
Copies of Selected Documents, 1947–52   HST

KRULAK, VICTOR
Specialist on Counterinsurgeny, Office of the Joint Chiefs of Staff, 1962–64
Oral History
(permission req)   JFK

LACY, WILLIAM S. B.
US Min, Consul of Embassy, Philippines, 1952–54
Amb to Korea, 1955
Spec Asst to the Sec of State for East–West Exchange, 1956–61
Oral History   DDE

LANDRY, ROBERT B.
Air Aide to the President, 1948–53
Files, 1948–52   HST

LAUKOFF, PERRY
US Foreign Serv officer
Sec of Mission, US Political Adviser for Fed Rep of Germany, 1945–49
Dir, Office of German Political Affairs,
Dept of State, 1949–52

Spec Asst to the Dir, Bureau of German Affairs, Dept of State, 1952
Oral History   HST

LEDDY, JOHN M.
Asst Sec of State for European Affairs
Amb to Organization of Economic Cooperation and Development, 1962–65
Oral History   LBJ

LeMAY, GEN. CURTIS
Chief of Staff, US Air Force
Oral History (restricted
during his lifetime and that
of all persons mentioned)   LBJ
(permission req)   PU

LEMNITZER, LYMAN
Deputy Chief for Plans and Research, Dept of the Army, 1952–55
Commander in Chief, US Far East Command, 1955–57
V Chief of Staff, 1957–59, and Chief of Staff, 1959–60, Dept of the Army
Chairman, Joint Chiefs of Staff, 1960–62
Supreme Allied Commander, 1963–69
Oral History   DDE
                                                    JFK

LEVA, MARX
Spec Asst and Gen Counsel to the Sec of Defense, 1947–49
Asst Sec of Defense, 1949–51
Oral History   HST

LEWIS, GEOFFREY W.
Deputy Chief, Div of German Economic Affairs, 1949–51
Deputy Dir, Bureau of German Affairs, Dept of State, 1950–55
Oral History   HST

LIGHTNER, E. ALLAN, JR.
US Foreign Serv officer, 1930–70
Deputy Dir, Office of Political Affairs, US High Commission, Fed Rep of Germany, 1949–51

Deputy Chief of Mission and Counsel of Embassy, Korea, 1951–53
Oral History   HST

LILIENTHAL, DAVID E.
Papers   PU

LINCOLN, FRANCIS F.
Member, US Mission to Greece, Economic Cooperation Admin, 1947–
50
Papers, 1945–67   HST

LIVERMORE, SHAW
Staff Member, Economic Coopera-
tion Admin, 1949–51
Asst to the Dir, Office of Defense
Mobilization, 1952–53
Oral History   HST

LOCKE, EDWIN A., JR.
Personal Rep of the President to
China, 1945
Spec Asst to the President, 1946–47
Amb in Charge of US Missiles to the
Near East, 1951–52
Papers, 1941–53   HST
Files, 1941–47   HST
Oral History   HST

LOCKE, EUGENE M.
Amb to Pakistan, 1966–67
Deputy Amb to S Vietnam, 1967–68
Oral History   LBJ

LODGE, HENRY CABOT
US Sen (R, Mass), 1947–53
Amb to S Vietnam, 1963–64, 1965–67
Oral History
   (portions closed)   JFK
   (permission req)   PU

LOEB, JAMES I.
National Dir, Americans for Demo-
cratic Action, 1947–51
Oral History   HST

LOVETT, ROBERT A.
Under Sec of State, 1947–49
Deputy Sec of Defense, 1950–51
Sec of Defense, 1951–53
Oral History   HST
                                           DDE
                                           JFK
                                           CU

LUCE, HENRY R.
Journalist
Papers, 1917–67   LoC
Oral History
   (permission req)   PU

MACARTHUR, DOUGLAS, II
Oral History
   (permission req)   PU

MACKNIGHT, JESSE M.
Spec Asst to the Sec of State, 1945–
56
US For Serv officer, 1956–72
Chargé d'Affaires, Surinam, 1956–
58
Chargé d'Affaires, Togo, 1959–60
UN Adviser, Bureau of African Af-
fairs, Dept of State, 1961–72
Papers, 1936–72   HST

MAKINS, SIR ROGER M. (LORD SHERFIELD)
Asst Under Sec of State for Foreign
Affairs, UK, 1947–48
Deputy Under Sec of State, 1948–52
UK Amb to US, 1952–56
Oral History   HST

MANN, THOMAS C.
US Foreign Serv officer, 1946–67
Deputy Asst Sec of State for Inter-
American Affairs, 1950–51
Diplomat in Greece, Guatemala, El
Salvador, 1953–57
Asst Sec of State for Economic Af-
fairs, 1957–60
Asst Sec of State for Inter–American
Affairs, 1960–61
Under Sec of State for Economic Af-
fairs, 1965–66
Oral History   HST
   (written permission)   DDE
                                           LBJ
                                           CU

MARA, CORNELIUS J.
Asst Military Aide to the President,
1949–52
Papers, 1944–50   HST
Oral History   HST

MARCY, CARL M.
Chief of Staff, US Sen Committee on
Foreign Relations, 1955–73
Oral History   JFK

MARTIN, EDWIN
Asst Sec of State for Economic Affairs, 1960–62
Asst Sec of State for Inter–American Affairs, 1962–63
Oral History
(permission req) JFK

MARTIN, EDWIN MCCAMMON
Deputy Dir, Office of Intl Affairs, Dept of State, 1948–49
Dir, Office of European Regional Affairs, Dept of State, 1949–52
Spec Asst to the Sec of State for Mutual Security Affairs, 1952–53
Oral History HST

MATLOCK, CLIFFORD C.
Political Officer, Dept of State, 1946–62
Political Adviser, European Coordinating Committee, 1949–50
Political Officer, US Delegation, North Atlantic Council, 1949–50
Political Officer and Dir, Plans and Policy Staff, Office of US Spec Rep in Europe, 1952–53
Oral History HST

MATTHEWS, FRANCIS P.
Sec of the Navy, 1949–51
Amb to Ireland, 1951–52
Papers, 1932–52 HST

MATTHEWS, H. FREEMAN
Member, US Delegation, Berlin Conf, 1945
Political Adviser, Council of Foreign Ministers Meetings, 1945–46
Amb to Sweden, 1947–50
Deputy Under Sec of State, 1950–53
Oral History HST

MCCARDLE, CARL W.
Asst Sec of State for Public Affairs, 1953–57
Papers, 1953–57 DDE

MCCLOY, JOHN J.
Asst Sec of War, 1941–45
US Military Gov and High Commander for the Fed Rep of Germany, 1949–52
Oral History DDE
(permission req) PU

MCCONE, JOHN A.
Chairman, Atomic Energy Commission, 1958–61
Dir, CIA, 1961–65
Papers, 1958–61 DDE
Oral History DDE
JFK

MCCONNELL, JOHN P.
V Commander in Chief, Strategic Air Command, 1961–62
Deputy Commander in Chief, US European Command, 1962–64
V Chief of Staff, US Air Force, 1964–65
Chief of Staff, US Air Force, 1965–69
Oral History LBJ

MCDUFF, ROBERT J.
Military Associate in the Office of the Chief of Staff, 1946–48
Papers, 1946–48 DDE

MCELROY, NEIL H.
Sec of Defense, 1957–59
Papers, 1948–62 DDE

MCGHEE, GEORGE C.
Asst Sec of State for Near Eastern, South Asian and African Affairs, 1949–51
Amb to Turkey, 1951–53
Under Sec of State for Political Affairs, 1961–63
Amb to Fed Rep of Germany, 1963–68
US Amb at Large, 1968–69
Copies of Papers HST
Oral History HST
JFK
LBJ

MCGUIRE, EDWARD PERKINS
Deputy Asst Sec of Defense for Intl Security Affairs, 1954–56
Asst Sec of Defense for Supply and Logistics, 1956–61
Oral History DDE

MCILVAINE, ROBINSON
Deputy Asst Sec of State for Public Affairs, 1954–56
Counsel, US Embassy, Lisbon, 1956–59
Counsel Gen, Congo, 1960–61
Oral History DDE

MCKEE, JOHN L.
US Army Office, Headquarters, European Command, 1949–53
Papers, 1917–54   HST

MCKEOGH, PEARLIE AND MICHAEL J.
Military Aides, 1942–45
Papers, 1941–48   DDE

MCNAMARA, ROBERT S.
Sec of Defense, 1961–68
Papers, 1961–68   LBJ
Oral History
    (portions closed)   JFK
        (restricted until 2000)   LBJ

MCNEIL, WILFRED J.
Spec Asst to the Sec of Defense, 1947–49
Asst Sec of Defense and Comptroller, Dept of Defense, 1949–59
Oral History   HST

MELBY, JOHN F.
2nd Sec, US Embassy, Chungking, China, 1945–46, and Nanking, China, 1946–48
Official, Office of Philippino and SE Asian Affairs, Dept of State, 1949–52
Spec Asst to the Sec of State for Mutual Security Affairs, 1952
Papers, 1938–52   HST

MEMOS TO THE PRESIDENT
FROM MCGEORGE BUNDY
AND WALT W. ROSTOW
National Security File, 1963–69   LBJ

MERCHANT, LIVINGSTON
US Foreign Serv officer, 1947–62
Counsel for Economic Affairs, US Embassy, Paris, 1945–46
Chief, Aviation Div, Dept of State, 1946–48
Deputy Asst Sec of State for Far Eastern Affairs, 1949–51
Deputy for Political Affairs to US Spec Rep in Europe, 1952–53
Asst Sec of State for European Affairs, 1953–56, 1958–59
Amb to Canada, 1961–63
Under Sec of State for Political Affairs
Oral History   HST
                                       DDE

MILLER, EDWARD G., JR.
Asst Sec of State for the American Representative Area, 1949–52
Papers, 1943–52   HST

MOCH, JULES
French Min of Defense, 1950–51
Oral History   HST

MOORER, THOMAS H.
Commander, 7th Fleet, 1962–64
Commander in Chief, Pacific, 1965
Chief of Naval Operations, 1967–70
Oral History   LBJ

MORRIS, CHARLES A.
Chief of Current Intelligence Establishment, Military Assistance Command, Vietnam, 1967–68
Oral History   LBJ

MUCCIO, JOHN H.
Amb to Korea, 1949–52
Envoy Extraordinary to Iceland, 1954
Oral History   HST

MURPHY, ROBERT D.
Amb to Japan, 1952
Asst Sec of State for UN Affairs, 1953
Deputy Under Sec of State, 1953–59
Under Sec of State for Political Affairs, 1959
Oral History   DDE

NATIONAL INTELLIGENCE ESTIMATES
National Security File, 1963–69   LBJ

NATIONAL SECURITY ACTION MEMORANDUMS
National Security File, 1963–69   LBJ

NATIONAL SECURITY COMMITTEE
Records, 1940–51   HST

NATIONAL SECURITY COUNCIL HISTORIES
National Security File, 1963–69   LBJ

NATIONAL SECURITY COUNCIL MEETINGS FILE
National Security File, 1963–69   LBJ

NAVAL AIDE TO THE PRESIDENT
Office Files, 1945–53   HST

NICHOLS, KENNETH D.
Chief of the Armed Forces Spec
    Weapons Proj, 1948–50
Deputy Dir of Guided Missiles in the
    Office of the Sec of Defense,
    1950–53
Gen Mgr of the Atomic Energy
    Commission, 1953–55
Member of the Army Scientific Ad-
    visory Panel, 1956–65
Oral History
    (written permission)   DDE

NITZE, PAUL H.
Asst Sec of Defense for Intl Security
    Affairs, 1961–63
Sec of the Navy, 1963–67
Deputy Sec of Defense, 1967–69
Oral History
    (permission req)   JFK
                                 LBJ

    **(restricted during his lifetime
    except w/permission)**   LBJ

NIXON, RICHARD M.
President of the US, 1969–74
Oral History
    (permission req)   PU

NOLTING, FREDERICK E., JR.
Dept of State Official, 1946–63
Under Sec of State, 1950–53
Amb to S Vietnam, 1961–63
Oral History   HST
                         LBJ

NORSTAD, LAURIS
Asst Chief of Staff and Chief of Staff
    for Operations, 12th Air Force
    and Med
Allied Air Force, 1942–44
Chief of Staff, 20th Air Force, 1944–
    46
Dir of Plans and Operations, War
    Dept, 1946–47
Deputy Chief of Staff for Opera-
    tions, US Air Force, 1950
Commander in Chief, US and Allied
    Air Forces, Central Europe, 1950–53
Air Deputy, Supreme Headquarters
    Allied Powers Europe, 1953–56

Supreme Allied Commander, 1956–
    63
Member, Presidential Committee on
    an All-Volunteer Force, 1969–72
Member, Gen Advisory Committee
    on Arms Control and Disar-
    mament, 1969–74
Papers, 1930–87   DDE
Oral History   DDE
                         PU

NOURSE, EDWIN G.
Chairman, Council of Economic Ad-
    visers, 1946–49
Papers, 1908–63
    (microfilm)   CU
Papers, 1946–49   HST
Oral History   HST

O'GARA, JOHN E.
Official, CIA, 1949–61
Papers, 1919–61   HST

OCKRENT, ROGER
Sec for the Admin of the Marshall
    Plan in Belgium, 1948–53
Oral History   HST

OHLY, JOHN H.
Spec Asst to the Sec of War, 1946
Spec Asst to the Sec of Defense,
    1947–49
Deputy Dir, Mutual Defense Assis-
    tance Prog, Dept of State, 1949–50
Asst Dir, Office for Intl Security Af-
    fairs, Dept of State, 1951
Spec Asst for Mutual Security Affairs
    in the Office of the Sec of State,
    1951–52
Oral History   HST

OPPENHEIMER, J. ROBERT
Dir Manhattan Proj, 1942–45
Papers, 1921–80   LoC

OSBORN, FREDERICK
US Deputy Rep to the UN Atomic
    Energy Commission, 1947–50
Papers, 1947–54   HST

PALMER, JOSEPH, II
Asst Sec of State for African Affairs
Oral History   LBJ

PANUCH, J. ANTHONY
Spec Counselor and Asst to the Administrator, Office of War Mobilization and Reconversion, 1945
Deputy Asst Sec of State for Admin, 1945–47
Adviser for the Military Governor, United States Occupation Zone of Fed Rep of Germany, 1947–49
Papers, 1931–73   HST

PARKS, LEWIS S.
US Navy officer
Exec Aide to the Asst Sec of the Navy, 1947, and to the Under Sec of the Navy, 1948–49
Commanding Officer, USS Manchester, 1950–51
Papers, 1944–80   HST

PARSONS, J. GRAHAM
US Foreign Serv officer, 1932–70
Spec Asst to the Personal Rep of the President to the Vatican, 1947–48
Papers, 1947–48   HST

PATTERSON, RICHARD C., JR.
Amb to Yugo, 1944–48
Amb to Guatemala, 1948–51
Min to Switzerland, 1951–53
Papers, 1918–66   HST

PATTERSON, ROBERT P.
Asst Sec, 1940
Under Sec, 1940–45
Sec of War, 1945–47
Papers, 1940–51   LoC

PAUL, ARTHUR
Asst for Intl Trade to the Sec of Commerce, 1945–47
Papers, 1944–47   HST

PAUL, NORMAN S.
Asst Sec of Defense
Under Sec of the Air Force
Oral History   LBJ

PELLA, GIUSEPPE
Prime Min, Italy, 1953–54
Oral History   HST

PESMAZOGLU, JOHN S.
Dir Gen, Min of Coordinating in Charge of Planning Economic Development, Greece, 1951–55
Oral History   HST

PHELPS, D. MAYNARD
US Rep, Allied Commission on Reparations, 1945–46
US Rep, Inter–Allied Reparations Agency, 1946
Papers, 1945–61   HST

PIKE, SUMNER T.
Member, Atomic Energy Commission, 1946–51
Papers, 1920–61   HST

PLOWDEN, EDWIN NOEL
Chairman, Economic Planning Board, UK, 1947–53
Oral History   HST

PORTER, PAUL A.
Chief, US Economic Mission to Greece, 1947
Papers, 1942–76   HST

PORTER, PAUL R.
Chief, Economic Cooperation Admin Mission to Greece, 1949–50
Papers, 1944–80   HST

REISCHAUER, EDWIN O.
Amb to Japan, 1961–66
Oral History   JFK

RENFROW, LOUIS H.
Asst Military Aide to the President, 1947–49
Asst to the Sec of Defense, 1949–50
Oral History   HST

RICE, EDWARD E.
US Foreign Serv officer in China, 1935–45
US Consul Gen, Stuttgart, Fed Rep of Germany, 1953–56
Member, Policy Planning Staff, Dept of State 1959–62
Oral History   DDE

RICHARDSON, ELLIOT L.
Under Sec of State, 1969–70
Sec of Defense, 1973
Papers   LoC

RICKOVER, HYMAN
Chief, Bureau for Nuclear Propulsion, Bureau of Ships, US Navy, 1947–81
Chief, Naval Reactors Branch, Atomic Energy Commission, 1953–81
Oral History   JFK

RIDDLEBERGER, JAMES W.
Chief, Div of Central European Affairs, Dept of State, 1944–47
Counsel of Embassy and Chief, Political Sect, American Military Govt, Berlin, 1947–50
Political Adviser to the Economic Cooperation Admin, 1950–52
Dir, Bureau of German Affairs, Dept of State, 1952–53
Oral History   HST

RIDGWAY, MATTHEW B.
US Army Chief of Staff, 1953–55
Oral History   PU

RIGDON, WILIAM M.
Asst Naval Aide to the President, 1942–53
Oral History   HST

RINGLAND, ARTHUR
Exec Dir, Advisery Committee on Voluntary Foreign Aid, 1946–52
Oral History   HST

RINGWAIT, ARTHUR R.
Chief, Div of Chinese Affairs, Dept of State, 1946–48
1st Sec, US Embassy, London, 1949–57
Oral History   HST

ROBERTSON OF OAKRIDGE, GENERAL LORD
UK Deputy Military Governor, 1945–48, and Commander in Chief and Military Gov, 1948–49, Fed Rep of Germany
UK High Commander, Allied High Commission, Fed Rep of Germany, 1949–50
Oral History   HST

ROBERTSON, WALTER
Asst Sec of State for the Far East, 1953–59
Oral History   DDE

ROCKWELL, STUART W.
2nd Sec and Consul, US Embassy, Ankara, 1946–48
Officer in Charge, Palestine-Israel-Jordan Affairs, Dept of State, 1948–50
Political Adviser to the Sec of the Air Force, 1950–52
1st Sec and Consul, US Embassy, Madrid, 1952–53
Oral History   HST

ROGERS, WILLIAM P.
Deputy Attorney Gen, 1953–57
Attorney Gen, 1957–61
Papers, 1938–62   DDE
Oral History   CU

ROSENMAN, SAMUEL I.
Spec Couselor to the President, 1945–46
Oral History   HST

ROSTOW, EUGENE V.
Under Sec of State for Political Affairs, 1966–69
Oral History   LBJ

ROSTOW, WALT W.
Deputy Spec Asst to the President for National Security Affairs, 1961
Chairman, Policy Planning Staff, Dept of State, 1961–66
Spec Asst to the President for National Security Affairs, 1966–68
White House Staff Files, 1961   JFK
Files, 1966–68   LBJ
Papers, 1950–84   LBJ
Oral History
   (portions closed)   JFK
**(restricted until March
   22, 1992)**   LBJ

RUSK, DEAN
Sec of State, 1961–69
Papers, 1961–63
   (microfilm)   JFK
Files, 1961–69   LBJ

Oral History
(portions closed)   JFK
                                            LBJ

(some passages subject
  to restrictions)   PU

SACHS, HANS-GEORG
Counselor of the Minister Deputy
  for the Marshall Plan, Fed Rep of
  Germany, 1949–52
Oral History   HST

SALINGER, PIERRE
Press Sec to the President, 1960–64
**White House Staff Files,
1960–64**   JFK

SALTZMAN, CHARLES E.
Asst Sec of State for Occupied Areas,
  1947–49
Oral History   HST

SATTERWAITE, JOSEPH C.
Deputy Dir, 1947–48, and Dir, 1948–
  49, Office of Near East and Afri-
  can Affairs, Dept of State
Amb to Ceylon, 1949–53
Oral History   HST

SCHLESINGER, ARTHUR M., JR.
Spec Asst to the President for Latin
  American Affairs, 1961–63
Papers, 1939–83   JFK
Oral History   JFK
                                            LBJ

SCHULTZE, CHARLES L.
Staff Member, Council of Economic
  Adv, 1952–58
Asst Dir, 1962–65, and Dir, 1965–68,
  Bureau of the Budget
Oral History   LBJ

SCOWCROFT, BRENT
Spec Asst to the President for National Security Affairs, 1974–77,
  1989–1991
Files, 1974–77   GRF

SEABORG, GLENN T.
Chairman, Atomic Energy Commission, 1961–71
Papers and Records, 1961–63
(permission req)   JFK

SERVICE, JOHN STEWART AND CHARLES E. RHETTS
**Papers Relating to Loyalty
  Investigation of Service,
  US Foreign Serv Officer,
  1950–63**   HST

SISCO, JOSEPH
Deputy Asst Sec of State for Intl Or-
  ganizations Affairs
Asst Sec of State for Near East and
  South Asian Affairs
Oral History   LBJ
                                            PU

SITUATION ROOM FILE
**National Security File,
1963–69**   LBJ

SMITH, GERARD C.
SALT I negotiator, 1970–72
Oral History
(permission req)   PU

SMITH, WALTER BEDELL
Chief of Staff, Allied Headquarters,
  North Africa, 1942–44
Chief of Staff, SHAEF, 1944–45
Chief of Staff, US Forces, European
  Theater, 1945
US Amb to the USSR, 1946–49
Commander Gen, 1st Army, 1949–
  50
Dir, CIA, 1950–53
Under Sec of State, 1953–54
Consultant, Spec Projects Office
  (Disarmament), Exec Office of the
  President, 1955–56
**Collection of World War II
  Documents, 1941–45**   DDE
Papers, 1942–61   DDE

SNOY, JEAN CHARLES
Chairman, Organization for European Economic Community,
  1948–50
Oral History   HST

SNYDER, JOHN W.
Sec of the Treasury, 1946–53
Papers, 1918–71   HST
Oral History   HST

SORENSEN, THEODORE C.
Spec Counsellor to the President,
  1961–64

STASSEN, HAROLD
    Oral History   PU

STEINHARDT, LAURENCE A.
    Amb to Peru, 1932–38
    Amb to USSR, 1939–41
    Amb to Turkey, 1942–45
    Amb to Czechoslovakia, 1945–48
    Amb to Canada, 1949–50
    Papers, 1929–50   LoC

STETTINIUS, EDWARD R., JR
    Sec of State, 1944–45
    Scrapbooks, 1944–45
        (microfilm)   UVa

STEVENS, JOHN M.
    Asst Sec of State for Far Eastern Affairs, 1959–62
    Amb to Afghanistan, 1962–66
    Oral History (closed)   JFK

STEVENSON, ADLAI E.
    Papers   PU

STIKKER, DIRK U.
    Dutch Min for Foreign Affairs, 1948–52
    Oral History   HST

STIMSON, HENRY L.
    Sec of War, 1940–45
    Diary, 1944–45
        (microfilm)   YU
    Oral History   CU

STINEBOWER, LEROY D.
    Economist, Dept of State, 1934–52
    Deputy Dir, Office of Intl Trade Policy, 1945
    Spec Asst to the Asst Sec of State for Economic Affairs, 1946–49
    Dir, Office of Financial and Development Policy, 1949–52
    Oral History   HST

STRAUSS, LEWIS L.
    Member, Atomic Energy Commission, 1946–50
    Chairman, Atomic Energy Commission, 1953–58
    Oral History   DDE
    (closed)   HST

SULLIVAN, JOHN L.

    Asst Sec of the Navy for Air, 1945–46
    Under Sec of the Navy, 1946–47
    Sec of the Navy, 1947–49
    Oral History   HST

SUMNER, JOHN D.
    Chief Economic Official, China Mission, Economic Cooperation Admin, 1948–49
    Papers, 1928–53   HST

SYMINGTON, STUART
    Asst Sec of War for Air, 1946–47
    Sec of the Air Force, 1947–50
    Papers, 1946–50
        (closed)   HST
    Oral History   HST

TANNENWALD, THEODORE, JR.
    Asst Dir and Chief of Staff to the Dir of Mutual Security, 1951–53
    Oral History   HST

TAYLOR, GEN. MAXWELL D.
    Military Rep to the President, 1961–62
    Chairman, Joint Chiefs of Staff, 1962–64
    Oral History
    (portions closed)   JFK
    (tape recordings of two
    interviews are restricted)   LBJ
    (permission req)   PU

THAYER, ROBERT H.
    Asst to the Amb to France, 1951–54
    US Min to Romania, 1955–58
    Asst Sec of State for Educational and Cultural Affairs, 1958–61
    Oral History   DDE

THOMAS, CHARLES
    Under Sec of the Navy, 1953
    Asst Sec of Defense for Supply and Logistics, 1953–54
    Sec of the Navy, 1954–57
    Oral History   DDE

THOMPSON, LLEWELLYN E.
    Amb to USSR, 1957–62
    US Amb–at–Large, 1962–66
    Oral History   JFK

THAYER, ROBERT H.
Asst to the Amb to France, 1951–54
US Min to Romania, 1955–58
Asst Sec of State for Educational and
Cultural Affairs, 1958–61
Oral History   DDE

THOMAS, CHARLES
Under Sec of the Navy, 1953
Asst Sec of Defense for Supply and
Logistics, 1953–54
Sec of the Navy, 1954–57
Oral History   DDE

THOMPSON, LLEWELLYN E.
Amb to USSR, 1957–62
US Amb–at–Large, 1962–66
Oral History   JFK

THOMSON, JAMES C., JR.
Spec Asst to the Under Sec of State,
1961
Spec Asst to the President, Rep for
Africa, Asia, and Latin America,
1961–63
Spec Asst to the Sec of State for Far
East Affairs, 1963–64
Member, National Security Council
Staff, 1964–66
Papers, 1960–66
(permission req)   JFK
Oral History   LBJ

THORNEYCROFT, LORD PETER
Min of Aviation, UK, 1960–62
Min of Defense, UK, 1962–64
Oral History
(portions closed)   JFK

THORP, WILLARD L.
Asst Sec of State for Economic Af-
fairs, 1946–52
Oral History   HST

TREVELYAN, SIR HUMPHREY
Deputy Under Sec, Foreign Office,
UK, 1962
UK Amb to Iraq, 1958–61
UK Amb to the USSR, 1962–65
Oral History   JFK

TRUMAN, HARRY S.
President of the US, 1945–53
Files (NSC), 1947–53   HST

Files (Presidential Sec),
1945–53   HST
Files (White House Cent),
1945–53 (part on microfilm)   HST

TSALDARIS, CONSTANTINE
Prime Min, Greece, 1946–47
Oral History   HST

TWINING, NATHAN F.
V Chief of Staff, 1950–53, and Chief
of Staff, 1953–57, Dept of the Air
Force
Chairman, Joint Chiefs of Staff,
1957–60
Oral History   DDE

TYLER, WILLIAM R.
Deputy Asst, 1961–62, and Asst Sec
of State for European Affairs,
1962–65
Oral History   JFK

UNITED STATES ARMS CONTROL
AND DISARMAMENT AGENCY
Records, 1961–63   JFK
(microfilm)   JFK
Records, 1964–68   LBJ
(microfilm)   LBJ

US CENTRAL INTELLIGENCE AGENCY
Printed materials, 1961–63   JFK
(microfilm)   JFK

US DEPARTMENT OF DEFENSE
Records, 1961–63   JFK
(microfilm)   JFK

US DEPARTMENT OF STATE
Records, 1961–63   JFK
(microfilm)   JFK

US PRESIDENT'S COMMISSION
ON FOREIGN AID
Records, 1947–48   HST

VAN DER BEUGEL, E. H.
Dir, Bureau for the Marshall Plan,
Foreign Affairs Office, Nether-
lands, 1947–52
Oral History   HST

VAN KLEFFENS, EELCO
Dutch Amb to the US, 1947–50
Oral History   HST

VANCE, CYRUS R.
Gen Counselor, Dept of Defense,
1961–62
Sec of the Army, 1962–63
Deputy Sec of Defense, 1964–67
Spec Rep of the President to Cyprus,
1967, to Korea, 1968
Negotiator, Paris Peace Talks on
Vietnam, 1968–69
Sec of State, 1977–80
Oral History LBJ

VAUGHAN, HARRY H.
Military Aide to the President, 1945–53
Papers, 1942–73
(part on microfilm) HST
Oral History HST

VON SUSSKIND, ALEXANDER
Deputy Chief, Mission to the Orga-
nization of the European Eco-
nomic Community, Fed Rep of
Germany, 1949–52
Oral History HST

VON SYDOW, ERIK
Head of the Swedish Delegation to
the Organization of the European
Economic Community, 1949–53
Oral HIstory HST

WALT, GEN. LEWIS W.
Sr Adviser, I Corps, Military Assistance
Command, Vietnam, 1966–67
Oral History LBJ

WALTERS, VERNON
Interpreter for the President, 1948–
Deputy Dir of the CIA, 1972–76
Amb to the UN, 1985–89
Amb to the Fed Rep of Germany,
1989–
Oral History DDE

WARNER, GEN. VOLNEY F.
Exec Officer and Sr Aide to Gen
Westmoreland, 1970–72
**Oral History (tape recording
is restricted)** LBJ

WARNKE, PAUL C.
Asst Sec of Defense for Intl Security
Affairs
Files, 1963–68 LBJ
Oral History LBJ

WAUGH, SAMUEL C.
Asst Sec of State, 1953–55
Deputy Under Sec of State, 1955
Papers, 1926–69 DDE

WEBB, JAMES E.
Under Sec of State, 1949–52
Papers, 1928–80 HST

WEIGLE, RICHARD D.
Exec Officer, Office of Far Eastern
Affairs, Dept of State, 1946–49
Oral History HST

WESTMORELAND, GEN. WILLIAM C.
Commander, US Military Assistance
Committee, Vietnam
Chief of Staff, US Army
Papers, 1962–73 LBJ

WHEELER, EARLE
Dir, Joint Chiefs of Staff, 1960–62
Commander Gen, European Com-
mand, 1962
Chief of Staff, US Army
Oral History JFK

WHITE HOUSE OFFICE
Office of the Spec Asst for Science
and Technology
Records, 1957–61 DDE

WHITE HOUSE OFFICE
Office of the Spec Asst for National
Security Affairs
Records, 1952–61 DDE

WHITE HOUSE OFFICE, NSC STAFF
Papers, 1948–61 DDE

WIESNER, JEROME B.
Spec Asst to the President for Sci-
ence and Technology, 1961–64
Papers, 1961–73 JFK

WILCOX, FRANCIS O.
Chief of Staff, US Sen Foreign Rela-
tions Committee, 1947–55
Asst Sec of State for Intl Organiza-
tion, 1955–61
Papers, 1930–85 HST
Oral History HST
DDE
PU

WILKINS, FRASER
  Asst Chief, Div of Near Eastern Affairs, Dept of State, 1948–49
  Officer in Charge, Palestine-Israel-Jordan Affairs, Dept of State, 1949
  Officer in Charge, Arabian Peninsula Affairs, Dept of State, 1950
  Dir, Office of Near Eastern Affairs, Dept of State, 1950
  1st Sec and Consul, US Embassy, New Dehli, 1950–52
  Oral History   HST

WILLIAMS, GEN. SAMUEL T.
  Deputy Corps Commander, Korea, 1952–54
  Commander, US Military Assistance and Advisory Group, Vietnam, 1955–60
  Oral History   LBJ

WILSON, EVAN M.
  US Foreign Serv officer, 1937–67
  Asst Chief, Div of Near Eastern Affairs, Dept of State, 1946–47
  2nd Sec and V Consul, and 1st Sec and Consul, US Embassy, Tehran, 1947–49
  Oral History   HST

WOOD, C. TYLER
  Deputy US Spec Rep in Europe, 1950–52
  Associate Deputy Dir, Mutual Security Agency, 1952–53
  Oral History   HST

WRIGHT, EDWIN M.
  Spec Asst to Loy W. Henderson, Bureau of Near Eastern and African Affairs, Dept of State, 1946–48
  Oral History   HST

YARMOLINSKY, ADAM
  Spec Asst to the Sec of Defense, 1961–64
  Deputy Asst Sec of Defense for Intl Affairs, 1965–66
  Papers, 1936–80   JFK
  Oral History   JFK
                                                            LBJ

YORK, HERBERT
  Member, Gen Advisory Committee, Arms Control and Disarmament Agency, 1962–69
  Oral History
  (portions closed)   JFK

YOST, CHARLES
  Minister-Counsel, US Embassy, Greece, 1950–53
  Deputy High Commander to Australia, 1953–54
  US Min to Laos, 1954–55
  Amb to Laos, 1955–56
  Min, US Embassy, Paris, 1956–58
  Amb to Syria, 1958
  Amb to Morocco, 1958–61
  Oral History   DDE
                                                            PU

ZUCKERMAN, EUGENE M.
  Chief Scientific Adviser to the Sec of State for Defense, UK, 1960–66
  Oral History   JFK

ZUCKERT, EUGENE M.
  Spec Asst to the Asst Sec of War for Air, 1946–47
  Asst Sec of the Air Force, 1947–52
  Member, Atomic Energy Commission, 1952–54
  Sec of the Air Force, 1961–65
  Oral History   HST
                                                            JFK
                                                            LBJ

Contributors

V. A. ....Vera Azar
C. S. B. ....Christopher S. Brown
M. B. ....Michael Brown
C. C. ....Campbell Craig
A. F. .... Amy Feldman
M. F. ....Mark Felipe
B. F. ....Benjamin Frankel
M. G. G. .... Mary G. Gotschall
M. H. ....Maija Harkonen
J. H. ....John E. Henson
B. D. K. ....Brian D. Kux
D. L. ....Dennis Lynch
P. M. ....Peter Macdonald
J. M. ....Joanna Mizgala
E. R. P. ....Erik R. Pages
S. M. P. ....Susan M. Peterson
J. R. ....James C. Raffel
J. R.-S. ....Joao Resende-Santos
J. W. .... John Webb

335

Index

Index

Bandung Conference, II 150, 244, 326; III 216

Bangladesh, II 31, 98

Bani-Sadr, Abul Hassan, II 173

Bank of Credit and Commerce International (BCCI), I 124

Bante, Teferi, II 218

Bao Dai, I 358; II 83, 84, 143, 144

Barker, Ray W., III 309

Barkley, Alben W., III 309

Bar-Lev defense line, III 107

Barnes, Donald F., III 309

Barnett, Robert W., III 309

Barrett, Edward W., III 309

Barrows, Leland, III 309

Baruch, Bernard, I 33–35, 4; II 129; III 101, 113, 309

Baruch Plan, I 4, 34, 128, 393, 505; III 57, 101, 225, 226

Basic Treaty, I 55

Bastovansky, St., III 132

Batista y Zaldívar, Fulgencio, II 24–25, 57, 63, 134; III 74, 146

Batt, William L., III 309

Battle, Lucius, III 309

Battle of Britain, I 114

Bay of Pigs invasion, I 30, 72, 139, 260, 352; II 18, 58; III 113, 74, 75, 126, 146, 210

Bazargan, Mehdi, II 173

Beach, Edward L., III 309

Becker, Nathan M., III 309

Begin, Menachem, II 15, 48

Belgian Congo, II 201

Belgium, I 6

Belk, Samuel E., III 309

Bell, Daniel, I 225

Bell, David E., III 309

Bell, Griffin, I 93

Bellows, Everett H., III 309

Ben Bella, Ahmed, II 25–27, 40

Bendetsen, Karl R., III 310

Bendjedid, Chadli, II 41

Benelux, III 60, 195

Benes, Eduard, I 329; II 122

Ben-Gurion, David, II 27–29, 93, 94, 216; III 309

Beria, Lavrenti P., II 51, 177, 186, 234, 324

Berlin blockade, I 24, 52, 329; II 323; III 59–60, 63

Berlin Crisis, I 158, 184, 209, 261, 434, 496; II 179; III 114, 74

Berlin Wall, I 28, 52, 261, 282, 487–488; II 179, 342; III 114–115, 74, 93, 159

Bernadotte Plan, I 330

Bernstein, Eduard, III 181

The Best and the Brightest (Halberstam), I 203

Bethe, Hans, III 310

Between Two Ages (Brzezinski), I 66

Bevan, Aneurin, I 35–39, 22, 25, 515

Bevin, Ernest, I 40–43, 6, 22, 25, 57; III 194, 218

Beyen, Jan, I 366

Bhutto, Zulfikar Ali, II 30–31, 369

Biafran war, I 517; II 123–124

Bidault, Georges, III 218

Biden, Joseph R., Jr., III 171

Bierut, Boleslaw, II 32–33, 110

Binh Xuyen, II 84

Biriuzov, Sergei, II 207

Bishop, Maurice, II 34–35, 60, 61

Bison bombers, III 116

Bissell, Richard M., I 138, 139; III 125, 310

Bitar, Salah al-Din, II 3

Blair, William, III 310

Blaisdell, Thomas C., Jr., III 310

Bloch, Emmanuel, I 427

Block, Herbert, III 198

Blundering into Disaster: Surviving the First Century of the Nuclear Age (McNamara), I 353

Blunt, Anthony, I 44–45, 75, 312

Board for International Broadcasting, III 242

Bohlen, Charles E., I 46–48, 8, 144, 188, 303, 329; III 133, 147, 192, 310

Bokassa, Jean-Bédel, I 192–193

Boland, Edward P., I 49–50, 416

Boland amendments, I 50, 101; II 266; III 142, 172

Bolivia, II 135

Bolshevik Military Revolutionary Committee, II 175

Bolsheviks, II 175, 319, 348

Bomber gap, III 116, 124, 200

Bonner, Elena, II 289, 290

Bonus Expeditionary Force, I 308

Borge Martínez, Tomás, II 36–37, 60

Bosch Gavino, Juan, I 176; II 38–39; III 77

Boston College, I 49

Boumédienne, Houari, II 40–41, 26, 340

Bourguiba, Habib, Jr., III 310

Bourguiba, Habib Ben Ali, II 42–43; III 310

Bowie, Robert R., III 310

Bowles, Chester, I 30; III 310

Bowles, Edward L., III 310

Bowsher, Charles, III 310

Brandeis, Louis D., I 3

Brandt, Willy, I 51–56, 268, 388, 447, 472; II 111; III 82, 232

Brazil, I 244; III 78, 226

Breaking Ranks (Podhoretz), I 403

Brerton, Lewis H., III 310

Brest-Litovsk Treaty, III 53, 245

Bretton Woods conference, I 358, 371; III 117–118

Bretton Woods system, III 160

Brezhnev, Leonid I., I 95; II 44–49, 12, 69, 224, 263, 328, 342, 344; III 118, 169, 176–177, 262, 283–284
  and arms reductions talks, I 60, 96, 323, 387; II 47, 48, 262
  and food program, II 113
  and Gromyko, II 125, 129–130
  and Kosygin, II 187, 188
  and Malinovsky, II 207
  and Ogarov, II 262, 263

Brezhnev Doctrine, II 47, 90, 328; III 118–121, 78, 92, 115

Bridges, Styles, III 61

Briggs, Ellis, III 310

Briggs, Ruth M., III 311

Brinksmanship, III 122

Broad Opposition Front, Nicaragua, II 318

Brodie, Bernard, I 258, 350

Brookings Institution, I 187

Brooks, Robert A., III 311

Brown, Edmond G. "Pat," I 411

Brown, George, I 57–58, 88

Brown, Harold, I 59–65, 67, 68, 96; III 311

Brown, Seyom, I 385

Brown, Winthrop, III 311

Browne, Malcolm, I 202

Brownell, Herbert, III 311

Bruce, David K. E., III 311

Brussels Pact, III 218

Brzezinski, Zbigniew, I 65–71, 60, 61, 63, 96, 97, 98, 188, 448, 500; II 293; III 85–86, 123, 210, 211, 311

"Budapest Appeal," III 205

Budenny, Semyon, II 176

Buganda, II 9

Bukharin, Nikolai, II 115, 175, 320

Bulganin, Nikolai, II 50–52, 177, 178, 223

Bulgaria, I 86, 115; II 72, 72–73, 85–86, 116, 305, 359–360; III 55, 184, 282

Bulgarian Communist party, II 72, 85, 86, 359

Bulgarian Democratic Forces, II 360

Bulgarian Socialist party, II 360

Bull, Harold R., III 311

Bullitt, William C., I 251

Bundy, McGeorge, I 71–73, 203, 274, 353, 430, 434, 469, 481; III 147, 154, 210, 311

Bundy, William P., I 137; III 311

Burgess, Guy, I 74–75, 44, 45, 312, 401

Burgess, W. Randolph, III 311

Burke, Arleigh A., III 311

Burma, I 466; II 329

Burnham, James, I 225

Burns, Arthur F., III 311

Burt, Richard R., III 169

Bush, George, I 76–81, 27, 28, 101, 107, 412; II 23, 82, 266; III 92, 128, 134, 212

Bush, Vannevar, III 101, 190

Butcher, Harry C., III 312

Butler, Rab, I 82–84, 132, 151, 314, 317, 318

Butterworth, W. Walton, III 312

Byrd, Robert C., III 171

Byrnes, James F., I 85–87, 4, 34, 116, 142, 490; III 57, 101, 239, 312

Cabot, John M., III 312

Cabot, Thomas, III 312

Cabral, Amílcar Lopes, II 53–55, 248

Cady, John F., III 312

Callaghan, James, I 88–89; III 222

Callaway, Howard H., III 312

Cambodia, I 386, 415; II 271–273, 292–293, 309–310; III 80, 119, 185, 197, 278, 280

Cambodian Communist party, II 271

Cambridge Cell, I 44, 74, 312

Campbell, John C., III 312

Camp David Accords, I 66, 96, 389, 500; II 15; III 83, 87

Canada, I 6; III 60, 229

Can America Stay Neutral? (Armstrong), I 18

Cannon, C. Craig, III 312

Cannon, Lou, I 411

"Can Nuclear Deterrence Last Out the Century?" (Iklé), I 231

Can We Be Neutral? (Armstrong), I 18

Cape Verde Islands, II 53–54

Cardenal, Pedro Joaquin Chamorro, II 318

Carlucci, Frank, I 90–91; III 212

Sunnis, II 20
Sun Yat-sen, II 74, 75, 209, 362
Supreme Revolutionary Council, Somalia, II 306
Surface-to-air missiles (SAMS), III 146
Suslov, Mikhail, II *327–328*, 11, 70, 80, 223, 358
Svechinsky, Vitaly, III 252
Svoboda, Ludvik, II 258
Symington, Stuart, I 189; III 200, 331
Symington amendment, III 226
Syria, I 157, 389; II 3–4, 19–23, 48, 244, 245; III 87, 106–108
Taft, Robert A., I *475–477*, 6, 129, 155, 323, 383; III 213
Taft-Hartley Act, I 356
Taiwan, I 309, 319, 386; II 76; III 62
Tanganyika African National Union (TANU), II 260
Tannenwald, Theodore, Jr., III 331
Tanzania, I 95; II 9, 10, 259–261
Taylor, Maxwell D., I *478–479*, 31, 259; III 76, 147, 331
Teheran Conference, 1943, I 47, 148, 209, 327, 331; II 128, 234, 322
Teller, Edward, I *480–482*, 59, 495; III 62, 90, 264
Terrorism, I 415
Tet Offensive, I 8, 31, 123, 246, 431; II 105–106, 106; III 79, 127, 279
Thailand, III 217
Thatcher, Margaret, I *483–486*, 213, 240; III 169, 171
Thayer, Robert H., III 331
Theater nuclear weapons (TNF), III 60
Third World, I 258, 259, 290, 414–415, 510; III 70, 165, 216, 220, 285
38th parallel, Korea, III 65, 178, 179
Thomas, Charles, III 331
Thomas, Norman, I 225
Thompson, Llewellyn E., Jr., I *487–488*; III 147, 331
Thomson, James C., Jr., III 332
Thor missile, III 167
Thorneycroft, Lord Peter, III 332
Thorp, Willard L., III 332
Tiananmen Square massacre, I 79; II 82, 159, 355, 356; III 92–93
Tigre People's Liberaton Front, II 219
Time, I 104, 304, 305
Timoshenko, Semyon, II 176
Titan missile, III 259
Tito, Josip Broz, I 254, 492; II *331–332*, 51, 87, 88, 122, 146, 188, 223, 283, 323, 326, 328; III 59, 120, 140, 182, 216
Tomahawk missile, I 379, 399
Tonkin Gulf resolution, I 31, 72, 176, 237, 245, 333; II 145; III 77, 268, 278
Toriello, Jorge, II 17
Tou Samouth, II 271
Towards the Understanding of Karl Marx (Hook), I 225
Tower, John, III 212
Tower Commission, III 128
Trade Expansion Act, 1962, I 30
Trade Reform Act, 1973, III 176–177, 188
Transport and General Workers Union, I 40, 57

Treaty of Moscow, I 54–55
Treaty of Paris, I 366; III 195
Treaty of Rome, 1957, I 12, 191, 366; III 158
Trevelyan, Humphrey, III 332
Triad, III *269*
Trident missile, I 292, 413, 485
Trident program, I 61
Trilateral Commission, I 60, 66; III 269
Trilateralism, III *269*
Trilling, Diana, I 225
Trilling, Lionel, I 103
Trotsky, Leon, I 225; II *333–336*, 115, 175, 233, 319; III 245, 246
The Troubled Partnership: A Reappraisal of the Atlantic Alliance (Kissinger), I 274
Trujillo Molino, Rafael Leonidas, I 110; II *336–337*, 38, 56; III 68, 127
Truman, Harry S, I *489–498*, 4, 22, 85–86, 116, 121, 136, 154, 221, 309, 337, 377, 475; II 51, 128, 143, 182; III 55, 64–65, 113, 114, 125, 139, 178, 179, 191, 199, 209, 238, 278, 332
  foreign policy of, I 115, 129, 476
  nuclear weapon policy of, I 23, 34, 481
Truman Doctrine, I 3, 4–5, 7, 24, 98, 121, 146, 172, 221, 253, 288, 330, 368, 434, 493–494; III *270–271*, 57–58, 63, 131, 156, 192, 287
Tsaldaris, Constantine, III 332
Tshombe, Moise-Kapenda, I 261; II *338–340*, 201, 226, 330
Tsiolkovsky, Konstantin, III 257
Tukhachevskii, M. N., II 346
Tunisia, I 358–359; II 42–43, 254, 278
Turkey, I 5, 6, 24, 41, 68, 172, 493; III 57, 58, 60, 70, 75, 83, 112, 139, 270
Turkish-Soviet defense system, I 4
Turner, Stansfield, I 101; III 128
Tuykhachevsky, Mikhail, III 246
Tverdokhlebov, Andrei, II 289
Twentieth Party Congress, USSR, II 52, 80, 178, 205, 223, 328, 364, 367; III *272–274*, 71, 183, 248
Twenty-Seventh Party Congress, USSR, III 234
Twinnig, Nathan F., III 332
"Two Camps" speech, Stalin, III 56
Two Tactics of Social-Democracy in the Democratic Revolution (Lenin), III 182
Tyler, William R., III 332
U-2 affair, I 217–218, 319, 407, 487; II 179; III *275–276*, 125–126
U-2 overflights, I 138–139; III 72, 73, 147, 162, 200
Uganda, I 95; II 9–10
Ukraine, II 176, 177
Ukrainian Communist party, II 233
Ulam, Stanislaw, I 481
Ulbricht, Walter, I 55; II *341–343*
Umansky, K. A., II 128
The Uncertain Trumpet (Taylor), I 259, 478; III 161
Union for the Total Liberation of Angola (UNITA), II 294, 295, 296, 297, 298
Union of Polish Patriots, II 32
Union of Soviet Socialist Republics, I 4; II 219; III 119, 282

and Albania, II 147
and Angola, II 249, 298
and atomic bomb, I 6
and Cuba, II 59, 61–62
and Egypt, III 70
and Korea, III 64
and Kuomintang, III 61
and Libya, II 277
and Syria, II 19, 22
and the Marshall Plan, III 193
and Vietnam, II 293
and West Germany, I 13
and WW II, II 321–322, 344
and Yugoslavia, II 87, 332
United Arab Emirates (UAE), III 230
United Arab Republic (UAR), II 3, 19, 245
United Front of Kampuchea, II 310
United Fruit Company, II 17; III 125
United Gold Coast Convention, II 254
United Mine Workers, I 356
United Nations Atomic Energy Commission, I 4; III 101, 113
United Nations Economic Commission for Africa, II 138
United Nations Organization, I 152, 206–207, 257, 270, 276, 434, 491; II 58, 74, 81, 128, 128–129, 129, 179, 182, 201, 234, 284, 285, 329–330, 338–339, 348–349, 363; III 277, 64, 178, 219, 288
  and Arab-Israeli war, 1973, III 107–108
United Nations Relief and Rehabilitation Agency, I 4
United Nations Security Council, I 7
United Nations Security Council Resolution 242, I 58
United Somali Congress, II 308
United States
  and Cambodia, II 310
  and Central America, II 17–18
  and Chiang Kai-shek, II 76
  and Cuba, II 25, 57, 58
  and Dominica, II 38–39
  and Egypt, II 245, 246
  and Iran, II 172
  and Iraq, II 156
  and Libya, II 278–279
  and Nicaragua, II 265
  and Somalia, II 307
  and Syria, II 23
  and the PRC, II 81–82, 151, 212, 363
  and Vietnam, II 106, 250
United States Air Force, III 208
United States Arms Control and Disarmament Agency, III 332
United States Central Command (USCENTCOM), III 242–243
United States Department of Defense, III 332
United States Department of State, III 332
United States Naval Academy, I *92–99*
United States President's Commission on Foreign Aid, III 332
United States-Soviet Nuclear Nonproliferation Treaty, I 243
The Unperfect Society: Beyond the New Class (Djilas), II 89
Urbanek, Karel, II 160